Democracy and Sovereignty

Democracy and Sovereignty

Rethinking the Legitimacy of Public International Law

Edited by

Daniel-Erasmus Khan, Evelyne Lagrange,
Stefan Oeter, and Christian Walter

BRILL
NIJHOFF

LEIDEN | BOSTON

Library of Congress Cataloging-in-Publication Data

Names: Democracy: Fundamental Building-Block of the International Order? (Conference) (2020 : Tutzing, Germany) | Khan, Daniel-Erasmus, editor. | Lagrange, Evelyne, editor. | Oeter, Stefan, editor. | Walter, Christian, 1966- editor. | Société française pour le droit international, sponsoring body. | Deutsche Gesellschaft für Völkerrecht, sponsoring body | Akademie für Politische Bildung (Tutzing, Germany), host institution.
Title: Democracy and sovereignty : rethinking the legitimacy of public international law / edited by Daniel-Erasmus Khan, Evelyne Lagrange, Stefan Oeter, and Christian Walter.
Description: Leiden ; Boston : Brill Nijhoff, [2023] | Includes index. | Identifiers: LCCN 2022037509 (print) | LCCN 2022037510 (ebook) | ISBN 9789004508705 (hardback) | ISBN 9789004508712 (ebook)
Subjects: LCSH: International law–Political aspects–Congresses.
Classification: LCC KZ1250 .D458 2020 (print) | LCC KZ1250 (ebook) | DDC 341–dc23/eng/20220919
LC record available at https://lccn.loc.gov/2022037509
LC ebook record available at https://lccn.loc.gov/2022037510

Typeface for the Latin, Greek, and Cyrillic scripts: "Brill". See and download: brill.com/brill-typeface.

ISBN 978-90-04-50870-5 (hardback)
ISBN 978-90-04-50871-2 (e-book)

This book is printed on acid-free paper and produced in a sustainable manner.

Contents

PART 3
Democracy Promotion in International Legal Practice

PART 4
Emerging Issues at the International Level

PART 5
Conclusions

Preface

At the time when this Preface is written, the foundations of international law are shattered in a way which seemed unimaginable only a few weeks before. The invasion of Ukraine ordered by Russia's President Putin on 24 February 2022, and his government's shallow justifications based on pure power-politics as well as the overt ambition to overthrow a democratic government, raise fundamental questions of the legitimacy of international law and of the delicate relationships between democracy and sovereignty within the international system. When we developed the overarching research question of this book, and when all its chapters were drafted and written, inquiring into the legitimacy of international law still seemed to many a largely theoretical exercise, driven by academics interested in a deeper understanding of their subject, namely the normative underpinnings of the international order and how they changed over time. In fact, it was not and is less than ever a speculative, purely academic enterprise.

While we acknowledge that some of the propositions presented in the contributions to the colloquium of Tutzing in September 2020 and published in this book may seem to stem from a time when the world of international law seemed relatively stable in comparison to today's uncertainties, with some dozens of states being reluctant to condemn a flagrant violation of the most basic rules of the United Nations Charter and jus contra bellum, we are firmly convinced that the tremendous challenges which the Russian aggression against Ukraine present to the international order, need to be addressed at a fundamental level. Against this backdrop, reflecting on possible strategies of legitimation that go beyond the existing state-centered approaches has become more pertinent, not less. In our view, the approach suggested here, which consists in comparing and, where possible, merging modern and traditional concepts of legitimation, continues to be of utmost relevance. This is backed by the fact that highly relevant current topics such as big data, climate change or investment protection demand new answers also with regard to the legitimation of international law.

The book is the result of a multilateral exercise in the sense that it lives off of the exchange between scholars from various countries which brings together different legal traditions and different intellectual approaches to international law. It is also inter-generational in the sense that it brings together renowned and experienced scholars as well as younger researchers. It is multilingual in the sense that three languages can be used, English, French, and German while the contributions are written either in English or French. Such is the spirit of the French-German colloquium taking place every other year within the framework of sister societies, the German Society for International Law and the French Society for International Law.

This book would not have been possible without the generous support of many institutions and persons. We thank the German Research Fund and the Université Franco-Allemande/Deutsch-französische Hochschule for supporting a German-French forum in which we had an intense discussion on drafts of the contributions, and the Politische Akademie in Tutzing, which hosted parts of the participants under difficult conditions created by the COVID-19 pandemic. LMU Munich and the Universität der Bundeswehr organized the forum consisting of two hybrid manifestations, a workshop for younger researchers and the biennial colloquium of the German and French Societies of International Law, with the support of the IREDIES (Université Paris 1 Panthéon-Sorbonne, Sorbonne Law School). We are very grateful to the organizational and technical support of Cathrine Crämer (LMU Munich) and David Schmidt (Universität der Bundeswehr Munich) both during the conference in Tutzing and when preparing the publication of the book. We are also indebted towards Catherine Botoko and Paul Heckler (IREDIES) for their support during the editing process, as well as towards Cornelia Schäffer (Universität der Bundeswehr München) for the preparation of the index.

We are currently living through truly dire days. It is, nevertheless, our sincere hope that the contributions to this book open new paths for creative thinking on the role and relevance of international law. Such perspectives are urgently needed in order to renew and strengthen the fundamental values enshrined in the UN Charter, which are peace, humanity and respect for the rule of law.

Daniel-Erasmus Khan *Evelyne Lagrange*
Stefan Oeter *Christian Walter*
Munich, Hamburg and Paris, 9 March 2022

Notes on Contributors

Markus P. Beham
is Assistant Professor at the Chair of constitutional and administrative law, public international law, European and international economic law at the University of Passau, Germany.

Christina Binder
is Professor of international law and international human rights law at the Universität der Bundeswehr Munich, Germany.

Laurence Burgorgue-Larsen
is Professor of public and comparative law at the Université Paris 1 Panthéon-Sorbonne, France and former Judge at the Constitutional Court of Andorra.

Emanuel Castellarin
is Professor of public law at the Université of Strasbourg, France.

Shehrazade El-Hajjar
is Ph.D. Candidate in public law at the Université Paris 2 Panthéon-Assas as well as Lecturer and Researcher in constitutional law, administrative law and international law at the Saint Joseph University of Beirut, Lebanon.

Kevin Grimmeiß
is Lecturer in European investment law at the University of Würzburg, Germany, and deputy head of unit at the Bavarian State Ministry of Health Care and Care, Germany.

Daniel-Erasmus Khan
is Professor of public law, public international law and European Law at the Universität der Bundeswehr Munich, Germany

Lando Kirchmair
is Deputy Professor for national and international public law with a focus on the protection of cultural heritage at the Universität der Bundeswehr Munich, Germany.

Yannick Mihnzou Kouassi
is Ph.D. Candidate in international law at the University of Strasbourg, France.

Evelyne Lagrange
is Professor of public international law at the Université Paris 1 Panthéon-Sorbonne, France.

Júlia Miklasová
is Postdoctoral Researcher at the University of Cologne, Germany.

Angelika Nußberger
is Professor of constitutional law, public international law and comparative constitutional law at the University of Cologne, Germany, and former Vice-President at the European Court of Human Rights, Strasbourg, France.

Stefan Oeter
is Professor of public law, public international law and foreign public law at the University of Hamburg, Germany.

Christian Pippan
is Assistant Professor of public international law and international relations at the University of Graz, Austria.

Ioannis Prezas
is Lawyer at the European Court of Human Rights (Strasbourg) and Associate Professor (Maître de conférences HDR) in public law at the Université Paris 1 Panthéon-Sorbonne, France (on leave).

Stephanie Schiedermair
is Professor of European law, public international law and public law at Leipzig University, Germany.

Christian Tomuschat
is Professor emeritus of public law, public international law and European law at Humboldt Universität zu Berlin, Germany.

Robert Uerpmann-Wittzack
is Professor of public and international law at the University of Regensburg, Germany.

Edith Vanspranghe
is Lecturer in public law at Aix-Marseille University, France.

Daniel Ventura
is Assistant Professor (Maître de conférences) of public law at the Université Côte d'Azur, France.

Christian Walter
is Professor of public international law and public law at Ludwig-Maximilians-Universität Munich, Germany.

CHAPTER 1

Democracy – Fundamental Building-Block of the International Order?

Stefan Oeter

1 Introduction: Democratic Governance in International Law – Perils and Pitfalls

Democracy has always been a contested concept, since the idea had come into existence in ancient Greece.[1] For ages, philosophers and political theorists tended to treat the concept with care, if not suspicion.[2] This started to change with enlightenment philosophy and the liberal constitutionalism movement of early 19th century, when the call for democratic governance became a slogan of 'progressive' forces.[3] After World War I, these forces seemed to have won the battle. Democratic constitutionalism had become the dominant paradigm.[4] In reality, democratic governance still was far from constituting the universal mode of political rule throughout the world. Colonialism was far from accepting that government should be based on the consent of the governed, and also Europe experienced strong backlashes in the inter-war period, where democratic constitutions were supplanted by new modes of authoritarian

1 See on the origins in ancient Greece the contributions in KA Raaflaub, J Ober and RW Wallace (eds.), *Origins of Democracy in Ancient Greece* (Univ. of California Press 2007) and J Ober, *The Athenian Revolution: Essays on Ancient Greek Democracy and Political Theory* (Princeton Univ. Press 1996).

2 See R Tuck, *The Sleeping Sovereign: The Invention of Modern Democracy* (CUP 2016) 1–62, 63–120.

3 See JT Kloppenberg, *Toward Democracy: The Struggle for Self-Rule in European and American Thought* (OUP 2016) 191–259, 252–408; see also the contributions of H Maier, 'Demokratie – V. die Demokratie als Indikator geschichtlicher Bewegung (19. Jahrhundert)' and W Conze, 'Demokratie – VI. Die 'Demokratie' in der modernen Bewegung' in O Brunner, W Conze and R Koselleck (eds), *Geschichtliche Grundbegriffe*, Vol. 1 (Klett-Cotta 1972), 861–873 and 873–895.

4 See S Oeter, 'Right to Self-Determination and the Creation of New States' in Société Française pour le Droit International (ed), *Le Traité de Versailles: Regards Franco-Allemands en Droit International à l'Occasion du Centenaire. 11ème Journées franco-allemandes* (Pedone 2020) 173–193.

 | DOI:10.1163/9789004508712_002

rule, culminating in fascism and nazism.[5] The 'new world order' of the United Nations was largely perceived as the final breakthrough for the paradigm of people's sovereignty.[6] It took some time until decolonization had ended the structures of foreign rule, and it remained contested what should be understood as the adequate meaning of democracy – 'people's democracy' based on 'democratic centralism' under the leadership of the 'vanguard of the people', or 'liberal democracy' based on representative government, separation of powers and rule of law.[7] The international order of the cold war period had to organize the coexistence of these competing concepts of democracy.

The demise of communist ideology and the end of the Soviet empire was generally construed, at least in the West, as the end of such ideological cleavage on the 'true meaning' of democracy.[8] A consensus had emerged – it seemed – that democracy could be seriously realized only in the forms of western 'liberal constitutionalism'. One state after the other freed from communist dictatorship gave itself a modern constitution according to the Western model, even Russia with its strong Soviet legacy, not to speak of many states of the 'Third World' that previously had tended to align with the Soviet block. Liberal democracy – thus was the impression – had finally gained and had become the only game in town. The famous 'end of history' slogan coined by Francis Fukuyama[9] was based on such understanding. International law did not remain untouched by that mood of victory of liberal democracy. The early 1990's saw a rising tide of writings in international law putting the principle of democracy at the center-stage of international legal requirements for the legitimacy of statehood and political authority.[10] The rights of political participation enshrined in the International Covenant of Civil and Political Rights gave a good anchor-point for such claims. The Covenant, ratified by a huge number of states across continents and political camps, seemed to express a growing consensus of founding blocks of democratic governance – and with the perceived victory of liberal democracy the trend seemed to go towards developing a shared understanding of what these requirements of political participation

5 See J-W Müller, *Contesting Democracy: Political Ideas in Twentieth-Century Europe* (Yale Univ. Press 2011) 49–90 and 91–124.

6 See M Mazower, *No Enchanted Palace: The End of Empire and the Ideological Origins of the United Nations* (Princeton Univ. Press 2009).

7 See J-W Müller, *Contesting Democracy: Political Ideas in Twentieth-Century Europe* (Yale Univ. Press 2011) 125–170.

8 See JC Goldfarb, *After the Fall: The Pursuit of Democracy in Central Europe* (Basic Books 1992).

9 F Fukuyama, *The End of History and the Last Man* (Penguin Books 1992).

10 See the genealogies of the democracy discourse of the 1990s given by F Ehm, *Das völkerrechtliche Demokratiegebot* (Mohr Siebeck 2013), 11–14.

should mean. The (extremely influential) article published in 1992 by Thomas Franck on the 'emerging right to democratic governance' expressed such understanding in a very refined form.[11] The article served as starting-point for a series of scholarly pieces in international legal academia on democracy as a (collective and individual) right and on the repercussions this 'right to democratic governance' might have for the international legal order and the details of international law.[12]

One might question why we took up that debate from the 1990s and made it the topic of the 2020 joint conference of the German and French societies of international law. A novel reading of the mentioned works from the 1990s shows us that our view on the topic has changed considerably.[13] There is a strong disillusionment with the 'right to democratic governance' discourse – we do not share any more the overwhelming optimism that liberal democracy had become a model without alternative, with a shared 'meaning-in-use' on

---

11 TM Franck, 'The Emerging Right to Democratic Governance' (1992) 86 *AJIL* 46–91.

12 See e.g. J Crawford, *Democracy in International Law* (CUP 1994); JA Frowein, 'Demokratie und Völkerrecht in Europa' in K Ginther et al. (eds), *Völkerrecht zwischen normativem Anspruch und politischer Realität – Festschrift für Karl Zemanek zum 65 Geburtstag* (Duncker & Humblot 1994), 365–375; CM Cerna, 'Universal Democracy: An International Legal Right or the Pipe Dream of the West?' (1995) 27 (2) NJIL 289–330; GH Fox and G Nolte, 'Intolerant Democracies' (1995) 36 (1) HILJ 1–70; AF Bayefsky, 'Democracy and the International Protection of Human Rights' (1996) 26 *Israel Yb. on Human Rights* 183–199; B Boutros-Ghali, 'Pour un droit international de la démocratie' in J Makarczyk (ed), *Theory of International Law at the Threshold of the 21st Century. Essays in Honour of Krzysztof Skubiszewski* (Kluwer 1996) 99–108; R Ezetah, 'The Right to Democracy' (1997) 22 (3) BJIL 495–534; H Köchler, *Neue Wege der Demokratie: Demokratie im globalen Spannungsfeld von Machtpolitik und Rechtsstaatlichkeit* (Springer 1998); B Bauer, *Der völkerrechtliche Anspruch auf Demokratie – zur Rolle internationaler Organisationen im weltweiten Demokratisierungsprozeß* (Lang 1998); A-M Slaughter, 'Building Global Democracy' (2000) 1 (2) CJIL 223–230; GH Fox and BR Roth (eds), *Democratic Governance and International Law* (CUP 2000); R Rich, 'Bringing Democracy into International Law' (2001) 12 (3) *Journal of Democracy* 20–34; GH Fox and BR Roth, 'Democracy and International Law' (2001) 27 RIS 327–352; S Wheatley, 'Democracy in International Law: A European Perspective' (2002) 51 (2) *ICLQ* 225–247; F Müller, *Demokratie zwischen Staatsrecht und Weltrecht* (Duncker & Humblot 2003); J Wouters, B De Meester and C Ryngaert, 'Democracy and International Law' (2003) 34 NYIL 137–198; J Ibegbu, *Right to Democracy in International Law* (Edwin Mellen Press 2003); J Kokott, 'Souveräne Gleichheit und Demokratie im Völkerrecht' (2004) 44 *ZaöRV* 517, 525–532; S Wheatley, *Democracy, Minorities and International Law* (CUP 2005), 127–150; T Bruha and K Alsen, 'Democracy and International Law. Reflections on Current Trends and Challenges' in G Gornig (ed), *Justitia et Pax. Gedächtnisschrift für Dieter Blumenwitz* (Duncker & Humblot 2008), 555–575; R Buchan, 'Developing Democracy through Liberal Informational Law' (2015) 4 (2) CJICL 319–343.

13 See S Marks, 'International Legal Encounters with Democracy' (2017) 8 (Issue 56) *Global Policy* 34–43.

what this would mean for the international order.[14] Democracy is again a contested concept – not only regarding its meaning, but also as far as its usefulness as a concept for international and constitutional law at all is concerned. Is there really a universal consensus that states should be organized along democratic principles? Phrasing the question in such a way immediately leads to a negative answer. The fierce dispute on how to assess normatively the notorious 'colour revolutions' is only an indicator of the fundamental dissent in the international community.[15] The principle of democratic governance has even become very much contested inside western liberal democracies – the rise of populist movements oriented towards identitarian 'illiberal democracy' in Europe and the surge of Trumpism in the United States, as an expression of a deep polarization in American society, deliver striking examples for such contestation.[16] Even in Western societies we do not have a clear consensus any more on what democracy really means and how it might make sense in future.

Viewed from that angle, it makes a lot of sense to review the old debates and to revisit what meaning a principle of democracy might have for current international law. The following essay should be understood as an introductory reflection starting our common endeavor to revisit the meaning and relevance of democracy for current discourses on international law. The presentation of my reflections has two major parts:

1) Post-Cold War international law and the rise of the 'emerging right to democratic governance': What were the theoretical foundations of the proclaimed 'democratic bias' in international law and what implications could be deduced from that paradigm in international law? Particular emphasis will be put here on (a) criteria for legitimacy of governments; (b) the concept of 'Democratic Peace'; (c) the requirements of 'good governance' in development aid; (d) issues of 'state-building and the promotion of transition to democracy.
2) Perils and pitfalls of a norm on democratic governance.

In a preliminary section, I will begin my reflections on the continuing relevance of the democratic governance discourse in international law with the question: Why should we deal (again) with the issue of democratic governance in international law? After the fall of the 'iron curtain', there was a significant

14 See, for example, A Magen, 'The Democratic Entitlement in an Era of Democratic Recession' (2015) 4 (2) CJICL 368–387.

15 See only S Stewart, *Democracy Promotion and the 'Colour Revolutions'* (Routledge 2012) and D Ó Beacháin and A Polese (eds), *The Colour Revolutions in the Former Soviet Republics: Successes and Failures* (Routledge 2010).

16 See A Schäfer and M Zürn, *Die demokratische Regression* (Suhrkamp 2021).

degree of euphoria in the air. The introductory remarks mentioned already the influential slogan of the 'end of history' (Fukuyama). The political model of liberal democracy seemed to have overcome all its competitors, no serious alternative was in sight any more.

The ensuing discussion on an 'emerging right to democratic governance' that came up as a result of Tom Franck's influential AJIL article from 1992 must be understood in light of that background. With no serious alternative model of political order in sight, people's sovereignty and the according legitimation of power by democratic elections seemed to be the only game in town that was still viable. "Increasingly, governments recognize that their legitimacy depends on meeting a normative expectation of the community of states" – democratic legitimacy.[17] Democratic elections, however, can only guarantee legitimacy if such elections are free and fair, so most scholars thought.[18] As a result, there seemed to have happened a change of 'shared meaning' in the international community. A formal guarantee of voting rights and a minimum of political participation had been listed in the provisions of the ICCPR from the beginning – but now this guarantee seemed to make sense and was perceived as being consented all over the world.[19] The existing right to regular and fair elections was seen as laying the ground for the proclaimed 'right to democratic governance'.

In the following years state practice concerning the safeguard of democratic elections and the way how to deal with 'undemocratic' coup governments was undergoing a visible change.[20] As a hallmark of such change one could see the reaction of the international community to the coup d'état in Haiti in 1991.[21] The world – governments as well as the global public – condemned the coup nearly unanimously and called for a return to democratic governance, insisting on handing power back to the elected President Aristide. The UN Security Council was taking measures under Chapter 7 pressuring the military junta in Port-au-Prince to restore democratic rule, which finally succeeded.[22] State

---

17 TM Franck, 'The Emerging Right to Democratic Governance' (1992) 86 *AJIL* 46.

18 Id., at 63–77.

19 Id., 64–69; see also GH Fox, 'The Right to Political Participation in International Law' (1992) 17 (2) *YJIL* 539–607.

20 See e.g. SD Murphy, 'Democratic Legitimacy and the Recognition of States and Governments' in GH Fox and BR Roth (eds), *Democratic Governance and International Law* (CUP 2000), 123–154.

21 This is also used by Tom Franck as a decisive argument – see TM Franck, 'The Emerging Right to Democratic Governance' (1992) 86 *AJIL* 46, 72–74.

22 See JR Ballard, *Upholding Democracy: The United States Military Campaign in Haiti, 1994–1997* (Praeger 1998) and RJ Perusse, *Haitian Democracy Restored: 1991–1995* (Univ. Press of America 1995).

practice, it thus seemed, was firm in its insistence on democratic legitimation of government and the integrity of the democratic process.[23]

In his seminal article, Tom Franck identified three foundations of the (now consolidating) right to democratic governance: internal self-determination, freedom of expression, and the right to elections and political participation.[24] The first was a new paradigm in the doctrine of self-determination, fusing the principle of people's sovereignty with the idea of self-determination and thus decoupling it from formation of a new state, instead insisting on inclusive modes of participatory models of governance giving each segment of the population a saying in political decision-making.[25] The second pillar, freedom of expression, constitutes one of the traditional freedoms essential for a liberal concept of a free society – a freedom that gained new significance as a guarantor of open public discourse constituting a pluralist society.[26] The third pillar, as a crowning piece, institutionalized the demands for participation of the people in government, via free and fair elections.[27]

The subsequent discourse on democratic governance as a structural requirement under international law had interesting – and quite different – phases:

- Tom Franck's 1992 article first started a very lively discussion throughout the 1990s, leading to a large body of literature on the 'emerging right to democratic governance'.[28]
- During the 2000s, an additional paradigm gained prominence that complemented the existing discourse on democratic governance – the concept of 'democratic peace'.[29] The underlying idea rested on the assumption that democratic regimes are the only type of government that does not lead war

23 See TM Franck, 'The Emerging Right to Democratic Governance' (1992) 86 *AJIL* 46, 76–79.

24 Id., at 52–60, 61–63, 63–77.

25 This is the core idea of the new concept of 'internal self-determination' coming up in these years – see A Eide, 'In Search of Constructive Alternatives to Secession' in C Tomuschat (ed), *Modern Law of Self-Determination* (Nijhoff 1993) 139–176, and A Rosas, 'Internal Self-Determination' in C Tomuschat (ed), *Modern Law of Self-Determination* (Nijhoff 1993) 225–252; see in addition K Senaratne, 'Internal Self-Determination in International Law: A Critical Third-World Perspective' (2013) 3/2 Asian JIL 305–339.

26 TM Franck, 'The Emerging Right to Democratic Governance' (1992) 86 *AJIL* 46, 61–63.

27 See in particular GH Fox, 'The Right to Political Participation in International Law' (1992) 17 (2) *YJIL* 539–607.

28 See the references above in n. 12.

29 See, e.g., B Russett, *Grasping the Democratic Peace: Principles for a Post-Cold War World* (Princeton Univ. Press 1993); WM Reisman, 'Humanitarian Intervention and Fledgling Democracies' (1995) 18 ILJ 794, 796–805; JM Owen IV, *Liberal Peace, Liberal War: American Politics and International Security* (Cornell Univ. Press 1997); JN Moore, 'Beyond the Democratic Peace: Solving the War Puzzle' (2004) 44 (2) VJIL 341–429.

against each other.[30] As a result, in order to create a peaceful world, modes of governance should be transformed to democracy. Only in a world of democracies would peace be secured, with the resulting drive that the spreading of democratic governance would be the primary recipe to secure peace.[31] The endeavors at regime change in Afghanistan and Iraq were argued in that sense, as well as the support for 'colour revolutions' in Serbia, Georgia and Ukraine.

- The following developments were not supporting the assumptions of 'democratic peace' and its missionary drive towards spreading democracy. In particular the development in Iraq after the 2003 invasion led to growing disillusionment – the drafting of a modern constitution incorporating all the attributes of Western democracy did not solve the problem, with Iraq becoming a fragmented state under the grip of sectarian militias (most of them financed and controlled by Iran).[32] The 'Arab spring' and its catastrophic aftermath corroborated the suspicions that democratic constitutions following the Western model might not be the perfect solution leading to peace and viable modes of governance.[33]
- Some efforts at revisiting the drive towards democratic governance were undertaken roughly twenty years after the euphoric beginnings of Tom Franck's 1992 article. In 2011–2014 some prominent authors – like Susan Marks,[34]

---

30 This narrative is argued already by Tom Franck in his 1992 article – TM Franck, 'The Emerging Right to Democratic Governance' (1992) 86 *AJIL* 46, 88; the controversial character of the 'democratic peace hypothesis' is revisited in ME Brown, SM Lynn-Jones and SE Miller (eds), *Debating the Democratic Peace* (MIT Press 1996).

31 In a radicalized logic, this leads to the justification of forcible 'regime change' – see, as a skeptical voice, WM Reisman, 'Why Regime Change is (Almost Always) a Bad Idea' (2004) 98 *AJIL* 516–525.

32 See, For example, J Stieb, *The Regime Change Consensus. Iraq in American Politics, 1990–2003* (CUP 2021); K Rittich, 'Occupied Iraq – Imperial Convergences?' (2018) 31 (3) LJIL 479–508; D O'Driscoll and D van Zoonen, 'The Future of Iraq – Is Reintegration Possible?' (2017) 24 (3) *Middle East Policy* 34–47; S Al-Kli, 'The On-Again, Off-Again State-Building Cycles in Iraq' (2015) 39 (2) *The Fletcher Forum of World Affairs* 133–148; S Power, 'The 2003–2004 Occupation of Iraq: Between Social Transformation and Transformative Belligerent Occupation' (2014) 19 (2) JCSL 341–380.

33 See, e.g., N Sultany, *Law and Revolution. Legitimacy and Constitutionalism after the Arab Spring* (OUP 2020); I Salamey, *The Decline of Nation-States after the Arab Spring* (Routledge 2017); R Grote, T Röder and AM El-Haj (eds), *Constitutionalism, Human Rights, and Islam after the Arab Spring* (OUP 2016); Z Akhtar, 'Arab Spring, Ancien Regimes and the Social Contract' (2013/2015) 18 *Yearbook of Islamic and Middle Eastern Law* 18–43.

34 S Marks, 'What has Become of the Emerging Right to Democratic Governance?' (2011) 22 (2) *EJIL* 507–524.

Jean d'Aspremont,[35] Jure Vidmar[36] and Hillary Charlesworth[37] – took up the issue again and revisited the question whether the imposition of criteria of democratic governance had contributed to a better world – an evaluation grounded in a huge dose of skepticism.

- In the years since 2015, there is not a complete silence on the topic. The limited amount of literature dealing with the 'democratic entitlement' in international law, however, remains grounded in the skepticism that has dominated the discussion since 2010.[38] The major debate on issues of democracy now takes place in political science and is focused on the endangerment of liberal democracy by populism and tendencies towards authoritarianism.[39]

The current debate on the endangerment of democracy shows a growing perception that democratic governance is now threatened even from the inside in liberal western democracies. A number of studies demonstrate that there is a growing rift between political and intellectual elites, on the one hand, and ordinary people on the other hand – a rift exploited by different strands of populists operating with the slogan "we are the people".[40] The populist narrative plays with the old myth of traditional nationalism imagining 'the people' as a homogeneous and united *body politic* – a narrative that is deeply antipluralist.[41] Such a populist version of identitarian imagination often goes along with an exaggerated emphasis of majoritarianism – an understanding that

35 J d'Aspremont, 'The Rise and Fall of Democracy Governance in International Law: A Reply to Susan Marks' (2011) 22 (2) *EJIL* 549–570.

36 J Vidmar, 'Democracy and Regime Change in the Post-Cold War International Law' (2013) 11 (2) NZJPIL 349–380; see J Vidmar, *Democratic Statehood in International Law. The Emergence of New States in Post-Cold War Practice* (Hart 2013).

37 H Charlesworth, 'Democracy and International Law' in *Hague Academy of International Law: Recueil des Cours* 371 (2014) 43–162; see also H Charlesworth, 'International Legal Encounters with Democracy' (2017) 8 (Issue 56) *Global Policy* 34–43.

38 See T Landman, *Human Rights and Democracy – The Precarious Triumph of Ideals* (Bloomsbury Academic 2013); C Marxsen, 'The Promise of Global Democracy: The International Impact of Civil Society' (2015) 47 (4) NYU JILP 719–782; D Thürer, 'Demokratie und Rule of Law im internationalen, staatlichen und transnationalen Recht' (2016) 26 (1) SRIEL 71–89; KA Alfadhel, *The Right to Democracy in International Law. Between Procedure, Substance and the Philosophy of John Rawls* (Routledge 2017); H Charlesworth, 'Democracy' in J. d'Aspremont (ed), *Concepts for International Law* (Edward Elgar 2019), 164–178.

39 See A Schäfer and M Zürn, *Die demokratische Regression* (Suhrkamp 2021).

40 See J-W Müller, *What is Populism?* (Penguin Books 2017).

41 See J-W Müller, *Democracy Rules* (Allen Lane 2021).

tends to construe democracy as a 'dictatorship of the majority' negating any legitimate right of minorities to live their difference.[42]

Such an understanding of democratic governance runs counter to the insights of modern political theory. Majority decisions are nothing more than a pragmatic arrangement to enable effective collective decision-making – an arrangement that is, in a contractarian perspective, acceptable only if basic interests of minorities are safeguarded by constitutional arrangements limiting the ability of majorities to impose their will on the whole of society.[43]

Accordingly, there is a need for a consensus of a higher order fixing the rules of the game – thus the importance of checks and balances, of counter-majoritarian institutions, of deeply entrenched arrangements securing the rule of law, an independent judiciary, a free civil society with a pluralist media system, and an enshrined set of fundamental rights and freedoms.[44]

Such an enriched understanding of democratic governance is very ambitious in institutional terms – and it is a construct severely challenged by populists of all kinds.[45] It may be perceived as an elitist and technocratic system that keeps the preferences of the people at bay and gives elites control of the system – but any other understanding of democracy, in particular if departing from an idea of a homogeneous people being able to express its will beyond representative institutions, risks nurturing authoritarian tendencies with a drive towards models of 'illiberal democracy'.[46]

---

42 See J Ober, *Demopolis: Democracy before Liberalism in Theory and Practice* (CUP 2017) 157–175.

43 See only – with impressive clarity on that point – JP Müller, *Demokratische Gerechtigkeit: eine Studie zur Legitimität politischer und rechtlicher Ordnung* (Deutscher Taschenbuch Verlag dtv 1993) 20–38.

44 See W Sadurski, 'Majority Rule, Democracy and Populism: Theoretical Considerations' in G Amato, B Barbisan and C Pinelli (eds), *Rule of Law vs Majoritarian Democracy* (Hart 2021), 189–198; M Bovens and T Schillemans, 'Non-Majoritarian Institutions and Representation' in R Rohrschneider and J Thomassen (eds), *The Oxford Handbook of Political Representation in Liberal Democracies* (OUP 2020) 511–525; C Saunders, 'Theoretical Underpinnings of Separation of Powers' in G Jacobsohn and M Schor (eds), *Comparative Constitutional Theory* (Edward Elgar 2018) 66–85; G Frankenberg, 'Democracy' in M Rosenfeld and A Sajó (eds), *The Oxford Handbook of Comparative Constitutional Law* (OUP 2012) 250, 257–258.

45 See also D Acemoglu and JA Robinson, *The Narrow Corridor – States, Societies, and the Fate of Liberty* (Penguin Random House 2020).

46 See J-W Müller, '«Illiberale Demokratie«?' in S Randeria (ed), *Rückkehr der illiberalen Demokratie?* (Verlag Neue Kritik 2016) 9–19.

2 Democratic Governance in Post-Cold War International Law

The paradigm shift that happened in the early 1990s is a remarkable development in itself. Seen from the background of a traditional understanding of sovereignty, with a marked neutrality of international law towards issues of internal organization of states,[47] the paradigm change of the early 1990s was nearly revolutionary.[48] The claim now made that international law has given up its neutrality towards issues of internal (constitutional) ordering, the 'fundamental right to choose and implement its own political, economic and social systems', was turning upside down the old understanding of an international law organizing coexistence of completely different ideological systems.

Tom Franck deduced his 'emerging right to democratic governance', in a very convincing assemblage of different bits and pieces from existing corner stones of positive international law. The main components of the construct were the following three key building blocks:

- The first, going back to the interwar period, was the principle of self-determination.[49] On his account, self-determination "postulates the right of a people organized in an established territory to determine its collective political destiny in a democratic fashion".[50] The idea of self-determination – he writes – "has evolved into a more general notion of internationally validated political consultation, one that is beginning to be applied even to independent (postcolonial) states".[51]
- The second, originating in the "antitotalitarianism born of World War II", was the right to free political expression. Protected through a multiplicity of international and regional regimes, rights to freedom of expression, assembly, and opinion constitute "the essential preconditions for an open electoral process".[52]
- The third, and newest, building block was the emerging entitlement to periodic elections which are free and fair. As Tom Franck explained, with a "substantial new majority of states [now] actually practicing a reasonably credible version of electoral democracy", stipulations in human rights treaties for a

---

47 As a paradigmatic understanding in that regard see E McWhinney, *"Peaceful Coexistence" and Soviet-Western International Law* (Sythoff 1964).

48 See GH Fox and BR Roth, 'Democracy and International Law' (2001) 27 RIS 327, 330–335.

49 TM Franck, 'The Emerging Right to Democratic Governance' (1992) 86 *AJIL* 46, 52–60.

50 Id., at 52.

51 Id., at 55; see also, however, concerning the antinomies of self-determination (at least in its traditional modes) and democracy RA Miller, 'Self-Determination in International Law and the Demise of Democracy' (2003) 41 (3) CJTL 601–648.

52 TM Franck, 'The Emerging Right to Democratic Governance' (1992) 86 *AJIL* 46, 61.

right to genuine periodic elections begin "to approximate prevailing practice and thus may be said to be stating what is becoming a customary legal norm applicable to all".[53]

These three components are – as Tom Franck saw it "closely interwoven strands of a single fabric. These three generations of democratic entitlement, reinforced by regional systems, not only share many of the same or similar norms, but also have developed common or comparable kinds of institutions, procedures and customs."[54] Tom Franck well recognized that democracy is not synonymous with elections, but his analysis placed considerable emphasis on this third and newest building block as the capstone of the edifice, and the latter part of his discussion was given over to the question of how to implement and enforce the democratic entitlement conceived as a right to free and fair elections.[55] He was impressed with the election-monitoring activities and institutions which had burgeoned in the early 1990s and deduced from that practice a universal pull towards an 'emerging' customary rule. "The entitlement to democracy in international law has gone through both a normative and a customary evolution. It has evolved both as a system of rules and in the practice of states and organizations. This evolution has occurred in three phases. First came the normative entitlement to self-determination. Then came the normative entitlement to free expression as a human right. Now we see the emergence of a normative entitlement to a participatory electoral process. The democratic entitlement, despite its newness, already enjoys a high degree of legitimacy, derived both from various texts and from the practice of global and regional organizations, supplemented by that of a significant number of non-governmental organizations."[56]

The number of such international documents expressing the idea of a democratic entitlement in international law is impressive. Greg Fox in his Max Planck Encyclopedia entry on the 'Right to Democracy' and its international protection[57] lists a long sequence of international legal documents, mostly from the 1990s and early 2000s:

- The Conference on Security and Cooperation in Europe ('CSCE') constitutes the institutional context in which the issue of democracy first came up as a prominent concern, immediately after the fall of the iron curtain.

53 Id., at 64.
54 Id., at 77.
55 Id., at 77–87.
56 Id., at 90.
57 GH Fox, 'Democracy, Right to, International Protection' in R. Wolfrum (ed), Max Planck Encyclopedia of Public International Law (OUP online ed. 2008).

In its 'Document of the Moscow Meeting of the Conference on the Human Dimension of the CSCE' from 3 October 1991, the member states "emphasize[d] that issues relating to human rights, fundamental freedoms, democracy and the rule of law are of international concern, as respect for these rights and freedoms constitutes one of the foundations of the international order".[58]

- In the framework of the United Nations, it took a bit longer until the issue gained some salience. The 'UN World Conference on Human Rights' of 1993 stated in its 'Vienna Declaration and Programme of Action' that "the international community should support the strengthening and promoting of democracy, development and respect for human rights and fundamental freedoms in the entire world".[59] The UN General Assembly can even be seen as a precursor to such insistence on democratic standards, if one takes for example the prominent 1990 resolution on 'Enhancing the effectiveness of the principle of periodic and genuine elections'.[60] The UN Commission on Human Rights continued with a series of resolutions adopted between 1999 and 2005, dealing with the importance of democracy.[61] Only the first of these resolutions speaks explicitly of a 'right' to democracy, although only in its title, whereas the operative text makes no mention of such right.
- The UN Secretary-General started roughly at the same time with mentioning democracy as an important structural principle in international order in his yearly reports on the work of the organization, submitted to the UN General Assembly.[62] The move towards promoting democracy had begun with the famous 1996 'Agenda for Democratization' of Secretary-General Boutros Boutros-Ghali.[63] Particularly interesting for the aftermath is Kofi Annan's 2006 'Report on the Work of the Organization'[64] where the UNSG, while repeating the supportive language used in earlier versions of the same document, declared the 'substantial progress for democratic governance' in the previous decade symbolized 'important gains in human rights, freedom and choice' (at para. 125).

58 'Document of the Moscow Meeting of the Conference on the Human Dimension of the CSCE' [done 3 October 1991] [1991] 30 ILM 1670, at para. I 1.

59 UN World Conference on Human Rights' [25 June 1993], UN Doc A/CONF.157/23, para. 8.

60 UNGA res. 45/150 (1990).

61 Fox in MPEPIL (n. 57), at para. 4.

62 Id. At para. 5.

63 Supplement to Reports on Democratization, UN Doc. A/51/761, 20 Dec. 1996.

64 UNGA, 'Report of the Secretary-General on the Work of the Organization' [16 August 2006] GAOR 61st Session Supp. 1.

- Also regional organizations were dealing with the issue of democracy in these years. This is especially true for the Council of Europe. The European Court on Human Rights, in the Case of the *United Communist Party of Turkey v Turkey*, decided in 1998 ([ECtHR] Reports 1998-I 1), declared that "democracy is without doubt a fundamental feature of the European public order" (at para. 45).[65] Any attempt towards undertaking a comprehensive review of the Council of Europe's efforts at democracy promotion teaches us some degree of modesty, however. An analytical survey of 2004 concludes that in European practice "democracy is not a settled idea or set of institutions. Rather than conceive of democracy as one form of best practice, or even as an ideal type to which imperfect political systems strive, it is necessary to see democracy as a complex of values and principles which interact in different ways in various contexts".[66]
- The other regional context in which the idea of a right to democracy was intensely debated may be found in the Americas. The 'Inter-American Democratic Charter', adopted by the OAS in 2001, declared in its Art. 1 that "[t]he peoples of the Americas have a right to democracy and their governments have an obligation to promote and defend it".[67]
- There are also other important organizations that were prominently mentioning the concept of a 'democratic entitlement'. The issue was at a very early phase discussed in the framework of the Commonwealth. In its Harare Commonwealth Declaration of 20 October 1991, the organization proclaimed in para. 4 the "individual's inalienable right to participate by means of free and democratic political processes in framing the society in which he or she lives".[68] In a comparable mood, the Inter-Parliamentary Union described in Art. 1 of the 'Universal Declaration on Democracy of the Inter-Parliamentary Union' democracy expressly as "a basic right of citizenship".[69]

A careful analysis of all these documents conveys a twofold lesson. First, there was a heightened awareness that issues of democracy had become a very

65 ECtHR, *United Communist Party of Turkey v Turkey* [ECtHR] Reports 1998-I 1, para. 45.

66 See L Pratchett and V Lowndes, *Developing Democracy in Europe – An Analytical Summary of the Council of Europe's Acquis* (Council of Europe Publ. 2004) 13.

67 OAS Doc OEA/Ser.P/AG/RES. 1 (XXVIII-E/01).

68 Commonwealth Secretariat, Report of the Commonwealth Secretary-General 1993 [Commonwealth Secretariat London 1993] 104.

69 Inter-Parliamentary Union, Universal Declaration on Democracy (Inter-Parliamentary Union [IPU]), Part 1 The Principles of Democracy, Art.1.

prominent topic at the international law and that normative development might go, as argued by Tom Franck, in the direction of establishing a 'right to democratic governance'. However, the wording in these documents remained often quite careful – it oscillates between the semantics of a 'right' to democracy, on the one hand, and the expression of mere political aspirations, on the other hand. Obviously there did not exist a clear-cut consensus among international lawyers, in doctrine as well as in practice, on the underlying question, namely what the new bias in favor of democratic governance might mean in detail.[70]

One basic problem which was not really solved at the time – and which remains open until today – is the disagreement over what the term 'democracy' really means.[71] In essence, there are two competing schools of thought, a '*procedural view*', mostly focusing on elections, and a '*substantive view*' insisting that democracy means much more than simply holding elections, that in substance it builds upon a whole cluster of rights and safeguards of an open and free society.[72]

The other basic question that remained open in the 1990s was the concrete normative status of the 'democratic entitlement' in international law. Even Tom Franck was careful enough to speak of an 'emerging right' – and not an existing one.[73] A series of authors embraced the idea of such normative progress and looked for indicators that it was in the process of consolidation.[74] Others remained skeptical – the claim of the existence of such a 'right' in positive international law was put into doubt by a number of prominent international lawyers, also in view of the significant divergence in acceptance of

70 See, for example, R Ezetah, 'The Right to Democracy: A Qualitative Inquiry' (1997) 22 Brooklyn JIL 495–534.

71 See Fox in MPEPIL (n. 57), at para. 3; see also J Dunn, 'Democracy, Globalization and Human Interests' (1998) 63 (3) *Il Politico* 353, 358–368.

72 See more in detail G Fox in MPEPIL (n. 57), at paras. 8–13.

73 See Franck (1992) 86 AJIL 46, 90–91; see also GH Fox and BR Roth, 'Democracy and International Law' (2001) 27 RIS 327, 337–338.

74 See, for example, J Crawford, 'Democracy and the Body of International Law' in GH Fox and BR Roth (eds), *Democratic Governance and International Law* (CUP 2000), 91–121; R Rich, 'Bringing Democracy into International Law' (2001) 12 (3) Journal of Democracy 20–34; GH Fox and BR Roth, 'Democracy and International Law' (2001) 27 RIS 327–352; S Wheatley, 'Democracy in International Law: A European Perspective' (2002) 51 (2) *ICLQ* 225, 227–235; see also, with much more critical nuances, R Müllerson, 'On Absolute and relative Universality of the Concept of Democracy' (2008) 38 Israel Yearbook on Human Rights 227–249.

democracy as a binding prerequisite for legitimate statehood across different regions of the world.[75]

What most authors of that 'high phase' accepted, however, was the existence of a *normative pro-democracy bias* in international law. The series of international documents listed above, with its broad range of UN, CSCE, OAS and AU practice, seemed to make this point evident. The following sections will revisit some of the most important emanations of such a pro-democratic bias in international legal practice.

2.1 *Criteria for Legitimacy of Governments*

One of the most important consequences of the argued 'pro-democratic bias' in international law may be its translation into a legal standard of regime legitimacy. Since 1990, a certain degree of practice in international law has developed denying the legitimacy of governments lacking the necessary democratic credentials.[76] The most obvious case in that regard results from military coups and the question of qualification of the resulting coup governments, but also from other violent modes of overthrowing a democratically elected government. UN practice following such a line started with the Security Council resolutions concerning the cases of Haiti 1991 and Sierra Leone 1997.[77] In these two cases, the respective de facto governments were qualified as illegitimate and the Security Council demanded a return to democratic governance.[78] Such a practice can be easily argued in terms of a 'pro-democratic bias', at least in cases where the military coups have ousted democratically elected governments.

---

75 See in particular GJ Simpson, 'Imagined Consent: Democratic Liberalism in International Legal Theory' (1994) 15 Australian Yb. of Int'l. L. 103–128; S Marks, 'The End of History? Reflections on Some International Legal Theses' (1997) 8 (3) EJIL 449–477; S Marks, *The Riddle of All Constitutions. International Law, Democracy, and the Critique of Ideology* (OUP 2000), 30–99; JHH Weiler, 'The Geology of International Law – Governance, Democracy and Legitimacy' (2004) 64 ZaöRV 547–562; A Coleman and J Maogoto, 'Democracy's Global Quest: A Noble Crusade Wrapped in Dirty Reality?' (2004) 28 (2) Suffolk TLR 175–242; LM Friedman, 'Roads to Democracy' (2005) 33 (1) JILC 51–69; L Morlino and A Magen, 'Scope, Depth and Limits of External Influence: Conclusions'. in A Magen and L Morlino (eds), *International Actors, Democratization and the Rule of Law: Anchoring Democracy?* (Routledge 2009), 224–256.

76 See e.g. SD Murphy, 'Democratic Legitimacy and the Recognition of States and Governments' in GH Fox and BR Roth (eds), *Democratic Governance and International Law* (CUP 2000), 123–154.

77 See SD Murphy, 'Democratic Legitimacy and the Recognition of States and Governments' in GH Fox and BR Roth (eds), *Democratic Governance and International Law* (CUP 2000) 123, 146–150.

78 See DL Donoho, 'Evolution or Expediency: The United Nations Response to the Disruption of Democracy' (1996) 29 (2) Cornell ILJ 329–382.

Comparable issues are coming up regularly in the context of the credentials committee of the UN General Assembly.[79] Between 1991 and 1998, the General Assembly (resp. its Credentials Committee) refused to accredit the representatives of some governments that were in effective control of national territory, like in the cases of Haiti, Sierra Leone, Cambodia, Liberia and Afghanistan. At the same time, five governments were accredited although the government they were representing lacked effective territorial control.[80] Such practice continued after 2000, finding a widely reported point of culmination in the 2021 accreditation battles concerning the representatives of the new Taliban government in Afghanistan and of the Myanmar military junta.[81] The picture is rather blurred if one looks more in detail in the practice concerning accreditation – in some cases the admission is refused due to the lack of constitutional credentials, whereas in others states do not raise any problem with representatives mandated by evidently non-democratic governments. As Jean d'Aspremont has summarized it in his thorough study from 2005, the "democratic character of a government does not seem to have played a crucial role in any of the credentials controversies which have gripped the United Nations".[82]

Practice of individual states goes even further, comprises also cases where authoritarian regimes were disregarding the results of elections, were too openly forging elections (with subsequent societal contestation) or disregard entirely democratic arrangements agreed prior to elections. Although state practice has given up the traditional mode of formally recognizing governments, practice cannot evade the issue of qualifying whether certain governmental representatives are legitimized to represent a state.[83] This is most obvious in cases of civil war where competing 'governments' contend to act

79 Concerning the role of the Credentials Committee see J-F Flauss and P Singer, 'La verification des pouvoirs de l'Assemblée générale des Nations Unies' (1985) 31 Annuaire Français de Droit International 620–652.

80 See M Griffin, 'Accrediting Democracies: Does the Credentials Committee of the United Nations Promote Democracy through its Accreditation Process, and Should It?' (2000) 32 (3) NJIL 725–788.

81 As to the Afghanistan case see the blogpost of LD Johnson, 'Expert Backgrounder: How Can The Taliban Be Prevented From Representing Afghanistan In The United Nations?' (*Just Security*, 18 August 2021) <https://www.justsecurity.org/77806/expert-backgrounder-how-can-the-taliban-be-prevented-from-representing-afghanistan-in-the-united-nations/> accessed 28 November 2021.

82 See J d'Aspremont, 'Legitimacy of Governments in the Age of Democracy' (2005) 38 (4) NJIL 877–618, at 605.

83 See Stefan Talmon, 'Recognition of Governments: An Analysis of the New British Policy and Practice' (1992) 63 BYIL 231, 246, and Charlesworth (n. 37) RdC 371 (2014) 43, at 77.

on behalf of the state; but even in other cases where a change of government happened in blatant disregard of normal constitutional procedure, third states must inherently qualify whether they recognize the resultant government.[84] States tend to be very reluctant to recognize governments that came to power as a result of a violent coup, although such recognition might be awarded if the coup government promises to hold elections soon (and thus commit in principle to the idea of democratic legitimacy).[85] Whereas the mentioned recognition practice is more or less exclusively based on what Jean d'Aspremont has called 'legitimacy of origin', the ways and means how a government exercises power (what Jean d'Aspremont calls 'legitimacy of exercise') may also play a role in certain regards.[86] This is visible in particular in cases where non-democratic governments call for military assistance in quashing an insurgency (the 'intervention by invitation' constellation); here governments, such as e.g. the French, routinely reject such intervention when such regimes were responsible for massive violations of human rights.[87]

The practice of denying legitimacy of coup governments has gained particular prominence in the context of the African Union and its sub-regional organizations, such as ECOWAS. There is now a standing practice of condemning violent overthrows of constitutional governments (and of putting pressure on the resultant coup governments to return, as soon as possible, to the democratic process).[88] This position has become quite solidified in the last two decades, with some more nuanced stance in cases where the legitimacy of the previous 'democratic' government is doubtful and the organization of democratic elections is promised for a near future.

More broadly, as mentioned above, there are situations where a government may be denied legitimacy on an international plane, although it did not come to power in a coup or violent overthrow of constitutional structures, but is rather a well-established government of the state in question. It is argued by some authors that international legitimacy in such circumstances should be

84 See J d'Aspremont, 'Legitimacy of Governments in the Age of Democracy' (2005) 38 (4) NJIL 877, 601.

85 Id., at 606.

86 Id., at 606–609.

87 Id., at 608.

88 See SA Dersso, 'The Status and Legitimacy of Popular Uprisings in the AU Norms on Democracy and Constitutional Governance' (2019) 63 (S1-May) *Journal of African Law* 107–30, in particular 113–115; P Manirakiza, 'Towards a Right to Resist Gross Undemocratic Practices in Africa' (2019) 63 (S1-May) *Journal of African Law* 81–105; KN Obse and C Pippan, 'Collectively Protecting Constitutionalism and Democratic Governance in Africa: A Tale of High Hopes and Low Expectations?' (2015) 4 (2) CJICL 344–67.

denied on the basis of gross human rights violations and a grave humanitarian situation, rather than a lack of democratic (electoral) practices.[89] This rarely happens, however, at least outside the contexts of invitations for intervention – and if it happens, it appears that denial of governmental legitimacy is linked at least as much with a partial loss of effective control over the territory as with the blatant violations of human rights and democratic standards.

In order to summarize the view on recognition practice, one can observe that state practice seems, all in all, to be rather inconclusive. There are some trends and practices, in particular on the African continent, that might be interpreted as being motivated by a concept of 'democratic entitlement'. Such practice is far from systematic, however, and does not find a thesis of a generalized 'pro-democracy bias'.

2.2 *'Democratic Peace'*

Even more ambivalent is our current perspective on the claims towards 'democratic peace' – debate that had started gaining prominence in the late 1990s.[90] In the years around 2000 there had developed a vivid debate on the 'democratic peace' paradigm.[91] The major essence of this paradigm was the assumption that democratic states are by definition prone to preserve peace.[92] As a result, only democratic states are to be qualified as 'peace-loving' and can be trusted in terms of preservation of peace, with the resulting quest that further

89 See, for example, J Vidmar, 'Democracy and Regime Change in the Post-Cold War International Law' (2013) 11 (2) NZJPIL 349–380.

90 See only B Russett, *Grasping the Democratic Peace: Principles for a Post-Cold War World* (Princeton Univ. Press 1993); WM Reisman, 'Humanitarian Intervention and Fledgling Democracies' (1995) 18 Fordham ILJ 794, 796–805; J Meernik, 'United States Military Intervention and the Promotion of Democracy' (2016) 33 (4) Journal of Peace Research 391–402; JM Owen IV, *Liberal Peace, Liberal War: American Politics and International Security* (Cornell Univ. Press 1997).

91 See J McMillan, *On Liberal Peace: Democracy, War and the International* Order (Tauris 1998); K Nowrot and EM Schabacker, 'The Use of Force to Restore Democracy: International legal Implications of the ECOWAS Intervention in Sierra Leone' (1998) 14 (2) AUILR 321–412; S Avineri, 'Democracy and the Ability to Intervene Internationally' (1998) 26 Israel Yb. on Human Rights 117–124; JR Oneal and B Russett, 'The Kantean Peace – The Pacific Benefits of Democracy, Interdependence, and international Organizations', 1885–1992' (1999) 52 (1) World Politics 1–37; P Margulies, 'Making Regime Change Multilateral – The War on Terror and transitions to Democracy' (2004) 32 (3) DJILP 389–420.

92 See, as a critical contestation of that assumption, A Geis and H Müller, 'Investigating 'Democratic Wars' as the Flipside of 'Democratic Peace', in A Geis, H Müller and N Schornig (eds), *The Militant Face of Democracy: Liberal Forces for Good* (CUP 2013) 3–23.

regime change towards democratic governance might be a necessity if peace should be secured.[93]

Radical apologists of the paradigm thus were drawing far-reaching conclusions, arguing for armed intervention in the service of pro-democratic regime change.[94] Would it not make sense to make aggressive states 'ready for peace', if needed ' for regime change'? I would like to mention here only Fernando Tesón as one of the most outspoken adherents of such position.[95]

The 'democratic peace' claim with its inherent call for pro-democratic regime change was taken up by the Bush administration after 2001, arguing a right to build 'peace-loving', democratic regimes in countries like Afghanistan and Iraq after the military intervention. The disillusionment followed a bit later – Afghanistan and Iraq are definitely no success stories of making the world 'ripe for democracy'.[96]

Academic debate on the democratic peace concept accordingly turned to a quite skeptical tone.[97] Even mere attempts at 'democracy promotion', aiding

---

93 From the beginning there were also skeptical voices – see, for example, H Leurdijk, 'The Challenge of Intervention on Behalf of Democracy' in M Castermans-Holleman (ed), *The Role of the Nation-State in the 21st Century Essays in Honour of Peter Baehr* (Kluwer 1998), 327–346; K von Hippel, *Democracy by Force. US Military Intervention in the Post-Cold War World* (CUP 2001).

94 See, e.g., D Wippman, 'Defending Democracy Through Foreign Intervention' (1997) 19 (3) HJIL 659–687, but also – more recently – R Buchan, 'Developing Democracy through Liberal Informational Law' (2015) 4 (2) CJICL 319–343.

95 See FR Tesón, 'Kantian Theory of International Law' (1992) 92 (1) Columbia Law Review 92 et seq.; FR Tesón, 'Collective Humanitarian Intervention' (1996) 17 (2) MJIL 323–371; FR Tesón, *Humanitarian Intervention: An Inquiry into Law and Morality* (3rd edn, Transnational Publ. 2005); FR Tesón, 'Ending Tyranny in Iraq' (2005) 19 (2) Ethics & International Affairs 1–20.

96 See, as to the Iraqi experience, the sarcastic description by Charlesworth (n. 37) *RdC* 371 (2014) 43, at 120–123; see also MA Hill, *Democracy Promotion and Conflict-Based Reconstruction: The United States and Democratic Consolidation in Bosnia, Afghanistan and Iraq* (Routledge 2011); D Ghanim, *Iraq's Dysfunctional Democracy* (Praeger 2011); Z Al-Ali, *The Struggle for Iraq's Future: How Corruption, Incompetence and Sectarianism Have Undermined Democracy* (Yale Univ. Press 2014).

97 See A. Geis, L. Brock and H Müller (eds), *Democratic Wars – Looking at the Dark Side of Democratic Peace* (Palgrave Macmillan 2006); W. Merkel and S Grimm (eds.), *War and Democratization: Legality, Legitimacy and Effectiveness* (Routledge 2008); A Buchanan, *Human Rights, Legitimacy, and the Use of Force* (OUP 2010); J Kane, 'Democracy and World Peace: The Kantian Dilemma of United States Foreign Policy' (2012) 66 (3) AJIA 292–312; D Peksen (ed), *Liberal Interventionism and Democracy Promotion* (Lexington Books 2014); Charlesworth (n. 37) RdC 371 (2014) 43, at 88–92; AW Bausch, 'Democracy, War Effort, and the Systemic Democratic Peace' (2015) 52 (4) Journal of Peace Research 435–447; S Reid-Henry, *Empire of Democracy. The Remaking of the West since the Cold-War, 1971–2017* (Simon & Schuster 2019).

and assisting in developing democratic structures in transition states, was more and more perceived with negative undertones. Clearly there was a danger of intervention, with institutions financed and directed by foreign powers trying to change the internal constitutional set-up.[98] Prominent authors were resuming already around 2005 that things evidently were going badly wrong. There was a 'backlash against democracy promotion', with governments in Russia and elsewhere expelling or harassing foreign NGOs and prohibiting local groups from receiving foreign funds. Western democracy and rule of law assistance was being publicly denounced as 'illegitimate political meddling'.[99]

2.3 *State-Building and Democracy Promotion*

Comparable problems are observable in the context of state-building that is happening in the framework of post-conflict peace-building.[100] There is a logic in the drive towards the construction of democratic institutional arrangements in cases where authoritarian regimes have broken down or have been destroyed by foreign military intervention. When international organizations or outside states are called in to assist in the reconstruction of statehood, there is not that much alternative. Should outside assistance go towards reconstructing authoritarian forms of rule? Quite naturally, international organizations and foreign states involved in the task of state-building opt for blueprints of democratic governance. This is true for the United Nations – practically all major UN peace-building missions of the early years of the 21st century have included significant democracy-building components.[101] And this is also true for the involvement of major western states in exercises of post-conflict state-building.[102]

'Democracy-building' has become a popular international remedy for states that are emerging from conflict. It is typically presented as an antidote to the

---

98 See S Boysen, 'Remnants of a Constitutional Moment: The Right to Democracy in International Law' in A von arnauld and K von der Decken (eds.), *The Cambridge Handbook of New Human Rights: Recognition, Novelty, Rhetoric* (CUP 2020), 465–480, at 473–479; see in addition S Marks, 'International Law, Democracy, and the End of History' in GH Fox and BR Roth (eds.), *Democratic Governance and International Law* (CUP 2000), 532–566.

99 See T Carothers, 'The Rule-of-Law Revival' in T Carothers (ed), *Promoting the Rule of Law Abroad: In Search of Knowledge* (Carnegie Endowment for International Peace 2006), 3–13.

100 See Charlesworth (n. 37) RdC 371 (2014) 43, at 112–130.

101 Id., at 114; see also, more in detail, S Chesterman, *You, the People. The United Nations Transitional Administration, and Statebuilding* (OUP 2003), at 4.

102 See T Carothers, *Aiding Democracy Abroad: The Learning Curve* (Carnegie Endowment for International Peace 1999).

causes of conflict and its attainment is propagated as marking the end of the troubled period. As a result, since the late 1990s, there have been quite a number of cases where such 'pro-democratic' state-building in post-conflict societies has been practiced, usually under the supervision of the UN Security Council – to name only the cases of Timor-Leste, Kosovo, Afghanistan, and Iraq. The achievements of such practice of post-conflict democracy promotion are more than mixed. if not a story of wholesale failure. There is no room here for discussing these cases in detail, but some of the major problems are evident. In the words of Hilary Charlesworth: "Most democracy-promotion and democracy-building projects take place in the non-Western world under the supervision of Western states or Western-dominated institutions. When democratization is on the agenda, international organizations tend to translate democracy into a checklist of processes and institutions such as elections, political parties, human rights, rule of law, legislative and judicial institutions, and free markets. Similarly, conceptions of democracy advanced internationally tend to mimic the governance structures of the proposers. They are generally technical and procedural and lack understanding of local contexts."[103] In other words: International organizations and aid agencies involved in state-building and democracy promotion tend to take recourse to established institutional solutions that seem to have been successful, exporting blueprints of democratic processes and institutions that work as 'constitutional transplants' in the target countries.[104] Constitutional transplants, however, as we know from studies, usually work quite differently than intended in their new contexts and produce unintended (and often counter-productive) results. "Overall, the restricted ideas of democracy that have informed much democracy-building have curtailed its promise. The focus has been on quick exits and building institutions familiar to Western democracies, while ignoring local forms of accountability and participation. The effect has been to shore up existing dispensations of power and privilege."[105]

The same experience, although in a more moderate form, has been made with the broader endeavors of democracy promotion in transition countries.[106]

---

103 See Charlesworth (n. 37) RdC 371 (2014) 43, at 116.

104 See also JR Schmidt, 'Can Outsiders Bring Democracy to Post-Conflict States?' (2008) 52 (1) Orbis 107–122.

105 See Charlesworth (n. 37), at 130.

106 Concerning the conceptual issues of democracy promotion see C Hobson and M Kurki (eds), *The Conceptual Politics of Democracy Promotion* (Routledge 2012); see also R Müllerson, *Democracy, a Destiny of Mankind? A Qualified, Contingent and Contextual Case for Democracy Promotion* (Nova Science Publ. 2009).

There is a wide-spread practice of international organizations and donor countries of promoting reforms intended to develop and consolidate modes of democratic governance.[107] This has gained some salience in particular in a number of regional organizations, such as the Council of Europe, the African Union and the Organization of American States (OAS)[108] – but also the United Nations are involved in the endeavor to promote tools of democratic governance.[109] In addition, a broad range of aid agencies, foundations and NGOs from Western countries are engaged heavily in the business of democracy promotion.[110] The problems resemble very much the basic problem of democracy-building in post-conflict societies – international organizations and aid agencies tend to use 'ready-made' solutions from the institutional horizon and experience of liberal Western and assume that these solutions will work in the (totally different) environments of the target countries. In addition, they are often interested in easily visible forms of 'success' with quick and easy exit. What one of the most renowned experts in the field of democracy and rule of law promotion, Thomas Carothers, has said for rule of law assistance is true also for democracy promotion: "Western nations and private donors have

---

107 See, e.g., T Carothers, *Critical Mission: Essays on Democracy Promotion* (Carnegie Endowment for International Peace 2004); R Müllerson, 'Democracy Promotion: Institutions, International Law and Politics' in *Hague Academy of International Law, Recueil des Cours* 333 (2008), 9–173; M McFaul, *Advancing Democracy Abroad: Why We Should and How We Can* (Bowman & Littlefield 2010); PJ Burnell, *Promoting Democracy Abroad: Policy and Performance* (Transaction Publ. 2011); M Kurki, *Democratic Futures: Revisioning Democracy Promotion* (Routledge 2013); D Huber, *Democracy Promotion and Foreign Policy: Identity and Interests in US, EU and Non-Western Democracies* (Palgrave Macmillan 2015).

108 See R Burchill, 'Regional Organizations and the Promotion and Protection of Democracy as a Contribution to International Peace and Security' in R Burchill (ed), *International Conflict and Security Law. Essays in Memory of Hilaire McCoubrey* (CUP 2005), 209–234; ER McMahon and SH Baker, *Piecing a Democratic Quilt? Regional Organizations and Universal Norms* (Kumarian Press 2006); D Hawkins and C Shaw, 'The OAS and Legalizing Norms of Democracy' in T Legler (ed), *Promoting Democracy in the Americas* (Johns Hopkins Univ. Press 2007), 21–39; H Tigroudja, 'The African Charter on Democracy, Elections and Governance' in A Yusuf and F Ouguergouz (eds), *The African Union: Legal and Institutional Framework* (Nijhoff 2012), 275–290; J Sarkin, The Need to Reform the Political Role of the African Union in Promoting Democracy and Human Rights in Domestic States, (2018) 26 (1) African Journal of International and Comparative Law 84–107.

109 See E Newman and R Rich (eds), *The UN Role in Promoting Democracy: Between Ideals and Reality* (United Nations Univ. Press 2004).

110 See KFF Quigley, *For Democracy's Sake: Foundations and Democracy Assistance in Central Europe* (Woodrow Wilson Center Press 1997); T Carothers, *Aiding Democracy Abroad: The Learning Curve* (Carnegie Endowment for International Peace 1999); M Cox, GJ Ikenberry and T Inoguchi (eds), *American Democracy Promotion: Impulses, Strategies, and Impacts* (OUP 2000).

poured hundreds of millions of dollars into rule-of-law reform, but outside aid is no substitute for the will to reform, which must come from within. Countries in transition to democracy must first want to reform and must then be thorough and patient in their legal makeovers. Meanwhile, donors must learn to spend their reform dollars where they will do the most good – and expect few miracles and little leverage in return."[111]

Probably the most successful tools of democracy promotion is the (nowadays very widespread) practice of election monitoring. Its singular focus on elections may again be problematic. As Hilary Charlesworth has phrased it, "a preoccupation with elections has become a feature of the international democracy-promotion industry in post-conflict societies. Its attractions are easy to understand: elections pass political and financial responsibility from an international intervener to local groups and allow a respectable exit".[112] At the same time, the limited (and rather technical) focus on the sober and successful organization of elections allows the accumulation of technical expertise and helps democratizing countries (or countries with fragile forms of democracy) to channel the political temptations at forging election procedures and results and to keep at bay the ensuing tendency to deny the validity of election results. The range of practices of election monitoring is impressive and deserves deeper analysis.[113]

2.4 *'Good Governance' in Development Aid*

The dilemma inherent in the practices of democracy promotion is further aggravated in the context of good governance conditionality in development aid. The usual modes of democracy promotion happen in concertation – and mostly in consent – with the state concerned. This is not always true for democracy promotion in post-conflict situations, in particular when state-building is filling the vacuum left by a military intervention, but in most contexts, democracy promotion rests on the consent of the state concerned. In the practices of

111 Carothers, 'The Rule-of-Law Revival' (n. 99), at 4.

112 See Charlesworth (n. 37) *RdC* 371 (2014) 43, at 128.

113 See C Binder and C Pippan, 'Election Monitoring, International' in R Wolfrum (ed) *Max Panck Encyclopedia of Public International Law* (OUP online ed. 2018); GH Fox, 'Election Monitoring: The International Legal setting' (2001) 19 (3) WILJ 295–319; E Bjornlund, *Beyond Free and Fair: Monitoring Elections and Building Democracy* (Woodrow Wilson Center Press 2004); C Binder, 'Two Decades of International Electoral Support' (2009) 13 Max Planck YB of United Nations Law 213–246; JG Kelley, *Monitoring Democracy. When International Election Observation Works, and Why it often Fails* (Princeton Univ. Press 2012); C Binder and L Kirchmair, 'Die Legitimität internationaler Wahlstandards' (2017) 55 (4) Archiv des Völkerrechts 383–413.

good governance conditionality in development aid this is different – the goal of promoting democracy is not endogenous but is imposed by the donor country or organization. This raises particular problems with the question whether there is really a domestic desire to adapt to institutional blueprints of Western democracy – and with the need to bring on board local knowledge on societal traditions of political ordering and prevailing value systems. Good governance conditionality tends – with other words – to impose specific Western values and institutional models upon societies governed by decidedly different traditions.

The concept of 'good governance' is a relatively new phenomenon.[114] It developed in the 1990s, being adopted over time by donor countries of development aid, by the European Union[115] as well as by international financial institutions such as the World Bank.[116] From its beginnings, the concept of 'good governance' rested on three pillars – human rights, rule of law and democracy. Externally imposed standards of democratic governance are particularly delicate since such requirements concern modes of societal coordination and organization that are inextricably linked with the inherited cultural traditions of social ordering. This might not raise severe problems if the concept of democratic governance would remain vague and flexible; if democracy conditionality requires specific adaptations according to Western models of liberal constitutionalism, such as representative democracy based on regular and free elections, such conditionality is much less innocent.

One might argue that such conditionality raises a concern that should be seen as trivial. The underlying rationale might be exemplified with the 2002 United Nations Development Programme's Human Development Report:[117]

---

114 See, for example, R Dolzer, 'Good Governance: Neues transnationales Leitbild der Staatlichkeit?' (2004) 64 (3) ZaöRV 535–546.

115 Concerning the EU's policy of democracy promotion and its practices of conditionality see F Hoffmeister, *Menschenrechts- und Demokratieklauseln in den vertraglichen Außenbeziehungen der Europäischen Gemeinschaft* (Springer 1998); R Youngs, *The European Union and the Promotion of Democracy* (OUP 2001); A Jünemann and M Knodt (eds), *European External Democracy Promotion* (Nomos 2007); D Kuon, *Good Governance im europäischen Entwicklungsrecht* (Nomos 2010); R Burchill, *The European Union, International Law and the Promotion and Protection of Democracy* (Hart 2012).

116 See D Gillies, Human Rights, Democracy and Good Governance – Stretching the World Bank's Policy Frontiers, in JM Griesgraber (ed), *The World Bank – Lending on a Global Scale* (Pluto Press 1996), 101–141; S Nelson and G Wallace, 'The International Monetary Fund and the Prospects for Democracy in the Developing World' in D Peksen (ed), *Liberal Interventionism and Democracy Promotion* (Lexington Books 2012), 87–114.

117 UNDP, Human Development Report 2002 – Deepening Democracy in a Fragmented World, to be found under: http://hdr.undp.org/sites/default/files/reports/263/hdr_2002_en_complete.pdf.

Referring to the 'new consensus' that 'governance matters for development', the report emphasized that what matters for human development is not just effective governance – important though that is – but democratic governance. This is in part because political freedoms are aspects of human development in their own right, but it is also because democracy can trigger a virtuous cycle of development, as political freedoms empower people to press for policies and priorities which expand the well-being of all.

In the terms of such thinking, democracy means more than merely holding elections. It requires the consolidation of democratic institutions and the strengthening of democratic practices with democratic values and norms embedded in all parts of society'. In particular, the report underlined the need for democratic values and norms to be embedded in the work of the military and police. The resulting temptation might lead to practices where donor countries and institutions impose very specific concepts and models upon the society that is seen to be in need of a democratic transformation. Such an externally induced transformation risks to end up in an assemblage of incoherent bits and pieces of Western models and institutions – incoherent due to the lacking fit of the bits and pieces as parts of a whole, but even more due to the missing linkage to institutional path-dependencies and inherited traditions of social ordering in the society doomed to be 'democratized'.

3 Perils and Pitfalls of a Norm on Democratic Governance

The preceding remarks have already pointed out that the high-flying hopes of a glorious avenue of institutional reform leading to 'democracy' all too often end up in failure and despair. 'Democratization' is not a direct way towards normative progress, but is a thorny endeavor fraught by many contradictions and significant perils that might end up in tragic choices. The following remarks are intended to shed some light on the (sometimes quite evident) pitfalls of any international attempt at promoting democracy, but also the more inherent perils hidden in the dark woods of post-conflict peace-building as well as institutional support for state-building in transition countries and development assistance dedicated to the promotion of democracy.

In a first step, we will take a closer look to the *obvious pitfalls* of post-cold war practice in support of democracy: This will take up issues which were raised already in some of the sections above, highlighting certain critical points of a too emphatic propagation of democracy as a tool of bettering the world.

– The ideology of 'Democratic Peace' that had moved a broad range of academic authors (and politicians) during the 1990s and early 2000s has proven to be a blueprint for catastrophe. The claims of an unfettered right of 'pro-democratic intervention' did not only erode the crucial rules of the prohibition of the use of force and collective security but proved to be ignorant of local conditions and did not contribute significantly to improve the fate of people in the countries concerned, plagued by extreme forms of repression, wide-spread insecurity and economic marginalization anyway. The text mentioned already the experiences made in Afghanistan, Iraq, and (lastly) Libya – in all three cases of interventions with fatal consequences for the stability and social order in the target countries. It became obvious that 'state-building' is an extremely challenging task where many things can (and often will) go wrong, leaving behind fragmented societies fraught by instability and extremely high levels of societal violence. The concept – this is probably not a hazardous statement – is now completely delegitimized.

– 'Democracy-building' in post-conflict peace-building, as well as too rigid strategies of democracy promotion, often linked with stringent modes of good governance conditionalities, are in a comparable danger of overpowering societies, leaving no genuine voice of the populations concerned.[118] Ignorance of the local conditions, cultural values and traditions, but also institutional path-dependencies of the inherited societal set-up risks producing institutional façades that do not fit to the societies upon which they are imposed. This all too often ends up in the trap described in comparative law literature as the phenomenon of 'legal transplants'.[119] There is a general lesson from studies on such 'transplants', which usually tend to result in counter-intuitive, 'perverse' transformations fitting to local power structures, but doing no favor to the ideal of a transformation towards more inclusive, 'democratic' forms of governance. These counter-productive shifts in context and meaning are barely foreseeable, due to the complex interactions with local contexts that are mostly not understood in their entirety, giving the transplanted institution a new meaning, transforming its role into something different. At the end, the use of such transplants resembles a lottery.

118 See Coleman and Maogoto (n. 75) (2004) 28 (2) Suffolk TLR 175, 217–221.

119 See A Watson, *Legal Transplants: An Approach to Comparative Law* (2nd edn, Univ. of Georgia Press 1993); P Legrand, 'The Impossibility of 'Legal Transplants' (1997) 4 (2) MJ 111–124; D Berkowitz, K Pistor and J-F Richard. 'The Transplant Effect' (2003) 51 (1) American Journal of Comparative Law 163–204; W Twining, 'Diffusion and Globalization Discourse' (2006) 47 (2) Harvard ILJ 507–516; J Fedtke, 'Legal Transplants' in JM Smits (ed) *Elgar Encyclopedia of Comparative Law* (Edward Elgar 2006), 434–437.

In addition, there are clear perils of post-cold war democracy promotion practices that do not that easily catch the attention of the observer, but which are nevertheless manifest if one engages in a detailed analysis:

- The technocratic practice of (externally dominated) 'democracy-building' is endangering genuine building-blocks of self-determination.[120] Self-determination shall safeguard the right of peoples to free choice of their political system and constitutional ordering. 'Democracy-building' dominated by actors from abroad tends to create an institutional straight-jacket that mirrors more the preferences of foreign actors than the preferences (and value-systems) of the populations concerned. The promise of participation of local population in most cases is more an empty promise than reality.[121] The resulting challenge was phrased by Andrew Coleman and Jackson Maogoto in the following words: "The wholesome abandonment of traditions cuts a society loose from its moorings. Democracy stands to gain from its position within the general socio-political landscape of a nation rather than possessing a reputation as a wholesale export of the West, which prescribes a specific Western template. The sense of ownership a citizen feels in a new political architecture contributes immensely to its support."[122]
- Empirical observation shows us an obvious temptation to limit 'democracy promotion' to technocratic issues of free elections.[123] The organization of an election process is a technically limited, manageable task suiting to the preferences of technocratic experts. It requires technical expertise, is limited in the amount of time and resources needed and grants an easy exit option after the election process has been finalized.[124] The observation is even more true for the practice of international election-monitoring, in practice the most widely used tool. But even other types of (seemingly technical) institution-building are much easier to handle than a 'holistic' attempt at transforming an entire society. As Nehal Bhutta remarked: "Merely designing an institution along liberal democratic lines is no guarantee that it will generate the political behavior characteristic of liberal democratic politics."[125]

---

120 See Charlesworth (n. 37) *RdC* 371 (2014) 43, at 132–135.

121 Id., at 133–134.

122 See Coleman and Maogoto (n. 75) (2004) 28 (2) Suffolk TLR 175, 218.

123 See O. Korhonen, "Post' as Justification: International Law and Democracy-Building after Iraq' (2003) 4 (7) German Law Journal 709, 723.

124 See Charlesworth (n. 37) *RdC* 371 (2014) 43, at 128.

125 N Bhutta, 'New Modes and Orders: The Difficulties of a *Jus Post Bellum* of Constitutional Transformation' (2010) 60 (3) UTLJ 799, 829.

Beyond these – rather open and still visible – perils of democracy promotion there exist also some more hidden, inherent perils of post-cold war pro-democracy practice. They are not really unknown – academic scholarship has identified these perils. They are, however, much less in the minds than the challenges and perils identified above.

- A particular problem arises with Western-style liberal democracy, usually based on a strong trait of majoritarianism, if this encounters ethnically and religiously divided societies. Elections in conditions of insecurity tend to polarize rather than unite societies. The ensuing mechanism of majoritarian forms of democracy tends to end up in the maxim 'the winner takes all'. This risks to "turn a multiethnic nation into a majoritarian dictatorship. Such a dictatorship can occur where a minority is effectively sidelined from actively participating in government, despite their ability to vote, by a majority whose dominance in government, and thus affairs of the State is guaranteed by the ballot. This is not an idle argument, since one need only look to Africa to see the effect of the straight application of one person, one vote in heterogeneous states dominated by one or two communities."[126] A systemic political, and in consequence often also economic, marginalization of significant segments of society often serves as a recipe for escalating conflicts. "An ethnic minority can be repressed or subject to discriminatory processes in a democratic system despite the appearance of political empowerment created by the electoral process; this can lead to an escalation of ethnic violence."[127] Michael Mann has even made a forceful argument that such dynamics of populist democracy constitutes one of the most important root causes of ethnic cleansing and genocide.[128]
- The 'democratic governance' built up by foreign actors, inspired by the institutional models of liberal Western democracies, tends to cast in iron the power of Western-educated elites, because these small urban elites are the only ones capable of managing the 'alien' institutional system in line with the expectations of the foreign actors, which enables them to channel the huge sums of foreign aid in the service of state-building to their own advantage. Such consolidation of power structures risks, in the end result, to block social change and to reinforce inequality – in circumstances structurally

126 See Coleman and Maogoto (n. 75) (2004) 28 (2) Suffolk TLR 175, 233.

127 Id., at 233.

128 See M Mann, *The Dark Side of Democracy: Explaining Ethnic Cleansing* (CUP 2005); see also A Chua, *World on Fire: How Exporting Market Democracy Breeds Ethnic Hatred and Global Instability* (Doubleday 2002).

characterized by extreme inequality and marginalization of large segments of society.[129]

- A specific problem exists with the structures of international administration preparing countries, in the context of an effort of post-conflict peacebuilding, for democratic statehood. The international institutions operating as drivers of democracy-building are themselves insulated from requirements of democratic accountability. They are part of an international bureaucracy following a very traditional hierarchical model, with a backstage control of national executives – no trace of 'democratic governance'. This feature of institutions of transitional administration in post-conflict peacebuilding reflects a more general problem of international governance. Critics argue that international institutions lack any democratic legitimacy at all, symbolize a 'democratic deficit' of the international system. That critique is difficult to refute – the lack of mechanisms of democratic accountability is obvious.[130] Academia has produced an enormous amount of scholarly writings on the question how to improve democratic legitimacy of international institutions. The challenge is undisputed – the answer remains open.

4 Conclusion: Why We Must Be Careful

We have seen in the preceding remarks, revisiting the strong calls for a 'pro-democratic bias' in international law, that the underlying 'liberal millenarianism'[131] rests on shaky ground and has produced a huge dose of unintended and counterproductive results. As a lawyer raised and socialized in a liberal democracy of the West, one cannot avoid to have an intuitive sympathy with the endeavor to make the world 'safe for democracy'. The understanding of democracy that is underlying the missionary attempts at 'democracy-building'

129 See also Coleman and Maogoto (n. 75) (2004) 28 (2) Suffolk TLR 175, 237–238.

130 See, for example, E Stein, 'International Integration and Democracy: No Love at First Sight' (2001) 95 (3) *AJIL* 489–534; JHH Weiler, 'The Geology of International Law – Governance, Democracy and Legitimacy' (2004) 64 *ZaöRV* 547–562; A Peters, 'Dual Democracy' in J Klabbers, A Peters and G Ulfstein, *The Constitutionalization of International Law* (OUP 2009), 263–340; S Wheatley, *The Democratic Legitimacy of International Law* (Hart 2010); T Christiano, 'Democratic Legitimacy and International Institutions' in S Besson and J Tasioulas (eds), *The Philosophy of International Law* (OUP 2010), 119–138; Charlesworth (n. 37) *RdC* 371 (2014) 43, 96–111.

131 The term was coined by Susan Marks – see S Marks, 'The End of History? Reflections on Some International Legal Theses' (1997) 3 (3) *EJIL* 449, 451–460.

and 'democracy promotion', however, has proven to be too simplistic and underdeveloped. Democracy can take very different shades and remains a heavily contested concept in detail. Working with an oversimplistic concept of democracy all too easily ends up, as we have seen, in a number of tragic perils and pitfalls. The last section of the paper tried to revisit these challenges and perils.

At the same time, it is far from clear whether the 'emerging right to democratic governance is still in a process of emergence. As Susan Marks remarked in her sarcastic account of the fallacies of 'liberal millenarianism' from 1997, "the international legal arguments are inclined to overstate the significance of the present moment, as an indication of the future. While the possibility of setbacks is certainly acknowledged, the evolutionary logic of the arguments tends to signal that contemporary trends will continue in a more or less linear fashion."[132] The trends which were contemporary in the 1990s, however, have definitely not continued. Liberal democracy is under assault. With China (and its decidedly authoritarian model of rule) the West has got an ideological competitor of quite some attraction for many countries of the 'Global South'. It would be difficult to find any serious scholar today who would argue that Western-style democracy is without alternative and is thus doomed to victory.

Just to the contrary, the normative consensus on democratic values has eroded even inside the West. Even internally, inside the traditional democracies of the West, the concepts of liberal democracy have lost clout. Political science literature experiences a wave of books and papers on the 'regression' of democracy, on the dangers of populism and the temptations of 'illiberal democracy'.[133] With other words: The West itself is not fully convinced of the virtues of traditional patterns of liberal democracy any more.

There is a widespread feeling that the limited focus on elections and representative institutions has left unanswered a lot of decisive questions. What is 'real democracy'? Some far-sighted authors argued already in 2004 that 'real democracy' "involves a complex relationship between the government and the governed. Direct replication of successful Western models does not necessarily result in successful transplants. For democracy to "work", it must evolve at the pace of the specific community rather than be imposed from above by a third party."[134] There are good arguments for 'democracy as a global value'[135] – but

132 Id., at 473.

133 See, as far as the consequences for international legal discourse are concerned, A Magen, 'The Democratic Entitlement in an Era of Democratic Recession' (2015) 4 (2) CJICL 368–387.

134 Coleman and Maogoto (n. 75) (2004) 28 (2) Suffolk TLR 175, 240.

135 See A Sen, 'Democracy as a Universal Value' (1999) 10 (3) *Journal of Democracy* 3 et seq.

the underlying value needs a quite different shape than the literature on a 'right to democratic governance' had implied. As Hilary Charlesworth remarked at the end of her magisterial Hague lecture, "international law should support a substantive definition of democracy tied to values, such as the accountability of political power and the creation of conditions of equality between participants in decisions."[136] Democracy in such an understanding is closely linked with human dignity, the desire of all human beings to be respected and not to be treated as a mere object of brute rule. "To characterize democracy as an ideal is to highlight that it is an engine of criticism and change necessarily at odds with prevailing realities."[137] Only if we take the ideal of democracy as an emancipatory force serious we will have a chance of democracy emerging as a global value. The current realities of the community of states and the international order are far away from such ideal – but that is not an argument against an enlightened concept of democracy. With a too limited, technocratic concept of 'democratic governance', that can be said with utmost certainty, the apologists of democracy as a global standard will not convince most people in the world that democratic governance is a virtue that should be adopted without any reservations.

136 Charlesworth (n. 37) *RdC* 371 (2014) 43, 144.
137 S Marks, 'The End of History?' (1997) 3 (3) *EJIL* 449, 476–77.

PART 1

The Democratic Principle – Conceptual Issues

CHAPTER 2

Pro-democratic Interventionism Revisited

Christian Pippan

1 Introduction

There is no denying. At the beginning of the third decade of the 21st century, debates about pro-democratic interventionism indeed have 'a dated feel'.[1] Almost instinctively, they call back to mind bold pronouncements, expressed in the glory days of the early post-Cold War era, about the 'universalization of Western liberal democracy',[2] the advent of a 'world of liberal states'[3] and the emergence of democratic governance as a 'global legal entitlement'.[4] As Thomas Franck, the main architect of the much debated democratic norm thesis, has famously stated in 1992:

> We are not quite there, but we can see the outlines of this new world in which the citizens of each state will look to international law and organization to guarantee their democratic entitlement.[5]

Today, almost exactly three decades later, it seems patently obvious that we are still not 'there'. All in all, the reconfiguration of the international (legal) order did not play out the way Franck and others had envisaged it in the early 1990s, at least not at the global level. While, formally, democracy still ranks high on the international community's 'value scale',[6] the overall tone of the concomitant

1 D Wippman, 'Pro-Democratic Intervention' in M Weller (ed), *The Oxford Handbook on the Use of Force in International Law* (OUP 2015) 797.
2 F Fukuyama, 'The End of History?' (1989) 16 The National Interest 3.
3 A-M Slaughter, 'International Law in a World of Liberal States' (1995) 6 EJIL 503.
4 T Franck, 'The Emerging Right to Democratic Governance' (1992) 86 AJIL 46.
5 Ibid 50.
6 According to the 2005 World Summit Outcome, adopted by Heads of State and Government of UN member states to mark the organization's 60th anniversary, democracy is 'a universal value based on the freely expressed will of people to determine their own political, economic, social and cultural systems and their full participation in all aspects of their lives'; UN Doc A/RES/60/1 (15 September 2005) para 135. Notably, this affirmation of democracy as a 'universal value' is instantly followed by the stipulation that, 'while democracies share common features, there is no single model of democracy'(ibid).

 | DOI:10.1163/9789004508712_003

scholarly discourse has, for the most part, taken on a decidedly more sober (or, as some may say, realistic) spin.[7] Concerns about the legal ramifications of democratic backsliding and the resurgence of authoritarian regimes in various corners of the world have recently even led some commentators to speculate about the dawn of a new era of 'authoritarian international law'.[8]

To say that, over the years, the general thrust of the debate on democracy and international law has become more nuanced and cautious is not to say that the debate as such has lost any of its attraction or relevance. Quite to the contrary, discussions about the meaning and place of democracy in international law and, particularly, the role of international actors in promoting and protecting democratic institutions and processes are well alive and continue to inspire legal scholars as well as practitioners.[9] To a certain (albeit lesser) extent, this also applies to the notion of 'pro-democratic intervention' (hereinafter: PDI) – a particularly controversial sub-section of the overall 'democracy and international law' discourse, which is predicated on the idea that, under certain circumstances, military force may lawfully be used by outsiders to preserve or restore democracy within a particular state.

When revisiting the notion, or concept, of PDI from the angle of international law, it is crucial to have a reasonable idea as to what is actually meant by it. Chapter 2, therefore, starts off by attempting to provide some conceptual clarifications, particularly by recalling the meaning of 'intervention' in international law and by distinguishing the specific notion of PDI from the broader concept of 'regime change'. Chapter 3 takes a quick look at the origins of the PDI thesis in the 1980s and early 1990s. The aim is not to present a detailed recount,

7 See eg S Marks, 'What has Become of the Emerging Right to Democratic Governance?' (2011) 22 EJIL 507; J d'Aspremont, 'The Rise and Fall of Democracy Governance in International Law' (2011) 22 EJIL 549; C Pippan, 'Democracy as a Global Norm: Has It Finally Emerged?' in M Happold (ed), *International Law in a Multipolar World* (Routledge 2012); H Charlesworth, 'Democracy and International Law' (2014) 371 RdC 42; A Magen, 'The Right to Democratic Governance in an Era of Democratic Recession' (2015) 4 CILJ 368; JS Dryzek, 'Can There Be a Human Right to an Essentially Contested Concept? The Case of Democracy' (2016) 78 Journal of Politics 357; KA Alfadhel, *The Right to Democracy in International Law: Between Procedure, Substance and the Philosophy of John Rawls* (Routledge 2017); A Horn, *The Human Right to Democracy. A Critical Evaluation* (de Gruyter 2019); S Boysen, 'Remnants of a Constitutional Moment: The Right to Democracy in International Law' in A v Arnauld, K v der Decken and M Susi (eds), *The Cambridge Handbook of New Human Rights* (CUP 2020).

8 T Ginsburg, 'Authoritarian International Law?' (2020) 114 AJIL 221.

9 The most recent collection of essays on the subject (containing contributions originally published elsewhere) is provided by GH Fox and BR Roth (eds), *Democracy and International Law* (E Elgar 2020). The volume can be seen as a 'sequel' to GH Fox and BR Roth (eds), *Democratic Governance and International Law* (CUP 2000).

but merely to highlight some of the basic premises of the 'original' PDI argument. Chapter 4 then turns to relevant international practice by zooming-in on four prominent cases of modern PDI: Haiti (1994), Sierra Leone (1997–1998), Côte d'Ivoire (2011), and The Gambia (2017). All of these cases were marked by the use of force, or the threat of it, by external actors to ensure compliance by recalcitrant domestic actors with the results of free and fair elections. Also, all of these cases involved activities both by (sub-)regional organizations and the UN Security Council (UNSC). As will be shown, though the UNSC has only rarely used its powers under Chapter VII of the UN Charter to authorize pro-democratic military action against unelected de facto regimes, the UNSC has also played a vital role in cases of PDIs (undertaken by regional organizations) were situated outside, or beyond, the UN Charter's collective security system. Chapter 5 will finally reflect on some of the implications derived from relevant post-Cold War practice on the issue of (il)legality of PDIs under contemporary international law.

2 Reflections on the Meaning of Pro-democratic Intervention

It is all but a truism that interferences by states in the domestic affairs of another state come in a variety of forms and may serve a multitude of possible objectives, including, obviously, political objectives. From the point of view of international law, however, such conduct raises legal issues only if it qualifies as an 'intervention' – in which case the relevant action or measure requires specific legal title, lest it be considered unlawful.[10] As the International Court of Justice (ICJ) has specified in a widely-cited passage of its decision in the *Nicaragua Case*, a prohibited intervention is one that (a) bears on matters 'in which each State is permitted, by the principle of State sovereignty, to decide freely' and (b) involves 'coercion' intended to bring about a policy change in the target state with regard to such matters.[11]

In *Nicaragua*, the ICJ also affirmed that under general international law (ie absent specific contractual commitments) the character of a state's political

10 As per Article 2(7) of the UN Charter, the UN, as an organization, is likewise required to respect the principle of non-intervention.

11 *Military and Paramilitary Activities in and against Nicaragua* (*Nicaragua v US*), Merits [1986] ICJ Rep 14 para 205. For a general discussion of the non-intervention norm see M Jamnejad and M Wood, 'The Principle of Non-Intervention' (2009) 22 LJIL 345; M Kohen, 'The Principle of Non-Intervention 25 Years after the Nicaragua Judgement' (2012) 25 LJIL 157.

system is profoundly a matter that belongs to its protected *domaine réservé*.[12] Arguably, limited exceptions to this appraisal already existed at the time of the Court's handing down of the judgment, particularly with respect to political systems built upon Nazi, fascist, or apartheid ideologies.[13] Eventually, however, it was the end of the all-embracive ideological antagonism of the Cold War – and the quickly evolving pro-democratic shift in various fields of international law and politics that came along with it – that began to more fundamentally challenge the traditional doctrine of international law's neutrality towards domestic regime type. In fact, proceeding from a fresh ('post-colonial') look at the right of peoples to self-determination and a progressive reading of the citizens' individual right to take part in genuine periodic elections, the democratic entitlement thesis revolves precisely around the argument that the adoption by states of a fairly specific political system – electoral democracy – 'is rapidly becoming, in our time, a normative rule of the international system'.[14]

To be sure, the controversial and multi-dimensional debate over the existence in international law of a global legal entitlement to democracy (or, rather, to a core procedural aspect of it) is only one factor to be considered when assessing the relevance of the non-intervention norm in the present context – and it is perhaps not even the most important. As the ICJ itself has emphasised, the decisive element 'which defines, and indeed forms the very essence of, prohibited intervention' is coercion.[15] Consequently, even if the choice of a political system is viewed as a matter situated squarely 'within the domestic jurisdiction of any state' – to use the wording of Article 2(7) of the UN Charter –, this by no means implies that every engagement by foreign actors with a state's political and constitutional dispensations will be tainted, under international law, with the stigma of illegality. Rather, to borrow from Oppenheim, relevant measures and actions constitute a prohibited intervention only if they can reasonably be characterized as 'forcible or dictatorial [...], in effect depriving the state intervened against of control over the matter in question' (here: the choice of its political system).[16]

There can be little doubt that uninvited military action by outsiders will normally fulfil the above-mentioned condition and, thus, represent an unlawful intervention[17] – unless, of course, such action can be justified on the basis

12 *Nicaragua* (n 11) paras 205, 263.

13 Pippan (n 7) 212.

14 Franck (n 4) 46.

15 *Nicaragua* (n 11) para 205.

16 R Jennings and A Watts, *Oppenheim's International Law* (9th edn, OUP 2008) 428.

17 As the ICJ has noted, again in *Nicaragua* (n 11), 'prohibited intervention is particularly obvious in the case of an intervention which uses force, either in the form of military

of an authorization by the UNSC under Chapter VII of the UN Charter or a valid claim to individual or collective self-defence in terms of Article 51 of the Charter.[18] The picture is markedly less clear when it comes to foreign interferences short of the threat or use of force. While it cannot be ruled out that (unilateral) financial and economic measures, including (targeted) sanctions, may under certain circumstances amount to coercion, state practice in this field is far from conclusive.[19] States confronted with such measures are typically quick in rejecting them as unlawful incursions in their internal affairs. Yet, more often than not, these states fail to demonstrate the 'subordination of the exercise of [their] sovereign rights' that is required by international law to support such a claim.[20]

Against this backdrop, it may not come as a surprise that the focus of the PDI debate has always been – and still is – on foreign military action. By contrast, to the extent that states and international organizations restrict themselves to non-forcible (diplomatic, financial, and/or economic) means of promoting or protecting democracy in a given state, relevant policies and measures are generally not regarded as manifestations of 'pro-democratic intervention(ism)' in the usual (narrow) meaning of the term.[21] As a result, it is less the opaque principle of non-intervention as such but rather the more specific prohibition of the use of force, as enshrined in Article 2(4) of the UN Charter and customary international law, which lies at the heart of legal discussions about the concept of PDI and its practical implications.

action, or in the indirect form of support for subversive or terrorist armed activities within another State' (ibid, para 205).

18 To state the obvious, any violation of the prohibition of the use of force will likewise result in a violation of the principle of non-intervention. Conversely, if a particular use of force can be justified under the UN Charter and/or customary international law, that justification will also render legally irrelevant any claim as to a violation of the principle of non-intervention.

19 Jamnejad and Wood (n 11) 367; see also H Neuhold, *The Law of International Conflict: Force, Intervention and Peaceful Dispute Settlement* (Nijhoff 2016) 159 (noting that 'the prohibition of intervention in the internal affairs of a state remains one of the most complex and controversial principles of international law to this day').

20 The phrase cited here first appeared in the UN General Assembly's 1965 Declaration on the Inadmissibility of Intervention in the Domestic Affairs of States and the Protection of Their Independence and Sovereignty, UN Doc A/RES/2131 (XX) para 2. Since then, the Assembly has reaffirmed it in numerous documents, including its seminal 'Friendly Relations Declaration' (24 October 1970) UN Doc A/RES/2625 (XXV).

21 D Wippman, 'Defending Democracy Through Foreign Intervention' (1997) 19 HJIL 659, 670.

Under what conditions, then, is an armed intervention to be considered 'pro-democratic'? Obviously, the relevant use of force, be it unilateral or collective in character, must be aimed at supporting democracy in the target state. To be more precise: The possible presence of other (supplementary) motives notwithstanding, cross-border military action, or the threat of it, only qualifies as a PDI if its primary purpose is to maintain or restore democracy in the state in which the action is, or is threatened to be, carried out.[22]

Though this, admittedly, is a rather straitforward definition of the concept, it is still useful to distinguish PDIs from other variations of the use of force in international relations, particularly when the consequence of such force is 'regime change'.[23] To be sure, if successful, a PDI will typically result in the removal of 'illegitimate' de facto rulers and their replacement by a *de jure* regime with adequate democratic credentials. Yet, while related, the concept of 'pro-democratic intervention' and that of 'foreign-imposed regime change' (FIRC)[24] is not necessarily identical. Simply put, a FIRC may well occur without the prefix 'pro-democratic' being attached to it. Depending on the specifics of the situation in question, this may become manifest, for instance, when the ouster of a state's regime at the hands of outsiders is ancillary to a lawful self-defense or (UN Security Council-authorized) responsibility to protect (R2P) operation.[25] Generally, in such scenarios, promoting or protecting democracy neither serves as the central motive nor as the purported normative foundation of the relevant intervention, even though hopes for some side-effects as to

22 See C Gray, *International Law and the Use of Force* (4th edn, OUP 2018) 449 (defining military operations as 'pro-democratic' when taken 'in support of the maintenance or restoration of a democratically elected government').

23 As commonly known, the term 'regime change' denotes the replacement by external actors of the government and/or system of government of a state by the use or threatened use of force; see GH Fox, 'Regime Change' in A Peters and R Wolfrum (eds), *Max Planck Encyclopedia of Public International Law* (online edn, OUP 2013).

24 D Reiter, 'Foreign-Imposed Regime Change', in W Thompson (ed) *Oxford Research Encyclopedia of Politics* (OUP 2017) <https://doi.org/10.1093/acrefore/9780190228637.013.335> accessed 15 February 2022.

25 On regime change in the context of self-defence see WM Reisman, 'Assessing Claims to Revise the Laws of War' (2003) 97 AJIL 82; Fox (n 23) para 34. On regime change as an intended or unintended by-product of R2P operations see AJ Bellamy and PD Williams, 'The New Politics of Protection: Côte d'Ivoire, Libya and the Responsibility to Protect' (2011) 87 International Affairs 825; M Beham and R Janik, 'Responsibility to Democratize? The "Responsibility to Protect" in Light of Regime Change and the "Pro-Democratic" Intervention Discourse' in RA Barnes and VP Tzevelekos (eds), Beyond Responsibility to Protect: Generating Change in International Law (Intersentia 2016).

the initiation or strengthening of democratic processes in the target state may be associated with it.[26]

A further aspect needs to be considered here. While regime change may be caused by an intervention that, as such, is not constitutively linked to pro-democratic considerations, the factual situation created by such an event may nevertheless pave the way for a reconstruction and state building program under the aegis of international actors, which may precisely be designed to lay the foundation for a democratic domestic political order. Regardless of the lawfulness, *vel non*, of the intervention that effectuated, directly or indirectly, the former regime's removal from power, the question of interest at this juncture pertains to the qualification of efforts by external actors to facilitate 'pro-democratic' state building in the aftermath of military conflict. Do such efforts qualify as a PDI, at least by implication?

While there appears to be a tendency among political scientists to respond to this issue in the affirmative,[27] an assessment from the vantage point of international law calls for a more nuanced approach. Importantly, the question, under which circumstances (if ever) force may lawfully be used by outsiders to preserve or restore democracy against the will of a regime in effective control over the state concerned, is fundamentally a matter of *jus ad bellum*. By contrast, international post-conflict reconstruction and state building is a matter of what in recent years has generally come to be known as *jus post bellum*.[28] Irrespective of the justification offered for any prior use of force within the context of international armed conflict, activities in this area require a separate legal basis. Typically, the latter is provided by host state consent, often in tandem with (or, if the situation so requires, substituted by) a Chapter VII

26 Given that military operations resulting in the disposal of a state's domestic regime represent an extremely far-reaching incursion into the internal affairs of a state, such action will of course routinely spark controversy, not just regarding its legality but also in respect of its morality and (political) reasonableness; see MW Reisman, 'Why Regime Change Is (Almost Always) a Bad Idea' (2004) 98 AJIL 516.

27 See eg NP Gleditsch, LS Christiansen and H Hegre, *Democratic Jihad? Military Intervention and Democracy*, Post-Conflict Transitions Working Paper No 15 (2007) <https://elibrary.worldbank.org> accessed 15 February 2022; R Rotte, '"A general loosing of the ties of civilized society ..." – *Democratic Interventionism* als legales oder legitimes außenpolitisches Instrument im 21. Jahrhundert?' in M Biegi *et al* (eds), *Demokratie, Recht und Legitimität im 21. Jahrhundert* (Springer 2008); R Merkel, 'Demokratischer Interventionismus?', in J Bung and A Engländer (eds), *Souveränität, Transstaatlichkeit und Weltverfassung* (Steiner 2017).

28 See eg E de Brabandere, 'The Concept of *Jus Post Bellum* in International Law' in C Stahn, JS Easterday and J Iverson (eds), *Jus Post Bellum: Mapping the Normative Foundations* (OUP 2014) 129.

UN Charter authorization by the Security Council.[29] Conversely, while modern post-conflict reconstruction and state building subscribes, virtually as a rule, to the vision of a democratic, inclusive, and rule-of-law-based domestic political system,[30] international action in this field does not redefine the purpose and character (let alone the purported justification) of any preceding use of force.[31] Overall, post-conflict state building is a complex and multi-facetted endeavour, which calls for a long-term commitment on the part of both external as well as domestic actors.[32] As such, it represents a distinct category of foreign engagement with a state's political and constitutional setup, which both for legal and conceptual reasons should be distinguished from the *jus ad bellum* concept of PDI.

3 A Cry from the Past: the Pro-democratic Intervention Thesis

As commonly known, the PDI debate started in the 1980s in the wake of the US-interventions in Grenada (1983)[33] and Panama (1989).[34] Prompted by the

29 UNSC authorization is regularly desired by foreign actors to enhance the legitimacy and local acceptance of post-conflict state building operations. It is legally required, however, when, in the aftermath of military conflict, it is unclear which faction has the authority (and legitimacy) to act on behalf of the state concerned; see M Saul, 'International Law and the Identification of an Interim Government to Lead Post-Conflict Reconstruction', in M Saul and J Sweeney (eds), *International Law and Post-Conflict Reconstruction Policy* (Routledge 2015). In light of Article 52 of the Vienna Convention on the Law of Treaties, explicit UNSC approval is likewise needed if the asserted host state consent has been produced by an illegal use of force; see GH Fox, *Humanitarian Occupation* (CUP 2008) 177.

30 M Cogen and E de Brabandere, 'Democratic Governance and Post-Conflict Reconstruction' (2007) 20 LJIL 669.

31 The establishment of UNMIK (the UN Interim Administration Mission in Kosovo) by the Security Council in the aftermath of NATO's *Operation Allied Force* against Serbia provides an early example in this context. While Resolution 1244 (1999) specifically entrusted UNMIK with overseeing the creation of democratic self-governing institutions in the former Serbian province, this certainly has not retroactively transformed NATO's intervention into a PDI. Moreover, by adopting Res 1244 (1999), the UNSC has not taken any position on the legality of NATO's unilateral action (though the UNSC did seem to acknowledge that what had been at stake in Kosovo was the resolution of 'a grave humanitarian situation'); UNSC Res 1244 (1999) UN Doc S/RES/1244 (10 June 1999) preamble, para 4.

32 See PR Williams and M Sterio (eds), *Research Handbook on Post-Conflict State Building* (E Elgar 2020).

33 In Grenada, following a request by the Organization of Eastern Caribbean States, US forces overthrew a leftist junta and replaced it by an interim government (which remained in office until elections a year later); see N Hajjami, 'The US Intervention in Grenada' in T Ruys, O Corten and A Hofer (eds), *The Use of Force in International Law. A Case-Based Approach* (OUP 2018).

34 In Panama, the US deposed General Manuel Noriega from power after he annulled the results of elections won by his opponent, Guillermo Endara (who, following Noriega's

fact that both operations were widely condemned – including by the UN – as flagrant violations of international law,[35] some US-American scholars proposed a re-reading of the non-intervention norms of the UN Charter, supposedly more in line with a modern understanding of the principle of sovereignty from which these norms ultimately derive their meaning and function. Pointing to the gradual acceptance in international doctrine and practice of a genuine link between popular sovereignty and the right of peoples to (internal) self-determination and, additionally, the growing body of international norms and standards embracing electoral democracy as the preferred model of governance, Michael Reisman – arguably the most prominent among these scholars – asserted that regimes whose claim to power is patently defying popular will can no longer invoke sovereignty (and the non-intervention norms associated with it) to shield their rule from international rebuke and remedy.[36] 'International law' Reisman writes in 1990, 'still protects sovereignty, but – not surprisingly – it is the people's sovereignty rather than the sovereign's sovereignty'.[37] According to this conception, a ruling elite which demonstrably ignores the freely expressed wishes of the people forfeits the right to speak for the state it purports to represent and, as a consequence, lacks the authority to object to foreign intervention designed to permit or facilitate the realization of popular will.[38] Ideally, such interventions would be mandated by 'centralized institutions, equipped with decision-making authority and the capacity

---

removal, was sworn in as Panama's new leader); see N Tsagourias, 'The US Intervention in Panama' in Ruys, Corten and Hofer (n 33).

35 See UNGA Res 38/7 (2 November 1983) UN Doc A/RES/38/7 (1983); UNGA Res 44/240 (29 December 1989) UN Doc A/RES/44/240 (1989).

36 MW Reisman, 'Sovereignty and Human Rights in Contemporary International Law' (1990) 84 AJIL 866. A slightly revised version of Reisman's 1990 contribution can be found in Fox and Roth (CUP, n 9) 239. See also for similar arguments A D'Amato, 'The Invasion of Panama was a Lawful Response to Tyranny' (1990) 84 AJIL 520; FR Tesón, 'The Kantian Theory of International Law' (1992) 92 Columbia Law Review 53.

37 Reisman (n 36) 869.

38 It should be noted that Reisman seemingly restricted this proposition to situations where the will of the people was ascertained in internationally monitored democratic elections. In a central passage of his 1990 editorial, he stipulated that, when the outcome of such elections is discarded 'by a local caudillo who either takes power by himself or assigns it to a subordinate he controls, a jurist rooted in the late twentieth century can hardly say that an intervention by outside forces to remove the caudillo and re-install the elected government is a violation of national sovereignty' (ibid 871).

to make it effective'.[39] However, Reisman concludes, since that solution will more often than not remain unlikely, 'effective international protection of fledgling democracies will depend on decisive action by the great industrial democracies'.[40]

At first glance, it appears as if Reisman's arguments were subsequently echoed in cases such as Haiti, Sierra Leone, Côte d'Ivoire, and The Gambia. Yet, as we shall see below, these cases were characterized by circumstances that, taken together, do not lend much support to any grand thesis of a customary legal right to unilateral military action in support of 'fledgling democracies'.[41] Indeed, upon closer inspection, one finds no precedent in post-World War II international practice where a state, or group of states, attempted to justify the use of armed force not authorized by the UN Security Council by reference to a purported stand-alone right to pro-democratic intervention.[42] Notably, this includes the 1989 US intervention in Panama, which has served as one of the main reference points for Reisman's PDI argument. While the restoration of democracy was indeed one (of several) stated objectives of US action against the Noriega regime, Washington's legal narrative was centered predominantly on a purported right to self-defence (to protect US citizens abroad) and the need to ensure the integrity of the 1977 Torrijos-Carter Treaties concerning the Panama Canal.[43]

A dozen years later, the narrative surrounding the US/UK intervention in Afghanistan, which led to the toppling of Afghanistan's first Taliban regime in December 2001, revealed a similar picture. Though *Operation Enduring Freedom* was accompanied by rhetoric pointing at the repressive and undemocratic character of the Taliban, the legal rationale offered by the US was grounded exclusively on a claimed right to self-defence against terrorist attacks (by Al-Qaeda) and a ruling elite 'unable and unwilling' to prevent such attacks.[44] Similarly, in the context of the 2003 invasion of Iraq, none of the

---

39 Reisman (n 36) 875.

40 MW Reisman, 'Sovereignty and Human Rights in Contemporary International Law' in Fox and Roth (CUP, n 9) 257; *id*, 'Humanitarian Intervention and Fledgling Democracies' (1995) 18 Fordham ILJ 794.

41 Reisman (n 40) 265 ('[t]he basic issue at stake here is customary international law').

42 M Byers and S Chesterman, '"You, the People": Pro-Democratic Intervention in International Law' in Fox and Roth (CUP, n 9) 279.

43 Ibid 274; Tsagourias (n 34).

44 Evidently, the US' invocation of a right to self-defence in the Afghanistan case constituted a rather progressive reading of Art 51 of the UN Charter, particularly as far as the toppling of the Taliban was concerned; see Gray (n 22) 109. But see Fox, according to whom the legality of FIRC under the banner of self-defence mainly hinges on a proportionality test. To pass it, the state claiming to act in self-defence must provide evidence that the

interveners – primarily the US, assisted by the UK and Australia – made any serious attempt to base the forceful ouster of Iraq's long-time leader, Saddam Hussein, on any general legal entitlement on the part of states to use force in order to promote or defend democratic institutions and processes in another state.[45]

Contrary to what is sometimes asserted in discussions of the interventions in Afghanistan and Iraq, it also seems rather implausible, even from a political perspective, that the idea of forcefully exporting 'Lockian' or 'Jeffersonian' democracy to nations governed by dictatorial regimes constituted the decisive motivation for the actions taken by the US and its allies.[46] Apparently, regime change was a central objective of both interventions, yet in the aftermath of '9/11' this was arguably driven, first and foremost, by domestic security concerns, the unfolding global war on terror and – in the case of Iraq – a specific US obsession (grounded in economic and strategic interests of the US industrial and military complex) with 'weapons of mass destruction' allegedly in the hands of a notoriously erratic national leader.[47]

4 From Port-au-Prince via Free Town to Banjul: Pro-democratic Intervention in Post-Cold War International Practice

Tellingly, the PDI thesis, as originally framed by Reisman and others, has not been employed to justify the thread or use of armed force by external actors even in those post-1989 cases, in which democratic considerations most likely did constitute the overriding *raison d'être* of international action. Among these

---

aggression against it is ongoing and that the threat of further armed attacks cannot be repelled effectively other than by ensuring the removal of the actual source of the threat – the regime of the aggressor state; Fox (n 23) para 34.

45 The liberation of the Iraqi people from the Baath regime and the creation of a democratic government in Iraq certainly played a role in political debates prior to the invasion, yet this aspect never made it into any of the official statements provided to justify *Operation Iraqi Freedom*. Instead, the intervening states relied on the extremely controversial argument that their action in 2003 was taken under the 'revived' authority of UNSC Resolution 678 (1990), which had been adopted by the Security Council in response to Iraq's invasion of Kuwait. For a critical discussion of the legality and wider implications of the operation see Gray (n 22) 367–72.

46 To be sure, following the end of major military combat, democracy promotion became a core element of post-conflict international state-building in Afghanistan as well as the US/UK occupation of post-Baathist Iraq.

47 For a detailed recount and assessment of both operations see L Moir, *Reappraising the Resort to Force: International Law, Jus ad Bellum and the War on Terror* (Hart 2010).

cases, the 1994 US-led *Operation Uphold Democracy* against the military junta in Haiti, which – three years earlier – had ousted Haiti's first democratically elected president, Jean-Bertrand Aristide, still stands out due to its explicit endorsement by the Security Council under Chapter VII of the UN Charter. In essence, UNSC Resolution 940 (1994), which authorized the use of 'all necessary means to facilitate the departure from Haiti of the military leadership' and 'the prompt return of the legitimately elected President',[48] can be seen as tacit acceptance on the part of the Council that utter disregard for the outcome of free and fair elections in a UN member state may, under certain circumstances, constitute a threat to international peace in terms of Article 39 of the UN Charter.[49] The 'under certain circumstances' caveat has to be taken seriously, however, given that the UNSC had described the situation in Haiti as 'unique' and its response to it as 'exceptional'.[50]

Though the Council did not specify as to what exactly accounted for the 'uniqueness' of the Haiti case, it may be inferred from the overall context of the episode that (at least) four factors played a critical role.[51] First, following the example set two years earlier by the UN General Assembly,[52] the Council continued to recognize Aristide as Haiti's legitimate leader, while denouncing the junta in Port-au-Prince as an 'illegal de facto regime'.[53] Second, as it became clear that international condemnation and economic sanctions failed to convince the junta to step aside, Aristide formally requested the UN to take 'prompt and decisive action'; a fact the Council explicitly took note of in Resolution 940 (1994).[54] Third, throughout the entire affair, the UNSC consistently highlighted the multiple efforts undertaken in support of Haiti's elected government within the framework of the Organisation of American States (OAS).[55] Lastly, while the Security Council left no doubt that the restoration

48 UNSC Res 940 (1994), UN Doc S/RES/940 (31 July 1994) para 4.

49 C Vandewoude, 'The Democratic Entitlement and Pro-Democratic Interventions: Twenty Years After Haiti' (2012) XII Anuario Mexicano de Derecho Internacional 779.

50 UNSC Res 940 (n 48) para 2.

51 See J Leininger, 'Haiti, Conflict' in A Peters and R Wolfrum (eds), *Max Planck Encyclopedia of Public International Law* (online edn, OUP 2008) para 29.

52 UNGA Res 46/7 (11 October 1991) UN Doc A/RES/46/7 (1991) para 2.

53 UNSC Res 841 (1993), UN Doc S/RES/841 (16 June 1993) para 4; UNSC Res 940 (n 48) para 3.

54 UNSC 'Letter Dated 30 July 1994 from the Permanent Representative of Haiti to the United Nations Addressed to the Secretary-General' (30 July 1994) UN Doc S/1994/910 Annex.

55 In Resolution 841 (n 53) the Council noted that any solution of the crisis should take the relevant decisions of the Organization of American States into account (para 1). On the OAS response to the coup in Haiti see BR Roth, *Governmental Illegitimacy in International Law* (Oxford 2000) 372–76.

of democracy in Haiti was the international community's primary objective,[56] Resolution 940 also pointed to the deteriorating humanitarian situation and a growing 'climate of fear', which the Council suspected 'could increase the number of Haitians seeking refuge in neighbouring Member States'.[57] Clearly, this (not entirely persuasive) hint at possible repercussions of the Haitian crisis on regional peace and stability was meant to heed the concerns of some Council members who remained sceptical that a rupture of a state's political and constitutional order would in itself justify the invocation of the UNSC's Chapter VII enforcement powers.[58]

The Haiti episode ushered in a new era with respect to the UNSC's approach to coups against duly elected governments, including, more recently, so-called 'self-coups' by incumbent leaders.[59] Over the past quarter-century, the Council has repeatedly rejected unconstitutional attempts to overturn the results of free and fair elections (though the UN organ remained conspicuously silent in some instances).[60] In a limited number of cases, the Council also followed the Haiti precedent and denied recognition to coup regimes.[61] Moreover, by invoking Chapter VII of the UN Charter, the Security Council has in some instances imposed coercive measures (such as arms embargos, travel bans,

56 UNSC Res 917 (1994), UN Doc S/RES/917 (6 May 1994) preamble; UNSC Res 940 (n 48) preamble.

57 UNSC Res 841 (n 53) preamble, para 11.

58 UNSC Res 940 (n 48) was finally adopted by a vote of twelve in favor, none against, with two abstentions; UNSC 'Provisional Verbatim Record of the 3413th Meeting' (31 July 1994) UN Doc S/PV.3413.

59 J d'Aspremont, 'Responsibility for Coups d'État in International Law' (2010) 18 TJICL451.

60 Notable examples of UNSC silence vis-à-vis coups against elected governments include the cases of Pakistan (1999) and Thailand (2006, 2014); see O Tansey, 'Lowest Common Denominator Norm Institutionalization: The Anti-Coup Norm at the United Nations' (2018) 24 Global Governance 287. More recently, the UNSC also responded in a rather lackluster fashion to the 2021 military takeover in Myanmar (following general elections in November 2020 which had resulted in a resounding victory of Aung San Suu Kyi's National League for Democracy). In a Presidential Statement issued six weeks after the military's seizure of power, the Council deplored the arbitrary detention of Suu Kyi and condemned the violence against peaceful protesters. However, at the behest of China and Russia, the UNSC avoided to label the events in Myanmar a 'coup' and desisted from mentioning even the possibility of more robust measures should the junta ignore its calls 'to uphold democratic institutions and processes' and to 'refrain from violence'; UN Doc S/PRST/2021/5 (10 March 2021).

61 On the general issue of non-recognition of coup-based regimes (and the prevailing selectivity displayed by the UN and the wider international community in this regard) see E de Wet, 'From Free Town to Cairo via Kiev: The Unpredictable Road of Democratic Legitimacy in Governmental Recognition' (2015) 108 AJIL Unbound 201.

and targeted economic sanctions) against coup perpetrators and their supporters.[62] While the Council continued to avoid the impression that a threat to international peace and security might be located exclusively in domestic disruptions of democracy, the inclusion of additional concerns in some of the respective Council resolutions clearly served no other purpose than to attribute some cross-border dimension to the situation at stake, however anecdotal or far-fetched.[63]

Overall, the UNSC has in recent years signalled a growing willingness to concern itself with illegal seizures of power from freely elected governments. Thus far, however, the Haiti case remained the only example in which the Council explicitly authorized a full military operation against a coup regime in order to safeguard the will of the people as expressed in democratic elections. In 1997, the UNSC used its Chapter VII powers to impose an oil and arms embargo against the military junta in Sierra Leone, which had acceded to governmental power as a result of a coup against elected President Ahmad Kabbah. Resolution 1132 (1997) also authorized the Economic Community of West African States (ECOWAS) to use force to ensure the implementation of the embargo by halting inward maritime shipping.[64] Yet, in January 1998, the Nigerian-led ECOWAS Monitoring Group (ECOMOG), whose presence in Sierra Leone had been approved by President Kabbah,[65] went beyond the Council's limited mandate to use force by engaging in an all-out attack on the military regime, which quickly resulted in the junta's defeat and removal from power. The UNSC, for its part, seemed rather untroubled by ECOMOG's unilateral move. In a statement by the President of the UNSC, ECOWAS was commended on its role in the resolution of the crisis, which, a month later, was followed by a Council resolution explicitly welcoming 'the return to Sierra Leone of its democratically elected President'.[66] While some have suggested that the Security Council's response to the events in Sierra Leone has effectively put a retroactive

62 For an overview see Tansey (n 60) 293.

63 Resolution 2048 (2012), adopted in response to the 2012 coup d'état in Guinea-Bissau, may be cited as a case in point. While the Council condemned the coup and explicitly invoked Art 41 of the Charter to impose an arms embargo as well es targeted sanctions against the coup regime, the resolution lacks almost any indication as to the peace-threatening transboundary effects of the case (other than a vague concern that the 'possible' increase in illicit drug trafficking as a result of the coup may negatively affect Guinea-Bissau 'and the subregion'); UNSC Res 2048 (2012), UN Doc S/RES/2048 (18 May 2012) preamble.

64 UNSC Res 1132 (1997) UN Doc S/RES/1132 (8 October 1997).

65 Gray (n 22) 439.

66 See UNSC 'Statement by the President of the Security Council' UN Doc S/PRST/1998/5 (26 February 1998); UNSC Res 1156 (1998) UN Doc S/RES/1156 (16 March 1998).

de jure seal on ECOMOG's military intervention,[67] it remains doubtful whether such a reading can in fact be reconciled with the wording of Article 53(1) of the UN Charter (which provides that the Council shall, where appropriate, utilize regional organizations for enforcement action 'under its authority'). Moreover, the Council's praise for the outcome of ECOMOG's intervention in Sierra Leone did not involve any of the language usually associated with UNSC authorizations pertaining to the use of force by states or regional organizations.[68]

Robust UN and (sub-)regional action in response to so-called 'self-coups' by incumbent rulers were at the centre of the more recent cases of Côte d'Ivoire (2011) and The Gambia (2017). In Côte d'Ivoire, political stability was already strained by persistent religious and ethnic cleavages when fresh conflict broke out in late 2010 as a result of President Laurent Gbagbo's refusal to hand over power to Alassane Ouattara, the winner of UN certified presidential elections. Gbagbo's self-coup was widely condemned by the international community, including the UN, the African Union (AU) and ECOWAS.[69] In December 2010, two weeks before Ouattara officially requested foreign military assistance to secure his electoral victory,[70] ECOWAS issued an ultimatum to Gbagbo and announced that, if he fails to heed it, the organization would be left with no alternative 'but to take other measures, including the use of legitimate force'.[71] The UNSC, for its part, took no position on this threat of force by ECOWAS. Rather, the Council affirmed the decision taken by ECOWAS and the AU to recognize Ouattara as President-elect and legitimate representative of the Ivorian people.[72] Moreover, the Council recalled its earlier authorization given to the UN peace-keeping force in Côte d'Ivoire (UNOCI) 'to use all necessary means to carry out its mandate to protect civilians under imminent threat of physical

---

67 See eg JI Levitt, 'Pro-Democratic Intervention in Africa' (2006) 24 WILJ 785, 801; BD Kreykes, 'A Case for Delegation: The UN Security Council, Regional Conflicts, and Regional Organizations' (2008) 11 Touro International Law Review 1.

68 K Nowrot and EW Schabacker, 'The Use of Force to Restore Democracy: International Legal Implications of the ECOWAS Intervention in Sierra Leone' (1998) 14 AUILR 312, 362. On the issue of UNSC *ex post facto* approval of military force see generally M Hakimi, 'To Condone or Condemn? Regional Enforcement Actions in the Absence of Security Council Authorization' (2007) 40 VJTL 643; I Johnstone, 'Condoning the Use of Force: The UN Security Council as Interpreter of the *Jus Ad Bellum*' (2018) 112 AJIL Unbound 113.

69 JD Gagnon, 'ECOWAS's Right to Intervene in Côte d'Ivoire to Install Alassane Ouattara as President-Elect' (2013) 3 Notre Dame JICL 51.

70 By a letter addressed to ECOWAS dated 6 January 2011 (ibid 65).

71 ECOWAS, Extraordinary Session of the Authority of Heads of State and Government on Côte d'Ivoire, Final Communiqué, ECW/CEG/ABJ/EXT/Fr./Rev. 0 (24 December 2010) para 10.

72 UNSC Res 1962 (2010) UN Doc S/RES/1962 (20 December 2010).

violence'.[73] In implementing its mandate, UNOCI received critical support by UNSC-authorized French forces, which were already present in Côte d'Ivoire (initially by agreement with the Ivorian government).[74] The French troops applied force to halt Gbagbo's increasing assaults on civilians and to stop his attacks on UNOCI. On 11 April 2011, following a decisive attack on military camps and the presidential palace in Abidjan by pro-Ouattara forces – backed both by UNOCI and French troops – Gbagbo was arrested and President-elect Ouattara finally took office.[75]

Despite its eventual outcome (the disposal of an illegitimate de facto ruler with the help of foreign and UN troops authorized by the Security Council), the Côte d'Ivoire episode must not be mistaken for a Haiti-style PDI. There can be no doubt that the military actions carried out by UNOCI and the French forces under the already existing humanitarian mandates provided to them by the Council contributed significantly to pro-democratic regime change in Côte d'Ivoire. But while the UNSC expressed support for the efforts by ECOWAS and the AU to resolve the post-electoral crisis[76] and imposed targeted sanctions against the Gbagbo regime, the Council never authorized military action specifically aimed at Gbagbo's removal from power and the installation of Ouattara as Côte d'Ivoire's new *de jure* leader.

In a sense, the Côte d'Ivoire episode is reminiscent of a further instance of regime change advanced, at least implicitly, by UNSC-authorized military action (although in this case without any linkage to UN peace keeping): NATO's *Operation Unified Protector*, which also happened to be implemented in 2011. Similar to the situation in Côte d'Ivoire, NATO's involvement in the Libyan crisis clearly accelerated the fall of the country's autocratic ruler, Muammar Gaddafi, at the hands of the Libyan rebels. Yet, while the UNSC at a later stage expressed its hope that, following the end of the conflict in Libya, the ensuing political transition will be 'underpinned by a commitment to democracy',[77] Resolution 1973 (2011) – which provided the legal basis for NATO's military engagement – strictly limited the use of force to the airborne protection of

---

73 UNSC Res 1975 (2010) UN Doc S/RES/1975 (30 March 2011).

74 The authorization provided to the French troops in Côte d'Ivoire to use force in order to assist UNOCI in the implementation of its mandate goes back to UNSC Res 1528 (2004) UN Doc S/RES/1528 (27 February 2004).

75 28th Report of the Secretary-General on the United Nations Operation in Côte d'Ivoire, UN Doc S/2011/387 (24 June 2011).

76 Whether the relevant endorsement by the UNSC was meant to also include the December 2010 ultimatum vis-à-vis Gbagbo by ECOWAS (and the threat of force that came with it) remains unclear.

77 UNSC Res 2009 (2011) UN Doc S/RES/2009 (16 September 2011) para 2.

'civilians and civilian populated areas under threat of attack'.[78] Hence, whatever one makes of the contentious debate as to whether NATO ultimately went beyond the limits set by the Council, it seems clear that what Resolution 1973 intended to sanction was exclusively a humanitarian (or R2P) operation, not an intervention to forcibly facilitate regime change and the formation of democratic government in Libya.[79]

The most recent cross-border military action that can reasonably be considered a PDI was the 2017 ECOWAS-led *Operation Restore Democracy* in The Gambia. Similar to the Côte d'Ivoire case, the episode was set off by a self-coup on the part of Gambia's former President, Yahya Jammeh, who saw himself unfit to accept the humiliation of having been defeated in democratic elections. Although he initially declared to respect the outcome of the December 2016 presidential elections, he changed his mind a few days later, professed to challenge the result before Gambia's Constitutional Court and requested Parliament to extent his term in office. The President's *volte-face* was immediately condemned by the UN, as well as regional organisations, and ECOWAS once again stood ready to secure – 'by all means necessary' – the winner of the elections, Adama Barrow, his rightful place in the presidential palace in Banjul.[80] ECOWAS' position was firmly supported by the African Union, which confirmed that, as of 19 January 2017 (the final date foreseen by the Gambian constitution for the swearing-in of a new head of state following presidential elections) 'outgoing President Jammeh will cease to be recognized as the legitimate President of The Gambia'.[81] As the deadline approached, ECOWAS troops massed around the country's borders. Barrow was sworn in on 19 January – albeit not in The Gambia but in the Gambian embassy in Senegal – and promptly requested military assistance to implement the will of the people as expressed in the December 2016 elections.[82] Almost simultaneously,

78 UNSC Res 1973 (2011) UN Doc S/RES/1973 (17 March 2011) para 4.

79 For detailed discussions of the case see C Pippan, 'The 2011 Libyan Uprising, Foreign Military Intervention, and International Law' (2011) 2 juridikum 159; M Payandeh, 'The UN, Military Intervention, and Regime Change in Libya' (2011–2012) 52 VJIL 355; G Wilson, 'The United Nations Security Council, Libya and Resolution 1973: Protection of Civilians or Tool for Regime Change' in C Panara and G Wilson (eds), *The Arab Spring: New Patterns for Democracy and International Law* (Nijhoff 2013).

80 ECOWAS, 50th Ordinary Session of the Authority of Heads of State and Government, Final Communiqué (17 December 2016) para 38.

81 African Union, Communiqué of the Peace and Security Council (13 January 2017) AU Doc PSC/PR/COMM (DCXLVII) para 5.

82 C Kreß and B Nußberger, 'Pro-Democratic Intervention in Current International Law: The Case of The Gambia' (2017) 4 Journal on the Use of Force and International Law 239, 241.

the UNSC adopted Resolution 2337 (2017), in which the Council unanimously endorsed the measures taken by ECOWAS and the AU, including their decisions to recognize Adama Barrow as the legitimate President of The Gambia.[83] While the resolution was not adopted under Chapter VII of the UN Charter and consequently did not include any specific authorization to use force, the Council called upon 'the countries in the region and the relevant regional organization to cooperate with President Barrow in his efforts to realize the transition to power'.[84] Two days later, following reports of ECOWAS troops having already crossed the Gambian border, Jammeh accepted to step down on the basis of a last-minute deal hammered out by ECOWAS, the AU, and the UN.[85]

5 PDI & International Law Thirty Years Post-Haiti: Where Do We Stand?

As the case of Haiti revealed, military action aimed at enforcing the results of internationally monitored elections may be authorized by the Security Council under the enforcement system contained in Chapter VII of the UN Charter provided that, in the opinion of the Council, some attendant transboundary effects of the case in question can be identified which carry at least a potential risk of threatening regional peace and security. In practice, however, the Security Council hardly ever makes use of this opportunity. To the extent that disruptions of domestic democratic processes were taken up by the UNSC in recent years, the Council did not revisit the vigorous, pro-active route chosen almost three decades ago against the Haitian junta. However, over the years, the Council adopted a remarkably lenient attitude towards pro-democratic threats or uses of force by regional actors. Tellingly, perhaps, the most prominent cases in this regard – Sierra Leone (1998), Côte d'Ivoire (2011), and The Gambia (2017) – all originated in Africa. All of them involved coups or self-coups against democratically elected governments. In each case, the use of force, or – in the Côte d'Ivoire case – the threat of it, was initiated by a subregional actor (ECOWAS, habitually supported by the African Union) without

83 UNSC Res 2337 (2017) UN Doc S/RES/2337 (19 January 2017) para 2.

84 Ibid, para 3.

85 Joint Declaration by ECOWAS, the African Union and the United Nations on the Political Situation of the Islamic Republic of The Gambia (Office of the Spokesperson of the UN Secretary-General, 21 January 2017) <https://www.un.org/sg/en/content/note-correspondents/2017-01-21/note-correspondents-joint-declaration-political-situation> accessed 15 February 2022.

prior UNSC blessing in terms of Article 53(1) of the UN Charter. Yet, none of these threats or uses of force were treated by the Council as transgressions of the Charter or general international law. Rather, the Security Council implicitly condoned or openly supported the military actions undertaken by African regional organisations.

What is one to make of this? Does the practice of the UNSC indicate confirmation on the part of the UN of the emergence of a customary PDI-norm, at least on a regional basis, which has altered the provisions of the UN Charter regarding the primacy of the Security Council over regional organisations in matters affecting international peace and security? Though supported by some authors, particularly with a view to the emerging African peace and security system,[86] such a reading of pertinent UN and regional practice is difficult to sustain. As Wippman points out, it is unclear 'how regional practice, even if tolerated and perhaps tacitly welcomed by the UN, can modify the UN Charter or *jus cogens* norms on the use of force'.[87] Moreover, the Security Council itself seems rather loath to accept that regional practice may be able to modify the basic tenets of the collective security system enshrined in the UN Charter. Thus, in a 2009 Presidential Statement regarding the resurgence of unconstitutional changes of government in parts of Africa, the Council welcomed the continuing efforts by the AU and sub-regional organisations to promote democracy and constitutional order in Africa but also recalled 'its primary responsibility for the maintenance of international peace and security' and that regional efforts must be 'consistent with Security Council resolutions and decisions'.[88]

Hence, to come to terms with the more recent PDIs in (Western) Africa, one needs to look beyond the UN Charter framework. Here, the focus quickly shifts to a further golden thread that runs through practically all of the relevant episodes mentioned above: In Sierra Leone, as well as in Côte d'Ivoire and The Gambia, each of the elected leaders who in one way or another had fallen victim to an unconstitutional seizure of power, issued a formal request for foreign military assistance at some point of the political and constitutional crisis that was generated by the disruption of the democratic processes in their respective countries. When they did so, each of them lacked effective control over the territory of the state they nonetheless claimed to represent. Pursuant

---

86 Levitt (n 67) 787. See also JM Iyi, *Humanitarian Intervention and the AU-ECOWAS Intervention Treaties Under International Law. Towards a Theory of Regional Responsibility to Protect* (Springer 2016).

87 Wippman (n 1) 814.

88 UN Doc S/PRST/2009/11 (5 May 2009).

to conventional doctrine, this would inevitably call into question the validity of such requests and, accordingly, the legality of any military action based on them.[89] Yet, in situations marked by a coup or reverse coup against a democratically elected regime, it has become increasingly doubtful whether conventional doctrine still holds.

As such, the concept of 'intervention by invitation' is widely recognized in international legal doctrine and practice as providing a legal basis for the deployment of foreign troops on the territory of a state whose recognized government has freely consented to it.[90] The underlying rationale proceeds from the assumption that, when military action is taken by states or international organizations with the valid consent of the state concerned, the element of coercion – a foundational aspect of the non-intervention norms of the UN Charter and general international law[91] – is simply absent.[92] In principle, a request for military assistance may be expressed ad hoc in response to a particular crisis in the requesting state or, perhaps, *ex ante* by way of a state's accession to a bi- or multilateral treaty entailing a 'pro-invasion clause' employable under the specific conditions laid down in the relevant treaty. The latter is clearly more controversial than the former and raises a number of vexing legal issues.[93] The best known modern examples of treaty-based pro-invasion clauses are Article 4(h) of the Constitutive Act of the African Union[94] and Article 25(e) of the 1999 ECOWAS Protocol on Conflict Prevention.[95] So far, both ECOWAS and the AU have refrained from basing military operations in their member states exclusively on treaty-based *ex ante* consent. Rather, as exemplified, inter alia, by the ECOWAS interventions in Sierra Leone (1998) and The Gambia (2017), such operations have consistently been implemented only after having obtained the additional ad hoc consent of the recognized *de jure*

89 G Nolte, 'Intervention by Invitation' in A Peters and R Wolfrum (eds), *Max Planck Encyclopedia of Public International Law* (online edn, OUP 2010) para 18.

90 GH Fox, 'Intervention by Invitation' in M Weller (ed), *The Oxford Handbook on the Use of Force in International Law* (OUP 2015) 816. For a detailed recent analysis see E de Wet, *Military Assistance on Request and the Use of Force* (OUP 2020).

91 Supra (at n 15).

92 See L Visser, 'May the Force Be with You: The Legal Classification of Intervention by Invitation' (2019) 66 NILR 21.

93 See BR Roth, 'The Illegality of "Pro-Democratic" Invasion Pacts', in Fox and Roth (CUP, n 9) 328; Wippman (n 1) 808–14.

94 Constitutive Act of the African Union (adopted 11 July 2000, entered into force 26 May 2001) 2158 UNTS 3, Art 4(h).

95 Protocol Relating to the Mechanism for Conflict Prevention, Management, Resolution, Peacekeeping and Security (adopted 10 December 1999, provisionally entered into force 10 December 1999) ECOWAS Doc A/P10/12/99, Art 25(e).

government or adequate authorization by the UNSC.[96] Overall, this appears to confirm the position, strongly supported in legal scholarship, that under general international law a state's 'standing invitation' to intervene expressed in a pro-invasion pact must be complemented by ad hoc consent given at the time that foreign military assistance actually takes place.[97]

As mentioned above, the authority to extend (or revoke) a request for military assistance rests with the recognized government of the state concerned. According to the traditional view, governmental recognition hinges first and foremost on 'effective control',[98] which would imply that the regime extending (or revoking) such a request needs to demonstrate a minimum of effectiveness over the territory of the state in question or at least a sufficiently representative part of it.[99] In light of recent (post-Cold War) institutional and state practice, however, the relevant question of agency in this context – namely: is the regime extending an intervention to intervene duly entitled to speak for the state? – can no longer be answered exclusively, or mechanically, on the basis of the effective control doctrine.[100]

Without venturing into details here,[101] it shall be recalled that in all of the relevant cases mentioned above the UNSC denied to afford recognition to coup regimes in effective control and approved, expressly or tacitly, requests for military assistance (addressed either directly to the UN or to a regional organisation) by elected leaders who, at the time of the issuing of the request, wielded no effective territorial control whatsoever. It is true that, in the Haiti case, the Council still seemed reluctant to treat exiled President Aristide's request for assistance as a sufficient legal basis for military action against the Haitian junta and instead relied on its own authority under Chapter VII of the UN Charter.[102] But such reluctance was no longer visible in later cases. Following the 1997 *coup d'état* in Sierra Leone, the UNSC condoned the PDI undertaken by ECOWAS upon request by exiled President Kabbah (who, despite his disposal from power, continued to be recognized as Sierra Leone's *de jure* head of

---

96 De Wet (n 90) 170–80.

97 Ibid 179. Eventually, this also resonates with the ICJ's general dictum according to which consent by states to foreign military operations on their territory must be 'revocable'; *Armed Activities on the Territory of the Congo (Democratic Republic of the Congo v Uganda)*, Merits [2005] ICJ Rep 168 para 46.

98 As per the classical *Tinoco Claims Arbitration (Great Britain v Costa Rica)* 1923 1 RIAA 369.

99 Roth (n 55) 185.

100 Fox (n 90) 833.

101 For further elaboration see D Wippman, 'Pro-Democratic Intervention by Invitation' in Fox and Roth (CUP, n 9) 299–311; Roth (n 55) 365–412; de Wet (n 90) 21–73.

102 See supra (at n 48).

state), even though ECOMOG's forcible removal of the military junta was not based on any prior Chapter VII authorization.[103]

The UNSC's response to the 2017 self-coup by incumbent President Jammeh in The Gambia is even more instructive: When Adama Barrow, the winner of the 2016 presidential elections, requested assistance from ECOWAS, he had never wielded any control over any part of Gambian territory.[104] While purposely refraining from addressing the situation under Chapter VII of the UN Charter, the UNSC nevertheless endorsed Barrow's recognition as Gambia's new president and supported the commitment by ECOWAS 'to ensure, *by political means first*, the respect of the will of the people of The Gambia'.[105] Notably, this came after the Gambian Parliament (which was still under control of Jammeh loyalists) had extended the incumbent President's term in office for ninety days beyond his original mandate and as Jammeh was still contesting the results of the 2016 elections before Gambia's Constitutional Court.[106] Yet, in the end, Barrow's clear democratic legitimacy, derived from elections he had won despite their attempted manipulation by Jammeh aides,[107] coupled with his collective recognition as Gambia's *de jure* leader by ECOWAS, the AU and – most importantly – the UNSC, evidently 'remedied' any concerns that otherwise might have been associated with the validity of the elected president's request for outside military assistance.

Ultimately, it is in such situations that the impact of the democratic legitimacy principle on the international law on the use of force becomes particularly tangible. Twenty-five years ago, commenting on *Operation Uphold Democracy* in Haiti, David Wippman remarked:

> If the Security Council seriously believed that Aristide constituted the only legitimate authority in Haiti and relied on Aristide's consent as a sufficient basis in itself for military intervention, that would have signalled a significant shift in international law.[108]

103 Nowrot and Schabacker (n 68) 396.

104 In fact, Barrow was sworn into office in the Gambian Embassy in Senegal only hours before he extended his request to ECOWAS (supra, at n 82).

105 UNSC Res 2337 (n 83) para 6 (emphasis added). Logically, the statement implied the Council's acceptance of military means should a political solution of the crisis remain unattainable.

106 Kreß and Nußberger (n 82) 248.

107 De Wet (n 90) 56.

108 Wippman (n 21) 677.

In light of the Council's subsequent practice, most notably in the cases of Sierra Leone and The Gambia, it might be suggested that this 'shift' in international law has, to a certain extent at least, become a reality. Of course, it is important not to overread the relevant (still highly selective) UN and regional practice in this regard. Instances, in which the principle of democratic legitimacy has replaced effective control as the decisive element in establishing the legal standing of a regime to exercise the state's sovereign rights in the international arena (including the right to extend a request for military assistance to foreign actors) have been limited to largely unambiguous cases of unconstitutional seizures of power in defiance of the will of the people, particularly when that will had been empirically ascertained in genuine elections.[109]

The international community's willingness to accept as lawful a 'PDI by invitation' in such scenarios strongly depends on the degree of collective validation of both the democratic pedigree and the *de jure* governmental status of the authority issuing the relevant request.[110] In order to minimize the risk of abuse, the relevant determinations cannot be left to individual states or sub-regional actors (who may be dominated by certain states) alone. Rather, for all practical purposes and in accordance with previous practice, this task primarily falls to the UNSC. Given the well-known deficiencies of the Council and its decision-making procedures, this approach certainly has its shortcomings; not least since the plurality of values and interests represented by its members will frequently prevent the Council from making the relevant determinations when faced with a 'recognition contest' following a coup or self-coup against a democratically elected regime.[111] That said, the solution's attractiveness lies in the fact that it reserves a crucial role for the Security Council in determining whether, in such situations, force may lawfully be used to restore an elected government to power, without the Council having to formally activate the collective security machinery under Chapter VII of the UN Charter.[112] This understanding is also in line with the underlying logic of the

109 Wippman (n 101) 308–11. See also BR Roth, 'Secession, Coups and the International Rule of Law: Assessing the Decline of the Effective Control Doctrine' (2010) 11 MJIL 2, 37.

110 Fox (n 23) para 31.

111 Arguably, in the absence of a UNSC position on the matter, the adoption of a broadly supported UN General Assembly resolution, entailing a declaration as to who shall be entitled to speak for a particular state, might offer an alternative route. The Assembly's response to the 'recognition contest' following the 2009 legislative coup against President Zelaya in Honduras perhaps provides an example in this regard; see GA Res 63/301 UN Doc A/RES/63/301 (1 July 2009). For a critical discussion of the Honduras case see Roth (n 109) 42–46.

112 Kreß and Nußberger (n 82) 250.

Charter, according to which – save for situations of self-defence – it shall be for the collective body of the UNSC, rather than for individual states or regional arrangements, to have the final word in matters involving the use of force in international relations.

6 Concluding Remarks

The debate on the (il)legality of pro-democratic armed intervention in international law is one of the remnants of the 'constitutional moment' often associated in international legal scholarship with end of the Cold War and the demise of 'old-school' East-West antagonism at the beginning of the 1990s.[113] Roughly thirty years later, one can hardly fight the impression that some of the defining early contributions to the debate were fuelled by the heat of the moment and an overly optimistic view of the direction into which the international legal order would inevitably advance. Not surprisingly, however, the hard-core version of the PDI thesis, which advocated the emergence of a new customary rule according to which even unilateral uses of force without any UN involvement would be lawful if their aim is to defend or restore 'fledgling democracies', did not stand the test of time. Rather, as relevant state and institutional practice from Haiti (1994) to The Gambia (2017) indicates, authorization by the UNSC under Chapters VII and VIII of the UN Charter, or consent to foreign military assistance by a state's legitimate government, remain the only viable, broadly accepted justifications for pro-democratic armed intervention.

To the extent that the notion of pro-democratic intervention is understood in the rather narrow terms applied in this contribution, the 1994 intervention in Haiti remains a singular event, as it so far represents the only PDI which was carried out by a multinational coalition based on an explicit prior 'Chapter VII mandate' provided by the Security Council. Subsequently, spurred by a growing number of pertinent cases, particularly in Africa, the focus of the PDI discourse shifted to the concept of 'PDI by invitation'; that is, the provision of pro-democratic military assistance by external actors upon request of the recognized government of the state concerned. The concept is no doubt ripe with tricky legal issues. Yet, as a general matter, recent practice by the UN as well as regional and sub-regional organisations implies that, when domestic actors attempt to reverse the will of the people, ascertained in internationally verified

113 Boysen (n 7).

free and fair elections, the deposed 'legitimate' (read: democratically elected) regime may retain the right to speak for the state and, hence, validly extend a request for military assistance against the illegitimate de facto rulers – notwithstanding that it lacks the kind of effective control normally required of *de jure* governments in international law.

In light of the undeniable risk of abuse, unilateral determinations as to the (continued) governmental status of an elected (yet ousted) regime are generally not viewed by the international community as providing a valid legal basis for foreign intervention, even in clear cases of unconstitutional disruptions of democracy. As a result, the permissibility of invited PDIs in international law ultimately hinges on an authoritative statement on the question of recognition by the UNSC (which would not necessarily have to be adopted under Chapter VII of the UN Charter), or, perhaps, the General Assembly (in case the Council is not seized with the matter or is effectively held hostage by one of its veto-holding permanent members).

As such, the concept of 'PDI by intervention' is situated beyond the collective security framework of the UN Charter. Reserving, nonetheless, a prominent position for the UN (particularly the UNSC) in this context means to accept that military assistance to defend or restore democracy in cases of unconstitutional seizures of power from duly elected governments will remain selective and dependent on political considerations of the major powers. Moreover, given that the supposedly outdated vision of a 'dichotomized world'[114] is seeming to gain traction again in world politics, it might well turn out that the growing influence of authoritarian states will further narrow liberal expectations about the role the UN in general and the Security Council in particular may be able to play when it comes to the protection of democratic institutions and processes within states.[115]

114 JHH Weiler, 'Armed Intervention in a Dichotomized World: The Case of Grenada' in A Cassese (ed), *The Current Legal Regulation of the Use of Force* (Nijhoff 1986).

115 See generally AS Weiner, 'Authoritarian International Law, the Use of Force, and Intervention' (2020) 114 AJIL Unbound 220.

CHAPTER 3

Democracy and the Rule of Law

Articulating the National and International Judiciary with Majoritarian Will: Some Thoughts Based on a Comparative Approach of the Regional Human Rights Courts (RHRC) Case Law

Laurence Burgorgue-Larsen

How do International and National Judiciaries take into account the Majoritarian Will of national societies in our globalised world? This is a complex question, affecting as it does the democratic foundations of our societies. In this respect, the notion has been subject to heavy criticism in academic and legal circles the world over. From Lord Sumption (an historian and former judge at the UK Supreme Court)[1] to Roberto Gargarella (an Argentinean legal theorist and political scientist),[2] to the leading scholar Jeremy Waldron (a well-known

1 Lord Sumption presented, in five *Reith Lectures* – organised by BBC Radio 4 – his vision of law in society and, in particular, his restrictive approach to the role of the judge in the City, defending 'a more politics, less law thesis' (see especially Reith Lectures No. 1 '*Law's Expanding Empire*'; No. 2 '*In Praise of Politics*'; and No. 3 '*Human Rights and Wrongs*'). The President of the ECtHR, Robert Spano, (without deviating from his adherence to the principle of subsidiarity and to the process-based review doctrine), skilfully defended the European Court's methods of interpretation. He simultaneously articulated, at a time of 'democratic deconsolidation', that: 'European societies established a structure of constitutional democracy in which certain fundamental rights and values were given normative status limiting majoritarian rule. In this manner, they attempted to make the political process itself more rational, less prone to being dominated by gut feelings, by fear, anger and hatred, all primitive human rights elements that have given life to populist and ultimately self-destructive tendency', see The Inaugural Bonavero Institute, *Annual Human Rights Lecture. The Democratic Virtues of Human Rights Law-A Response to Lord Sumption's Reith Lectures*, (*ECHR*, 20 February 2020) https://www.echr.coe.int/Documents/Speech_20200220_Spano_Lecture_London_ENG.pdf.

2 In an article entirely focused on the *Gelman* case (IACtHR, *Gelman v. Uruguay*, Merits, Reparations and Costs, Series C No. 22 (Feb. 24, 2011), R Gargarella radically rejects the Inter-American Court's case law on amnesties. The starting point of his analysis– its philosophical foundation – is the State and its processes of deliberation, rather than the individual and the principle of protection *pro homine*. He believes instead that the Court should have drawn a distinction between the different kinds of amnesties in Latin America, for example by taking into consideration their varying degrees of democratic legitimacy. He criticizes how little importance the Court seems to give to 'majorities', especially when their will runs counter to human rights, see 'Sin lugar para la soberania popular. Democracia, derechos y castigo en el caso Gelman', Latin-American Seminar on Constitutional Theory and Policy,

 | DOI:10.1163/9789004508712_004

NYU professor of Constitutional Law),[3] the activism of the Judiciary is seen as a disproportionate attack on democracy; a principle which is supposed to be embodied by the people's representatives in legislative assemblies.

It is nonetheless the case that the role of national courts and the primary role of constitutional courts (CC) is, broadly speaking, to protect the rights of minorities. Democracy itself is, then, at stake here. The subject becomes further complicated when international courts (IC) – and more specifically, due to their functions, the regional human rights courts (RHRC), which will be the focal point of this article[4] – come into play. These courts must 'reconcile' their juridical control with that of national courts, which are the first to examine the conformity between laws adopted by political majorities, and constitutional rules.

Several scenarios are then conceivable. I will touch on two classic ones here. In the first scenario, the RHRC exercise their control by considering and approving the solutions proposed by domestic courts, which had themselves approved the legislative choices of the majority. In this instance, there is consistency between the two judicial solutions, and jurisdictional peace is thus achieved. This in turn avoids political uproar in the legal and political arenas. In the second scenario, RHRC call into question the decisions of national courts which had been respectful of the national legislative power, *i.e*, the Majoritarian Will. This specific scenario of discordance between national and international judicial solutions gives rise to the 'democratic question' *par excellence.*

Opponents of international judicial review will not hesitate to utilise the argument of democratic usurpation in order to lambast the International Judiciary's decisions – particularly when they call into question previous decisions taken by a domestic court that validate the legislative choices of the majority. At the other end of the spectrum, advocates of international scrutiny will emphasise the importance of the last resort principle, because a healthy democracy is one which, ultimately, protects the rights of minorities.

(Yale University 2013), https://law.yale.edu/sites/default/files/documents/pdf/sela/SELA13_Gargarella_CV_Sp_20120924.pdf, accessed 27 October 2021.

3 J Waldron, *Law and Disagreement* (OUP 1999).

4 I will focus principally on RHRC given the broad effects of their rulings on the functioning of societies that occupy various positions on the spectrum between 'democratic' and 'undemocratic'. I have deliberately integrated the case law of the Inter-American and African Human Rights Courts alongside European case law. While the latter has been important, and even taken centre-stage for over 60 years, it must nowadays be combined with the case law of other regional courts in order to produce a comprehensive picture of the topic, rather than a eurocentric one.

RHRC thus act as guardians of these rights and of the rule of law more generally.[5] The International Judiciary, however, is well aware that by exercising this control over the expression of the majority's political will, approved by domestic courts, they find themselves engaged in a particularly delicate balancing act.

Building on these specific examples, the aim of his article is to highlight and demonstrate that RHRC are trying to articulate their review in two ways, which are representative of the democratic challenge that threatens the *raison d'être* of their office.[6] The first way in which RHRC' attempt to achieve this is the more cautious of the two approaches, designed to avoid rush and disproportionately defy internal political authorities. This is known as articulation through deference (1). It is worth noting that this trend is very European. Indeed, the Inter-American and the African Court have not developed such a relationship with domestic judiciaries, though certain voices in the academic[7] and political[8] arenas are calling for change. The second way is underpinned by the *raison d'être* of RHRC, that of the ultimate protection of minority rights. In this case, the articulation is characterised by greater intransigence, inflexibility, rigidity. Although the three regional human rights courts use the latter approach, we can observe important differences in the ways in which they exercise it. (2). Articulation through deference and articulation through inflexibility are therefore the two major trends, which will be critically presented and discussed in the following developments.

---

5 Another important question is how 'to guard the guardian of the rule of law'? For some proposals, see. A Follesdal, 'International human rights courts and the (international rule of law): Part of the solution, part of the problem, or both?' (2021) 10 (1) Global constitutionalism 118.

6 Rather than approaching the question of articulating different kind of legitimacies from a purely theoretical standpoint, the analysis proposed in this article is based exclusively on case law. An immersion in case law and its nuances is often skimmed over, or, if given attention, is analysed in a mediated manner (via the work of other researchers). It is, nevertheless, a crucial analytical tool.

7 P A Acosta Alvarado, M Núñez Poblete (eds), *El Margen de Apreciación en el Sistema Interamericano de Derechos Humanos: Proyecciones Regionales y Nacionales* (Mexico, IIJ, UNAM, 2012).

8 In a Declaration signed on 11 April 2019 in Santiago de Chile, the governments of Argentina, Brazil, Chile, Colombia, and Paraguay called on the Inter-American Commission and Court to exercise greater judicial restraint, in particular by adopting the doctrine of national margin of appreciation.

1 Articulation through *Deference*

By introducing new concepts, such as the margin of appreciation doctrine (MoA), and by launching new procedural review – which gives credit to both the internal procedure of parliamentary deliberation (the 'process-based review') and the internal procedure of judicial deliberation – the ECtHR is trying to spare sovereign sensibilities, and more particularly the internal spaces in which democratic deliberation takes shape. Conceptual Engineering (deference through the creation of concepts) (1.2) and Procedural Engineering (deference through the creation of new procedural relationships) (1.3) are, therefore, the two main elements of the general trend towards judicial restraint in the realm of the sole European human rights system. This is a truly European way of taking into account the will of the national judiciary.

It is crucial to note here that such a trend has not always characterised the case-law of the European Court. It has become increasingly prevalent since 2010 amidst the high-level discussions that launched an ongoing process of reform.[9] This trend therefore corresponds to a particular moment in the history of the European system; faced with deep and persistent mistrust, the European Court has strategically reconfigured its jurisprudential policy. This reconfiguration has been urged and legitimised by the Icelandic president of the ECtHR, R. Spano, in several notable academic contributions.[10] This is not currently the approach of the other two RHRC. In spite of often opposing stances taken by States[11] (and/or some institutions of the Organisation of American States and the African Union), the Inter-American and African Human Rights Courts – even if they may in specific cases show judicial restraint – have not made it a structural marker of their case law. On the contrary, the Inter-American Court

9 See the Conferences in Interlaken (18–19 February 2010); Izmir (25–27 April 2011); Brighton (18–20 April 2012); Brussels (26–27 March 2015; and Copenhagen (11–13 April 2018). The main challenges facing the European System since the reform process are well presented *in* L Robert, H Surrel (eds), *Quel avenir pour le système européen de protection des droits de l'homme?* (Nemesis-Anthemis 2020).

10 R Spano, 'Universality or Diversity of Human Rights? Strasbourg in the Age of Subsidiarity' (2014) 14 (3) HRLR 1; R Spano 'The Future of the European Court of Human Rights – Subsidiarity, Process-Based Review and the Rule of Law' (2018) 18 (3) HRLR 1.

11 Thus, the denunciation of the jurisdiction of the Inter-American Court by Trinidad and Tobago (1998) and Venezuela (2012), on the one hand, and the denunciation of the jurisdiction of the African Court to examine cases presented by individuals and NGOs from Rwanda (2016), Tanzania (2019), Benin and Côte d'Ivoire (2020), on the other, demonstrate that states are always in control of the extent of their obligations as a last resort; for more details, I refer to my last book, *Les 3 Cours régionales des droits de l'homme in context. La justice qui n'allait pas de soi* (Pedone 2020).

launched its famous theory of 'conventionality control' in 2006 in the landmark ruling *Almonacid Arellano*,[12] according to which domestic judges must directly apply the Inter-American standard, even when it conflicts with national legislation and practice.[13] As for the African Court, it does not yet follow a pattern of judicial restraint,[14] even though some of its members request it in specific cases.[15]

1.1 *Deference through the Creation of Concepts*

1.1.1 Conceptual Engineering

Creating concepts in the course of a jurisprudential policy, which are designed specifically to avoid conflict with national authorities, and, in particular, national judges, has been the hallmark of the European Commission of Human Rights (EComHR) and, subsequently, of the European Court of Human Rights (ECtHR).[16]

The margin of appreciation is one such concept, created from scratch by the bodies of the European system. It has become a so-called 'star concept', although its interpretation generates controversy, and in some cases, ambiguity. Its origin, moreover, remains obscure. It does not appear to derive from international law *stricto sensu* and does not appear as such in the preparatory work for the Convention. According to Javier García Roca, no one wants to assume authorship of it: continental lawyers attribute its authorship to common law lawyers, and vice versa.[17] It is certain, however, that for Anglo-Saxon (particularly British) lawyers, the idea of a margin of appreciation granted to State bodies is new, whereas for French lawyers, it may appear familiar if one considers administrative law and the case law of the *Conseil d'Etat* on the discretionary nature of administrative action.

---

12 IACtHR, *Almonacid Arellano et al v. Chile*, Merits, Reparations and Costs, Series C No. 154 (Sept. 26, 2006).

13 For greater detail on the subject, complete with an extensive bibliography, as well as all the critics launched by diverse doctrinal sectors see: L Burgorgue-Larsen, 'Conventionality control: the Inter-American Court of Human Rights' in Max Planck Encyclopedia of International Procedural Law [MPEiPro], December 2018.

14 For more details, see the annual chronicle on the African Court case law written since 2018 and published at the RTDH by L. Burgorgue-Larsen and G-F. Ntwari.

15 See the dissenting opinion of Justice B. Tchikaya in the *Jebra Kambole* case: IACtHPR, *Jebra Kambole v. Tanzania* n°018/2018 (July 15, 2020).

16 This was done well before it was incorporated into the preamble of the Convention by Protocol No. 15, which entered into force on 1 August 2021 in the aftermath of its ratification by Italy.

17 J García Roca, *El margen nacional de la interpretación del Convenio europeo de derechos humanos : soberanía e integración* (Civitas-Thomson Reuters 2010).

What is certain, however, is that margin of appreciation is a notion which, historically, has been forged by the European Commission of Human Rights in the sensitive field of the use of Article 15 ECHR,[18] *i.e.* that of derogation from rights in time of war or public emergency 'threatening the life of the nation'.[19] This said, it is well known that the concept as used by the Court has continued to spread to the point where it is no longer confined to Article 15.

1.1.2 Margin of Appreciation in 'Derogation Cases'

Following the doctrine created by the European Commission, the European Court (ECtHR) has used, for the first time *expressis verbis* the formula 'national margin of appreciation' in an Inter-State case brought by Ireland – alleging violation of Articles 3 (prohibition of torture), 5 (Right to liberty) and 15 (Derogation) by the United Kingdom in the context of the latter's fight against Irish Republican Army (IRA) terrorism.[20] The guiding thread between the case-law of the European Commission and Court concerning the emergence of the concept is therefore the existence of a danger threatening the life of the nation, the assessment of which – in order to trigger the procedure for derogation from rights – is left to the discretion of the States.

For a long time, the fight against terrorism was at the origin of the doctrine's mobilisation; it was deployed with regard to the Kurdish terrorism of the PKK in Turkey,[21] and Islamist terrorism in the United Kingdom[22] as well as France.[23] Before 2020, eight states had triggered Article 15.[24] This changed with the shock of the COVID-19 pandemic. A divide thus emerged between the States that mobilised Article 15 as early as March 2020[25] and other countries, mostly

18 Article 15 establishes a double obligation of information on States: they must inform the Secretary General of the Council of Europe not only of the measures taken in the context of the state of emergency and the reasons for them, but also of the end of their implementation (Article 15 para. 3). In addition to this procedural obligation, States have substantive obligations: on the one hand, to keep non-derogable rights out of reach and, on the other, to continue to protect the other rights and freedoms guaranteed by the Convention in spite of these emergency measures.

19 EComHR, *Greece v. United Kingdom* (Sept. 26, 1958); EComHR, *Lawless c. Irlande* (Dec. 19, 1959).

20 ECtHR, *Ireland v. the United Kingdom* (Jan. 18, 1978) para. 207.

21 ECtHR, *Aksoy v. Turkey* (Dec.18, 1996); ECtHR, *Demir v. Turkey* (Sept. 23, 1998).

22 After the Twin Towers attacks, see in particular, ECtHR, GC, *A. v. the United Kingdom* (Feb. 19, 2009).

23 After the Paris attacks of Jan. and Nov. 2015, and then of Nice in Jul. 2016.

24 Albania, Armenia, France, Georgia, Greece, Ireland, Turkey and the UK.

25 In chronological order, Latvia, Romania, Armenia, the Republic of Moldova, Estonia, Georgia, Albania, Northern Macedonia, Serbia and San Marino.

in Western Europe, which – although they had also adopted legislation that infringed on many rights and freedoms – did not want to trigger the derogation mechanism. This East-West divide was telling; it revealed a grey area, or at least a disagreement, amongst the Council of Europe States between restrictions on rights – notably those on the right of association and assembly (Art 11 ECHR) and movement (Art. 2 para 4) – and the removal of some of the freedoms of individuals. The picture is further complicated by the fact that some countries which have activated the Article 15 mechanism have adopted less restrictive laws than those which have not.[26]

In any event, the case law shows that the Court intends – whatever the circumstances which have triggered Article 15 – to maintain its jurisprudential policy characterised by restraint.[27] The national margin of appreciation granted to States is particularly 'wide', so much so that the qualification of 'danger threatening the life of the nation' was refused only once by the European Commission of Human Rights. This occurred when the colonels' junta took power in Greece and cynically invoked the existence of a danger in order to justify measures which infringed on freedoms.[28]

With the exception of non-derogable rights,[29] all other 'conditional' rights may be subject to derogatory measures, which must be adopted 'to the extent strictly required by the demands of the situation' (Art. 15 §1 ECHR). One might think that this expression would encourage the Court to exercise thorough control of the proportionality of the measures adopted. However, this is far from the case. The ECtHR systematically recalls that 'it grants States a wide margin of appreciation in determining the nature and scope of the derogatory measures which they consider necessary to avert the danger invoked'.[30] This in turn

26 S Wallace, 'Derogation from the European Convention on Human Rights: The Case for Reform' (2020) 20 (4) HRLR 769.

27 However, this minimal control is increasingly criticised in academic circles because states of emergency are, historically, the contexts in which human rights violations are most likely to occur, see: O Gross, F Ní Aoláin, 'From discretion to Scrutiny: Revisiting the Application of the Margin of Appreciation Doctrine in the Context of Art.15 ECHR' (2001) 23 (3) HRQ 625.

28 EComHR, *Denmark, Norway, Sweden and the Netherlands v. Greece* (Nov. 5, 1969). Council of Europe, The Greek Report: Report of the Sub-Commission, vol. 1, Part 1, 1969, p.70.

29 Articles 2, 3, 4 §1, 7 of the ECHR and Art. 4 of Protocol 7, Art. 1 of Protocol 6 and 13. These are therefore six rights which, in the European conventional field, are not subject to derogation. The Court has constantly highlighted the importance of not modifying these – in particular the prohibition of torture – despite the extraordinary difficulty of effectively combating acts of terror (ECtHR, *A. v. United Kingdom* (Feb. 19, 2009), para.127; ECtHR, *Saadi v. Italy* (Feb. 28, 2008); ECtHR, *M.S. v. Belgium* (Jan. 31, 2012).

30 ECtHR, *A. v. United Kingdom* (Feb. 19, 2009) para. 184; ECtHR, *Mehmet Hasan Altan v. Turkey* (March, 20, 2018) para. 89.

justifies such an approach by mobilising the mantra of non-substitution of its point of view in lieu of that of the governments, because the former are 'directly responsible for striking a balance between the adoption of effective measures to combat terrorism on the one hand and respect for individual rights on the other'.[31] The same deference applies to national judges 'unless it can be established that they have misinterpreted the Convention or the Court's case-law or that its conclusions are manifestly unreasonable'.[32] However, this deference is becoming increasingly problematic in the current context of democratic deconsolidation and authoritarianism that is sweeping across Europe, where, increasingly, many judicial systems are coming under the direct control of the Executive branch of government. Thus, when the Court, in several chamber judgments against Turkey, departs from long-established principles in order to validate *in casu* that it is impossible for a detainee to access their investigation file, we are entitled to affirm, alongside the dissenting judges, that 'the Court cannot tolerate that a very specific case law, which disregards the principles established by the Grand Chamber and by the Court's established case-law as a whole [...] be developed in respect of a single High Contracting Party'.[33] In other words, deference in principle to measures adopted within the derogation framework should not be supplemented by *ad hoc* deference to a particular country which all observers (including the Council of Europe Commissioner for Human Rights) agree no longer respects elementary democratic principles. Nevertheless, derogation does not permit everything and the Court still performs judicial review in order to safeguard against arbitrariness.[34]

---

31 ECtHR, Pl, *Brannigan and McBride v. United Kingdom* (May 23, 1993) para. 59.

32 ECtHR, *A. v. United Kingdom* (Feb. 19, 2009) para. 182.

33 Dissenting opinion of Judges Bosnjak, Ranzoni and Koskelo (para. 57) in the *Atila Tas v. Turkey case*, 19 Jan. 2021 (personal translation from the original in French).

34 When, after 11 September 2001, the UK government derogated from Article 5 para. 1 f) and introduced a system of indefinite pre-trial detention of foreign terrorist suspects who were not deportable under Article 3 (see *Anti-terrorism, Crime and Security Act 2001*, 14 Dec. 2001), the Court – following the House of Lords – held that the measure was disproportionate in that it unjustifiably discriminated against those who were not British citizens. Similarly, when, after the attempted coup in Turkey on 15 July 2016, a state of emergency was declared and repeatedly extended, the Court found violations of Articles 5 para. 1 and 10 of the Convention in a case where the applicants – in this case, journalists known for their critical analysis of the actions of Recep Tayyip Erdogan's government – were arrested and imprisoned. The Court seems to be unwilling to weaken its control over both the continued detention of the applicants, and the infringement on their freedom of expression (ECtHR, *Mehmet Hasan Altan v. Turkey,* March 20, 2018; same day, *Sahin Alpay v. Turkey*). It was furthermore relayed, at the political level, by the vigilance of the Parliamentary Assembly (Res. 2209, pt 18.3).

1.1.3 Expansion of Margin of Appreciation in the Overall Case Law

Since 1984, the Court has identified three criteria for assessing the scope of the Margin, declaring that it 'will vary according to the circumstances, the subject matter, and its background'.[35] This formulation, which attempts to theorise or at least rationalise the use of the margin, is deliberately vague so as not to find itself disproportionately bound by it. For this reason, the Court has continued to operate on a case-by-case basis, giving significant weight to what is at stake for the applicant (circumstances), to the rights at stake (the subject-matter) and above all, to the existence or lack of a 'European consensus' (background). This last criterion has taken on considerable importance over time, since its presence is supposed to result in a 'narrow' margin of appreciation for the States and, conversely, its absence is supposed to grant them a wider – even broad – margin.

This is not the occasion to go back over the numerous academic discussions that have mobilised scholars over the last fifteen years in relation to the methodological problems that the use of the European consensus has generated. Only the areas in which the doctrine has been deployed will be mentioned here, in order to highlight the extent of deference which the Court has afforded to States on particularly sensitive issues. The historical and sociological construction of States democratic governance, economic, and social questions as well as societal issues, are therefore predilection areas where the MoA has been used by the Court.

All the issues that reveal the history of the political construction of states are areas in which the European Court has little intention of imposing any 'European' point of view. In this way, the specificities of secular states (such as France),[36] or of States with close ties to the Catholic Church (such as Spain),[37] are preserved. Beyond the relationship of states to religion,[38] their relationship to 'democratic governance' – in other words, to elections – is also preserved. It is well known that the Court, from 1987 onwards, with the *Mathieu Mohin*

---

35 ECtHR, *Rasmussen v. Denmark* (Nov. 28, 1984) para. 40. In French, the formula is written as follows: '*L'étendue de la marge d'appréciation varie selon les circonstances, les domaines et le contexte*.' In the ground-breaking judgment related to the statutory duty of vaccination – ECtHR, GC, *Vavrička and others v. The Czech Republic,* April 8, 2021 – the Court summarised some of the most salient aspects of the MoA doctrine (para. 273). Similarly, see the case concerning the disenfranchisement of persons divested of legal capacity, see ECt , *Strøbye and Rosenlind v. Denmark* (Feb., 2, 2021) para. 129.

36 ECtHR, GC, *S.A.S. v. France* (July 1, 2014) para. 155.

37 ECtHR, GC, *Fernández Martínez v. Spain* (June 12, 2014) para. 152.

38 R Uerpmann-Wittzack, E Lagrange, S Oeter (eds), *Religion and International Law* (Brill 2018).

and Clerfayt judgment[39] transformed the scope of Article 3 of Protocol n° 1: it went from being a simple political clause (placing on States the sole obligation to organise free legislative elections at regular intervals), to becoming the legal basis for enshrining subjective rights for the benefit of individuals. This transformation constituted a major upheaval. Nevertheless, in this broader framework, the Court's jurisprudential policy has been characterised by significant caution. It has always moved forward in a balanced manner: any progress made has been balanced by strategic restraint. This is evident on three levels: the identification of the legislature,[40] its election,[41] and any disputes that might arise from it.[42] Economic and social issues are typically conducive to the mobilisation of the margin of appreciation doctrine. The Court grants States control over their economic policy irrespective of what these policies are: from countries which have moved from a centralised and planned political

39 ECtHR, *Mathieu Mohin and Clerfayt v. Belgium* (March 2 1987).

40 With regard to the identification of the 'legislature', the Court has always given due consideration to the functioning of each political system, while simultaneously refusing to distort the concept of the legislature. Thus, it has always refrained from applying it to electoral processes that are not parliamentary.

41 ECtHR, *Podkolzina v. Latvia* (April 9, 2004). In this case, the applicant was struck out of the list of candidates which makes ineligible persons who do not have a command of Latvian at the 'upper' level. In the Government's submission, the obligation for a candidate to understand and speak Latvian was warranted by the need to ensure the proper functioning of Parliament, in which Latvian is the sole working language. They emphasised in particular that the aim of this requirement was to enable MPs to take an active part in the work of the House and effectively defend their electors' interests. At the para. 34, the Court emphasizes the MoA due to historical elements: '[The Court] considers that the interest of each State in ensuring that its own institutional system functions normally is incontestably legitimate. This applies all the more to the national parliament, which is vested with legislative power and plays a primordial role in a democratic State. Similarly, regarding the principle of respect for national characteristics enunciated above, the Court is not required to adopt a position on the choice of a national parliament's working language. *That decision, which is determined by historical and political considerations specific to each country*, is in principle *one which the State alone has the power to make. Accordingly, regarding the respondent State's margin of appreciation, the Court concludes that requiring a candidate for election to the national parliament to have sufficient knowledge of the official language pursues a legitimate aim*'. (Italics added).

42 The European Court's deference with regard to post-electoral disputes has been vividly enshrined in the Grand Chamber judgment of 10 July 2020, *Mugemangango v. Belgium*. In the context of a challenge that arose in the wake of the 2014 elections to the Walloon Parliament, the Court had to examine the Belgian constitutional system, which does not allow any room for judicial review of electoral disputes. The Court was sensitive to the arguments raised by domestic authorities about the historical aspect of this peculiarity, based on the State's argument regarding the constitutional identity of its system dealing with post-election disputes.

and economic regime to a liberal one (such as Romania),[43] to those which approach the right of trade unions to strike in a liberal manner.[44] The economic crisis of 2008 has only confirmed this approach, in which a wide margin of appreciation has been granted to States in adopting austerity measures by legislative or other means.[45] Moreover, the European Court also grants leeway to its Member States with regard to sensitive and complex societal issues. These include, for instance, the legal effects of gender reassignment surgery,[46] sexual abuse in church-run educational institutions,[47] or same-sex marriage.[48]

The second way of articulating the International Judiciary with Majoritarian Will is creating new procedural techniques.

1.2 *Deference through the Creation of New Procedural Relationships*

1.2.1 Procedural Engineering

The European Court has launched new procedural reviews – which give credit both to the internal procedure of parliamentary deliberation (the so-called 'process-based review') on the one hand, and the internal procedure of judicial deliberation on the other. With this clear-cut approach, the European Court is trying to spare sovereign sensibilities, and more particularly the internal spaces where democratic deliberation takes shape. Such deference to the legislator and the judiciary has not yet developed within Inter-American and African case law.

1.2.2 Taking into Account the Parliamentary Deliberation (*The 'Process-Based Review'*)

The 'process-based review' appeared clearly in the European field with the *Animal Defenders* judgment in 2013.[49] This technique consists of conferring a particularly strong presumption of conventionality on a law that would have been debated at length within a parliament, where all opinions would have been expressed and discussed, and where the national courts, through possible advisory functions, would have had a say in the making of the law. There are specific consequences for this method of tackling the domestic process: 'The

43 ECtHR, *Preda and Others v. Romania* (April 29, 2014) para. 129.

44 ECtHR, *National Union of Rail, Maritime and Transport Workers v. the United Kingdom* (April 8, 2014) para. 86.

45 ECtHR, *Mamatas and Others v. Greece* (July 21, 2016) para. 88.

46 ECtHR, GC, *Hämäläinen v. Finland* (July 16, 2014).

47 ECtHR, GC, *O'Keeffe v. Ireland* (Jan. 28, 2014).

48 ECtHR, dec., *Manenc v. France* (Sept. 21, 2010); ECtHR, dec., *Gas and Dubois, v. France* (March 15, 2012).

49 ECtHR, GC, *Animal Defenders International v. The United Kingdom* (April 22, 2013).

more convincing the general justifications invoked in support of the general measure, the less importance the Court attaches to the impact of that measure in the particular case before it'.[50]

This technique has since been used regularly – sometimes in a questionable, or at least contested way – by the Court. The most striking example is the *Garib* judgment,[51] in which three dissenting opinions were signed by five judges in this Grand Chamber case.[52] They critically discussed the harsh consequences for the applicant, which were the direct consequence of how the proportionality test was used by the Court.

The case was unusual in that it brought to light a 'societal issue', *i.e.* an issue that reveals similar phenomena in diverse societies, who consequently do not treat them similarly. In this case, the Netherlands had decided to combat the impoverishment of specific neighbourhoods in large urban conglomerates. It is known that large cities in Europe – and indeed throughout the world – are confronted with a similar phenomenon: the impoverishment of certain neighbourhoods resulting from a complex accumulation of factors (the relocation of prosperous commercial activities; the persistent unemployment of residents; the dilapidation of public and private buildings, and so on). However, each State tries, as best as it can, through urban policies aimed at promoting social diversity, to find the keys to remedy the subsequent 'ghettoisation' of such neighbourhoods. This phenomenon was tackled by the Dutch legislator who, on 1 January 2006, adopted a law on special measures for urban areas, which empowered certain municipalities to 'take measures in certain classified areas, specifically to grant partial tax exemptions to owners of small businesses and to select new residents according to their sources of income'.

On the basis of the possibilities offered by the Urban Agglomerations Act, the municipality of Rotterdam – a port city representing the industrial heart of the Netherlands – classified several of its neighbourhoods as 'sensitive'. One of these neighbourhoods was the Tarwewijk district, where the applicant – a Dutch national and single mother raising her two minor children – had been living in a one-room flat since 2005. While her landlord wanted to take back this flat 'in order to renovate it for his own use', he offered her a three-room flat with a garden in the same Tarwewijk neighbourhood. In accordance with the new regulations that had just come into force in 2006, Mrs Garib submitted

50 *Ibid.*, para. 109.

51 ECtHR, GC, *Garib v. The Netherlands* (Nov. 6, 2017).

52 The Georgian judge Nona Tsotoria and the Maltese judge Vincent De Gaetano signed one; the Portuguese judge Paulo Pinto de Albuquerque joined by the Bosnian judge Faris Vehabović signed another and, the third was signed by the Lithuanian judge Egidijus Kūris.

an 'application for residence authorisation', which was rejected in 2007 by the Mayor's office on the grounds that she had not lived in the municipality of Rotterdam for six years and that she received only social security benefits as a source of income – both criteria which are expressly provided for by the legislation.

The generality of the Grand Chamber's reasoning in validating the prohibition on Mrs Garib's continuing to live in the Tarwewijk district was the main focus of the dissent.[53] The core of the challenge was that the Court had made a general assessment of the interests at stake (as laid down in the 2006 Act), rather than a precise analysis of the effects of the Act on the applicant's individual situation. After recalling the general principles of its case law on the preferred areas for mobilising the national margin of appreciation,[54] and after insisting that the area of economic and social policies allowed for a wider margin,[55] the examination of the proportionality of the measure was deployed at the level of 'the relevant legislation and public policies', in nineteen paragraphs.[56] The Court went on to dissect the architecture of the law, its history, and the balances ultimately achieved by the legislator (in particular following the intervention of the Dutch Council of State in the process of drafting it), and finally recognised the conventionality to the law at stake. Afterwards, the Court dealt with the applicant's 'personal situation' in a mere nine paragraphs, thus activating an examination of proportionality *stricto sensu* that turned out to be totally truncated. One by one, the European Court discarded the specific factual elements of the case that should or could, in any case, have tipped the analysis in favour of Ms Garib. Worse still, according to Kūris J., it deliberately failed to mention to the reader that the applicant had to move into another flat which was 'just a stone's throw away, figuratively and even literally …' (point 7 of the dissent) from the original one. Although the applicant posed no threat to public order and was already living in the Tarwewijk neighbourhood, the Court gave no weight to these elements, while simultaneously emphasising that the system put in place 'did not deprive anyone of accommodation or force anyone to leave their home'.[57] This last statement is surprising since the facts of the case showed the exact opposite: the applicant had been living in Tarwewijk since 2005, and the new legislation forced her to leave the area! The

53 Paragraph 3 of the opinion of Judges Tsotoria and Gaetano; paragraphs 10, 12, and 14 of the opinion of Judge Pinto de Albuquerque; paragraph 1 of Judge Kūris.

54 ECtHR, GC, *Garib v. The Netherlands* (Nov. 6, 2017) paras. 136–141.

55 Ibid., para. 139.

56 *Ibid.*, paras. 142–157.

57 *Ibid.*, para. 144.

Court also imposed paternalistic obligations on the applicant, such as having to justify her preference for a particular neighbourhood and revealing private information to public authorities.[58] In other words, it *de facto* reversed the burden of proving the proportionality of the State's interference with the applicant's right (point 12 of the opinion of Judge Pinto de Albuquerque).

Despite these harsh criticisms by insiders and scholars,[59] the turn to process-based review is now a well-established fact in European case law. The *M.C*[60] case proves it beyond doubt in a subject matter concerning mandatory disclosure of convictions. Its para 49 is clear proof of this statement:

> The Court reiterates that a State can, consistently with the Convention, adopt general measures which apply to pre-defined situations regardless of the individual facts of each case even if this might result in individual hard cases (see *Animal Defenders International v. the United Kingdom* [GC], §§ 106–107 (…). Such general measures may be in the form of a single, absolute prohibition (as in *Animal Defenders International* itself) or may, as in the present case, be in the form of a criterion which, if met, carries particular consequences. *The central issue in both kinds of cases is not whether less restrictive rules should have been adopted but whether, in adopting the general measure in question and striking the balance it did, the State acted within the margin of appreciation afforded to it* (see *Animal Defenders International*, cited above, § 110).

Another deferential technique consists of making the most of national case law, and thus validating it, when it has itself taken into account the standards set at the level of the European court.

1.2.3 Taking into Account the Domestic Judicial Deliberation (the Judicial-Based Review)

'Taking into account' is not always a guarantee of conventionality. Numerous judgments of the European Court have highlighted the clumsy, inappropriate, erroneous, or non-existent use of conventional standards by domestic courts.[61]

58 *Ibid.*, paras. 162 and 166.

59 J García Roca, 'Entre stabilisation et régression du standard ou le temps de la déférence internationale, de l'imprécision de la marge nationale d'appréciation et de la procédure raisonnable de décision' (2020) 121 RTDH 71.

60 ECtHR, *M.C. v. The United Kingdom* (March, 3, 2021).

61 ECtHR, *Saber and Boughassal v. Spain* (Dec. 18, 2018); ECtHR, *Otegi Mondragon v. Spain* (March 15, 2011).

However, when the standard is *duly* taken into account and carries a proper proportionality review, then the European Court is obviously deferential, as it values this use of the conventional standard by national courts and particularly by Constitutional courts. Such an approach has manifested itself in two types of situations: one in which the interpretation of rights and the balancing of different interests are key, and the second in cases where the authority of Constitutional courts' decisions is in fact no longer accepted internally and, in sum, democratic stability is at stake.

When all national courts – and more precisely Constitutional and Supreme Courts with constitutional competences – have duly exercised the proportionality review among several interests, assuming their function as *juges conventionnels de droit commun* without ambiguity, finding a violation is no longer the aim of the European Court's decision. It instead intends to transform the guardians of the constitutions into guardians of the Convention by encouraging them to import conventional standards into their reasoning by setting them up as interpretative parameters of constitutional rights. All actors on the European judicial scene are familiar with this trend.[62] The *López Ribalda*[63] case – which involved recording employees on surveillance cameras without their knowledge – clearly demonstrates the European Court's deference to domestic courts when they have *all* duly applied the criteria identified in a famous Strasbourg case in the area of staff members surveillance by video: the *Barbulescu* case.[64]

In an ideal world in which Constitutional courts are the undisputed guarantors of the preservation of the separation of powers and fundamental rights, their decisions should be duly respected by all national authorities, be they executive, legislative, or judicial. It turns out that this ideal is not always in line with reality. The European Court will then come to the rescue of the constitutional judges by validating their decisions[65] *a posteriori* and, at the same time, exposing those national authorities that have ignored them. This approach is valid in different contexts: from the fragile situation of democratic transitions, to more established democratic regimes, which regularly suffer from deficiencies of varying degrees of seriousness.

62 For an example of an order of the Chamber of Appeals of the Constitutional Court of Karlsruhe that takes due account of the European Court case law in assessing the excessive length of proceedings in a case before it, see German Constitutional Court, Order, August 28, 2015, 1 BvR 2781/13 – Vz 11/14.

63 ECtHR, GC, *López Ribalda et al. v. Spain* (Oct. 7, 2019) para. 132.

64 ECtHR, GC, *Barbulescu v. Romania* (Sept. 5, 2017).

65 Ibid., para. 139.

The situation in many Eastern European countries has given rise to what might be called a 'democratic transition case law'. Though fascinating – as it bears witness to the political developments that took place in Europe following the fall of the Berlin Wall – it is equally delicate, as it reveals how fragile the processes of democratic implantation in fact are. In this context, when Constitutional courts exercised their functions in accordance with democratic principles but saw their authority bypassed and thus weakened by political authorities, the last democratic bulwark turned out to be the European Court. Although this situation reveals the weakness of constitutional justice at a given moment in the context of complex political circumstances, it also reveals the major support that the European Court gives to constitutional guardians by validating their positions *a posteriori*. The *Kurić*[66] case, which gave the European Court the opportunity to address the issue of 'The Erased of Slovenia', is a paradigmatic example of this. Once independent, Slovenia implemented a nationality policy that undermined the *modus vivendi* that had existed under the former Socialist Federal Republic of Yugoslavia (SFRY) – where many minorities lived peacefully – and helped to 'erase' the existence of over 25,000 people. Suddenly, citizens of the former SFRY and permanent residents of Slovenia no longer had a legal existence. In defiance of customary international law – which requires the avoidance of statelessness and the improvement of the situation of those who become stateless, particularly in the case of state succession – the young sovereign state created a massive number of stateless persons, with the aim of creating an 'ethnically pure' state. In this context, the European Court valued the various decisions of the Slovenian Constitutional Court, which had used the weapon of law to challenge such a policy, which they found amounted purely to orchestrating 'legalistic ethnic cleansing'. The Slovenian judge, in his concurring opinion, emphasised the position of the Constitutional Court:

> In fairness to the national legal system, we must consider *the honourable and courageous stance – faced with the continuity of this appalling situation – taken twice by the Constitutional Court in Slovenia*. This proves all over again that the national defence of constitutional rights is the best antechamber for our own protection of human rights. *The relevant judgments of the Constitutional Court in Ljubljana were snubbed by both the executive and the legislative branches at the time*. The price will now be paid by the Slovenian taxpayer. As per recent information, the rest of the

66 ECtHR, GC, *Kurić and al. v. Slovenia* (June 26, 2012).

> judicial branch, owing to its characteristic post-communist legal formalism, has likewise failed to compensate the aggrieved for the continuing violations such as we have established in the cases before us.
>
> This case also proves that legal mills do grind slowly – but unremittingly. Precisely because of international jurisdiction, at least here, justice will have been done. Moreover, while justice as such cannot be defined, injustice is easily recognisable. The broader question is, therefore, why it was not recognised in the domestic legal system. Indeed, in post-communist legal systems there seems to be an irreconcilable mutual exclusion between mechanical legal formalism on the one hand and the simple sense of justice on the other. Often enough, we encounter this irreconcilability – *summum ius, summa iniuria!* – in other cases, including Western ones, except that in this colossal instance the Constitutional Court had identified the injustice. *It was the malevolent political will that impeded the rule of law and blocked the proper judicial remedy.* (italics added)

Identical scenarios – in which decisions of the guardians of the Constitution have been ignored – have also appeared in the workings of older democracies, where both the functioning of justice in general[67] and of political coexistence in particular can be called into question. A key example of this can be found, for instance, in the so-called 'Catalonian self-determination' case.[68]

This quick overview of case law unambiguously shows that the precautions taken by the European Court are designed not to collide head-on with the points of view of the national courts, which are themselves grappling with the political and sociological realities of their country. In a nutshell, deference is very often at stake in its review. However, this is not systematically the case. Intransigence and inflexibility can also be the main features of the Judiciary International's case Law. This is what we will see in the second part of this

---

67 ECtHR, *García Mateos v. Spain* (Feb. 19, 2013).

68 ECtHR, dec., *Aumatell i Arnau v. Spain* (Sept. 11, 2018). This decision of inadmissibility is quite striking because it clearly demonstrates that the European Court here came to reinforce the Spanish Constitutional Court, whose decisions were systematically ignored by the Catalan authorities that organized an illegal referendum for self-determination, without respecting the wording of the Constitution. The Court highlighted the importance, in democratic societies, of the enforcement of the decisions of constitutional courts, recalling an opinion of the Venice Commission (3 March 2017) at para. 37: 'When a public official refuses to execute a judgment of the Constitutional Court, he or she violates the principles of the rule of law, the separation of powers and the loyal cooperation of the organs of the state'.

article, where Inter-American and African case law, on the one hand, will be compared with European case law on the other.

2 Articulation through *Intransigence*

The scenarios of conventional intransigence carried out by RHRC are imposing. Not only can the Courts go against the decisions of the domestic courts that have validated the choices of the legislators, but they can also directly oppose the choices of the constituent powers (both primary and derived). However, while this conventional intransigence is common to all three regional human rights systems on issues of democratic governance (albeit with important procedural peculiarities) (2.1), this concordance breaks down when it comes to important societal issues (2.2). In such contexts, it is reasonable to ask whether we are still in a scenario where there is an 'articulation' of judicial competence (internal and international). Does intransigence leave room for articulation or is the latter simply of a different type?

2.1 *The* Common Intransigence *in Democratic Subject Matters*

RHRC' are in unison in defending certain main elements of democratic governance at all costs and doing so in different contexts (2.1.1). However, this common approach to the defence of democracy will take specific turns, and will trigger different effects in various regional systems. In this case, it is the African Court of Human and Peoples' Rights, which is able to carry out an extensive review thanks to its large *ratione materiae* jurisdiction (2.1.2).

2.1.1 Different Contexts: One Single Intransigence

Whether State societies are trying to rebuild themselves or, conversely, are experiencing dangerous processes of democratic backsliding, the courts will be inflexible in preserving major elements of what they consider to be part of the rule of law. While some frequently contrast democracy (in short, the people's will) with human rights, regional courts show that both must go hand in hand. Human rights are part of the democratic set-up, and when the 'Majoritarian will' forgets this, regional courts are there to remind them of this vital element.

2.1.1.1 *Democratic Building and Transitional Justice*

Several countries in Europe, as well as in Latin America, have experienced internal armed conflicts, which have in some cases led to legal proceedings before regional courts. Several scenarios have given the courts the opportunity to demonstrate their inflexibility when it comes to protecting certain red lines in these transitional justice processes. The first scenario is when the ECtHR disavowed an overall framework made by an 'internationalized' constituent power. The second scenario is when the IACtHR disavowed the enactment of amnesty laws – whether approved by parliament or referendum. Let us turn now to the presentation of both scenarios.

While the *Mathieu Mohin and Clerfayt* judgment[69] gave the Court the opportunity, by 13 votes to 5, to give primacy to political imperatives (of serene coexistence between different linguistic communities) over individual rights (of some Walloon political personalities seeking equal treatment), this initial caution was largely overtaken in two 'Bosnian cases' in the specific context of democratic re-building. In the two groundbreaking *Sedjic*[70] and *Zornic*[71] judgments, the ECtHR considered the equal treatment of citizens – irrespective of ethnic belonging – more important than the wording of the Constitution – the 'Dayton Agreement'[72] – which, from the perspective of achieving peace and stability, have organized institutionalized discrimination among the different peoples of Bosnia and Herzegovina. These cases have been heavily discussed, and indeed criticised, by influential scholarly voices specialising in power-sharing matters among several ethnic, religious, and cultural communities.[73] Additionally, these cases have been criticised by certain insiders (e.g.- Judge Bonello in his separate opinion); nevertheless, despite their different provenances, these criticisms have all given precedence to the subjective individual right of non-discrimination over the political imperative of trying to ensure lasting peace in Bosnia and Herzegovina, the latter stemming from the Dayton Agreements. To put it differently and somewhat schematically, between the two pillars of liberal democracy, the way in which voting is organised and the preservation of individual rights (in this case the rights of ethnic minorities), the Court's jurisprudential policy has tended towards the preservation of the

69 ECtHR, *Mathieu Mohin and Clerfayt v. Belgium* (March 2, 1987).

70 ECtHR, GC, *Sejdic and Finci v. Bosnia and Herzegovina* (Dec. 22, 2009).

71 ECtHR, *Zornic v. Bosnia and Herzegovina* (July 14, 2014).

72 In 1995, the General Framework Agreement for Peace, the 'Dayton Agreement', was signed. This Framework contains in its fourth annex the constitution of Bosnia and Herzegovina. One of the major objectives of this instrument was to put an end to the war and to deal with the strong ethnic conflicts among Serbs, Croats and Bosniaks. This text was drafted in secret diplomatic negotiations under pressure from international negotiators. The lack of representativity and transparency in the constitution-making process cast doubt on the internal legitimacy of the Bosnian constitution, see C Steiner, N Ademovic, *Constitution of Bosnia and Herzegovina, Commentary* (Konrad Adenauer Stiftung Sarajevo 2010).

73 S Graziadei, '*Democracy v. Human Rights*? The Strasbourg Court and the Challenge of Power Sharing' (2016) 12 (1) ECLR 54; C Mc Crudden, B O'Leary, *Courts and Consociations* (OUP 2013).

second pillar. While the Constitutional Court of Bosnia and Herzegovina had declined twice its competence – finding it could not review a constitutional provision as well as the legislation implementing it[74] – the ECtHR, for the first time in its history, declared a constitutional provision unconventional.

In Latin America, since 2001, the IACtHR has deemed unconventional any kind of Amnesty laws, no matter what the circumstances of their adoption had been.[75] By equating self-amnesties (that of Fujimori in Peru, with the *Barrios Altos* ruling in 2001)[76] and Salvador Allende in Chile (with the *Almonacid Arrellano* ruling in 2006),[77] with amnesties voted by parliaments (as in Brazil with the *Gomes Lund* case in 2011),[78] and those adduced by the people *via* referendum as in Uruguay (in the very dramatic and paradigmatic *Gelman case* in 2011),[79] authors such as Roberto Gargarella have considered that the IACtHR has usurped democratic power.[80] Nevertheless, the Court has continued along this path, with a slight inflexion, but one that, in reality, has nothing to do with the criticisms levelled by authors who over-invest the people and their representatives with absolute democratic legitimacy. While the general trend is the prohibition of amnesties for all serious human rights violations, the Inter-American Court, in the case of *El Mozote Massacre* in 2012,[81] introduced an exception relating to reconciliation processes following internal armed conflicts. Indeed, while the Court recalled the prohibition of amnesties for massive human rights violations – in particular when war crimes and crimes against

74 Constitutional Court of Bosnia and Herzegovina, *Elections to the Presidency and the House of Peoples*, U 5/04, 31 March 2006; U 13/05 *Electoral Law*, 26 May 2006, with the concurring opinion of judge Feldmann and the dissenting opinions of judges Palavric and Grewe.

75 C Binder, 'The Prohibition of Amnesties by the Inter-American Court of Human Rights' (2011) 12 (5) GLJ 1204; L Burgorgue-Larsen, 'Le bannissement de l'impunité: décryptage de la politique jurisprudentielle de la Cour interaméricaine des droits de l'homme' (2012) 89 RTDH 3; N Kiriakou, 'Rights Cast into Oblivion? Amnesties in the Case-Law of the Inter-American Court of Human Rights', *in* Y Haeck, C Burbano-Herrera, O Ruiz-Chiriboga (eds), *The Inter-American Court of Human Rights: Theory and Practice, Present and Future* (Human Rights Centre of Ghent, Intersentia 2015); C Martín, 'Catching up with the Past: Recent Decisions of the Inter-American Court of Human Rights Addressing Gross Human Rights Violations Perpetrated during the 1970–1980s' (2007) 7 (4) HRLR 777.

76 IACtHR, *Barrios Altos v. Peru*, Series C No. 75 (March 14, 2001).

77 IACtHR, *Almonacid Arellano et al v. Chile*, Merits, Reparations and Costs Series C No. 154 (Sept. 26, 2006).

78 IACtHR, *Gomes Lund et al. [Guerrilha do Araguaia] v. Brazil*, Preliminary Objections, Merits, Reparations and Costs Series C No. 219 (Nov. 24, 2010).

79 IACtHR, *Gelman v. Uruguay*, Merits, Reparations and Costs, Series C No. 221 (Feb., 24, 2011).

80 See footnote n°3.

81 IACtHR, *El Mozote and Nearby Places v. El Salvador*, Merits, Reparations and Costs, Series C No. 252 (Oct., 25, 2012).

humanity have been committed – it attached importance for the first time to the specific political context in which an amnesty law could be enacted: *in casu*, the settlement of the end of an armed conflict. It paid attention to the course of the peace negotiations, the content of the 1992 peace agreements, and the rules of international humanitarian law. Article 6 § 5 of Protocol II of the Geneva Conventions became essential in assessing the compatibility of the 'General Amnesty Law for Peacebuilding' with the obligations under the American Convention.[82] Although in this case the Salvadoran amnesty law was ultimately declared unconventional, this new approach demonstrates that the automatic unconventionality of amnesty laws is no longer the case, especially when transitional justice mechanisms are at stake.

2.1.1.2 *Democratic Backsliding and Independence of the Judiciary*

RHRC have become, by necessity, the ultimate bulwark against arbitrariness. They have found themselves at the forefront of the defence of liberal democratic values in an increasingly uncertain world, where there are many signs of 'democratic deconsolidation'.[83] In this respect, the three continents are confronted with the same challenges: faced with increasingly authoritarian governments – which do not hesitate to manipulate democratic rules – regional courts have become spokespersons for the preservation of the separation of powers and by extension the independence of justice.

The first regional court to face major challenges to judicial independence was the Inter-American Court. It builds up a body of case law in the context of the so-called 'removal of judges' litigation (which, moreover, is part of the wider context of the often arbitrary removal of public servants). From the mobilisation of Articles 8 and 25 of the American Convention – which relate, respectively, to the right to a fair trial and to an effective remedy – it enshrined in its judgments a right for the judge to have his independence guaranteed by the State. Such a turning point appears in the *Supreme Court of Justice*

82 This provision stipulates that 'upon the cessation of hostilities, the authorities in power shall endeavour to grant the widest possible amnesty to persons who have taken part in the armed conflict'.

83 The formula is from Y Mounk and S Foa' work, 'The signs of deconsolidation' (2017) 28 *Journal of democracy* 5. For some comparative insights, I permit myself to refer to L Burgorgue-Larsen, 'Populism and Human rights. From Disenchantment to Democratic Riposte' in C Izquierdo-Sans, C Martínez-Capdevila, M Nogueira-Guastavino (eds), *Fundamental Rights Challenges. Horizontal Effectiveness, Rule of Law and Margin of National Appreciation* (Springer 2021).

(*Quintana Coello et al.*)[84] judgment on the removal by parliamentary resolution of twenty-seven judges of the Supreme Court of Justice of Ecuador. It is worth presenting paragraph 153 of the ruling, which is particularly enlightening in this regard:

> The foregoing serves to clarify some aspects of the Court's jurisprudence. Indeed, in the case of *Reverón Trujillo v. Venezuela*, the Court concluded that the right to be heard by an independent tribunal, enshrined in Article 8(1) of the Convention, only implied that a citizen has a right to be judged by an independent judge. However, it is important to point out that judicial independence should not only be analysed in relation to justiciable matters, given that the judge must have a series of guarantees that allow for judicial independence. *The Court considers it pertinent to specify that the violation of the guarantee of judicial independence, as it relates to a judge's tenure and stability in his position, must be examined in light of the conventional rights of a judge who is affected by a State decision that arbitrarily affects the term of his appointment*. In that sense, the institutional guarantee of judicial independence is directly related to *a judge's right to remain in his post*, as a consequence of the guarantee of tenure in office. (italics added)

This case-law was confirmed in two further judgments, namely *Constitutional Tribunal* (*Camba Campos et al.*)[85] and *López Lone et al.*[86] Thus, in the view of the Inter-American Court, it is now established that Article 8 § 1 of the American Convention recognises not only the right of persons appearing before a court to an independent judge but also the right of judges themselves to have their independence safeguarded and respected by the State.[87]

The Court's entire case law on 'removal' and disciplinary measures is geared towards the objective of guaranteeing the independence and stability of democratic institutions. It has specified that judges have specific guarantees due to the necessary independence of the Judiciary, which has been understood

---

84 IACtHR, *Supreme Court of Justice* (*Quintana Coello et al.*) *v. Ecuador*, Prel. objection, Merits, Reparations and Costs Series C No. 266 (Aug. 23, 2013) para. 84.

85 IACtHR, *Constitutional Tribunal* (*Camba Campos et al.*) *v. Ecuador*, Prel. objections, Merits, Reparations and Costs Series C No. 268 (Aug. 28, 2013).

86 IACtHR, *Ecuador and López Lone et al. v. Honduras*, Prel. objection, Merits, Reparations and Costs Series C No. 302 (Oct. 5 2015).

87 Such a jurisprudential policy continued: the Inter-American Court took advantage of new cases to deepen the multiple facets of Article 8 for all kind of civil servants facing arbitrary removal and/or disciplinary measures.

as 'essential for the exercise of the judicial function'.[88] In this sense, the Inter-American Court has affirmed *expressis verbis* that one of the main objectives of the separation of public powers is the guarantee of judicial independence.[89] This autonomous exercise must be guaranteed by the State both in its institutional aspect, that is, in relation to the judiciary as a system, and in its individual aspect, that is, in relation to an individual judge. In any case, the objective of protection lies in preventing the judicial system in general, and its members in particular, from being subjected to possible undue restrictions on the exercise of their function by bodies outside the judiciary or even by those exercising review or appeal functions. The Court has pointed out that judicial independence derives from the respect of three guarantees: an adequate appointment process, non-removability from the position, and protection against external pressures.[90] In the *Martínez Esquivia*[91] case, the Court reiterated the guarantee of security of tenure and proceeded to extend this guarantee in two ways: to prosecutors and to provisionally appointed prosecutors. In the same vein, the Court does not focus on the formal membership of the applicants in the judiciary to apply these specific guarantees. Thus, in the *Schonenberg* case,[92] the fact that the applicant belonged to the Supreme Electoral Court (*Tribunal Federal Electoral*), which was not part of the judiciary in El Salvador, did not prevent the Court from considering him functionally as a fully fledged judge, thus benefiting from reinforced guarantees.[93]

As democratic deconsolidation reached Europe, the European Court also had to build a body of case law to preserve judicial independence. It all started

88 IACtHR, *Rico v. Argentina*, Prel. objection, Merits, Reparations and Costs Series C No. 383 (Sept. 2, 2019) para. 52.

89 *Ibid.*, para. 53.

90 IACtHR, *Constitutional Tribunal (Camba Campos et al.) v. Ecuador*, Prel. objections, Merits, Reparations and Costs Series C No. 268 (Aug. 28, 2013) para. 83. With regard to the guarantee of stability and irremovability of judges, the Court has considered that it implies the following: (a) removal from office must be exclusively on the permitted grounds, either through a process that complies with judicial guarantees or because the term or period of their mandate has been completed; (b) judges can only be removed for serious disciplinary offences or incompetence; and (c) any proceedings followed against judges must be resolved in accordance with established standards of judicial conduct and through fair procedures that ensure objectivity and impartiality according to the Constitution or the law. See, *Rico v. Argentina, prec.*, para. 55.

91 IACtHR, *Martínez Esquivia v. Colombia,* Prel. objection, Merits, Reparations and Costs Series C No. 412 (Oct. 6, 2020).

92 IACtHR, *Colindres Schonenberg vs. El Salvador,* Prel. objection, Merits, Reparations and Costs Series C No. 373 (Feb. 4, 2019).

93 *Ibid.*, para. 67.

with the important *Baka* judgment. Faced with the arbitrary dismissal of the President of the Hungarian Supreme Court[94]– revealing Hungary's slow drift from democracy since the early 2010s – the Court was intransigent: it declared, on two occasions,[95] albeit with analytical variations, the unconventionality of such a manoeuvre, both from the point of view of Article 6 § 1 (because the applicant was unable to gain access to the Constitutional Court) and from the point of view of Article 10 (because he was removed from office following remarks he had made in the context of his professional duties as President of the National Council of Justice). The European Court did not hesitate to point out that the transitional law of impeachment was an *ad hominen* law and, as such, lacked a 'legitimate purpose'.[96] It particularly emphasised the requirement of the rule of law, reviving the methodological fundamentals laid down in the *Golder* judgment.[97] The *Broda and Broja* judgment extended the *Baka* ruling in an important way by establishing a subjective right to security of tenure.[98] In a case involving the premature termination of the mandates of vice-chairmen of courts, without review by an ordinary court or by 'another body exercising judicial functions', the Court found that the 'very substance' (*le contenu essentiel*) of the right of access to a judge had been infringed.[99]

In general terms, the European Court of Human Rights has deemed that 'in a democratic society, both the courts and the investigating authorities must remain free from any political pressure'.[100] Similarly, in the *Kövesi* case, the ECtHR noted that the dismissal of a prosecutor before the end of her term of office, as well as the reasons justifying the decision, 'can hardly be reconciled with the particular consideration to be given to the nature of the judicial function as an independent branch of State power and to the principle of independence of prosecutors, which [...] is a key element in the maintenance of

94 A former judge at the European Court between 1991 and 2008.

95 ECtHR, *Baka v. Hungary* (May 27, 2014); ECtHR, GC, *Baka v. Hungary* (June 23, 2016).

96 This case is also essential because the Court – although it was not explicit in this respect – is in fact reviewing constitutional legislation, which, for the Portuguese (Pinto de Albuquerque) and Russian (Dedov) judges, confirms the Court to be, in fact, a European constitutional court (a subject already addressed in doctrine. See J-P Costa, 'La Cour européenne est-elle une Cour constitutionnelle européenne ?' in *Mélanges en l'honneur de J. Gicquel* (Montchrestien 1997); J-F Flauss, 'La Cour européenne est-elle une Cour constitutionnelle?' in M de Salvia, J-F Flauss, *La Convention européenne des droits de l'homme: développements récents et nouveaux défis*, (Bruylant 1997); A Stone Sweet, 'Sur la constitutionnalisation de la Convention européenne' (2009) 80 RTDH 923.

97 ECtHR, Pl, *Golder v. the United Kingdom* (Feb. 21, 1975), para. 34.

98 ECtHR, *Broda and Bojara v. Poland*, (June 29, 2021).

99 *Ibid.*, para. 149.

100 ECtHR, *Petrović v. Serbia* (Oct. 15, 2014), para. 73.

judicial independence'.[101] Besides the question of arbitrary removal of judges and prosecutors, the appointment process as such has been at the core of the case law. An important step was taken in a ground-breaking judgment against Iceland,[102] in which the European Court gave a new meaning to one of the formulae of Article 6 §1 in order to account for the appointment of judges. In other words, after access to the courts (*Golder* case)[103] and the enforcement of judgments (*Hornsby* case),[104] the content of Article 6 has been enriched:

> Having regard to its fundamental implications for the proper functioning and the legitimacy of the judiciary in a democratic State governed by the rule of law, *the Court considers that the process of appointing judges necessarily constitutes an inherent element of the concept of 'establishment' of a court or tribunal 'by law'*, and an interpretation to the contrary would defy the purpose of the relevant requirement. The Court reiterates in this connection that the Convention 'is intended to guarantee not rights that are theoretical or illusory but rights that are practical and effective.[105] (Italics added)

Once this assertion of principle had been made, the Court immediately declined the correlative possibility of providing for limits because 'a *certain* margin of appreciation should be afforded to the states'. In order to be able to examine the conventionality of such limits, the Court established a methodological triptych around the notion of a 'seriousness threshold'.[106] This

101 ECtHR, *Kövesi v. Romania* (Aug. 20, 2020) para. 208.

102 ECtHR, GC, *Guomundur Andri Astraosson v. Iceland* (Dec. 1, 2020).

103 ECtHR, Pl, *Golder v. the United Kingdom* (Feb. 21, 1975).

104 ECtHR, *Hornsby v. Greece* (March 19, 1997).

105 ECtHR, GC, *Guomundur Andri Astraosson v. Iceland* (Dec. 1, 2020) para. 227.

106 *Ibid.*: In the first instance, there must, in principle, be 'a *manifest* breach of domestic law, in the sense that the breach must be objectively and genuinely identifiable as such' (para. 244); secondly, 'the breach in question must be assessed in the light of the object and purpose of the requirement of a 'tribunal established by law', namely to ensure the ability of the judiciary to perform its duties free of undue interference and thereby to preserve the rule of law and the separation of powers' (para. 246); thirdly, the Court considered that the review conducted by national courts, if any, as to the legal consequences – in terms of an individual's Convention rights – of a breach of a domestic rule on judicial appointments plays a significant role in determining whether such breach amounted to a violation of the rights to a 'tribunal established by law', and thus forms part of the test itself (para. 248). The European Court tried clearly here to keep the balance between two competing interests: respect for the integrity of the appointment process on the one hand, and the preservation of principles of legal certainty and irremovability of judges during their term of office on the other.

approach has been implemented with intransigence with regard to political appointments of judges in Poland, both to the Constitutional Court and to the Supreme Court.[107]

The African Court is no exception to the rule. It emphasised the need for independent justice – regardless of the jurisdiction involved (ordinary or constitutional) – and, in the process, it identified the key elements for organising the impartiality of judges. Contrary to the European and American Conventions, the Banjul Charter has a very specific stance on this matter. Indeed, Article 26 states that 'States Parties to the present Charter shall have the duty to guarantee the independence of the courts'. Thus, in one of the *Sébastien Ajavon* cases, the Court affirmed that 'the guarantee of the independence of the courts imposes on States not only the duty to enshrine such independence in their legislation but also the obligation to refrain from any interference in the affairs of justice at all levels of the judicial process'.[108] Similarly, in another *Sébastien Ajavon* case,[109] the Court opted for a comprehensive approach to independence, noting that Article 26 'enshrines not only the independence of the courts taken separately, as judicial bodies, but also that of the judiciary as a whole, like the executive and the legislature'.[110]

As we observed, the intransigence of the regional fight for judicial independence and against the arbitrariness of appointment or removal of judges and prosecutors is indicative of the International Judiciary's will to preserve at all costs the rule of law as a fundamental component of a democratic society. While this defence of elements inherent to the liberal foundations of democracies is common to all three effective regional human rights systems, the African system is singularly different in one respect.

2.1.2 One Intransigence, Different Effects

The Arusha Court, in the wake of the 'substantive decompartmentalization' (*décloisonnement matériel*) instituted by the Ouagadougou Protocol (Art. 3 § 1 and 7),[111] has been called upon to apply international instruments – adopted at the sub-regional and continental levels – in the area of good democratic

107 ECtHR, *Xero Flor w Polsce sp. Zo.o. v. Poland* (May 7, 2021); ECtHR, *Reczkowicz c. Poland* (July 22, 2021).

108 ACtHPR., *Sébastien Germain Ajavon v. Benin* (March 29, 2019) para. 280.

109 ACtHPR, *Sébastien Germain Ajavon v. Benin* (Dec. 4, 2020).

110 *Ibid.*, para. 310. *In casu,* Article 26 was declared infringed because 'the presence of the President of the Republic as President of the CSM and that of the Minister of Justice constitute clear evidence that the judiciary is not independent' (para. 322).

111 As I called it in the book: L Burgorgue-Larsen, *Les 3 Cours régionales des droits de l'homme in context. La justice qui n'allait pas de soi* (Pedone 2020), 245, 260, 276 et s.

governance. In its landmark judgment *Action pour la protection des droits de l'homme,*[112] the African Court considered the Economic Community of West African States Protocol on Democracy and Good Governance (2001) and the African Charter on Democracy, Elections and Governance (2007)[113] to be 'human rights instruments', according to the meaning of Article 3 of the Ouagadougou Protocol.

Although political issues had appeared before the Court early on in proceedings against Tanzania[114] – by means of, in particular, Article 13 of the Charter concerning political rights – it was the judgment handed down in 2016 against Côte d'Ivoire that profoundly and durably accelerated the transformation of 'democratic disputes' before the Court. The Court thus increasingly became the receptacle for the manipulation of the electoral game by the political majorities in place who obstinately refuse the principle of political alternation. The overall case law concerning these democratic subject-matters highlights the impressive powers of the African Court; it reviews not only the content of the Constitutions (as established by the original constituent power or by the derived constituent power), but also the ways in which these are modified. This last element is clearly illustrated by the *X.Y.Z.*, *Sébastien Ajavon,* and *Eric Noudehouenou* cases which bring to light the chronicle of democratic backsliding in Benin under Patrice Talon's regime. Here, the Court directly disavowed the manner in which the Beninese Constitution of 11 December 1990 was urgently amended, in total contradiction with the principle of 'national consensus', guaranteed not only in Article 10 § 2 of the African Charter on Democracy, but which was also intrinsically linked to the political history of the country. While the competence of constitutional and/or supreme courts to review constitutional amendments is a contentious issue that divides doctrine and leaves a disparate constitutional *praxis* in Africa (and beyond),[115] the

112 ACtHPR, *Action pour la Protection des Droits de l'Homme (APDH) v. Côte d'Ivoire* Merits, req. No 001/2014 (Nov, 18 2016).

113 PJ Glen, 'Institutionalizing Democracy in Africa : A Comment on the African Charter on Democracy, Elections and Governance' (2012) 5 African Journal of Legal Studies, 170 ; B Tchikaya, 'La Charte africaine de la démocratie, des élections et de la gouvernance' (2008) 54 AFDI 515.

114 ACtHPR, *Révérend Christopher R. Mtikila v. Tanzania & Tanganyika Law Society et Human Rights Centre v. Tanzania,* Merits req. n° 009/2011 et n° 011/2011 (June 14, 2013).

115 A significant part of contemporary doctrine justifies the limitation of the constitutional revision power in order to combat 'unconstitutional amendments'. In the Anglo-Saxon world, the writings of R Dixon, M Landau, 'Transnational Constitutionalism and a Limited Doctrine of Unconstitutional Constitutional Amendments' (2015) 13 (3) *I.CON* 606, and those of R Albert – *Constitutional Amendments. Making, Breaking, and Changing Constitutions* (OUP 2019) are key. For a presentation of such an issue in the African realm,

African Court – thanks to the instruments on good governance – was able to establish itself as a continental 'super' constitutional court, to use Adem Kassie Adebe's formula.[116]

There are two areas in which the inter-conventional consensus – which is actually an inter-continental consensus – among RHRC is ground-breaking: the first relates to issues of economic and social rights and the second to the rights of sexual minorities.

2.2 *A Different Kind of Inflexibility in the Social and Societal Domains*

Social justice on the one hand, and sexual justice on the other, are two fields in which the three RHRC differ. The courts are inflexible with regard to these two issues, but not in the same way. Whereas the European inflexibility aims to preserve the political choices made by states and their executive and legislative powers, the African and American inflexibility aims to make social justice a reality. Notwithstanding, in so doing, the African Court is not an activist body: it follows the State's will as stated in the African Charter's provisions, in which economic, social, and cultural rights are protected (as well as in other African instruments). By contrast, the Inter-American Court is innovative, using borderline interpretative methods to tackle inequalities which go beyond domestic (legislative and judicial) pusillanimity. As for the question of 'sexual justice', – a formulation whose purpose is to highlight the search of equality between same-sex and opposite-sex couples – an important divide, for now, exists only between the ECtHR and the IACtHR; indeed, for the time being, the ACtHPR has not yet ruled on this issue.

2.2.1 Social Justice

The protection of economic and social rights is quite diverse among Human Rights Systems in general. Either social rights are noticeably absent (as is the case with the European Convention on Human Rights), or they fall victim to the 'syndromes of progressiveness' (i.e., their realization is subject to the State's having sufficient financial resources, as per article 26 of the American

---

see RN Sandje, 'Le droit de la révision constitutionnelle dans le nouveau constitutionnalisme africain' (2016) 4 RDP 1209. For a broader discussion, see R Ben Achour (ed), *Les changements anticonstitutionnels de gouvernement : approches de droit constitutionnel et de droit international* (PUAM 2014).

116 AK Adebe, 'Taming Regressive Constitutional Amendments: The African Court as a Continental (super) Constitutional Court' (2019) 17 (1) I.CON 89; for more details, see our paper published in 2020 in AFDI: 'La Cour africaine des droits de l'homme et des peuples à la croisée des chemins'.

Convention) or conditionality (in which they acquire normative status only after intervention by the legislature, as with the 'Principles' in the European Union's Charter of Fundamental Rights at the core of Chapter IV on Solidarity). When social rights do have pride of place in the texts (International Covenant on Economic, Social and Cultural Rights, European Social Charter), it is the very structure of the protection mechanisms that reduces their scope, either by setting up committees with no function as courts of law and whose jurisdiction is optional,[117] or by limiting justiciability to certain rights. This can be seen in the case of the San Salvador Protocol to the American Convention on Human Rights (which was adopted in 1988 and came into force in 1999), which makes only two rights justiciable: the right to form trade unions (article 8), and the right to education (article 13).[118] Only the African Commission on Human and People's Rights (ACHPR) stands out in this regard. The ACHPR is particularly generous concerning social rights: the Right to work (Art. 15); to health (Art. 16) and to education (Art. 17) are all justiciable. In the same vein, references to development are present in other provisions concerning peoples and duties (*e.g.,* Article 22).

If we shift the analysis from texts to case law, we see an opposition between Africa and the Americas on the one hand, and Europe on the other. While in Europe the European Court has highlighted the MoA in the field of economic and social issues so as not to disavow the political choices of States in this area, the Inter-American Court has developed a case law that tends to disavow any national legislation that has the effect of preserving, and sometimes even reinforcing, social inequalities on the continent. In this regard, the case-law of the Inter-American Court markedly deviates from the more cautious European approach. While the scope of article 26 of the American Convention had long been at the centre of multiple doctrinal *disputatio*, and the Court of San José had warily opened up a new horizon in 2009 by considering the principle of 'no-backsliding' on social rights justiciable,[119] it brought about a real conceptual revolution in a major judgment against Peru in *Lagos del Campo*.[120] The Court came up with a new interpretation of article 26, considering that 'the economic and social standards' it refers to derive both from the OAS Charter

117 This is the case of the Committee on Economic and Social Rights created by the optional protocol of the International Covenant on Economic, Social and Cultural Rights and of the European Committee of Social Rights.

118 O Ruiz-Chiriboga, 'The American Convention and The Protocol of San Salvador: Two Intertwined Treaties. Non Enforceability of Economic, Social and Cultural Rights in the Inter-American System' (2011) 31 (2) NQHR 159.

119 IACtHR, *Acevedo Buendía et al. [Discharged and retired employees of the Comptroller]*, Prel. Objections, Merits, Reparations and Costs, Series C no 198 (July 1, 2009).

120 IACtHR, *Lagos del Campo v. Peru*, Prel. Objections, Merits, Reparations and Costs Series C no 340 (Aug. 31, 2017). The case concerned the dismissal of a worker for serious

and the American Declaration on the Rights and Duties of Man (two texts with important social provisions). Having asserted the justiciability of article 26 – cutting short years of controversy – and having used the technique of 'derivation', the Court will be able as and when cases arise to address and protect an unprecedented number of economic and social rights.[121]

The incipient African case law on this matter is taking a similar route. Whether in its contentious (*Ogiek case*)[122] or advisory function (*PALU opinion*),[123] the African Court is working to use the full potential of the Banjul Charter. The *Ogiek* case provides an opportunity for it to rule for the first time in its young history on so-called 'indigenous' litigation. At issue was the eviction of the Ogiek from their ancestral territory, the Mau Forest, a forest complex in southwestern Kenya that is among the largest in East Africa and is also the watershed for more than seven lakes, including Lake Victoria. The Ogiek judgment is a landmark ruling in the African system: in addition to complementing the 'quasi-jurisprudence' of the African Commission on Human

misconduct further to his public statements as a workers' representative. Domestic courts, and more specifically the Supreme Court, overturned the trial court's ruling and approved the dismissal on elliptic grounds. Having been fired, he was unable to draw a pension and could not find other work. His family life and health were affected (para.152). Peru was found (by five votes to two) to have infringed both the right to 'job security' (*el derecho a la estabilidad laboral*), as recognised by article 26 (in conjunction with articles 1para. 1, 13, 8, and 16 of the Convention), and the right of freedom of association of workers, as recognised by articles 16 and 26 (in conjunction with articles 1para.1, 13, and 8 of the American Convention.

121 In the six months that followed the revolution of the *Lagos del Campo* decision, the Court confirmed its new approach drawn from the derivation of rights both in the *Petroperú* case and its advisory opinion at the request of Colombia (IACtHR, *Environment and Human Rights*, Nov. 15, 2017, OC-23/17). In the case involving Peru, the Court declared that the right to work had been violated with respect to more than a hundred workers because they had no access to an effective legal remedy pursuant to article 8 para. 1 and 25 (IACHR, *Dismissed Employees Petroperú et al. v. Peru*, Prel. Objections, Merits, Reparations and Costs, Nov. 30, 2017, Series C no 344, para. 195). Following the request for an advisory opinion presented on 14 March 2016 by the Colombian government, the Court, when asked about the obligations of states with respect to the protection of the environment in the Caribbean region under the text of the treaty, took the opportunity to enshrine the justiciability of the right to a healthy environment (para. 57). This was then was further considered as an 'autonomous' right. Jurisprudential policy seems to be well implanted and the Court takes every opportunity it has to further it: IACtHR, *San Miguel de Sosa et al. v. Venezuela*, Merits and Reparations and Costs, Series C no 348 (Feb. 8, 2018); IACtHR, *Poblete Viches et al. v Chile*, Merits and Reparations and Costs, Series C no 349 (March 8, 2018).

122 ACtHPR, *African Commission on Human Rights v. Kenya* ('Ogiek case'), Merits, req. n° 006/ 2012 (May 26, 2017).

123 ACtHPR, *Request for an Advisory Opinion by The Pan African Lawyers Union (PALU) on The Compatibility of the Vagrancy laws with the African Charter on Human and Peoples Rights and others human rights instruments applicable in Africa*, req. n°001/2018 (Dec., 4, 2020).

Rights on these issues, the Court decided to start from the analysis of the right to property (Article 14), in order to devote *ad hoc* developments to the notion of 'indigenous population'.[124] Having recognised the Ogiek as an indigenous population, the Court was then able to examine the rights enshrined in Articles 2 (non-discrimination), 4 (right to life), 8 (freedom of conscience and religion), 17 (right to culture), and last but not least, 21 (right to the free disposal of natural resources) and 22 (right to development). In addition to taking a position on major issues for the African continent, the Court was given the opportunity to align itself with the Inter-American standard.[125]

The opinion of 4 December 2020 on the so-called vagrancy laws is also significant. For the first time, the African Court had the opportunity to make important statements, thanks to its advisory function, on a problem that runs through many African societies: the criminalisation of disadvantaged people, who are stigmatised by terminology dating back to the colonial era and which in turn generates a 'presumption of delinquency'. Thus, 'ruffians', 'lunatics', 'wanderers', 'idlers', and 'vagrants' are all terms which, according to the Court, 'reflect an outdated and largely colonial perception of individuals without any rights and the use of these terms dehumanises and demeans these persons, who are perceived as having an inferior status'.[126] After this welcome exercise in contextualisation, the African Court declared the incompatibility of vagrancy laws with several provisions of the Banjul Charter (2, 3, 5, 6, 7, 12, and 18); the African Charter on the Rights of the Child (3, 4 § 1 and 17); and the Maputo Protocol (Article 24). Most importantly, in answering the last question posed by PALU, the Court set out 'the positive obligation [of States] to repeal or amend their laws on vagrancy', which 'requires them to take all necessary measures, as soon as possible, to revise all their legislation, in particular those laws which provide for offences related to vagrancy'.[127]

124 ACtHPR, *Ogiek case, op.cit.*, paras. 103–113.

125 Indeed, we know that the Inter-American Court was the first international court, in 2001, to take on board the specificity of the 'indigenous fact' (*le fait autochtone*). If on the whole the interpretative consistency with the inter-American system is there – Kenya was unanimously condemned for the violation of almost all the rights invoked – the only exception concerned the conception of the right to life. The 'Arusha Court' developed a convoluted argument on the concept of 'dignified life' and did not recognise, *in casu*, its violation.

126 ACtHPR, *Request for an Advisory Opinion by PALU, op.cit.*, para. 79.

127 In so doing, it put into effect the effective the obligation set out in Article 1 of the African Charter, according to which 'Member States (…), recognise the rights, duties and freedoms set forth in this Charter and undertake to adopt legislative or other measures to give effect to them'. It linked this obligation to similar ones in the African Charter on the Rights of the Child (Article 1) and the Maputo Protocol on the Rights of Women (Article 26). Although they are written in the same register, there are variations in the terminology used between the two. While the *mantra* of adopting 'legislative or other measures' and/or 'necessary measures' is common to both, the Maputo Protocol is bold in requiring states to allocate 'adequate budgetary resources'. In any event, this common thread enabled the African

2.2.2 'Sexual Justice'

We have seen in the first part of this article that the European Court has always been attentive to historical, social, cultural, and religious sensitivities on societal issues and has never ventured to impose a specific legislative policy on States in accordance with the MoA doctrine. This was the case with regard to same-sex marriage: although the ECtHR has always fought against discrimination on the basis of sexual orientation,[128] it has never ventured to impose this legal figure on States. In short, it does not seek to replace national legislators.[129] Its Inter-American counterpart, however, did not bother with such restraint;[130] rather, it required States to institute marriage for same-sex couples.[131]

Court to affirm in para 153 that State Parties were obliged, 'inter alia, (to) amend or repeal their laws and regulations on vagrancy in accordance with these instruments'.

128 *Ad. exemplum*, ECtHR, *Dudgeon v. Ireland* (Oct. 22 1981); ECtHR, *Norris v. Ireland* (Oct. 26, 1988); ECtHR, *Modinos v. Cyprus* (Apr. 22, 1993); ECtHR, *Salgueiro da Sila Mouta v. Portugal* (Dec. 21, 1999); ECtHR, *Schalk and Kopf v. Austria,* (June 24, 2010); ECtHR, GC, *X and others v. Austria* (Feb. 19, 2013); ECtHR, *Vallianatos and others v. Greece* (Nov. 7, 2013); ECtHR, *Sabalic v. Croatia* (Jan. 14, 2021); ECtHR, *Case of Association Accept and others v. Romania* (June 1st, 2021); ECtHR, *Yartsev v. Russia* (July 20, 2021).

129 ECtHR, dec., *Manenc v. France* (Sept. 21, 2010); ECtHR, *Gas and Dubois v. France* (March 15, 2012).

130 The same policy exists concerning 'reproductive rights': IACtHR, *Artavia Mutillo and al (Fertilisatio in vitro) v. Costa Rica,* Prel. objection, Merits, Reparations and Costs, Nov. 28, 2012. The Court examined, for the first time, the question of whether Costa Rica may, under the American Convention on Human Rights, protect human embryos from destruction by banning *in vitro* fertilization (IVF) in its jurisdiction. *In casu,* the applicants challenged a decision of the Supreme Court of Costa Rica, issued in 2000, declaring it to be incompatible with the American Convention (ACHR). According to this domestic court, IVF constitutes an attack on the person, because it treated the embryo as an object, and entails a high rate of embryonic death. In response to the applicants' request, the IACtHR decided that the Costa Rica Supreme Court's prohibition of IVF violated the applicant's rights to personal integrity (art.5), personal liberty (art.7), privacy (art. 11) and the right to family (art. 17). Regarding IVF and the pre-implantational embryo – the key issue – the ACtHR rules that the latter could not be understood as a person; in others words, the right to life (art.4) cannot be extended to an embryo and to unborn persons. The Court noted the diverse biological, medical, ethical, moral, philosophical and religious perspectives, and accepted that there is no single agreed-upon definition of the beginning of life. However, for the purposes of Article 4 para.1 and taking into account the scientific evidence presented, the Court noted that, even though a fertilised egg gives rise to a cell with sufficient genetic information for the potential development of a 'human being', the fact is that development is precluded until the embryo is implanted in a woman's body. An embryo which is never implanted could not develop, for the lack of necessary nutrients or a suitable environment. Conception therefore occurs *from the moment of implantation* and an embryo alone cannot be granted the status of a 'person'. In so doing, the IACtHR gives a very novel interpretation to Article 4 para. 1 of the ACHR which states '*Every person has the right to have his life respected. This right shall be protected by law and, in general, from the moment of conception*'.

131 IACtHR, *State Obligations Concerning Change of Name, Gender Identity, and Rights Derived from a Relationship Between Same-Sex Couples (Interpretation and Scope of Articles 1 para. 1,*

In a ground-breaking advisory opinion delivered in November 2017, the IACtHR 'became the first international tribunal to find that same-sex marriage is a fundamental right under international law'.[132] This finding was a response to a request from Costa Rica filed in 2016 that asked the Court to review whether the country's failure to grant the same economic rights to same-sex couples violated the American Convention, and asked the Court for guidelines on appropriate domestic mechanisms that could guarantee same-sex couples' economic rights.[133]

In a critical passage, the Court called to all OAS States, including those which are not party to the American Convention and therefore not subject to the Court's jurisdiction, to adopt measures in the direction of legalizing same-sex marriage. The passage below is striking:

> [The Court] urges states to promote, in good faith, the legislative, administrative and judicial reforms required to adapt their domestic laws, and internal interpretations and practice (…) [states] are obliged not to violate the provisions that prohibit discriminating against [same-sex couples] and must, consequently, ensure them the same rights derive from marriage in the understanding that this is a transitional situation.[134]

Beyond the fact that the Court ruled by advice, using the conventionality control doctrine within the realm of its advisory function,[135] it holds that Member States of the American Convention have an obligation to recognize same-sex marriage, to permit transgender individuals to change their name and gender on identity documents, and to ensure the economic rights of those in same-sex relationships. Such developments in the case law have given rise to a great deal

3, 7 11para.2, 13, 17, 18 and 24, in relation to Art.1, of the American Convention on Human Rights), Advisory Opinion OC-24/17, Série A n°24 (Nov. 24, 2017).

132 J Contesse, 'The Rule of Advice in International Human Rights Law', (2021) 115 (3) AJIL 381.

133 IACtHR, *State Obligations Concerning Change of Name …, op.cit.*, para. 2. Specifically, Costa Rica asked: (1) whether states must 'recognize and facilitate the name change of an individual in accordance with his or her gender identity'; (2) whether the lack of administrative procedures for name change in such circumstances could be considered contrary to the American Convention on Human Rights; (3) whether the American Convention requires states to recognize all economic rights that derive from a same-sex relationship; and (4) whether there must be a specific mechanism to govern relationships between persons of the same sex for the state to recognize all the economic rights that derive from that relationship.

134 IACtHR, *State Obligations Concerning Change of Name …, op.cit.*, paras. 225–226.

135 On this point, see J Contesse, *op.cit., passim.*

of criticism. For instance, jurists linked to Catholic universities,[136] supported by powerful conservative movements,[137] have criticised this conception of marriage.[138] Others, more generally, have criticised the way in which the Court has used international and domestic developments to impose on States the obligation to recognise marriage for all[139] from a technical standpoint. This issue of same-sex marriage leads to a stark European-American divide. European restraint is contrasted with Inter-American activism. So far, the African Court has not yet been called upon to rule on societal issues of this magnitude. At this stage, the question is as follows: what will the ACtHPR do in due course on a subject where Africa's own states are fighting diplomatic battles against the demands of the LGBT community?[140]

3 Conclusion

Rather than presenting yet another theoretical analysis in order to address the issue of the articulation of the Majoritarian Will with domestic and international judicial powers, this article has sought to decipher the major jurisprudential trends that are emerging in Strasbourg, San José, and Arusha. The intercontinental picture shows that it is not possible to draw definite conclusions across the board. The relationship to the majority will be different for each system depending on the political context in which it was created and has since evolved, the structure of the texts that govern it, and the members who make

136 *Ad exemplum*, A Paul, 'La Corte Interamericana *in Vitro*: Comentarios sobre su proceso de Toma de Decisions a Propósito del caso Artavia' (2013) Revista Derecho Público Iberoamericano, 303; LM De Jesus, '*Artavia Murillo v. Costa Rica*: The Inter-American Court on Human Rights' Promotion of Non-Existent Human Rights obligations to authorize Artificial Reproductive Technologies' (2014) 18 UCLA Journal of International Law and Foreign Affairs 275.

137 R Urueña, 'Evangelicals at the Inter-American Court of Human Rights', (2019) 113 AJIL UNBOUND 360.

138 As well as the conception of life in the *Artavia Murillo* case (*Artavia Murillo v. Costa Rica*, Preliminary Objections, Merits, Reparations and Costs, Série C No. 257 (Nov. 28, 2012) and the conception of family in the *Atala Riffo* case (*Atala Riffo and Daughters v. Chile,* Merits, Reparations and Costs, Serie C No. 239 (Feb. 24, 2012).

139 On that point, the presentation of the main technical critics related to the use of external sources is well discussed by J Contesse, *op.cit.,* spec. 390–393.

140 O Nwarchok, A Sylla, 'La question homosexuelle en Afrique : entre droit, politique et éthique' (2020) AHRY/AADH 213.

up the courts and their willingness to change the structural defects of national societies. At this stage, it is certain that the three RHRC unanimously agree on an essential element which is in reality at the basis of their creation: the will to safeguard the democratic bases of the States at all costs. Thus, while social and societal issues are dealt with differently, those relating to the preservation of judicial independence and the separation of powers share common ground.

CHAPTER 4

On the Importance of a Sense of Truth for a Democratic Legal Culture and the International Order

Lando Kirchmair

1 Introduction*

Many scholars hold that the rule of law and democracy are in crisis.[1] International law plays an important role in this. We even witness on the one hand that leaders are seeking to use international law to extend their power.[2] On the other hand, however, international law might also contribute to prevent democratic backsliding.[3] This chapter proposes to engage with *Gustav Radbruch* in order to shed light on the crucial problem of this crisis. It is claimed that *Radbruch* provided a diagnosis which is also of relevance for our current crisis. We may conclude, relying on *Radbruch*, that a sense of truth is of utmost relevance for our current crisis in particular and a democratic legal culture in general. Even though post-truth has become an issue of debate, this chapter holds with *Radbruch* that we still underestimate the danger of "alternative facts" and the value of truth for democracy. Going beyond *Radbruch*, we will look at two different philosophical conceptions of truth in order to show how,

* An early version of this paper has been presented at the workshop "Rethinking the Legitimacy of Public International Law: Democracy, Digitalisation and Climate Change as Challenges for the Traditional Concept of Sovereignty?", organized by the Société française pour le droit international and the German Society for International Law at the Akademie für Politische Bildung, Tutzing on 23 September 2020. The author is grateful to the participants of this event and to Jane Hofbauer for discussions, comments and stimulating criticism.

1 See, eg, S Levitsky and D Ziblatt, *How Democracies Die* (Crown 2018); D Runciman, *How Democracy Ends* (Profile 2018); Y Mounk, *The People vs. Democracy: Why Our Freedom is in Danger and How to Save It* (Harvard University Press 2018); T Ginsburg and A Z Huq, *How to Save a Constitutional Democracy* (University of Chicago Press 2019).

2 See T Ginsburg, 'The Machinery of International Law and Democratic Backsliding: The Problem of Term Limits' (2020) 14 Law & Ethics of Human Rights 1.

3 See ibid 18 stating that "[w]e are beginning to observe two contradictory and related trends: the abuse of human rights law to facilitate incumbent bypass of term limits, and the hints of a thicker normative framework in international law, still incompletely enforced, to make this more difficult".

 | DOI:10.1163/9789004508712_005

within the realm of discourse theory (*Jürgen Habermas* and *Robert Alexy*) and Wittgensteinian (constitutional) games of justification (*Dennis Patterson* and *Julian Nida-Rümelin*), a sense of truth – in a different, but fundamental sense – is relevant for a democratic legal culture. The argument holds that truthfulness, as we will see, is indispensable for a democratic legal culture. This might play out as *Peter Häberle* has argued in a "constitutional prohibition to tell lies" for officials in particular. Truthfulness is, however, also relevant for the international legal order in general. Finally, this chapter will argue that the importance of truthfulness for a democratic legal culture should also be reflected in the discourse on a (human) right to democracy in international law.

2 The Importance of a Sense of Truth for a Democratic Legal Culture

2.1 *Gustav Radbruch on the Importance of a Sense of Truth for the Democratic Constitutional State*

Gustav Radbruch has provided an important insight into the current crisis of the rule of law and democracy.[4] This might be surprising as *Radbruch* is mainly famous for his justice formula which aims at resolving the "conflict between justice and legal certainty". According to *Radbruch* "flawed law", which does not meet the standard of justice to a tolerable degree, "must yield to justice".[5] While this formula was directed at dealing with National Socialist injustice in the post-WW II era in Germany, *Radbruch* also offered a largely neglected diagnosis as to why the creation of his justice formula had become necessary in the first place. His diagnosis reads as follows:

> The most conspicuous characteristic of Hitler's personality, which became through his influence the pervading spirit of the whole of National Socialist 'law' as well, was a complete lack of any sense of truth

4 For a more extensive analysis of this section (2.) see, L Kirchmair, 'What Gustav Radbruch Teaches Us about (Authoritarian) Populism: Lies by Officials Should Not Be Referred to as Populism Because They Are a Genuine Threat to the Democratic Legal Culture', in S Kirste and N Paulo (eds), *Populism, Democracy and the Rule of Law* (ARSP-Beiheft 2021) 86 ff.

5 G Radbruch, 'Statutory Lawlessness and Supra-Statutory Law' (2006) 26 Oxford Journal of Legal Studies 1, 7. Cf on this M Borowski and S L Paulson (eds), *Die Natur des Rechts bei Gustav Radbruch* (Mohr Siebeck 2015); S Kirste, 'Rechtsidee und Elemente der Gerechtigkeit bei Gustav Radbruch' in W Pauly (ed), *Rechts- und Staatsphilosophie des Relativismus. Pluralismus, Demokratie und Rechtsgeltung bei Gustav Radbruch* (Nomos 2011) 57 discussing the formula with reference to Radbruch's idea of law; as well as B Bix, 'Radbruch's Formula and Conceptual Analysis' (2011) 56 American Journal of Jurisprudence 45.

> or any sense of right and wrong. Because he had no sense of truth, he could shamelessly, unscrupulously lend the ring of truth to whatever was rhetorically effective at the moment. And because he had no sense of right and wrong, he could without hesitation elevate to a statute the crudest expression of despotic caprice.[6]

This diagnosis is not only relevant for the past. It is also – as this chapter claims – of utmost relevance for our current crisis.[7] However, *Radbruch* only mentioned the importance of a sense of truth for a democratic constitutional state in passing. Nowadays, post-truth has become an issue and "alternative facts" do concern us to some extent.[8] However, this chapter holds with *Radbruch* that the importance of a sense of truth for the democratic constitutional state has been underestimated so far.[9] Moreover, this chapter suggests that we should place a sense of truth at the centre of our concerns when speaking about a crisis of the rule of law and democracy these days.

Radbruch's diagnosis, holding that a lack of a sense of truth is troublesome for a democratic constitutional state, has some intuitive virtue of

---

6 Radbruch (n 5), 7. The German original G Radbruch, 'Gesetzliches Unrecht und übergesetzliches Recht' (1946) 1 Süddeutsche Juristenzeitung 105, 107 reads as follows: "Die hervorstechendste Eigenschaft in Hitlers Persönlichkeit, die von ihm aus zum Wesenszug des ganzen nationalsozialistischen 'Rechts' geworden ist, war sein völliger Mangel an Wahrheitssinn und Rechtssinn: weil ihm jeder Wahrheitssinn fehlte, konnte er dem jeweils rednerisch Wirksamen ohne Scham und Skrupel den Akzent der Wahrheit geben; weil ihm jeder Rechtssinn fehlte, konnte er ohne Bedenken die krasseste Willkür zum Gesetz erheben".

7 Literature on the crisis of democracy, the rule of law and the crisis of the democratic constitutional state is increasing quickly. Cf above n 1. See also for current debates under the umbrella of populism, the Symposium on Public Law and the New Populism (2019) 17 International Journal of Constitutional Law; Public Law and Populism (2019) 20 German Law Journal; as well as the special section on Populism and Constitutionalism (2019) 15 European Constitutional Law Review.

8 Oxford Dictionaries chose "post-truth" as word of the year in 2016, available at https://en.oxforddictionaries.com/word-of-the-year/word-of-the-year-2016 accessed 30 April 2021. "Post-truth" is defined as "relating to or denoting circumstances in which objective facts are less influential in shaping public opinion than appeals to emotion and personal belief". *Donald Trump* spearheaded this phenomenon with more than 20,000 false or misleading claims as the fact checker by the Washington post has shown, G Kessler, S Rizzo and M Kelly, 'President Trump has made more than 20,000 false or misleading claims' (*The Washington Post*, 13 July 2020) <https://www.washingtonpost.com/politics/2020/07/13/president-trump-has-made-more-than-20000-false-or-misleading-claims/> accessed 30 April 2021.

9 Compare, e.g., S Jasanoff and H R Simmet, 'No funeral bells: Public reason in a "post-truth" age' (2017) 47 Social Studies of Science 751, who argue as follows: "Debates about public facts are necessarily debates about social meanings, rooted in realities that are subjectively experienced as all-encompassing and complete, even when they are partial and contingent".

persuasiveness. Without a sense of truth, there is no democratic constitutional state. This claim was already made by *Kant*, when he maintained that lies spoil reciprocal trust.[10] Trust is necessary for a society. Yet, if we take a closer look, it becomes difficult to classify this rather simple and accurate diagnosis. What is the concrete significance of the importance of a sense of truth for a democratic constitutional state?

This question is hard to answer because scholars even dispute what truth actually means. The essence of truth is a major philosophical controversy, which cannot be resolved in this brief chapter. Neither is this chapter interested in what truth means in an epistemological manner. Rather – and *Gustav Radbruch* can also be understood in this way – a sense of truth means truthfulness.[11] Such a synonymous understanding of a sense of truth and truthfulness also seems to be covered by a passage in *Radbruch's* work which explicitly relates to his sense of truth thesis. The passage is in the epilogue to his *Philosophy of Law*, which he wrote probably in 1947. There *Radbruch* writes:

> Truthfulness is the sister of justice.[12]

This statement is catchy. However, it is also in need of explanation. If we continue reading we learn that

> also truthfulness, also good faith [...] have not only been continuously violated by National Socialism, but they were also fundamentally denied.

---

10 I Kant, 'Über ein vermeintliches Recht zu lügen' in W Weischedel (ed), *Werke* Vol 8 (Suhrkamp 1977) 425.

11 Kant (n 10), differentiated between the epistemological notion of truth and truthfulness: "Weil Wahrhaftigkeit eine Pflicht ist, die als die Basis aller auf Vertrag zu gründenden Pflichten angesehen werden muß, deren Gesetz, wenn man ihr auch nur die geringste Ausnahme einräumt, schwankend und unnütz gemacht wird". It follows according to Kant: "Es ist also ein heiliges, unbedingt gebietendes, durch keine Konvenienzen einzuschränkendes Vernunftgebot; in allen Erklärungen wahrhaft (ehrlich) zu sein". Compare also P Häberle, *Wahrheitsprobleme im Verfassungsstaat* (Nomos1995) 81, who argues in connection with the quest for truth in the constitutional state, "[d]aß darin keine Garantie objektiv erreichter Wahrheit steckt [...]. Letztlich kommt es wohl mehr auf die Wahrhaftigkeit von Personen als auf Institutionen an".

12 Epilogue to G Radbruch, *Rechtsphilosophie. Studienausgabe*, ed by R Dreier and S L Paulson (Mohr Siebeck 2nd ed 2003) 199 in German: "Schwester der Gerechtigkeit ist die Wahrhaftigkeit". English translations – if not indicated otherwise – are those of the author.

> It was routine in National Socialism to use words which obviously contradicted their cause.[13]

Radbruch gives examples to illustrate his point. He refers among other things to the fact that reasons for military interventions were consciously and artificially created. In this regard, *Radbruch* points to a declaration by *Hitler* on 22 September 1938 in which he assured *Chamberlain* repeatedly that if the problem of the Sudetenland were solved, Germany would not make any more territorial claims in Europe. On 29 September 1938 the Sudetenland was handed over to Hitler in the Munich agreement and yet at the very beginning of October, *Hitler* instructed General *Keitel* to draw up plans to destroy the rest of Czechoslovakia. In fact, as early as 22 April 1938,[14] *Hitler* had already agreed to a proposal by General *Jodl* which said that the "initiative green" (against Czechoslovakia) would be triggered by an incident in Czechoslovakia which would allow Germany to intervene militarily. Determining the precise date and time of this incident was of great importance in the planning. Finally, *Radbruch* refers to a speech made by *Hitler* on 22 August 1939, before the *Blitzkrieg* against Poland. *Hitler* said:

> I will find a propagandistic reason for starting a war, no matter whether this is credible or not. The victor will not be asked whether he told the truth. When starting and waging war, it is not right that matters but victory. [...] The strongest man is right![15]

---

13 Radbruch (n 12), 199 in German: "Auch die Wahrhaftigkeit, auch Treu und Glauben wurden vom Nationalsozialismus nicht nur fortdauernd verletzt, vielmehr grundsätzlich verleugnet. Es gehörte zur Uebung des Nationalsozialismus, Worte zu gebrauchen, die der Sache offenkundig widersprechen".

14 "Studie Grün" is available at <https://www.ns-archiv.de/krieg/1938/tschechoslowakei/fall-gruen-22-04-1938.php> accessed 30 April 2021. Note that Radbruch in the afterword talked about 30 August 1938.

15 Radbruch (n 12), 199 [Footnotes have been omitted. Further evidence can be found in the *Studienausgabe*.] in German: "ein Gesetz, das zur Freimachung und parteimäßigen Neubesetzung der Amtsstellen dienen sollte, hieß 'Gesetz zur Wiederherstellung des Berufsbeamtentums', die Ausrottung von Geisteskranken als unnötiger Esser wurde 'Gnadentod' genannt. Feierliche Erklärungen, daß von Deutschland weitere territoriale Ansprüche nicht mehr erhoben würden, wurden abgegeben und zugleich solche territorialen Machterweiterungen schon geplant und vorbereitet. Ja, es werden Anlässe zu kriegerischem Eingreifen bewußt und künstlich geschaffen: am 22.9.1938 erklärte Hitler, er habe Chamberlain versichert und wiederhole es jetzt, 'daß es – wenn dieses Problem (Sudetenland) gelöst ist – für Deutschland in Europa keine territorialen Probleme mehr gibt', am 29.9. wurde ihm im Münchner Abkommen das Sudetenland ausgeliefert, schon zu Anfang Oktober beauftragt er General Keitel mit der [...] Planung zur 'Zerschlagung

Especially the last two sentences are by far not solitary events. *Peter Häberle*, for instance stated that also former Yugoslavia painfully taught us that the first victim of war is truth.[16] Lies after all played also a central role in deliberately misleading the general public before and during the war in Iraq in 2003.[17] Another association is the re-emergence of the misnomer "*Lügenpresse*" ("lying press"), which was already used during the time of National Socialism in order to discredit critical news.[18]

Radbruch is often referred to as the most influential German legal philosopher of the last century. His work and the interpretation of his work are, accordingly, substantial. This chapter cannot deal with this richness in any comprehensive way. Yet, the above cited rather brief passages raise suspicion. Attempts to locate the sense of truth thesis in *Gustav Radbruch's* understanding of law are not really promising. The sense of truth thesis by *Radbruch* cannot be integrated easily into his understanding of law.[19] Instead of reconstructing for instance Neo-Kantian origins of *Radbruch*, this chapter will look at modern conceptions of a democratic legal culture in order to validate the sense of truth thesis. Two conceptions, which however both do not refer to *Gustav Radbruch*, particularly come to mind as they also offer sophisticated philosophical backup on the question of what is truth.

---

der Rest-Tschechei'. Am 30.8.1938 stimmte Hitler einem Vorschlag Jodls zu, in dem es heißt: 'Die Aktion "Grün" (gegen die Tschechei) wird ausgelöst durch einen Zwischenfall in der Tschechei, der Deutschland den Anlaß zu militärischem Eingreifen gibt. Die Bestimmung des Zeitpunkts dieses Zwischenfalls nach Tag und Stunde ist von größter Bedeutung'. In einer Ansprache am 22. August 1939 (vor dem Polenkrieg) sagte der Führer: 'Ich werde propagandistischen Anlaß zur Auslösung des Krieges geben, gleichgültig, ob glaubhaft. Der Sieger wird später nicht gefragt, ob er die Wahrheit gesagt [hat] oder nicht. Bei Beginn und Führung des Krieges kommt es nicht auf das Recht an, sondern auf den Sieg. [...] Der Stärkere hat das Recht!'".

16 Häberle (n 11), 32, n 33: "Der Krieg in Ex-Jugoslawien belehrt schmerzlich, daß das erste Opfer von Kriegen die Wahrheit ist – die Kriegsberichterstattung aller am Bürgerkrieg beteiligten Seiten zeigt es".

17 See, eg, D Miller (ed.), *Tell me lies. Propaganda and Media Distortion in the Attack on Iraq* (Pluto Press 2nd ed 2003).

18 For a more recent publication, see V Lilienthal and I Neveria, *Lügenpresse: Anatomie eines politischen Kampfbegriffs* (Kiwi 2017).

19 See, again, Kirchmair (n 4).

2.2 *The Importance of a Sense of Truth for the Discourse Theory of Law*

Jürgen Habermas has constructed a comprehensive edifice, from the consensus theory of truth[20] to the discourse theory of law.[21] What role is there for a sense of truth within the discourse theory of law?

Habermas fundamentally distinguishes between communicative action and strategic action. Communicative action is oriented towards understanding while egoistic interests drive strategic action.[22] Communicative action, in turn, can be distinguished according to assertions in propositional truth, normative correctness and subjective truthfulness. The latter means that "the manifest intention of a speech act is meant as it is expressed".[23] The discourse theory of law builds on these insights. As a theory of truth, it is a theory about truth as correctness.[24] The truth is what can be claimed in a non-coercive general and justified consensus. For participants in a rational discourse, we have to assume pragmatic prerequisites, which are a sort of aspiration; in *Habermas'* words, they are "an unavoidable supposition, reciprocally made in discourse".[25] From

---

20 See J Habermas, 'Wahrheitstheorien' in H Fahrenbach (ed), *Wirklichkeit und Reflexion. Walter Schulz zum 60. Geburtstag* (Neske 1973), 211; id, *Wahrheit und Rechtfertigung. Philosophische Aufsätze* (Suhrkamp 1999). For early criticism see A Beckermann, 'Die realistischen Voraussetzungen der Konsenstheorie von J. Habermas' (1972) 3 Zeitschrift für allgemeine Wissenschaftstheorie 63. Cf for criticism, N Rescher, *Pluralism: Against the Demand for Consensus* (Oxford University Press 1993); for criticism of this criticism, see S O'Neill, 'Book Review: Nicholas Rescher, Pluralism Against the Demand for Consensus' (1995) 7 Utilitas 340. See, however, also J Habermas, 'Kommunikatives Handeln und detranszendentalisierte Vernunft' in id, *Zwischen Naturalismus und Religion. Philosophische Aufsätze* (Suhrkamp 2005), 27; and id, 'Zur Architektonik der Diskursdifferenzierung. Kleine Replik auf eine große Auseinandersetzung', in: ibid 84.

21 See J Habermas, *Between Facts and Norms. Contributions to a Discourse Theory of Law and Democracy* (MIT Press 1996, translated by W Rehg from the German original *Faktizität und Geltung – Beiträge zur Diskurstheorie des Rechts und des demokratischen Rechtsstaats* (Suhrkamp 1992)); R Alexy, 'Probleme der Diskurstheorie' (1989) 43 Zeitschrift für philosophische Forschung 81.

22 J Habermas, *The Theory of Communicative Action: Reason and the Rationalization of Society* Vol 1 (Beacon Press 1985, translated by T McCarthy from the German original *Theorie des kommunikativen Handelns* Vol 1 (Suhrkamp 1981)); as well as id, *The Theory of Communicative Action: Lifeworld and System: A Critique of Functionalist Reason* Vol 2 (Beacon Press 1985, translated by T McCarthy from the German original *Theorie des kommunikativen Handelns* Vol 2 (Suhrkamp 1981)).

23 J Habermas, Erläuterungen zum Begriff des kommunikativen Handelns (1982), reprinted in id, *Vorstudien und Ergänzungen zur Theorie des kommunikativen Handelns* (Suhrkamp 1995), 588 in German: "die manifeste Sprechintention so gemeint ist, wie sie geäußert wird".

24 See Alexy (n 21).

25 Habermas (n 20), Wahrheitstheorien, 258 quoted in T McCarthy, *The Critical Theory of Juergen Habermas* (MIT Press 1978), 310. In German: "eine in Diskursen reziprok vorgenommene Unterstellung".

an observer's perspective we see that rational discourse is rarely to be found in a pure form and this supposition can be counterfactual, with the prerequisites only anticipated. Yet, if we find ourselves in fundamentally different situations we are confronted with problems in such a conception. Hence, conscious manipulations and lies cannot be brought in line with the prerequisites of a communicative competence.[26] This is of utmost relevance, because according to *Habermas'* discourse principle "just those norms deserve to be valid that could meet with the approval of those potentially affected, insofar as the latter participate in rational discourses".[27]

I do not wish to engage either critically or affirmatively with the discourse theory of law.[28] Rather is it enough for my purpose to show that a complete lack of any sense of truth is a fundamental problem from the perspective of the discourse theory of law. This should have become clear even after such a brief analysis. Lies cannot be brought in line with discourse theory's prerequisites.[29]

---

26 See J Habermas, 'Was heißt Universalpragmatik?' in K-O Apel (ed), *Sprachpragmatik und Philosophie* (Suhrkamp 1976), 174. Compare also a recent talk given by *Jürgen Habermas* at the "New Perspectives for Europe" conference at the Goethe University Frankfurt, published as an online article in *Social Europe* on 22.10.2018 under the title "'New' Perspectives For Europe" <https://www.socialeurope.eu/new-perspectives-for-europe> accessed 30 April 2021. The talk starts as follows: "I am invited to talk about New Perspectives on Europe, but new ones fail me, and the Trumpian decay afflicting even the core of Europe makes me seriously question my old perspectives". This, I think, is alarming, even though *Habermas* talks about European Integration (and not about the requirements of communicative competence to which truthfulness belongs): "if the suspected link between the economic drifting apart of the eurozone member economies on the one hand and the strengthening of right-wing populism on the other hand in fact holds, then we're sitting in a trap in which the necessary social and cultural preconditions for a vital and safe democracy face further damage". See also a current interview with *Jürgen Habermas* in A Bächtiger, J S Dryzek, J Mansbridge and M E Warren (eds), The Oxford Handbook of Deliberative Democracy (Oxford University Press 2018), 871. Compare also K-O Apel, *Transformation der Philosophie*, Vol. 2, *Das Apriori der Kommunikationsgemeinschaft* (Suhrkamp 1973), 400 in German: "Lügen z. B. würde offenbar den Dialog der Argumentierenden unmöglich machen, aber dasselbe gilt schon auch für die Verweigerung des kritischen Verständnisses bzw. der Explikation und Rechtfertigung von Argumenten. Kurz: In der Argumentationsgemeinschaft ist die wechselseitige Anerkennung aller Mitglieder als gleichberechtigte Diskussionspartner vorausgesetzt".

27 Habermas (n 21), 127. For a critical view see S Benhabib, 'In the Shadow of Aristotle and Hegel: Communicative Ethics and Current Controversies in Practical Philosophy in Hermeneutics in Ethics and Social Theory' in id, *Situating the Self: Gender, Community, and Postmodernism in Contemporary Ethics* (Routledge 1992) 53–54.

28 Neither will we focus on the differences in the conceptions of *Habermas* and *Alexy*.

29 Note, however, that in his most recent discourse theory of justice, *Alexy* holds that the problems of ideal discourse (with the requirement of empirical truth among other requirements) need to be answered by institutionalization (and problems of

In order to avoid the criticism that the importance of a sense of truth for the democratic legal culture is only relevant for the discourse theory of law, another conception shall be analysed. In what follows we will briefly show that a sense of truth is also of utmost importance for Wittgensteinian (constitutional) games of justification in the realms of law and democracy.

2.3 *The Importance of a Sense of Truth for Wittgensteinian (Constitutional) Games of Justification*

Regarding the "legal" reading of *Wittgenstein* we will refer to the work of *Dennis Patterson*.[30] The "democratic" reading of *Wittgenstein* will rely on arguments advanced by *Julian Nida-Rümelin*.[31]

Dennis Patterson deals with the question as to "What does it mean to say that a proposition of law is true?"[32] After outlining the debate in legal philosophy against the background of the philosophical debate between so-called realists and anti-realists, *Patterson* concludes that it is not convincing to explain the truth of legal propositions by reference to some state of affairs.[33] For him it is not the interpretation but the understanding of an activity which is central for judging whether a legal proposition is true. According to *Patterson*, argumentative practice in a Wittgensteinian sense is key to judging whether a legal proposition is true. He refers to the example of constitutional debates on the legitimacy of judicial review, in order to demonstrate that argumentative figures, which are recognized in the discourse, show that a constitutional proposition

---

proceduralization by a theory of substance). See R Alexy, 'Gerechtigkeit als Richtigkeit', paper presented at the JKU interdisciplinary masterclass on 21 February 2019, 6 (on file with the author). Given that human rights are in place (especially freedom of thought and freedom of the press), 7 "anything is exposed to the fire of arguments" ("Alles ist dem Feuer der Argumente ausgesetzt".). Concerning the ideal and the real discourse in the conception of Alexy, compare also C Bäcker, 'Rationality without Ideality. Outlines of a Relativistic Discourse Theory of Law' in J A de Oliveira, S L Paulson and A Travessoni Gomes Trivisonno (eds), *Alexy's Theory of Law* (ARSP Beiheft 2015), 11.

30 D Patterson, *Law and Truth* (Oxford University Press 1996), especially ch 7 and 8 with references to L Wittgenstein, *Tractatus Logico-Philosophicus* (translated by D Pears and B McGuinnes 1974); id, *Philosophical Investigations* (translated by G E M Anscombe [1953] 2001; id, *The Blue and Brown Books* (Basil Blackwell 2nd ed 1960)); as well as id, *Notebooks 1914–1916* (translated and ed by G H von Wright and G E M Anscombe, 2nd ed 1979).

31 J Nida-Rümelin, *Wahrheit und Demokratie* (CH Beck 2006), especially ch 1 with references to L Wittgenstein, *Über Gewißheit. Werkausgabe* Vol 8, *Bemerkungen über die Farben. Über Gewißheit. Zettel. Vermischte Bemerkungen* (Suhrkamp 1984); and id, *Philosophische Untersuchungen* (Suhrkamp 1995).

32 Patterson (n 30), 3.

33 Patterson (n 30), 151.

is true.[34] His answer to the question as to what makes legal propositions true is not whether a legal proposition designates a relation between a statement and a state of affairs. Rather, according to *Patterson*, "normativity in law arises from linguistic practices". Thus, legal propositions are true if a competent legal actor can justify the proposition.[35]

Although such relevant argumentative figures, in other words the rules of the particular game, are flexible in a certain way, it is not possible to ignore those rules or make them up. The process is, thus, not arbitrary but relies on competent actors. The complete ignorance of relevant actors and their justifications in such a process are, therefore, not irrelevant but must be problematized as a lack of a sense of truth within this conception.

"Democracy without truth claims is empty", says *Julian Nida-Rümelin*.[36] He too refers to *Wittgenstein's* later works when he bases his conception of truth not on "final certainty" but on "daily justifications by our empirical and normative convictions".[37] According to *Nida-Rümelin*, the rules of justification are a) "pre-given to our lifeworld and not invented or posited", b) "not comprehensibly explicable" and c) "not rigid".

Neither is it possible to distinguish clearly between meta-rules which characterize our game of justification and between those rules which control our daily games of justification. Moreover, these rules are d) "ineluctable" and they contain the perspective of e) "[a] gradualism of justification". The transition from the "ineluctable basis" and "yet to be justified single convictions" is also fluent. Lastly *Nida-Rümelin* highlights that f) "[there] is no final certainty in observing the good and especially there is no certainty in the abstraction from all perception and the trust in all empiricism and all rationality detached from life-world practice".[38] Against a threatening "postmodern radicalization" of this perspective, *Nida-Rümelin* holds that different games of justification are cross-linked in a "common practice". Moreover, these games do not only refer to this "common practice" but also to a "common knowledge". It is precisely these commonalities that cannot be questioned "in toto". Only a "local scepticism" is possible.[39]

34 Patterson (n 30), ch 7.

35 Patterson (n 30), 179.

36 Nida-Rümelin (n 31), 7 "Demokratie ist ohne Wahrheitsansprüche inhaltsleer".

37 Nida-Rümelin (n 31), 7 in German he does not speak about "endgültige Gewissheiten" but about "alltägliche Begründungen unserer empirischen wie normativen Überzeugungen".

38 Nida-Rümelin (n 31), 30–31.

39 Nida-Rümelin (n 31), 35–36 he also refers to this as "pragmatic unity" ("pragmatische Einheit") and "epistemic unity" ("epistemische Einheit"). Moreover, he adds at this

Against this background *Julian Nida-Rümelin* develops the "relationship between democracy and truth". Interestingly he refers to his personal experience in politics and grants that what *Habermas* calls "strategic communication" is of relevance to politics.[40] Yet, he argues that "strategic communication, which undermines understanding in the long run, which, thus, can only exist as a parasite of truthful, trustful and reliable communication, runs against robust realities of the life-world".[41]

This is of great significance for the claimed importance of a sense of truth for a democratic legal culture. A certain degree of strategic communication seems to be tolerable. However, this tolerance is not endless. *Nida-Rümelin*, for instance, mentions the dangers of impairing deliberative democracy through the evolution of the media, which "leaves less and less space for well-conceived and differentiated political argument".[42] Hence, we come to conclude from this perspective as well that a sense of truth is of utmost importance for a democratic legal culture.

3 Consequences Following from the Importance of a Sense of Truth for a Democratic Legal Culture and the International Order

So far, this chapter has claimed that the importance of a sense of truth for a democratic legal culture as argued by *Gustav Radbruch* is still valid today. We have also seen that different conceptions of the law based on different philosophical perspectives (i.e. the discourse theory of law as well as Wittgensteinian (constitutional) games of justification) rely on the importance of a sense of truth.

---

stage (36) that the postmodern interpretation of *Wittgenstein's* perspective has to reject life-world essentials, which gives it – precisely from a Wittgensteinian perspective – little reliability ("[d]ass die postmoderne Interpretation der Wittgenstein'schen Perspektive lebenswelchtliche Essentialia zurückweisen muss, macht sie gerade aus einer Wittgenstein'schen Perspektive wenig vertrauenswürdig".). Compare also Nida-Rümelin (n 31), 70 ff.

40 Nida-Rümelin (n 31), 37 ff.

41 Nida-Rümelin (n 31), 38 "strategische Kommunikation, die die Fundamente der Verständigung langfristig unterminiert, die also nur als Parasit wahrhaftiger, vertrauensvoller und verlässlicher Kommunikation bestehen kann, [...] sich an robusten Realitäten der Lebenswelt [stößt]".

42 Nida-Rümelin (n 31), 44 "dem durchdachten und differenziert vorgetragenen politischen Argument immer weniger Raum gibt".

This chapter has spoken of *a* sense of truth (instead of *the* sense of truth). The reason for this is that the importance of a sense of truth has to be argued consistently depending on the conception of truth and democracy we choose. In a next step we will take a closer look at potential consequences following from the importance of a sense of truth for a democratic legal culture. Firstly, by looking at a potential "constitutional prohibition to tell lies" for officials as argued by *Peter Häberle* and secondly, at the international order and its handling of truth.

3.1 *A Sense of Truth, a "Constitutional Prohibition to Tell Lies" and the Difference between "Factual" and "Rational Truth"*

Peter Häberle has pondered the question asked here in an inimitable fashion.[43] After giving an overview of truth in philosophical discourse, he refers to famous writers who have written on truth. He highlights many passages in the works of *Johann Wolfgang von Goethe* and *William Shakespeare*.[44] Of particular interest is his quest for truth in the constitutional state. The constitutional state, according to *Häberle*, does not "possess eternal given truths". Rather it is "continuously involved in processes of merely *searching* for truth".[45] This very quest for truth becomes possible "according to *three fundamental freedoms* of the constitutional state: the freedom of *religious belief*, *art* and *science*".[46] *Häberle* divides up the question of truth in a pluralistic democracy into three areas of concern, namely the dispute about the relationship between "truth and the majority", an "understanding of the shaping of public societal opinion", and "as part of that, a restriction on the freedom of the press in the interests of other objects worthy of protection and an orientation towards 'truthful' media coverage".[47] For this chapter, his claim for a "constitutional prohibition to tell lies" is of particular interest.[48]

---

43 Häberle (n 11). See also P Häberle, '"Wahrheitsprobleme im Verfassungsstaat" – eine Zwischenbilanz' in J Bohnert et al (eds), *Verfassung – Philosophie – Kirche. Festschrift für Alexander Hollerbach* (Duncker & Humblot 2001), 15.

44 See Häberle (n 11), 52 ff and 58 ff.

45 Häberle (n 11), 79 [*italics* original]: the constitutional state is not "im Besitz ewiger vorgegebener Wahrheiten" but "stets auf Wegen der bloßen Wahrheits*suche*".

46 Häberle (n 11), 82 [*italics* original] in German: "von den *drei Grundfreiheiten* des Verfassungsstaates aus möglich: von der Freiheit der *Religions*ausübung, der *Kunst* und der *Wissenschaft* her".

47 Häberle (n 11), 86: the three areas of concern are "Wahrheit und Mehrheit", "[das] Verständnis der öffentlichen gesellschaftlichen Meinungsbildung" and "als Teil davon bei der Begrenzung der Pressefreiheit im Interesse anderer Schutzgüter und ihrer Ausrichtung auf die 'wahrheitsgemäße' Berichterstattung".

48 Häberle (n 11), 90 ff: "[das] verfassungsstaatliche Verbot der Lüge".

Is every lie prohibited? According to *Kant*, morally speaking, there is a duty to truthfulness.[49] And *Häberle* holds that the constitutional state assumes that its citizens "set out on a journey to 'seek the truth'". Yet, objective truths cannot be guaranteed, only "subjective truths".[50] Thus, we can only expect truthfulness, in *Radbruch's* words a sense of truth, which requires that claims are oriented towards the truth. Hence, they must be free from fraudulent intentions.[51] According to *Häberle* we have a "human right to err",[52] which is implicitly included in our quest for truth. Even though political lies are often not sanctioned or even revealed, political ethics condemning these lies are indispensable.[53] Therefore, *Häberle* claims with reference to *Kant*[54] and in line with *Böhme*, that: "By lying we insult the humanity in our communication partner and in ourselves. Hence, especially the powerful, which includes politicians, do not have a right to lie".[55]

Generalizing these thoughts, we can hold that we should differentiate between private and public actions. While "private lies" do not affect a democratic legal culture (except, of course, when specific legal duties are being performed, such as the duty of witnesses, etc., to be truthful), "public lies" are

49 See Kant (n 10), 427: "Wahrhaftigkeit eine Pflicht ist, die als die Basis aller auf Vertrag zu gründenden Pflichten angesehn werden muß, deren Gesetz, wenn man ihr auch nur die geringste Ausnahme einräumt, schwankend und unnütz gemacht wird. Es ist also ein heiliges, unbedingt gebietendes, durch keine Konvenienzen einzuschränkendes Vernunftgebot; in allen Erklärungen *wahrhaft* (ehrlich) zu sein". [*italics* original] Compare also O Höffe, *Kant* (C H Beck 7th ed 2007), 199–200. Note, however, that *Kant* also postulates that there is no right to a truth which is harmful to others.

50 Häberle (n 11), 9 speaks of humans or citizens who "sich auf den Weg der 'Wahrheitssuche' begeben".

51 For a distinction between lies and bullshit, see D Lanius and R Jaster, 'Ist Donald Trump ein Lügner? Fake News, Lügen und Bullshit' (*praefaktisch*, 18 December 2018) <https://www.praefaktisch.de/postfaktisch/ist-donald-trump-ein-luegner-fake-news-luegen-und-bullshit/> accessed 30 April 2021 referring to H G Frankfurt, *On Bullshit* (Princeton University Press 2005).

52 Häberle (n 11), 92 "Menschenrecht auf Irrtum" (with further reference to B Guggenberger). Cf also K Schmalenbach, 'Wahrheit und Lüge unter der Herrschaft der Grundrechte' (2005) 37 Juristische Arbeitsblätter 749 on the morally questionable, but nevertheless, by fundamental rights protected lie in the German Basic Law of citizens.

53 Häberle (n 11), 92.

54 Kant (n 10).

55 G Böhme, 'Die Sozialstruktur der Lüge' in P Kemper (ed), *Opfer der Macht. Müssen Politiker ehrlich sein?* (Suhrkamp 1993), 84 "Durch Lügen beleidigt man die Menschheit im Kommunikationspartner und in sich selbst. Daraus folgt, daß insbesondere die Mächtigen, das heißt auch die Politiker kein Recht auf Lüge haben".

banned by the "constitutional prohibition to tell lies". Officials are prohibited to tell lies.

The quest for truth and the constitutional prohibition to tell lies is "indispensable for the constitutional state as a *value of culture*, particularly against the backdrop of experiences with its totalitarian counterpart".[56] *Häberle* goes on by arguing that politics in the constitutional state cannot flourish without certain truth claims.[57] This, however, still remains vague.[58] This chapter, too, refrains from making concrete claims about concrete definitions of truthfulness. The reason behind this reluctance lies in the insight that this difficult topic does not allow for generalized claims. Rather, the constitutional prohibition for officials to tell lies in the form of a duty to truthfulness is claimed to be of utmost importance for a democratic legal culture. *Radbruch's* sharp diagnosis has been used to give weight to this claim. Beyond that, this chapter argues that we must justify the constitutional prohibition to tell lies according to our specific understanding of law and the philosophical background to that which we advocate. Hence, in the examples used here, the constitutional prohibition to tell lies for officials very likely changes depending on whether a discourse theoretical or a Wittgensteinian conception is taken as the starting point. Consequently, it seems difficult to speak of an international obligation for states to guarantee a specific national constitutional prohibition for officials to tell lies.

Before jumping to premature conclusions on the importance of a sense of truth for a democratic legal culture, however, we need to acknowledge furthermore the – at first glance seemingly – sceptical view expressed by *Hannah Arendt*. To her "truthfulness has never been counted among the political virtues, and lies have always been regarded as justifiable tools in political dealings".[59] This is quite astonishing as she is nevertheless convinced that a liar

56 Häberle (n 11), 94 [*italics* original]. The quest for truth and the constitutional prohibition to tell lies is as a "*Kulturwert* für den Verfassungsstaat, gerade auch nach den Erfahrungen mit dem totalitären Gegenmodell unverzichtbar".

57 Häberle (n 11), 97 "Politik im Verfassungsstaat kann m.E. ohne gewisse Wahrheitsansprüche auf Dauer nicht gedeihen".

58 For one such criticism of *Häberle*, see W Brugger, 'Rezension' (1995) 50 JuristenZeitung 1005, 1005–1006.

59 H Arendt, 'Lying in Politics: Reflections on The Pentagon Papers' (*The New York Review of Books*, 18 November 1971) <https://www.nybooks.com/articles/1971/11/18/lying-in-politics-reflections-on-the-pentagon-pape/ accessed 30 April 2021> republished as id, 'Die Lüge in der Politik' in id, *Wahrheit und Lüge in der Politik. Zwei Essays* (Piper 2nd ed 1972), 8 "Wahrhaftigkeit zählte niemals zu den politischen Tugenden, und die Lüge galt immer als ein erlaubtes Mittel in der Politik". Similarly id, 'Wahrheit und Politik' in id, *Wahrheit und Lüge in der Politik. Zwei Essays* (Piper 2nd ed 1972) 44 "niemand hat je die Wahrhaftigkeit zu den politischen Tugenden gerechnet". This, however, becomes

cannot succeed against reality for which there is no replacement.[60] This is, according to her, a lesson to be learned from totalitarian experiments and the alarming trust totalitarian rulers placed in lies.[61] And, thus, to *Arendt* too organised lies are an eminent problem as they destroy the capacity of human beings to differentiate between the truth and the untruth.[62]

For our purpose it is interesting to learn that *Arendt* followed *Leibniz* in differentiating between a "rational truth", which includes mathematical, scientific and philosophical truths, and a "factual truth".[63] Precisely the latter is important to the political process because it can endanger the whole processes while the "rational truth" cannot.[64] Besides, also the European Court of Human Rights amounts to a distinction between "facts" and "value judgments".[65]

Her core concern is to argue for an understanding of politics in flux. Therefore, she argues, with *Madison*, that every aspiration to an absolute truth which claims to be independent from opinions "strikes at the very roots of all politics and all governments".[66] Instead of absolute truths, it is important to

---

understandable later when Arendt (ibid 74–75) explains that truthfulness is not a virtue of politics, because articulating a truth claim does not actually belong to the political process for it does not aim at changing the world and the circumstances under which we are living. However, lies are always political, because they necessarily aim at changing something. Arendt adds (ibid 75), that this changes only if a community uses lies as a political weapon.

60 Arendt (n 59), 10.

61 Arendt (n 59), 10.

62 Arendt (n 59), 10 "Das prinzipielle Lügen der Terror-Regime kann nur erreichen, daß die Unterscheidung von Wahrheit und Unwahrheit überhaupt aus dem Bewußtsein der Menschen verschwindet".

63 Arendt (n 59), 48–49 speaking of "Vernunftwahrheiten" und "Tatsachenwahrheiten" while explicitly emphasizing that she will not bother about the legitimacy of this differentiation. For an insightful discussion see J Zinsmaier, 'Hannah Arendt und das "postfaktische Zeitalter"' (*praefaktisch*, 16 August 2016) <https://www.praefaktisch.de/postfaktisch/hannah-arendt-und-das-postfaktische-zeitalter/#_ftn11> accessed 30 April 2021.

64 Arendt (n 59), 48.

65 *Lingens v Austria* (ECtHR Judgment from 8 July 1986) Application no 9815/82, para 46 "In the Court's view, a careful distinction needs to be made between facts and value-judgments. The existence of facts can be demonstrated, whereas the truth of value-judgments is not susceptible of proof". Cf, *Dalban v Romania* (ECtHR Judgment from 28 September 1999, GC), Application no 28114/95, para 4, where the Court held that "it would be unacceptable for a journalist to be debarred from expressing critical value judgments unless he or she could prove their truth".

66 H Arendt, 'Truth and Politics' (*The New Yorker*, 25 February 1967). In German Arendt (n 59), 51 "'Jede Regierung', sagt Madison, 'beruht auf Meinung', da ohne die Unterstützung Gleichgesinnter nicht einmal die Tyrannenherrschaft an die Macht kommen oder sich an ihr halten könnte. Das aber heißt, daß innerhalb des Bereichs menschlicher Angelegenheiten jeder Anspruch auf absolute Wahrheit, die von den Meinungen der

have a vibrant process with open results. For such a process, it is important to allow for a variety of opinions instead of a somewhat undiscussable truth.[67]

In addition, *Arendt* acknowledges that in our times, the last traces of the ancient philosophical differentiation between philosophical truth and simple opinion have vanished.[68] While in ancient times there was a dispute between the rational truth and politics, this dispute did not vanish with the dissolution of opinion and truth. Instead, the dispute between truth and politics still goes on. However, now the dispute between politics and truth is directed at factual truths instead of the rational truth.[69] This shift is of utmost relevance because if historical facts, such as the fact that a majority of Germans supported *Hitler*, become mere opinions, our factual reality erodes. This is a political problem of great importance.[70] Precisely this problem might force us to reconsider the contradiction of truth and opinion.[71] Yet, this does not mean that factual truths and opinions are antagonisms. Factual truths also have a political nature. Facts are subject to opinion, and opinions can serve various interests and passions, fall far apart and, yet still be legitimate. However, integrity must always be guaranteed. For if this is not the case, in *Arendt's* words, "freedom of opinion becomes a farce, if the information on facts is not guaranteed".[72] As a direct consequence thereof, we lose the basis for exchanging opinions (which must be related to factual truths in order to be legitimate according to *Arendt*) and, thus, the basis for politics.[73] For the rational truth has as its antagonist error, illusion or mere opinion. The opposition of the factual truth is outright lies.[74]

Menschen unabhängig zu sein vorgibt, die Axt an die Wurzeln aller Politik und der Legitimität aller Staatsformen legt".

67 Arendt (n 59), 48. Note, that also for Arendt opinions are only legitimate if they refer to truth facts.

68 Arendt (n 59), 54 (with a pointed reference that this was unimaginable to Hegel in Fn. 12).

69 Arendt (n 59), 54–55 mentioning as an example that in "Hitler-Germany" or "Stalin's Russia" it was more dangerous to talk about concentration- and extinction camps, whose existence was not a secret at the time, than to voice "heretical" views about the respective ideologies – anti-Semitism, racism, communism.

70 Arendt (n 59), 55.

71 Arendt (n 59), 56.

72 Arendt (n 59), 57–58 "Tatsachen sind der Gegenstand von Meinungen, und Meinungen können sehr verschiedenen Interessen und Leidenschaften entstammen, weit voneinander abweichen und doch alle noch legitim sein, solange sie die Integrität der Tatbestände, auf die sie sich beziehen, respektieren. Meinungsfreiheit ist eine Farce, wenn die Information über die Tatsachen nicht garantiert ist".

73 See also Zinsmaier (n 63) with the assessment that precisely this is a problem of our current crisis.

74 Arendt (n 59), 72.

Because the liar can invent facts as she wishes, she can adjust her lies to whatever her audience would like to hear.[75] This seems to be a pertinent issue of what is referred to as "alternative facts" nowadays. This brings us back to the importance of a sense of truth and the constitutional prohibition for officials to tell lies for a democratic legal culture which holds, also against the apparent scepticism of *Hannah Arendt*. The pivotal question concerning the constitutional prohibition for officials to tell lies is, however, who passes judgement on a violation of that prohibition. Even if we argue consistently within a chosen theory, it remains open to interpretation. This question does not render impossible the constitutional prohibition to tell lies for officials. Yet, this problem suggests that we should be careful when arguing for a potential international obligation in this regard. Rather this seems to favour a push towards transparency as a basic prerequisite for trust in a democratic legal culture.[76]

3.2 *Truth and the International Legal Order*

Finally, we will briefly discuss what role there might be for international law in promoting truth for a democratic legal culture. This quest in turn is of relevance for the legitimacy of international law too.[77] There are several candidates to investigate the potential role of international law in promoting truth for a democratic legal culture.[78]

The International Declaration on Information and Democracy, signed on 11 November 2018 in Paris,[79] includes principles on the information and communication space which are promising tools for our endeavor. Concerning the right of information, for instance, this Declaration stipulates that "[f]reedom of opinion is guaranteed by the free exchange of ideas and information *based on factual truths*".[80] The truth, it goes on, "may take many forms", and

75 Arendt (n 59), 75.

76 See in this vein, Kirchmair (n 4), 103 ff.

77 For a brief overview of the notion of legitimacy in general, in international law and international relations in particular, see C Binder and L Kirchmair, 'Die Legitimität internationaler Wahlstandards: Völkerrechtliche Defizite und eine politikwissenschaftliche Perspektive' (2017) 55 Archiv des Völkerrechts 383, 385–389.

78 For an important differentiation between false and distorted (or tendentious) news, see B Baade, 'Fake News and International Law' (2019) 29 EJIL 1357, 1358 with further references on such usage by the League of Nations as well as the United Nations.

79 Published on 2 November 2018 and unanimously adopted by the members of the Information and Democracy Commission chaired by Christophe Deloire, the secretary general of Reporters Without Borders (RSF), as well as the first female Peace Prize Laureate from the Islamic World, Shirin Ebadi <https://rsf.org/sites/default/files/international_declaration_on_information_and_democracy.pdf> accessed 30 April 2021.

80 Ibid [*italics* LK].

"is grounded on the correspondence between reality and perceptions or on the best available evidence from established methods of scientific, academic, journalistic or other professional practices designed to produce trustworthy information and knowledge".[81] Hence, this Declaration does not hinge upon a simplified account of truth, but pays tribute to what was labelled here by relying on Radbruch "a sense of truth", when asking for "principles of commitment to truth, plurality of viewpoints and rational methods of establishment and verification of facts".[82] The essence of this declaration, which also refers to the potential harm done by dissemination of misleading information, is that comprehensive and free information is a *conditio sine qua non* for democracy.[83] This declaration is thus important for us even though we have to admit that it is not legally binding.[84] In fact, it is based upon the initiative of the non-governmental organization Reporters without Borders. Yet, also 12 Heads of State and Government, among them Emmanuel Macron and Justin Trudeau, launched a political process based on this declaration which arouse also the interest of the UN Secretary General, the Director-General of UNESCO, the Secretary General of the Council of Europe as well as the G7.[85]

Not by accident, this declaration has been signed 70 years after the installment of the Universal Declaration of Human Rights, which enshrines in Article 19 the right to freedom of opinion and expression. While the Universal Declaration is neither legally binding, Article 19 of the International Covenant on Civil and Political Rights as well as Article 10 of the European Convention on Human Rights provide for some sort of normative guidance for truthfulness in international law – and both instruments are, in contrast to the declarations mentioned before legally binding. In as much as that the right to freedom of speech which is guaranteed by these norms can be measured against

81 Ibid.

82 Ibid.

83 See G Lutz, *Participation, Information and Democracy: The Consequences of Low Levels of Participation and Information for the Functioning of Democracy* (LIT 2006), who shows that low levels of information have an effect on elections.

84 See on this issue of the declaration A Heldt, 'Internationales Abkommen über das Internet als Raum des Gemeinwohls' (*JuWissBlog*, 8 November 2018) <https://www.juwiss.de/92-2018/> accessed 30 April 2021.

85 See C Deloire, 'How an initiative on information and democracy came to the attention of the G7 in just one year' (*OECD The Forum Network*, 4 November 2019) <https://www.oecd-forum.org/posts/55510-how-an-initiative-on-information-and-democracy-came-to-the-attention-of-the-g7-in-just-one-year> accessed 30 April 2021, who points also to an "International Partnership on Information and Democracy" on the initiative of French president Emmanuel Macron which has been signed by 30 countries at the UN General Assembly on 26 September 2019.

the touchstone of truth: untrue statements are not protected by the right to freedom of speech.[86] We have, thus, at least a negative protection of truth in international human rights law.

The European Court of Human Rights for instance stated that even

> [w]here a statement amounts to a value judgment, the proportionality of an interference may depend on whether there exists a sufficient factual basis for the impugned statement, since even a value judgment without any factual basis to support it may be excessive.[87]

Another, already briefly mentioned, issue of relevance is the question as to how international law responds to disinformation and propaganda which both endanger a sense of truth and thus also a democratic legal culture.[88] In the

86 So for instance Article 19, General Comment No.34: Article 19: Freedoms of opinion and expression, 21 July 2011 <https://www.refworld.org/docid/4e38efb52.html> accessed 30 April 2021 para 50 states only that "At least with regard to comments about public figures, consideration should be given to avoiding penalising or otherwise rendering unlawful untrue statements that have been published in error but without malice". Cf similarly the Joint Declaration on Freedom of Expression and "Fake News", Disinformation and Propaganda by The United Nations (UN) Special Rapporteur on Freedom of Opinion and Expression, the Organization for Security and Co-operation in Europe (OSCE) Representative on Freedom of the Media, the Organization of American States (OAS) Special Rapporteur on Freedom of Expression and the African Commission on Human and Peoples' Rights (ACHPR) Special Rapporteur on Freedom of Expression and Access to Information (2017) "Stressing that the human right to impart information and ideas is not limited to "correct" statements, that the right also protects information and ideas that may shock, offend and disturb, and that prohibitions on disinformation may violate international human rights standards, while, at the same time, this does not justify the dissemination of knowingly or recklessly false statements by official or State actors".

87 *Feldek v. Slovakia* (ECtHR Judgment from 12 July 2001), Application no 29032/95, para 76; *Kuliś and Różycki v Poland* (ECtHR Judgment from 6 October 2009), Application no 27209/03. Cf A Sardo, 'Categories, Balancing, and Fake News: The Jurisprudence of the European Court of Human Rights' (2020) 33 Canadian Journal of Law & Jurisprudence 435; S Smet, 'Freedom of Expression and the Right to Reputation: Human Rights in Conflict' (2010) 26 American University International Law Review 183; as well as for an overview on the Strasbourg case law on media as 'public watchdog', see R Uerpmann-Wittzack, 'Public Watchdogs and Democratic Society: The Role of the Media and of the Strasbourg Court' in K S Ziegler, E Wicks and L Hodson (eds), The UK and European Human Rights: A Strained Relationship? (Hart 2015), 441.

88 For an overview, see H Lahmann, 'Information Operations and the Question of Illegitimate Interference under International Law' (2020) 53 Israel Law Review 189 who also points out (at 191) the difference between disinformation (which is "deliberately false or misleading") against misinformation (which is "factually wrong information yet not intentionally so") with reference, among others, also to European Commission, 'A Multi-Dimensional

Joint Declaration on Freedom of Expression and "Fake News", Disinformation and Propaganda the United Nations (UN) Special Rapporteur on Freedom of Opinion and Expression, the Organization for Security and Co-operation in Europe (OSCE) Representative on Freedom of the Media, the Organization of American States (OAS) Special Rapporteur on Freedom of Expression and the African Commission on Human and Peoples' Rights (ACHPR) Special Rapporteur on Freedom of Expression and Access to Information (2017) elaborated on Standards on Disinformation and Propaganda:

> Firstly, they hold that "a) General prohibitions on the dissemination of information based on vague and ambiguous ideas, including "false news" or "non-objective information", are incompatible with international standards for restrictions on freedom of expression, as set out in paragraph 1(a), and should be abolished".

However, they add that

> c) State actors should not make, sponsor, encourage or further disseminate statements which they know or reasonably should know to be false (disinformation), or which demonstrate a reckless disregard for verifiable information (propaganda).
> d) State actors should, in accordance with their domestic and international legal obligations and their public duties, take care to ensure that they disseminate reliable and trustworthy information, including about matters of public interest, such as the economy, public health, security and the environment.

While these qualifications remain rather suggestions, the prohibition of intervention guaranteed by customary international law provides for some relief as it includes false reporting, at least when it is directed towards revolution.[89] The non-intervention principle grounded in customary international law is

Approach to Disinformation' (30 April 2018) Final report of the High Level Expert Group on Fake News and Online Disinformation 10; cf also Baade (n 78); European Parliament, 'Resolution on EU Strategic Communication to Counteract Propaganda against It by Third Parties' (23 November 2016) Doc. 2016/2030(INI).

89 See, eg, E De Brabandere, 'Propaganda' in R Wolfrum (ed), *Max Planck Encyclopedia of Public International Law* (Oxford University Press November 2012), para 11 arguing that states must refrain from subversive propaganda aiming at civil disobedience. Cf also M J Kearney, 'Propaganda for War, Prohibition' in R Wolfrum (ed), *Max Planck Encyclopedia of Public International Law* (Oxford University Press May 2009).

also likely to be breached in case of "deliberately false and intended to produce dissent or encourage insurgents".[90] Such a qualification, however, is also criticized in the literature which draws upon the doctrinal question as to whether adversarial information operations may qualify as "coercion" as pointed out by the Nicaragua judgment of the ICJ.[91] According to the ICJ an "[i]ntervention is wrongful when it uses methods of coercion in regard to such choices, which must remain free ones".[92] By pointing to the UN Friendly Relations Declaration, the ICJ stipulated that "[t]he element of coercion, which defines, and indeed forms the very essence of, prohibited intervention, is particularly obvious in the case of an intervention which uses force, either in the direct form of military action, or in the indirect form of support for subversive or terrorist armed activities within another State".[93] Critical voices now hold, that "deceptive manipulation by way of a disinformation campaign cannot be conceived as coercion".[94] While convincing arguments argue in favour of a broad understanding of what amounts to a coercive act in this regard, for instance by stating "if the degree of manipulation is so deceptive that it destroys voluntarism",[95] state practice carried by opinio juris indeed seems not to be fully supportive in this regard.[96] However, the aggravating circumstances in proving adversarial disinformation campaigns of foreign states needs also to be taken into account when speaking of a reluctance of states in condemning foreign

90 See Baade (n 78), 1363 quoting M Jamnejad and M Wood, 'The Principle of Non-Intervention' (2009) 22 Leiden Journal of International Law 345, 374.

91 *Military and Paramilitary Activities in and against Nicaragua* (*Nicaragua v US*) (Merits) [1986] ICJ Rep 14 para 205. For an overview on the different positions in the literature, see Lahmann (n 88) 200 ff.

92 ICJ Nicaragua (n 91) para 205.

93 ICJ Nicaragua (n 91) para 205.

94 See Lahmann (n 88) while stating (216) that "it might be high time to broaden the notion" of coercion and yet finding that there is no uniform state practice and opinio juris to underpin such claims, he points (202) to the criticism expressed by J D Ohlin, 'Election Interference: The Real Harm and the Only Solution' (2018) Cornell Law School Research Paper 7; and N Tsagourias, 'Electoral Cyber Interference, Self-Determination and the Principle of Non-Intervention in Cyberspace' (*ejiltalk*, 26 August 2019) <https://www.ejiltalk.org/electoral-cyber-interference-self-determination-and-the-principle-of-non-intervention-in-cyberspace> accessed 30 April 2021 in this regard.

95 See J Nye, 'Protecting Democracy in an Era of Cyber Information War' (*Governance in an Emerging New World*, 13 November 2018) <https://www.hoover.org/research/protecting-democracy-era-cyber-information-war> accessed 30 April 2021 quoted after Lahmann (n 88) 200.

96 For an overview, see Lahmann (n 88) 206 ff who rather suggests (at 189) to "focus on deceptive and manipulative conduct of information operations as the most viable path to outlaw such state behaviour in the future".

information intervention and a potential prohibition in customary international law.

Finally, fact-finding and truth commissions are yet other important tools in international law.[97] Especially "[t]he right to the truth about gross human rights violations and serious violations of human rights law" has been considered to be

> an inalienable and autonomous right, linked to the duty and obligation of the State to protect and guarantee human rights, to conduct effective investigations and to guarantee effective remedy and reparations. This right is closely linked with other rights and has both an individual and a societal dimension and should be considered as a non-derogable right and not be subject to limitations.[98]

Particularly in times of transformation such commissions can contribute to beware the sensitive balance between peace and justice, precisely by bringing the facts to light so that the whole truth can be told.[99] In this vein, these commissions might also contribute – even though under special circumstances – to the development of a prosperous democratic legal culture.[100]

---

97 Compare, eg, C E M Harwood, *The Roles and Functions of Atrocity-Related United Nations Commissions of Inquiry in the International Legal Order* (Brill 2019); C Henderson (ed), *Commissions of Inquiry. Problems and Prospects* (Hart 2017).

98 Summary of the United Nations, ECOSOC, Commission on Human Rights, Promotion and Protection of Human Rights: Study on the Right to Truth – Report of the Office of the United Nations High Commissioner for Human Rights, E/CN.4/2006/91, 8 February 2006; for discussion, see after O Ben-Naftali and R Peled, 'How Much Secrecy Does Warfare Need?' in Anne Peters and Andrea Bianchi (eds), *Transparency in International Law* (Cambridge University Press 2013), 358ff with further references; cf also Yasmin Naqvi, 'The right to the truth in international law: fact or fiction?' (2006) 88 International Review of the Red Cross 245 concluding "it may be argued that the right to the truth stands somewhere on the threshold of a legal norm and a narrative device".

99 See, eg, S Krebs, 'Facts, Alternative Facts, and International Law' (*ejiltalk*, 29 May 2017) <https://www.ejiltalk.org/facts-alternative-facts-and-international-law> accessed 30 April 2021 holding that "[i]n our 'post truth' era, where 'alternative facts' are often produced to counter unwelcomed facts and narratives, it is more important than ever to seek new and better ways to produce and introduce information".

100 See J A Sweeney, 'The Elusive Right to Truth in Transitional Human Rights Jurisprudence' (2018) 67 International & Comparative Law Quarterly 353 providing a critique of how 'the right to truth' is justified.

4 Conclusion

A sense of truth in *Radbruch*'s words, which equals truthfulness, is still vital for today's democratic legal culture. For both the discourse theory of law (as advanced by *Jürgen Habermas* and *Robert Alexy*) and the Wittgensteinian (constitutional) games of justification (as argued by *Dennis Patterson* and *Julian Nida-Rümelin*), a sense of truth is of utmost importance. While *Peter Häberle* argues for a constitutional prohibition to tell lies which has been interpreted here as a duty of officials to be truthful, *Hannah Arendt* importantly pointed out the distinction between "rational" and "factual truths". Each conception of a democratic constitutional state, must respect – depending on the conception – a sense of truth since a complete lack of any sense of truth would make our democratic legal culture implode. Therefore, the discourse in international law on a (human) right to democracy should consider the importance of a sense of truth.[101] Truthfulness is indispensable for a democratic legal

---

101 See, eg H J Steiner, 'Political Participation as a Human Right' (1988) 1 Harvard Human Rights Journal 77; cf T Franck, 'The Emerging Right to Democratic Governance' (1992) 86 AJIL 46, 46 identifying an "emerging right to democratic governance" protected by "collective international processes"; or G Fox, 'The Right to Political Participation in International Law' (1992) 17 Yale Journal of International Law 539; as well as G H Fox and G Nolte, 'Intolerant Democracies' (1995) 36 Harvard International Law Journal 1 arguing for an international assessment of democratic government; assembled in G H Fox and Brad R Roth (eds), *Democratic Governance and International Law* (Cambridge University Press 2000). Revisiting the "democracy and international law puzzle" 20 years after the publication of Tom Francks above cited article holding that "it may well be concluded that its [the Franckian conception of the democratic entitlement] ascendance into 'fully word made law' is now almost complete". C Pippan, 'Democracy as a global norm. Has it finally emerged?' in M Happold (ed), *International Law in a Multipolar World* (Routledge 2012) 221 reprinted in G H Fox and B R Roth (eds), *Democracy and International Law* (Edward Elgar 2020). Pippan also states that "an international regime on democratic governance would also seem to embrace criteria generally associated with the notion of 'good governance'", listing among other criteria also "transparency". To this end, however, he considers that "since these standards are still largely undefined and only incoherently applied by international actors, they are [...] effectively useless as global normative benchmarks for a meaningful evaluation of state behaviour". Cf also S Wheatley, *Democracy, Minorities and International Law* (Cambridge University Press 2006), speaking of the emergence of democracy as a legal obligation of states particularly focusing on the resolution of "cultural conflicts"; Restating the "requirements of democratic legitimacy in terms of the deliberative ideal developed by Jürgen Habermas", S Wheatley, *The Democratic Legitimacy of International Law* (Hart 2010); N Petersen, *Demokratie als teleologisches Prinzip. Zur Legitimität von Staatsgewalt im Völkerrecht* (Springer 2009) arguing that states have the international legal obligation to democratize (but not to democracy); see also F Ehm, *Das völkerrechtliche Demokratiegebot. Eine Untersuchung zur schwindenden Wertneutralität des Völkerrechts gegenüber den staatlichen Binnenstrukturen* (Mohr

culture, both at the national and at the international level. The briefly consulted international soft- and hard law instruments such as the International Declaration on Information and Democracy form an important component of a topos of truth of the international order. We have seen that especially in relation to potential disinformation campaigns led or attributed to foreign states, international (customary) law might offer some protection. This is of great importance as evinced, for instance, by the recent accusations of Russian interferences with the 2020 United States presidential elections as well as the lies spread in realm of the illegal war of aggression of Russia against Ukraine.[102]

Siebeck 2013); as well as more recently H Charlesworth, 'International Legal Encounters with Democracy' (2017) 8 Global Policy 34.

102 See, for instance, D O'Sullivan, 'Facebook: Russian Trolls Are Back. And They're Here to Meddle with 2020' (*CNN.com*, 22 October 2019) <https://edition.cnn.com/2019/10/21/tech/russia-instagram-accounts-2020-election/index.html> accessed 30 April 2021. Concerning the 2016 United States presidential elections, see only R S Mueller, *The Mueller Report: Report on the Investigation into Russian Interference in the 2016 Presidential Election* (Melville House 2019).

CHAPTER 5

La relation contrariée entre souveraineté et démocratie au prisme des approches critiques du droit international

Edith Vanspranghe

La présente contribution cherche à analyser l'articulation entre « souveraineté » et « démocratie » en tant que concepts de droit international, en mobilisant pour ce faire le cadre théorique des approches critiques du droit international. En retour, cette étude contribuera à enrichir ce paradigme.

Le concept de souveraineté a été analysé, parmi d'autres auteurs affiliés à une approche critique, par Monique Chemillier-Gendreau, qui invite à confronter la promesse théorique portée par la notion de souveraineté, selon laquelle les Etats sont souverains et, partant, égaux, avec la réalité. D'après cette auteure en effet, « [l]a notion de souveraineté est loin (…) de correspondre en toutes circonstances au contenu annoncé. (…) Cette doctrine n'est énoncée que pour être immédiatement contredite »[1]. La contradiction fondamentale du concept de souveraineté tiendrait plus exactement au postulat d'une souveraineté nécessairement égale entre Etats, alors qu'en réalité, les Etats sont dans une position non seulement d'inégalité matérielle évidente, mais aussi d'inégalité juridique dans l'ordre international – les deux types d'inégalité étant liés. R. P. Anand affirme ainsi que:

> [n]or in the class-ridden international society is there any other principle which on its face asserts a greater contrast between so-called law and the facts of life. States are overwhelmingly unequal, not only in resources and influence, but in the voting power and other rights conferred on them by international instruments[2].

Au-delà de l'exemple le plus connu de l'inégalité juridique des Etats dans l'ordre international – à savoir l'existence de membres permanents au Conseil

1 M Chemillier-Gendreau, 'Démocratie globale : Un continent inexploité' (2007) 5 Nouvelles FondationS 51.

2 R P Anand, 'Sovereign Equality of States in International Law' (1976) 197 Collected Courses of the Hague Academy of International Law, 103, voir aussi 190–191.

 | DOI:10.1163/9789004508712_006

de sécurité des Nations Unies (articles 23 §1 et 27 §3 de la Charte des Nations Unies) – le présent article s'intéressera à d'autres manifestations de l'inégalité entre Etats, démontrant ainsi le caractère fallacieux de la notion de souveraineté telle qu'entendue en droit international.

L'étude s'intéresse à plusieurs dimensions de la souveraineté : la souveraineté internationale en tant qu'elle s'applique aux relations entre Etats, et la souveraineté des Etats dans leur ordre juridique interne. Ainsi, la souveraineté est, d'une part, définie comme la capacité d'action juridique et la libre détermination des Etats sur la scène internationale et, d'autre part, comme l'exclusivité du pouvoir, y compris juridique, sur leur propre territoire, selon les acceptions proposées dans le *Dictionnaire de droit international public*[3]. Pour reprendre de nouveau les termes de Monique Chemillier-Gendreau :

> [d]'une part, l'Etat ne peut exercer son pouvoir souverain que s'il est reconnu par les autres Etats, sans quoi il reste en guerres incessantes pour accéder à cette souveraineté à laquelle il prétend. D'autre part, les relations internationales ne cessant de se développer ont porté atteinte de manière croissante aux pouvoirs des Etats. (...) Les fonctions régaliennes (...) sont altérées partout, mais dans des proportions très différentes selon les sociétés[4].

Poursuivant son analyse, Monique Chemillier-Gendreau envisage le concept de souveraineté comme l'un des ressorts par lesquels le droit international peut constituer un outil de domination pour les Etats les plus puissants de l'ordre international[5]. Dans le même sens, Anthony Anghie a mis en lumière l'héritage impérialiste qui caractérise selon lui, de façon intrinsèque et non pas fortuite, le concept de souveraineté et, au-delà, le droit international depuis sa genèse[6].

---

3 « A. Notion qui, dans l'ordre interne, exprime la puissance suprême (*suprema potestas*) de gouverner, de commander et de décider et qui, liée à l'apparition de l'Etat moderne, est inséparable de celui-ci (...) ; B. Dans l'ordre international, caractère de l'Etat signifiant qu'il n'est soumis à aucun autre pouvoir de même nature », liée à la définition selon laquelle la souveraineté internationale est « C. Aptitude légale de l'Etat, pleine et entière, qui lui permet, du moins potentiellement, d'exercer tous les droits que l'ordre juridique international connaît, et en particulier la faculté de décider, d'accomplir un acte, de poser des règles », J Salmon, *Dictionnaire de droit international public* (LGDJ 2001) 1045.

4 M Chemillier-Gendreau, 'Démocratie globale : Un continent inexploité' (2007) 5 Nouvelles FondationS 52–53.

5 M Chemillier-Gendreau, *Humanité et souverainetés* (La Découverte 1995), 100.

6 A Anghie, Imperialism, Sovereignty and the Making of International law (Cambridge University Press 2004).

Le concept de démocratie en droit international a lui aussi été abondamment analysé par les auteurs critiques, pour, bien souvent, en démontrer la dimension hégémonique, ou à tout le moins l'usage à cette fin qui en est fait[7]. Anthony Anghie décrit la démocratie comme étant « *used as a means of furthering imperialism* »[8]. Pour sa part, Monique Chemillier-Gendreau s'est saisie du concept de démocratie pour tenter de lui redonner un sens en le rattachant à la protection et à l'autodétermination des peuples,[9] dimensions justement contredites aujourd'hui par la manière dont la norme est promue et mise en œuvre.

La norme démocratique est envisagée ici comme « contrainte axiologique »[10] : la démocratie n'est pas, en tant que telle, une norme de droit international général, dans le sens positif du terme[11]. Certes, certains éléments concourant à l'organisation démocratique d'un régime sont consacrés dans des règles de droit international, conventionnelles (par exemple celles qui sont contenues dans le Pacte international relatif aux droits civils et politiques, à l'article 25 en particulier), ou, pour certains auteurs, de nature coutumière[12]. En revanche, l'établissement d'un régime démocratique interne ou d'une « démocratie », par ailleurs dépourvue d'une définition arrêtée en droit international, n'est pas prescrit par une règle de droit international positif[13].

---

7 W P Alford, 'Exporting the pursuit of happiness' (2000) 113 Harvard Law Review 1677; M Mutua, *Human Rights Standards: Hegemony, Law, and Politics* (State University of New York Press 2016), et de nouveau A Anghie, *Imperialism, Sovereignty and the Making of International law* (Cambridge University Press 2004).

8 A Anghie, Imperialism, Sovereignty and the Making of International law (Cambridge University Press 2004), 320.

9 M Chemillier-Gendreau, 'Démocratie globale : Un continent inexploité' (2007), 5 Nouvelles FondationS 51, 52–53 ; M Chemillier-Gendreau, *Régression de la démocratie et déchaînement de la violence* (Textuel 2019).

10 Ce sont les termes de Jacques Chevallier à propos de l'Etat de droit, voir J Chevallier, *L'Etat de droit* (5e édition, Montchrestien 2010), 116.

11 Elle est envisagée comme telle dans le cadre européen (Union européenne et Conseil de l'Europe), voir sur ce point G Cahin, "Reconstruction et construction de l'Etat en droit international' (2020), 411 RCADI, 128.

12 Jean d'Aspremont défend l'existence d'une règle coutumière relative à l'organisation d'élections libres, J d'Aspremont, *L'Etat nondémocratique en droit international. Étude critique du droit international positif et de la pratique contemporaine* (Pedone 2008), 291–298. En revanche, d'autres auteurs s'opposent à cette conception, dont N Petersen, *DemokratiealsteleologischesPrinzip. Zur LegitimitätvonStaatsgewaltimVölkerrecht* (Springer 2009), 124.

13 L A Sicilianos, L'ONU et la démocratisation de l'Etat : Systèmes régionaux et ordre juridique universel (Pedone 2000) ; A Abuhamoud, La démocratie en droit international. Etude critique sur le statut juridique de la démocratie en droit international et la légitimité de l'imposer par la force (L'Harmattan 2017).

La norme démocratique n'est pas, pour autant, sans effets sur le comportement des Etats et sur l'organisation même de l'ordre international, raison pour laquelle le terme de « contrainte axiologique » est retenu. Elle sera, par facilité, désignée comme norme, au sens large, dans les lignes ci-dessous.

Des interrogations sur les deux concepts mentionnés ci-dessus ressort nettement la grille de lecture critique retenue dans la présente étude. Les approches critiques proposent en effet une lecture hégémonique de l'ordre international consistant à avancer que l'ordre international est caractérisé par une forme de domination de certains Etats sur d'autres. Cette domination est, selon une définition néo-Gramscienne, fondée sur la légitimation idéologique de cet ordre des choses plutôt que sur le seul usage de la force[14]. Le droit international constitue alors un outil déterminant du phénomène de légitimation et d'acceptation de la situation[15]. La présente étude se propose d'explorer plus précisément le rôle de la souveraineté et de la démocratie dans ce phénomène.

Ce rôle tient à la contradiction susmentionnée, qu'il s'agira de démontrer, à savoir que la souveraineté est une fiction qui véhicule une lecture erronée de l'ordre international. Ce concept, tout à la fois masque et permet des rapports de domination légitimés, et donc une situation d'hégémonie telle que définie plus haut. La démonstration de l'inégale souveraineté des Etats se fondera sur l'analyse du fonctionnement et des usages de la norme démocratique, en ce qu'elle illustre la façon dont la souveraineté des Etats moins puissants peut être limitée. Le propos n'est pas de s'interroger sur la mesure dans laquelle l'idéal démocratique en tant que tel, ou même les droits humains, exerceraient, depuis l'ordre international, une contrainte sur la souveraineté, essentiellement interne, des Etats[16]. Une telle approche laisse en effet de côté la dimension hégémonique de ce processus pour la présenter comme touchant

---

14 « L'hégémonie désigne à l'origine une position de *prédominance* d'un acteur sur tous les autres, au point de conférer à celui qui en bénéficie la capacité de dicter aux autres leur conduite et de pouvoir définir jusqu'aux règles du jeu. On parlera ainsi d'une *position* hégémonique », G Hermet*et al.*, *Dictionnaire de la science politique et des institutions politiques* (8e édition, Armand Colin 2015), 141. Dans le mêmesens, « [*h*]*egemony can be defined as capabilities that are matched by influence over other states in the international system* », E Krahmann, 'American Hegemony or Global Governance? Competing Visions of International Security' (2005) 7 International Studies Review531,533.

15 Voir entre autres J Alvarez, 'Hegemonic International Law Revisited' (2003) 97 AJIL 973, B Rajagopal, 'Counter-Hegemonic International Law' (2006) 27 Third World Quarterly 767, et plus récemment R Bachand, *Les subalternes et le droit international: une critique politique* (Pedone 2018).

16 Voir par exemple les propos de M Virally, 'Panorama du droit international contemporain: cours général de droit international public' (1983), 183 RCADI, 124, d'après lequel « la souveraineté va désormais se trouver arrêtée par des droits appartenant à d'autres sujets de droit que les Etats », en l'occurrence les individus.

« les Etats » en général alors que, comme le souligne Monique Chemillier-Gendreau, cela concerne certains Etats plus que d'autres : « [c]e que l'on nomme aujourd'hui les contraintes externes pèse de plus en plus sur les décisions étatiques, davantage naturellement pour les pays faibles que pour ceux qui sont forts. Il en résulte une hiérarchie entre les Etats qui fait mentir le principe de l'égalité souveraine »[17]. Il s'agit donc plutôt de s'intéresser aux usages faits de la norme démocratique.

Cette analyse contribuera ainsi à alimenter les travaux critiques sur le droit international. Les termes de « pouvoir », de « puissance » ou de « faiblesse », (sur)utilisés dans les approches critiques pour catégoriser les Etats ne renvoient en effet pas toujours à des situations concrètes ; de même, le terme « hégémonie » revêt de nombreuses acceptions et dimensions. Il est donc important, pour étoffer ce cadre théorique, de caractériser, de façon concrète, en quoi peut consister cette hégémonie. En l'occurrence, le caractère hégémonique de l'ordre international est ici envisagé comme restriction de la souveraineté de certains Etats, au profit d'autres Etats, dont la position de domination se trouve ainsi renforcée. La démonstration permettra donc à la fois de confirmer la pertinence de ce cadre théorique, de lui donner une dimension plus spécifique en le rattachant au concept de souveraineté, et de l'appuyer sur des manifestations concrètes à travers l'analyse de la norme démocratique et de ses usages.

La méthode retenue s'apparente délibérément à de la sociologie du droit en ce qu'elle ne se limite pas à l'étude du droit positif, mais prend en compte les conditions matérielles (au sens large, dans le sens de réalité) dans lesquelles le droit international évolue, suivant en cela les préceptes de l'Ecole de Reims, selon laquelle « *it is impossible to create and analyse norms without reference to the concrete conditions of their formation as well as the structure of the international institutions and international relations.* (…) [*W*]*e need to analyse reality to understand the norms* »[18].

Reprenant cette proposition méthodologique, il s'agira donc de démontrer l'inégale souveraineté des Etats en prenant en compte les réalités matérielles caractérisant l'ordre international. Cette démonstration se fondera sur l'analyse du fonctionnement et des usages de la norme démocratique sur la scène internationale, en ce que cette dernière constitue l'un des ressorts du caractère inégal de la souveraineté affectant aussi bien les relations entre Etats (1), que leur souveraineté interne (2).

---

17 M Chemillier-Gendreau, 'Démocratie globale : Un continent inexploité' (2007), 5 Nouvelles FondationS 52–53.

18 M Chemillier-Gendreau, 'Contribution of the Reims School to the Debate on the Critical Analysis of International Law. Assessment and Limits' (2011) 22 EJIL 3 649, 651.

1 L'inégalité des Etats face à la norme démocratique au plan international

La façon dont la norme démocratique s'articule avec la souveraineté internationale est double : la norme démocratique marque à la fois l'inégalité politique « initiale » des Etats, c'est-à-dire qu'elle constitue en tant que telle un facteur d'inégalité entre Etats (1.1), et dans le même temps, elle fonctionne comme une entrave à l'exercice de la souveraineté des Etats, engendrant davantage d'inégalités (1.2). Ces deux dimensions constituent les deux faces d'une même pièce qui est celle de l'inégale souveraineté des Etats au plan international au regard de la norme démocratique.

1.1 *Les obstacles à l'élaboration et à l'interprétation de la norme démocratique*

Plusieurs éléments montrent que les Etats ne contribuent pas de manière égale au droit international général et à l'élaboration de la norme démocratique (1.1.1). En tout état de cause, les Etats ne disposent pas de la même capacité à faire de cette norme un usage correspondant à leurs intérêts (1.1.2.).

1.1.1 Les obstacles à l'élaboration de la norme démocratique

Deux problèmes distincts, quoique liés, se posent quant à l'élaboration par les Etats de la norme démocratique : s'ajoute à la (non-)participation de certains Etats à la formation du droit international en général, la question plus spécifique du modèle de démocratie constituant la norme démocratique au plan international.

La question de la (non-)participation des Etats issus de la décolonisation à la formation du droit international a été très abondamment traitée[19]. Sans rouvrir le débat, il suffit de retenir ici que ces Etats n'ont pas participé à l'élaboration des normes coutumières et conventionnelles antérieures à leur indépendance, et n'ont pu ensuite que se soumettre aux premières et adhérer aux secondes. Le problème peut partiellement être résolu, d'un point de vue volontariste, par cette acceptation des règles existantes[20] – et par la création

19 Voir parmi d'autres références, G Abi-Saab, 'The Newly Independent States and the Rules of International Law: An Outline' (1962) 8 Howard Law Journal, 95.

20 Le caractère « démocratique » des sociétés est déjà affirmé dans la Déclaration universelle des droits de l'homme de 1948, art. 29 § 3, en complément de l'affirmation selon laquelle « toute personne a le droit de prendre part à la direction des affaires publiques de son pays » et que « la volonté du peuple est le fondement de l'autorité des pouvoirs publics », art. 21.

de nouvelles règles. En ce qui concerne la norme démocratique, la quasi-totalité des Etats reconnaît aujourd'hui, dans ses discours, la démocratie en tant que « valeur universelle ». Elle est en effet très fréquemment présentée comme telle dans les résolutions de l'Assemblée générale des Nations Unies[21], y compris dans les déclarations phares telles que celles du Sommet mondial de 2005[22]. Mais le terme « valeur » ne signifie pas règle et, comme rappelé en introduction, la démocratie ne constitue pas une règle de droit positif en droit international. Pour autant, comme cette présentation va chercher à le démontrer, le fait de correspondre, ou non, à la norme, n'est pas sans effets juridiques pour les Etats.

L'autre point de tension a trait au contenu de la norme démocratique. A ce sujet, il est évident que le droit international est, en général, le fruit d'un héritage juridique européen[23]. Ceci est d'autant plus vrai pour la norme démocratique telle qu'elle existe en droit international aujourd'hui : elle reprend pour l'essentiel un modèle politique ayant émergé autour du XVIIIème siècle en Europe. En conséquence, la norme démocratique est particulièrement marquée par l'absence de participation à son élaboration de nombreux Etats (Etats issus de la décolonisation et plus largement Etats non-Européens ou non liés à l'héritage européen). Ces derniers incluent les Etats actuellement les moins puissants de l'ordre international (sans y être limités), en particulier si la puissance est ici envisagée dans un sens hégémonique, donc fondée non pas sur la capacité militaire ou même économique, mais sur la capacité à déterminer les valeurs et normes de l'ordre international. La conséquence en est l'exclusion *a priori* d'Etats ne correspondant pas au modèle de démocratie promue, et qui doivent donc faire la démarche d'y correspondre, alors que tel n'est pas le cas des Etats sur lesquels le modèle est calqué et qui y correspondent automatiquement.

Reste alors la question de « l'appropriation » de la norme démocratique par les Etats qui en sont exclus *a priori*, faute d'y correspondre initialement.

1.1.2 L'appropriation de la norme démocratique

Non seulement certains Etats se trouvent initialement exclus de la norme démocratique dans le sens où ils ne correspondent pas au modèle de démocratie promu, mais cette exclusion perdure dans l'évolution et l'appropriation de

---

21 Voir parmi de nombreuses autres, les résolutions A/RES/75/199 (2020), A/RES/74/158 (2019), etc.

22 A/RES/60/1 (2005).

23 G Abi-Saab, 'The Newly Independent States and the Rules of International Law: An Outline' (1962) 8 Howard Law Journal, 96.

la norme. Ce phénomène est tout à la fois une cause et une manifestation de l'inégale souveraineté des Etats. C'en est une cause puisque la non-conformité avec la norme démocratique permet de mettre en place des mesures et mécanismes limitant la souveraineté des Etats concernés (*infra*, 1.2 et 2). Et c'en est une manifestation puisque c'est le fait que la souveraineté des Etats soit limitée qui les empêche de s'approprier la norme démocratique, dans le sens où ils n'ont pas la « puissance juridique » pour en faire évoluer le contenu. Comme l'explique Malcolm Shaw :

> it would not strictly be accurate to talk in terms of the equality of states in creating law. The major states will always have an influence commensurate with their status, if only because their concerns are much wider, their interests much deeper and their power more effective[24].

La norme démocratique est, en droit international, caractérisée par une forte indétermination : de statut (*supra,* Introduction), mais aussi de contenu. Martti Koskenniemi a mis en avant, dans sa thèse sur l'indétermination du droit international, qu'une norme floue est plus propice à faire l'objet d'une « récupération » par les Etats pourvus de la capacité politique et juridique pour ce faire. En d'autres termes, son contenu, et son interprétation pourront être modelés de manière à favoriser lesdits Etats[25]. Concrètement, dans le cas de la norme démocratique, cela se fait par deux mécanismes principaux. Premièrement, comme on l'a vu, la norme est calquée sur un modèle émanant directement des Etats puissants, qui ont été capables de l'imposer. Deuxièmement, son contenu est également alimenté par la pratique de promotion et de mise en œuvre dont elle fait l'objet, par ces mêmes Etats.

Les mesures et programmes internationaux de promotion de la démocratie tendent à se baser sur un modèle dit formel de démocratie, voire sur un modèle « électoral » encore plus minimal. Ce dernier tient pour démocratique un gouvernement arrivé au pouvoir à l'issue d'élections correspondant à certains critères minimaux (transparence, etc.)[26]. Si ce seul élément semble pour de nombreux acteurs internationaux désormais insuffisant, il continue

24 M Shaw, *International Law* (6ème édition, Cambridge University Press 2008), 193.

25 M Koskenniemi, '*The Politics of International Law – 20 years later*' Voir aussi J Salmon, 'Les notions à contenu variable en droit international public' in C Perelman et R Vander Elst (ed), *Les notions à contenu variable en droit,* (Bruylant 1984).

26 Voir sur ce point, J d'Aspremont, 'The Rise and Fall of Democracy Governance in International Law: A Reply to Susan Marks' (2011) 22 EJIL 2, 549.

de fonder une large pratique, notamment onusienne, de soutien à l'organisation d'élections[27]. L'approche formelle ajoute à cette conception strictement électorale un ensemble d'institutions (au sens large) fonctionnelles et transparentes, caractérisant un gouvernement représentatif. Elle est souvent couplée, dans le discours et la pratique internationaux, au respect d'un nombre limité de droits fondamentaux et/ou relatifs à la participation politique[28]. Sans la présenter comme une définition, l'Assemblée générale des Nations Unies déclare que :

> les éléments essentiels de la démocratie comprennent le respect des droits de l'homme et des libertés fondamentales, notamment la liberté d'association et de réunion pacifique, la liberté d'expression et d'opinion, et le droit de participer à la conduite des affaires publiques, directement ou par l'intermédiaire de représentants librement choisis, de voter et d'être élu dans le cadre d'élections authentiques, périodiques et libres, au suffrage universel et égal et au scrutin secret garantissant la libre expression de la volonté populaire, ainsi qu'un système pluraliste de partis et d'organisations politiques, le respect de l'état de droit, la séparation des pouvoirs, l'indépendance du pouvoir judiciaire, la transparence et l'obligation pour l'administration publique de rendre des comptes, de même que des médias libres, indépendants et pluralistes[29].

Plusieurs auteurs ont avancé que cette conception de la démocratie prédomine sur la scène internationale[30], et qu'elle est reprise lorsque la démocratie est promue et exportée dans le cadre de ce qu'il est convenu d'appeler la « coopération » internationale[31]. Les classements internationaux de la démocratie élaborés par des *think tanks* occidentaux le confirment également : il en est

---

27 Voir ainsi le rapport du Secrétaire général portant sur l'« Affermissement du rôle de l'Organisation des Nations.

Unies aux fins du renforcement de l'efficacité du principe d'élections périodiques et honnêtes et de l'action en faveur de la démocratisation », A/74/285 (2019), en particulier l'annexe II.

28 Les programmes et projets de promotion de la démocratie mis en œuvre par les acteurs internationaux consistent généralement à l'organisation d'élections, à la mise en place d'institutions et structures type « Ombudsman » et organismes de lutte contre la corruption, et à la promotion de droits politiques à travers un soutien à la société civile.

29 A/RES/59/201 (2004) para 1.

30 J d'Aspremont, L'Etat non-démocratique en droit international. Étude critique du droit international positif et de la pratique contemporaine (Pedone 2008), titre préliminaire.

31 T Carothers, Aiding Democracy Abroad: The Learning Curve (Carnegie 1999).

ainsi des explications méthodologiques de *The Economist* qui produit le principal classement en la matière, et du *Democracy index*, indiquant que « *[t]he condition of having free and fair competitive elections, and satisfying related aspects of political freedom, is clearly the basic requirement of all definitions* »[32].

Or, il est possible d'identifier deux motifs pour lesquels ce modèle de démocratie formelle présente un intérêt pour les Etats puissants : d'une part, ils correspondent déjà à ce modèle, d'autre part, c'est un modèle plus facile à promouvoir qu'une conception plus substantielle, voire matérielle de la démocratie.

A l'inverse, une conception plus étoffée de la démocratie inclurait les conditions matérielles permettant l'exercice des droits politiques et fondamentaux susmentionnés et le libre choix par le peuple des éléments constituant la démocratie formelle (élections, institutions, système politique, économique et social en général). Cette conception, nettement plus exigeante, mettrait les Etats puissants en difficulté, tant pour ce qui est de s'y conformer, que de la promouvoir dans la sphère internationale. Dans les deux cas en effet, cela nécessiterait des moyens, y compris financiers, plus conséquents. Pour autant – et c'est en cela que l'analyse ci-dessus reste réductrice –, le même constat vaut également pour les autres Etats : il leur sera plus aisé de se conformer à un modèle moins exigeant. En outre, si le modèle prédominant était celui de la démocratie matérielle, sa promotion ou son imposition aux Etats concernés serait pour eux plus intrusive, en ce qu'elle offrirait un « droit de regard » plus étendu aux acteurs internationaux impliqués dans sa promotion.

Face à cette inégalité initiale des Etats vis-à-vis de la norme démocratique, les Etats considérés comme ne se conformant pas – ou mal – à la norme démocratique tentent d'insister sur l'importance du respect et de la préservation des particularités nationales en opposition à un modèle uniforme et/ou émanant de certains Etats. Ce rappel – fréquent dans les résolutions de l'Assemblée générale des Nations Unies[33] – n'est certes pas contesté, mais il n'a pas non plus permis la remise en cause du modèle prédominant.

La norme démocratique révèle donc certains des mécanismes à travers lesquels le droit international peut être un outil avantageant les Etats capables

32 L Kekic, 'The Economist Intelligence Unit's index of democracy' (The Economist 2007) <https://www.economist.com/media/pdf/DEMOCRACY_INDEX_2007_v3.pdf> consulté le 21 mai 2021.

33 Voir par exemple la déclaration du Sommet mondial de 2005, A/RES/60/1 (2005) para 135. L'Assemblée générale des Nations Unies réaffirme dans nombre de ces résolutions sur le sujet que « si les démocraties ont des caractéristiques communes, il n'existe pas de modèle unique de démocratie, que la démocratie n'est pas l'apanage d'un pays ou d'une région », voir entre autres A/RES/74/158 (2019).

de l'utiliser en leur faveur. Ce processus est double : le fait même de promouvoir la démocratie au rang de norme avantage les Etats déjà démocratiques, et ce d'autant plus que le modèle de démocratie mis en avant correspond au modèle existant dans ces Etats. Ainsi, en dépit de son extranéité pour de nombreux Etats et du fait que ceux-ci sont difficilement à même de la modeler à leur convenance, la norme démocratique semble être globalement acceptée. Le fait qu'elle ne constitue pas à ce jour une règle de droit positif peut également être interprété comme une forme de résistance de la part des Etats initialement non-conformes à la norme. Cette résistance ne protège toutefois pas les Etats concernés d'un usage hégémonique de la démocratie puisque, même réduite à une valeur, la norme démocratique n'est pas seulement une manifestation, mais également une cause des limites pesant sur la souveraineté des Etats les moins à même d'en faire un usage avantageux.

1.2 *L'application de la norme démocratique comme limitation de la souveraineté des Etats dans l'ordre international*

La non-conformité initiale de certains Etats avec la norme démocratique a pour conséquence leur catégorisation comme « non démocratiques ». Cette catégorisation engendre elle-même une marginalisation multiforme : une marginalisation idéologique non officielle qui discrédite le discours des Etats concernés, et donc leur participation à la formation de l'ordre international et de son droit (1.2.2.), et des formes d'exclusions plus officielles (1.2.1.). Les cas de figure présentés dans cette section concernent avant tout la souveraineté internationale des Etats, c'est-à-dire leur libre capacité d'action juridique dans la sphère internationale. Cependant, certaines de ces limites ont également des conséquences directes sur la souveraineté des Etats au plan interne, qui seront abordées dans la seconde partie de l'étude.

1.2.1 L'encadrement officiel de la souveraineté internationale des Etats par la norme démocratique

Il existe plusieurs cas de figure dans lesquels la catégorisation d'un Etat comme présentant des insuffisances sur le plan démocratique a pour conséquence une limitation de sa souveraineté internationale. On distinguera ici les limites indirectes, c'est-à-dire les limites auxquelles les Etats ont le choix de se soumettre ou non, des limites imposées ou sanctions permises par la norme démocratique eu égard à la souveraineté internationale des Etats.

La possibilité d'adhérer aux traités et conventions internationales, et de coopérer avec (et « bénéficier » de l'aide des) organisations internationales, constitue l'une des manifestations de la souveraineté internationale des Etats. Or, cette possibilité est fréquemment encadrée par la norme démocratique.

Ainsi, certaines organisations internationales exigent, par leur statut, la conformité avec un certains nombres de critères apparentés à une forme démocratique de gouvernement. C'est le cas de l'Organisation des Etats américains (OEA) qui requiert de ses membres « une organisation politique basée sur le fonctionnement effectif de la démocratie représentative » (art. 3d de la Charte de l'OEA), et qui suspend les Etats dont le gouvernement démocratique est renversé (art. 9 de la même Charte). C'est également le cas bien connu de l'Union européenne qui mentionne explicitement la « démocratie » comme « valeur » que les Etats membres sont tenus de respecter[34]. Les critères d'adhésion à l'Union relatifs à l'organisation démocratique des régimes concernés sont extrêmement étoffés[35], et l'Union dispose en outre d'un mécanisme de suspension en cas de « violation grave et persistante par un État membre des valeurs visées à l'article 2 » (art. 7 du Traité sur l'Union européenne (TUE)), parmi lesquelles la démocratie.

Le cas de l'Union européenne est plus particulièrement intéressant en ce que l'exigence démocratique touche non seulement les Etats membres de l'organisation, mais également les Etats souhaitant entretenir, à un titre ou à un autre, des relations économiques avec celle-ci, que ce soit via les accords de partenariat économique avec les Etats « Afrique Caraïbe Pacifique » dits ACP, ou dans le cadre du Système de Préférence Généralisée obligeant les Etats « bénéficiaires » à ratifier un ensemble de conventions internationales en matière de droits humains, y inclus des droits politiques propres à un régime démocratique, et encourageant plus largement la bonne gouvernance[36].

Bien qu'elle ne soit pas désignée par ce terme, cette conditionnalité démocratique est encore plus manifeste pour les Etats nouveaux ou pour les Etats recouvrant leur indépendance, en particulier dans le cadre d'une « reconstruction » internationale menée par l'Organisation des Nations Unies et d'autres Etats ou

34 L'article 2 du Traité sur l'Union européenne stipule que l'« Union est fondée sur les valeurs de respect de la dignité humaine, de liberté, de démocratie, d'égalité, de l'État de droit, ainsi que de respect des droits de l'homme, y compris des droits des personnes appartenant à des minorités. Ces valeurs sont communes aux États membres dans une société caractérisée par le pluralisme, la non-discrimination, la tolérance, la justice, la solidarité et l'égalité entre les femmes et les hommes ».

35 En plus d'adhérer à l'article 2 TUE cité ci-dessus, les Etats candidats doivent remplir le critère politique énoncé par le Conseil européen de Copenhague de 1993 selon lequel « l'Etat candidat doit présenter des institutions stables garantes de la démocratie, de l'Etat de droit, des droits de l'homme et du respect et de la protection des minorités », décliné au sein de plusieurs « chapitres » autorisant l'adhésion. Voir sur ce point, parmi d'autres, C Boutayeb, *Droit institutionnel de l'Union européenne* (6ème édition, LGDJ 2020), 146–147 et 156.

36 Voir sur ce sujet, F Petiteville 'La coopération économique de l'Union européenne entre globalisation et politisation' (2001) 51 Revue française de sciences politiques 3, 431.

organisations[37]. Les Etats concernés par une telle intervention internationale, qui a sauf exception lieu avec leur consentement formel, ne peuvent recouvrer l'entièreté de leur souveraineté internationale, qu'à la condition d'adopter une forme démocratique de régime. Ce fut en particulier le cas du Timor Leste et du Kosovo[38]. Dans le même sens, Jean d'Aspremont souligne le cas d'Etats aspirant à l'indépendance, par exemple le Soudan du sud et, de nouveau, le Kosovo, dont on exige en échange de leur reconnaissance internationale une certaine conformité à la norme démocratique, qui n'est pas imposée aux Etats déjà existants[39]. C'est alors l'existence même de l'Etat, donc la seule *possibilité* de sa souveraineté, qui est ici conditionnée par la norme démocratique.

Par ailleurs, plusieurs types de restrictions et sanctions peuvent être imposés aux Etats eu égard à leur défaut de démocratie perçu. Ainsi, le Conseil de sécurité des Nations Unies peut, en cas de menace contre la paix et la sécurité internationales, décider de sanctions contre des Etats[40], y compris dans le cas de violations des droits humains. De telles mesures ont été prises à l'encontre d'une trentaine d'Etats depuis les années 1960. Si le motif pro-démocratique est rarement expressément mentionné dans les résolutions, ce fut tout de même le cas pour certains, dont le premier cas de sanction qui condamne les « mesures de répression politique » prises par le « régime illégal » de Rhodésie du sud en 1968[41] ou l'évocation parmi d'autres motifs de la « répression de [l]a population civile » en Irak en 2002[42]. De façon plus explicite, le Conseil de sécurité a également pris des sanctions contre le gouvernement *de facto* en Sierra Leone afin de « permettre le rétablissement du gouvernement démocratiquement élu et le retour à l'ordre constitutionnel »[43]. On peut d'ailleurs lire sur le site de l'ONU que « [d]e plus en plus, les sanctions sont également

37 Voir *infra*, 2. Ces interventions déploient avant tout leurs effets dans l'ordre interne des Etats concernés et seront donc abordées dans la seconde partie de cette étude.

38 *Idem*.

39 J d'Aspremont, L'Etat non démocratique en droit international. Étude critique du droit international positif et de la pratique contemporaine (Pedone 2008), 79.

40 Incluant « l'interruption complète ou partielle des relations économiques et des communications ferroviaires, maritimes, aériennes, postales, télégraphiques, radioélectriques et des autres moyens de communication, ainsi que la rupture des relations diplomatiques », article 41 de la Charte des Nations Unies.

41 S/RES/253 (1968). Voir aussi le document d'information public du Conseil de sécurité (2021) <https://www.un.org/securitycouncil/sites/www.un.org.securitycouncil/files/subsidiary_organs_factsheets.pdf> consulté le 24 mai 2021.

42 S/RES/1441 (2002), préambule. Voir aussi la résolution S/RES/1500 (2003) dans laquelle le Conseil de sécurité se félicite de la mise en place du « Conseil de gouvernement de l'Iraq, largement représentatif, qui marque une étape importante vers la formation par le peuple iraquien d'un gouvernement représentatif internationalement reconnu » para 1.

43 S/RES/1132 (1997), para 1.

utilisées pour (…) assurer que des élections aient lieu »[44]. Ainsi, en 2011, le Conseil de sécurité leva une partie des sanctions adoptées contre la Libye à la suite de l'accession au pouvoir du « *first democratically constituted national unity government* »[45].

L'Union européenne peut elle aussi prendre des sanctions contre des « acteurs étatiques » en cas de violation de certains droits humains, dont des droits politiques (liberté d'association et d'expression)[46], sur la base de l'article 29 du Traité sur l'Union européenne. Comme l'expose une décision récente du Conseil en la matière, « [c]es mesures restrictives ciblées poursuivront les objectifs de la politique étrangère et de sécurité commune énoncés à l'article 21 du traité UE et contribueront à l'action de l'Union pour consolider et soutenir la démocratie (…) »[47].

La non-conformité d'un Etat à la norme démocratique peut donc constituer une forte contrainte sur l'exercice de sa souveraineté internationale, et peut aller jusqu'à conditionner son existence même. D'autres formes moins explicites de marginalisation dans la sphère internationale sont également à l'œuvre en sus de celles présentées ci-dessus.

1.2.2 La dépréciation insidieuse de la souveraineté des Etats considérés comme non démocratiques et ses conséquences

La démocratie étant « assurément devenue un critère fondamental de légitimation des gouvernements à l'époque contemporaine »[48], les Etats perçus comme non ou insuffisamment démocratiques sont délégitimés dans l'ordre international. Si l'on définit la légitimité comme « système référentiel intersubjectif influençant la réaction des acteurs d'un ordre social face à une action de l'un d'entre eux »[49], les Etats perçus comme non démocratiques se verront opposer des attitudes ou réactions différentes de celles dont bénéficieront les « bons élèves », qui sont également les Etats qui ont été capables d'établir leur propre modèle comme norme. De manière plus diffuse et moins directement

44 ONU (2016) <https://news.un.org/fr/story/2016/05/334492-sanctions-de-lonu-comment-ca-marche-et-qui-les-utilisent> consulté le 22 mai 2021.

45 Conseil de sécurité (2021) <https://www.un.org/securitycouncil/sites/www.un.org.securitycouncil/files/subsidiary_organs_factsheets.pdf> consulté le 24 mai 2021.

46 Décision PESC 2020/1999 consolidée concernant des mesures restrictives en réaction aux graves violations des droits de l'homme et aux graves atteintes à ces droits (2020), art. 1.

47 *Ibid*, préambule.

48 J d'Aspremont, L'Etat nondémocratique en droit international. Étude critique du droit international positif et de la pratique contemporaine (Pedone 2008), 180.

49 R Bachand, Les subalternes et le droit international (Pedone 2018), 209.

contraignante que les mesures décrites plus haut, mais aussi de façon plus difficilement contournable, les Etats non démocratiques sont tenus, pour éviter cette marginalisation, d'adhérer à une norme à laquelle ils ne correspondent pas et ne souhaitent pas nécessairement correspondre. Ce phénomène permet en même temps de légitimer la norme elle-même puisqu'il induit une adhésion quasi-générale à celle-ci. Tous les Etats, promeuvent effectivement, dans leur discours, la démocratie[50]. Cette dynamique correspond à la définition néo-Gramscienne de la situation de domination caractérisant l'ordre international, qui repose non pas sur l'usage de la force, mais sur l'acceptation d'un ordre hiérarchique sur la base de motifs idéologiques.

Ainsi, la construction et le contenu de la norme démocratique, et sa fonction de « contrainte axiologique », sont à la fois des manifestations et des causes des restrictions pesant sur la souveraineté internationale des Etats les moins capables de faire valoir leurs intérêts, ce qui assoit et perpétue le système hégémonique qui caractérise l'ordre international. A bien des égards, la restriction de la souveraineté internationale des Etats se manifeste également par une restriction de leur souveraineté interne, *a fortiori* lorsque la norme mobilisée comme outil d'hégémonie porte précisément sur le régime des Etats, comme c'est le cas de la norme démocratique.

2 Les restrictions à la souveraineté des Etats et des peuples au plan interne à travers la norme démocratique

Les restrictions quant à la souveraineté interne des Etats concernés par les phénomènes décrits ci-dessus ne sont que le pendant ou la continuation de la dynamique présentée en première partie. La norme démocratique touchant directement l'organisation interne des Etats, l'intrusion dans l'ordre interne des Etats, autorisée par le processus de marginalisation et de dépréciation présenté plus haut, prend de multiples formes qui affectent tant l'exercice de la souveraineté par les Etats sur leur territoire (2.1) que la souveraineté des peuples qui constituent théoriquement les bénéficiaires finaux de la norme démocratique (2.2). La question du consentement des concernés à la promotion voire à l'imposition des mesures visant à réaliser la norme démocratique sera, dans les deux cas, discutée.

50 En plus de la consultation des débats sur le sujet à l'Assemblée générale des Nations Unies ou à la Sixième Commission, voir de nouveau, sur ce point, *ibid.*, 282, et *supra*, 1.1.1. Les limites à l'élaboration de la norme démocratique.

2.1 *La souveraineté de l'Etat face à l'instauration d'un régime démocratique dans un contexte internationalisé*

Certaines des mesures décrites dans la première partie de cette étude comme entamant la souveraineté internationale des Etats ont également des conséquences pour la souveraineté interne des Etats. Elles consistent en effet en l'adoption d'une législation et d'institutions internes devant correspondre au modèle de démocratie retenu par les promoteurs internationaux (organisations internationales ou Etats).

Les programmes d'« aide » mis en œuvre par des organisations internationales (dont l'ONU et ses agences, au premier rang desquels le Programme des Nations Unies pour le développement (PNUD)[51], la Banque Mondiale, les organisations régionales, etc.) et par des Etats dans un cadre bilatéral, tels que les Etats-Unis (entre autres à travers leur agence de « coopération » USAID[52]) proposent aux Etats une aide financière et technique afin de « renforcer » leur régime démocratique. Il est alors attendu des Etats concernés, en sus d'organiser régulièrement des élections correspondant aux critères établis de transparence, qu'ils modifient leur législation et leurs institutions, parfois leur Constitution, en vue d'accroître leur conformité à un modèle donné de démocratie. A titre d'exemple, le PNUD insiste sur le soutien qu'il a fourni aux « processus de réforme constitutionnelle » dans les pays concernés[53].

Toutefois, ces programmes reçoivent, sur le plan formel, le consentement des Etats concernés, et ne peuvent donc être analysés comme une restriction à la souveraineté de ceux-ci. En effet, ces programmes sont validés avec les partenaires internationaux[54], dont la présence elle-même fait l'objet d'accords formels. Il en va de même, techniquement, pour ce qui est des interventions onusiennes de « reconstruction » d'un Etat à la suite d'un conflit[55]

51 Ainsi en matière de « gouvernance démocratique », « [l]e PNUD aide les pays à entreprendre des réformes constitutionnelles », https://www.undp.org/content/undp/fr/home/democratic-governance-and-peacebuilding.html.

52 Voir le site de l'agence https://www.usaid.gov/democracy.

53 Voir par exemple le descriptif des activités du PNUD sur la page consacrée à la gouvernance démocratique, et les projets y relatifs, PNUD (2021) <https://www1.undp.org/content/undp/fr/home/democratic-governance-and-peacebuilding/inclusive-political-processes.html> consultée le 26 mai 2021.

54 Les « Prodoc » ou documents de projets sont cosignés par un représentant de l'acteur international et par un représentant gouvernemental, voir à titre d'exemple les documents du PNUD disponibles en ligne, par exemple <https://info.undp.org/docs/pdc/Documents/ETH/PRODOC.%20-SEEDS-2019-22.pdf>, consultés le 26 mai 2021.

55 Voir *infra*, 2.1.2. Ces interventions qui s'articulent très directement avec la souveraineté des peuples concernés, seront analysées plus en détail dans la section consacrée ci-dessous.

(telles qu'elles ont eu lieu, entre autres, au Timor Leste, au Kosovo, mais aussi en Afghanistan, en Irak, etc.), qui reçoivent le consentement de l'Etat hôte[56]. Dans ce dernier cas, cependant, le contrôle qu'exercent les Etats sur la mise en œuvre concrète et des détails de l'exécution des programmes peut être limité. On peut alors s'interroger sur la mesure dans laquelle ces Etats pourraient se retrouver face à une « intervention qui se retourne contre la souveraineté ou la volonté de l'Etat « invitant » »[57], ou qui dépasse les limites de son consentement[58].

Les mesures de conditionnalité démocratique de l'Union européenne sont d'un autre ordre puisqu'il s'agit, en échange d'un partenariat économique censé être avantageux pour les Etats concernés, associé au financement de projets de développement, de se conformer à certaines exigences démocratiques[59] nécessitant réformes et révisions internes. Le non-respect de ces exigences peut entraîner la suspension de l'accord[60]. Les mêmes pratiques sont également mises en œuvre par les Etats puissants (et catégorisés « démocratiques ») de façon bilatérale avec leurs partenaires économiques, quoique de façon moins systématique et constante : ainsi des Etats-Unis[61], de la France[62], etc. Toutefois, de nouveau, l'Etat reste en théorie libre d'accepter le partenariat économique.

---

56 Selon la « doctrine Capstone » élaborée par l'ONU en 2008, les opérations de maintien de la paix doivent respecter trois principes, dont celui du consentement. Voir le document disponible en ligne <https://peacekeeping.un.org/sites/default/files/capstone_doctrine_fr.pdf> consulté le 28 mai 2021.

57 K Bannelier-Christakis et T Christakis, 'Volenti non fit injuria ? Les effets du consentement à l'intervention militaire', (2004) 50 AFDI 1 102, 135.

58 *Ibid.*, 136.

59 Accord de partenariat entre les membres du groupe des Etats d'Afrique, des Caraïbes et du Pacifique et la Communauté européenne et ses Etats membres, signé à Cotonou, Bénin, le 23 juin 2000 (dit Accord de Cotonou), article 8 para 4, article 9, article 20 para 1 d, article 33.

60 *Ibid*, article 96. Voir sur les sanctions prises par l'Union européenne dans ce cadre, R Youngs, *'The end of democratic conditionality: good riddance?'* (2010) FRIDE Working papers <https://www.files.ethz.ch/isn/130596/WP102_The_end_democratic_conditionality_ENG_set10.pdf>consulté le 18 mai 2021.

61 En effet les Etats catégorisés démocratiques ou en démocratisation n'ont pas nécessairement davantage d'aide de la part des Etats-Unis dans les années 1990, voir l'article de S Hook, "Building democracy' throughforeignaid: The limitations of United States politicalconditionalities, 1992–96', (1998) 5 Democratization 150.

62 Voir la thèse d'A Sadio, Conditionnalité politique de l'aide publique au développement des partenaires occidentaux à l'Afrique : analyse des actions françaises en Afrique subsaharienne (2019) <https://tel.archives-ouvertes.fr/tel-02279173/file/fix_cA9aINxH.pdf>consultée le 21 mai 2021. Voir aussi le rapport du Haut Conseil de la coopération internationale, 'Gouvernance démocratique et coopération internationale' (2002) <https://www.vie-publique.fr/sites/default/files/rapport/pdf/034000027.pdf> consulté le 21 mai 2021.

Ces mesures sont donc, formellement tout du moins, adoptées avec le consentement de l'Etat concerné. Monique Chemillier-Gendreau parle toutefois de « contraintes externes » que l'on peut identifier ici comme étant économiques et politiques[63], dans la même ligne que ce qui a été développé dans la première partie de cette étude. Parmi les contraintes économiques, il faut prendre en compte le fait que les programmes d'aide vont de pair avec un soutien financier et des projets de développement économique dans divers domaines, bénéficiant par ailleurs à l'Etat concerné (voire nécessaires à son maintien). De même, pour ce qui est des accords entre l'Union européenne et les pays ACP, le « choix » est, si ce n'est contraint, du moins orienté par le fait que l'Union européenne fournit aux mêmes Etats de l'aide au développement, à quoi il faut ajouter la difficulté, déjà mentionnée, à rester en marge du commerce mondial. De façon moins directe, Dario Battistella note que

> [l]a plupart du temps, les Etats non démocratiques sont incités à adopter le modèle démocratique par la voie douce du *soft power*, c'est-à-dire par l'intermédiaire de la force d'attraction que les démocraties exercent sur les Etats désireux de se rapprocher d'elles dans l'espoir de bénéficier d'une prospérité comparable[64].

Les influences d'ordre politique pesant sur le comportement de l'Etat en matière d'acceptation de la norme démocratique en son sein sont multiples et complexes. Parmi elles, le gain de légitimité de l'Etat « bon élève » en matière de démocratie sur la scène internationale peut également influencer son acceptation de la mise en œuvre de certaines mesures. De façon plus déterminante, les Etats acceptant la présence d'une mission de maintien de la paix sont souvent dans une position où une intervention onusienne constitue la condition pour le régime de se maintenir au pouvoir, ou d'y (ré)accéder le cas échéant. Le consentement des Etats doit donc être regardé comme essentiellement formel, masquant les rapports de pouvoir ayant influencé, voire dicté, le comportement de l'Etat concerné.

Enfin, plusieurs « cas limites » d'intervention dans les affaires internes d'un Etat ont consisté à faire usage de la force avec un objectif pro-démocratique plus ou moins explicite. En 1994, le Conseil de sécurité de l'ONU a ainsi autorisé

---

63 Et qui avaient déjà été rappelées il y a plus de soixante ans par , G Abi-Saab, 'The Newly Independent States and the Rules of International Law: An Outline' (1962) 8 Howard Law Journal 95, 118–119.

64 D Battistella, 'L'Occident, exportateur de démocratie' (2011) Politique étrangère 4 813, 816–817.

une intervention internationale « à utiliser (...) tous les moyens nécessaires pour faciliter le départ d'Haïti des dirigeants militaires, eu égard à l'Accord de Governors Island, et le prompt retour du président légitimement élu »[65]. Si ce cas est une exception[66], il n'en reste pas moins qu'il s'agit d'une intervention armée sur le territoire d'un Etat en vue de rétablir la démocratie.

L'intervention militaire en Libye en 2011, autorisée par le Conseil de sécurité dans sa résolution 1973, s'est quant à elle fondée sur l'argumentaire de « protection des populations civiles »[67] mais aussi sur l'importance d'« apporter une solution à la crise, qui satisfasse les revendications légitimes du peuple libyen » y compris par le biais de « réformes politiques nécessaires »[68]. Cette intervention a été critiquée au motif qu'elle aurait outrepassé son mandat et facilité la chute du régime (considéré comme non-démocratique) en place au moment de l'intervention[69]. Le Conseil de sécurité, rappelant que « la période de transition doit être ancrée dans l'attachement à la démocratie » a ensuite autorisé l'envoi d'une mission onusienne de paix ayant entre autres pour mandat de « lancer la rédaction de la constitution et le processus électoral »[70]. De nouveau, il s'agit ici d'un exemple, certes critiqué, de recours à la force à la fois initialement non consenti, fondé en partie sur un argumentaire démocratique et débouchant sur un processus d'établissement de la démocratie par les acteurs internationaux.

La souveraineté interne de l'Etat peut donc être limitée de façon plus ou moins contrainte par le biais de la mobilisation de la norme démocratique. De manière plus paradoxale, il en va de même de la souveraineté du peuple.

2.2 *Le respect de la volonté du peuple dans l'instauration d'un régime démocratique dans un contexte internationalisé*

L'ONU et les autres acteurs internationaux présents dans les Etats en « reconstruction » jouent un rôle conséquent dans la mise en place des institutions et dans l'adoption des Constitutions des Etats concernés. Or, si ces Etats ont, dans le cadre d'une lecture positiviste du droit international, exprimé leur

---

65 S/RES/940 (1994) para 4.

66 O Corten, 'La résolution 940 du Conseil de sécurité autorisant une intervention militaire en Haïti: la consécration d'un principe de légitimité démocratique?' (1995) 6 EJIL 116.

67 S/RES/1973 (2011).

68 *Ibid.*, para 1 et 2.

69 N Ameur, 'La Libye entre les intérêts de l'Occident et la résistance de Kadhafi', (2011) 29 Outre-Terre 3 299, 301 ; N Andersson et D Lagot (dir.), *Responsabilité de protéger et guerres « humanitaires ». Le cas de la Libye* (L'Harmattan 2012), 99.

70 S/RES/2009 (2011) para 12 b).

consentement formel à l'action des acteurs internationaux, la question se pose du respect de la volonté des peuples concernés eux-mêmes, étant donné l'objectif démocratique annoncé. Il s'agit ici d'interroger la mesure dans laquelle les peuples concernés peuvent exprimer et expriment effectivement leur volonté en matière de régime politiquedans le cadre de la mise en œuvre de la norme démocratique[71].

Formellement, les Constitutions et institutions élaborées dans le contexte d'une présence internationale dans l'Etat concerné sont adoptées par les peuples selon deux types de modalités. Soit par un organe représentatif (par exemple, la Constitution timoraise (voir ci-dessous), la Constitution afghane adoptée en 2004 par la *Loya Jirga*, ou encore la Constitution du Kosovo adoptée en 2008 par l'Assemblée) soit, plus rarement, par référendum (comme en Irak en 2005). Ces modalités d'adoption masquent cependant le rôle et l'influence des acteurs internationaux dans ces processus.

Tout d'abord, la question du type de régime lui-même (démocratique ou non) est exclue du choix laissé au peuple concerné, étant donné que la norme démocratique constitue un prérequis pour les acteurs internationaux. Le présupposé démocratique est évident dans la résolution 1244 relative à la mission des Nations Unies au Kosovo en 1999[72], dans la résolution établissant la mission des Nations Unies en Irak en 2003[73] et dans l'ensemble des résolutions ou accords établissant des missions ou des programmes onusiens dans les Etats concernés.

Plus paradoxalement encore au regard d'une compréhension de la démocratie comme choix par le peuple, dans plusieurs cas, ce sont les Nations Unies elles-mêmes qui sont en charge de mettre en œuvre la norme démocratique dans ses manifestations concrètes. Au Timor Leste, le Conseil de sécurité a chargé l'Administration transitoire des Nations Unies au Timor oriental (ATNUTO) de « créer des institutions locales démocratiques »[74] afin de leur transférer le pouvoir. Les élections ayant désigné l'Assemblée constituante au Timor Leste en 2001 ont ainsi été organisées par l'ATNUTO sur la base du règlement établi par cette dernière[75]. L'Assemblée a rédigé puis adopté la future

71 La question se pose également de la mesure dans laquelle le consentement donné par le régime de l'Etat peut être considéré comme représentatif de la volonté du peuple, dans un contexte souvent caractérisé par une forte défiance de celui-ci vis-à-vis de celui-là. Pour y répondre, il serait nécessaire de fournir un historique et une analyse détaillée des forces en présence pour chaque cas, ce qui n'est pas l'objet de cette étude.

72 S/RES/1244 (1999) para 11 c.

73 S/RES/1511 (2003) para 7.

74 S/RES/1272 (1999) para 8.

75 UNTAET/REG/2001/2 (2001).

Constitution timoraise, conseillée en cela par l'ATNUTO[76], contre l'opinion de certains représentants politiques qui avaient appelé à une consultation populaire[77]. Cette même Assemblée a ensuite été transformée en Parlement alors que tel n'était pas son mandat initial, afin d'éviter les frais d'un nouveau processus électoral financé par les acteurs internationaux[78].

Le cas du Kosovo manifeste également un très fort contrôle de la part des acteurs internationaux du processus d'adoption de la Constitution de 2008. Décrite comme ayant été « [p]réparée par les services juridiques de l'ONU assistés d'experts occidentaux », elle a été approuvée par le Représentant civil international avant d'être promulguée par le Président et formellement adoptée par l'Assemblée, quoique sans réel vote[79]. Le Représentant civil international conserve par ailleurs un rôle décisionnaire important, au point de pouvoir annuler une loi adoptée par les institutions kosovares[80].

Le rôle laissé au peuple concerné semble bien limité dans le cadre d'une telle approche, les institutions « démocratiques » étant conçues et mises en place, voire contrôlées, par un acteur international. Ainsi, la mise en œuvre du présupposé démocratique reste pour une bonne part entre les mains des acteurs internationaux, en contradiction avec la conception de la démocratie comme concrétisation de l'expression de la souveraineté du peuple concerné.

Si, sur le plan formel, on peut estimer que le consentement tant de l'Etat que de son peuple est respecté, de fortes contraintes pèsent donc sur le comportement de l'Etat et rognent le plein exercice de sa souveraineté. Le présupposé démocratique, bien qu'il soit précisément censé coïncider avec la volonté des peuples, leur est toutefois imposé. Si cela peut ne pas poser de problème théorique puisque la volonté du peuple n'est censée s'exprimer que dans un contexte démocratique, la mise en œuvre concrète de la norme démocratique peut elle-même s'avérer assez peu démocratique. En outre, la volonté initiale de certains acteurs, au premier rang desquels les Etats-Unis, de faire « tout ce qui est en [leur] pouvoir pour apporter l'espoir de la démocratie, du développement, du marché libre et du libre-échange aux quatre coins de la planète »,

---

76 « Un certain nombre d'articles ont été amendés pour refléter les suggestions faites par l'ATNUTO », V Huet, 'La première constitution du Timor oriental', (2003) 56 Revue française de droit constitutionnel 4 865, 867.

77 S Dovert et F Durand, 'Les élections à Timor-Est, 2001–2012 : la démocratique au risque des tensions' (2012) *Echo* Géo, Sur le Vif, para 18–21.

78 *Ibid.*

79 O Perrot, 'Les perspectives incertaines de la Constitution du Kosovo' (2008) Esprit 7 164.

80 Plan Ahtisaari pour le statut du Kosovo (2007) art. 2.1.c. Voir aussi D Doli et F Korenica, 'Calling Kosovo's Constitution: A Legal Review' (2010) 22 Denning Law Journal 51.

ainsi qu'ils l'annoncent eux-mêmes dans leur stratégie nationale de sécurité[81], jette le doute sur le degré de consentement laissé aux Etats concernés. La norme démocratique révèle de nouveau de fortes inégalités dans la capacité des Etats, et même de leurs peuples, à exercer pleinement leur souveraineté.

3 Conclusion

La présente étude a cherché à montrer les mécanismes par lesquels la norme démocratique en elle-même, et les usages qui en sont faits, peuvent avoir pour effet de restreindre la souveraineté des Etats tant sur le plan international que sur le plan interne et, paradoxalement, également celle des peuples. S'il est communément admis que certaines règles de droit international peuvent effectivement limiter la souveraineté des Etats sur leur territoire, la norme démocratique se distingue de ce phénomène à plusieurs titres : d'une part, parce qu'il ne s'agit pas d'une règle positive de droit international et que les Etats n'y ont donc pas souscrit ; d'autre part, parce que leur souveraineté internationale, c'est-à-dire leur capacité d'action juridique sur la scène internationale, se trouve également affectée, et ce de façon très inégale selon les Etats. Pour parvenir à ce constat, le choix a été fait de replacer le droit international dans sa réalité matérielle, c'est-à-dire de prendre en compte les inégalités factuelles entre Etats, de même que les mécanismes et phénomènes non juridiques à l'œuvre, en termes de légitimité par exemple.

L'étude constitue ainsi une pierre supplémentaire dans l'entreprise de déconstruction de la souveraineté comme concept fondateur du droit international, en révélant la contradiction dont ce concept est porteur. La souveraineté suppose, et est en même temps censée formaliser, l'égalité des Etats, ne serait-ce qu'en termes de capacité d'action juridique dans l'ordre international. Or, cela s'avère être un « camouflage » de la réalité[82].

Il ressort de cette analyse que certains Etats ont la capacité d'imposer leur volonté à d'autres, et ce par le biais de mécanismes idéologiques, dans le sens où ces mécanismes reposent sur des idées, telle la norme démocratique. Comme le souligne Gérard Cahin,

> [i]l est vrai que le recours fait par les Etats aux instruments et aux techniques du droit international pour projeter vers l'extérieur leur

81 Stratégie nationale de sécurité des Etats-Unis de 2002, citée par D Battistella, 'L'Occident, exportateur de démocratie' (2011) Politique étrangère 4, 813.

82 M Chemillier-Gendreau, 'Contribution of the Reims School to the Debate on the Critical Analysis of International Law. Assessment and Limits' (2011) 22 EJIL 3 649, 652.

> puissance, leur domination économique et leur hégémonie politique a toujours bénéficié, et continue ô combien de bénéficier à l'heure de la mondialisation, à ceux qui sont déjà les plus puissants. (…) [L]a reconstruction ou la construction de la souveraineté des uns [peut] comme dans bien des domaines favoriser l'expansion de la souveraineté des autres et l'exportation de leurs modèles politiques et économiques[83].

Cette approche est même délibérément défendue par certains auteurs qui se trouvent être également acteurs des relations internationales, explicitant clairement l'inégale souveraineté caractérisant en réalité les Etats dans l'ordre international. Ainsi, Robert Cooper, diplomate britannique ayant occupé diverses fonctions au sein des institutions européennes, explique qu'il

> [f]aut s'habituer au fait qu'il y a deux poids deux mesures en matière de normes. Entre eux, les États postmodernes [occidentaux] fonctionnent grâce à des règles établies et à l'existence d'une sécurité fondée sur la coopération et l'ouverture. Cependant, lorsqu'ils ont affaire à des Etats étrangers à ces conceptions, les Européens doivent recourir à des méthodes d'une époque antérieure – force, attaque préventive, ruse, tous ces artifices qu'il est nécessaire d'utiliser contre ceux qui vivent encore dans un monde où prévalent, comme au XIXème siècle, les règles du chacun pour soi. Dans la jungle, ils doivent appliquer les lois de la jungle[84].

Ce constat vient donc confirmer le cadre théorique critique décrivant l'ordre international comme un ordre hégémonique, et précise en même temps en quoi peuvent consister certains des ressorts et dynamiques d'une telle situation.

---

83 G Cahin, 'Reconstruction et construction de l'Etat en droit international' (2020), 411 RCADI, 50–51.

84 R Cooper, *La Fracture des nations. Ordre et chaos au XXIe siècle* (Denoël 2004), 84 (italique ajouté).

PART 2

Democracy and Human Rights

CHAPTER 6

Journalists in Danger and the Possibilities of International Law

Stephanie Schiedermair

> The moment we no longer have a free press, anything can happen. What makes it possible for a totalitarian or any other dictatorship to rule is that people are not informed.[1]
>
> HANNAH ARENDT, 1978

Summary

The article analyses the protection international law provides for the media with a focus on the individual journalist as the key player in the media landscape.

1 Introduction: From Where the Bombs Come

The media, as an indispensable precondition of stable democratic systems, increasingly falls victim to attacks from different sides. In 2020, 49 journalists worldwide were killed for their activities,[2] while 305 journalists and 100 citizen journalists are still imprisoned.[3] The 2020 World Press Freedom Index issued by Reporters Without Borders notes that we are "entering a decisive

1 See https://www.nybooks.com/articles/1978/10/26/hannah-arendt-from-an-interview/ (30.8.2022).

2 Cf. *Reporter without Borders*, Violations of Press Freedom Barometer 2020, https://rsf.org/en/barometer?year=2020 (30.8.2022).

3 See *Reporter without Borders*, Violations of Press Freedom Barometer 2021, https://rsf.org/en/barometer?year=2021 (30.8.2022).

 | DOI:10.1163/9789004508712_007

decade for journalism, exacerbated by coronavirus".[4] The reasons for this lie in the actions of aggressive authoritarian regimes, the fundamental changes of the media landscape due to the technical development, the accompanying economic problems and a deep suspicion or even hatred towards the media.[5] Authoritarian states in particular are tightening restrictions on freedom of expression and information, for example through centralised state access to the internet, as is happening with the "Great Firewall" of China[6] and the Runet project in Russia.[7] In Europe,[8] the systematic reshaping of media landscapes in Hungary[9] and Poland[10] and the accompanying repression of media workers bear witness to comparable tendencies as do the events after the 2016 coup in Turkey.[11] On the other side of the Atlantic, the storming of the Capitol showed how the permanent incitement of violent sections of the population by the former US president turned into physical violence against democratic institutions and media representatives.[12] But even in countries with a stable constitutional state, there is a discernible trend towards accepting restrictions on

4 Cf. *Reporter without Borders*, 2020 World Press Freedom Index, https://rsf.org/en/2020-world-press-freedom-index-entering-decisive-decade-journalism-exacerbated-coronavirus (30.8.2022).

5 See *Reporter without Borders*, 2020 World Press Freedom Index, https://rsf.org/en/2020-world-press-freedom-index-entering-decisive-decade-journalism-exacerbated-coronavirus (30.8.2022).

6 Cf. *Kuo*, China's Great Firewall descends on Hong Kong internet users, July 8 2020, https://www.theguardian.com/world/2020/jul/08/china-great-firewall-descends-hong-kong-internet-users (30.8.2022).

7 See *Wakefield*, Russia 'succesfully tests' its unplugged internet, December 24, 2019, https://www.bbc.com/news/technology-50902496 (30.8.2022).

8 For the general situation in Europe see *Renate Schroeder*, Media, Freedom of Speech, and Democracy: Journalists under pressure in Europe, in: Angelos Giannakopoulos (ed.), Media, Freedom of Speech, and Democracy in the EU and Beyond, 2019, p. 25.

9 Cf. *Attila Batorfy*, Hungary: A Country on the Path towards an Authoritarian Media System, in: Angelos Giannakopoulos (ed.), Media, Freedom of Speech, and Democracy in the EU and Beyond, 2019, p. 31. See also the Memorandum of the Council of Europe´s Commissioner for Human Rights concerning Hungary, https://rm.coe.int/memorandum-on-freedom-of-expression-and-media-freedom-in-hungary/1680a1e67e (30.8.2022).

10 See *Reporter without Borders*, Poland, https://rsf.org/en/poland (30.8.2022).

11 See the report concerning Turkey of Reporters Without Borders, https://rsf.org/en/news/turkey-press-freedom-figures (March 9 2021) and the Council of Europe's Platform to promote the protection of journalism and safety of journalists, https://fom.coe.int/en/accueil (30.8.2022).

12 'Murder the Media' was scratched into a door of the Capitol, cf. https://www.nytimes.com/2021/01/06/business/media/media-murder-capitol-building.html (30.8.2022).

freedom of expression for security and other reasons.[13] For the member states of the European Union, this is exemplified by the draft of an EU regulation aimed at combating the dissemination of terrorist content on the Internet and imposing comprehensive monitoring obligations on Internet providers (Terrorist Content Online Regulation).[14] Moreover, the Commission's proposal for an e-evidence regulation, which would allow the judicial authorities of each member state to access user data directly from the provider (possibly located in another EU state) within six hours in individual cases, is likely to pose problems for the protection of editorial secrecy.[15] After criticism from the European Federation of Journalists,[16] the European Parliament, the Council and the Commission have now started trilogue negotiations on the e-evidence package.[17]

The repressive measures taken by many states due to the SARS-CoV-2 virus further aggravate the situation.[18] Authoritarian governments withhold information about contagions and deaths, try to manipulate reporting and prevent the dissemination of information by independent journalists.[19] The understandable concern to curb the spread of false information about the virus has led to massive official restrictions on press freedom in numerous countries. Honduras, for example, has suspended the constitutional article on press

13 Cf. *Posetti, Bell, and Brown,* Journalism & The Pandemic: A Global Snapshot of Impacts, 2020; *European Centre for Press & Media Freedom,* Feindbild Journalist – Bedrohung als Normalzustand, 2020.

14 See *European Commission,* Proposal for a Regulation of the European Parliament and of the Council on preventing the dissemination of terrorist content online, 12.9.2018, COM/2018/640 final, https://eur-lex.europa.eu/legal-content/EN/ALL/?uri=CELEX:52018PC0640 (30.8.2022).

15 Cf. *European Commission,* Proposal for a Regulation of the European Parliament and of the Council on European Production and Preservation Orders for electronic evidence in criminal matters, 17.4.2018, COM/2018/225 final, https://eur-lex.europa.eu/legal-content/EN/TXT/?uri=COM:2018:225:FIN (30.8.2022).

16 See *European Federation of Journalists,* Joint letter: 'e-evidence' regulation must protect journalists, September 17, 2020, https://europeanjournalists.org/blog/2020/09/17/joint-letter-e-evidence-regulation-must-protect-journalists/ (30.8.2022).

17 See *Thomas Wahl,* New E-Evidence Legislation: Trilogue Started – Criticism on EP Stance, March 25, 2021, https://eucrim.eu/news/new-e-evidence-legislation-trilogue-started-critics-on-ep-stance/ (30.8.2022).

18 Cf. *Posetti, Bell, and Brown,* Journalism & The Pandemic: A Global Snapshot of Impacts, 2020.

19 See *Reporters without Borders,* 2021 World Press Freedom Index, https://rsf.org/en/2021-world-press-freedom-index-journalism-vaccine-against-disinformation-blocked-more-130-countries (30.8.2022).

freedom;[20] in Armenia, journalists are only allowed to publish official information on COVID-19;[21] and in China, seven journalists are still imprisoned after reporting critically on the conditions in Wuhan.[22] Additionally, in multiple countries, for example in Russia, there is an expansion of digital surveillance, the collection of location data of individual profiles, the censorship of social media and the uncontrolled use of facial recognition software.[23] Moreover, the COVID-19 pandemic has fuelled a culture of disinformation on the internet,[24] which makes the struggle against fake news even more urgent, while also reinforcing the trend of stifling critical journalism. The closure of borders can also restrict journalism as it prevents persecuted media workers from fleeing to a safe neighbouring country.

The attacks on free journalism stem from state authorities on the one hand and from private individuals on the other. At the anti-racism demonstrations in the USA triggered by the murder of George Floyd, journalists were arrested and attacked by state authorities with tear gas and rubber bullets, a television team from Deutsche Welle was shot at with rubber bullets on camera in Minneapolis.[25] But the number of cases of physical attacks on journalists by political radicals has increased significantly as well.[26] Defamation and inflammatory campaigns repeatedly lead to violent attacks, especially at demonstrations.[27] Other subtle influences on journalistic work add to a sceptical or even hostile attitude towards journalists, such as the increase of so called preventive lawyer strategies that can be observed in Germany as a targeted means of

---

20 Cf. *Comité pol la Libre Expresión*, Emiten decreto que restringe libertad de expresión en crisis por COVID-19, 17.3.2020, http://www.clibrehonduras.com/index.php/portada-alertas/1125-emiten-decreto-que-limita-libertad-de-expresion-en-crisis-por-covid-19 (30.8.2022).

21 Vgl. *Mejlumyan*, Armenia takes hard line against media reporting on COVID-19, 23.3.2020, https://eurasianet.org/armenia-takes-hard-line-against-media-reporting-on-covid-19 (30.8.2022).

22 S. *Reporters without Borders*, https://rsf.org/en/news/china-one-year-after-covid-19-outbreak-seven-journalists-still-detained-reporting-issue (30.8.2022).

23 Cf. https://www.theguardian.com/world/2020/apr/02/cybergulag-russia-looks-to-surveillance-technology-to-enforce-lockdown (30.8.2022).

24 The UNESCO speaks of a "disinfodemic" accompanying the Corona pandemic, cf. https://en.unesco.org/sites/default/files/unesco_covid_brief_en.pdf (30.8.2022).

25 See https://www.nytimes.com/2020/06/04/world/attacks-press-george-floyd.html (30.8.2022).

26 Cf. *Council of Europe*, Parliamentary Assembly, Threats to media freedom and journalists' security in Europe, Report January 3 2020, Doc. 15021, p. 11.

27 See the study of the European Centre for Press & Media Freedom, Feindbild Journalist – Bedrohung als Normalzustand, p. 3 et seq.

preventing critical reporting even before it is published ("If you write this, I'll sue you!").[28]

In some cases, further factors add to the threat. Female journalists can present a double target because they are journalists and women, as the killing of three journalists – targeted in part for being women – in Afghanistan in March 2021 shows.[29] Journalists themselves may be discriminated against or threatened on the basis of their gender, age, religion, origin, sexual identity, culture, health status, living situation or social status. This is on top of journalists being threatened for the topics of their work. The latter becomes relevant for Europe regarding reporting on the "LGBT-free zones" in eastern Poland[30] and the proposed amendment to the Polish constitution in Hungary which wants to ban adoption by homosexual couples.[31]

All these developments occur in a time where the media landscape and journalism are in transition, with the classical media world being turned upside down by digital age phenomena.[32] The process provides manifold challenges for media companies and for journalists because conditions for the media are in constant change. It also sets new issues on the legal agenda, such as the regulation of hate speech on the internet.[33] The law is right in the middle of this transition process. The law still adheres to the classical media categories such as the press, film and broadcasting, yet jurisprudence seeks to adjust the classical categories to new phenomena and legislators are increasingly trying to find answers to the challenges, for example by making internet

28 Cf. the interesting study concerning the situation in Germany: *Gostomzyk and Moßbrucker*, „Wenn Sie das schreiben, verklage ich Sie!" – Studie zu präventiven Anwaltsstrategien gegenüber Medien, Frankfurt am Main 2019.

29 The Islamic State has claimed responsibility for the shootings, see https://www.nytimes.com/2021/03/05/world/asia/afghanistan-women-journalists.html (30.8.2022).

30 Cf. *Douglas*, How the EU can stop Poland's 'LGBT-free zones', 25.9.2020, https://www.dw.com/en/how-the-eu-can-stop-polands-lgbt-free-zones/a-55042896 (30.8.2022).

31 Cf. https://www.nbcnews.com/feature/nbc-out/pandemic-rages-hungary-ramps-anti-lgbtq-legislation-n1248659 (16.03.2021); https://ejc.net/uploads/downloads/EJC_LGBTQI_communities_a_reporters_guide.pdf (30.8.2022). As a reaction to the ongoings in Poland and Hungary the EU Commission has presented a strategy for equality for which it needs the consent of all member states, https://ec.europa.eu/commission/presscorner/detail/en/qanda_20_357 (30.8.2022).

32 For an overview see *Witschge/Anderson/Domingo/Hermida* (ed.), The SAGE Handbook of Digital Journalism, 2016.

33 Cf. *Schieb/Preuss*, Studies in Communication and Media 7 (2018), p. 583; *Brown*, Models of Governance of Online Hate Speech, 2020, https://rm.coe.int/models-of-governance-of-online-hate-speech/16809e671d (30.8.2022).

providers accountable[34] and by elaborating mechanisms to fight fake news on the internet.[35]

In this situation of change and threat, the urgent question arises how law can contribute to the protection of free media – and it can only be a contribution since a consensus on the need of an independent, free media as an essential precondition for any democracy ultimately cannot be enforced by law.[36]

2 The Protection of the Media under International Law

2.1 *International Treaties*

In addition to the mechanisms existing in democratic states, such as the classic protection of the informant as a part of the constitutional guarantee of freedom of the press and broadcasting, international law as well provides mechanisms for the protection of the media. These mechanisms are increasingly coming into focus for various reasons: on the one hand, the Internet as a worldwide communication system forces a broadening of the view beyond national borders, while on the other hand, the increasing failure of domestic protection mechanisms raises the question in individual cases of whether it is possible to take legal action outside the national legal system.

2.1.1 Global Protection: International Covenant on Civil and Political Rights (ICCPR)

The global human rights norm for the protection of journalists is article 19 of the International Covenant on Civil and Political Rights. Following art. 19 of the Universal Declaration of Human Rights (UDHR), art. 19 ICCPR protects the

34 See, e. g., the EU Commissions proposal for a Digital Services Act (DSA), https://ec.europa.eu/digital-single-market/en/news/proposal-regulation-european-parliament-and-council-single-market-digital-services-digital (30.8.2022) and Digital Markets Act (DMA), https://ec.europa.eu/info/sites/info/files/proposal-regulation-single-market-digital-services-digital-services-act_en.pdf (30.8.2022), which aim at uniform rules governing digital services in the EU.

35 See the strategy of the EU Commission to tackle online disinformation, https://ec.europa.eu/digital-single-market/en/tackling-online-disinformation (30.8.2022).

36 The former German Federal Constitutional Court's judge Ernst-Wolfgang Böckenförde coined the phrase that the "the free, secular state lives on preconditions that it cannot guarantee itself", see *Böckenförde*, Die Entstehung des Staates als Vorgang der Säkularisation, in: Säkularisation und Utopie. Ebracher Studien, Ernst Forsthoff zum 65. Geburtstag (1967), p. 75–94; cf. also Christian Rath, „Freiheit ist ansteckend", September 23 2009, https://taz.de/!576006/ (30.8.2022). A free media landscape constitutes one of these essential preconditions.

freedom to hold and to express opinions without interference, rejecting both state and private interference.[37] The question of whether and to what extent art. 19 ICCPR also covers freedom of the media was raised explicitly in two complaints under the 1st Optional Protocol,[38] but both complaints were dismissed as inadmissible.[39] In its General Comment on article 19, the Human Rights Committee has taken a clear position though, stating that "a free, uncensored and unhindered press or other media is essential in any society to ensure freedom of opinion and expression and (…) constitutes one of the cornerstones of a democratic society."[40] The right to access media reporting is seen by the Committee as a corresponding right of the public[41] and is closely linked to the right to vote and the participation in public affairs.[42] The Comment also stresses the rights of media users of ethnic and linguistic minorities and calls upon states to encourage an independent and diverse media.[43] In relation to public broadcasting, the Committee demands the independence of the media particularly editorial freedom, and warns of influencing the media via their funding mechanisms.[44]

The report also elaborates on possible restrictions on freedom of the media according to article 19 para. 3 ICCPR. At the beginning, the General Comment makes clear that a reversion between norm and exception is not allowed.[45] It also stresses that the restricions must be provided by law and must stay within the borders drawn by article 19 para. 3 ICCPR.[46] The endangerment of

37 See *Taylor*, Article 19: Freedom of Expression, in: Taylor, A Commentary on the International Covenant on Civil and Political Rights, Cambridge 2020, p. 538, 542 et seq.

38 Optional Protocol to the International Covenant on Civil and Political Rights, Adopted and opened for signature, ratification and accession by General Assembly resolution 2200A (XXI) of 16 December 1966, https://www.ohchr.org/Documents/ProfessionalInterest/ccpr-one.pdf (30.8.2022).

39 *UN Human Rights Committee*, A Newspaper Publishing Company v. Trinidad and Tobago, Communication No. 360/1989, 14.7.1989, CCPR/C/36/D/360/1989 und *UN Human Rights Committee,* A Publication and a Printing Company v. Trinidad and Tobago, Communication No. 361/1989, 14.7.1989, CCPR/C/36/D/361/1989.

40 *UN Human Rights Committee*, General Comment No. 34, 12.9.2011, CCPR/C/GC/34, p. 3; cf. also communication No. 1128/2002, Marques v. Angola, Views, 29 March 2005.

41 *UN Human Rights Committee*, General Comment No. 34, 12.9.2011, CCPR/C/GC/34, p. 4; cf. also communication No. 1334/2004, Mavlonov and Sa'di v. Uzbekistan.

42 *UN Human Rights Committee*, General Comment No. 34, 12.9.2011, CCPR/C/GC/34, p. 5.

43 *UN Human Rights Committee*, General Comment No. 34, 12.9.2011, CCPR/C/GC/34, p. 4.

44 *UN Human Rights Committee*, General Comment No. 34, 12.9.2011, CCPR/C/GC/34, p. 4; see also Concluding observations on Republic of Moldova (CCPR/CO/75/MDA).

45 *UN Human Rights Committee*, General Comment No. 34, 12.9.2011, CCPR/C/GC/34, p. 5.

46 *UN Human Rights Committee*, General Comment No. 34, 12.9.2011, CCPR/C/GC/34, p. 5 et seq.

journalists because of their activities is adressed explicitly by the Comment.[47] The scope of protection includes full-time reporters as well as bloggers.[48] An essential part of the protection of article 19 according to the Comment consists of the "limited journalistic privilege not to disclose information sources".[49] The Comment calls for states to prosecute the perpetrators and to grant victims and (in the case of death) their bereaved an appropriate form of redress.[50] Special attention is drawn to restrictions due to national security.[51] The Comment admonishes that treason laws and other similar provisions may not be used as a means to suppress the dissemination of information by journalists.[52] Concerning the principle of proportionality, the Committee highlights that public debate in a democratic society especially calls for free and unhindered media coverage.[53] It therefore critizes laws punishing the criticism of public figures,[54] the disrespect for authority,[55] flags and symbols and the defamation of the head of state,[56] the protection of the honour of public officials[57] and the prohibition of criticism of institutions such as the administration and the army.[58] The Committee clearly points out that punishing a media outlet, publisher or journalist only on account of critical reporting on the government or the political system can *never* be considered a necessary restricion of article 19 ICCPR.[59] The ECtHR has further articulated the crucial role of the media as

47 *UN Human Rights Committee*, General Comment No. 34, 12.9.2011, CCPR/C/GC/34, p. 6.

48 Ibid., p. 11.

49 Ibid., p. 11; Concluding observations on Kuwait (CCPR/CO/69/KWT).

50 Ibid.; Communication No. 1353/2005, Njaru v. Cameroon; Concluding Observations on Nicaragua (CCPR/C/NIC/CO/3); Concluding Observations on Tunisia (CCPR/C/TUN/CO/5); Concluding Observations on the Syrian Arab Republic (CCPR/CO/84/SYR); Concluding Observations on Colombia (CCPR/CO/80/COL); Concluding Observations on Georgia (CCPR/C/GEO/CO/3); Concluding Observations on Guyana (CCPR/C/79/Add.121).

51 *UN Human Rights Committee*, General Comment No. 34, 12.9.2011, CCPR/C/GC/34, p. 7 et seq.

52 Cf. also Concluding Observations on Hong Kong (CCPR/C/HKG/CO/2); Concluding Observations on the Russian Federation (CCPR/CO/79/RUS).

53 *UN Human Rights Committee*, General Comment No. 34, 12.9.2011, CCPR/C/GC/34, p. 8 et seq.; Communication No. 1180/2003, Bodrozic v. Serbia and Montenegro, Views adopted on 31 October 2005.

54 See Communication No. 1180/2003, Bodrozic v. Serbia and Montenegro, Views adopted on 31 October 2005; Communication No. 1128/2002, Marques v. Angola.

55 Concluding observations on Honduras (CCPR/C/HND/CO/1).

56 See concluding observations on Zambia (CCPR/ZMB/CO/3), para.25.

57 Concluding observations on Costa Rica (CCPR/C/CRI/CO/5), para. 11.

58 See ibid.; Concluding Observations on Tunisia (CCPR/C/TUN/CO/5), para. 91.

59 *UN Human Rights Committee*, General Comment No. 34, 12.9.2011, CCPR/C/GC/34, p. 11; Concluding Observations on Peru (CCPR/CO/70/PER). This is also confirmed for

a *public watchdog* for public debate, especially when public debate itself is at stake. In contrast to the ECtHR, the Committee explicitly rejects the margin of appreciation doctrine,[60] a constant in the ECtHR's jurisprudence. It seems as if the Committee fears that states could use this doctrine to argue non-interference in domestic affairs, a traditional argument against human rights, and the doctrine would make it easier for violator states to escape the pressure to justify their actions.

Concerning the transformation of the media landscape, the General Comment, which originates from 2011, points out that States parties should foster the independence of new media and ensure access of individuals to it. In this context, the Committee reaffirms its rejection of state media monopolies and calls upon states to promote plurality of the media and be careful with government subsidies.[61] Discussing a possible regulation of the spread of fake news on the internet, the Comment remarks that no general prohibition of expressions of an erroneous opinion or an incorrect interpretation of past events could become appropriate. The Comment also calls it *normally incompatible* with article 19 para. 3 to restrict the entry of a foreign journalist to a country, to hinder journalists to travel out of a country and to restrict the journalist's freedom of movement within the country.[62] The fact that some reporters due to the closed borders on account of the COVID-19 pandemia can not leave the country they stay in, may therefore get in conflict with the right provided by article 19 ICCPR.

In addition to art. 19 ICCPR, other human rights also provide protective effect for journalists, such as the prohibition of torture.[63] The protection against arbitrary killing under art. 6 ICCPR can also become relevant for journalists as the case of the Slovak journalist Ján Kuciak exemplifies. Kuciak had uncovered connections between the mafia and the head of government, Robert Fico,

---

the publication on a website, cf. Concluding observations on the Syrian Arab Republic (CCPR/CO/84/SYR).

60 *UN Human Rights Committee*, General Comment No. 34, 12.9.2011, CCPR/C/GC/34, p. 9; Communication No. 511/1992, Ilmari Länsman, et al. v. Finland, Views adopted on 14 October 1993.

61 *UN Human Rights Committee*, General Comment No. 34, 12.9.2011, CCPR/C/GC/34, p. 10.

62 *UN Human Rights Committee*, General Comment No. 34, 12.9.2011, CCPR/C/GC/34, p. 11.

63 *UN General Assembly*, Convention against Torture and Other Cruel, Inhuman or Degrading Treatment or Punishment, 10.12.1984, A/RES/39/46. For the interaction between article 19 and other Covenant provisions see Taylor, Article 19: Freedom of Expression, in: Taylor, A Commentary on the International Covenant on Civil and Political Rights, Cambridge 2020, p. 540 et seq.

and probably fell victim to a contract killing together with his fiancée.[64] The right to personal freedom under art. 9 of the ICCPR and the protection against arbitrary arrest are also sadly topical, as the imprisonment of journalists after the attempted coup in Turkey shows.[65] In this context, the interpretation of *arbitrariness* represents a crucial issue. As a rule, the detentions are based on a legal provision since the journalists are regularly accused of committing criminal offences. Given that autocratic states use police investigations as a tool against critical journalists, it cannot be said that these deprivations of liberty are not arbitrary simply because they are in accordance with legal provisions. The Committee also points to the chilling effect of measures that create a situation of uncertainty or intimidation for journalists, as in Sri Lanka where the case of a journalist accused of criminal defamation of high officials was pending for six years.[66]

Finally, the right to privacy under article 17 ICCPR functions as a catch-all right in the sense of freedom of decision and action.[67] For the work of journalists, the protection of the home and correspondence, but also of the spoken word, can become crucial. In cases where a journalist is imprisoned, the extensive adjudication practice of the Human Rights Committee on article 17 concerning the treatment of prisoners becomes relevant as well.[68]

2.1.2 Regional Protection

2.1.2.1 *Africa*

The global protection provided by the ICCPR is complemented by regional human rights treaties. In Africa, starting from the Banjul Charter (1981)[69] a separate system of regional human rights protection with specific characteristics has developed.[70] Article 9 of the Banjul Charter guarantees every individual the right to receive information (para. 1) and to express and disseminate his opinions within the laws and regulations (para. 2). The African Court has dealt with

64 See *Reuters*, Slovak journalist's murder was contract killing, prosecutor says, https://www.reuters.com/article/us-slovakia-crime-police-idUSKBN1H2207 (30.8.2022).

65 Cf. Turkey sentences 25 journalists to jail for 'coup links', https://www.bbc.com/news/world-europe-43337655 (30.8.2022).

66 *UN Human Rights Committee*, Kankanamge v. Sri Lanka, CCPR/C/81/D/909/2000, 27 July 2004 [9.4].

67 See *Schiedermair*, Der Schutz des Privaten als internationales Grundrecht, p. 95 et seq.

68 Cf., for example, *UN Human Rights Committee*, Pinkney v. Canada, Communication No. Nr. 27/1977, 29 October 1981, CCPR/C/14/D/27/1977, 35.

69 The African Charter on Human and Peoples' Rights was concluded in Nairobi on 27 June 1981 and came into force on 21 October 1986, UN Treaty Series No. 26363, 1988, p. 217.

70 Cf. *Manisuli Ssenyonjo* (ed.), The African Regional Human Rights System, 2011.

article 9 in its fundamental judgement of December 5th, 2014.[71] The Applicant had been imprisoned for twelve months and sentenced to a US $3,000 fine, $9000 damages and $500 court costs for having written an article in which he accused the Prosecutor of Burkina Faso of corruption. The Court systematically analyzed article 9 referring to the UN Human Rights Committee, the jurisdiction of the European Court of Human Rights, the jurisprudence of the Inter-American Court and the statements of the African Commission on Human and Peoples' Rights.[72] It assumed that the restrictions based on the Burkina Faso Penal Code had been "provided by law" within international standards. The Court acknowledged that *the honour and reputation of a person or a profession* provide a legitimate purpose.[73] In this case, the Court saw the honour of Magistrates, jurors and assessors in the performance of their duties as a *perfectly legitimate objective*.[74] The focus on the judgement laid on whether the restrictions were necessary. The Court referred to the context of a democratic society and to the fact that according to article 19 para. 3 of the Charter, the enjoyment of freedom entails duties and responsibilities as well. As a guideline for the necessitiy test, the Court invokes questions the African Commission has posed, namely if a less restrictive solution exists and if the restriction destroys the essence of the right in question.[75] In line with the Commission, the Court observes that a *public figure* like the Prosecutor must endure a higher degree of criticism.[76] Quoting the ECtHR, the Inter-American Court, the UN Human Rights Commission and the UN Human Rights Committee as authorities, the African Court notes that defamation constitutes an offense punishable by imprisonment in Burkina Faso that can in general and in the specific case not be considered a necessary limitation to freedom of expression.[77] The Court

71 See African Court on Human and Peoples' Rights, Lohé Issa Konaté v. Burkina Faso, 004/2013, December 5th 2014, https://www.african-court.org/afc_home/ (30.8.2022).

72 Cf. African Court on Human and Peoples' Rights, Lohé Issa Konaté v. Burkina Faso, 004/2013, December 5th 2014, https://www.african-court.org/afc_home/ (30.8.2022), p. 33 et seq.

73 Cf. Cf. African Court on Human and Peoples' Rights, Lohé Issa Konaté v. Burkina Faso, 004/2013, December 5th 2014, https://www.african-court.org/afc_home/ (30.8.2022), p. 136 et seq.

74 See African Court on Human and Peoples' Rights, Lohé Issa Konaté v. Burkina Faso, 004/2013, December 5th 2014, https://www.african-court.org/afc_home/ (30.8.2022), p. 36.

75 Cf. African Court on Human and Peoples' Rights, Lohé Issa Konaté v. Burkina Faso, 004/2013, December 5th 2014, https://www.african-court.org/afc_home/ (30.8.2022), p. 39.

76 See African Court on Human and Peoples' Rights, Lohé Issa Konaté v. Burkina Faso, 004/2013, December 5th 2014, https://www.african-court.org/afc_home/ (30.8.2022), p. 42.

77 Cf. African Court on Human and Peoples' Rights, Lohé Issa Konaté v. Burkina Faso, 004/2013, December 5th 2014, https://www.african-court.org/afc_home/ (30.8.2022), p. 44 et seq.

points to very exceptional circumstances in which it might consider imprisonment necessary, e.g. incitement to international crimes, public incitement to hatred, or discrimination or violence against a person or group on account of their race, colour, religion or nationality.[78] Finally, the Court declared the preceding judgements of the Burkina Faso Courts disproportionate and therefore came to an infringement of article 9 and 19 of the Charter. The Court unanimously ordered Burkina Faso to amend its legislation on defamation to make it compatible with international law.[79]

The decision shows that the African Court is willing to offer protection for journalists in danger. However, the African human rights system faces the great challenge of a high standard of human rights codified in substantive law on the one hand and a sobering reality of the human rights situation in Africa on the other. The enthusiasm associated with the commencement of the work of the African Human Rights Court in Arusha has gradually given way to increasing disillusionment in view of the fact that African states are increasingly refusing to cooperate with the Court.[80] The Corona pandemic has aggravated the situation for journalists in Africa severely as authoritarian states are trying to suppress information concerning the virus and the policy implemented (or not implemented) in the context of the pandemic.[81]

2.1.2.2 *America*

For Central and South America, the American Convention on Human Rights (ACHR)[82] contains a detailed regulation on freedom of expression within article 13. The media are mentioned in article 13 para. 3 as possible victims of abusive control by state authorities or private individuals and thus expressly included in the scope of protection. Prior censorship is prohibited in article 13 para. 2, where the respect for the rights or reputations of others, the protection of national security, public order, public health or morals are enumarated as reasons for limitations. In its case law, the Inter-American Court of Human

78 Cf. African Court on Human and Peoples' Rights, Lohé Issa Konaté v. Burkina Faso, 004/2013, December 5th 2014, https://www.african-court.org/afc_home/ (30.8.2022), p. 165.

79 See African Court on Human and Peoples' Rights, Lohé Issa Konaté v. Burkina Faso, 004/2013, December 5th 2014, https://www.african-court.org/afc_home/ (30.8.2022), p. 49.

80 Cf. Africa's Court of Human Rights on the brink of collapse, https://www.dw.com/en/africas-court-of-human-rights-on-the-brink-of-collapse/a-53776946 (30.8.2022).

81 See https://www.dw.com/en/is-the-coronavirus-killing-press-freedom-in-africa/a-53061431 (30.8.2022).

82 Cf. American Convention on Human Rights, adopted at the Inter-American Specialized Conference on Human Rights, San José, Costa Rica, 22 November 1969, https://www.cidh.oas.org/basicos/english/basic3.american%20convention.htm (30.8.2022).

Rights has emphasized the complementary nature of the rights of article 13 as the individual right to expression implies a collective right to receive any information whatsoever and to have access to the thoughts expressed by others.[83] The Court sees the crucial role of the media in this process[84] and builds the bridge to article 10 ECHR when linking freedom of expression with the needs of a democratic society.[85] The Court points out that despite the different wordings of article 13 ACHR and article 10 ECHR concerning limitations, both norms require restrictions to be strictly proportional and tailored to the accomplishment of the legislative goal.[86]

In its jurisprudence, the Court has always made clear that the individual journalist is in the centre of protection of article 13 ACHR. The protection of freedom of expression is granted to nationals of a state member of the Organization of American States (OAS) and to journalists with another citizenship acting within the territorial scope of the OAS countries as well.[87] In a ruling of 2 July 2004, the Court ordered Costa Rica to pay US $20,000 damages to a journalist for his criminal prosecution. The journalist had written a series of articles citing European press reports alleging corruption by a former Costa Rican diplomat. The newspaper and the journalist had been ordered to pay the diplomat a fine equivalent to 120 days' wages and US $200,000 in damages. The Inter-American Human Rights Court stated that the prosecution of the journalist violated article 13 ACHR and pointed to the ECtHR's jurisprudence that a public figure (such as the diplomat in this case) would have to endure a higher risk of being criticized in public.[88] In this context, the Court explicitly referred to its own jurisprudence that also upholds "a reduced margin for any restriction on political debates or on debates on matters of public interest."[89]

---

83 Inter-American Court of Human Rights, Advisory Opinion OC-5/85 of November 13, 1985, para. 30 et seq.

84 Inter-American Court of Human Rights, Advisory Opinion OC-5/85 of November 13, 1985, para. 34 ("It is the mass media that make the exercise of freedom of expression a reality."). And Inter-American Court of Human Rights, Ivcher Bronstein Case, Judgement of February 6, 2001, Series C No. 74, para. 150 ("[Keeping society informed] is an indispensable requirement to enable society to enjoy full freedom.").

85 See ibid., p. 11 et seq.

86 For a comparison of the two norms see *Eduardo Andrés Bertoni*, The Inter-American Court of Human Rights and the European Court of Human Rights: A Dialogue on Freedom of Expression Standards, European Human Law Review Issue 3, 2009, p. 332.

87 Cf. Resolution of the Inter-American Commission on Human Rights in the case of the US citizen Stephen Schmidt, Nº 17/84, Case Nº 9178, COSTA RICA, October 3, 1984.

88 Inter-American Court of Human Rights, Case of Herrera-Ulloa v. Costa Rica, Judgment of July 2, 2004, https://www.corteidh.or.cr/docs/casos/articulos/seriec_107_ing.pdf (30.8.2022), p. 67 et seq.

89 Ibid., para. 127.

The Committee to Protect Journalists who wrote an *amicus curiae* brief in the case welcomed the decision of the Inter-American Court of Human Rights.[90]

The jurisprudence of the Court has always made an effort to strengthen free journalism in Central and South America.[91] In the case "The Last Temptation of Christ"[92] concerning the prohibition of prior censorship, the Court's decision led to an exemplary constitutional reform in Chile.[93] In a case presented to the Court by the Inter-American Commission on Human Rights on July 16, 2019, a judgement of the Court is yet to be made:[94] The Colombian journalist Jineth Bedoya had been abducted, tortured and raped in 2000. She was supposed to interview a member of a far-right paramilitary group in the Modelo prison in Bogotá in the course of an investigation of arms trafficking network operating out of the Modelo prison.[95] The promised interview turned out to be a trap. The journalist was drugged and driven outside of town where she was beaten and gang-raped. Her attackers told Bedoya that the violence inflicted on her was meant to be a message to the Colombian press. While three of her attackers have been sentenced so far, Bedoya, who has been pursuing justice for more than 20 years and now campaigns against sexual violence, argues that others were involved, including state officials. Her hearing in front of the Inter-American Court of Human Rights was accompanied by great public attention as the procedure is seen as a possible precedent for sexual violence victims in Colombia.[96] In the hearing, the Colombia state official apologized for the crimes committed,[97] but shortly after Colombia's representatives withdrew from the hearing on the case declaring five of the six judges biased.[98] The

90 See https://cpj.org/2004/08/court-overturns-costa-rican-defamation-sentence-cp/ (30.8.2022).

91 Cf. for example the list of cases in http://oea.org/en/iachr/expression/jurisprudence/si_decisions_court.asp (30.8.2022).

92 Cf. Inter-American Court of Human Rights, Olmedo-Bustos et al. v. Chile, Judgment of February 5, 2001, https://corteidh.or.cr/docs/casos/articulos/seriec_73_ing.pdf (30.8.2022).

93 See http://oea.org/en/iachr/expression/jurisprudence/si_decisions_court.asp (30.8.2022).

94 Cf. https://www.oas.org/en/iachr/expression/showarticle.asp?artID=1148&lID=1 (30.8.2022).

95 Cf. https://thewire.in/world/colombia-journalist-jineth-bedoya-victim-sexual-violence-quest-justice (30.8.2022).

96 See https://www.theguardian.com/global-development/2021/mar/15/jineth-bedoya-colombian-journalist-sexual-violence (30.8.2022).

97 Cf. https://www.globaltimes.cn/page/202103/1219354.shtml (30.8.2022).

98 See https://cpj.org/tags/jinethbedoya/ (30.8.2022).

process shows that the fight for free journalism in Central and South America is often closely connected to the fight against corruption with all its highs and lows[99] and that the endangerment of journalists reporting on it is serious.

2.1.2.3 *Asia*

There is no comprehensive regional treaty on human rights protection for Asia, which is owed to the enormous political and cultural heterogeneity of the continent.[100] The League of Arab states adopted the Arab Charter on Human Rights in 2004,[101] yet the states maintain a sceptical approach to international human rights protection. The intransparent adopting process of the Statute of the envisaged Arab Court of Human Rights and the fact that the Court shall only be open to human rights claims of state parties and not of individuals show that the Arab Charter is not an effective step ahead for human rights in Asia.[102] The same is true for the ASEAN Human Rights Declaration adopted at the 21st ASEAN Summit in 2012[103] with the ASEAN Intergovernmental Commission on Human Rights (AICHR)[104] as a framework institution.

2.1.2.4 *Europe*

In Europe, the media are protected by a network of fundamental rights watched over by the ECtHR, the CJEU and national courts.[105] In addition to the case law of national constitutional courts, the ECtHR has developed a differentiated jurisprudence around article 10 ECHR, whereas the CJEU has not yet had the chance to develop more in-depth case law concerning article 11 of the Charter

---

99 Cf. https://www.oas.org/JURIDICO/spanish/RepoBM.htm (30.8.2022).

100 Cf. *Schiedermair*, Der Schutz des Privaten als internationales Grundrecht, p. 102 f.

101 For the text see https://digitallibrary.un.org/record/551368 (30.8.2022); *Wael Allam*, The Arab Charter on Human Rights: Main Features, Arab Law Quarterly 2014, p. 40.

102 Cf. *International Commission of Jurists*, The Arab Court of Human Rights: A Flawed Statute for an Ineffective Court, Geneva 2015; Sandkühler, MenschenRechtsMagazin 1/2012, p. 5 et seq.

103 See ASEAN Human Rights Declaration, November 19th, 2012, https://asean.org/asean-human-rights-declaration/ (30.8.2022). See also the reaction of the UN High Commissioner for Human Rights, https://news.un.org/en/story/2012/11/426012 (30.8.2022) and Doyle, The ASEAN Human Rights Declaration and the Implications of Recent Southeast Asian Initiatives in Human Rights Institution-Building and Standard-Setting, International & Comparative Law Quarterly Vol. 63, Issue 1, January 2014, pp. 67–101.

104 Cf. https://aichr.org (30.8.2022).

105 See *Voßkuhle*, 'Pyramid or Mobile? – Human Rights Protection by the European Constitutional Courts' Opening of the Judicial Year 2014 at the European Court of Human Rights Strasbourg, 31 January 2014, https://www.echr.coe.int/Documents/Dialogue_2014_ENG.pdf, p. 36.

of Fundmantal Rights of the European Union, but so far has rather focused on the right to privacy and data protection.

2.1.2.4.1 European Convention on Human Rights

2.1.2.4.1.1 *Freedom of Expression and the Media*

Art. 10 ECHR guarantees freedom of expression, information, the press and broadcasting. Although the press is not mentioned explicitly in article 10,[106] the ECtHR has consistently emphasised the fundamental importance of a free press for democratic societies in view of the function of the press as a *public watchdog*[107] in its extensive jurisprudence on art. 10 ECHR and has interpreted its scope of protection broadly.[108] In addition to journalistic research,[109] editorial secrecy[110] and the protection of sources,[111] the organisational framework conditions for the press and broadcasting[112] are also covered by the protection of art. 10 ECHR. All parties involved in the production and dissemination of the press also enjoy the protection of art. 10 ECHR.[113] Non-governmental organisations that contribute to the formation of public opinion can also invoke art. 10 ECHR in individual cases.[114] Journalistic broadcasting contributions are treated according to the principles developed for freedom of the press[115] with the ECtHR emphasising the particularly intensive effect of audiovisual content on the viewer.[116] In view of the broad interpretation of the scope of protection of art. 10 ECHR and the dynamic interpretation generally characteristic of the ECtHR's case law, journalistic contributions in all traditional and digital media are covered by the protection of art. 10 ECHR.[117] This is particularly relevant

106 Only article 6 para. 1 ECHR explicitly mentions the press which can be excluded from a trial under certain circumstances.

107 See, for example, ECtHR, 27 March 1996 – 17488/90 – Goodwin, para. 39.

108 Cf. *Schiedermair*, in: *Pabel/Schmahl* (ed.), Internationaler Kommentar zur EMRK, art. 10 para. 67 et seq.

109 See ECtHR, 77551/01, 25 April 2006, para. 52.

110 Cf. ECtHR, 20477/05, 27 November 2007.

111 See ECtHR 38224/03, 14 September 2010 – Sanoma Uitgevers, para. 50; ECtHR, 27 March 1996 – 17488/90 – Goodwin, para. 39.

112 Cf. ECtHR, 17 September 2009 – 13936/02 – Manole a. o. v. MDA, para. 104 et seq.

113 See ECtHR, 11 January 2000 – 31457/96 – News Verlags-GmbH & Co. KG v. Austria, para. 40.

114 See ECtHR v. 14.4.2009 – 37374/05 – Society for Civil Liberties, para 27; see also ECtHR v. 22.4.2013 – 48876/08 – Animal Defenders International, para 103.

115 Cf. ECtHR 23 September 1994 – 15890/89 – Jersild.

116 See ECtHR 17 September 2009 – 13936/02 – Manole, para. 97.

117 See, in this respect, the transfer of the protection of "correspondence" to the interception of telecommunication ECHR 6 September 1978 – 5029/71 – Klass et al, para. 49 et seq.; see ECtHR 17 May 2016 – 33677/10 and 52340/10 – Fürst-Pfeiffer v. Austria (on the obligations

as critical journalists in autocratic states are often driven out of conventional daily newspapers and shift their activities to digital platforms.

The core component of press freedom is the protection of press secrecy, i.e., the protection of journalistic sources of information, as the ECtHR fundamentally stated in the 1996 *Goodwin v. United Kingdom* judgment.[118] If a state requires a journalist to disclose his or her source of information, the ECHR requires the state to claim an overriding public interest.[119] The Court expressly recognizes the protection of national security as a possible justification for interventions in press freedom, but called for an intensive proportionality test in each individual case.[120] The privileged treatment of journalists when balancing freedom of the media with other legal interests is subject to the condition, that the journalists concerned have obtained the information in good faith, on the basis of carefully researched facts and in accordance with the standards of journalistic ethics.[121] The responsibility associated with the exercise of freedom of the press, which finds a normative basis in the wording of art. 10 (2) (which refers to "duties"), applies not only to journalists but also to publishers.[122] The ECtHR grants freedom of opinion and freedom of the press particularly broad scopes in cases where a *debate of public interest* is involved.[123] The interpretation of the *public interest* therefore is a central element of the proportionality test and has the power to influence the outcome of the decision. The Court thus clearly regards the rights enshrined in art. 10 as freedoms committed to democratic decision-making. Accordingly, it interprets these freedoms more narrowly if it is only a matter of satisfying the curiosity of a particular readership about the private life of celebrities.[124] That way, the Court ties a strong knot between freedom of the media and their function

of the publisher of an internet news portal), para. 26; ECtHR v. 5 October 2017 – 21272/12 – Becker v. Norway (on the protection of sources), para. 5, 42, 59, 65 et seq.

118 See ECtHR, 27 March 1996 – 17488/90 – Goodwin, para. 39. See also Grabenwarter, Article 10 – Freedom of Expression, European Convention on Human Rights, Commentary, 2014, p. 286 et seq.

119 Ibid.

120 Cf. ECtHR, 9 February 1995 – 16616/90 – Vereniging Weekblad Bluf! v. Netherlands, para. 36; ECtHR, 14 September 2010 – 38224/03 – Sanoma Uitgevers, para. 59 et seq.

121 Cf., for example, ECtHR, 1 July 1997 – 20834/92, Oberschlick (no. 2) v. Austria, para. 29; ECtHR 23 September 1994 – 15890/89 – Jersild v. Danmark (GC), para. 31.

122 ECtHR, 8 July 1999 – 26682/95 – Sürek v. Turkey (GC), para. 63; ECtHR 15 January 2009 – 20985/05 – Orban a.o. v. France, para. 47.

123 Cf., for example, ECtHR 2 October 2008 – 36109/03 – Leroy v. France, para. 41; 15 December 2009 – 821/03 – Financial Times Ltd. et al., para. 59.

124 ECtHR, 24 June 2004 – 59320/00 – Von Hannover v. Germany – para. 65.

for a democratic system. Whether the phenomenon of citizen journalism[125] falls under the general guarantee of freedom of expression or is subject to the special protection of media freedoms is not yet clear. The fact that the ECtHR interprets article 10 with a strong connection to its democratic function speaks in favor of extending the special protection to citizen journalists as well. Yet citizen journalists would have to fulfill the duties imposed on professional journalists as well to enjoy the media privilege relevant for the balancing in the proportionality test. Whether this is an adequate and realistic approach is not yet clear.

Art. 10 not only contains a right to respect that prohibits state interference but also a duty to protect, which obliges the state to protect press and broadcasting enterprises and journalists if they are exposed to attacks, e.g., on account of their critical reporting.[126] Generally, the Court grants the national authorities a certain margin of appreciation.[127] The state interventions in the Polish and Hungarian media landscape show the explosive nature of the question of the extent Member States have a positive duty to protect diversity in broadcasting from article 10 ECHR.

2.1.2.4.1.2 *Right to Liberty and Security and Right to a Fair Trail*

The cases against journalists in Turkey illustrate the importance of the right to liberty and security under art. 5 ECHR for journalistic work. Freedom in para. 1 entails freedom of physical movement,[128] paras. 2–4 list specific rights of detained persons, such as the right to know the reasons for an arrest. In the proceedings in Turkey, the state authorities often claim a link to national security, which entails the application of special national secrecy rules, making it difficult to follow up on the state's interference with the rights of the detainees.[129] The consequences for the journalists are an excessively long period of pre-trial detention and only limited monitoring of the conditions of detention.

125 For the term see https://www.britannica.com/topic/citizen-journalism (30.8.2022); *Axel Springer Akademie*, Bürgerjournalismus oder partizipativer Journalismus, https://www.axel-springer-akademie.de/info/buergerjournalismus-partizipativer-journalismus.html (30.8.2022).

126 Cf. ECtHR 16 March 2000 – 23144/93 – Özgür Gündem v. Turkey, para. 42 et seq.; ECtHR, 14 September 2010 – 2668/07 – Dink, para. 106.

127 See *Grabenwarter*, Article 10 – Freedom of Expression, European Convention on Human Rights, Commentary, 2014, p. 292 et seq. For the applicable margin of appreciation see ECtHR 12 September 2011 – 28995/06 – Polomo Sánchez et al. (GC), para. 53 et seq.

128 See ECtHR 2 August 2001 – 44955/98 – Mancini, para. 16.

129 Cf. Scott Griffen, Let Turkey's Journalists Report Freely, https://euobserver.com/stakeholders/150385 (30.8.2022).

The cases in Turkey also show the importance of the right to a fair trial. Art. 6 para. 1 concretises the fair trial principle through individual rights, such as the right to be tried by an independent and impartial court, the right to a public trial and the right to be tried within a reasonable time. At the same time, the rights of the defendant in para. 3 are violated, for example, by limited contact with a lawyer. Lastly, the presumption of innocence guaranteed by article 6 para. 2 can become undermined by a deliberately controlled public prejudgement of journalists.

2.1.2.4.1.3 *Emergency: Art. 15 ECHR*

The threat to journalists in Turkey raises the question of whether and under what conditions restrictions on journalistic freedoms are possible in the case of a national emergency. In this case art. 15 para. 1 ECHR allows interventions that could normally not be justified under the limits of the individual Convention right. The provision has become practically relevant after the failed coup attempt on 15 July 2016 in Turkey. In the course of the investigations against the masterminds of the coup attempt, numerous journalists were imprisoned and the government also used the coup attempt as a pretext to crack down on opposition individuals and groups.[130] The ECtHR has given its opinion on the legal consequences of a state of public emergency in the cases of *Altan v. Turkey* and *Alpay v. Turkey*.[131] The Court ruled that the arrests of Mehmet Altan and Sahin Alpay violated article 5 and article 10 ECHR, stressing that "the existence of a 'public emergency threatening the life of a nation' must not serve as a pretext for limiting freedom of political debate, which is at the very core of the concept of a democratic society".[132] The ECtHR stated that mere criticism of the government could not attract criminal sanctions, let alone accusations of membership of a terrorist organisation or attempting to overthrow the government.[133] The Court stressed that the detention of journalists prior to trial is only permissible in exceptional circumstances and after all other means have been exhausted and points to the *chilling effect* on the social climate of the whole society.[134] In both judgments, the ECtHR has made it very clear that even special circumstances such as a public emergency do not allow disproportionate and arbitrary restrictions of journalistic freedoms. The

130 Vgl. etwa *Can Dündar*, A Gift of God for Erdogan, https://www.dw.com/en/a-gift-of-god-for-erdogan/av-49599913 (30.8.2022).

131 See ECtHR 20 March 2018 – 13237/17 – Altan and 16538/17 – Alpay.

132 ECtHR 20 March 2018 – 13237/17 – Altan, para. 210.

133 Cf. ECtHR 20 March 2018 – 13237/17 – Altan, para. 211.

134 Ibid., para 212.

clarity of the Court's ruling is hard to beat and constitutes a landmark decision for freedom of individual journalists in Europe.

2.1.2.4.2 EU Fundamental Rights Charter

Unlike the ECHR, the Charter of Fundamental Rights of the European Union (CFR) explicitly regulates freedom of the media in art. 11 para. 2 thus taking into account the importance of the media in the modern information society.[135] The term 'media freedom' indicates that all types of media are covered and signals openness to future developments.[136] Furthermore, media plurality is explicitly postulated as a basic prerequisite of a functioning democracy in article 11 para. 2 CFR. Art. 11 CFR entails positive obligations as well, e.g., the freedom of the media has to be balanced against the right to privacy.[137] The question of positive obligations of the member states to guarantee a diverse free media landscape as the basis of their obligations under art. 2 Treaty on European Union will turn up in practice if the restructuring of the media landscapes in Hungary and Poland becomes relevant before the European Court of Justice or the German Federal Constitutional Court.[138] At the same time, the question arises which procedures can be used at the Union level to exert pressure on member states whose media landscapes can no longer be described as diverse in the sense of article 11 para. 2 CFR. The fact that the competence for the media rests with the member states is in a certain tension with the obligations of the member states under art. 2 TEU and art. 11 CFR.

2.2 *Decisions of International Organisations*

In view of the threat to journalists worldwide, international organisations have sounded the alarm. Numerous resolutions at international and European level explicitly deal with the protection of journalists. From a legal perspective, the resolutions represent non-binding *soft law* of primarily political significance. Yet their importance should not be underestimated as they make problems

135 Apart from that, the scope and the meaning of article 11 CFR are parallel to art. 10 ECHR according to article 52 para. 3 CFR, cf. also Lock, art. 11, in: Kellerbauer/Klammert/Tomkin (ed)., The EU Treaties and the Charter of Fundamental Rights, 2019, para 1.

136 See *Bernsdorff*, in: Meyer/Hölscheidt, GrCh, art. 11, para. 18.

137 Cf. Lock, art. 11, in: Kellerbauer/Klammert/Tomkin (ed)., The EU Treaties and the Charter of Fundamental Rights, 2019, para 7.

138 In its decision Right to be Forgotten II of 27.11.2019, https://www.bundesverfassungsgericht.de/SharedDocs/Pressemitteilungen/EN/2019/bvg19-084.html (30.8.2022) the German Constitutional Court applies the CFR as a standard for the fundamental rights review in the area determined by Union law, which may also lead to an interpretation of Art. 11 GRC by the German Constitutional Court in the future.

visible to the world public, and in the course of time, standards formulated in soft law can become legally binding by becoming customary international law or by being incorporated into international treaties.[139] Besides, soft law can be used to interpret treaties and thus have an immediate practical effect.[140]

2.2.1 United Nations

At the global level, the Security Council of the United Nations, the General Assembly and the Human Rights Council have adopted a number of resolutions on the protection of journalists in recent years.[141] In resolutions 1738 (2006) and 2222 (2015), the Security Council has called for the protection of journalists in armed conflicts.[142] The General Assembly has highlighted attacks and acts of violence faced by journalists worldwide in resolution A/69/488[143] and urged member states to respect human rights obligations in the fight against terrorism in resolution A/70/489.[144] The Human Rights Council addressed the safety of journalists and condemned violent attacks on them in resolutions A/HRC/RES/21/12[145] and A/HRC/27/L.7.[146] On this basis, the United Nations tries to keep the protection of journalists in the awareness of the public worldwide. To foster this goal, the UN also declared the *International Day to End Impunity for Crimes against Journalists* on 2 November 2020 and called upon states to end the *existing culture of impunity* in this area.[147]

2.2.2 Council of Europe/Parliamentary Assembly

On a regional level, the Parliamentary Assembly of the Council of Europe has also addressed the threat to journalists in numerous political resolutions and, in that way, flanked the case law of the ECtHR. Resolution 2141 from 2017 follows up on the creation of a platform for the protection of journalists in 2015

139 For the nature and effects of soft law cf. *Schiedermair*, ZRP 2/2019, 48, 49 et seq.

140 Cf. v. *Arnauld*, Völkerrecht, para. 278.

141 See https://www.ohchr.org/EN/Issues/SafetyOfJournalists/Pages/resolutions.aspx (30.8.2022).

142 *UN Security Council*, Resolution 1738 (2006), 23 December 2006, *UN Security Council*, Resolution 2222 (2015), 27 May 2015, S/RES/1738; S/RES/2222.

143 *UN General Assembly*, The safety of journalists and the issue of impunity, 11 February 2015, A/RES/69/185.

144 *UN General Assembly*, Protection of human rights and fundamental freedoms while countering terrorism, 25 February 2016, A/RES/70/148.

145 *UN General Assembly Human Rights Council*, Safety of journalists, 9 October 2012, A/HRC/RES/21/12.

146 *UN General Assembly Human Rights Council*, The safety of journalists, 19 September 2014, A/HRC/27/L.7.

147 See https://en.unesco.org/commemorations/endimpunityday (30.8.2022).

and calls for action by designated Council of Europe member states in specific individual cases, such as the release of various named journalists in Turkey, Russia and Azerbaijan.[148] Another resolution from 2017 deals with political interference in independent journalists and media.[149] The resolution calls on member states to better protect the safety and freedom of journalists and the independence and diversity of the media requires political forces in member states to condemn targeted incitement against journalists and counter the growing distrust of the media.[150] Resolution 2254 (2019) addresses freedom of the media as a basic condition for democratic elections and calls on Member States to adopt strategies to protect their democratic elections from targeted manipulation and propaganda in the social media. The overall picture shows that the Council of Europe, and thus also the majority of the Council of Europe states, are aware of the dangers for the media landscape in Europe.

2.2.3 EU Commission

The EU supports the Council of Europe's efforts in protecting journalists.[151] Moreover, the European Parliament has issued its own Resolution on Strengthening Media Freedom: the Protection of Journalists in Europe, Hate Speech, Disinformation and the Role of Platforms,[152] which adresses the main legal concerns the EU is dealing with in various forms, e.g., the Digital Services Act and the Digital Markets Act.[153] For journalists, the fight against disinformation is of high importance. In the course of the pandemic, disinformation about the emergence and consequences of the COVID-19 virus was repeatedly put into the world and its existence denied.[154] The partly targeted disinformation campaigns also provide potential dangers for journalistic reporting, which depends on truthful information. The EU Commission has adopted a catalogue of measures to combat disinformation in connection with the

148 *EU Parliamentary Assembly,* Attacks against journalists and media freedom in Europe, 25 January 2017, Resolution 2141 (2017).

149 *EU Parliamentary Assembly,* Political influence over independent media and journalists, 29 July 2017, Resolution 2179 (2017).

150 See *EU Parliamentary Assembly,* Political influence over independent media and journalists, 29 July 2017, Resolution 2179 (2017) para. 7, 8.

151 Cf. https://eeas.europa.eu/delegations/council-europe/87859/safeguard-our-democracies-we-must-protect-journalists-world-day-end-impunity-crimes-against_en (30.8.2022).

152 *European Parliament,* 2020/2009 (INI), 25 November 2020, https://www.europarl.europa.eu/doceo/document/A-9-2020-0205_EN.html (06.05.2021).

153 See Fn. 34.

154 Cf. Spread of coronavirus fake news causes hundreds of deaths, https://www.dw.com/en/coronavirus-misinformation/a-54529310 (30.8.2022).

COVID-19 pandemic.[155] This includes, for example, the expansion of strategic communication within and outside the EU, better cooperation between the EU institutions, the achievement of greater transparency on online platforms and the strengthening of freedom of opinion.

2.3 *Monitoring and Procedural Enforcement*

The overview of the international legal protection of journalistic work and the political efforts to raise awareness of the difficult situation journalists find themselves in, inevitably raise the question of monitoring and enforcing the protection provided by international law. The procedural enforcement of human rights in general provides the greatest challenge in practice.[156] Even though the ICCPR is a binding international treaty that has been ratified by most states, procedural enforcement of the substantive standards formulated in the Covenant remains difficult. The obligation to report to the UN Human Rights Committee and the individual complaints procedure regulated in the 1st Optional Protocol to the Covenant offer procedural enforcement possibilities, but in practice their effects are limited. On a regional level, the ECHR and the ACHR provide comparably effective legal instruments in the form of the individual complaints giving citizens of a signatory state the opportunity to appeal after exhausting domestic legal remedies. This possibility explains the success of human rights protection by the ECtHR and the IACtHR and is also the reason why the system of individual complaint has become a global model for the enforcement of human rights standards. But even in Europe, the question of whether and to what extent ECtHR rulings in which the Court found violations of journalists' Convention rights actually led to the corresponding measures being lifted in the member state remains a matter of serious discussion.[157] Although one should not underestimate that international legal proceedings at least result in attacks against journalists receiving worldwide attention, the partly ineffective enforcement of the protection provided remains a matter of legal and political concern.

155 See *European Commission*, https://ec.europa.eu/info/sites/default/files/corona_fighting_disinformation.pdf (30.8.2022).

156 Cf. *Douglas Donoho*, Human Rights Enforcement in the Twenty-First Century, Georgia Journal of International and Comparative Law vol. 35 2006, p. 1.

157 Cf. the pesimistic assessment of *George Stafford*, The Implementation of Judgments of the European Court of Human Rights: Worse Than You Think – Part 2: The Hole in the Roof, https://www.ejiltalk.org/the-implementation-of-judgments-of-the-european-court-of-human-rights-worse-than-you-think-part-2-the-hole-in-the-roof/ (30.8.2022).

3 Concluding Remarks

Journalists worldwide enjoy a high level of protection with international law shielding their work from interference by state and private actors. Although the level of material guarantees is high, the lack of effective procedural enforcement reveals the gap between material norms and a harsh reality. Yet, there is hope: despite the ongoing attacks against the media from state authorities and private actors and the manifold challenges the media are confronted with, the international community consistently and strongly affirms freedom of the media as a common international value reflected in national and international regulation. The procedural enforcement of this consensus in each case depends heavily upon the will of the states, though, and therefore has to be accompanied by a political process not only on an international but on a national level as well. This is in the interest of each state because, as UN Secretary General António Guterres put it, "When journalists are targeted, societies as a whole also pay the price. The kind of news that gets silenced – corruption, conflicts of interest, illegal trafficking – is exactly the kind of information the public needs to know."[158]

158 Statement from UN Secretary General António Guterres, on 2 November 2017, the day United Nations General Assembly Resolution 68/163 designated to be the International Day to End Impunity for Crimes Against Journalists, https://ifex.org/how-can-un-resolutions-make-it-safer-to-be-a-journalist/ (30.8.2022).

CHAPTER 7

Freedom of Association

The Shrinking Space of Civil Society

Robert Uerpmann-Wittzack

1 Introduction*

Freedom of association is a core guarantee of international human rights law. Together with the freedom of assembly, freedom of association complements freedom of expression. Article 20 of the Universal Declaration of Human Rights (UDHR), Article 22 of the International Covenant on Civil and Political (ICCPR) and Article 11 of the European Convention on Human Rights (ECHR) guarantee freedom of association. Article 22(2) ICCPR and Article 11(2) ECHR both allow restrictions, which must have, however, a legal basis, serve an enumerated legitimate aim and be "necessary in a democratic society". The ECHR uses the same formula in Articles 8–11 with regard to the protection of private and family life, freedom of expression, freedom of thought, conscience and religion, and freedom of assembly. By contrast, the ICCPR reserves the reference to a democratic society for freedom of assembly (Article 21 ICCPR) and freedom of association, thus emphasizing the specific nexus between these two collective guarantees and democracy.

While freedom of expression allows individuals to expose their ideas, and freedom of assembly enables them to do so collectively,[1] freedom of association permits them to create a stable framework for pursuing common goals over a long time. Hence, freedom of association is the very basis of civil society commitment.

Freedom of association gained ground in Europe and worldwide in the 1990s, after the Cold War had ended. The backlash followed since the beginning of the new millennium.[2] After the terrorist attacks of 11 September 2001,

* I owe thanks to Charlotte Wicke for preparatory research and valuable comments.

1 See Human Rights Committee (HRC) 'General comment No. 37 (2020) on the right of peaceful assembly (article 21)' (2020) UN Doc CCPR/C/GC/37 paras 1, 4.

2 See D Rutzen, 'Civil Society under Assault' (2015) 26 Journal of Democracy 28–39; C F Swiney, 'Counter-Associational Revolution: The Rise, Spread, and Contagion of Restrictive Civil Society Laws in the World's Strongest Democratic States' (2019) 43 Fordham International Law Journal 399–456.

 | DOI:10.1163/9789004508712_008

restrictive laws were enacted with a view to fighting international terrorism and money laundering. Simultaneously, the enthusiasm for common, global values yielded again to thinking in terms of national sovereignty and self-determination. Freedom of association is being restricted in many countries worldwide, and restrictions take various forms. Associations are compelled to submit to strict registration requirements, funding is restricted, and activists are prosecuted. Associations face severe sanctions and even forced dissolution in case of minor non-compliance, or they are stigmatized by public authorities.

Examples are manifold. In 2012, Russia enacted a law on foreign agents obliging associations that receive any funding from abroad to register as a "foreign agent" if the association participates in political activities.[3] The term "political activities" is both broad and vague. It covers, inter alia, activities in the field of human rights, democracy and the rule of law.[4] In principle, a single rouble or Euro, which a foreign citizen sends to the association's bank account, would suffice to turn the NGO into a foreign agent.[5] The qualification as a "foreign agent", which must be indicated on all materials issued or distributed by the association,[6] bears a negative and stigmatizing connotation.[7] According to the UN Special Rapporteur on the rights to freedom of peaceful assembly and of association, the Russian expression is equivalent to "foreign spy".[8] Moreover, the status of a foreign agent implies enhanced monitoring obligations, which are burdensome and costly.[9]

In a similar vein, the Hungarian Transparency Law of 2017 obliges any association receiving a certain amount of funding from abroad to make a declaration and to indicate on its homepage as well as in its publications and other press products that it has been classified as an organization in receipt of support from abroad.[10] Non-compliance may be sanctioned by a fine or by forced

3 Venice Commission, 'Opinions no. 716-717/2013 on Federal Law N. 121-FZ on non-commercial organisations ("Law on foreign agents"), on Federal Laws N. 18-FZ and N. 147-FZ and on Federal Law N. 190-FZ on making amendments to the Criminal Code ("Law on treason") of the Russian Federation' (27 June 2014) CDL-AD (2014) 025 paras 9, 44 ff.

4 ibid, para 83.

5 ibid, para. 70.

6 ibid, para 48.

7 ibid, paras 54 ff.

8 UN Special Rapporteur on the rights to freedom of peaceful assembly and of association '[Second] Report' (2013) UN Doc A/HRC/23/39 para 28.

9 Venice Commission (n 3) paras 91–92.

10 Case C-78/18 *Commission v. Hungary* ECLI:EU:C:2020:476 paras 1–5, 54; see also Venice Commission, 'Opinion 889/2017 on the Hungarian Draft Law on the transparency of organisations receiving support from abroad' (20 June 2017) CDL-AD(2017)015.

dissolution.[11] The European Court of Justice (ECJ) found these requirements to be deterrent and stigmatizing.[12] According to the Court, they were based on a mere presumption that any foreign funding would invariably jeopardise Hungary's "political and economic interests ... and the ability of its institutions to operate free from interference".[13]

The Kavala case illustrates the problem of criminal prosecution for engaging in civil society activities. In Kavala, the European Court of Human Rights (ECtHR) did not only find a violation of the right to liberty under Article 5(1)(c) ECHR because Turkey had arrested the applicant without a "reasonable suspicion".[14] Rather, the Court also engaged in an analysis of Article 18 ECHR, which prohibits applying restrictions for "any purpose other than those for which they have been prescribed". Eventually, the Court found Article 18 ECHR to be violated because Turkey had used unconvincing charges to prosecute the applicant for his legitimate activities as an NGO leader, to reduce him to silence and to dissuade others from following his example.[15] Angelika Nußberger has compared such a condemnation under Article 18 ECHR with showing the red card.[16]

This chapter shall analyse the role of freedom of association and civil society from two perspectives: Section 2 takes the perspective of liberal human rights law, while Section 3 explores the democratic dimension. Whereas liberal human rights law protects global civil society, democracy builds upon a civil society formed by the citizens constituting the people of a given country. Tensions between both approaches arise, when civil society organisations are funded or operate in a transnational way. Against this backdrop, Section 4 outlines standards for the justification of restrictions on freedom of association before some conclusions will be drawn in Section 5.

The chapter draws on United Nations and Council of Europe practice comprising the work of political, expert and judicial bodies. Within the United Nations, contributions made by the Human Rights Committee and the Special Rapporteur on the rights to freedom of peaceful assembly and of association[17]

---

11 ibid, para 56, 58.

12 ibid, para 118.

13 ibid, para 86, 93.

14 *Kavala v. Turkey* App no 28749/18 (ECtHR, 10 December 2019) paras 135–160.

15 *Kavala v. Turkey* App no 28749/18 (ECtHR, 10 December 2019) paras 222–224, 231–232.

16 A Nußberger, 'Europa, deine Menschenrechte' (2020) 47 Europäische Grundrechte Zeitschrift 389, 393; see also H Keller and S Bates, 'Article 18 ECHR in Historical Perspective and Contemporary Application' (2019) 39 Human Rights Law Journal 2, 12, who highlight the relevance of Article 18 ECHR as a codification of the doctrine of abuse of rights.

17 See UN Special Rapporteur on the rights to freedom of peaceful assembly and of association 'Ten years protecting civic space worldwide' (2020) UN Doc A/HRC/44/50.

are particularly relevant. On the European level, the case law of the European Court of Human Rights[18] is corroborated and complemented by documents issued by the so-called Venice Commission, i.e. the European Commission for Democracy through Law,[19] and by the Committee of Ministers.[20]

2 Human Rights Liberalism

From a human rights perspective, freedom of association is important because it enables individuals to pursue common goals collectively and in an enduring way. The ECtHR has emphasized the link between freedom of association and freedom of expression by pointing out that freedom of association has, inter alia, the objective of protecting opinions and the freedom to express them.[21] Since 1976, the ECtHR holds that "pluralism, tolerance and broadmindedness" characterize a "democratic society"; therefore, freedom of expression covers not only "'information' or 'ideas' that are favourably received or regarded as inoffensive or as a matter of indifference, but also … those that offend, shock or disturb".[22] Given the close relationship between freedom of expression and freedom of association, the Court has applied the same formula to associations "whose views offend, shock or disturb".[23] The Court's willingness to interpret freedom of association in the light of the principle of personal autonomy[24] confirms its liberal approach.

Freedom of association does not only protect the right to establish an association,[25] but also the whole functioning of an association including its

18 For an overview see ECtHR, 'Guide on Article 11 of the European Convention on Human Rights, Freedom of assembly and association, updated on 31 May 2020' paras 105–222.

19 See Venice Commission, 'Compilation of Venice Commission opinions concerning freedom of association (revised in December 2019)' (3 December 2019) CDL-PI(2019)007.

20 See Council of Europe Committee of Ministers, 'Recommendation CM/Rec(2007)14 on the legal status of non-governmental organisations in Europe' (1006th meeting of the Ministers' Deputies 10 October 2007).

21 *Freedom and Democracy Party (ÖZDEP) v. Turkey* [GC] App no 23885/94 (ECtHR, 8 December 1999) para 37; *Vörður Ólafsson v. Iceland* App no 20161/06 (ECtHR, 27 April 2010) para 46.

22 *Handyside v. United Kingdom* App no. 5493/72 (ECtHR, 7 December 1976) para 49; see also S Dollé and C Ovey, 'Handyside, 35 years down the road' in J Casadevall, E Myjer, M O'Boyle and A Austin (eds), *Freedom of Expression. Essays in Honour of Nicolas Bratza* (Wolf Legal Publishers 2012) 544–545.

23 *Redfearn v. United Kingdom* App no 47335/06 (ECtHR, 6 November 2012) para 56.

24 *Vörður Ólafsson v. Iceland* App no 20161/06 (ECtHR, 27 April 2010) para 46.

25 *Sidiropoulos and others v. Greece* App no 26695/95 (ECtHR, 10 July 1998) para 40.

funding.[26] In fact, proper funding is essential for the success of any civil society organisation. In his 2020 report, the UN Special Rapporteur on the rights to freedom of peaceful assembly and of association has underlined the importance of cross-border funding for the continued operation of civil society organisations.[27]

Hence, the right to seek for and to accept funding from other States, international organisations, NGOs or private individuals is covered by freedom of association.[28] Registration requirements, restrictions on funding and sanctions applied in case of non-compliance with these rules all constitute interferences with the right to freedom of association. They may be justified only under the conditions laid down in Article 22(2) CCPR and Article 11(2) ECHR.[29]

In sum, the liberal approach to freedom of association has a cosmopolitan dimension. This is in line with freedom of expression, which comprises, according to the relevant human rights instruments, the right to "receive and impart information and ideas … regardless of frontiers".[30] Liberal human rights practice has extended the transnational dimension to freedom of association, thus laying ground for a global, cosmopolitan civil society. It should be kept in mind, however, that international human rights instruments highlight the importance of trans-border speech and information. Trans-border financial influence does not necessarily enjoy the same degree of protection.

3 The Perspective of Democratic Self-Determination

Analysing freedom of association from the perspective of democratic self-determination may lead to other results. In his concept of an ideal democracy, Jean Jacques Rousseau was hostile towards any associations regrouping some citizens.[31] According to Rousseau, such partial associations would compromise the *volonté générale*. This concept stands in sharp contrast with freedom of association as guaranteed by Article 22 ICCPR and Article 11 ECHR. From the perspective of international human rights law, democracy must be a pluralist

26 Special Rapporteur (n 8) para 16.
27 Special Rapporteur (n 17) para 51.
28 Committee of Ministers (n 20) para 50; see also Special Rapporteur (n 8) para 16–17.
29 See above, Section 1.
30 Article 19 UDHR, Article 19(2) ICCPR, Article 10(1) ECHR.
31 Jean Jacques Rousseau, *Du contrat social*, Livre II, Chapitre III (1762) 57–59.

one.[32] Hence, the freedom to establish political parties[33] and other civil society organisations is an essential element of democracy.

Freedom of association is important for any pluralist democracy, because it enables groups of citizens to organize and to collectively promote their goals and pursue a given agenda.[34] According to the European Court of Human Rights, there is a direct relationship between democracy, pluralism and freedom of association.[35] Still according to the Court, the way in which freedom of association is secured under domestic law and in which domestic authorities apply it in practice are benchmarks for the state of democracy in a given State.[36] Like the media,[37] civil society organisations may serve as watchdogs,[38] as Transparency International does. They may raise concerns for human rights issues, for the situation of minorities or other disadvantaged groups or for common concerns such as environmental degradation and climate change. According to the HRC, the existence and operation of such associations, "including those which peacefully promote ideas not necessarily favourably viewed by the Government or the majority of the population, is a cornerstone" of democratic societies as referred to in Article 22(2) ICCPR.[39] Hence, admitting associations that "offend, shock or disturb"[40] is not only a liberal demand but also a democratic one.

In a democratic context, freedom of association is a right of citizens.[41] Article 25 ICCPR guarantees the right to take part in the conduct of political affairs, to vote and to be elected to all citizens. Likewise, Article 3 of the First Protocol to the ECHR obliges States parties to hold free elections permitting

32 *Freedom and Democracy Party (ÖZDEP) v. Turkey* [GC] App no 23885/94 (ECtHR, 8 December 1999) para 37; *Refah Partisi and others v. Turkey* [GC] App no 41340/98 and others (ECtHR, 13 February 2003) para 89; HRC (n 1) para 40, also confirms the link between democracy and political pluralism.

33 See S Wheatley, 'Democracy in international law: a European perspective' (2002) 51 ICLQ 225, 240.

34 See Venice Commission (n 19) 4, 13; see also Special Rapporteur (n 17) para 1.

35 *Gorzelik and others v. Poland* [GC] App no 44158/98 (ECtHR, 17 February 2004) para 88; confirmed by Case C-78/18 *Commission v. Hungary* ECLI:EU:C:2020:476 para 112.

36 *Gorzelik and others v. Poland* [GC] App no 44158/98 (ECtHR, 17 February 2004) para 88.

37 See *von Hannover v. Germany* (No. 2) [GC] App nos 40660/08, 60641/08 (ECtHR, 7 February 2012) para 102.

38 See HRC 'Views' *Toktakunov v. Kyrgyzstan* (28 March 2011) UN Doc CCPR/C/101/D/1470/2006 paras 6.3, 7.4.

39 HRC 'Views adopted by the Committee at its 112th session (7–31 October 2014)' *Kalyakin v. Belarus* (10 October 2014) UN Doc CCPR/C/112/D/2153/2012 para 9.2.

40 See above n 23.

41 See Venice Commission (n 19) 4, 13.

"the free expression of the opinion of the people". Both provisions correspond to Article 1 ICCPR, which grants "all peoples" the right of self-determination. All these provisions connect democracy to the self-determination of a certain group, i.e. to citizens that constitute a people.

It is true that the concept of citizenship and, even more, the concept of peoples may appear vague and indeterminate. At the local level, for instance, there may be good reasons to grant the right to vote and to be elected to foreigners residing in a country as suggested by Article 6(1) of the European Convention on the Participation of Foreigners in Public Life at Local Level.[42] This would detach elements of citizenship from nationality and create partial citizenship of non-nationals at the local level. In any case, however, citizenship, as understood by existing international human rights law, presupposes special ties to a certain community.

If freedom of association is to serve democratic self-determination, its point of reference will be the respective people. The Venice Commission has elaborated this point in an Opinion regarding Azerbaijan:

> Freedom of association should form the basis of any pluralist democracy. All groups in society should therefore have the freedom to participate in associative life as this contributes towards the development of a strong democratic civil society.[43]

This corresponds to Article 16 ECHR, which permits state parties to restrict the political activity of aliens also with regard to freedom of association. Even though Article 16 ECHR is applied narrowly,[44] it confirms the basic idea that democracy means self-determination of and within a given group.

From this perspective, a pluralist democracy demands that citizens are able to establish both political parties and civil society organisations and that they are free to engage in these associations. Foreign interference by contrast, may appear as a challenge to democratic self-determination. From a democratic

---

42 Convention on the Participation of Foreigners in Public Life at Local Level (adopted 5 February 1992, entered into force 1 May 1997) ETS No. 144.

43 Venice Commission, 'Opinion no. 636/2011 on the compatibility with human rights standards of the legislation on non-governmental organisations of the Republic of Azerbaijan' (19 October 2011) CDL-AD(2011)035 para 79; see also Venice Commission (n 19) 4.

44 See *Perinçek v. Switzerland* [GC] App no 27510/08 (ECtHR, 15 October 2015) para 122; Lukas Meyer, 'Der Ausländervorbehalt in der Rechtsprechung des EGMR' (2018) 56 Archiv des Völkerrechts 258–267.

point of view, admitting foreign or transnational associations does not seem obvious.

Questions of funding are ambivalent from a democratic point of view. Any association wishing to raise its voice in a pluralist democracy needs appropriate funds. Therefore, proper funding is crucial in a democratic society. On the other hand, those who support an association with important funds may do so in order to implement their own agenda and to give particular weight to their own goals. A democratic society, by contrast, is based on the principle of democratic equality of all citizens. Therefore, neither economic power nor external actors should bias elections and public debate.

Hence, it is recognized that a State may outlaw foreign funding of political parties.[45] According to the Common Rules against Corruption in the Funding of Political Parties and Electoral Campaigns adopted by the Committee of Ministers of the Council of Europe in 2003, "States should specifically limit, prohibit or otherwise regulate donations from foreign donors".[46] For the ECtHR, there was no doubt that a ban on financing by foreign States was "necessary for the preservation of national sovereignty".[47] The Court was less convinced with regard to funding by a foreign non-State actor, but it saw the ban covered by the State's margin of appreciation.[48]

The complete ban on foreign financial influence is seen as an exception that only applies to actors directly involved in the election of a people's representatives.[49] Other civil society organisations should, as a rule, retain the possibility to receive foreign funding. A similar tendency to reduce measures against foreign influence to the core of democratic participation appears in the case law concerning Article 16 ECHR. The article allows States to limit "the political activity of aliens". The ECtHR tries to restrict the exception clause to activities

45 See Venice Commission, 'Opinion No. 366/2006 on the prohibition of financial contributions to political parties from foreign sources' (31 March 2006) CDL-AD(2006)014 para 33 and passim.

46 Articles 7 and 8 of the Common Rules, Appendix to: Council of Europe Committee of Ministers, 'Recommendation Rec(2003)4 on common rules against corruption in the funding of political parties and electoral campaigns' (835th meeting of the Ministers' Deputies 8 April 2003).

47 *Parti nationaliste basque – Organisation régionale d'Iparralde v. France* App no 71251/01 (ECtHR, 7 June 2007) para 47; see also M Jamnejad and M Wood, 'The Principle of Non-intervention' (2009) 22 Leiden Journal of International Law 345, 368 according to whom State funding of a party in another country may amount to unlawful intervention.

48 *Parti nationaliste basque – Organisation régionale d'Iparralde v. France* App no 71251/01 (ECtHR, 7 June 2007) para 47.

49 Venice Commission, 'Study No. 895/2017, Report on funding of associations' (18 March 2019) CDL-AD(2019)002 para 78.

that "directly affect the political process",[50] thus leaving space for foreigners engaging in public debates. Nevertheless, it may be retained that democracy does not militate in favour of accepting outward interference. If activities of non-domestic associations and foreign funding of associations is protected, this stems from the liberal dimension of international human rights law, not from democratic principles.

4 Standards for Justifying Restrictions

The liberal approach underlying freedom of association as well as its democratic implications set the framework for permissible restrictions. International bodies have developed a series of standards for the justification of interferences with Article 22 ICCPR and Article 11 ECHR.

First, any restriction must pursue a legitimate aim. Under Article 22(2) ICCPR, freedom of association may only be restricted "in the interest of national security or public safety, public order (*ordre public*), the protection of public health or morals or the protection of the rights and freedoms of others". Article 11(2) ECHR replaces the interests of public order by "the prevention of disorder and crime". These lists are exhaustive and must not by extended.[51] According to the ECtHR, they must be construed narrowly.[52]

While the fight against international terrorism and money laundering are recognized aims,[53] justifying restrictions with the interest to protect state sovereignty from foreign interference seems problematic. State sovereignty and non-interference as such are not listed in Article 22(2) ICCPR or Article 11(2) ECHR.[54] In *Parti national basque*, the ECtHR held that national sovereignty might justify a ban on foreign state funding of political organisations but not necessarily on funding by foreign private actors.[55] The European Court refrained, however, from referring to any of the aims listed in Article 11(2) ECHR.[56] In another context, the ECtHR has held that certain restrictions imposed on civil servants could be justified by the "right of others ... to

50 *Perinçek v. Switzerland* [GC] App no 27510/08 (ECtHR, 15 October 2015) para 122.
51 Special Rapporteur (n 8) para 30.
52 *Sidiropoulos and others v. Greece* App no 26695/95 (ECtHR, 10 July 1998) para 38.
53 Venice Commission (n 19) para 53.
54 See also Special Rapporteur (n 8) para 30.
55 *Parti nationaliste basque – Organisation régionale d'Iparralde v. France* App no 71251/01 (ECtHR, 7 June 2007) para 47.
56 For a deeper analysis see Venice Commission (n 49) paras 74–76.

effective political democracy"[57] even in the absence of any concrete "threat to the stability of the constitutional or political order".[58] In this context, the ECtHR emphasised the fundamental character of democracy for the European public order.[59]

Hence, exercising a certain control over the funding of civil society organisations in general and political parties in particular may be justified under the headings of the rights of others, i.e., the rights of all citizens, or of public order, where the proper functioning of democracy is at stake. Here, the ambivalent character of funding has to be kept in mind: While adequate funding is essential for the functioning of any association, financially strong actors may use their financial means in order to push their goals at the expense of others.[60] Even in a liberal democracy, there are good reasons to limit the influence of economic power on democratic process in favour of the democratic equality of all citizens. This may justify quite strict regulations on the funding of political parties that directly participate in the election of the people's representatives, and it may justify at least transparency obligations with regard to civil society organisations that participate in public debates. It is true that the Venice Commission has condemned any public disclosure obligation for civil society organisations others than political parties as "a drastic measure".[61] This is certainly true if the disclosure obligation stigmatizes like labelling an association as "foreign agent".[62] However, simply making resources transparent hardly seems stigmatizing or "drastic" unless public opinion strongly condemns any foreign influence. If public opinion is fundamentally opposed to any foreign influence, however, it seems problematic to circumvent this problem by concealing even substantial foreign influence. It may be discriminating, though, to impose public disclosure obligations on foreign funded associations alone and not on all associations.[63]

Aims that are, in principle, legitimate must not be abused as a pretext for restricting freedom of association. Such an abuse may be presumed if the restriction at hand is not fitted to realize the legitimate aim or contradictory. In the fight against money laundering, for instance, it would be incoherent and discriminating to impose stronger reporting obligations on civil society

57 *Ahmed and others v. United Kingdom* App no 22954/93 (ECtHR, 2 September 1998) para 54.
58 ibid, para 52.
59 ibid, para 54.
60 See also Venice Commission (n 49), para 38, in the context of lobbying.
61 Venice Commission (n 49) para 106; but see Venice Commission (n 746) paras 52–53.
62 See above n 7.
63 Venice Commission (n 49) para 127.

organisations than on business corporations, given that the latter are at least as exposed to money laundering activities.

Furthermore, any restriction must be necessary for achieving the aim pursued. Restrictions on foreign funding, for example, would be excessive if they applied even to minor donors and negligible sums.[64] Hence, the German Statute on Political Parties exempts donations not exceeding 1000 Euro from the ban on foreign funding of political parties.[65] Moreover, lawful activities must not be stigmatized.[66]

Finally, any restriction must stand a strict proportionality test. Thus, reporting obligations must not be overly burdensome and costly.[67] This is particularly true for small NGOs that would be overburdened and deterred by excessive bureaucracy. Dissolving an association must be reserved for the most extreme cases.[68] While it is legitimate to require transparency, liquidating an association for not fully complying with complicated reporting requirements will hardly meet a serious proportionality test.

5 Conclusions

To sum up, democracy, as understood by international human rights law, is a pluralist one. Freedom of association is essential for any pluralist democracy. There is, however, an inherent tension between liberal human rights cosmopolitanism and democratic self-determination of a given group. If domestic associations receive relevant foreign funding or if powerful transnational associations come into play, their financial power may shift the balance within a given group. Of course, this does not only apply to external actors but also to financially powerful domestic actors that may dominate debates in contradiction to the idea of democratic equality of citizens, which implies that all voices should have the same impact. While external voices must be heard in a liberal democracy, there are good reasons to control the impact of financial power.

---

64 See Venice Commission (n 49) para 13; Venice Commission (n 3) para 70.

65 Section 25(2)(3)(c) Parteiengesetz.

66 See also Venice Commission (n 3) para 87.

67 Venice Commission and OSCE Office for Democratic Institutions and Human Rights, 'Joint Opinion on Ukrainian Draft Law No. 6674 on introducing changes to some legislative acts to ensure public transparency of information on finance activity of public associations and of the use of international technical assistance' (16 March 2018) CDL-AD(2018)006 para 40.

68 *Tebieti Mühafize Cemiyyeti and Israfilov v. Azerbaijan* App no 37083/03 (ECtHR, 8 October 2009) para 63, 82; Venice Commission (n 3) para 116.

It would be excessive, however, to prohibit all foreign funding of civil society organisations. While some monitoring and transparency requirements may be imposed on civil society organisations, they must be neither overly costly or burdensome nor stigmatizing. During the last twenty years, many States have enacted laws that go far beyond what would be acceptable in a pluralist democracy, thus shrinking the space for civil society. This development reveals a fundamental scepticism towards liberalism and pluralism, which form the very basis of international human rights law. At the same time, the growing aversion against foreign influence reflects a dwindling transnational consent on which values should be promoted.[69] In the absence of a real consent on common values, investing funds in the promotion of values abroad may be perceived as hegemonic.

69 See also Nußberger (n 16) 397.

PART 3

Democracy Promotion in International Legal Practice

CHAPTER 8

Democracy Promotion and Development Cooperation

Between Business as Usual and the End of the "End of History"

Emanuel Castellarin

1 Introduction*

Since World War II, democracy promotion has been increasingly linked to development. The seminal experiences of US-led German and Japanese reconstruction played a major role in linking democracy and economic State (re) building. Decolonisation and the Cold War created a new context for this nexus. The concept of development emerged in the 1950s, essentially in the economic sense, but it has evolved to include a social and cultural dimension and the idea of meeting the needs of the present without compromising the ability of future generations to meet their own needs.[1] The correlation between democracy and development has been much debated since the 1960s, both from the empirical and from the normative point of view.[2] These debates have also been related to longstanding controversies on the relationship and respective priority of political and civic rights or of economic, social and cultural human rights. It is worth noting that, for the purposes of these debates, democracy and development have mainly been analysed in the framework of the State, with a regional dimension, but without any special attention to cosmopolitan or transnational democracy.

Since the end of the Cold War, the existence of a correlation between democracy and development has been widely accepted, both in social sciences and in political and legal instruments. Examples of the awareness of this correlation include the 1993 Vienna Declaration and Programme of Action adopted

---

* The paper was completed, websites were last consulted, and data were collected on 10 June 2021.

1 G. H. Brundtland, Our Common Future: Report of the World Commission on Environment and Development. Geneva, UN doc. A/42/427, p. 41–42.

2 366 books or articles in Peace Palace Library catalogue include both "democracy" and "development" in their title.

 | DOI:10.1163/9789004508712_009

by the World Conference on Human Rights[3] and the 2002 UNDP Human Development Report *Deepening Democracy in a Fragmented World*.[4] In 1998, UNESCO established the International Panel on Democracy and Development, whose final report of 2002 underlined the correlation between development and with democracy, defined as embodying four basic principles (freedom, justice, free participation of citizens, and human rights).[5] As shown by this example, development is often explicitly linked to concepts similar to democracy, such as human rights, the rule of law, good governance, political participation, etc.[6] Hence, democracy promotion unavoidably overlaps in part with the promotion of similar values.

Unsurprisingly, the development-democracy nexus is also taken into account in development policies, including the activity of multilateral development banks and external policies aimed at promoting development abroad.[7] Depending on the point of view, democracy promotion in development policies can be seen as based on shared values or inspired by a form of legal imperialism. However, most studies on democracy promotion in development cooperation are at least implicitly placed in the conceptual context of the "end of history". In the wake of the end of the Cold War, Francis Fukuyama used this expression to argue that liberal democracy is the final form of human government.[8] He described democracy (at least as a normative model) as an unsurpassable horizon, so that its expansion, although sometimes slow or

3 Article 1, § 8: "Democracy, development and respect for human rights and fundamental freedoms are interdependent and mutually reinforcing".

4 See also *Human development: economic growth and democracy. The role of parliaments in ensuring the necessary links between freedoms, citizen involvement, economic growth, and social investments*, Resolution adopted by the 86th Inter-Parliamentary Conference, 12 October 1991.

5 B. Boutros-Ghali (ed.), *The Interaction Between Democracy and Development*, Paris, UNESCO, 2002. On the role of the United Nations, M. Tommasoli (ed.), *Democracy and Development: The Role of the UN*, IDEA, UN, UNDP, 2013.

6 The 1986 United Nations General Assembly Declaration on the Right to Development already defined development by reference to the full realisation of human rights and all fundamental freedoms: "The right to development is an inalienable human right by virtue of which every human person and all peoples are entitled to participate in, contribute to, and enjoy economic, social, cultural and political development, in which all human rights and fundamental freedoms can be fully realized" (A/RES/41/128, 4 December 1986, article 1, § 1). See also World Bank, OECD, *Integrating Human Rights into Development*, 2nd edition, 2013, <https://openknowledge.worldbank.org>.

7 When referring to bilateral relations between industrialised and developing countries, the traditional expression "development aid" has been generally replaced by "development cooperation", to signal the quest for a shift from a paternalistic to an egalitarian relationship.

8 F. Fukuyama, *The End of History and the Last Man*, New York, Free Press, 1992.

difficult in practice, is unavoidable in the linear progression of human history. However, in recent years, democratic fatigue and democratic backsliding have notoriously challenged this unidirectional view of history, so that a debate has emerged on whether democracy is in crisis.[9] These phenomena are not just effects of the well-known gap between normative models and social reality in facade democracies: they are the result of a more profound doubt on the meaning, rationale, and attractiveness of democracy, which can be witnessed not only in fragile democracies, but also in well-established ones.[10]

Legal instruments of development cooperation policies need to be assessed against this background to understand to what extent and by what means they include democracy promotion. The existing legal instruments will be analysed in Part 2, where it will be shown that democracy promotion permeates today's Western development cooperation policies, a refined version of instruments which emerged at the end of the Cold War. However, development cooperation policies also include a-democratic features, especially at the multilateral level and in non-Western programmes. A-democratic development cooperation will be analysed in Part 3, before some concluding remarks.

2 The Importance of Democracy Promotion in Western Development Cooperation Policy

Democracy promotion is an important objective of Western development cooperation policies, as shown by its integration in French, German and US instruments (2.1), in the activity of the Development Aid Committee of the Organisation for Economic Co-operation and Development (OECD DAC) (2.2) and in European Union instruments (2.3). This study does not aim at a thorough analysis of the effects of Western development cooperation policies on democracy in developing countries. This issue has been under the scrutiny of

9 E.g., J. Rupnik, "From Democracy Fatigue to Populist Backlash", *Journal of Democracy*, 2007, 18 (4), p. 17–25; Roland Rich, *Democracy in crisis: why, where, how to respond*, Boulder, Lynne Rienner, 2017; T. Ginsburg, "International Courts and Democratic Backsliding", *Berkeley journal of international law*, 2019, 37(2), p. 265–288. Fukuyama himself has identified internal forces leading to the possible political decay of liberal democracies (*Political Order and Political Decay: From the Industrial Revolution to the Present Day*, New York, Farrar, Straus and Giroux, 2014).

10 E.g., A. Wuttke, K. Gavras, H. Schoen, "Have Europeans Grown Tired of Democracy? New Evidence from Eighteen Consolidated Democracies, 1981–2018", *British Journal of Political Science*, 2020, p. 1–13.

political scientists, economists, and experts of international relations.[11] From the point of view of international law, the most noteworthy feature of democracy promotion in Western development cooperation policies is the conditionality of some instruments. This controversial practice will be analysed through the example of the EU external action (2.4).

2.1 *Democracy Promotion in National Development Cooperation Policies*

Development cooperation is not the only vector of democracy promotion in the foreign policy of Western countries. Other democracy promotion initiatives are usually carried out under the leadership of ministries of foreign affairs, both at the bilateral level (e.g., political dialogue) and the multilateral level, within international organisations. The relevant issues are often dealt with by specific structures of ministries of foreign affairs, whether their name explicitly refers to democracy, like the Bureau of Democracy, Human Rights, and Labor of the United States State Department, or not.[12] Depending on the legal and political framework of each State, other non-profit organisations may play a significant role, such as the National Endowment for Democracy in the United States[13] and foundations of German political parties.[14]

Development agencies and ministries of Western countries, such as the US Agency for International Development (USAID), the French *Agence France Développement* and the German Federal Ministry for Economic Cooperation and Development (*Bundesministerium für wirtschaftliche Zusammenarbeit und Entwicklung*), communicate on democracy promotion as an important feature of the development cooperation policies.[15] To be sure, democracy is

---

11 E.g., S. Knack, "Does Foreign Aid Promote Democracy?", *International Studies Quarterly*, 2004, 48(1), p. 251–266. The paper concludes that no evidence is found that aid promotes democracy.

12 E.g., the French Ministry of Europe and of foreign affairs includes a *Sous-direction des droits de l'homme et affaires humanitaires*, while the German *Auswärtiges Amt* includes a *Beauftragte für Menschenreche, internationale Entwicklung und Soziales*.

13 On US democracy promotion, Thomas O. Melia, *The Democracy Bureaucracy. The Infrastructure of American Democracy Promotion*, 2005, <https://pdf.usaid.gov>.

14 Friedrich-Ebert-Stiftung, Friedrich-Naumann-Stiftung für die Freiheit, Hanns-Seidel-Stiftung, Heinrich-Böll-Stiftung Konrad-Adenauer-Stiftung, and Rosa-Luxemburg-Stiftung. For a comparison of US and German democracy promotion, J. Wolff, H.-J. Spanger, H.-J. Puhle, *Comparative International Politics of Democracy Promotion*, London, Routledge, 2013.

15 <https://www.usaid.gov/democracy>; <https://www.bmz.de/de/entwicklungspolitik/demokratie>; Agence France Développement, "L'AFD, les processus démocratiques et les medias", <https://www.afd.fr>. Other implementing agencies also integrate democracy promotion in their activity. Examples include, in France, Canal France International, the French Agricultural Research Centre for International Development (*Centre international*

often presented in connection with human rights and good governance and is far from being the only objective of development cooperation policies. Others cross-cutting issues, such as climate change, diversity, migrations, peace and stability are arguably even more crucial in the overall presentation of national development cooperation policies. However, democracy promotion is a significant dimension of the activity of the relevant agencies and ministries. The French development cooperation policy is an example. The La Baule speech by president François Mitterrand held in 1990 at the 16th conference of Heads of State of Africa and France, where African countries were called on to launch a democratisation process, was a turning point after the end of Cold War.[16] The democracy-development nexus was reaffirmed as a key factor in a 2002 report by the High Council of International Cooperation, a consultative body,[17] and in the 2006 policy paper setting the general strategy of French development cooperation policy for the following years.[18] More recent strategy papers are centred on other concepts, such as climate change and gender equality,[19] but the importance of democracy promotion has never been explicitly called into question.

Sometimes, democracy promotion also corresponds to specific organs and instruments, which contribute to greater continuity over time. USAID is the most significant case. The trend towards the integration of democratic governance into development cooperation started in the 1980s and dramatically increased in the 1990s.[20] The USAID Center for Democracy, Human Rights and

de recherche agricole pour le développement), *Expertise France*, *France Volontaires*, and the French National Research Institute for Development (*Institut de recherche et de développement*); in Germany, the German Technical Cooperation (*Deutsche Gesellschaft für Technische Zusammenarbeit*), the German Development Service (*Deutscher Entwicklungsdienst*), the German Agency for International Cooperation (*Deutsche Gesellschaft für Internationale Zusammenarbeit*) and the *Kreditanstalt für Wiederaufbau* Development Bank.

16 "La situation économique de l'Afrique, les possibilités d'aide des pays les plus riches et la position française en matière de coopération et d'aide financière", La Baule, 20 juin 1990, <www.vie-publique.fr>.

17 Haut Conseil de la Coopération Internationale, *Gouvernance democratique et cooperation internationale*, 2002, <www.vie-publique.fr>.

18 French Ministry of Foreign Affairs, *Stratégie gouvernance de la coopération française*, 2006, <www.diplomatie.gouv.fr>. The policy paper was followed by a more scholarly reflection on the same topic: S. Bellina, H. Magro, V. de Villemeur, *Democratic Governance: A New Paradigm for Development?*, Paris, French Ministry of Foreign Affairs, 2008.

19 Agence France Développement, *Pour un monde en commun. Plan d'orientation stratégique 2018–2022*, <www.afd.fr>.

20 T. Carothers, *Revitalizing U.S. democracy assistance. The challenge of USAID*, Washington, Carnegie Endowment for International Peace, 2009, p. 9–12; J. Brian Atwood, "Human

Governance supports field missions and is at the core of a network of academic partners and implementing organisations. Among its ten teams, at least two ("Countering Authoritarianism" and "Democratic Elections and Political Processes") are specifically devoted to the promotion of the core of democracy, but all others (ranging from "Justice, Rights, and Security" to "Counter Trafficking in Persons") are also directly or indirectly related to democracy promotion. Since its creation in 2012, the Center for Democracy, Human Rights and Governance has issued several policy documents, in particular the 2013 USAID *Strategy On Democracy Human Rights and Governance* and the 2017 USAID *Democracy, Human Rights and Governance Learning Agenda*. The 2021 *Electoral Assessment Framework*[21] exemplifies the Center's approach on a more technical issue.

2.2 *Democracy Promotion within the Development Assistance Committee of the OECD*

At the international level, unilateral approaches to development cooperation are coordinated to some extent, in particular within the Development Assistance Committee of the OECD. Created as Development Assistance Group by and OECE Ministerial Resolution in 1960[22], the DAC is a forum for discussion and coordination among donors. It currently has 30 members (29 States and the EU). Seven other States are participants and six international institutions (the IMF, the World Bank, 3 regional development banks, and the United Nations Development Programme) are observers. Following the usual working methods of the OECD,[23] its functioning relies on peer review and non-binding standard-setting based on good practices. Democracy-related issues form a significant part of the activity of one the DAC subsidiary bodies, the DAC Network on Governance (GovNet), created in 1995. GovNet also covers political economy analysis and anti-corruption issues, but the importance of democracy promotion in its activity is reflected in the 2014 *Accountability and Democratic Governance: Orientations and Principles for Development*. This document is a reference study without legally normative effect, but its collection

rights, democracy, and development: partners at last", *Open Global Rights*, 11 November 2013, <www.openglobalrights.org>.

21 Center for Democracy, Human Rights and Governance (USAID), *The Electoral Assessment Framework: A Tool to Assess Needs, Define Objectives, and Identify Program Options*, 2021.

22 On the history of the DAC, H. Führer, *The Story of Official Development Assistance*, OCDE/GD(94)67, 1996.

23 On the normative power of the OECD, SFDI, *Le pouvoir normatif de l'OCDE*, Paris, Pedone, 2014.

of good practices is influential within the DAC institutional framework. Based on country studies, these non-binding guidelines aim at contributing to the emergence of consistency in the practice of donors. From the theoretical point of view, the main point of interest is the use of accountability as the key concept to streamline support to different actors of democracy (parliaments, political parties, media) or to act in specific settings (electoral assistance revenue matters).

Even more importantly, data collected within the DAC provide a picture of the financial weight of democracy promotion in Official Development Assistance (ODA) and allow comparisons between donors. The overview of data from 2009 to 2018 provides a useful picture of how governance is taken into account in ODA.[24] Funding for governance increased from $10.98 billion in 2009 to $12.95 billion in 2018. In relative terms, it fell from 10.7% of total ODA in 2009 to 8.5% in 2015, before rebounding to 9.7% in 2018, when total ODA reached $133.5 billion.[25] The United States is the largest single governance ODA provider, but the EU and its Member States, considered together, are larger donors.[26] Interestingly, governance is not equally prioritised by all ODA providers: while Australia and Sweden devote over 18% of ODA to governance, this share falls at 1% or below for Greece and Hungary, while the Unites States (12.1%) and the EU (10.1%) are around the average.[27] As to channels of disbursements, the respective role of the public sector, multilateral organisations, and NGOs remained stable, respectively above 40%, around 20% and around 25%. Disbursements through private actors increased from 0% to 7%.[28] South and Central Asia, sub-Saharan Africa, and the Middle East are the largest recipient regions of governance ODA. Flows to several individual countries remained stable between 2009 and 2018, in particular to Afghanistan, which is the top recipient. Some flows declined over time (Iraq, India, Kosovo, Lebanon, Sudan), while others increased (Colombia, Jordan, Mexico, Pakistan, Papua New Guinea, Ukraine).[29]

Governance ODA serves three main purposes, which are relatively stable in spite of significant variation from year to year: "public sector policy and administrative management", "legal and judicial development", and "democratic

24 OECD, *DAC Official Development Assistance to Governance: An Overview (2009–2018)*, DCD/DAC/GOVNET(2021)5, 22 January 2021.

25 *Ibid.*, p. 6–7.

26 *Ibid.*, p. 12.

27 *Ibid.*, p. 12–13.

28 *Ibid.*, p. 10.

29 *Ibid.*, p. 10–11.

participation and civil society".[30] As shown by these entries, democracy promotion *stricto sensu* is difficult to distinguish from human rights and other governance issues. Taken at face value, available data do not allow to conclude that democracy as such is a top priority of ODA. Democracy is not explicitly mentioned in the DAC's mandate for the period 2018–2022[31] and has not even been chosen as a topic for an edition of the yearly Development Co-operation Report so far. However, these facts do not show a lack of interest, but can rather be explained by the mainstreaming of governance issues within a broader holistic approach. Indeed, around one-quarter of ODA disbursements have a governance dimension,[32] which suggests that democracy promotion is seen as a relevant cross-cutting issue in ODA.

2.3 *Democracy Promotion in the European Union's Development Cooperation Policy*

Among Western development cooperation policies, that of the European Union is particularly structured and legalised. It is based on solid constitutional foundations: completing a trend started by the Maastricht Treaty,[33] article 21(1) of the Treaty on European Union includes democracy among the principles that should guide the EU's external action. By virtue of article 21(2)(b) TEU, the consolidation and support of democracy, the rule of law, human rights, and the principles of international law are among the cross-cutting objectives of the EU's external action. Under article 21(3) TEU, the Union shall respect democracy as a principle and an objective of its external action, in a spirit of consistency throughout its external action, which includes development cooperation policy based on article 208 TFEU. This provision states that "Union development cooperation policy shall have as its primary objective the reduction and, in the long term, the eradication of poverty", but also recalls that "Union policy in the field of development cooperation shall be conducted within the framework of the principles and objectives of the Union's external action".

30 *Ibid.*, p. 8.

31 https://www.oecd.org/dac/thedevelopmentassistancecommitteesmandate.htm.

32 *Ibid.*, p. 14–19.

33 The Maastricht Treaty established democracy promotion as a general objective of EU common foreign and security policy (Article J.1) and EU development cooperation (Article 130, u of the Treaty on the European Community).

Democracy promotion by the EU has attracted significant attention both in general[34] and regarding development cooperation.[35] The Council,[36] the Parliament,[37] the Commission, and the High Representative of the Union for Foreign Affairs and Security Policy[38] have consistently reaffirmed the need for

---

34 For an overview, European Parliament, *EU support for democracy and peace in the world*, 2019, doc. PE 628.271; *Promoting democracy and observing elections*, <www.europarl.europa.eu>; N. Vandeputte, L. Luciani, *European Union democracy assistance: an academic state of play*, Bruxelles, European Partnership for Democracy, 2018; J. D. Saltnes, *The EU's Human Rights Policy. Unpacking the literature on the EU's implementation of aidconditionality*, Arena Working Paper no. 2, 2013, <www.sv.uio.no>.

35 G. Crawford, "Promoting democratic governance in the south", *European Journal of Development Research*, 2000, 12(1), p. 23–57; K. Del Biondo, "Democracy Promotion Meets Development Cooperation: The EU as a Promoter of Democratic Governance in Sub-Saharan Africa", *European Foreign Affairs Review*, 2011, 16(5), p. 659–672; K. Del Biondo, J. Orbie, "The European Commission's implementation of budget support and the Governance Incentive Tranche in Ethiopia: democracy promotor or developmental donor?", *Third World Quaterly*, 2014, 35(3), p. 411–427; W. Hout, "Governance and Development: Changing EU Policies", *Third World Quaterly*, 2010, 31(1), p. 1–12; International Institute for Democracy and Electoral Assistance, *Democracy in Development: Global consultations on the EU's role in democracy building*, Stockholm, 2009; C. Pierobon, "Civil Society in the EU Development and Human Rights Agenda: The Case of DG DEVCO-EIDHR", in R. Marchetti (ed.), *Partnerships in International Policy-Making: civil society and public institutions in European and Global Affairs*, London, Palgrave Macmillan, 2017, p. 195–214.

36 Council conclusions on Democracy Support in the EU's External Relations, doc. 16081/09, 17 November 2009; Council Conclusions on the roots of Democracy and sustainable development: Europe's engagement with Civil Society in external relations, doc. 14535/12, 15 October 2012; Council Conclusions on the Action Plan on Human Rights and Democracy 2015 – 2019, doc. 10897/15, 20 July 2015; Council Conclusion on EU engagement with civil society in external relations, doc. 10279/17, 19 June 2017; Council Conclusions on Democracy, doc. 12836/19, 14 October 2019; Council Conclusions on EU Action Plan on Human Rights and Democracy 2020–2024, doc. 12848/20, 18 November 2020.

37 European Parliament, *Global Democracy Support*, <www.europarl.europa.eu> Zitation ausreichend?

38 *The inclusion of respect for democratic principles and human rights in agreements between the community and third countries*, COM (95) 216, 23 May 1995; *Democratisation, the rule of law, respect for human rights and good governance: the challenges of the partnership between the European Union and the ACP States*, COM (98) 146, 12 March 1998; *Democracy building in EU external relations. Joint paper Commission/Council General Secretariat*, SEC (2009) 1095, 17 July 2009; *A partnership for democracy and shared prosperity with the Southern Mediterranean*, COM (2011) 200, 8 March 2011; *Joint Communication on 'Human Rights and Democracy at the Heart of EU External Action: Towards a more effective Approach.* COM (2011) 886, 12 December 2011; *Increasing the impact of EU Development Policy: an Agenda for Change*, COM (2011) 637, 13 October 2011; *The Roots of Democracy and Sustainable Development: Europe's Engagement with Civil Society in External Relations*, COM (2012) 492, 12 September 2012; *Action Plan on Human Rights and Democracy (2015–2019)*. Keeping human rights at the heart of the EU agenda, *JOIN* (2015) 16, 28 April 2015; *EU Action Plan on Human Rights and Democracy 2020–2024*, JOIN (2020) 5, 25 March 2020; *On the European democracy action plan*, COM (2020) 790, 3 December 2020.

democracy promotion in the Union's external action. This steady political support makes the EU one of the most vocal actors of democracy promotion in the international society.

The Union's scheme of generalised tariff preferences (SGP) is arguably the most significant unilateral legal instrument that puts these ambitions into practice.[39] Although adopted on the basis of article 207 TFEU (common commercial policy), the SGP regulation, which explicitly recalls Article 21 TEU in its recitals, is intimately related to development cooperation: since its inception in 1971, it has aimed at granting trade preferences to developing countries. However, the EU's development cooperation policy is also implemented on the basis of international agreements, the most important of which is the Cotonou Agreement with 79 African, Caribbean and Pacific (ACP) countries. Following on from the Lomé conventions, the first of which was signed in 1975, this agreement was concluded in 2000 for 20 years and was revised in 2005 and 2014.[40]

Democracy promotion plays a prominent role in the agreement, which inspired similar, although less strict, clauses in other EU agreements, most notably trade agreements. As stated in article 1, the promotion of a stable and democratic political environment and the improvement of the institutional framework necessary for the functioning of a democratic society are among the objectives of the agreement, and therefore must be taken into account in the definition of priority areas of cooperation through the political dialogue established by article 8. Article 9 is an "essential elements" clause. Respect for human rights, democracy based on the rule of law, and transparent and accountable governance are considered as an integral part of sustainable development (article 9(1)). Democratisation, development, and the protection of fundamental freedoms and human rights are presented as interrelated and mutually reinforcing.[41] Democratic principles are seen as universally recognised principles that underpin the organisation of the State, even if each country may develop its democratic culture (article 9(2)). Most importantly, democratic principles are defined as essential elements of the agreements, which triggers

39 Regulation (EU) No 978/2012 of the European Parliament and of the Council of 25 October 2012 applying a scheme of generalised tariff preferences, OJ 2012 L 303/1, applicable until 31 December 2023.

40 Partnership agreement between the members of the African, Caribbean and Pacific Group of States of the one part, and the European Community and its Member States, of the other part, signed in Cotonou on 23 June 2000, *OJ 2000 L 317/3*.

41 The 2012 Sipopo declaration, adopted at the 7th summit of ACP heads of State and government, also "recognizes that sustainable development can only be achieved in an environment of [...] respect for human rights, democratic principles and the rule of law" (ACP/28/065/12, 14 December 2012).

specific procedures in case of violations (article 96). A similar but distinct legal regime is set for good governance (article 97). The 2010 amendments clarified that political conditionality can be applied reciprocally.[42]

The applicability of the agreement, which was initially due to expire in February 2020, was extended until 30 November 2021. On 3 December 2020, the EU and the Organisation of African, Caribbean and Pacific States (OACPS) reached a political deal on a new agreement to succeed the Cotonou Partnership Agreement.[43] The 'post-Cotonou' EU/Africa-Caribbean-Pacific Partnership Agreement was initialled on 15 April 2021. Its final text is not available at the time of writing, but democracy promotion can be expected to remain a priority: the Commission,[44] the Council,[45] and the European Parliament[46] have all expressed their wish to maintain democracy as an essential element of the agreement. In somewhat looser terms that do not refer to the "essential elements" clause, ACP States also confirmed that commitment to democracy is among the specific objectives that should underpin the post-Cotonou agreement.[47] The most important expected evolution in the post-Cotonou agreement in this respect is the strengthening of regular political dialogue to prevent Article 96 consultation.[48]

Support to democracy promotion by the EU in third countries is not limited to legal instruments but also relies on a set of financial instruments. The European instrument for democracy and human rights (EIDHR) was a fund specifically devoted to the promotion of democracy-related issues in third countries in the framework of the 2014–2020 Multiannual Financial Framework.[49] In the framework of the 2021–2017 Multiannual Financial

42 Article 9(4)(4) of the Cotonou Agreement.

43 EU Council, *Cotonou Agreement*, <www.consilium.europa.eu>.

44 *Joint communication – A renewed partnership with the countries of Africa, the Caribbean and the Pacific*, JOIN (2016) 52, 22 November 2016, p. 25–26. The joint communication refers to the "Cotonou acquis" and recommends the conclusion of a new umbrella agreement and not a substantially revised partnership or full regionalisation.

45 Negotiating directives for a partnership agreement between the European Union and its Member States on the one part, and with countries of the African, Caribbean and Pacific group of States, of the other part, doc. 8094/18 ADD 1, 21 June 2018, p. 8 and 21, with several other references to democracy.

46 European Parliament resolution of 14 June 2018 on the upcoming negotiations for a new Partnership Agreement between the European Union and the African, Caribbean and Pacific Group of States, 2018/2634(RSP), § 8.

47 ACP negotiating mandate for a Post–Cotonou Partnership Agreement with the European Union, ACP/00/011/18, 30 May 2018, § 21(b).

48 J. D. Saltnes, "A Break from the Past or Business as Usual? EU-ACP Relations at a Crossroad", Arena Working Paper no. 3, 2021, <www.sv.uio.no>, p. 12–18.

49 Regulation (EU) 235/2014 establishing the European instrument for democracy and human rights (EIDHR), OJ 2014 L 77/85.

Framework, the EIDHR and nine other instruments have been merged into the Neighbourhood, Development and International Cooperation Instrument (NDICI). Although the regulation has not been adopted at the time of writing, the political agreement outlining its main features was endorsed by the European Parliament and the Council in March 2021.[50] While the overall allocation is of €79.5 billion, €6.36 billion are reserved to thematic programmes, as opposed to geographic programmes.[51] More than €1 billion is specifically devoted to human rights and democracy promotion,[52] which is also a horizontal objective irrigating other programmes. Moreover, the evolution of EU budget programmes is without prejudice to the European Endowment for Democracy (EEF), established in 2013 by the EU and its Member States as a non-profit association under Belgian private law, which targets primarily the EU's neighbourhood.[53]

Democracy promotion also relies on operational instruments, in particular administrative arrangements between the EU and other multilateral or regional institutions. The New Partnership for Africa's Development (NEPAD) is specifically relevant, as it was launched in 2001 with an explicit reference to the democracy-development nexus. NEPAD was integrated in the African Union's Commission as the African Union's Development Agency in 2018. Although it has not had a high-profile activity so far, it has benefitted from the EU's political support.[54]

50 Communication from the Commission to the European Parliament pursuant to Article 294(6) of the Treaty on the Functioning of the European Union concerning the position of the Council on the adoption of a Regulation of the European Parliament and of the Council on the Neighbourhood, Development and International Cooperation Instrument – Global Europe for the period 2021–2027, COM (2021) 267, 28 May 2021.

51 At least 93% of the funding under the EU NDICI should contribute to actions designed in such a way that they fulfil the criteria for ODA as established by the DAC of the OECD (Position of the Council at first reading with a view to the adoption of a regulation of the European Parliament and of the Council establishing the Neighbourhood, Development and International Cooperation Instrument – Global Europe, amending and repealing Decision No 466/2014/EU of the European Parliament and of the Council and repealing Regulation (EU) 2017/1601 of the European Parliament and of the Council and Council Regulation (EC, Euratom) No 480/2009, doc. 6879/1/21 REV 1, 27 May 2021, recital 21 and article 3(4).

52 At the time of writing, the Council position is to devote €1.36 billion euros to the Human Rights and Democracy thematic programme, 200 million euros more than in the Commission's proposal (doc. 6879/1/21 REV 1, article 6(2)(b)).

53 The statutes are available at <www.democracyendowment.eu>. The choice of this legal form, probably inspired by the US National Endowment for Democracy, has the advantage of allowing more flexible support to political and civil society actors.

54 See, however, H. Lynge Ottosen, *NEPAD's Contribution to Democracy and Good Governance in Africa*, Stockholm, International Institute for Democracy and Electoral Assistance,

2.4 *Democratic Conditionality in the EU's Development Cooperation Policy*

One of the most significant features of some EU development cooperation instruments is to be conditioned upon the respect of democratic principles. Conditionality is the set of conditions attached to the provision of benefits of development programmes. Its role in development policies has been largely discussed,[55] as it is at the core of bilateral North-South agreements[56] and of the lending activity of multilateral institutions such as development banks.[57] Like other Western development policies, the EU external policies include several examples of political conditionality, including democratic conditionality,

2010. The paper acknowledges that the NEPAD has shown few concrete results, but argues that it an innovative mechanism which has helped to increase the importance of democracy and good governance in Africa's development agenda. According to the author, the EU could have done more to share its own experience with democracy promotion within regional policy integration. See also F. C. Asogwa, A. A. Akachuku, "Global African Unity in the Era of Globalization: an Assessment of the Place of the New Partnership for Africa's Development (NEPAD)", in C. Quist-Adade, V. Dodoo (eds), *Africa's many divides and Africa's future: pursuing Nkrumah's vision of Pan-Africanism in an era of globalization, Cambridge*, Cambridge Scholars, 2015, p. 34–50; D. Gnamou, "Le NEPAD: cadre institutionnel de l'appui international à la paix et au développement en Afrique", in SFDI, *Droit international et développement*, Paris, Pedone, 2015, p. 137–153.

55 E.g., J. K. Boyce, "Development Assistance, Conditionality, and War Economies", in K. Ballentine, H. Nitzschke (eds), *Profiting from Peace: Managing the Resource Dimensions of Civil War*, Boulder, Lynne Rienner, 2005, p. 287–314; G. Sorensen (ed.), *Political Conditionality*, London, Routledge, 1993; O. Stokke, *Aid and Political Conditionality*, London, Routledge, 1995; A. Shah, *Development Assistance and Conditionality: Challenges in Design and Options for More Effective Assistance*, Paris, OECD, 2018.

56 E.g., P. R. Baehr, "Problems of aid conditionality: The Netherlands and Indonesia", *Third World Quarterly*, 1997, 18(2), pp. 363–376; H. Selbervik, "Aid and conditionality. The role of the bilateral donor: A case study of Norwegian–Tanzanian aid relationship", 1999, <www.oecd.org>.

57 F. O. Anunobi, *The Implications of Conditionality: The International Monetary Fund and Africa*, Lanham, University Press of America, 1992; L. F Guder "IMF and World Bank Conditionality and Concessional Development Financing", *Griffin's view on international and comparative law*, 2005, 6(2), p. 114–135; K. Havnevik, *The IMF and the World Bank in Africa: conditionality, impact and alternatives*, Uppsala, Scandinavian Institute of African Studies, 1987; R. Hopkins, A. Powell, A. Roy, "The World Bank, conditionality and the comprehensive development framework", in C. L. Gilbert, D. Vines (eds), *The World Bank: structure and policies*, Cambridge, Cambridge University Press, 2000, p. 282–298; J. Jones, "Conditionality and the World Bank: a Story of Domination", in A. Bendaña, G. Heiene, J. Jones (eds), *Global justice – the white man's burden? Essays on development and justice in honor of Øystein Tveter*, Bergen, Fagbokforlaget, 2007, p. 135–150; C. Santiso, "Good Governance and Aid Effectiveness: The World Bank and Conditionality", *Georgetown Public Policy Review*, 2001, 7(1), p. 1–22.

which have been widely analysed as features of EU external relations,[58] of the EU neighbourhood policy[59] and, as membership conditionality, in the framework of the EU enlargement process.[60] Following a well-established distinction, conditionality can be *ex-ante*, when conditions must be met for the programme to be triggered, or *ex-post*, when compliance with the conditions is verified during the programme. Conditionality can manifest itself in the form of incentives (positive conditionality) or in the form of withdrawal of benefits (negative conditionality).[61] *Ex-ante* positive conditionality can take the form of aid selectivity, where sufficient levels of democratic governance are a precondition for more benefits, so that additional benefits are allocated to the countries that have the best performance on certain criteria, including the quality of democracy.[62]

The GSP+ programme is an example of *ex-ante* positive conditionality, which can become *ex post* negative conditionality. The special incentive arrangement for sustainable development and good governance is provided for in Chapter 3 of the GSP Regulation and is currently applied to nine vulnerable low- and lower-middle-income countries.[63] In order to be eligible, a State must have

58 For a sociological point of view, T. Bodenstein, J. Faust, "Who Cares? European Public Opinion on Foreign Aid and Political Conditionality", *Journal of common market studies*, 2017, 55(5), p. 955–973. From a legal point of view, T. P. Holterhus, "The Legal Dimensions of Rule of Law Promotion in EU Foreign Policy: EU Treaty Imperatives and Rule of Law Conditionality in the Foreign Trade and Development Nexus", in T. P. Holterhus, *Law behind Rule of Law Transfers. On Rule-based Interactions of Legal Orders in a Globalized World*, Baden-Baden, Nomos, 2019, p. 73–112.

59 F. Schimmelfennig, H. Scholtz, "EU Democracy Promotion in the European Neighbourhood: Political Conditionality, Economic Development and Transnational Exchange", *European Union Politics*, 2008, 9(2), p. 187–215.

60 K. Barrett, "Has EU Conditionality Made a Difference to Democratic Reforms and Human Rights Development on Montenegro?", H. F. Carey (ed.), *European Institutions, Democratization, and Human Rights Protection in the European Periphery*, Lanham, Lexington, 2014, pp. 153–180.

61 S. Koch, "A Typology of Political Conditionality Beyond Aid: Conceptual Horizons Based on Lessons from the European Union", *World Development*, 2015, 75(3), p. 97–108, p. 99.

62 A traditional example of aid selectivity is the US Millennium Challenge Corporation, a development fund established in 2004. (*ibid.*).

63 Armenia, Bolivia, Cape Verde, Kyrgyzstan, Mongolia, Pakistan, the Philippines, and Sri Lanka. Uzbekistan joined on 9 April 2021. Paraguay ceased to benefit from GSP+ on 1 January 2019, as it was classified by the World Bank as an upper-middle income country for three consecutive years. Armenia and Sri Lanka could leave the scheme by 1 January 2022 and 1 January 2023 respectively (European Commission and High Representative of the Union for Foreign Affairs and Security Policy, *Report on the Generalised Scheme of Preferences covering the period 2018–2019*, JOIN (2020) 3, 10 February 2020, p. 15). However, other countries (Bangladesh, Bhutan, Lao People's Democratic Republic, Kiribati,

ratified, without any prohibited reservations and without any serious failure to effective implementation, 27 international conventions.[64] These conventions include the International Covenant on Civil and Political Rights, whose article 25 refers to three essential components of democracy, i.e. the right to take part in the conduct of public affairs, directly or through freely chosen representatives; the right to vote and to be elected at genuine periodic elections which shall be by universal and equal suffrage and shall be held by secret ballot, guaranteeing the free expression of the will of the electors; and the right to have access, on general terms of equality, to public service in his country. The benefit is the reduction of EU tariffs to 0%, which is more favourable than the partial or full removal of customs duties on two third of tariff lines (standard GSP). The benefit of the GSP+ programme is similar to the special arrangement for the least-developed countries (Everything But Arms), which provides duty-free, quota-free access for all products except arms and ammunition to least developed countries.[65] However, GSP+ beneficiary countries programmes are not eligible for this programme, as they are not least developed countries.

All preferential arrangements set in the GSP programme may be withdrawn temporarily in case of serious and systematic violation of principles laid down in the listed conventions.[66] This implies steady monitoring by the EU, although not specifically focused on democracy.[67] Although not all investigations lead to benefit withdrawal, benefits were withdrawn on some occasions: Myanmar/ Burma in 1997 (GSP; forced labour), Belarus in 2007 (GSP; freedom of association and on collective bargaining) and Sri Lanka in 2010 (GSP+; civil and political rights, torture, rights of the child). Preferences were re-established for Myanmar/Burma (2013) and Sri Lanka (2016), but not for Belarus.[68] Bangladesh, Cambodia and Myanmar have been under enhanced scrutiny in the last few years,[69] and Everything But Arms benefits were partially withdrawn to Cambodia in February 2020. Cambodia's situation is directly relevant for democracy promotion, as the withdrawal of benefits was based on

Myanmar, Nepal, São Tomé and Principe, Tajikistan, Timor-Leste) could join the scheme in the next years (*ibid.*, p. 4).

64 Article 9 and Annex VIII of the regulation.

65 Chapter 4 of the regulation. 48 countries are currently beneficiaries of this scheme.

66 Article 19(1)(a) of the regulation.

67 *Report on the Generalised Scheme of Preferences covering the period 2018–2019*, p. 7–9.

68 I. Zamifir, *Human Rights in EU Trade Policy. Unilateral Measures Applied by the EU*, European Parliamentary Research Service, 2018, doc. PE 621.905.

69 *Ibid.*, p. 2–3.

breaches of rights to political participation, alongside with the freedoms of assembly, expression and association.[70]

The Cotonou Agreement is the most analysed example of *ex-post* negative conditionality in the EU's development cooperation policy. Democratic and human rights conditionality have been introduced in several agreements concluded by the EU, far beyond development cooperation policy.[71] However, agreements with ACP countries are those through which the EU became a world leader regarding democratic conditionality in development cooperation agreements.[72] Although already present in the Lomé III Agreement of 1984, political conditionality became an actionable legal principle in the Lomé IV-bis Agreement of 1995.[73] The main legal effect of the "essential elements" clause of article 9 is to enable each party to take appropriate measures in case of serious breaches by the other party. Accordingly, article 96 sets a consultation procedure in case of breach, which can lead to "appropriate measures", including the unilateral suspension of benefits, either in the field of development cooperation or in the field of economic and trade relations.[74] Moreover, a breach of the "essential elements" clause of the Cotonou Agreement can lead to the suspension of trade preferences in Economic Partnership Agreements with ACP

70 Commission Delegated Regulation (EU) 2020/550 of 12 February 2020 amending Annexes II and IV to Regulation (EU) No 978/2012 of the European Parliament and of the Council as regards the temporary withdrawal of the arrangements referred to in Article 1(2) of Regulation (EU) No 978/2012 in respect of certain products originating in the Kingdom of Cambodia, OJ 2020 L 127/1.

71 L. Bartels, "The Application of Human Rights Conditionality in the EU's Bilateral Trade Agreements and Other Trade Arrangements with Third Countries", European Parliament Think Tank, 2008, doc. PE 406.991; M. Giorello, "The Clauses of Democratic Conditionality in the European Union's External Relations", in C. Cosgrove-Sacks, *Europe, Diplomacy, and Development. New Issues in EU Relations with Developing Countries*, London, Palgrave Macmillan, 2001, p. 79–95. For a recent example, see articles COMPROV.4(1), COMPROV.12 and INST.35 of the Trade and Cooperation Agreement between the European Union and the United Kingdom, OJ L 2020 444/14.

72 L. Christoph, *Menschenrechts- und Demokratieklauseln in den Außenbeziehungen der Europäischen Union zu den AKP-Staaten*, Baden-Baden, Nomos, 2020; H. Cuyckens, "Human Rights Clauses in Agreements between the Community and Third Countries. The Case of the Cotonou Agreement", Institute for International Law Working Paper no. 147, <www.law.kuleuven.be>.

73 P. Hilpold, "Human Rights Clauses in EU-Association Agreements", in S. Griller, B. Weidel (eds), *External Economic Relations and Foreign Policy in the European Union*, Vienna, Springer, 2002, p. 359–383.

74 J. Mackie, J. Zincke, "When Agreement Breaks Down, What Next? The Cotonou Agreement's Article 96 Consultation Procedure", European Centre for Development Policy Management Discussion Paper No. 64A, 2005, <https://ecdpm.org>.

countries, which refer to the Cotonou agreement.[75] Also taking into account the equivalent procedure of the Lomé IV-bis convention, the consultation procedure of article 96 of the Cotonou agreement has been triggered in 24 cases between 1995 and 2018. Most cases were directly related to democracy promotion: the procedure was triggered by undemocratic regime change in 15 cases and by severe procedural deficiencies in democratic elections in nine cases (sometimes in addition to human rights or rule of law concerns).[76] Not all consultations resulted in the suspension of benefits, but when this occurred, the suspended benefits were based on development cooperation schemes framed by the Cotonou agreement, as opposed to economic and trade cooperation.

The EU's democratic conditionality has been criticised for several reasons. The Cotonou agreement drew most attention, but, to some extent, lessons to be learnt in this framework also apply to other mechanisms. Besides usual debates on political conditionality in general, some authors have criticised the inherent ambiguity of democratic principles as a benchmark for conditionality.[77] Taken in its most radical form, this criticism seems excessive, as the very nature of democratic principles is to operate as standards and not as specific rules. The Cotonou agreement, with the relatively detailed account of article 9, and the subsequent practice contribute to shape the content of these principles. However, it is true that the boundaries of democratic principles are not totally clear. The EU practice has essentially focused of single-event breaches, most notably coups d'état. Although egregious and relatively easy to identify, these breaches are far from being the only hurdles to democratisation: other serious breaches of democratic principles, which can even be more dangerous in the long run as they are systematic in a given country and common to several countries, stayed under the radar.

The most common criticism of the EU's democratic conditionality is that its application is based on double standards.[78] Overall, it cannot be denied that the EU's democratic conditionality mechanisms are relatively effective, in the sense that they were applied in several cases, which creates an objective incentive for partner countries to comply with democratic principles in

75 L. Bartels, *Human Rights Provisions in Economic Partnership Agreements in Light of the Expiry of the Cotonou Agreement in 2020*, Strasbourg, European Parliament, 2017, doc. PE 578.011.

76 J. D. Saltnes, "The European Union's Human Rights Policy: Is the EU's Use of the Human Rights Clause Inconsistent?", *Global Affairs*, 2018, 4(2–3), p. 277–289.

77 A. Zimelis, "Conditionality and the EU–ACP Partnership: A Misguided Approach to Development?", *Australian Journal of Political Science*, 2011, 46(3), p. 389–406, p. 403.

78 *Ibid.*, p. 404.

the future. However, the vast majority of article 96 consultations (22) occurred before 2010. Consultations and scholarly studies became rare in recent years, but these phenomena do not seem to be due to a dramatic improvement in the respect of democratic principles. Moreover, it is well documented that the EU practice is inconsistent.[79] Between 1995 and 2018, seven coups d'état in ACP countries and 11 electoral processes with major flaws according to the election observers were not followed by article 96 consultations.[80] A significant comparator is the UN Human Rights Committee, which is more prone to address human rights violations than the EU.[81]

Some authors have tried to identify the reasons of this inconsistency. EU interest dependent on political circumstances, especially due to security interests (but also to economic interests or historical ties), is a common explanation. Nonetheless, it has also been argued that some cases of inaction were due to the finding that, depending on the circumstances, democracy promotion might not always be the best option for development. Following this line of reasoning, the withdrawal of benefits could hinder ongoing economic and social development and create instability in relatively stable, although not very democratic countries. It can be rebutted that less effective democracy promotion might be expedient in the short term, but is not a good option for sustainable development in the long term, especially if democracy is considered by nature one of its components. Nevertheless, it is undisputable that democratic conditionality is a source of dilemmas. Moral and constitutional arguments militate in favour of democratic conditionality and of its systematic and consistent application. At the same time, selective application and opacity, although political expedient in some cases, hinder the effectiveness of democracy promotion. As acknowledged by the Commission and by the High Representative of the of the Union for Foreign Affairs and Security Policy, the picture is mixed with regards to the respect of the essential elements of the Cotonou agreement by ACP partners.[82]

The likely retention of democratic conditionality in the post-Cotonou agreement is logical: radical change in the core conception of the "essential elements" clause and of the legal consequences of its breach is not advisable. At the same

79 K. Del Biondo, "EU Aid Conditionality in ACP Countries: Explaining Inconsistency in EU Sanctions Practice", *Journal of Contemporary European Research*, 2011, 7(3), p. 380–395.

80 J. D. Saltnes, *op. cit.* fn 76.

81 A. Moberg, "The Condition of Conditionality – Closing in on 20 Years of Conditionality Clauses in ACP-EU Relations", *Scandinavian studies in law*, 2015, 60, p. 275–305, p. 295–302.

82 *Joint communication – A renewed partnership with the countries of Africa, the Caribbean and the Pacific*, JOIN (2016) 52, 22 November 2016, p. 6.

time, article 96 consultations and other more flexible forms of political dialogue need to be revitalised. Arguably, a slightly different, less confrontational perspective can be useful to encourage democratisation while drawing consequences from serious breaches of democratic principles. A potential solution to existing shortcomings would be the strengthening of positive conditionality over negative conditionality. This option does not seem to be at the core of the post-Cotonou agreement, but the EU followed an approach of democratic aid selectivity after the Arab Spring(s) in relations with MENA countries in the framework of the European Neighbourhood Policy. The so-called "more for more" approach aimed at sustaining deep and sustainable democracy by rewarding best democratic and human right performers through additional benefits.[83]

Overall, the outcome of this approach was not a success. It has been argued that this is due to the discrepancy between theory and practice: the situation in the first half of the 2010s would have been better described as 'less of the same', as the rate of funds disbursed actually worsened.[84] Others insisted on the persistence of negative conditionality, as the EU policy also included a "less for less" approach, and argued that the EU should continue the support of democracy in spite of intermediate setbacks, as satisfying democratic standards in the MENA regions cannot reasonably be reached immediately.[85] Be it as it may, the form of aid selectivity embodied in the "more for more" approach for MENA countries was not effective: as acknowledged by the European Parliament, "the initial efforts after the Arab Spring (or Arab Springs) to introduce stricter conditionality and delivery incentives for beneficiary countries through the 'more for more' principle did not lead to greater leverage on the part of the EU in its ability to promote real change in the areas of democracy, the rule of law, human rights [etc.]".[86]

Although some flaws are probably contingent on the experimental post-Arab Spring(s) programmes and could be corrected in the future, more positive conditionality is not a panacea for the intrinsic difficulties of democratic

83 European Commission and High Representative of the of the Union for Foreign Affairs and Security Policy, *A new response to a changing Neighbourhood*, COM (2011) 303, 25 May 2011, p. 2 and 28.

84 F. Bicchi, "The Politics of Foreign Aid and the European Neighbourhood Policy Post-Arab Spring: 'More for More' or Less of the Same?", *Mediterranean Politics*, 2014, 19(3), p. 318–332.

85 J. C. Völkel, "More for More, Less for Less – More or Less: A Critique of the EU's Arab Spring Response à la Cinderella", *European Foreign Affairs Review*, 2014, 19(2), p. 263–281.

86 European Parliament resolution of 27 March 2019 on the post-Arab Spring: way forward for the MENA region, 2018/2160(INI), § 8.

conditionality. Existing mechanisms have undoubtedly contributed to the mainstreaming of democracy promotion, but they have not always contributed to stable democracies. Most importantly, the real added value of existing mechanisms is difficult to assess in comparison with other endogenous and exogenous factors. All in all, it is not certain that in the future they would be decisive in curbing a possible widespread erosion of democracy. This is a significant grey area of the democracy-development nexus. On the one hand, democratic conditionality shows a potential hiatus between the specific objectives of development policy and the general objectives of the EU's external action: even some those who criticise the selectivity of the EU's democratic conditionality, which has a direct negative impact on its effectiveness as a development policy tool, recognise that it is an effective and persuasive foreign policy tool.[87] On the other hand, the relative ineffectiveness of democracy promotion through conditionality does not necessarily hinder economic development in all the affected countries.

The limits of democratic conditionality are related to the longstanding debate on whether democracy is a necessary condition, a component, a necessary implication or an independent variable with respect to development. Democracy promotion in Western development cooperation policies is based on instruments whose main features are, to a large extent, inherited from the end the Cold War. In spite of the apparent worldwide consensus on the democracy-development nexus, a-democratic development policies also exist and are arguably more and more competitive.

3 A-Democratic Development Cooperation Policies

Several features of today's development cooperation policies show indifference or even reluctance to democracy promotion. On the one hand, democracy is often seen in a purportedly utilitarian way in multilateral development policies, which are therefore compatible with both democratic and with non-democratic approaches (3.1). On the other hand, Western development cooperation policies increasingly face the competition of policies where democracy plays no role, such as the Chinese one (3.2).

87 A. Moberg, *op. cit.* fn 81, p. 303.

3.1 *The Utilitarian Approach to Democracy in Multilateral Development Policies*

Development cooperation policies in general are largely inspired by other objectives than democracy promotion. Development cooperation and democracy promotion have become increasingly interconnected, but cooperation between them is only partial and its future remains uncertain.[88] As such, this remark is a truism. However, the a-democratic features of development cooperation sometimes result in a utilitarian approach to democracy, in the sense that democracy is not promoted as a value per se, but only inasmuch it is instrumental to the achievement of other objectives, which are seen as overarching within a given framework.

World Bank development policies can be seen an example of this approach. At first sight, democratic principles are not totally absent from the organisation's activity. One of the components of World Bank conditionality is good governance.[89] This concept includes necessary features of any democratic system: accountability, transparency access to information, the role of stakeholders and civil society, the independence of the judiciary, and more generally a certain legal security.[90] However, several core features of the concept of democracy, such as those addressed in the 2014 DAC guidelines (party and media pluralism, electoral processes, institutional design) are not explicitly included in the concept of good governance.

Most importantly, governance is a performance-oriented concept: in World Bank documents, it is presented as "an essential complement to sound economic policies. Efficient and accountable management by the public sector and a predictable and transparent policy framework are critical to the efficiency of markets and governments, and hence to economic development".[91] Indeed, "[b]ehind the emphasis on PSM [Public Sector Management] as a key dimension of governance is the growing conviction that an efficient government is a *sine qua non* for sustainable economic growth".[92] The concept of good governance is not necessarily biased or flawed: its development within the

88 T. Carothers, "Democracy Support and Development aid: The elusive synthesis", *Journal of Democracy*, 2010, 21(4), p. 12–26.

89 K. S. Lateef, *Evolution of The World Bank's thinking on Governance*, International Bank for Reconstruction and Development, 2016, <https://openknowledge.worldbank.org>.

90 World Bank, *Governance and Development*, 1992, <https://documents.worldbank.org> p. 13 and ff.

91 L. T. Preston, "Foreword" in World Bank, *Governance and Development*, 1992, <https://documents.worldbank.org>, p. v.

92 World Bank, *Governance. The World Bank's Experience*, 1994, <https://documents.worldbank.org>, p. viii.

World Bank was also part of a reflection on the limits of the dominant emphasis on markets under the Washington consensus of the 1980s,[93] sometimes referred to as the lost decade of development (especially for Latin America). Moreover, some non-economic concerns, such as environmental issues or gender equality, are taken into account in an increasingly visible way, particularly since the 2000s. However, democracy as such is only present incidentally, or even accidentally, as a factor of efficiency and not as a criterion of legitimacy. The timid and indirect references to democracy in existing documents can be seen as a starting point for discreet promotion and future progress, but to a certain extent, the current situation is the result of political and legal constraints which are difficult to circumvent.

From the political point of view, the need for political neutrality of the World Bank can be easily explained by the diversity of its members and the power relations between them. This is all the more understandable in a universal international organisation, whose functionalist logic is strengthened by the operational and financial nature of its activity. Good governance should not be seen as a substitute for democracy, but as a strategic concept that allows some consensus. To some extent, constructive ambiguity on the exact role of democracy within good governance allows forms of indirect promotion that would be more controversial within full-fledged democracy promotion. Nonetheless, development cooperation is to a large extent depoliticised. This situation, which has been observed even for the EU's development cooperation,[94] is the result of technicisation, which aims at avoiding potentially controversial topics and at focusing on poverty reduction. Even more than other similar issues such as human rights, democracy can be, perhaps paradoxically, divisive.

From the legal point of view, the constitutive treaties of the relevant international organisations provide a weak basis for explicit democracy promotion. For example, according to section 10 of article IV of the International Bank for Reconstruction and Development Articles of Agreement, "[t]he Bank and its officers shall not interfere in the political affairs of any member; nor shall they be influenced in their decisions by the political character of the member or

93 K. S. Lateef, *op. cit.* fn 89, p. 22. See also I. Shihata, "The World Bank and "Governance" Issues in Its Borrowing Members", in I. Shihata, *The World Bank in a Changing World. Selected Essays*, Dordrecht, Martinus Nijhoff, 1991, p. 53–96.

94 I. Heidlmayr-Chegdaly, *Technocratisation and Depoliticisation of Democracy Promotion and Development Aid. The European Union and the African Development Bank in Morocco*, Baden-Baden, Nomos, 2020; A. Pallotti, "The European Union and Africa: Depoliticised Development and the Elusive Quest for Democracy and Security", Globus Research papers no 13, 2018, <https://papers.ssrn.com>.

members concerned. Only economic considerations shall be relevant to their decisions, and these considerations shall be weighed impartially in order to achieve the purposes [of the organisation]". As acknowledged by the World Bank President in 1991, at that time even the concept of governance produced "some apprehension among our borrowing members that our staff might exceed the Bank's mandate in ways which could be interpreted as interfering in the political affairs of our borrowers".[95] Among the statutes of international development banks, article 1 of the Agreement Establishing the European Bank for Reconstruction and Development is exceptional, as it states that the Bank only operates in "countries committed to and applying the principles of multiparty democracy".[96] The concept of good governance also stems from statutory constraints, as it allows to elude debates on whether democracy promotion would constitute prohibited political activity.

Caution in dealing with democracy promotion as such does not only characterise development banks, but is also manifested in the UN definition of the objectives of development policies. While the concept of democracy was absent from the seven Millennium Development Goals of 2000, it is only indirectly taken into account in the 17 Sustainable Development Goals of 2015. The United Nations General Assembly declared that "democracy, good governance and the rule of law, as well as an enabling environment at the national and international levels, are essential for sustainable development, including sustained and inclusive economic growth, social development, environmental protection and the eradication of poverty and hunger".[97] However, only objectives that are indirectly related to democracy are mentioned in Goal 16 ("Promote peaceful and inclusive societies for sustainable development, provide access to justice for all and build effective, accountable and inclusive institutions at all levels").[98] The indicators adopted by the United Nations

95 B. B. Conable, "Memorandum to Bank managers", 29 August 1991, reproduced in World Bank, *Managing Development. The Governance Dimension*, 1992, <https://documents.worldbank.org>.

96 Agreement establishing the European Bank for Reconstruction and Development, OJ 1990 L 372/4, article 1. The provision was amended, but the reference to "principles of multiparty democracy, pluralism and market economics" was left unchanged. See also the *Procedures to Implement the Political Aspects of the Mandate of the European Bank for Reconstruction and Development*, originally adopted in 1991 and revised in 2013, with an addendum in 2018 (EBRD, "Multiparty democracy and pluralism", <www.ebrd.com>). The EBRD follows a "more for more, less for less" approach to democracy promotion (*ibid.*).

97 United Nations General Assembly, *Transforming our world: the 2030 Agenda for Sustainable Development*, A/RES/70/1, 21 October 2015, § 9.

98 "16.3. Promote the rule of law at the national and international levels and ensure equal access to justice for all.

General Assembly in 2017 make it clear that, at best, democracy is incidentally promoted. In fact, it is not democracy as such that is promoted, as indicators are either independent from the kind of political regime[99] or based on the perception of population.[100] The only indicator that has a direct relation to democracy is proportional representation of groups of the population in institutions,[101] which is nonetheless far from being sufficient to assess the quality of democracy. All in all, multilateral development policies are to a large extent a-democratic. Western development cooperation policies are compatible with this approach, but so are other national development cooperation policies where democracy promotion is absent.

3.2 *The Competition of Programmes Where Democracy Promotion Plays No Role: the Example of Chinese Development Cooperation*

Among development cooperation policies where democracy promotion plays no role, the Chinese one is the most important, both financially and politically.[102] It has attracted significant interest, but limited scholarly studies, especially on legal issues. Several significant features are still difficult to assess precisely, including the structure and the overall amount of Chinese

---

16.6. Develop effective, accountable and transparent institutions at all levels.

16.7. Ensure responsive, inclusive, participatory and representative decision-making at all levels" (*ibid.*, § 59).

99 "16.3.1. Proportion of victims of violence in the previous 12 months who reported their victimization to competent authorities or other officially recognized conflict resolution mechanisms / 16.3.2. Unsentenced detainees as a proportion of overall prison population / 16.6.1. Primary government expenditures as a proportion of original approved budget, by sector (or by budget codes or similar)" (United Nations General Assembly, *Work of the Statistical Commission pertaining to the2030 Agenda for Sustainable Development*, A/RES/71/313, 6 July 2017, annex).

100 "16.6.2. Proportion of population satisfied with their last experience of public service.

16.7.2. Proportion of population who believe decision-making is inclusive and responsive, by sex, age, disability and population group" (*ibid.*).

101 "16.7.1. Proportions of positions (by sex, age, persons with disabilities and population groups) in public institutions (national and local legislatures, public service, and judiciary) compared to national distributions" (*ibid.*).

102 The expression "development cooperation" has recently replaced the traditional expression "foreign aid" in Chinese official documents (Chinese Council of State, *China's International Development Cooperation in the New Era*, 10 January 2021, <http://english.www.gov.cn>). On recent development of Chinese development cooperation, including the establishment of the Forum for China–Africa Cooperation in 2000 and of the China International Development Cooperation Agency in 2018, see C. Cheng, "The Logic Behind China's Foreign Aid Agency", Carnegie Endowment for International Peace, 21 May 2019, <https://carnegieendowment.org>; E. Tjønneland, "The changing role of Chinese development aid", Chr. Michelsen Institute insight no 2, 2020, <www.cmi.no>.

development cooperation programmes.[103] While concessionality is an essential feature of the DAC ODA definition,[104] not all Chinese foreign aid is concessional.[105] According to an estimate, Chinese foreign aid totalled $354.4 billion between 2000 and 2014, including about $75 billion in concessional aid and about $275 billion in low concessional loans.[106] OECD estimates are significantly different: China's total concessional finance for development only reached $3.1 billion in 2015.[107] Moreover, non-concessional loans are channelled through different entities, including private (State-controlled) entities, State entities, and international organisations: available data only rely on known information, which is limited.[108]

In any case, it is not disputed that, in the eyes of recipient countries, Chinese development cooperation programmes can be a complement or an alternative to traditional ODA and traditional regional or multilateral programmes. Crucially, Chinese programmes officially aim at avoiding political conditionality: "no strings attached" is the motto which is most commonly associated to Chinese development cooperation policy. First elaborated in the Chinese government's 1964 *Eight Principles for Economic Aid and Technical Assistance to Other Countries*,[109] the (official) lack of political conditionality is recalled in the Council of State's white papers on development cooperation, including the one issued in January 2021.[110] These documents carefully avoid any reference to

---

103 See L. Lynch, S. Andersen, T. Zhu, "China's Foreign Aid: A Primer for Recipient Countries, Donors, and Aid Providers", Center for Global Development, 9 July 2020, <www.cgdev.org>.

104 This implies, in DAC statistics, the requirement of a minimum grant component depending on the applicable financial scheme (OECD, "Official development assistance – definition and coverage", <www.oecd.org>).

105 F. Wan, "How 'unconditional' is China's foreign aid?", *Deutsche Welle*, 15 May 2018, <www.dw.com>.

106 A. Dreher, A. Fuchs, B. Parks, A. M. Strange, "Aid, China, and Growth: Evidence from a New Global Development Finance Dataset", AidData Working Paper no. 46, 2017, <http://docs.aiddata.org>.

107 OECD, "Development Co-operation of the People's Republic of China", <www.oecd.org>.

108 A. Dreher, A. Fuchs, B. Parks, A. M. Strange, *op. cit.* fn 106, p. 10–11. E.g., at least at the beginning, the Belt and Road Initiative was mainly financed through the China Export and Import Bank and the China Development Bank, while the Asian Infrastructure Investment Bank (created in 2015) only played a limited role (J. Lo, "Why isn't China's Belt and Road Initiative acting through the Asian Infrastructure Bank?", *IR Theory in Practice*, 25 October 2015, <https://irtheoryinpractice.com>).

109 Principle 2: "In providing aid to other countries, the Chinese government strictly respects the sovereignty of recipient countries, and never attaches any conditions or asks for any privileges" (<www.china.org.cn>).

110 Chinese Council of State, *China's Foreign Aid* (*2011*), <http://english.www.gov.cn>, § 1: "China upholds the Five Principles of Peaceful Coexistence, respects recipient countries' right to independently select their own path and model of development, and believes

concepts that could be seen as immediately related to democracy promotion. Like in all development cooperation policies, this position is based on domestic constitutional foundations. It is well known that the Popular Republic of China followed a specific path towards development and democracy, whose result is difficult to fit in traditional analytical category: depending on the framework of analysis, China can be seen as a democratic developing country or as an undemocratic developed country, with all possible intermediate qualifications. The lack of political conditionality is presented as a corollary of equality and non-interference in internal affairs, two of the five principles of peaceful coexistence enshrined in the preamble of the 1982 Constitution.[111]

From a policy perspective, discussions revolve around whether this approach simply coexists or also competes with Western development cooperation policies, which include democracy promotion and traditional multilateral development policies. Empirical data do not seem to be conclusive. When individual cases are studied, the assessment is highly dependent on the interest at play for China, and therefore on its efforts and strategy.[112] Using broader sets of data, some argue that the claim that Chinese programmes systematically impairs the effectiveness of Western development cooperation is unsubstantiated.[113] According to the other studies, Chinese programmes undermines democratic governance[114] and weakens the democratising effects of DAC ODA.[115] However,

---

that every country should explore a development path suitable to its actual conditions. China never uses foreign aid as a means to interfere in recipient countries' internal affairs or seek political privileges for itself". *China's Foreign Aid* (2014), <http://english.www.gov.cn>, preface. Chinese Council of State, *China's International Development Cooperation in the New Era*, *op. cit.* fn 102, § 1.3: "When cooperating with other countries for development, no country should interfere in their efforts to find a development path suited to their own national conditions, interfere in their internal affairs, impose its own will on them, attach political strings, or pursue political self-interest".

111 Chinese Council of State, *China's Foreign Aid* (2011), *op. cit.* fn 110, § 1.

112 D. Chen, K. Kinzelbach, "Democracy promotion and China: blocker or bystander?", *Democratization*, 2015, 22(3), p. 400–441, which compares the cases of Myanmar and Hong Kong; C. Hackenesch, "Not as bad as it seems: EU and US democracy promotion faces China in Africa", *Democratization*, 2015, 22(3), p. 419–437, which studies the cases of Ethiopia and Angola and concludes that domestic factors are determinant for the success of Western development cooperation policies.

113 A. Dreher, A. Fuchs, B. Parks, A. M. Strange, *op. cit.* fn 106, p. 23–26.

114 E. Kersting, C. Kilby. "Aid and Democracy Redux", *European Economic Review*, 2014, 67(3), p. 125–143, p. 137 and 139.

115 X. Li, "Does Conditionality Still Work? China's Development Assistance and Democracy in Africa", *Chinese Political Science Review*, 2017, 2(2), p. 201–220, p. 216; A. Sharshenova, G. Crawford, "Undermining Western democracy promotion in Central Asia: China's countervailing influences, powers and impact", *Central Asian Survey*, 2017, 36(4), p. 453–472.

these analysis diverge on the final consequences of this phenomenon: while some conclude that traditional development cooperation has a positive and statistically significant effect on democracy in the long run,[116] others consider that the democratising effect of aid conditionality works only when recipient countries do not have alternative sources of aid.[117]

From the legal point of view, it is worth noting that international law plays a very limited role in the Chinese approach to (the lack of) democracy in development cooperation. While Western policies rely on references to international instruments and on international co-ordination within the OECD DAC, Chinese development cooperation mainly relies on national law instruments.[118] The direct link between the non-interference in internal affairs and the rejection of a democratic dimension of development cooperation shows that international law is only used to underscore its limits. To be sure, Chinese programmes are also embedded in a network of international agreements, but the "no strings attached" approach has excluded any reference to international instruments related to democracy so far. What remains to be seen in the next years is whether the Chinese approach will remain essentially a domestic law approach or whether it will increase its interaction with international norms and institutions. The establishment of the Asian Infrastructure Investment Bank in 2015 showed that China is growingly willing to invest on the international structures underpinning development policies. Some forms of dialogue with the West already exist, such as the China-DAC Study Group.[119] Moreover, the Chinese Council of State's white paper of January 2021 on development cooperation seems to show an ever stronger commitment to multilateralism.[120] However, the Chinese approach, even in its "internationalised" version, will essentially be parallel to Western-based international organisations and policies as long as it does not aim at influencing general international law and universal international institutions.

While provisions like article 9 of the Cotonou agreement contribute to international practice on the democracy-development nexus, furthering the possible evolution of customary law at the universal level, Chinese development cooperation is a non-practice in this respect. This does not mean that it has no

116 E. Kersting, C. Kilby, *op. cit.* fn 114, p. 139.

117 X. Li, *op. cit.* fn 115, p. 217.

118 Inasmuch as contracts are used for loans, the applicable law is not necessarily Chinese law, but is not public international law.

119 OECD, "Development Co-operation of the People's Republic of China", <www.oecd.org>.

120 Chinese Council of State, *China's International Development Cooperation in the New Era*, *op. cit.* fn 102, §§ III.4, V.2, VI.2, VIII.1, VIII.2.

influence on the evolution of international policies, in particular within multilateral international organisations. Empirical studies suggest that the availability of "unconditional" aid influences the way in which the World Bank applies its own conditionality: it has been shown that the World Bank delivers loans with significantly fewer conditions to recipient countries which also receive Chinese aid,[121] even if this phenomenon does not affect governance conditionality specifically but conditionality in general. Arguably, the World Bank's practice can be explained by the will to remain competitive when development resources are abundant.[122] Unsurprisingly, as the Western and the Chinese approach to democracy in development cooperation policy are different, each approach can shape international law in a different way.

4 Concluding Remarks

In the last 30 years, democracy promotion has become a significant component of development cooperation, with a remarkable continuity since the end of the Cold War. Although challenged by alternative models and not directly integrated in multilateral development policies, it is deeply rooted in Western development cooperation policies, where it has been mainstreamed. In spite of its limits, the EU's development cooperation policy is particularly explicit in this respect, which constitutes an important difference with respect to multilateral institutions. At the same time, compared with Western development cooperation policies, the neutrality of multilateral development policies shows that democracy promotion can be divisive. One can wonder whether this situation reflects a form of benevolence towards active democracy promotion or whether it ends up hindering it. There is no hint that democracy promotion is declining in development cooperation and that the Western approach is becoming wishful exceptionalism. However, all involved actors are aware of the growing competition by national development cooperation programmes with "no strings attached".

The current context should encourage a renewal of democracy promotion in Western development cooperation policies. Although their financial instruments remain a great source of influence, these policies cannot simply rely on a "business as usual" approach, but need to adapt to the lessons of the last few years. In particular, democratic conditionality is not always effective: in

121 D. Hernandez, "Are "New" Donors Challenging World Bank Conditionality?", *World Development*, 2017, 96(3), p. 529–549, p. 544–545.

122 *Ibid.*, p. 545.

the case of the EU's development cooperation policy, the practice of EU institutions does not allow a sufficient level of predictability of the consequences of breaches of democratic principles in partner countries. Enhanced political dialogue can be useful, but it should not lead to lowering democratic standards. The overall aim should be the prevention of broader erosion of democratic achievements and the reinstatement of liberal-democratic societies as attractive models, in a context where the "end of history" and the lack of alternatives are not certainties anymore.

CHAPTER 9

Election Observation and Assistance

Their Potential for Democracy Promotion with Special Focus on Challenges in Times of COVID-19

Christina Binder

1 Introduction*

The contribution of international electoral assistance and observation to democracy promotion is very topical: Electoral support activities have skyrocketed since the beginning of the 1990s. Numerous international organizations engage in these activities today, among them the United Nations (UN), the Organization of American States (OAS), the Organization for Security and Cooperation in Europe (OSCE), the European Union (EU), the Council of Europe (CoE) and, more recently, the African Union (AU) and the Commonwealth of Independent States (CIS).[1] The relevance also shows in concrete figures: As of April 2021, ODIHR has conducted close to 390 election activities;[2] the EU has deployed over 120 Election observation missions to all continents (since 2000);[3] and the UN provided electoral assistance to more than 50 countries between 2017 and 2019 alone.[4]

---

* This contribution is partly based on C Binder, 'International Electoral Support: Challenges and Added Value' (2009) 13 Max Planck UNYB 213–46; see also C Binder/C Pippan, 'Election Monitoring, International', in R Wolfrum (ed), Max Planck Encyclopedia of Public International Law, 2018, https://opil.ouplaw.com.

1 In Africa, also sub-regional organizations, such as the Economic Community of West African States (ECOWAS) and the Southern African Development Community (SADC), are increasingly becoming involved in election-related activities. Likewise, numerous NGOs such as the Carter Center, the National Democratic Institute, the European Network of Election Monitoring Organizations (ENEMO), or IFES are frequently engaged in EOMs and relevant electoral assistance projects.

2 See OSCE/ODIHR Website <https://www.osce.org/odihr/infographic-election-follow-up>.

3 See EU External Action Service, 'Election Observation Missions' <https://eeas.europa.eu/topics/election-observation-missions-eueoms_en/421/Election%20observation%20missions%20(EUEOMs)>.

4 UN SG Report electoral Assistance (2019) <https://dppa.un.org/sites/default/files/sg-electoral_assistance_report_final_2019114_e.pdf>.

 | DOI:10.1163/9789004508712_010

The remarkable increase of election related activities goes hand in hand with a renewed understanding of national sovereignty in international law, which is no longer insensible to the way, how a regime is formed. Some refer to an 'emerging right to democracy',[5] others to a right to the 'emergence of democratic governance'.[6] An individual right to participate in elections, including electoral guarantees, is incorporated in international human rights instruments (*e.g.* Art 25 ICCPR).[7] At the 1993 World Conference on Human Rights, the representatives of 171 states underlined *inter alia* the responsibility of the international community to 'support the strengthening and promotion of democracy […] in the entire world'.[8] Thereby, the commitment to democracy and the recognition of the right to political participation seems to be almost universally shared and accepted.

At the same time, the realisation of democracy, the implementation of the right to political participation is far from perfect. For example, Freedom House, in its survey measuring political and civil liberties, found 'freedom in retreat' in 2020 for the 15th consecutive year in a row; constating thus a deepening democratic recession.[9] Particular concerns were raised in relation to the detrimental impact of the COVID-19 pandemic, which seems to have furthered authocratic tendencies and put additional constraints on democracies and democracy promotion worldwide.

Against that background, one may thus ask after roughly three decades of electoral support activities: what is their impact on democracy promotion? Or, more precisely, can they contribute to improve the quality of electoral processes in general and particularly in difficult times as the current COVID-19 pandemic? In doing so, we understand elections as essential part of democracy promotion – in line with former UN Secretary General Kofi Annan's

5 T Franck, 'The Emerging Right to Democratic Governance' (1992) 86 AJIL 46; T Franck, 'The Emerging Right to Democratic Governance' in R Falk (ed) 2 Human Rights: Critical Concepts in Political Space (2008) 171.

6 N Petersen, 'The Principle of Democratic Teleology in International Law', (2008) 34 Brooklyn Journal of International Law, 33.

7 As of May 2021, the ICCPR was ratified by 173 states, the International Convention on the Elimination of Racial Discrimination (CERD) by 182 states, the Convention on the Elimination of All Forms of Discrimination against Women (CEDAW) by 189 states, the Convention on the Rights of Persons with Disabilities by 182 States. (See UN Human Rights Office of the High Commissioner <https:// indicators.ohchr.org>).

8 Vienna Declaration and Programme of Action, 25 June 1993, para I/8.

9 Freedom in the World 2021, S Reducci, 'Democracy under Siege' <https://freedomhouse.org/report/freedom-world/2021/democracy-under-siege>.

statement: 'While democracy must be more than free elections, it is also true [...] that it cannot be less'.[10]

In the following, this contribution will start with an overview of relevant electoral support activities and also refer to the international standards at stake (Part 2). On that basis, it turns to the potential of international electoral support and discusses to what extent it is an adequate tool to improve the quality of elections, therewith contributing to democracy promotion (Part 3). Then, the limitations and challenges faced will be examined (Part 4). A brief appreciation concludes (Part 5).

2 Generalities on International Electoral Support

2.1 *Overview*

Electoral support activities are conducted by an always increasing number of international organizations. Some of them, as the OAS, the OSCE, the CoE, the AU, the CIS and the Commonwealth of Nations limit their engagement to Member States, whereas the EU is the only organization that observes elections and conducts electoral assistance projects exclusively in non-member countries. Unlike Eurasia, the Americas and Africa, Asia lacks a regional organization engaging in electoral support.[11]

International electoral support activities can take place during all phases of the electoral cycle, i.e. voter and candidate registration, election campaign, election day, complaints and appeals as well as, more generally, in relation to the drafting of the legal framework governing elections. The difference between electoral observation and assistance relates to the role they play for the electoral process. While electoral observation is based on the principle of non interference and – in the end – issues a statement whether the elections were conducted in line with international standards;[12] electoral assistance

10 UN Secretary General Kofi Annan, address at the International Conference 'Towards a Community of Democracies', Warsaw, 27 June 2000. See Press Release SG/SM/7467 <http://www.un.org/News/Press/docs/2000/sgsm7467.htm>. Obviously, for true democracy promotion a more holistic approach is needed. This will be discussed at the end of this contribution.

11 To be sure, in recent years both the CIS and the Shanghai Cooperation Organization (SCO) have begun to deploy election observers to countries in Eastern Europe and Central Asia. However, since the respective missions are frequently accused of deviating from established international standards, election monitoring by these organizations has so far remained a rather controversial exercise.

12 Election observation is generally defined as the 'purposeful gathering of information regarding an electoral process, and the making of informed judgements on the conduct

directly supports national electoral authorities – eg through legal and logistical advice, poll worker training or civic education – but will not publically comment on the quality of the electoral process.

2.2 *Framework for the Support Activities: Applicable Standards*

A detailed set of international standards and best practices governs electoral support activities. They are set out in two bodies of international law: general human rights instruments and the election observation/assistance practice of international organizations.

In international human rights law, the right to political participation and related political freedoms seem most important. The right to political participation is provided, eg, in Art 25 of the Covenant on Civil and Political Rights (ICCPR), which details its elements as follows:

> Every citizen shall have the right and the opportunity, without any of the distinctions mentioned in article 2 and without unreasonable restrictions: [...] b) To vote and to be elected at genuine periodic elections which shall be by universal and equal suffrage and shall be held by secret ballot, guaranteeing the free expression of the will of the electors; [...].

Similar guarantees are incorporated in the Universal Declaration of Human Rights (UDHR) (Article 21.3) and in regional human rights treaties (Article 3 of Protocol 1 to the European Convention on Human Rights (ECHR), Article 23 of the American Convention on Human Rights (ACHR) as well as Article 13 of the African Charter on Human and Peoples' Rights).

These provisions, as further developed in the practice of the respective human rights monitoring bodies, generally provide that elections have to be periodic and genuine (e.g. with a level playing field for all candidates/incumbents and the opposition), based on universal and equal suffrage and held by secret ballot.[13] Moreover, elections must allow for the free expression of the will of the electorate which outrules, at least, practices such as an intimidation or coercion of voters. Further standards are established in specialised

---

of such a process on the basis of the information collected, by persons who are not inherently authorized to intervene in the process [...]'. International IDEA, 'Glossary of Electoral and Related Terms' <http://wwwold.idea.int/publications/ace/electoral_glossary.htm#e>. See also the similar but more detailed definition of 'international election observation' of the Declaration of Principles for International Election Observation, New York, 27 October 2005.

13 See also HRC, General Comment No 25/57, 12 July 1996, UN Doc CCPR/C/21/Rev.1/Add.7.

treaties such as the International Convention on the Elimination of All Forms of Racial Discrimination (CERD, Art 5.c), the Convention on the Elimination of all Forms of Discrimination against Women (CEDAW, Art 7 and 8) as well as the Convention on the Rights of Persons with Disabilities (CRPD, Art 29) with the aim of eliminating discrimination based on race, gender and disability in elections.

The binding standards in human rights instruments are further developed by non-binding standards and political commitments adopted in the context of international organizations,[14] particularly the UN, the OSCE, the CoE, the OAS and the AU. Although formally, these commitments are not legally binding, they serve as common standards of reference and are supposed to foster implementation in a similar way as obligatory standards. The regulatory framework so developed varies in detail and concreteness. The biannual General Assembly Resolutions 'Enhancing the effectiveness of the principle of periodic genuine elections' ('Enhancing Resolutions') are rather vague on relevant standards and also stress the necessary autonomy of states by affirming that the primary obligation to organize elections is with governments (see eg UNGA Res 60/162 of 16 December 2005). At regional level, likewise the Inter-American Democratic Charter (Arts. 23–25)[15] remains rather vague. The 1990 CSCE/OSCE Copenhagen Document (paras. 6–8),[16] the 2002 OAU/AU Declaration on the Principles governing Elections in Africa (paras II–IV) as well as the 2007 African Charter on Democracy, Elections and Governance (Art 17)[17] conversely, outline the election related commitments of member states in considerable detail. Very comprehensive and detailed is likewise 2002 Code of Good Practice in Electoral Matters[18] in which the Venice Commission of the Council of Europe assembled principles of European heritage at expert/technical level.

Drawn from the above, among the standards and best practices that guide relevant electoral support activities (election observation and assistance) are the following: universal and non-discriminatory voter registration; effective guarantee of equal voting rights; creation of a level playing field for parties and

14 See also Binder/Pippan, note ♣, para 21.

15 Inter-American Democratic Charter, 12 September 2001, (2001) 40 ILM 1289.

16 Conference on Security and Co-operation in Europe, 'Document of the Copenhagen Meeting of the Conference on the Human Dimension of the CSCE', 29 June 1990, (1990) 29 ILM 1305. The CSCE was renamed OSCE in 1994.

17 Organization of African Unity, 'OAU/AU Declaration on the Principles Governing Democratic Elections in Africa', 8 July 2002, AHG/Decl 1 (XXXVIII).

18 European Commission for Democracy Through Law (Venice Commission), 'Code of Good Practice in Electoral Matters', 5–6 July and 18–19 October 2002, CDL-AD(2002)023.

candidates, including adequate access to the media and to public funds; existence of a transparent legal framework and a neutral and impartial election administration, usually implying the establishment of an independent electoral commission; freedom of voters to form and express their opinion without intimidation; secrecy of the vote; correct counting of votes and publication of the results; guarantee of an effective complaints and appeals procedure; and due installation in office of those validly elected. At the same time, however, these standards and best practices must always be considered against the background of diverging country situations and countries' varying stages in the process of democratic transition. This contextualisation allows for a certain flexibility and opens a possibility to accommodate different domestic situations.[19]

In addition, political freedoms, as the freedoms of expression, assembly, association and movement establish basic preconditions for genuine elections.[20] These rights are of relevance for the entire electoral process: during the pre-election period (e.g. as regards the election campaign or the establishment of political parties); on election-day; and in the post-election phase (e.g. in case of public demonstrations or manifestations; or public criticism of the results).[21]

Electoral support activities may draw upon these standards and best practices, which also serve as yardsticks to assess a country's electoral performance. This raises specific questions during the current COVID-19 pandemic. Indeed, electoral standards/political rights and freedoms come under considerable pressure in times of pandemic when quarantines/containment measures impose restrictions of movement and assembly therewith preventing, for example, election rallies and making it harder if not impossible for contestants to convey their message to the electorate during election campaigns. Even more directly may the right to political participation be encroached upon: Universal suffrage is at stake in times of pandemic, for instance, when voters do not dare to cast their vote for fear of infection; voting secrecy and freedom when states rely increasingly on remote voting methods as postal voting, thus moving out of the controlled environment of the polling stations, to reduce the risk of spreading the disease. Electoral support activities, especially election observation missions, need to take these difficulties/restrictions into account when conducting their assessments.

19 A country is thus assessed not only against the scale of absolute values but also as to its proper progress made.

20 See *e.g.* Arts 19, 21, 22 ICCPR.

21 Fair trial standards as contained in Art 14 ICCPR are crucial for the assessment of specific aspects of the electoral process, such as for election disputes resolution mechanisms.

What are the features of electoral support activities? – Focus will lie on the OSCE and EU as regards election observation missions (EOMs) and on the UN with respect to electoral assistance.

2.3 *International Election Observation: Methodology and Organisation of an EOM*[22]

EOMs for a particular election are deployed on the invitation of the country concerned.[23] Mostly, observation missions observe direct elections for state institutions at the national level. While organisations traditionally have focused on new democracies and countries in transition, more recently (targeted) missions have been sent[24] also to long standing democracies.[25] Limited missions may likewise be deployed either because the legal framework or the overall conditions for genuine democratic elections are not in place, because security factors do not permit the necessary minimum conditions for effective election observation or because certain aspects of an election are considered of particular relevance. Also in face of the COVID-19 pandemic, more limited missions have been deployed to account for the constraints imposed on EOMs by the pandemic (see below).

Indeed, the mandate of election observation missions diversified over time. In recent observation practice, limited (technical) or targeted missions are frequently deployed. They look into areas of particular interest in a specific country, such as voter registration, e-voting, campaign finance or absentee, early, or postal voting. Conversely, in order to arrive at an accurate and comprehensive assessment of the respective election, the mandate of traditional/full-scale international monitoring missions is generally broad in terms of subject matter, time frame and geography.

'Full fledged' EOMs generally consist of two components: long term and short term observation; also equalling a qualitative and a quantitative part.[26] The Core Team (8–12 persons) and a limited number of Long Term Observers

22 See also C Binder 'International Election Observation by the OSCE and the Human Right to Political Participation' (2007) 13 EPL 133, 145.

23 For instance, all OSCE participating states have been requested to inform the ODIHR of their upcoming elections and to issue an official invitation to the ODIHR in a timely manner. (OSCE/ODIHR Election Observation Handbook (6th ed, 2010) 13).

24 These assessment missions usually comprise a team of experts who visit a country shortly before an election and on election-day. They focus on specific issues and the implementation of best practices. (See *ibid.*, 14).

25 For a comprehensive overview see the website of OSCE/ODIHR <https:// www.osce.org/odihr/elections>.

26 For details see Election Observation Handbook, note 23, 25 *et seq.*

(LTOs) (usually around 14–20) are deployed already several weeks before election-day.[27] The Core Team is composed of experts in different areas, including a legal, an electoral and a political expert, a media analyst and in some cases, also a gender or a minority expert. It will assess the overall framework for and the conduct of the elections from the respective capital city. LTOs are deployed in teams of two in different regions throughout the country to observe the various phases of the election (pre-election phase, election-day, the immediate post-election phase and the extended post-election phase) country-wide.[28]

A large number of Short Term Observers (STOs) (up to 1300;[29] the number depends on the organisation[30] and on the country situation) is deployed immediately before the election. They visit various polling stations on election-day, and, guided by questionnaires, render a primarily statistical/quantitative assessment of the elections.[31]

Immediately after election-day, a statement of preliminary findings and conclusions[32] presents a mission's assessments to the public in a press conference. A comprehensive final report, with an in depth analysis and country specific recommendations for future elections follows a few weeks after the election.[33] The implementation of these recommendations has recently been furthered by increased follow-up activities of organizations such as the OSCE/ODIHR, the CoE and the EU; recommendations may also be the starting point for future electoral assistance. This reflects a holistic view of elections which covers the whole electoral cycle. Such a comprehensive 'electoral cycle approach' is an essential component of modern election observation/monitoring methodology.

27 A needs assessment mission will assess extent, needs and context of the intended EOM 2–3 months prior to the effective deployment of the mission (See *ibid.*, 23–4).

28 For further details, see *ibid.*, 29 *et seq.*

29 1.300 STOs observed the Repeat Second Round of the Ukraine Presidential Elections on 26 December 2004.

30 For instance, the OSCE tends to deploy more STOs than the EU.

31 The questions asked refer to the polling station committee (composition, preparedness), the setting of the polling station (presence of campaign material etc.), the presence of local observers, party representatives and unauthorized persons such as the police or the military. Further questions concern the accuracy of the voter lists and the conduct of the polling.

32 For more details, see Election Observation Handbook, note 23, 66–7.

33 See in this sense *ibid.*, 77.

2.4 *Electoral Assistance*

Electoral/technical assistance missions tend to be smaller than EOMs. Being targeted expert missions, especially missions with a long term component remain in the country considerable time. The UN provides electoral assistance to an annual average of 40 to 50 countries as diverse as Armenia, Bhutan, Cambodia, Democratic Republic of the Congo (DRC), Mexico, Timor-Leste, Togo, Yemen and Zambia.[34] Of this assistance, approximately half is focused on an election event and half on longer-term support.

Possible types of assistance range from technical advice as regards the most appropriate information technology for the establishment of voter and candidate lists or for the tabulation and transmission of results, to legal advice, the logistical and operational support during all phases of the electoral cycle, poll worker or domestic observer training. Specific forms of assistance support countries in addressing the challenges of COVID-19, e.g. as regards the introduction of new technologies for remote voting. Technical assistance may also include the provision of direct funding. It can take place throughout the entire electoral cycle and will not only focus on electoral authorities but also address other electoral stakeholders, such as political parties, civil society, domestic observers and the media.

2.5 *Electoral Support and COVID-19*[35]

The COVID-19 pandemic put considerable constraints on electoral support activities, most notably on election observation. Indeed, the physical deployment of election observers is generally difficult, if not impossible, when elections are held in times of pandemic. Threats to life and health of observers are huge and the practical feasibility of deploying a mission may be insurmountable. At the same time, it may be necessary to have certain international observation for the sake of the integrity of the electoral process. Thus, during the ongoing COVID-19 pandemic, limited election observation missions under tightened security measures have been deployed for example, to Serbia, Croatia, North Macedonia, Poland and Montenegro.[36]

34 UNDP, 'Electoral Assistance Implementation Guide' (2007) <http://www.undp.org/governance/docs/UNDP-Electoral-Assistance-Implementation-Guide.pdf> 5.

35 See also CoE Congress of Local and Regional Authorities, 'Local and Regional Elections in Major Crisis Situations', CG-FORUM(2020)01-05, 22.

36 OSCE/ODIHR, 'Elections in 2020' <https://www.osce.org/odihr/elections/2020>. Note that most of these missions were composed only of the core team of experts and no systematic observation of Election Day was conducted. However, for example during the recent parliamentary elections in Montenegro, also long-term observers were deployed to observe the electoral process in the regions. Additionally, note that at some

The physical presence of an election observation mission in a limited format in times of COVID-19 is conditioned by various factors. First, travel restrictions may be in place that do not allow international observers to come to the country or allow only certain nationals to do so, thus limiting the composition of a mission.[37] Second, international observers may be required upon the arrival in the country to stay in quarantine or take a test to minimize the risk of importing the virus. It is then up to the inviting state's authorities to facilitate solutions that are conducive to the conduct of observation activities. Third, the personal composition of the mission needs to be adjusted in light of the pandemic. For example, in times of COVID-19, it is not recommended for persons from vulnerable groups to participate in missions due to related health risks.[38] Further, social distancing should be adhered to both during meetings with interlocutors and on the Election Day and personal protective equipment like face masks should be provided and used. In any case, the number of observers on the ground should be limited.[39]

Default options and alternative strategies may be necessary when the physical presence of observers in the country is not possible, including remote meetings with key stakeholders (eg the Central Election Commission, candidates, political parties, civil society, domestic observers, the media) as well as a co-operation with domestic NGOs and international partners who are in the country on election day to allow for some physical observation of the electoral process. While such alternative strategies obviously cannot replace the deployment of an election observation mission, it at least allows for remote presence, some degree of observation, maintains a platform for the dialogue with local authorities and domestic stakeholders and therefore should have some beneficial effects as regards the integrity of the electoral process even when done remotely. In any case, the COVID-19 pandemic requires a certain adaptation of electoral support.

---

of these missions, for example in the presidential elections in Poland, observers from the Parliamentary Assembly of the Council of Europe were present. CoE PACE, 'PACE to assess the Presidential election in Poland', <http://assembly.coe.int/nw/xml/News/News-View-EN.asp?newsid=7932&lang=2>. Reportedly, social distancing measures were observed during meetings with interlocutors and personal protective equipment like face masks was used.

37 World Politics Review, 'How Election Observers Are Adapting to COVID-19' (2020) <https://www.worldpoliticsreview.com/trend-lines/28902/how-election-observers-are-adapting-to-covid-19>.

38 EFOR Policy Brief no. 89, 'Planning election observation during the COVID-19 pandemic> (2020) <https://expertforum.ro/en/files/2020/08/PB-89-observation.pdf>.

39 *Ibid.*

2.6 *Resume*

The appraisal above evidences the complementary function of international election observation and assistance activities. Problem areas, which are indicated in the reports of EOMs may, for instance, subsequently be taken up and addressed by means of technical assistance. In doing so, electoral assistance activities can use the recommendations of EOMs as orientation and guidance during the assistance project. Subsequent EOMs, in their findings and reports, may then assess the impact of the relevant electoral assistance activity.

This leads to the added value of electoral support. How may electoral support enhance the quality of electoral processes? – Through various means, indeed.

3 Potential of International Electoral Support

International electoral support may enhance the quality of electoral processes/democracy in particular by means of 1) precise standards and best practices; 2) the very presence of obervers; 3) technical and/or financial assistance; 4) a (de-)legitimation of results by observers who assess the elections; and 5) detailed recommendations and according follow up activities.

3.1 *Precise Standards and Best Practices*

Electoral support (election observation and technical assistance) has produced an extensive set of standards and best practices which influence and further detail general human rights standards (i.e. the right to political participation). For instance, general human rights law does not establish which electoral system (majority, semi-proportional or proportional representation system) should be adopted. Best practices nonetheless maintain that developing democracies should ideally choose a system which stimulates the development of political parties and thus prefer a proportional representation system to a strict majority system.[40] Moreover, excessively high threshold degrees for parties to enter parliament are not considered appropriate in proportional representation systems set up in young democracies.[41] Relevant best practices also guide electoral processes in time of the COVID-19 pandemic: they call

40 See for instance OSCE/ODIHR, Assessment of the Law on Election of the President, Republic of Tajikistan, 26 July 2006.

41 For instance, a six percent threshold to enter parliament was considered high in Moldova. (OSCE/ODIHR, Final Report, Republic of Moldova, Parliamentary Elections, 25 February 2001, 3).

for mitigation measures (face-masks and disinfectants, measures to prevent crowding in polling stations as a move to bigger locations or the extension of voting over several days) as well as an increased use of alternative/remote voting methods (e.g. postal- or internet-voting)[42] to balance health risks with respect for electoral standards.[43]

Such detailed standards and best practices facilitate exact recommendations as well as targeted electoral assistance activities. They make it also easier for national governments to improve their electoral performance.

3.2 *Presence of Observers & Public Attention*

Furthermore, the very presence of EOMs should improve the quality of the election process. International observers strengthen the position and further the security of local actors; including civil society and opposition candidates.[44] On election-day, the presence of international observers in polling stations deters overt acts of electoral fraud.[45] Furthermore, the publication of an EOM's preliminary findings usually attracts considerable media attention. This focus on a country's election is a strong instrument to pressure national authorities to conduct elections in conformity with international standards. Accordingly, in most cases, the electoral process as such is improved by the presence of an impartial and objective third party which observes how elections are conducted. This seems indeed particularly necessary in times of COVID-19, when health considerations and according restrictions overshadow the conduct of elections which may be abused by incumbants to gain unfair advantages accordingly.

3.3 *Technical and/or Financial Assistance and Support*

The provision of electoral assistance facilitates the implementation of international electoral standards in a more direct way.[46] The broad knowledge of the electoral assistance teams may be a precious help for a country to bring its electoral process in line with international standards.[47] Financial assistance,

---

42 See CM/Recommednation (2017) on standards for e-voting, <https://www.coe.int/en/web/electoral-assistance/elections-and-covid-19?fbclid=IwAR2NXNG5hsHaf5q7m_1KyQRghoNkw-ija4tAWX7pQFZ-xCfiXmDfw8S7olU>.

43 See CoE, Elections in Major Crisis situations, note 35.

44 See e.g. H Balian, 'Ten Years of International Election Assistance and Observation' (2001) 3 Helsinki Monitor 197, 199–200.

45 See *ibid.*

46 Various reports directly refer to the possibility of electoral assistance. (See for instance the OSCE/ODIHR, Final Report, Russian Federation, Presidential Election, 14 March 2004, 2).

47 For further information on election assistance see e.g. OSCE/ODIHR's website, <http://www.osce.org/odihr-elections/13411.html>.

on the other hand, delivers funds, which particularly evolving democracies might need. Such assistance seems most relevant in challenging times as COVID-19.[48] For true democracy promotion, especially a long term approach to electoral assistance should prove beneficial and further an election process in the sense of Suksi's ideal view: 'Each turn of the electoral cycle should bring the process to a higher level of perfection so that the election elements are ever better implemented and realised'.[49]

3.4 *(De-)Legitimating Process and Results*

International election observers should also contribute to the electoral process by means of their independent judgements: The missions' findings enjoy considerable credibility due to the multinational character of EOMs.[50] Accordingly, depending on whether a mission signals compliance with international standards or states the contrary, they may either legitimate or de-legitimate the elections.[51] Elections found to be conducted in accordance with international standards will raise public confidence and encourage political actors to accept the outcome of an election. In the case of the contrary, the mission's findings will give voice and weight to allegations of national actors who claim that electoral fraud has occurred. Moreover, findings of election observation missions may be – and already are occasionally – drawn upon as evidence by international human rights monitoring institutions as the European Court of Human rights.[52] Accordingly, international election observation has value to add particularly in the aftermath of an election. A mission's findings may either facilitate a peaceful installation in office of fairly elected candidates or support the

48 See eg the assistance provided by the CoE to Ukraine for the 2020 local elections, <https//www.coe.int/en/web/electoral-assistance/-/preparation-and-conduct-of-2020-local-elections-in-ukraine-in-context-of-quarantine-restrictions>.

49 M Suksi, 'The Electoral Cycle: On the Right to Participate in the Electoral Process', in M Suksi, J Lindblad (eds), *Election Elements: On the International Standards of Electoral Participation* (2003) 1, 34.

50 Normally OSCE member states second their observers. Since not all states have sufficient funds at their disposal, a voluntary fund for EOMs was established in 2001 in order to diversify EOMs. The fund proved particularly useful to include observers from Central and Eastern Europe as well as from the CIS (Election Observation Handbook, note 23, 25). In EU missions, the European Commission pays the observers. It is attempted that observers from as many as possible of the 27 member states participate.

51 As to this objective of election observation, see A Tostensen, 'Election Observation as an Informal Means of Enforcing Political Rights', (2004) 22 Nordisk Tidsskrift for Menneskerettigheter 330, 335 *et seq*. See also International IDEA, note 12.

52 M Suksi, 'The Use of Election Observation Reports in Regional Human Rights Jurisprudence', (2016) 34 Nordic Journal of Human Rights, 229.

contestation of results in cases of fraud.[53] Ideally, this contributes to democracy promotion.

3.5 *Detailed Recommendations*

EOMs, furthermore, support national authorities to improve future electoral processes. Especially the recommendations contained in final reports indicate deficiencies and serve as valuable basis to bring election processes in line with international standards.[54] To boost the positive impact of recommendations, organisations as OSCE/ODIHR have indeed set up comprehensive and searchable recommendation databases.[55] This should assist domestic authorities and civil society to follow up on recommendations and also make it easier to track their implementation. Likewise in times of COVID-19, recommendations may valuably guide domestic actors. For example, relevant recommendations concerning the stability of the electoral law or election campaigning in times of pandemic were made in relation to various elections (see eg the 2020 Serbian parliamentary elections).[56] It is hoped that they will be implemented accordingly.

Ideally, the findings of an election observation mission likewise serve as starting point to follow up activities by international organisations (EU, CoE, OSCE/ODIHR) and the provision of technical assistance. Election observation and electoral assistance may thus go hand in hand. In sum, international electoral support has considerable value to add, especially when a country is willing to bring its electoral process in line with international standards. However, a number of obstacles may hinder effective support or reduce its impact.

---

53 In this sense Balian, note 44, 200.

54 This is well evidenced by the Ecuadorian electoral cycle with elections (including one referendum) in 2007, 2008 and 2009. Problem areas concerning the formula for the assignation of seats (*'factor ponderador'*), the disenfranchisement of prisoners without conviction and security forces, and the disproportionate powers of the election administration were criticised in the 2007 final report. In the following, these areas/issues were addressed by the national authorities. As a result, the EU EOM which observed the 2009 general elections was able to ascertain the implementation of their previous recommendations. See EU EOM Ecuador, Presidential and Parliamentary Elections, 26 April 2009, Statement of Preliminary Findings and Conclusions, Quito, 28 April 2009, 1.

55 OSCE/ODIHR, Electoral Recommendations Database <https://paragraph25.odihr.pl>.

56 See eg OSCE/ODIHR ODIHR Special Assessment Mission Final Report, Republic of Serbia, 21 June 2020 Parliamentary Elections. See also CoE Venice Commission, 'Respect for Democracy, Human Rights, the Rule of Law during states of Emergency', CDL-AD(2020)014-e.

4 Limitations/Challenges to International Electoral Support

The limitations encountered by electoral support activities may be divided into five main areas: 1) general considerations of national sovereignty; 2) obstacles which are related to the political situation in the country, 3) the detrimental impact of the COVID-19 pandemic; 4) intra-organisational problems in the respective organisation and 5) inter-organisational problems between different international organisations which are active in the field of election observation.

4.1 *General Considerations of National Sovereignty*

Assertions of national sovereignty and a rejection of international/external actors potentially affecting electoral support activities exist at two levels. First, electoral support may – as a matter of principle – be rejected as 'undue interference' with countries' national sovereignty. Such general rejection of electoral support may indeed be read into certain resolutions of the General Assembly, which evidence some states' concern regarding a potential interference in their internal affairs. In these so called 'Respect Resolutions' the GA calls upon 'Respect for the principles of national sovereignty and non-interference in the internal affairs of States in their electoral process'.[57] Were these Resolutions shared by too many countries, such statements could challenge the very basis of electoral support. Still, no further 'Respect Resolution' was tabled since 2005, while the Assembly continues to adopt the opposite 'Enhancing Resolutions' on a biannual basis. Thus, positively, the general resistance to international democracy promotion seems to gradually loose importance.

A government's punctual rejection of international electoral support as undue interference or for alleged partiality is a more widespread problem. Angola, for example, has not consented to the conditions set by EU observers to enable a credible observation in 2017; nor did Venezuela in 2015, therewith preventing the deployment of EOMs. Rwandese authorities criticized the findings of the EU EOM final report on the 2008 Rwandan elections as biased; as did Ethiopian stakeholders concerning the 2005 EU EOM assessment of the Ethiopian elections. Likewise, the Nigerian electoral commission rejected the EU EOM's assessment of the Nigerian 2007 elections and accused EU observers to be 'electoral tourists'. Such rejections, if not carefully handled, may seriously affect the (positive) impact of a report/an EOM, which in the perception of the

57 These affirm, *inter alia*, 'the right of peoples to determine methods and to establish institutions regarding electoral processes and, consequently, that there is no single model of democracy or of democratic institutions' A/RES/60/164 of 16 December 2005, para 3.

domestic population and relevant electoral stakeholders, lose their credibility. While an EOM can never prevent allegations of bias or 'hidden agendas', diligently drafted assessments with due reference to international standards are a certain safeguard against criticisms.

4.2 *Political and Human Rights Situation in the Country*

Further challenges stem from the overall political and human rights situation in a country. The lack of political will of a country's government to improve the electoral process is much more difficult to overcome than technical insufficiencies or a lack of experience of national authorities. In extreme cases, EOMs have not been deployed at all because the minimum conditions for democratic elections were not in place and a deployment of observers would have given false and unintended legitimacy to the process. For example, OSCE/ODIHR did not send election missions to Turkmenistan until 2007 and has only deployed limited missions to the country since then because preconditions essential to free and fair elections were lacking. No EU or OAS observers were sent to the 2020 Venezuelan Parliamentary elections boycotted by the opposition because the national situation did not meet international standards. The EU withdrew missions from the 2002 Zimbabwe presidential elections and the Côte d'Ivoire for similar concerns.

Still, the risk of giving undeserved legitimacy to a flawed electoral process has to be balanced against the potential benefits of engaging in a dialogue with a country's authorities and of keeping the domestic electoral process under international scrutiny. As a middle course, international organizations have at times opted for reduced missions, comprised of only a small number of long term observers, such as OSCE/ODIHR in case of the presidential elections in Uzbekistan in 2015 or electoral experts (eg OSCE/ODIHR in case of the 2017 elections in Turkmenistan). In worse cases where the international organisation does not want to comment on the electoral process at all, there is always the possibility to offer a minimum component of electoral assistance (such as media advice or poll worker training). Therewith, the organisation avoids issuing a statement on the elections (and therefore giving false legitimacy to a flawed process) without cutting all communication channels with the country concerned.[58]

58 See also R Ludwig, 'The UN's electoral assistance: Challenges, accomplishments, prospects', in E Newman, R Rich, *The UN Role in Promoting Democracy. Between Ideals and Reality* (2004) 169, 182.

More generally, an erosion of human rights when encountered in a country hampers the impact of electoral support activities.[59] If basic human rights such as the freedoms of expression, assembly, association and movement are not guaranteed, the electoral process will be seriously tainted and the presence of observers or the provision of technical advice of only limited added value. To exemplify, the training of political parties and candidates is of no use, where the right to freedom of assembly is lacking; and support concerning operational needs on e-day will be worthless if voters are not free when casting their vote for reasons of intimidation. An 'illustrative' example are the major human rights violations in the context of the 2020 Presidential elections in Belarus.[60] Unequal campaign conditions were likewise criticized during the 2020 early parliamentary presidential elections in Azerbaijan where a tightly controlled political environment was observed.[61] And the 2007 elections in Nigeria were criticized for their 'very poor organisation, lack of essential transparency, widespread procedural irregularities, substantial evidence of fraud, widespread voter disenfranchisement at different stages of the process, lack of equal conditions for political parties and candidates and numerous incidents of violence' as 'falling far short of international standards'.[62] In all these cases, the presence of independent observers neither impeded electoral fraud nor did it prevent human rights violations.

In sum, the 'success' of electoral support activities depends to a large extent on the national situation and, also, the receptiveness and willingness of the national authorities to hold elections in accordance with international standards. Where the political will and the basic pre-conditions for free and fair elections in a country are missing, electoral support activities have little possibility to increase the quality of the elections, and, therefore, to further democratic governance. In some countries, the COVID-19 pandemic seems to have aggravated this situation.

59 See in this sense Balian, note 44, 203.

60 No election observation mission was deployed to these elections. However, see already the 2004 Belarus elections: in the pre-election period, where the police conducted raids on campaign offices of opposition candidates and even detained a candidate. OSCE/ODIHR, Final report, Republic of Belarus, Parliamentary Elections, 17 October 2004, 2.

61 OSCE/ODIHR, Final Report, Republic of Azerbaijan, Early Parliametary Elections, 9 February 2020, 13.

62 EU EOM, Nigeria, Final Report, Gubernatorial, State Houses and Assembly Elections, 14 April 2007 and Presidential and National Assembly Elections, 21 April 2007, 1.

4.3 *Detrimental Impact of COVID-19*

COVID-19 and the detrimental impact of the related health emergency on domestic electoral processes have indeed imposed additional challenges on international electoral support. Often, the transparency of elections is significantly reduced due to the contingencies of the pandemic at hand. Similarly, deadlines may be shortened and domestic authorities take decisions in face of the pandemic abruptly without due deliberation. Moreover, limitations of the freedoms of assembly and movement are regularly adopted to contain the disease. The pandemic related restrictions of political freedoms seem to have conferred an unfair advantage to incumbants in some countries, eg when campaign related restrictions prevented the opposition to convey their message to the electorate (see eg Serbian Parliamentary elections 2020). Possible impacts of state-of-emergency measures on observation activities, if effective, need to be also taken into consideration.[63] Moreover, new ways of observation may need to be explored. When alternative voting modalities like postal voting are in place, observation activities need to be adjusted to follow these new realities.[64] Remote analysis may become necessary in some cases.[65] The COVID-19 pandemics thus poses challenges to both, a country's electoral processes and election missions which are required to adapt their observation strategies.

4.4 *Intra-organisational Problems*

Also, intra-organisational problems reduce the impact of electoral support activities. First, international standards and best practices – though gradually refined and expanded in recent years – still fail to tackle the totality of ongoing processes as well as emerging challenges. Critical areas include, for example, the misuse of administrative resources, campaign and political party finance, as well as the full inclusion of vulnerable groups, such as disabled persons, persons belonging to national minorities and internally displaced persons. Additional standards are likewise necessary to cope with the challenges arising from an increased use of new technologies (eg internet voting) and the growing reliance on alternative/remote voting methods as postal (or internet) voting. Since remote voting takes place outside the controlled environment of the polling station, it is more open to fraud and/or coercion and to violations of the secrecy of the vote. This became particularly apparent during the COVID-19

63 Global Network of Domestic Election Monitors, 'Guidance on Election Monitoring During the COVID-19 Pandemic' (2020) <https://gndem.org/stories/guidance-on-election-monitoring-during-the-covid-19-pandemic/>.

64 *Ibid.*

65 World Politics Review, 'How Election Observers Are Adapting to COVID-19' (2020).

pandemic where, to contain the spread of the disease, countries have resorted frequently to postal voting (less so to internet voting which requires a sophisticated technology). Accordingly, a continuous development of standards including an adaptation of election observation and assistance methodology seems necessary. International electoral support activities have only started to tackle these problems and deal with their consequences for the election process (see eg the 2013 OSCE/ODIHR Handbook for the Observation of New Voting Technologies).

Further questions relate to the still insufficient follow-up which is given to the reports and recommendations issued by EOMs: It may hamper the due implementation of a mission's findings and considerably reduce the mission's potential to improve the quality of domestic electoral processes. One may distinguish roughly between a political and an operational/technical side. From a more political side, the follow-up – if there is any – depends on the international organisation (and its legal capacities) as well as on the international community. In the framework of organizations as the OSCE or the OAS, the findings of EOMs are reported to the respective Permanent Council. While, in theory, the latter should discuss and follow up to the reports of the missions, in practice, this mechanism has proved insufficient and adequate follow-up is not provided. The EU enters into a political dialogue with the country concerned which – although rather successful with respect to the ACP states – is conducted in a fairly informal manner. Only exceptionally, targeted measures such as the visa ban and freezing of assets which were adopted by the EU Council in response to the flawed 2020 presidential elections and the ensuing violent repression of the opposition in Belarus are taken.[66] Further examples include sanctions imposed by the US government following Venezuela's ban of election observers in the context of the country's 2017 Constituent Assembly elections, as well as targeted US measures against the head of Nicaragua's Supreme Electoral Council in response to alleged electoral fraud in the context of the country's 2016 presidential elections.[67] Thus, a more consistent political follow up, including pressure in problematic cases would be useful. Also, an election mission's findings could and should increasingly be taken up by international human rights monitoring mechanisms, at regional and at universal level.[68]

66 See eg European Council, 'Belarus: EU prolongs sanctions for a year', 25 February 2021. Note that, as stated above, no election observation mission had been sent to the Belarus elections.

67 See Binder/Pippan, note ♣, para 29.

68 For stronger links and reporting from election observation missions into the Universal Periodic Report and the UN treaty body system, see A Davis-Roberts and DJ

From a more technical/operational side, there are certain positive trends as regards follow up activities to missions by international organizations such as the EU, OSCE/ODIHR, and the CoE especially recently. Such activities range from searchable election recommendation databases[69] to follow-up visits in countries to scrutinize the implementation of a mission's recommendations, possibly linked to concrete offers of technical assistance. All this seems particularly important when a mission's overall assessment of the election was negative. Notwithstanding these positive developments, a systematic follow-up to problematic elections is still missing which may reduce the impact of an election mission's findings and its benefits for democracy promotion.

Finally, the reproach made especially to EOMs – being more 'apprehended' by the countries concerned than technical assistance for their public assessment of the electoral process – was a selectivity of the countries where they were deployed to. In particular election observers' focus on developing democracies was criticized since also 'older/more established' democracies are said to have blind spots. Such selectivity may be detrimental to an organisation's reputation and discredit the observation process. The (positive) impact of EOMs on the process of democratic consolidation is likely to be reduced accordingly. While positively, in response to this criticism, the range of countries EOMs are sent to has been enlarged (see above), to enhance the EOMs' credibility and avoid the reproach of applying 'double standards', international organisations might consider to further diversifying the range of countries to which EOMs are deployed.

4.5 *Inter-organisational Problems*

There are also inter-organisation problems. The variety of organisations which engage in election support activities call for a good cooperation and division of tasks in order to avoid duplications and contradictions, among international actors as well as between international and domestic organisations. Recently, the cooperation between the different international actors has improved. Arrangements include a division of tasks already in the forefront of an election (*e.g.* the referral of requests to competent regional organisations by the UN which concentrates on the provision of electoral assistance); or forms of cooperation for particular observation missions, in form of information sharing arrangements (*e.g.* on deployment plans); in an institutionalized form, with

---

Carroll, 'International Election Observer Recommendations and UN Human Rights Mechanisms: Toward a More Robust System of Global Accountability on Democracy and Human Rights', in (2017) 35 Nordic Journal of Human Rights 311; see also Suksi, note 52.

69 See note 55.

a secretariat/ office established by one organisation to coordinate the observers; or, as the closest form, joint observation missions where the organisations speak with one voice and issue joint statements.

While these arrangements have proven beneficial, diverging methodologies, capacities and expectations, a fight for visibility as well as different political agendas of monitoring organisations still lead to cooperation failures, with, as most crucial, diverging assessments of the election process. These diverging assessments enable the respective governments to 'forum shop' and to rely on those statements which are the most convenient for them. This reduces the impact of EOMs and prevents the beneficial effect these missions may have for democracy promotion. Examples include the diverging statements of CIS and OSCE/ODIHR observers with regard to parliamentary elections in Uzbekistan (2004), Tajikistan (2005) and Russia (2011); conflicting statements of SCO and OSCE/ODIHR observers concerning the presidential elections in Uzbekistan (2016); and the differing assessments by European and certain African observer groups of the 2016 general elections in Uganda.[70] As regards the coordination between electoral assistance and observation, tensions may arise when an EOM comments negatively on an electoral process which was implemented according to the advice and with the aid of electoral assistance.

What is more, the relationship between international and domestic observers also remains in need of improvement. Despite the important role of domestic observers in promoting a broader understanding of the basic requirements of genuine elections in their societies, and notwithstanding recent efforts by some organizations (particularly the EU) to further reach out to domestic groups, domestic observers do, in most cases, still not receive sufficient attention and support from international organizations.

4.6 *General Limits of International Electoral Support*

There are also certain general limits of international electoral support. Electoral processes in line with international standards, to be sure, greatly enhance the chance of a peaceful hand over of powers and contribute to a country's democratic consolidation. However, the impact of electoral support activities is, in the end, uncertain. Post electoral violence in countries such as Kenya (2007/2008) and Belarus (2020/21) as well as authoritarian overthrows of democratically elected regimes in Fiji (2007), Mauritania (2008) and Myanmar (2020/21) raised doubts about the possible sustainability of electoral support. In a worrying trend, autocratic tendencies seem to have been fostered in some states

70 See Binder/Pippan, note ♣.

(Turkey, Hungary) during the COVID-19 pandemic with restrictions of political freedoms and constraints imposed on democratic space through pandemic related emergency powers.

These doubts about the impact of electoral support are increased in cases of a disproportionate emphasis on election day rather than on the longer term process of democratic institution building. Indeed, such disproportionate (or even exclusive) emphasis on elections cannot answer the question of good governance and the quality of democracy.[71] There are 'limits of electoralism' as it provides inadequate criteria for categorizing regimes as democratic and distinguishes between 'the ritual of democracy' and its 'substance', given that 'many African leaders are learning to play the election game – giving aid donors an election barely clean enough to receive a low – passing grade, but dirty enough to make it difficult for the opposition to win'.[72] For this reason, scholars[73] have repeatedly criticized an exaggerated focus by international actors on elections rather than on the long term democratization process.

There are welcome efforts by international actors to counter these criticisms through the adoption of a longer term approach to electoral support.[74] Changes in the observation and assistance methodology and an increased focus on the more comprehensive 'so called' electoral cycle approach are promising developments respectively. Such long term approach should further the process of democratic institution building and thus enhance the sustainability of electoral support activities. It needs to be further developed in the future.

5 Concluding Remarks

Despite its limitations and challenges, international electoral support has proved to be a valuable instrument to improve the quality of electoral processes. The comprehensive documentation of the entire election process, the immediate political pressure exercised by a mission's findings and/or the technical and financial assistance offered to countries truly present an 'added

71 See e.g. G O'Donnell, 'Human Development, Human Rights, and Democracy', in G O'Donnell, G Cullell *et al* (eds), *The Quality of Democracy. Theory and Applications* (2004) 9; L. Diamond, L. Morlino, *Assessing the Quality of Democracy* (2005).

72 M Ottaway, 'Should Elections Be the Criterion of Democratization in Africa?' (1993) 145 CSIS Africa Notes, 3 *et seq.*

73 *Ibid.*

74 This general statement does not apply to cases where electoral assistance is provided on a punctual basis to improve specific shortcomings of the electoral process.

value'. In particular in 'evolving democracies' and in countries in transition, appropriate electoral support should thus constitute a viable tool for democracy promotion.[75]

Still, it is always to be kept in mind that elections do not equate democracy. Elections are an essential, but only one of the elements which are constitutive for a functioning democracy. Other relevant elements include human rights, the rule of law and the separation of powers. This becomes particularly apparent in times of COVID-19 with severe limitations of political freedoms. It remains therefore essential to link electoral support to the broader process of democratic institution building, which presupposes long term approaches. To return to the statement by UN Secretary General Kofi Annan: 'While democracy must be more than free elections, it is also true [...] that it cannot be less'.[76] An integrated approach to electoral support, which effectively combines election observation with long term technical assistance programs, allows also to address the 'more' of democracy. It then, and without neglecting the crucial importance of elections, truly turns to be 'democracy promotion and support'.

---

75 See in this sense Tostensen, note 951, 335.

76 Kofi Annan, note 10.

CHAPTER 10

Democratic Sanctions and International Law

Ioannis Prezas

1 Introduction

Unlike sanctions, "democratic sanctions", an expression coined and widely used by political science scholars specialized in international relations, is not a term of art in international law. In view of the exponential expansion of sanctions in contemporary practice, identifying the phenomena that fall within this concept and thus attaching a useful legal meaning to it appears at first blush to be a futile intellectual exercise. This is so for two reasons. First, because it is almost impossible to define "democracy" in either political or legal terms. However, for present purposes, it is safe to assume that the existence and the quality of a democracy can be assessed in light of many interconnected factors such as free and fair elections, respect for human rights, especially freedom of expression, including the absence of repression of the opposition, and more generally respect for the separation of powers and the rule of law. Indeed, it is clear that there exists no watertight distinction between democracy as a political system and the rule of law and human rights.[1] Democracy is thus not only about how a government comes to power in the first place but also about how it maintains and exercises such power. Second, because sanctions may be imposed by various senders on various targets for various reasons and they sometimes pursue more than one goal simultaneously. How is it then possible to single out democratic sanctions? An attempt to find a working definition of the concept would arguably be to insist on the main purpose of the sanction. While sanctions have been imposed on some stable and more or less powerful authoritarian regimes, such as North Korea, Iran, Syria, or Russia, their main, albeit not exclusive, purpose is not to promote, at least openly, regime change or to enforce democracy (this would be too much to ask), but to prevent (not to say punish) nuclear proliferation, support for terrorism, massive violations of human rights and humanitarian law during an internal conflict, or other threats to international peace and security. In contrast, and perhaps more

1 A Jakab, 'What Can Constitutional Law Do against the Erosion of Democracy and the Rule of Law? On the Interconnectedness of the Protection of Democracy and the Rule of Law' (2020) 6 Const Stud 5.

 | DOI:10.1163/9789004508712_011

modestly, democratic sanctions are coercive tools that are primarily designed to put pressure on governments and individuals in order to bring about policy changes more in line with democratic principles within a given country. Thus, unlike other softer means of promoting democracy such as electoral assistance and monitoring or democratic conditionality in the field of financial aid, democratic sanctions are conceived as hard democratization means. Having said that, the purpose of this contribution is not to offer an exhaustive analysis of all instances that would qualify as democratic sanctions under this definition. Instead, focusing on more recent cases, it provides an overview of the problems these sanctions raise as a matter of international law. To this end, it first identifies the grounds for potentially triggering democratic sanctions (2), and then discusses the contemporary features of institutional (3) and unilateral democratic sanctions (4), before offering some brief concluding remarks (5).

2 Grounds for Triggering Democratic Sanctions: from Coups d'état to Democratic Backsliding and Erosion

Sanctioning undemocratic practices presupposes in theory that these are unlawful under international law. While the existence of a duty to respect democracy in customary law remains perhaps controversial, as we will see in section 4, international institutional law clearly supports such an idea. First of all, though the United Nations Charter does not contain any reference to democracy, collective security mechanisms may occasionally serve as sanctioning devices in the case of undemocratic changes of government or other undemocratic practices, as we will see in a moment. Moreover, it is undoubtful that most regional institutions adopt democracy, human rights, and the rule of law as a gold standard for government such as, to name a few, the European Union (EU),[2] the Council of Europe,[3] the Economic Community of West African States (ECOWAS),[4] the African Union (AU),[5] and the Organization of

2 Article 2 of the Treaty on European Union provides that the Union is founded, among others, on the values of respect for democracy, the rule of law, and human rights.

3 See preambular paragraph 2 read in conjunction with Articles 1 a) and 3 of the Statute of the Council of Europe (1949).

4 Protocol on Democracy and Good Governance supplementary to the Protocol relating to the Mechanism for Conflict Prevention, Management, Resolution, Peacekeeping and Security (2001), entered into force in 2008, Article 1, d).

5 Constitutive Act of the African Union (2000), entered into force in 2001, Article 4, m) and p). Promotion for "democratic principles and institutions, popular participation and good governance" is also one of the objectives of the Union, see Article 3, g).

the American States (OAS).[6] Hence, by joining these institutions and ratifying relevant legal instruments containing democracy clauses, States, governments, and leaders are no more free to act as they wish. Indeed, as the Court emphasized in the Nicaragua Case, there is nothing to prevent a State from accepting a limitation on its sovereignty by agreement in relation to a question of domestic policy such as the holding of free elections on its territory.[7] Still, the fact that democracy is proclaimed as a fundamental principle or value, especially on a regional level, would be an empty shell if there is no mechanism to enforce it. At the same time, only situations meeting a seriousness threshold, at least in the opinion of the sanctioning entities, usually attract democratic sanctions. One has therefore to identify, without any conceptual *a priori*, the grounds that trigger or are likely to trigger democratic sanctions in international law and practice. It is submitted here that these grounds are based on three closely interrelated situations: accessing, maintaining, and exercising power.

As a means of accessing power by militarily overthrowing a democratically elected government, coups d'état are presumably at the top of the conceivable seriousness scale of undemocratic practices. Military coups in the traditional sense are inconsistent with many regional legal instruments addressing situations where a "democracy is abruptly brought to an end by any means"[8] or where a "democratically constituted government has been overthrown by force".[9] The AU Charter on Democracy, Elections and Governance, adopted in 2007 and entered into force in 2012, offers a more comprehensive approach in that respect. Building on Article 30 of the AU Constitutive Act of 2000, which provides for sanctions against "Governments which shall come to power through unconstitutional means",[10] the Charter is intended to encompass all possible scenarios of undemocratic behavior under the generic expression "unconstitutional changes of government". Indeed, according to its Article 23:

6 Article 2 b) of the OAS Charter and the Inter-American Democratic Charter of 2001 proclaiming in its Article 1 that the "peoples of the Americas have a right to democracy and their governments have an obligation to promote and defend it".

7 *Case concerning Military and Paramilitary Activities in and against Nicaragua* (*Nicaragua v United States of America*) (Merits) [1986] ICJ Rep 4, para 259.

8 Protocol A/SP1/12/01 on Democracy and Good Governance supplementary to the Protocol relating to the Mechanism for Conflict Prevention, Management, Resolution, Peacekeeping and Security (2001), entered into force in 2008, art 45, para 1.

9 Article 9 the OAS Charter, inserted by the Protocol of Washington of 1992. On the ambiguities of the Inter-American Democratic Charter see infra.

10 Article 30.

> State Parties agree that the use of, inter alia, the following illegal means of accessing or maintaining power constitute an unconstitutional change of government and shall draw appropriate sanctions by the Union:
> 1. Any putsch or coup d'Etat against a democratically elected government.
> 2. Any intervention by mercenaries to replace a democratically elected government.
> 3. Any replacement of a democratically elected government by armed dissidents or rebels (…)
> 4. Any refusal by an incumbent government to relinquish power to the winning party or candidate after free, fair and regular elections; or
> 5. Any amendment or revision of the constitution or legal instruments, which is an infringement on the principles of democratic change of government.

Keeping in mind that the list is not exhaustive, this provision deals with "illegal means" of both accessing or maintaining power, though it is not always clear whether this illegality stems from the violation of domestic (constitutional) law or international law, or both. We will come back later to the last two situations regarding means of maintaining power. As far as the first three are concerned, it is clear that they cover different forms of a coup d'état against a democratically elected government, but it may be a matter of contention whether the government which is a victim of such practices would genuinely qualify as a democratically elected government, *i.e.* resulting from free and fair elections, preferably conducted under international monitoring. Moreover, a coup against a dictator, such as the one removing from power Omar al-Bashir in Soudan (2019) would not be an unconstitutional change of government under this provision. Yet, Soudan was temporality suspended by the AU, as we will see below. At the same time, other situations are more complex. The incumbent president of Tchad Idriss Deby, in power since 1990, supported by some undeniably democratic States such as France, and running for a sixth mandate, was reelected in April 2021 from the first round with about 80% of the votes. However, his reelection, similarly to the previous ones, was contested because it took place in a context of well-documented political repression. An attack launched on the day of the election by the Front for Change and Concord in Chad (FACT), based mainly in Libya, eventually led to the death of the newly re-elected president. Even if one admits that this regime was democratically elected, the aftermath was manifestly unconstitutional. While Article 81 of the constitution provides that in case of vacancy the duties of the president are provisionally exercised by the president of the National Assembly and that new presidential elections must be organized ninety days at most after the vacancy, a transitional Military Council chaired by the son of the deceased took power instead. The parliament and government were dissolved and the constitution was replaced by a new transition charter. The Military Council appointed the head of the civilian-led transitional government and pledged to restore democracy within 18 months. What is more striking, however, is that, unlike other recent cases, the Peace and Security Council (PSC) of the AU did not immediately suspend Tchad from its participation in the activities of this institution due to political disagreements among AU member States, some of which believed that a suspension would fuel the country's instability.[11] In a communiqué adopted on 14 May 2021, while it reiterated its total rejection of any unconstitutional change of government on the continent, the PSC only strongly condemned the use of violence by mercenaries, foreign fighters, and rebels in pursuit of political power in Chad and underscored the utmost necessity that the transition to democratic rule should be completed within the 18-month period.[12] In other words, the PSC decided to give some time to the putschists. The reason was probably that this putsch against, for the sake of argument, a democratically elected government was the lesser evil compared to the two other forms of undemocratic change of government, *i.e.* intervention by foreign mercenaries, armed dissidents, or rebels (in a word, the FACT) to replace the government. As a result, a coup may be temporarily and exceptionally tolerated if there is a broader threat to the peace and stability of the region in the view of the competent institution (that is to say in the view of the majority of its member States).

Having said that, a coup may attract sanctions even when there is no express provision on the matter, provided that the applicable instrument clearly imposes broad democratic duties on member States, such as for instance Article 2 of the Treaty on European Union (TEU) or the Statute of the Council of Europe. Moreover, beyond regional law, UN law also supports the idea that coup d'états may be triggering grounds for democratic sanctions. Indeed, collective security mechanisms under chapter VII of the Charter may occasionally serve as sanctioning devices designed to restore democracy as shown by the emblematic, but perhaps "outlier cases",[13] of

11 'AU balancing act on Chad's coup sets a disturbing precedent', available at: https://issafrica.org/iss-today/au-balancing-act-on-chads-coup-sets-a-disturbing-precedent.

12 Peace and Security Council of the African Union 'Communiqué' PSC/BR/COMM.(CMXCVI)., adopted at its 996th meeting, 14 May 2021.

13 B Roth, 'Secessions, Coups, and the International Rule of Law: Assessing the Decline of the Effective Control Doctrine' (2010) Melb. J. Int'l. L. 393, 430.

Haiti[14] and Sierra Leone[15] in the 90s. Of course, it would be naive to believe that the United Nations Security Council (UNSC) reacts automatically to all coup d'états or other forms of disruption or erosion of the democratic order within a given State. In some more recent cases, the UNSC has indeed condemned coups under chapter VII, and demanded the restoration of democracy, as with regard to Guinea-Bissau in 2012[16] or the "mutiny" that occurred in Kati, Mali, on 18 August 2020.[17] On the other hand, as far as the recent coup in Myanmar on 1 February 2021 is concerned, the President of the UNSC issued a carefully balanced statement on behalf of its members which were once more divided on the issue especially because of the Chinese and Russian unwillingness to support a more robust approach. Without using the word coup, but condemning 'the violence against peaceful protestors", the UNSC expressed "its continued support for the democratic transition in Myanmar", and stressed "the need to uphold democratic institutions and processes, refrain from violence, fully respect human rights and fundamental freedoms and uphold the rule of law".[18] The UNSC has not yet reacted to the situation in Tchad either. From a legal point of view, scholars have debated the rather academic issue of whether a coup d'état may as such be qualified as a threat to international peace and security.[19] In principle the UNSC has a wide, albeit perhaps not unlimited discretionary power when it comes to the finding of a threat to the peace under Article 39 of the UN Charter. In addition to being contrary to treaty provisions as seen above, a coup, as a means of accessing power, may thus also be occasionally inconsistent with the UN Charter insofar as the UNSC determines that it constitutes a threat to the peace justifying sanctions.[20]

14 UNSC Res 940 (31 July 1994) UN Doc S/RES/940.

15 UNSC Res 1132 (8 October 1997) UN Doc S/RES/1132.

16 UNSC Res 2048 (18 May 2012) UN Doc S/RES/2048.

17 UNSC Res 2541 (31 August 2020) UN Doc S/RES/2541 (2020).

18 UNSC Statement by the President of the Security Council on Myanmar (10 March 2021) UN Doc S/PRST/2021/5.

19 For an affirmative view see LA Sicilianos, *L'ONU et la démocratisation de l'Etat, Systèmes régionaux et ordre juridique universel* (Pedone 2000), 182–216, 206.

20 According to one view, even if "it does not seem unreasonable to hold that coups constitute a violation of the rules of international law pertaining to democracy", it would be "very difficult to attribute the coup d'état to the state that has sustained an unconstitutional change in government" and as a result the coup d'état "cannot be considered an internationally wrongful act, and no state incurs international responsibility", see J d'Aspremont, Responsibility for Coups in International Law' (2010) 18 Tulane J Int & Comp L 451, 467–470. Still, attribution of conduct is a precondition for assessing its lawfulness under international law. Consequently, if a conduct is not attributable to a State, its international lawfulness becomes irrelevant. Moreover, at least as a matter of UN law, this does not preclude the conduct in question from being attributable to illegitimate

Having said that, coups are far from being the only threats to democracy likely to trigger sanctions in contemporary practice. As seen above, the AU Democratic Charter mentions two other situations going beyond traditional coups as means of accessing power to encompass means of maintaining power. The first one, *i.e.* the refusal by an incumbent government to relinquish power to the winning party or candidate after free, fair, and regular elections, sometimes attract sanctions or at least international condemnations. For instance, the UNSC and the AU have supported the winner of the elections against the refusal of incumbent presidents to transfer power, such as in the Gambia in 2016–2017[21] or in Côte d'Ivoire in 2010–2011.[22] The second, *i.e.* amendments or revision of the constitution or legal instruments, which is an infringement on the principles of democratic change of government, is more difficult to assess. As everyone knows, governments, even presumably democratic ones, very often try to change the rules of the game in order to reinforce their position and remain in power. But what are the admissible limits of such practices even when carried out by, at least in theory, democratically elected governments? For instance, was the controversial 2020 constitutional referendum in Guinea, reportedly organized in a context of repression and fraud, which deleted the two-term limit in order to allow Alpha Condé to be reelected for a third time, consistent with these provisions? And, beyond Africa, what about the referendum in Turkey (2017) that transformed a parliamentary regime into an authoritarian presidential one? In a similar vein, authoritarian governments remaining in power by manipulating elections and repressing political opposition offer another ground for triggering democratic sanctions. In such cases, it is almost impossible to distinguish between accessing, maintaining, and exercising power. Belarus is one typical example of this scenario. Without going into the long history of sanctions against the regime in place, the presidential elections of 9 August 2020 that allowed Alexander Lukashenko, often nicknamed the last dictator in Europe, to be reelected for a sixth term with the official – not to say fabulous – result of 80%, have been severely denounced especially by the EU and the US. The EU considered that

governments or individuals, and this appears to be true of some other undemocratic practices as well, as shown by the development of targeted sanctions.

21 UNSC Res 2337 (19 January 2017) UN Doc S/RES/2337 (without reference to chapter VII, however).

22 UNSC Res 1975 (30 March 2011) UN Doc S/RES/1975 para 1, urging under chapter VII all the Ivorian parties and other stakeholders to respect the will of the people and the election of Alassane Ouattara as President of Côte d'Ivoire, as recognized by ECOWAS, the African Union and the rest of the international community.

these elections "were found to be inconsistent with international standards and marred by the repression of independent candidates and a brutal crackdown on peaceful protesters" and therefore were neither free nor fair.[23] Likewise, the US took sanctions against persons that undermine democratic processes or institutions in Belarus.[24] In a similar context, both the US and the EU have adopted unilateral sanctions in relation to the situation in Venezuela over the past years. In particular, the US sanctions are justified by the "continued usurpation of power by Nicolás Maduro and persons affiliated with him, as well as human rights abuses, including arbitrary or unlawful arrest and detention of Venezuelan citizens, interference with freedom of expression, including for members of the media, and ongoing attempts to undermine Interim President Juan Guaido and the Venezuelan National Assembly's exercise of legitimate authority in Venezuela".[25] For its part, the Council of the EU declared itself deeply concerned "at the continuing deterioration of democracy, the rule of law and human rights in Venezuela",[26] and maintained that the elections held in Venezuela in May 2018[27] as well as in December 2020 were neither free nor fair as they failed to comply with the international standards for a democratic process.[28] Furthermore, the muzzling of political opponents, independent media, and civil society in Nicaragua since 2018 triggered EU[29] and US sanctions, the latter being for instance justified by the Ortega regime's "systematic dismantling and undermining of democratic institutions and the rule of law and its use of indiscriminate violence and repressive tactics against civilians".[30]

---

23 Council Decision (CFSP) 2021/353 of 25 February 2021 amending Decision 2012/642/CFSP concerning restrictive measures against Belarus.

24 Treasury Sanctions Additional Belarusian Regime Actors for Undermining Democracy, 23 December 2020, available at https://home.treasury.gov/news/press-releases/sm1222.

25 Executive Order 13884 of August 5 2019, Blocking Property of the Government of Venezuela. All relevant documents are available at https://home.treasury.gov/policy-issues/financial-sanctions/sanctions-programs-and-country-information/venezuela-related-sanctions.

26 Council Decision (CFSP) 2017/2074 of 13 November 2017 concerning restrictive measures in view of the situation in Venezuela.

27 Council Decision (CFSP) 2018/901 of 25 June 2018 amending Decision (CFSP) 2017/2074 concerning restrictive measures in view of the situation in Venezuela.

28 Council Decision (CFSP) 2021/276 of 22 February 2021 amending Decision (CFSP) 2017/2074 concerning restrictive measures in view of the situation in Venezuela.

29 Council Decision (CFSP) 2019/1720 of 14 October 2019 concerning restrictive measures in view of the situation in Nicaragua (as amended by Council Decision (CFSP) 2020/1467 of 12 October 2020).

30 Executive Order 13851 of November 27, 2018, Blocking Property of Certain Persons Contributing to the Situation in Nicaragua.

Inadmissible means of accessing, maintaining, or exercising power, such as coups, refusals to step down, manipulation of electoral and constitutional laws, along with repression of political opposition all constitute triggering grounds for democratic sanctions in international law and practice. Still, in apparently more demanding – in terms of democratic requirements – institutions, gradual policy changes leading to a creeping democratic backsliding and erosion from within, *i.e.* resulting from the manner in which a democratically elected government exercises its prerogatives may also trigger sanctions as shown by the rule of law crises in Hungary and Poland to which we will return below. Having established the different grounds for triggering democratic sanctions, it is now necessary to take a closer look at the scope of these sanctions, which may be institutional or unilateral in nature.

3 Institutional Democratic Sanctions

3.1 *Military and Economic Sanctions*

As a matter of principle, prodemocratic military intervention in order to restore democracy remains the prerogative of the UNSC acting under Chapter VII of the UN Charter. Still, this is a rather exceptional course of action. After the economic sanctions against the military junta in Haiti had proved unsuccessful, the UNSC authorized member States, acting within the framework of a multinational force, to "use all necessary means to facilitate the departure from Haiti of the military leadership".[31] On the other hand, the military action of the ECOWAS – which had, however, only been authorized under Chapter VIII the UN Charter to ensure the strict implementation of the embargo using ECOMOG troops[32] – leading to the departure of the junta, was according to the prevailing view, implicitly and *post facto* approved by the Council.[33] But it remains very doubtful whether the UNSC also implicitly approved the ECOWAS operation "Restore Democracy", which successfully intervened in January 2017 in order to force the recalcitrant incumbent president of the Gambia to step down, since it only expressed, without any reference to chapter VII, "its full support to the ECOWAS in its commitment to ensure, *by political means first*, the respect of the will of the people".[34]

31 UNSC Res 940 (31 July 1994) UN Doc S/RES/940 para 4.

32 UNSC Res 1132 (8 October 1997) UN Doc S/RES/1132 para 8.

33 As inferred by the Statement by the President of the Security Council (26 February 1998) UN Doc S/PRST/1998/5 and also UNSC Res 1162 (17 April 1998) UN Doc S/RES/1162 para 2.

34 UNSC Res 2337 (19 January 2017) UN Doc S/RES/2337 para 6 (emphasis added).

Beyond military action to restore democracy, both in the Haiti[35] and Sierra Leone[36] cases, the UNSC imposed more or less comprehensive economic sanctions, including an oil and arms embargo and a naval blockade in relation to Haiti, while at the same time adopting targeted sanctions (assets freeze or travels bans) against military junta members. As is well known, the UNSC has abandoned comprehensive economic sanctions that had devastating effects on the population of the countries concerned and uses only targeted individual sanctions against the authors of a coup, such as in relation to Guinea-Bissau in 2012. In this case, the UNSC strongly condemned the military coup, which undermined the conclusion of the democratic electoral process and, acting under Article 41 of the UN Charter but without, surprisingly, finding a threat to the peace, demanded "that the Military Command takes immediate steps to restore and respect constitutional order, including a democratic electoral process" before imposing a travel ban to individuals "seeking to prevent the restoration of the constitutional order or taking action that undermines stability in Guinea-Bissau, in particular those who played a leading role in the coup d'état and who aim, through their actions, at undermining the rule of law, curtailing the primacy of civilian power and furthering impunity and instability in the country".[37] Similarly, in the aftermath of the controversial 2010 elections in Côte d'Ivoire, the UNSC reiterated its targeted sanctions against individuals who obstructed peace and reconciliation in this country.[38] The UN's shift from comprehensive sanctions to targeted or smart ones had not only the merit to spare innocent civilians, but also probably suggests that States, including their populations, are victims and not authors of the conduct of their illegitimate rulers. Still, some regional organizations do not hesitate to impose comprehensive economic sanctions along with targeted ones, as did ECOWAS following the coup d'état of 18 august 2020 in Mali.[39] In that case, the sanctions were lifted less than two months later after the establishment of a civilian government and thus the normalization of the constitutional order in this country.[40]

35 UNSC Res 873 (13 October 1993) UN Doc S/RES/873; UNSC Res 875 (16 October 1993) UN Doc S/RES/875; UNSC Res 917 (6 May 1994) UN Doc S/RES/917 (1994).

36 UNSC Res 1132 (8 October 1997) UN Doc S/RES/1132 paras 5, 6, 8.

37 UNSC Res 2048 (18 May 2012) UN Doc S/RES/2048 paras 4, 6, and 9.

38 UNSC Res 1975 (30 March 2011) UN Doc S/RES/1975 (2011) para 12.

39 Declaration of ECOWAS Heads of State and Government on Mali (20 August 2020), available at: https://www.ecowas.int/declaration-of-ecowas-heads-of-states-and-governmenet-on-mali-2020/).

40 Declaration of ECOWAS Heads of State and Government on Mali (5 October 2020), available at: https://www.ecowas.int/declaration-of-ecowas-heads-of-state-and-government-on-mali/.

3.2 *Political Sanctions*

In addition to military and economic democratic sanctions, which are more intrusive and coercive, suspension is the main political sanction of democracy within regional international institutions. When "democracy is abruptly brought to an end by any means", the ECOWAS protocol on Democracy and Good Governance, provides, among others, for suspension of the Member State concerned from all ECOWAS decision-making bodies,[41] as it happened in Mali in 2020 until the restoration of the conditional order[42] and once again after the new coup of May 2021.[43] Likewise, according to the Constitutive Act of the African Union, "Governments which shall come to power through unconstitutional means shall not be allowed to participate in the activities of the Union". The African Union systematically applies this provision, along with the relevant provisions of its Charter on Democracy, Elections and Governance of 2007 which entered into force in 2012,[44] in the case of coups d'états, for instance with regard to Soudan in 2019[45] and to Mali which was suspended for a first time in August 2020,[46] returned a few months later in view of the establishment of a civilian led-government, before being again suspended after the new coup that took place in May 2021.[47] In the case of the Gambia in 2016, a State that was interestingly not a party to the African Charter, the PSC of the AU, acting under the relevant provisions of the African Charter on Democracy but without imposing suspension, supported the newly-elected president against the incumbent president refusing to cede power.[48] This seems to suggest that suspension is an action reserved for the most serious forms of undemocratic

41 Protocol on Democracy and Good Governance, supra, Article 45 paras 1 and 2 (the latter providing that these sanctions may take various forms "in increasing order of severity", including the refusal to support the candidates presented by the Member State concerned for elective posts in international organizations, to organize ECOWAS meetings in the Member State concerned, and finally suspension).

42 See declarations above.

43 ECOWAS 'Communiqué' Extraordinary Summit on the Political Situation in Mali ACCRA, 30 May 2021.

44 See Articles 23–26 of this instrument. See also K D Magliveras, G J Naldi, *The African Union* (2nd edn, Wolters Kluwer 2018) 125–127 and 192–215.

45 Peace and Security Council of the African Union 'Communiqué' PSC/PR/COMM.(DCCCXLIV), adopted at its 854th meeting on the situation in Sudan, 6 June 2019.

46 Peace and Security Council of the African Union 'Communiqué' PSC/PR/COMM.(CMXLL) adopted at its 941st meeting, 19 August 2020.

47 Peace and Security Council of the African Union 'Communiqué' PSC/PR/COMM. (1001(2021)), adopted at its 1001st meeting, 1 June 2021.

48 Peace and Security Council of the African Union'Communiqué' PSC/PR/COMM. (DCXLVII), adopted at its 647th meeting, 13 January 2017 paras 4 et 5.

changes of government. Still, as seen above, the PSC did not suspend Tchad following the death of the president and the instauration of a military transition regime.

The situation in the Americas is perhaps a bit more complex. The Protocol of Washington of 1992, which amended the OAS Charter, includes an Article 9 according to which "A Member of the Organization whose democratically constituted government has been overthrown by force may be suspended from the exercise of the right to participate" in the activities of the Organization. However, this provision has never been applied as such, perhaps because some member States have never ratified the Protocol, but also because it only envisages coups d'état, while other forms of disruption of the democratic order were emerging.[49] In response to this situation, the Inter-American Democratic Charter (2001), a soft law instrument whose exact legal scope remains uncertain,[50] seems to offers a more comprehensive set of grounds for democratic sanctions. According to its Article 19, "an unconstitutional interruption of the democratic order or an unconstitutional alteration of the constitutional regime that seriously impairs the democratic order in a member state, constitutes, while it persists, an insurmountable obstacle to its government's participation in sessions of the General Assembly and other bodies of the Organization". Article 20 provides for diplomatic initiatives in the event of an unconstitutional alteration of the constitution, though the Permanent Council and the General Assembly may also take the "decisions they deem appropriate". The scope of these decisions is not otherwise specified. On the other hand, according to Article 21 of the same instrument when a special session of the General Assembly "determines that there has been an unconstitutional interruption of the democratic order of a member state, and that diplomatic initiatives have failed, it shall take the decision to suspend said member state from the exercise of its right to participate" in the OAS by an affirmative vote of two-thirds of the member States. This suspension, according to the same provision, "shall take effect immediately". However, these provisions raise a number of problems. Does the expression "unconstitutional interruption" go beyond the cases where the "democratically constituted government has been overthrown by force" as

49 J M Arrighi, 'The "Democracy Clause" in the Americas' in B Bonafè, J Combacau, P d' Argent (eds), *The limits of international law. Essays in Honour of Joe Verhoeven* (Bruylant 2015) 223, 227.

50 According to one view, the Democratic Charter, adopted by consensus during a session of the General Assembly, is an authoritative interpretation of the OAS Charter, including its Article 9, see V Saranti, 'A System of Collective Defense of Democracy: The Case of the Inter-American Democratic Charter' (2011) 3 Goettingen J Int'l L 675, 695 ff.

provided for in Article 9 of the OAS Charter? And, if so, what is an unconstitutional alteration of the constitutional regime? In sum, what are the specific criteria for defining when the state's democratic institutions have been altered or interrupted?[51] The only case of application of the Charter to this day, regarding Honduras, illustrates this ambiguity. Following the 2009 coup d'état against the constitutional government of President Zelaya, the OAS General Assembly condemned the coup "which has produced an unconstitutional alteration of the democratic order",[52] and decided to suspend "the Honduran state from the exercise of its right to participate in the Organization of American States, in accordance with Article 21 of the Inter-American Democratic Charter".[53] However, while the General Assembly found in the preamble of its suspension resolution, as in its first resolution, that the coup d'état "produced an unconstitutional alteration of the democratic order", it decided to act in accordance with Article 21 which arguably only covers cases of unconstitutional interruptions of the democratic order. Moreover, in its suspension resolution, the same organ instructed the Secretary-general to step up all diplomatic initiatives for the restoration of democracy and the rule of law, while at the same time clarifying that such initiatives would not "imply recognition of the regime that emerged from this interruption of the constitutional order".[54]

Within the OAS, the case of Venezuela is even more intriguing. In response to growing pressure from the organization since the beginning of the crisis, Venezuela formally notified its intention to withdraw from it in 2017. The withdrawal should have come into effect in 2019. However, the Permanent Council of the OAS, reaffirming the right of the peoples of the Americas to democracy and the obligation of their governments to promote and defend it as reflected in Article 1 of the Inter-American Democratic Charter, and acknowledging "that Nicolás Maduro's presidential authority lacks legitimacy"[55] decided, by a divided vote, to accept the appointment of the agent of the leader of the opposition Guaido as representative of Venezuela at the organization. Many States, naturally including Venezuela, voted against this resolution on the ground that the OAS had no authority to recognize or refuse to recognize the governments

51 See e.g. J M Arrighi, supra, 234.

52 Resolution on the Political Crisis in Honduras (July 1, 2009) AG/RES. 1 (XXXVII-E/09) rev. 1 para 1.

53 Resolution adopted by the XXXVII OAS Special General Assembly (July 5, 2009), OEA/Ser.P AG/RES.2 (XXXVII-E/09) rev. 1, 16 July 2009 para 1.

54 Ibid. para 3. The Spanish versions of these resolutions use the same terms.

55 CP/RES. 1117 (2200/19), 10 January 2019, and corresponding footnotes.

of its member States and that this was, therefore, contrary to its Charter.[56] This schizophrenic situation explains why the OAS approved a resolution rejecting "the fraudulent elections held in Venezuela on December 6, 2020", deciding "to not recognize its results, for being neither free nor fair in accordance with the conditions established in international law" and condemning "in the strongest terms the consistent and deliberate strategy of the illegitimate regime of Nicolás Maduro to undermine the democratic system and the separation of powers" with the affirmative vote of … Venezuela.[57] As a result, Venezuela is still a member of the Organization albeit represented by a government that enjoys no effective authority.[58]

At this point, some brief, albeit rather banal remarks appear appropriate. Suspension and non-recognition, as collective means of reaction against coups or other undemocratic situations, are not automatic. They depend on the political will of the competent intergovernmental organ of the organization, that is to say usually the will of the majority of its member States. Some of these States, for their own reasons (e.g. special political "alliance" with the State whose government undergoes some kind of undemocratic change, or security interests and stability considerations) may not be willing to vote in favor of more robust resolutions. In addition, political sanctions of this kind display a rather symbolic or even platonic character if they are not backed by more coercive tools.

Having said that, in Europe, the Statute of the Council of Europe goes beyond suspension as it allows, under its Article 8,[59] for exclusion in case a member State "has seriously violated Article 3", which imposes on member States to respect the principles of the rule of law and of the enjoyment by all persons of human rights, both stemming from the democratic principle. Nevertheless, it is not a secret that exclusion is not very frequent in international practice for

56 OEA/Ser.G, CP/RES. 1124 (2217/19), 10 April 2019, adopted by eighteen states voting in favor, nine against, six abstentions, and one state absent.

57 OEA/Ser.G, CP/RES. 1164 (2309/20) rev. 1, 10 December 2020.

58 See also for a critical appraisal, H P Aust, 'Die Anerkennung von Regierungen: Völkerrechtliche Grundlagen und Grenzen im Lichte des Falls Venezuela' (2020) 80 ZaöRV 73, 79 ss.

59 "Any member of the Council of Europe which has seriously violated Article 3 may be suspended from its rights of representation and requested by the Committee of Ministers to withdraw under Article 7. If such member does not comply with this request, the Committee may decide that it has ceased to be a member of the Council as from such date as the Committee may determine". In the Greek Case, which remains exceptional, brought before the Council of Europe but also the Human Rights Commission and the Court, the Greek junta decided to withdraw from the Council of Europe in 1969 before a suspension or a request to withdraw could be made. Greece was readmitted in 1974 after the fall of the military regime.

obvious political (not to stigmatize the State) and legal (not to release it from its obligations) reasons. By contrast, the EU establishes a more sophisticated mechanism while at the same time ignoring exclusion. Article 7 of the TUE provides for a two-fold procedure of a preventive and sanctioning character respectively.

The preventive limb is found in paragraph 1 of this provisions which provides that on a reasoned proposal by one-third of the Member States, by the European Parliament, or by the European Commission, "the Council, acting by a majority of four-fifths of its members after obtaining the consent of the European Parliament, may determine that there is a clear risk of a serious breach by a Member State of the values referred to in Article 2. Before making such a determination, the Council shall hear the Member State in question and may address recommendations to it, acting in accordance with the same procedure". This provision constitutes a kind of early warning political procedure and has been triggered in two cases. The first concerns the rule of law in Poland and the procedure was triggered in December 2017 when the European Commission published its reasoned proposal where it expressed its concerns about the lack of an independent and legitimate constitutional review and the adoption by the Polish Parliament of new legislation relating to the Polish judiciary which raises grave concerns with regards to judicial independence and significantly increases the systemic threat to the rule of law in Poland. More particularly, the Commission observed that within a period of two years, more than thirteen consecutive laws have been adopted affecting the entire structure of the justice system in Poland and whose ordinary pattern has been that "the executive or legislative powers have been systematically enabled to interfere significantly with the composition, the powers, the administration and the functioning of these authorities and bodies. The legislative changes and their combined effects put at serious risk the independence of the judiciary and the separation of powers in Poland which are key components of the rule of law".[60] The second case concerns Hungary and was triggered in September 2018 by the European Parliament which in its reasoned proposal to the Council expressed several concerns related, among many others, to the functioning of the constitutional and electoral system, the independence of the judiciary and

---

60 European Commission, Proposal for a Council Decision on the determination of a clear risk of a serious breach by the Republic of Poland of the rule of law, COM (2017) 835 final, 20 December 2017 para 173. See also for an account of the Polish rule of law crisis and the failures of EU institutions to take effective action L Pech, P Wachowiec, D. Mazur, 'Poland's Rule of Law Breakdown: A Five-Year Assessment of EU's (In)Action' (2021) *Hague J Rule Law*, https://doi.org/10.1007/s40803-021-00151-9.

of other institutions, and to many basic human rights. It considered that the different facts and trends taken together represented a systemic threat to the values of Article 2 TEU and constituted a clear risk of a serious breach thereof by Hungary.[61] However, to this day, the Council of the European Union has not taken a decision either on Poland or on Hungary. As far as the sanctioning limb is concerned, it is detailed in the following paragraphs of Article 7 TUE. Unlike its preventive counterpart, which is based on a finding of a clear risk of a serious breach of Article 2 values by the Council of the European Union, here the European Council, acting unanimously, may determine "the existence of a serious and persistent breach by a Member State" of these values. When such a determination has been made, "the Council, acting by a qualified majority, may decide to suspend certain of the rights deriving from the application of the Treaties to the Member State in question, including the voting rights of the representative of the government of that Member State in the Council".[62]

It is not possible to discuss here in detail this highly political mechanism and its well-known shortcomings.[63] Suffices to say that given the voting requirements it would seem that while the preventive limb is very difficult to trigger, as in the case of Hungary and Poland, the sanctioning limb seems almost impossible to trigger. Hence, a number of questions come to mind. First, what would the EU do in the event of a military coup in one of its member States? Admittedly, this is not very likely but, still, the mechanism for dealing with situations where one or more member States disregard the values of Article 2 remains the same – that is to say probably incapable of producing any concrete effect – regardless of the nature and gravity of the undemocratic conduct in question. Second, unless there is a convincing and legitimate *distinguo* to make, is it not somewhat contradictory, not to say hypocritical, for the EU to unilaterally adopt democratic sanctions against some States (as we will see

61 European Parliament resolution of 12 September 2018 on a proposal calling on the Council to determine, pursuant to Article 7(1) of the Treaty on European Union, the existence of a clear risk of a serious breach by Hungary of the values on which the Union is founded (2017/2131(INL)). It is noteworthy that the Court of Justice dismissed on 3 June 2021 Hungary's action against this Parliament resolution by ruling that, while the contested resolution adopted under Article 7, para 1 of the TUE may be subject to judicial review under Article 263 TFEU, MEPs' abstentions do not have to be counted in order to determine whether the majority of two-thirds of the votes cast, referred to in Article 354 TFEU, has been reached, see Case C-650/18, Hungary v Parliament.

62 Ibid. paras 2 and 3.

63 See for a thorough discussion K Scheppele, D Kochenov, B Grabowska-Moroz, 'EU Values Are Law, after All: Enforcing EU Values through Systemic Infringement Actions by the European Commission and the Member States of the European Union' (2020) *Yearbook of European Law* 3, 32 ff (with many further references).

below) while at the same time it remains unwilling or unable to sanction its own member States? Third, is there anything to be done for economic integration and interdependence factors and considerations to give way to political values such as democracy?

3.3 *Judicial Sanctions?*

As with military and economic sanctions, political measures adopted by international institutions against non-democratic governments, such as suspension or even (controversially) non-recognition, as in the case of Venezuela, ultimately depend on a discretionary decision of the competent instances of these institutions, which may be difficult to reach due to the divergence of opinion among member States as mentioned above. It might thus be necessary to look for other, *seemingly* less politicized means for enforcing democracy. For that reason, in addition to the role domestic courts and tribunals could play in that respect, international tribunals may also be called upon to rule on the compatibility of undemocratic practices with international law. Judicial democratic sanctions of this kind are becoming more and more common in contemporary practice. They may be directed against either backsliding governments violating fundamental political rights and the rule of law or, more exceptionally, individuals whose criminal responsibility for undemocratic behavior could be established by a competent international tribunal.

Judicial sanctions of the first type have flourished in the old continent especially over the past few years. Admittedly, the European Court of Human rights promotes democracy when it finds that measures interfering with the enjoyment of human rights are not necessary in a democratic society and thus not in accordance with, for instance, Articles 8 to 11 of the European Convention. Yet such measures are not usually related to some kind of democratic erosion in the defendant State. Is it even necessary to remind readers that France and Germany, among many other unquestionably democratic States, are found in breach of the European Convention almost every day? However, in some cases, democratic backsliding and erosion give rise to systematic violations of political freedoms and other rights. To give some recent examples, in the case Baka v Hungary concerning the premature removal from office of the president of the Supreme Court of Hungary (as a consequence of the entry into force of several constitutional and legislative reforms), the Court found a violation of Article 10 (freedom of expression), considering that his removal was linked to his publicly expressed and very critical opinion with respect to these reforms.[64] In the

64 Baka v. Hungary, App no 20261/12 (ECtHR, GC, 23 June 2016) paras 168–176.

context of the persecution of political opponents in Turkey since the beginning of the Erdogan era, an important recent case is that of an opposition politician who was one of the co-chairs of the Peoples' Democratic Party (HDP) and a member of the National Assembly for the HDP, arrested and detained on suspicions of having committed many offenses, including terrorism-related. The Grand Chamber found, among other violations, not only that the fact that the applicant was unable to take part in the activities of the National Assembly on account of his pre-trial detention constituted an unjustified interference with the free expression of the opinion of the people and with his own right to be elected and to sit in Parliament recognized by Article 3 of Protocol No. 1 to the Convention (para 397),[65] but also that his detention, especially during two crucial campaigns relating to the referendum and the presidential election "pursued the ulterior purpose of stifling pluralism and limiting freedom of political debate, which is at the very core of the concept of a democratic society", concluding that there has been a violation of Article 18[66] of the Convention in conjunction with Article 5.[67] In another judgment, which is, however, not final, after a thorough examination of relevant materials related to the reforms of the justice system in Poland, the Court found a violation of Article 6 § 1 of the Convention on the ground that the Disciplinary Chamber of the Supreme Court, which heard the applicant's complaints, was not an independent tribunal established by law due to irregularities in the appointment process of its members.[68]

Beyond these human rights-based judicial sanctions in cases of democratic backsliding affecting the independence of the judiciary or the freedom of expression of political opponents, the EU legal order adopts a more proactive stance under the principle of the rule of law. The Court of Justice of the EU indeed goes beyond the protection of the human rights of judges when it comes to measures affecting their status, such as disciplinary proceedings or

65 *Selahattin Demirtaş v. Turkey* (no. 2) App no 14305/17 (ECtHR, GC, 22 December 2020) para 397.

66 This provision, entitled, "Limitation on use of restrictions on rights", provides that "The restrictions permitted under this Convention to the said rights and freedoms shall not be applied for any purpose other than those for which they have been prescribed". It thus prohibits abuse of power.

67 *Selahattin Demirtaş v. Turkey* (no. 2) App no 14305/17 (ECtHR, GC, 22 December 2020) para 437. See also *Navalnyy v Russia* App nos 29580/12 and 4 others (ECtHR, GC, 15 November 2018), with respect to the detention of a political opponent in Russia where the Court found a violation of Article 18 in conjunction with both Article 5 and Article 11 of the Convention.

68 *Reczkowicz v Poland* App no 43447/19 (ECtHR, 22 July 2021).

premature removal from office, to encompass a more thorough understanding of the rule of law as a fundamental pillar of a democratic society. Without entering into the details of the relevant case law,[69] the EU legal order protects judicial independence as such. Mobilizing Article 19 (1) TEU second subparagraph[70] in conjunction with Article 47 of the Charter (right to an effective remedy and to a fair trial), the Court of Justice held the view that this provision, which gives concrete expression to the value of the rule of law affirmed in Article 2 of the same treaty, requires member States to provide remedies that are sufficient to ensure effective legal protection in fields covered by EU law.[71] On that basis, it decided in an infringement case against Poland that lowering the retirement age of the judges of the Supreme Court in a retroactive manner and granting the President of the Republic the discretion to extend the period of judicial activity of judges of that court beyond the newly fixed retirement age constituted a violation of Article 19 (1) TEU.[72] European States, therefore, have a duty to ensure that their national justice system as a whole is fair and especially independent from the other branches of government. As a result, abusive constitutional and legislative reforms undermining the rule of law and the separation of powers, as in Poland and Hungary over the past years, may entail judicial sanction. The manifest ineffectiveness of purely political mechanisms mentioned above combined with the arguably limited effect of judicial sanctions in infringement or preliminary cases under Article 19 of the TUE which, in passing, exclusively deal with judicial independence and the rule of law, has, however, prompted some authors to propose a more robust judicial approach aiming at fully enforce EU values. According to this approach, infringement actions, both under Article 258 and 259 TFEU could be adapted as instruments for enforcing EU values by bundling a set of specific violations into a single general infringement action. The idea would be to show, the argument goes, how a pattern of unlawful activity rises to the level of being a systemic violation calling for systemic compliance. Going further, they even suggest the use of Article 260 Treaty on the Functioning of the EU (TFEU) to deduct fines from

69 See K Lenaerts 'The Two Dimensions of Judicial Independence in the EU Legal Order' in R Spano, I Motoc, B Lubarda, P Pinto de Albuquerque, M Tsirli (eds) assisted by A Lazana, *Fair Trial: Regional and International Perspectives / Procès équitable: perspectives régionales et internationales. Liber Amicorum Linos-Alexandre Sicilianos* (Brussels Anthemis 2020) 333.

70 "Member States shall provide remedies sufficient to ensure effective legal protection in the fields covered by Union law".

71 C-619/18, Commission v Poland (Independence of the Supreme Court), 24 June 2019 paras 54–55.

72 Ibid. para 96.

EU funds due to be received by backsliding member States.[73] Still, one may wonder whether the Court of Justice is really the appropriate forum to enforce compliance in cases where what is at stake is the overall decline of democratic institutions in a given country. While such an international (or better supranational) government of judges would perhaps not be a threat to democracy, quite to the contrary, it remains that the erosion of democracy is not only a legal but also a political problem that accordingly warrants a political solution. This is not to say that judicializing democratic values is a bad thing, but simply that the courts should not substitute for the ineffective political institutions of the EU.

Beyond judicial sanctions against governments responsible for democratic backsliding and erosion, another more radical form of judicial sanction would be to hold persons engaging in undemocratic behavior accountable before an international criminal tribunal. As a matter of principle, coups d'états or other forms of undemocratic changes of government, including democratic backsliding and erosion, do not, as such, constitute international crimes within the meaning of the Statute of the International Criminal Court (ICC). However, in some cases, undermining democracy may be linked to massive human rights violations and especially trigger crimes against humanity including persecution on political grounds under the jurisdiction of the ICC according to Article 7 of its Statute in connection with any of the other acts referred to in the same provision, such as murder, extermination, torture, enforced disappearance, or rape. The same provision defines persecution as 'the intentional and severe deprivation of fundamental rights contrary to international law by reason of the identity of the group or collectivity". Nonetheless, to entail individual responsibility, these acts must be committed "as part of a widespread or systematic attack directed against any civilian population, with knowledge of the attack", attack meaning "a course of conduct involving the multiple commission" of these abovementioned acts "against any civilian population, pursuant to or in furtherance of a State or organizational policy to commit such attack". Therefore, undemocratic situations, including infringements of the right to political participation, may be contextual factors when determining issues of individual criminal responsibility for core crimes.[74] This said, a 'course of conduct" is obviously a strict condition to be met. For instance, the Office of the

73 See K Scheppele, D Kochenov, B Grabowska-Moroz, supra, 59ff.

74 See also T Wood, 'Domestic Politics, International Crimes: Gross Violations of the Right to Political Participation' (2016) 16 Int'l Crim L Rev 730.

ICC Prosecutor found that the situation in Honduras was a "borderline case",[75] since the violence following the coup d'état of 2009 was not only owed "to the political turmoil triggered by the coup", but was also the result of common criminal activity in the country.[76] More particularly, the alleged killings did not occur "primarily in locations that could be perceived as being more associated with the political opposition" as the information available was "insufficient to establish that the alleged victims of killings were targeted owing to their political affiliation or professional activities", a circumstance which pointed to the absence of a "course of conduct" because "the alleged crimes fail to evidence a certain pattern of behaviour indicating that they were committed as part of a campaign or operation carried out against the civilian population".[77] On the other hand, post-electoral violence amounting to crimes against humanity, allegedly committed by an incumbent president unwilling to step down and his followers, may entail international criminal responsibility as shown in the case of L. Gbagbo in Cote d'Ivoire, although his subsequent acquittal decision of 15 January 2019 was ultimately confirmed by the Appeals Chamber on 31 March 2021. More interestingly, on 8 February 2018, the Prosecutor opened a preliminary examination of the situation in Venezuela since the beginning of the constitutional crisis in April 2017.[78] In 2020, the Office completed its preliminary assessment and concluded that there is a reasonable basis to believe that since at least April 2017, civilian authorities, members of the armed forces, and pro-government individuals had committed several crimes against humanity such as imprisonment, torture, rape, and persecution on political grounds.[79]

While undemocratic practices as such do not constitute international crimes under the ICC Statute, African Union law is far more ambitious. Building on the Charter on Democracy mentioned above, whose Article 25, § 5 provides that "perpetrators of unconstitutional change of government may also be tried before the competent court of the Union", the yet to be established African Court of Justice and Human Rights will have criminal jurisdiction over many

75 ICC, The Office of the Prosecutor, Report on Preliminary Examination Activities (2015) para 288.

76 Ibid. para 272.

77 Ibid. paras 276 and 278.

78 It is noteworthy that on 27 September 2018 the Office of the Prosecutor also received a referral from a group of States Parties to the Rome Statute (Argentina, Canada, Colombia, Chile, Paraguay, and Peru), requesting the Prosecutor to initiate an investigation on crimes against humanity allegedly committed in Venezuela since 12 February 2014, *i.e.* the first day of major opposition protests against the Maduro government.

79 ICC, The Office of the Prosecutor, Report on Preliminary Examination Activities (14 December 2020) para 204.

other crimes such as piracy, terrorism, or corruption, as well as over perpetrators of an unconstitutional change of government by virtue of the Malabo Protocol of 2014.[80] By specifying that "unconstitutional change of government" means committing or ordering to be committed "with the aim of illegally accessing or maintaining power", Article 28 E of this instrument criminalizes the same set of acts that may trigger suspension of illegitimate governments as seen above, while adding a new one, *i.e.* "any substantial modification to the electoral laws in the last six months before the elections without the consent of the majority of the political actors". The African Court will therefore be the first international criminal tribunal vested with jurisdiction over such crimes. This exponentially extended criminal jurisdiction clearly reflects the disenchantment of the African Union with the selective and even, as sometimes suggested, neocolonialist targeting of the continent by the ICC. However, this ambitious approach raises a number of complex issues.[81] While it seems that this new crime does not infringe a supposed right of popular rebellion against an authoritarian regime, the exact scope of criminally prohibited conducts remains rather vague especially when it comes to "constitutional amendments infringing the principles of democratic change of government or inconsistent with the constitution", as well as with respect to "the substantial modification of electoral laws". For instance, as noted by some scholars, "what if an amendment to a national constitution is inconsistent with the constitution, but the aim is indeed to make it more democratic?"[82] This and other challenges to the principle of legality, including foreseeability, should have been more thoroughly addressed. Furthermore, the apparent dissociation between these conducts and core crimes could potentially lead to purely political trials. It is thus rather doubtful that this new instrument, once in force, will truly serve as a deterrent tool for current or potential dictators in Africa, as it just adds yet another layer of complexity to a democratic project whose realization still remains a far-away dream. Should criminalization, as judicialization in the

---

80 The Malabo protocol is not yet in force as it has been signed by only 15 States out of 55 AU Member states and ratified by none to this date (15 ratifications being necessary for entry into force in accordance with its Article 11).

81 For an overview see H van der Wilt, 'Unconstitutional Change of Government. A New Crime within the Jurisdiction of the African Criminal Court' in C Jalloh, K Clarke and V Nmehielle (eds), *The African Court of Justice and Human and Peoples' Rights in Context* (Cambridge University Press 2018) 619; G Kemp, S Kinyunyu. 'The Crime of Unconstitutional Change of Government (Article 28E)' in G Werle and M Vormbaum (eds), *The African Criminal Court, A Commentary on the Malabo Protocol* (TMC Asser Press 2017) 57.

82 G Kemp, S Kinyunyu, supra, 67.

EU legal order, be an ersatz for collective political response against undemocratic governments and their leaders? Perhaps not. In any case, such political response can only come from governments and leaders that respect democratic values themselves.

4 Unilateral Democratic Sanctions: Lawful Reactions or Violations of International Law?

Compared to institutional democratic sanctions, which are presumably both legitimate and lawful, unilateral democratic sanctions, especially economic sanctions imposed without UNSC endorsement, are far more controversial in international law.[83] These sanctions may be targeted or more or less comprehensive. Targeted sanctions or smart sanctions are aimed specifically at listed persons and entities ('targeted individual sanctions'), such as asset freezing and travels bans, or at particular sectors of the economy of the targeted State ('sector-wide' or 'sectoral sanctions'). Like UN targeted sanctions, their unilateral avatars tend to minimize the effects on the population of the targeted state as they are designed to affect only those allegedly responsible, that is, leaders or entities in close association with the regime, for engaging in nuclear proliferation activities, supporting terrorist networks, otherwise threatening peace and security, or in our case undermining democracy and the rule of law. Comprehensive unilateral sanctions, on the other hand, are aimed at the whole economy including the financial system of the targeted State and tend to be more indiscriminate and thus to have adverse effects on the lives of the whole population living therein. Without going further into the details of this seemingly clear-cut dichotomy, which does not always reflect the complex reality of sanctions, recent examples of unilateral democratic sanctions include Belarus. In this case, the EU adopted targeted restrictive measures (assets freeze and travel ban) against persons and entities "responsible for serious violations of human rights or the repression of civil society and democratic opposition, or whose activities otherwise seriously undermine democracy or the rule of law in Belarus, or any person associated with them",

83 At the outset, it should be emphasized that despite some opinion to the contrary, unilateral prodemocratic military intervention is prohibited in international law, see in detail J Wouters, B De Meester, and C Ryngaert, 'Democracy and International Law' (2003) NYIL 139, 165–177 (with many references) and H Charlesworth, 'Democracy and International Law' (2015) 371 Recueil des cours de l'Académie de droit international 88–92.

including the president.[84] More sophisticated targeted sectoral sanctions have however been introduced by the EU following the unlawful forced landing of an intra-EU Ryanair flight in Minsk, Belarus, on 23 May 2021. These measures expand the arms embargo previously in place while strengthening the trade restrictions in relation to equipment, technology, or software intended primarily for use in the monitoring or interception by the Belarusian authorities of the internet and of telephone communications on mobile or fixed networks. Moreover, they provide for further trade restrictions concerning, among others, petroleum products along with financial restrictions on access to EU capital markets by the Belarusian Government as well as Belarusian state-owned financial institutions and entities.[85] Likewise, the US adopted targeted sanctions against individuals and entities "for their roles in the fraudulent August 9, 2020, presidential election in Belarus and the subsequent violent crackdown on peaceful pro-democracy protests", including those responsible for "actions or policies that undermine democratic processes or institutions in Belarus" such as the members of the Central election commission and police officials responsible for the crackdown.[86] Similarly, the EU has, since 2017, imposed targeted restrictive measures against those "undermining democracy or the rule of law and those responsible for serious violations of human rights" in Venezuela along with an embargo on arms and equipment which might be used for internal repression or surveillance.[87] Following the December 2020 legislative elections, the Council decided to adopt additional targeted restrictive measures.[88] For its part, the US sanctions program against Venezuela is broader. It has

84 Council Decision (CFSP) 2021/353 of 25 February 2021 amending Decision 2012/642/CFSP concerning restrictive measures against Belarus; Council Implementing Regulation (EU) 2020/2129 of 17 December 2020 implementing Article 8a(1) of Regulation (EC) No 765/2006 concerning restrictive measures in respect of Belarus.

85 Council Decision (CFSP) 2021/1031 of 24 June 2021 amending Council Decision 2012/642/CFSP concerning restrictive measures in view of the situation in Belarus; Council Regulation (EU) 2021/1030 of 24 June 2021 amending Regulation (EC) No 765/2006 concerning restrictive measures in respect of Belarus.

86 Executive Order 13405 of 2006 as updated, see Treasury Sanctions Additional Belarusian Regime Actors for Undermining Democracy, 23 December 2020, available at https://home.treasury.gov/news/press-releases/sm1222.

87 Council Decision (CFSP) 2017/2074 of 13 November 2017 concerning restrictive measures in view of the situation in Venezuela; Council Regulation (EU) 2017/2063 of 13 November 2017 concerning restrictive measures in view of the situation in Venezuela.

88 Council Decision (CFSP) 2021/276 of 22 February 2021 amending Decision (CFSP) 2017/2074 concerning restrictive measures in view of the situation in Venezuela; Council Implementing Regulation (EU) 2021/275 of 22 February 2021 implementing Regulation (EU) 2017/2063 concerning restrictive measures in view of the situation in Venezuela.

imposed, along with targeted individual sanctions, a comprehensive blockage of all property and interests in property belonging to Venezuela located in the United States.[89] Moreover, after the recent coup in Myanmar, the US[90] and the EU adopted targeted individual sanctions against natural and legal persons, entities, and bodies "whose activities undermine democracy and the rule of law in Myanmar/Burma", namely individuals responsible for the military coup and the subsequent military and police repression against peaceful demonstrators, including the Myanmar Armed Forces Commander-in-Chief.[91]

However, unilateral democratic sanctions, as part of the wider policy of "unilateral coercive measures" (in the UN jargon) or "restrictive measures" (in the EU jargon) of an economic character, raise a number of issues, especially when they are very extensive or even comprehensive in nature. Designed to coerce a State, a government, or its leaders to change domestic policies so as to respect or restore democracy, unilateral democratic sanctions may potentially be contrary to international law. For more than two decades now the United Nations General Assembly (UNGA) and more recently the Human Rights Council (HRC) have annually rejected unilateral coercive measures as being incompatible with "international law, international humanitarian law, the Charter of the United Nations and the norms and principles governing peaceful relations among States" and as "impeding the full realization of the rights set forth in the Universal Declaration of Human Rights and other international human rights instruments, in particular the right of individuals and peoples to development".[92] Moreover, the HRC urges states "to avoid the use of economic, political or other measures to coerce another State

89 Executive Order 13884 of August 5, 2019, Blocking Property of the Government of Venezuela. All relevant documents are available at https://home.treasury.gov/policy-issues/financial-sanctions/sanctions-programs-and-country-information/venezuela-related-sanctions.

90 See U.S. Department of the Treasury press release of 11 February 2021, available at https://home.treasury.gov/news/press-releases/jy0024.

91 Council Decision (CFSP) 2021/482 of 22 March 2021 amending Decision 2013/184/CFSP concerning restrictive measures against Myanmar/Burma; Council Decision (CFSP) 2021/483 of 22 March 2021 amending Decision 2013/184/CFSP concerning restrictive measures against Myanmar/Burma; Council Regulation (EU) 2021/479 of 22 March 2021 amending Regulation (EU) No 401/2013 concerning restrictive measures in respect of Myanmar/Burma; Council Implementing Regulation (EU) 2021/480 of 22 March 2021 implementing Regulation (EU) No 401/2013 concerning restrictive measures in respect of Myanmar/Burma.

92 UNGA 'Human rights and unilateral coercive measures' (16 December 2020) UN Doc A/RES/75/181 para 1 and UNCHR Res 46/5 'The negative impact of unilateral coercive measures on the enjoyment of human rights' (23 March 2021) UN Doc A/HRC/RES/46/5 para 1.

with regard to the exercise of its sovereign rights",[93] while the UNGA establishes an inextricable link between non-intervention and human rights by rejecting unilateral sanctions not only "as being tools for political or economic pressure" against targeted countries "adopted with a view to preventing those countries from exercising their right to decide, of their own free will, their own political, economic and social systems", but also "because of the negative effects of those measures on the realization of all the human rights of vast sectors of their populations".[94] However, while one might be tempted to agree with the idea that "the entitlement to democracy can only be expected to flourish if it is coupled with a reiterated prohibition on such unilateral initiatives",[95] whether unilateral coercive measures of an economic and financial character, including those intended to promote or enforce respect for democratic principles, are consistent with the principle of non-intervention and human rights remains an open issue. It is premature to draw the conclusion that the above-mentioned UN resolutions reflect in their entirety an emergent rule of customary international law, as shown by the heavily divided voting records.[96] Still, this should not prevent us from briefly discussing these issues.

4.1 *Non-intervention*

With regard to the principle of non-intervention, an apt starting point is of course the Nicaragua case. There the International Court of Justice (ICJ) clarified that the principle of non-intervention, which is "part and parcel of customary international law", "involves the right of every sovereign State to conduct its affairs without outside interference". More particularly, the Court held that "a prohibited intervention must (…) be one bearing on matters in which each State is permitted, by the principle of State sovereignty, to decide freely. One of these is the choice of a political, economic, social and cultural system, and the formulation of foreign policy. Intervention is wrongful when it uses methods of coercion in regard to such choices, which must remain free ones", before adding that "the element of coercion, which defines, and indeed

93 UNHCR Res 46/5 'The negative impact of unilateral coercive measures on the enjoyment of human rights' (23 March 2021) UN Doc A/HRC/RES/46/5 para 4.

94 UNGA Res 181 'Human rights and unilateral coercive measures' (16 December 2020) UN Doc A/RES/75/181 para 6.

95 T M Franck, 'The Emerging Right to Democratic Governance' (1992) 86 Am J Int'l L 46, 85.

96 See also A Hofer, 'The Developed/Developing Divide on Unilateral Coercive Measures: Legitimate Enforcement or Illegitimate Intervention?' (2017) 16 Chinese Journal of International Law 175, 192–7.

forms the very essence of, prohibited intervention, is particularly obvious in the case of an intervention which uses force (…)".[97]

Therefore, to find a violation of the principle in the case of unilateral democratic sanctions, two conditions must be met. First, that the matter is not covered by international law, *i.e.* it falls within the *domaine réservé* of the targeted State. Second, that the latter is coerced to change its behavior on such a matter.

It is not necessary here to linger over the recurring question of whether there exists a customary duty for States (or their governments and leaders) to respect democracy. If such a duty existed, the issue would cease to fall within the exclusive domestic jurisdiction of the State concerned and the principle of non-intervention would become irrelevant. While it is rather unquestionable that such a duty forms part of many regional orders as seen above, the traditional view expressed by the ICJ in the Nicaragua case is that "a State's domestic policy falls within its exclusive jurisdiction, provided of course that it does not violate any obligation of international law. Every State possesses a fundamental right to choose and implement its own political, economic and social systems".[98] On its face, this statement would seem to exclude any customary duty for States to be democratic. Even less, this duty would be of an *erga omnes* character allowing for third States to adopt democratic sanctions against the responsible State.[99] However, this is perhaps not what the Court meant to say. "Domestic policy" which falls within the *domaine réservé* of a State must not violate any obligation of international law. Political individual rights, as part of both treaty and perhaps also customary international law should thus be respected even when a State exercises its own fundamental right to choose and implement its political, economic, and social systems. It is one thing to choose a political system, it is another to breach fundamental political rights. Accordingly, it is rather artificial to separate democracy as a political model from respect for fundamental political rights.[100] Admittedly, as the Court put

---

97 *Case concerning Military and Paramilitary Activities in and against Nicaragua* (*Nicaragua v United States of America*) (Merits) [1986] ICJ Rep 4 paras 202 and 205.

98 *Case concerning Military and Paramilitary Activities in and against Nicaragua* (*Nicaragua v United States of America*) (Merits) [1986] ICJ Rep 4 para 258.

99 The issue of collective or third-party countermeasures will not be discussed further here. Suffices to say that unilateral sanctions including democratic ones are not always in breach of obligations due to the responsible State. Indeed, trade embargoes or other economic or financial sanctions are not in principle prohibited by general international law. Unless they breach bilateral treaties of commerce, WTO law, or some other specific rule binding the sanctioning State to the targeted State, they cannot qualify as countermeasures but simply as measures of retorsion.

100 As one author does when he observes that "while the violation of fundamental human rights surely amounts to an internationally wrongful act *erga omnes*, it seems highly

it, it is not possible to "contemplate the creation of a new rule opening up a right of intervention by one State against another on the ground that the latter has opted for some particular ideology or political system".[101] Nevertheless, in almost all situations triggering democratic sanctions, the link between democracy and respect for political rights is unbreakable. After all, democracy is not only about respecting abstract and theoretical political models, but also the will of the people as expressed through the unhindered exercise of its political freedoms. Moreover, the sacrosanct sovereign freedom of the State seems caught in a vicious circle as a State cannot but act through its government. But what if the government is or becomes undemocratic? To get out of this logical deadlock, one must assume that the principle of freedom of choice of the political regime is only applicable when the government enjoys democratic legitimacy. This legitimacy covers both accession to power and the exercise thereof, including the absence of political repression. For these reasons, the *domaine réservé* defense would seem to be utterly irrelevant in contemporary international law.

However, even if one maintains that it is possible to separate democracy and human rights, do democratic sanctions breach the principle of non-intervention in such "domestic" affairs? And what is the degree of unlawful coercion triggering the principle of non-intervention? If is it clear that unilateral military coercion satisfies this condition, what about economic or political coercion? It should be recalled in that respect that in relation to the trade embargo imposed by the US on Nicaragua, the Court simply stated that it was "unable to regard such action on the economic plane as is here complained of as a breach of the customary-law principle of non-intervention".[102] But this does not mean that economic coercion can never reach this threshold. Still, international law does not appear to give a clear answer to this question. One might thus be tempted to think that unilateral democratic sanctions of a more or less comprehensive economic nature, such as those that the US imposes on Venezuela or on other States such as Syria or Iran, are likely to violate the principle "when they amount to an overwhelming pressure causing the target State to be forced to make (or not to make) certain decisions falling within the

questionable that the breach of democratic values also gives rise to such a wrongful situation", see G Puma, 'The principle of non-intervention in the face of the Venezuelan crisis' (2021) QIL, Zoom-in 79, 5, 14.

101 *Case concerning Military and Paramilitary Activities in and against Nicaragua* (*Nicaragua v. United States of America*), (Merits)[1986] ICJ Rep14, 133, para 263.

102 *Case concerning Military and Paramilitary Activities in and against Nicaragua* (*Nicaragua v. United States of America*), (Merits)[1986] ICJ Rep14, 133, para 245.

scope of its domestic jurisdiction". In other terms, there must exist a causal link in the sense that the targeted government "has changed, because of sanctions as such, the 'ordinary' course of its political action both in its domestic sphere and in its international relations with other States".[103] This threshold would therefore not seem to be met in the case of Venezuela since the policy has not yet changed there.[104] But according to the same view, the premature recognition by the US (and some EU member States, but not the EU as such) of opposition leader Guaido, claiming to be the president as head of parliament, following the disputed re-election of Nicolás Maduro in 2018 and financial support given to him by the US, would clearly breach the principle and also entail the unlawfulness of economic sanctions since all these actions form part of a course of conduct with the declared purpose of contributing to overthrowing Maduro.[105] However, this argument is not convincing for two reasons. First, it conflates coercion with its effectiveness. Admittedly, coercion has to be significantly strong and overwhelming. In our view, however, it does not necessarily have to be successful. Put differently, from a legal point of view, it is irrelevant whether unilateral democratic sanctions, similarly to other unilateral coercive measures, cause the desired or intended effect, *i.e.* respect for democracy. Second, it is also contradictory because if a policy change is the criterion of unlawful coercion when it comes to economic sanctions, how can one admit that premature recognition of an ineffective government, which is perhaps less coercive as one might think, could be qualified as unlawful intervention – and even entail the unlawfulness of economic measures which taken separately seem perfectly lawful – since, once more, despite all this pressure policy has not (yet) changed in Venezuela? Needless to add that if the situation changes, non-intervention would probably become irrelevant.

Having said that, the assessment of the fulfillment of the threshold condition must take into account various factors such as how difficult it is for the targeted government to find economic or political support elsewhere in order to satisfy not only its own needs but also those of its population. Of course, source entities insist on the fact that their democratic sanctions "are designed not to harm" the population of the target State.[106] The general assumption is also that smart sanctions are a far more humane foreign policy tool than more or less comprehensive sanctions. This type of sanction implicitly suggests

103 G Puma, supra, 21.

104 G Puma, supra, 21.

105 G Puma, supra, 26.

106 See for instance Council Conclusions on Venezuela, Brussels, 25 January 2021 (OR. en) 5582/21 COLAC 5 CFSP/PESC 48 para 6.

that the only real affected State is the one that is a victim of the breach of the democratic duty, *i.e.* the one whose government no longer satisfies democratic standards. Thus, it would not be impossible to assume that in view of the development of targeted individual or smart sanctions, this democratic duty is only binding on the illegitimate leaders as such. However, more or less comprehensive economic sanctions, albeit abandoned by the UN after the criticisms of the humanitarian impact of what has been called the 'sanctions decade',[107] continue to be used by the US and, to a lesser extent, by the EU. When this happens, there is no easy way to separate the targeted State or government from its population. After all, the population is an element inherent in the existence of a State. If there is no population, there is no State. Inflicting suffering, whether by design or not, on the population of the targeted State probably produces global coercion on this State. Yet, coercion is irrelevant if one assumes, as seen above, that respecting democracy and human rights are no longer in the realm of domestic jurisdiction. This brings us to the second issue.

4.2 *Human Rights*

While targeted individual democratic sanctions, whether UN or unilateral, raise a number of specific human rights concerns in terms of due process, the right to property, or the freedom of movement, they are now subject to a more clearly defined legal framework and remedies.[108] By contrast, the issue of the compatibility with international law, including human rights law, of comprehensive unilateral sanctions affecting, in one way or another, the entire population of the targeted State remains more complex and controversial. This is of course also true of democratic sanctions. If trade embargoes can breach bilateral treaties of commerce or WTO law, while assets freeze of foreign state-owned banks and other entities can disregard sovereign immunities, is it possible to argue that comprehensive sanctions are also inconsistent with human rights law? Admittedly, the negative impact of unilateral democratic sanctions is well-documented with regard to Venezuela.[109] Still, as the present

---

107 D Cortright and GA Lopez, *The Sanctions Decade: Assessing UN Strategies in the 1990s* (Lynne Rienner 2000).

108 See on EU restrictive measures, C Beaucillon, *Les mesures restrictives de l'Union européenne* (Bruylant 2014).

109 HRC, 'Negative impact of unilateral coercive measures on the enjoyment of human rights, Report of the Special Rapporteur on the negative impact of unilateral coercive measures on the enjoyment of human rights' (5 July 2019) UN Doc paras 16–35; see also HRC, 'Report of the Independent Expert on the promotion of a democratic and equitable international order on his mission to the Bolivarian Republic of Venezuela and Ecuador' (3 August 2018) UN Doc A/HRC/39/47/Add.1 paras 34–39 (on economic sanctions); M Weisbrot, J

author tried to demonstrate elsewhere,[110] there exist many substantive and procedural hurdles to be overcome in order to make accountability possible for unilateral sanctions, including democratic ones, affecting the lives of people living in the targeted States. First of all, it is far from obvious that sanctioning entities are under a duty to respect human rights, such as the right to life and especially the economic and social rights of persons living in the targeted State. A negative answer to this question seems to be based on the fact that despite some opinion to the contrary, the extraterritorial applicability of most human rights instruments relies on extraterritorial conduct (*i.e.* when a State acts on the territory of another State), but not on extraterritorial effect, *i.e.* on account of the effects democratic sanctions may produce on the enjoyment of rights in the targeted country. For this reason, it would seem that most human rights bodies and courts do not have jurisdiction to hear complaints about such effects, since the source entity does not formally exercise jurisdiction over individuals adversely affected by sanctions. What is more, even if one extend the notion of extraterritorial human rights obligations and jurisdiction through cause-and-effect considerations, it would just move the problem to an even more complex level of analysis. Indeed, unlike targeted individual sanctions, unilateral comprehensive economic sanctions raise an issue that is crucial to establishing accountability: the existence of a causal link between these sanctions and the violation of specific rights of identified groups or individuals. Assessing the harmful impact of comprehensive democratic sanctions targeting the economy as a whole rather than identified individuals (such as illegitimate leaders etc.) through the lens of causality is a herculean task. As a matter of fact, establishing causality and thus accountability would require a case-by-case analysis. Such an analysis would have to take into account a complex chain of events involving not only multiple alternative causes attributed to the sanctioning entities, to the targeted State, and to private actors but also an assessment of the foreseeability of the consequences of their respective actions and omissions for the human rights of individuals and groups living in the targeted State. As a result, it seems that existing international human rights law and quasi adjudicative mechanisms are not suitable for addressing this problem. Substantive and procedural obstacles, coupled with the causality

Sachs, 'Economic Sanctions as Collective Punishment: The Case of Venezuela', (Center for Economic and Policy Research April 2019).

110 I Prezas, 'From targeted states to affected populations: exploring accountability for the negative impact of comprehensive unilateral sanctions on human rights' in C Beaucillon (ed), *Research Handbook on Unilateral and Extraterritorial Sanctions* (Edward Elgar 2021).

conundrum, all seem to militate against accountability for what may certainly look like 'collateral damages' of democratic sanctions.

For similar reasons, using international criminal law to challenge democratic sanctions is perhaps doomed to fail. On 13 February 2020 Venezuela referred the situation on its own territory to the Prosecutor of the ICC, alleging that crimes against humanity had been committed therein "as a result of the application of unlawful coercive measures adopted unilaterally" by the US against Venezuela, since at least 2014. For Venezuela, the severe humanitarian consequences of these sanctions amounted to a widespread or systematic attack upon a civilian population pursuant to Article 7(1) of the Rome Statute and were imposed by the US for the purpose of promoting regime change.[111] However, it seems rather unlikely that the Office of the Prosecutor will establish subject-matter jurisdiction. Among many other factors militating against this scenario, not to mention the US hostility towards the ICC, the most convincing view is that "given the silence of the Statute about effects jurisdiction, there are compelling arguments in favour of a strict construction of Article 12 and the exclusion of such a concept".[112] As a result, the extraterritorial effects of domestically adopted legislative measures intended to promote democracy in another State would not appear to amount to crimes "committed on the territory" of that State.

Last but not least, beyond human rights, Venezuela is currently challenging some provisions of EU Regulation 2017/2063 imposing an arms embargo as seen above. In support of its action, it relies on four pleas of law: that its right to be heard has been violated, that the Council infringed its obligation to state the reasons and to provide sufficient evidence for the adoption of the restrictive measures, that it committed a manifest error of assessment in that respect, and, more interestingly, that these measures constitute unlawful countermeasures under customary international law. While this action was dismissed on 20 September 2019 by the General Court of the EU on the ground that the applicant lacked *locus standi* as it was not directly affected, as required by Article 263 TFUE, by the contested restrictive measures,[113] the Court of Justice of the European Union (Grand Chamber), following the Advocate General's Opinion, took the opposite view in his 22 June 2021 judgment and referred the case back to the General Court for a final judgment to be given on the merits.[114]

---

111 ICC, The Office of the Prosecutor, Report on Preliminary Examination Activities (14 December 2020) paras 90–104.

112 W Schabas, *An introduction to the ICC* (5th edn,,Cambridge University Press 2017) 68.

113 Case T-65/18 *Bolivarian Republic of Venezuela v Council*, ECLI:EU:T:2019:649.

114 CJEU (Grand Chamber), judgment of 22 June 2021, Case C-872/19 P, *Bolivarian Republic of Venezuela v Council*, ECLI:EU:C:2021:507.

The battle over the lawfulness of unilateral democratic sanctions is now heading towards an almost entirely unchartered territory.

5 Concluding Remarks

Instead of concluding by synthesizing what has already been said above, it is perhaps preferable to recall that beyond strict legal considerations, democratic sanctions, and arguably all sanctions for that matter, raise two fundamental policy issues. The first one is that of their effectiveness. Indeed, if democratic sanctions, especially of an economic and financial nature, are coercive devices intended to promote, restore, or strengthen democratic institutions in a given country, do they achieve this purpose? Political science scholars are divided on this issue,[115] and dealing with it is beyond the scope of a legal inquiry. At the same time, it is necessary to point out the obvious: that every case is unique. Recent cases where democratic sanctions were imposed do not obey a general rule because everything depends on the situation in the targeted country and above all on its external support, including by what is usually termed a "black knight" such as Russia in relation to Belarus.[116] The second policy issue, closely related to the first one, is selectivity. As seen above, in some instances, competent international institutions fail to agree on the course of action that should be taken in order to tackle undemocratic practices in a given member State. In addition, it is no secret that the main actors in the field of unilateral democratic sanctions, *i.e.* the EU and the US, do not sanction each and every coup d'état or other form of erosion of democracy any more than the UNSC or other regional institutions. Why? Because imposing sanctions is a policy decision based less on legal considerations than on other more practical factors such as domestic and global pressure to that end, the target vulnerability, and the anticipated costs of such an action. Put differently, it is sometimes easier to target poor and vulnerable States than stable authoritarian regimes and the

115 See, *ex multis*, von C von Soest and M Wahman, 'Are democratic sanctions really counterproductive?' (2015) Democratization 957 (arguing in favor of limited effectiveness). See also European Parliament, Extraterritorial sanctions on trade and investments and European responses, STUDY Requested by the INTA committee, November 2020, 44 ff (for an inconclusive survey of the empirical research studies in relation to democratic sanctions).

116 K Shyrokykh, 'Human rights sanctions and the role of black knights: Evidence from the EU's post-Soviet neighbours' (2021) Journal of European Integration, DOI: 10.1080/07036337.2021.1908278.

decision is usually taken after a careful cost-benefit calculation.[117] Finally, the interplay between sovereignty-oriented and human rights-oriented critiques of unilateral democratic sanctions relies on a paradox since we usually tend to think of State sovereignty as a threat to human rights protection. For that reason, introducing sovereignty-oriented arguments in UN resolutions allegedly destined to promote respect for human rights overshadows the basic idea that human rights should not become the accessory of a sovereignty discourse. Sanctioning entities such as the US and the EU conceive democratic sanctions as enforcement mechanisms serving legitimate purposes including the defense of their own conception of democracy, comprising *political rights*. By contrast, targeted States condemn unilateral democratic sanctions as an illegitimate intervention in their domestic affairs and they usually tend to overplay and thus instrumentalize the impact of comprehensive sanctions on the *economic and social rights* of their populations. Ultimately democracy and human rights seem to serve as a pretext for a profoundly political conflict between sanctioning entities and targeted States with both using them to promote their respective policy agendas and interests.[118]

117 See C von Soest and M Wahman, 'Not all dictators are equal: Coups, fraudulent elections, and the selective targeting of democratic sanctions' (2015) Journal of Peace Research 17.

118 See I. Prezas, supra.

CHAPTER 11

Council of Europe as the Guardian of Democracy

The Venice Commission

Angelika Nußberger and Júlia Miklasová

1 Introduction

Democracy is mentioned in all the treaties of the Council of Europe (CoE) as a basic structural principle of the state. The same goes for the constitutions of the Council of Europe's member states. In fact, in the preamble of the European Convention on Human Rights (ECHR), the contracting parties explicitly reaffirm 'their profound belief in those fundamental freedoms which are the foundation of justice and peace in the world and are best maintained … by an *effective political democracy*';[1] the statute of the CoE speaks in its preamble of '*genuine democracy*'.[2] This explicit reliance on and endorsement of democracy as 'the only acceptable form of government' can be considered as a trademark of the geographical space of the Council of Europe.[3]

But this consensus can be misleading. It is possible to label a box by the etiquette of democracy even when its content does not match such a description. Painting with a broad brush, two basically different models may be distinguished. On the one hand, democracy may be seen as a system where the majority's will is unconditionally accepted. On the other hand, it may be argued that power has to be vested in different actors and balanced in order to ensure that the interests of the minority (or minorities) are adequately taken into account despite the majority's right to decide on the basic political questions. The latter model is the one propagated by the Venice Commission. Its credo is that despite a 'large variety of political systems and practices across

1 European Convention for the Protection of Human Rights and Fundamental Freedoms (adopted 4 November 1950, entered into force 3 September 1953) 213 UNTS 221, preamble (*emphasis added*) ('ECHR' or 'Convention').

2 Statute of the Council of Europe (adopted 5 May 1949, entered into force 3 August 1949) 87 UNTS 103.

3 CoE (Venice Commission), 'Opinion on the Balance of Powers in the Constitution and the Legislation of the Principality of Monaco' (14–15 June 2013) CDL-AD(2013)018, para 7 ('Opinion on Monaco').

 | DOI:10.1163/9789004508712_012

states' there is a 'European consensus on the core components of what a democracy is'.[4]

Based on this assumption the Venice Commission' mission is to decide on a case-by-case basis on what rules and mechanisms are democratic and at the same time to have the courage to criticize what is not democratic. This task is also reflected in its name: 'The European Commission for Democracy through Law'. It is embedded in its Revised Statute, according to which the Venice Commission's 'own specific field of action shall be the guarantees offered by law in the service of democracy'.[5]

This paper traces the Venice Commission's contribution to the upholding of democracy in the geographical space of the Council of Europe and beyond. It does so first by outlining its origins and evolution. Then, the paper focuses on the geographical scope of the Commission's activities seen through the prism of its role as the guardian of democracy. Third, it examines the substantive standards that the Commission applies in its work, followed by the examples of key outputs of the Commission in the area of the functioning of democratic institutions. Then, the paper discusses the impact of the Commission's work and different facets through which it is achieved. It also analyses challenges and paradoxes stemming from the Commission's innovative nature. Lastly, the paper offers conclusions.

2 Looking Back at Thirty Years of Evolution

In January 2020, the Venice Commission celebrated its 30th anniversary. Undeniably, this moment offers an appropriate occasion for the reflection on the Commission's evolution through three decades of activities and its contribution to the development of democracy in Europe.

2.1 *Creative Period (1990–2000)*

The origins of the idea to set up an advisory body for constitutional matters had preceded the fall of the Berlin Wall, but it was this event that created an undeniable momentum for its establishment.[6] The Venice Commission – named after

4 ibid para 8.

5 CoE (Committee of Ministers) Res (2002) 3 (27 February 2002) Adopting the Revised Statute of the European Commission for Democracy through Law, art 1(1) ('Revised Statute').

6 G Buquicchio and S Granata-Menghini, 'The Venice Commission Twenty Years On: Challenge Met But New Challenges Ahead' in M van Roosmalen and others (eds), *Fundamental Rights and Principles – Liber Amicorum Pieter van Dijk* (Intersentia 2013) 241.

the city, in which its four plenary sessions a year take place – was established on an Italian initiative in January 1990.[7] In May the same year, the Council of the Committee of Ministers adopted a resolution creating the Venice Commission through a partial agreement within the CoE.[8]

This first phase of the Commission's work was inextricably linked with the assistance to the ex-communist states of Central and Eastern Europe in drafting new constitutions and in transferring best practices.[9] In fact, '[a]ll of them, from the Baltic States via the then Soviet Union to Albania, had approached the Venice Commission for advice'.[10] The guidance was built on the results of the comparative analysis; this period can be characterized as the golden age of constitutionalism and of constitutional comparative law.

2.2 *Realist Period (2000–2010)*

In the second decade of its activities, the Venice Commission had to come to terms with the realization that it was not easy to create new constitutional systems simply imitating models of other States. It understood the need to pay more attention to all the internal difficulties and to be more sensible with respect to the cultural context of each individual state. There is no one-size-fits-all model of constitutional engineering.[11]

In this period, a relative success occurred when the former communist States – Poland, Hungary, Czech Republic, Slovakia, the Baltic States, Slovenia, Romania, and Bulgaria – acceded to the European Union (EU). This was meant to crown a successful transition of these states from the communist regimes to democracy based on the respect for the rule of law and human rights. Indeed, the Venice Commission's assistance was instrumental in this process.

An apparent end to the Central and Eastern European transitions might have brought an existential crisis for the Venice Commission – the end of its *raison d'être*.[12] Nevertheless, the institution managed to reinvent itself by

---

7 H Steinberger, 'Venice Commission' in *Max Planck Encyclopaedia of International Law* (online edn, OUP 2007), para 1.

8 CoE (Committee of Ministers) Res (90)6 (10 May 1990) On a Partial Agreement Establishing the European Commission for Democracy through Law.

9 Steinberger (n 7) para 8.

10 ibid.

11 See on this issue P Craig, 'Transnational Constitution-Making: The Contribution of the Venice Commission on Law and Democracy' (2017) 2 UC Irvine JICTL 56, 80.

12 Buquicchio and Granata-Menghini, 'The Venice Commission Twenty Years On' (n 6) 252; V Volpe, 'Drafting Counter-Majoritarian Democracy: The Venice Commission's Constitutional Assistance' (2016) 76 ZaöRV 811, 816.

opening itself up to a non-European spectrum of members through the adoption of an enlarged agreement in 2002.[13]

During this time period, a number of revolutions took place – in particular in Ukraine, Kyrgyzstan and Georgia. These events were followed by constitutional revisions, which were submitted to and reviewed by the Venice Commission. On the other hand, Russia under president Vladimir Putin started to trace its own path following the second war in Chechnya, the replacement of the elected and powerful governors, and the 'domestication' of the Constitutional Court, which had been very powerful in the 1990s. 'Democracy' was reinvented and given the name of 'managed democracy' or 'sovereign democracy'.[14] On balance, the second decade was defined by the shared feelings of optimism as well as pessimism.

2.3 *Period without Illusions (2010–2020)*

In the third decade, the Commission has had to face up to a new profound challenge. The anti-liberal model of government has become more and more attractive in some of the states within the EU such as Hungary and Poland and beyond.[15] The anti-liberal tendencies have also flourished in 'established' liberal democracies as the anti-democratic and anti-liberal parties have celebrated previously unseen electoral successes and popularity. Hungary's president Viktor Orbán's speech in 2014 was emblematic of these developments as he declared that:

> the Hungarian nation is not simply a group of individuals but a community that must be organised, reinforced and in fact constructed. And so in this sense the new state that *we are constructing in Hungary is an illiberal*

13 Volpe (n 12) 816; Revised Statute (n 5); Buquicchio and Granata-Menghini, 'The Venice Commission Twenty Years On' (n 6) 252–253. See for more *infra*.

14 The concept of 'sovereign democracy' was coined in 2006 by V Surkov, the then First Deputy Chief of Staff of the Russian Presidential Administration. In an article published that year Surkov defined the term of 'sovereign democracy' as 'the way of political life of society, in which the authorities, their bodies and actions are elected, formed and directed exclusively by the Russian nation in all its diversity and integrity for the sake of achieving material well-being, freedom and justice for all citizens, social groups and peoples that form it.' V Surkov, 'Nationalization of the Future' (*Expert*, 20 November 2006) <https://web.archive.org/web/20061205211300/http://www.expert.ru/printissues/expert/2006/43/nacionalizaciya_buduschego/> accessed 5 July 2021 (*unofficial translation from Russian*); see M Mommsen, *Putins „gelenkte Demokratie": „Vertikale der Macht" statt Gewaltenteilung* (Beck Verlag 2007).

15 See I Krastev and S Holmes, *The Light that Failed: Why the West is Losing Its Fight for Democracy* (Pegasus Books 2020).

> *state, a non-liberal state*. It does not reject the fundamental principles of liberalism such as freedom, and I could list a few more, but it does not make this ideology the central element of state organisation, but instead includes a different, special, national approach.[16]

The term 'illiberal democracy' originally coined by Fareed Zakaria in 1997[17] is the phenomenon defined by a number of features, which do not operate in a black and white fashion, but rather flourish within different shades of grey. In particular, the governing power suppresses the opposition; in elections, there are no viable alternatives to the governing party; and generally, the phenomenon is linked to the lack of established and stable political parties. Moreover, the idea of 'personalities above programmes' is typical for illiberal democracy. This entails the president who is above the political fighting, governs for the benefit of the people and profits from a special interpretation of separation of powers. Moreover, the ruling party gradually abolishes all the constitutional checks of power. Ultimately, the question mark hangs above the possibility of a peaceful change of power in such a regime.

In these challenging conditions, the Venice Commission has been a tireless motor for the advancement of a liberal democracy in Europe. It has issued opinions on all the questions raised in this context. In certain situations its views have become central to the broader processes in other European institutions dealing with these developments, especially in Hungary and Poland.[18]

3 Geographical Scope of Operation

The bulk of the Venice Commission's work is the adoption of opinions on draft laws amending the constitutions or other bills in the area of constitutional law

16 Prime Minister Viktor Orbán, 'Speech at the 25th Bálványos Summer Free University and Student Camp' (*Tusnádfürdő* (Băile Tuşnad), Romania, 26 July 2014) <http://2010-2015.miniszterelnok.hu/in_english_article/_prime_minister_viktor_orban_s_speech_at_the_25th_balvanyos_summer_free_university_and_student_camp> accessed 28 June 2021 (*emphasis added*).

17 F Zakaria, 'The Rise of Illiberal Democracy' (1997) 76 Foreign Affairs 22.

18 For Hungary see L Bode-Kirchhoff, 'Why the Road from Luxembourg to Strasbourg Leads through Venice: The Venice Commission as a Link between the EU and the ECHR' in K Dzehtsiarou and others (eds), *Human Rights Law in Europe: The Influence, Overlaps and Contradiction of the EU and the ECHR* (1st edn, Routledge 2014) 66–69; for Poland and Hungary see R Clayton, 'The Venice Commission and the Rule of Law Crisis' (2019) 3 Public Law 450, 456–460. See for more *infra*.

submitted for evaluation either voluntarily or on request of the CoE bodies with respect to member states of the CoE.[19] This in fact resembles 'an abstract constitutional review' – however, without binding judgments at its end.[20] The Commission also drafts *amicus curiae* for the European Court of Human Rights (ECtHR) and national constitutional courts (upon request), undertakes research studies and publishes guidelines and codes of conducts in selected areas.[21] Furthermore, it functions as a focal point for the dialogue among constitutional courts. While it can undertake general studies on its own initiative, it does not have the competence to issue an opinion *proprio motu*.[22] Within the Council of Europe, the Venice Commission functions as a 'more generalized intervention ex ante' – prevention being at the core of its mission.[23]

The 2002 Revised Statute does not delimit the scope of the Venice Commission's operation *ratione loci*.[24] As said, the Commission's activities originally focused primarily on the assistance to the Central and Eastern European ex-communist states in their transition to democracy. But this geographical focus persisted – even after three decades of work, almost all the opinions of the Venice Commission still concerned the Central and Eastern European states. According to De Visser, until 2015, only seven seasoned democracies have asked for the services of the Commission and one was subject to the Commission's opinion upon the request of the Parliamentary Assembly.[25] The most prominent examples concerning 'established' democracies include Luxembourg, Finland and Monaco.[26]

---

19 I Cameron, 'Russian Constitutional Law and Judgments of the European Court of Human Rights' in E Bylander, A Jonsson Cornell and J Ragnwaldh (eds), *Forward! Вперёд! Framåt!: Essays in Honour of Prof Dr Kaj Hobér* (Iustus 2019) 58; W Hoffmann-Riem, 'The Venice Commission of the Council of Europe – Standards and Impact' (2014) 25 EJIL 579, 580.

20 Cameron (n 19) 58.

21 Clayton (n 18) 451.

22 ibid 451–452.

23 Craig (n 11) 70.

24 S Granata-Menghini, 'La Commission de Venise du Conseil de l'Europe: méthodes et perspectives de l'assistance constitutionnelle en Europe' (2017) 2 Les Nouveaux Cahiers du Conseil constitutionnel 69, 72; Revised Statute (n 5).

25 M de Visser, 'A Critical Assessment of the Role of the Venice Commission in Processes of Domestic Constitutional Reform' (2015) 63 American Journal of Comparative Law 963, 1005–1006. See also A-L Chané and others, *EU Engagement with other European Regional Organisations* (FRAME 2016) 111, ftn 549; Granata-Menghini (n 24) 72.

26 CoE (Venice Commission), 'Interim Opinion on the Draft Constitutional Amendments of Luxembourg' (11–12 December 2009) CDL-AD(2009)057; CoE (Venice Commission), 'Luxembourg: Opinion on the Proposed Revision of the Constitution' (15–16 March

This misbalance may contribute to the psychological perception that the West always 'lectures' the East,[27] which may in turn reinforce an apparent East-West divide in a seemingly united Europe.[28] The Commission's advice might be perceived as patronising and paternalistic in the recipient Eastern European states. This can in turn inadvertently fuel the resentment and disillusionment in some Central and Eastern European states (as the echo of the past when these countries were subjected to the diktat of the communist centre) and drive the anti-liberal wave there. The solution cannot be the abandonment of advice and critique where and when it is needed, but it should entail the opening up of the Venice Commission to the West and raising the awareness about its work and expertise even in more seasoned 'older' member states of the CoE.[29]

Today, the Venice Commission has 62 member states, including all 47 Member States of the CoE as well as member states from different corners of the world – Middle East and North Africa (for example Morocco, Algeria, Tunisia), North and Latin America (for example the USA, Mexico, Chile, Brazil, Peru), Asia (for example South Korea, Kazakhstan, Kyrgyzstan).[30] Belarus – not a member state of the CoE – is an associate member of the Venice Commission.

Thus, the Commission can now use its know-how acquired with respect to transitions in Central and Eastern Europe in other similar situations beyond the European context.[31] The Commission's advice regarding the drafting of a new constitution in Tunisia in the wake of the Arab Spring revolution exemplifies its capacity and potential in this area.[32] Nevertheless, this type of expansion naturally raises the questions of the standards used and the risk of Euro-centrism.[33] So far, such problems have not been particularly acute given

2019) CDL-AD(2019)003; CoE (Venice Commission), 'Opinion on the Constitution of Finland' (14–15 April 2008) CDL-AD(2008)010; Opinion on Monaco (n 1124).

27 Similarly De Visser (n 26) 1005–1006.

28 See on the East-West divide within the European Union S Lehne, 'Europe's East-West Divide: Myth or Reality?' (*Carnegie Europe*, 11 April 2019) <https://carnegieeurope.eu/2019/04/11/europe-s-east-west-divide-myth-or-reality-pub-78847> accessed 29 June 2021; T Valášek, 'Why Can't the EU's West and East Work as One?' (*Carnegie Europe*, 8 November 2019) <https://carnegieeurope.eu/2019/11/08/why-can-t-eu-s-west-and-east-work-as-one-pub-80300> accessed 29 June 2021.

29 De Visser (n 26) 1006–1007.

30 Cameron (n 19) 58. See 'Members of the Venice Commission' <https://www.venice.coe.int/WebForms/members/countries.aspx?lang=EN> accessed 29 June 2021.

31 Volpe (n 12) 816.

32 Clayton (n 18) 456; Buquicchio and Granata-Menghini, 'The Venice Commission Twenty Years On' (n 6) 253.

33 Volpe (n 12) 817, ftn 15.

a consensual nature of any seizure of the Commission by the member states from beyond the CoE. By participating in the Commission's work as members or by requesting the opinions from it, the non-CoE states implicitly agree with the standards applied by the Venice Commission.[34] Nevertheless, the tension persists – as pointed by Hoffmann-Riem – with a growing and more heterogeneous membership, the question becomes 'explosive' for the Commission.[35]

4 Substantive Standards

As to the yardstick for the evaluation of pieces of legislation, the Venice Commission refers to the 'European standards'. In formulating these standards, the Commission relies on various sources. First, it is the classical 'hard law' of public international law (in particular the ECHR and the case law of the ECtHR).[36] In fact, the ECHR is the minimum standard for the Venice Commission.[37] In formulating best practices, the Commission aims higher than the ECtHR.[38] While the Commission is reluctant to mention EU case law, it has already occasionally referred to the jurisprudence of the Court of Justice of the European Union (CJEU).[39] Second, the Commission also builds on 'soft law' instruments (especially the documents produced by various bodies of the CoE). It also refers to its own previous opinions and general studies in a self-referential manner.[40] Last, but not least, the Commission derives its standards from the results of the comparative constitutional law analysis.[41]

34 Hoffmann-Riem (n 19) 581–582.

35 Hoffmann-Riem points to a need of redefinition of the idea of individual self-determination and the concept of social justice. Hoffmann-Riem (n 19) 583–584.

36 Bode-Kirchhoff (n 18) 57–58; Hoffmann-Riem (n 19) 581–582.

37 Hoffmann-Riem (n 19) 581, ftn 13. See CoE (Venice Commission), 'Opinion on the Constitutional and Legal Provisions Relevant to the Prohibition of Political Parties in Turkey' (13–14 March 2009) CDL-AD(2009)006, para 62.

38 G Buquicchio and S Granata-Menghini, 'The Interaction between the Venice Commission and the European Court of Human Rights: Anticipation, Consolidation, Coordination of Human Rights Protection in Europe' in L-A Sicilianos and others (eds), *Regards croisés sur la protection nationale et internationale des droits de l'homme / Intersecting Views on National and International Human Rights Protection: Liber Amicorum Guido Raimondi* (Wolf Legal Publishers 2019) 38.

39 Bode-Kirchhoff (n 18) 70; CoE (Venice Commission) and OSCE/ODIR, 'Guidelines on Freedom of Peaceful Assembly, 2nd edn' (4 July 2010) CDL-AD(2010)020, para 80, ftn 128.

40 G Buquicchio and S Granata-Menghini, 'Conseil de l'Europe: Commission de Venise' (2014) Rép Eur 1, 10; Hoffmann-Riem (n 19) 582.

41 Bode-Kirchhoff (n 18) 57–58; Hoffmann-Riem (n 19) 582.

The Commission's key substantive areas of focus include protection of human rights and fundamental freedoms, democracy and rule of law.[42] Compared to the field of human rights, there is no special and detailed Convention and related case law concerning the functioning of democratic institutions; therefore the soft law plays a more prominent role in this area.[43] In any case, the Commission builds on the existence of a 'European consensus' on the key essential features of the definition of democracy.[44]

5 Impact of the Commission's Opinions

The Venice Commission is not a court; it is an advisory body. Its opinions are formally non-binding. In its endeavour, the Commission relies on the power of persuasion and dialogue.[45] From this perspective, its outputs can be characterized as soft law and thus can be generally examined through the prism of theorization relevant to soft law.[46] Indeed, '[t]he Venice Commission is not only a consumer but also a producer of soft law.'[47] There are three areas where the Commission's soft law interacts with other, 'harder' modes of law-making.[48] These are the channels through which the Commission's work achieves the greatest impact.

First, the Commission's opinions are an important factor in internal politics. The request for an opinion can come amid a heated political debate and the involvement of the Commission might have appeasing effects – resolving the issue solely along the legal lines.[49] However, because of the lack of a binding

42 See Revised Statute (n 5), art 1.

43 Buquicchio and Granata-Menghini, 'Conseil de l'Europe: Commission de Venise' (n 40) 10. Craig (n 11) 78.

44 Opinion on Monaco (n 1124), paras 7–25; Buquicchio and Granata-Menghini, 'Conseil de l'Europe: Commission de Venise' (n 40) 10.

45 Clayton (n 18) 452; Bode-Kirchhoff (n 18) 57.

46 Hoffmann-Riem (n 19) 580–581.

47 Buquicchio and Granata-Menghini, 'The Interaction between the Venice Commission and the European Court of Human Rights' (n 38) 38.

48 On the interaction between soft and hard law see D Shelton, 'Soft Law' in D Armstrong (ed), *Routledge Handbook of International Law* (Routledge 2009) 72; A Nußberger, 'Hard Law of Soft Law – Does it Matter?' in A van Aaken and I Motoc (eds), *The European Convention on Human Rights and General International Law* (OUP 2018) 44; G Shaffer and MA Pollack, 'Hard and Soft Law' in JL Dunoff and MA Pollack (eds), *Interdisciplinary Perspectives on International Law and International Relations: State of the Art* (OUP 2013) 207–213.

49 Granata-Menghini (n 24) 75–76.

character, it is also relatively easy for a state to ignore the opinion.[50] While the Commission does not have a systematic compliance monitoring or impact assessment,[51] scholars claim that especially when the state itself requests the opinion, it implements it.[52] In any case, not only country-specific opinions, but also general studies and guidelines serve as models within the process of municipal law-making.[53] 'Once soft law norms are created, they provide the frame for future reaffirmation or elaboration.'[54]

Second, soft law of the Venice Commission can produce effects when it becomes the reference point within processes at the EU level – whether it is during the accession process[55] or the new EU rule of law procedure.[56] In these processes, the Commission's recommendations lose its non-binding character to a great extent as their violation can be followed by significant political consequences, if not sanctions.[57] Nevertheless, this process is also linked to the risk of de-legitimation – the recipient states can perceive the Commission more as the arm of the EU than a consultative body.[58]

Third, the ECtHR frequently mentions the works of the Commission. The first time when it cited a Venice Commission document was in the *Banković* case, referring to the 'Report on the Preferential Treatment of National Minorities by their Kin-State'.[59] By February 2021, the Strasbourg court has referred to Venice Commission documents in some 250 judgments and decisions.[60] Moreover, since 2001 the Venice Commission has also made seven *amicus curiae* as third party before the Court.[61] The Court refers both to the

50 See Hoffmann-Riem (n 19) 592–595 for the example of Russia and for a complicated dialogue between the Commission and Hungary.

51 Clayton (n 18) 452; Undeniably, there is a need to improve impact assessment.

52 Clayton (n 18) 452–453. Other observers claim that a great majority of opinions is followed. Granata-Menghini (n 24) 75. Hoffmann-Riem offers a more nuanced picture Hoffmann-Riem (n 19) 589.

53 D Thürer, 'Soft Law' in *Max Planck Encyclopaedia of International Law* (online edn, OUP 2009), para 32.

54 ibid.

55 See with respect to Serbia Bode-Kirchhoff (n 18) 63–66.

56 Granata-Menghini (n 24) 76.

57 See ibid 76–77.

58 Hoffmann-Riem (n 19) 597.

59 *Banković and Others v Belgium and Others* App no 52207/99 (Decision as to the Admissibility) (ECtHR, 12 December 2001) para 60. Bode-Kirchhoff (n 18) 59.

60 'References to the Work of the Venice Commission' <https://www.venice.coe.int/WebForms/pages/?p=02_references&lang=EN> accessed 29 June 2021.

61 *Jeličić v Bosnia and Herzegovina* ECHR 2006-XII 253 (CDL-AD(2005)020); *Parti Nationaliste Basque v France* ECHR 2007-II 349 (CDL-AD(2006)014); *Bijelić v Montenegro and Serbia*

general studies and country-specific opinions.[62] Undeniably, not all the references have the same quality as the references are made in different parts of judgments,[63] but in certain cases, for example in *Baka v Hungary*,[64] *Big Brother Watch v UK*[65] and others, the works of the Commission were instrumental for the decision itself.[66]

Thus, soft law, including that of the Venice Commission, can serve as an element for the evolutive interpretation of the Convention ('European consensus'), as 'general guidelines for interpretation and filling in gaps in the text of the Convention'.[67] More broadly, in referring to the opinions, studies and *amicus curiae* submissions, the Court seeks to reinforce the legitimacy and acceptance of its decisions.[68] Thus, the soft law standards elaborated by the Commission can gain the force of hard law when endorsed by the ECtHR.[69]

App no 11890/05 (ECtHR, 28 April 2009) (CDL-AD(2008)021); *Sejdić and Finci v Bosnia and Herzegovina* ECHR 2009-VI 273 (CDL-AD(2008)027); *Rywin v Poland* App nos 6091/06, 4047/07, 4070/07 (ECtHR, 18 February 2016) (CDL-AD(2014)013); *Berlusconi v Italy* App no 58428/13 (Decision on Striking the Application out of the List of Cases) (ECtHR, 27 November 2018) (CDL-AD(2017)025) and *Mugemangango v Belgium* App no 310/15 (ECtHR, 10 July 2020) (CDL-AD(2019)021). See Buquicchio and Granata-Menghini, 'The Interaction between the Venice Commission and the European Court of Human Rights' (n 38) 42–46; Bode-Kirchhoff (n 18) 59–62.

62 Buquicchio and Granata-Menghini, 'The Interaction between the Venice Commission and the European Court of Human Rights' (n 38) 47.

63 See Hoffmann-Riem (n 19) 585–586.

64 *Baka v Hungary* App no 20261/12 (ECtHR, 23 June 2016), paras 57–60 (referring to country-specific opinions on Hungary), paras 82–83 (referring to country-specific opinions on judiciary in Armenia and Georgia), para 117 (referring to the position of the Venice Commission when assessing violation of Article 6(1) ECHR), para 148 (referring to the position of the Venice Commission when assessing violation of Article 10 ECHR).

65 *Big Brother Watch and Others v UK* App nos 58170/13, 62322/14, 24960/15 (ECtHR, 25 May 2021), paras 196–201 (referring to the Report of the Venice Commission on the Democratic Oversight of Signals Intelligence Agencies (CDL-AD(2015)011), paras 330 and 350 (relying to the position of the Venice Commission when assessing violation of Article 8 ECHR).

66 See for more Buquicchio and Granata-Menghini, 'The Interaction between the Venice Commission and the European Court of Human Rights' (n 38) 46–49; Council of Europe 'References to the Work of the Venice Commission' (https://www.venice.coe.int/WebForms/pages/?p=02_references&lang=EN, accessed 21 February 2022).

67 Nußberger (n 48) 49; 'The Court is, in this context however, free to decide which rules of soft law it wants to accept as guidelines and which ones it rather puts aside as not to the point, be they outdated or too far-reaching. Due to the "soft" character of these norms, the Court does not necessarily have to justify its position.' ibid. This is in line with the observations of Hoffmann-Riem with respect to references of the ECtHR to Venice Commission. Hoffmann-Riem (n 19) 587–588.

68 Hoffmann-Riem (n 19) 585 and 587.

69 Buquicchio and Granata-Menghini, 'The Interaction between the Venice Commission and the European Court of Human Rights' (n 38) 49.

Similarly, even the CJEU has recently referred to the Venice Commission's work in the area of rule of law[70] and independence of the judiciary.[71]

6 Examples of the Commission's Influence in Shaping Democracy in Stress Situations

6.1 *Report on 'Respect for Democracy, Human Rights and the Rule of Law during States of Emergency: Reflections'*

The COVID-19 pandemic has in many instances led states to adopt emergency powers.[72] According to the Commission, the pandemic requires 'great democratic resilience in order to avoid that emergency powers curtail fundamental rights and conflict with the rule of law'.[73] The Venice Commission's report issued in June 2020 examines this topic from different perspectives. First, it is close to the Court's jurisprudence. The report highlights the margin of appreciation of states regarding the grounds for declaring a state of emergency, but nevertheless states, '[a]lthough states have a wide margin of discretion in this area, their powers are not unlimited'.[74] Naturally, the report focuses on the state of emergency from the perspective of human rights:

> In addition to providing for grounds for restrictions of human rights in order to protect public health, it should be recalled that "Article 2 [ECHR] requires the State to take appropriate steps to safeguard the lives of those within its jurisdiction"… in the public-health sphere, these positive obligations require States to make regulations compelling hospitals, whether

70 Case T-290/17 *Edward Stavytskyi v Council of the European Union* [2019] ECLI:EU:T:2019:37, para 68; Case T-348/14 *Oleksandr Viktorovich Yanukovych v Council of the European Union* [2016] ECLI:EU:T:2016:508, para 99; Case T-346/14 *Oleksandr Viktorovich Yanukovych v Council of the European Union* [2016] ECLI:EU:T:2016:497, para 98; Case T-340/14 *Andriy Klyuyev v Council of the European Union* [2016] ECLI:EU:T:2016:496, para 88 (all referring to the Rule of Law Checklist (CDL-AD(2016)007rev). See also Case T-731/15 *Sergiy Klyuyev v Council of the European Union* [2018] ECLI:EU:T:2018:90, para 141 in connection with para 96 (referring to Venice Commission's opinions on Ukrainian 'Law on Purging the Government').

71 Case C-619/18 *European Commission v Republic of Poland* [2019] ECLI:EU:C:2019:531, para 82 (referring to the Opinion No 904/2017 (CDL-AD(2017)031).

72 CoE (Venice Commission), 'Report: Respect for Democracy, Human Rights and the Rule of Law during the States of Emergency: Reflections' (19 June 2020) CDL-AD(2020)014, para 1.

73 ibid para 1.

74 ibid para 43.

private or public, to adopt appropriate measures for the protection of patients' lives.[75]

However, the report also goes beyond the 'human rights' aspects, highlighting the inter-institutional elements in the context of state of emergency. The report provides for solutions to the risks of concentration of decision-making powers in the government or in one sole minister during the state of emergency.[76] 'A solution which combines respect for the supremacy of the legislature with the need for speed and decisive action is to provide that all government ordinances issued under delegated powers are speedily (or within a specified period of days) put before the legislature either for approval, or to give it an opportunity to disapprove these'.[77] The parliament must be allowed to approve or not specific provisions of the ordinance, not only to pass or reject the ordinance as a whole.[78] This in turn presupposes that the parliament continues to sit: 'dissolution of the parliament should not be possible during the state of emergency. If the mandate of the parliament expires in the course of the state of emergency and if it is not possible to hold regular elections, the mandate should be extended till the end of the state of emergency'.[79] Similarly, the legal effects of disapproval or approval must also be specified.[80] 'Where the government relies heavily on its medical experts in issuing measures, which will usually be the rational approach in a pandemic, the parliament might consider organizing hearings with these, and other independent experts, to obtain as full a picture as possible of the problems and their possible solutions'.[81]

According to Venice Commission, in order for the emergency powers to comply with the requirements of the rule of law, they must have in-built guarantees against abuse, specifically 'the principles of necessity, of proportionality and of temporariness'.[82] Moreover, the Venice Commission adds, '[r]espect of these principles must be subject to effective, non-partisan parliamentary control and to a meaningful judicial control by independent courts'.[83]

75 ibid para 45 (*footnotes omitted*).
76 ibid paras 70–71.
77 ibid para 71.
78 ibid.
79 ibid.
80 ibid.
81 ibid.
82 ibid para 121 and see paras 10–13.
83 ibid para 121 and see para 14.

6.2 *The 2016 Opinion on Emergency Decree Laws in Turkey*

Upon the request of the Chair of the Monitoring Committee of the Parliamentary Assembly of CoE (PACE), the Venice Commission also issued an opinion on the compatibility of the implementation of the state of emergency in Turkey following the failed coup in July 2016 with the CoE standards.[84] The opinion recalled, 'that the main purpose of the state of emergency is to restore the democratic legal order'.[85] Moreover, [t]he emergency regime should not be unduly protracted; if the Government rules through emergency powers for too long, it will inevitably lose democratic legitimacy'.[86]

The Commission expressed its concerns with respect to the implementation of the state of emergency in Turkey. In particular, it held that '[t]he Government took permanent measures, which went beyond a temporary state of emergency'.[87] Specifically, '[c]ivil servants were dismissed, not merely suspended, organisations and bodies were dissolved and their property confiscated instead of being put under the temporary State control'.[88] Moreover, according to Commission, the government introduced several structural changes to the legislation, which should normally be adopted under the ordinary legislative procedure outside state of emergency.[89] The government also used its emergency powers through *ad hominem* legislation.[90]

6.3 *Other Examples*

Other works of the Venice Commission can be mentioned in the context of contribution to the working of democratic institutions. For example, already in 2001, the Venice Commission adopted the Guidelines and Report on the Financing of Political Parties.[91] In these documents, the Commission held that it would be useful to clarify the competences of several supervisory bodies, so as to ensure the coordination and information sharing, and to avoid the duplication of responsibilities.[92]

---

84 CoE (Venice Commission), 'Opinion on Emergency Decree Laws Nos 667–676 Adopted Following the Failed Coup of 15 July 2016' (9–10 December 2016) CDL-AD(2016)037, para 1 ('The 2016 Opinion on Emergency Decree Laws in Turkey').

85 ibid para 229.

86 ibid.

87 ibid para 227.

88 ibid.

89 ibid.

90 ibid.

91 CoE (Venice Commission), 'Guidelines and Report on the Financing of Political Parties' (9–10 March 2001) CDL-INF(2001)08.

92 ibid 13–14.

In 2013, upon the request of PACE, the Commission adopted a Report on the Role of Extra-Institutional Actors in the Democratic System (Lobbying), which provided an overview of strategies aimed to strengthen the role that these actors can have in the support of democracy.[93] This report was prepared as a contribution to the Committee of Ministers' assessment of the feasibility of a legal instrument in this field.

The practice of political responsibility of governments within the framework of the parliamentary systems has also been of a particular interest for the Venice Commission. It examined the separation of political and criminal responsibility of ministers in the proper functioning of a parliamentary system in the report devoted to 'The Relationship between Political and Criminal Ministerial Responsibility' adopted in 2013.[94] The Commission stressed that the criminal proceedings should not be used to punish political error or disagreements.[95]

In the country-specific Opinion on Azerbaijan adopted in 2016, the Commission mostly focused on the system of checks and balances and the strengthening of the presidential powers vis-à-vis the powers of parliament, which were already very weak in the then Constitution.[96] Opinion also examined '(the lack of)' the involvement of the parliament in the constitutional amendment procedure.[97]

7 Democratic Deficit Doubts, Procedure, Innovativeness

The preamble of the Revised Statute singles out the Commission's independence and its flexible working methods as sources of its success.[98] Nevertheless, the issues of membership and procedure also raise some concerns particularly for an institution given the task to contribute to the functioning of democratic institutions.

93 CoE (Venice Commission), 'Report on the Role of Extra-Institutional Actors in the Democratic System (Lobbying)' (8–9 March 2013) CDL-AD(2013)011.

94 CoE (Venice Commission), 'Report on the Relationship between Political and Criminal Ministerial Responsibility' (8–9 March 2013) CDL-AD(2013)001.

95 ibid para 106.

96 CoE (Venice Commission), 'Azerbaijan: Opinion on the Draft Modifications to the Constitution Submitted to the Referendum of 26 September 2016' (14–15 October 2016) CDL-AD(2016)029, para 49ff and paras 85–86 ('The 2016 Opinion on Azerbaijan').

97 ibid paras 10–16 and para 83.

98 Revised Statute (n 5) preamble.

First, each member state of the Commission appoints one member and one substitute for a term of four years.[99] 'The members of the Commission shall serve in their individual capacity and shall not receive or accept any instructions'.[100] The members are experts 'who have achieved eminence through their experience in democratic institutions or by their contribution to the enhancement of law and political science'.[101] Thus, the members are unelected experts who issue non-binding, but influential opinions for democratically elected governments on the very core matters of sovereignty. Volpe in this context refers to a seeming 'paradox' of non-democratic technocratic institutions teaching democracy to democratically accountable governments.[102] An expertocracy is another term used in this context.

The involvement of expert bodies in global (regional) governance is frequently assessed in terms of input and output legitimacy. While the input legitimacy refers to government *by the people*, the output legitimacy refers to the government *for the people*.[103] Input legitimacy presupposes belief that '*citizens* have a fair chance (however understood) to influence decision-making and scrutinize the results'.[104] Output legitimacy refers to the efficiency and quality of decisions that render them legitimate.[105] The two concepts are inter-related in the sense that a contested input legitimacy of a decision-making process may make it easier to challenge its output legitimacy.[106]

At first sight, the processes of the Venice Commission – an unelected body of experts – could be seen to suffer from deficiencies namely on the side of input legitimacy. Nevertheless, according to Hoffmann-Riem, since the Commission's non-binding opinions are applied by the states subjected to democratic decision-making, 'this does not constitute a substantial deficit'.[107] Another aspect is that the Venice Commission is set up as an enlarged

---

99 ibid art 2(2) and 2(3).

100 ibid art 2(1).

101 ibid.

102 Volpe (n 12) 841–842.

103 M Bovens, D Curtin and P Hart, 'The Quest for Legitimacy and Accountability in EU Governance' in M Bovens, D Curtin and P Hart (eds), *The Real World of EU Accountability* (OUP 2010) 20–21 (*emphasis in original*).

104 ibid 21 (*emphasis in original*).

105 M Ambrus and others, 'The Role of Experts in International and European Decision-Making Processes: Setting the Scene' in M Ambrus and H Raulus (eds), *The Role of 'Experts' in International and European Decision-Making Processes: Advisors, Decision Makers or Irrelevant Actors?* (CUP 2014) 6.

106 ibid 6.

107 Hoffmann-Riem (n 19) 582–583.

agreement; its members are states that preserve the power to renew or not the appointment of the experts of the Commission.[108]

Another problematic aspect relates to a rather loose procedural framework of the Commission's operation, which according to De Visser 'may inadvertently undermine the quality and usefulness of its assistance'.[109] The Statute contains almost no regulation concerning the preparation of the opinions; it only determines actors that can request an opinion.[110] The Rules of Procedure are also rather minimalistic regarding the rules governing the preparation of opinions.[111] This document states that the opinions and reports of the Commission 'are as a general rule prepared by one or more rapporteurs appointed by the President'.[112] The working method is developed over time and is personalized: 'Aucun formalisme dans les procédures'.[113] In 2010, the Venice Commission adopted 'Guidelines Relating to the Working Methods of the Venice Commission',[114] but retained a rather minimalistic approach allowing for a maximum of flexibility.[115]

De Visser argues that while this approach had merits in the early stages of the Commission's work, today it is 'outweighed by a combination of reasons that militate in favour of a comprehensive procedural framework to govern the Commission's functioning'.[116] De Visser calls for a number of formal changes to be made to the Rules of Procedure including the procedural obligation to undertake state visits, the right of state authorities to comment on the draft opinion following the visit, the composition of working groups and the position of the investigated state with respect to the composition of the working

108 ibid 582. See for similar arguments with respect to the UN Special Procedures SP Subedi, 'Human Rights Experts in the United Nations: A Review of the Role of United Nations Special Procedures' in M Ambrus and H Raulus (eds), *The Role of 'Experts' in International and European Decision-Making Processes: Advisors, Decision Makers or Irrelevant Actors?* (CUP 2014) 251–252.

109 De Visser (n 26) 965.

110 ibid 971–972.

111 ibid 971.

112 CoE (Venice Commission), 'Rules of Procedure' (8–9 March 2002 as amended) CDL-AD(2018)018, art 14 and see also art 14a.

113 J Robert, L'ingénierie constitutionnelle et l'Europe de l'est: Le rôle de la Commission européenne pour la démocratie par le droit' in S Milacic (ed) La réinvention de l'État: Démocratie politique et ordre juridique en Europe centrale et orientale (Bruylant 2003) 197.

114 CoE (Venice Commission), 'Guidelines Relating to the Working Method of the Venice Commission' (15–16 October 2010) CDL-AD(2010)034.

115 Buquicchio and Granata-Menghini, 'Conseil de l'Europe: Commission de Venise' (n 40) 11.

116 De Visser (n 26) 992.

group.[117] According to De Visser, these changes would bring a higher level of credibility to the Commission and ensure that the principle of legal certainty is fulfilled in its functioning.[118] However, while other observers admit that the procedural framework may be improved, they do not find the entirety of De Visser's critique justified, in particular with regard to the right of national authorities to comment on the preliminary draft opinions.[119]

The Venice Commission was set up as an experimental project, which achieved success not least because of its not too rigid approach and its ability to deliver immediate response to urgent matters. This pragmatism fits well to situations when the guidance on the content of the concepts is needed urgently. On the one hand, there is no complicated procedure of a court. On the other hand, it is still an *aliud* in comparison with a political process.

8 Conclusion

The idea of creating the Venice Commission preceded the fall of the Berlin Wall, but was met with suspicion as too encroaching on the fundamentals of sovereignty and internal affairs of each individual state.[120] It was only the watershed moment of the fall of communism that created the momentum for setting up this innovative and in many aspects pioneering institution.[121]

In the last three decades, the Venice Commission has functioned as a true guardian of the democratic principles in Europe and beyond. This key objective is translated in its name, mission and the core of its DNA. During these three decades, the Commission has also faced up to new challenges and changing political climates, but it has always managed to self-innovate and to remain relevant. Flexibility and pragmatism have defined its working methods; its soft law outputs blur the distinction between binding and non-binding and its membership no longer centres on Europe solely. In many aspects, the Commission as a consultative body of experts of a European regional

117 ibid 994–998.

118 ibid 993.

119 Craig (n 11) 75–77.

120 Buquicchio and Granata-Menghini, 'Conseil de l'Europe: Commission de Venise' (n 40) 3; Buquicchio and Granata-Menghini, 'The Venice Commission Twenty Years On' (n 6) 241.

121 Buquicchio and Granata-Menghini, 'The Venice Commission Twenty Years On' (n 6) 241.

organisation encapsulates the modern forms of governance and law-making and related challenges.

The Commission has grown from an innovative experimental project in the early 1990s into a 'reputation-enhancing community'[122] in the second decade of 21st century. However, it is indispensable today when the very idea of a liberal democracy has been questioned on multiple fronts. In these circumstances, the Venice Commission continues to offer a platform for responding to such challenges and to the needs of a rapidly changing world in transition that seems to be losing its central focus.

122 Hoffmann-Riem (n 19) 596.

PART 4

Emerging Issues at the International Level

CHAPTER 12

Democracy through the Lens of Digital Surveillance

An Assessment of the Legitimacy of General Principles of Law

Daniel Ventura

In* the realm of convincing examples illustrating an exclusive display of State competences, secret surveillance measures have long been construed as an arbitrary means to conduct secret interference with the rights to privacy, freedom of expression, and peaceful assembly, thus undermining the tenets of a democratic society.

In France, for instance, it was not until 1991 that a legal framework reduced the arbitrariness of administrative measures of telephone tapping – so-called 'security administrative interceptions' – motivated by 'national security, the safeguarding of essential elements of France's scientific and economic potential, or the prevention of terrorism, organised crime and delinquency'.[1] Despite the progress that the 1991 law constituted, the activity report of the Parliamentary Delegation on Intelligence for the year 2014 – prior to the adoption of Law No. 2015–912 of 24 July 2015 on intelligence – still deplored the detrimental absence of a general legal framework for the activities of intelligence services, noting that this absence '[left] our services in a state of complete legal destitution, exposing the civil servants who work in this field and creating the conditions for possible infringements of fundamental freedoms for citizens'.[2]

Earlier, in the symbolically significant year 1984, the European Court of Human Rights strongly condemned the United Kingdom for its practice of intercepting personal data under a Home Secretary's warrant based on a largely unfettered custom that stemmed from a government report dating back

* The author would like to express his gratitude to Paul Heckler (PhD student and research assistant at University Paris 1 Pantheon-Sorbonne) for his helpful and insightful review of this contribution.

1 French Law n°91–646 of 10 July 1991 *relative au secret des correspondances émises par la voie des communications électroniques* art 3.

2 French Parliamentary Delegation on Intelligence, '*Rapport relatif à l'activité de la délégation parlementaire au renseignement pour l'année 2014 par M. Jean-Jacques Urvoas*' para 65, as quoted in the explanatory memorandum of the Law n°2015–912 of 24 July 2015 on intelligence (our translation) <https://www.legifrance.gouv.fr/dossierlegislatif/JORFDOLE000030375694/> accessed 15 May 2021.

 | DOI:10.1163/9789004508712_013

to 1957. The Court found that such warrant did not meet the 'minimum degree of legal protection required by the rule of law in a democratic society'.[3]

More recently, the shockwaves caused by the revelation, in 2013,[4] of the US intelligence programmes *PRISM* (for the acquisition of data by intelligence services from internet service providers) and *Upstream* (for the direct interception of data from undersea fiber-optic cables) quickly forced many European States to reveal the existence of their own surveillance programmes in the context of the fight against terrorism. According to the United Nations Conference on Trade and Development (UNCTAD), as many as 128 States around the world had set up legislation to secure the protection of data and privacy in 2021,[5] although with dramatic discrepancies, especially as far as the interference caused by public authorities are concerned.

These various examples demonstrate, on the one hand, how national security, as a *domaine réservé* of States, is an undeniable ground for derogatory interference with the right to privacy for the purpose of implementing covert surveillance measures and thus entails a wide margin of appreciation in favour of States in this regard. Yet, on the other hand, they are symptomatic of the fact that secret surveillance has gradually entered the field of legality and judicial review and it is in this way that international law has gradually become relevant as well for assessing the compatibility of such interference with internationally recognised and binding human rights such as the right to privacy.

No comprehensive rules of international law have ever governed domestic surveillance practices, not to mention foreign intelligence gathering and digital surveillance as a whole. The Convention of the Council of Europe for the Protection of Individuals with regard to Automatic Processing of Personal Data (Convention n°108) of 28 January 1981 remains the only specific and binding international instrument governing digital privacy, including States' interference through surveillance channels. Its amending protocol adopted in May 2018 (commonly referred to as Convention 108+) substantially developed the safeguards inferred from the general principles for data protection, extended the scope of protected data, and the obligations of transparency

3 ECtHR (Plenary), *Malone v. United Kingdom*, req. n° 8691/79 (2 August 1984) para 79.

4 G Greenwald, 'NSA collecting phone records of millions of Verizon customer daily' (*The Guardian*, 6 June 2013) <https://www.theguardian.com/world/2013/jun/06/nsa-phone-records-verizon-court-order> accessed 15 May 2021.

5 UNCTAD, *Data Protection and Privacy Legislation Worldwide*, <https://unctad.org/fr/node/27563> accessed 15 May 2021. Among these 128 legislations, 28 were listed in Africa (and 9 draft legislation) out of 54 countries; 34 in the Asia-Pacific region (and 6 draft legislation) out of 60 countries; 24 in America (and 4 draft legislation) out of 35 countries, and 43 in Europe (1 draft legislation) out of 45 countries listed.

and accountability of data controllers in the context of new information and communication technologies.[6] Although open for signature by any States, this Convention has been poorly ratified aside from the Contracting States of the Council of Europe.[7]

At the universal level, the main binding conventional rule applying to surveillance practices is to be found in the International Covenant on Civil and Political Rights (ICCPR) of 1966, whose Article 17 forbids in general terms 'arbitrary or unlawful interference with [...] privacy' and restates the right of anyone to 'the protection of the law against such interference'. This provision is at the heart of several recent UN General Assembly resolutions on 'the right to privacy in the digital age' calling upon all States to respect and protect the right to privacy as well as to put an end to its violations 'including by ensuring that relevant national legislation complies with their obligations under international human rights law'.[8] Such 'obligations' have been gradually uncovered through the work of the UN Human Rights Committee (HRC) which recognised as soon as 1988 that Article 17 protected individual privacy against undue interference by public authorities through electronic means.[9] For instance, many of its recent Concluding observations as part of its Universal Periodic Review dwell upon the shortcomings of various States' legislation governing online surveillance activities with respect to Article 17 ICCPR.[10] Similarly, many reports made by the UN High Commissioner for Human Rights under the auspices of the UN Human Rights Council also interpreted this disposition in the context of both domestic and extraterritorial surveillance, including on a mass scale.[11]

Although deprived of a binding character, the existing guidelines and soft law principles on digital surveillance measures are largely concordant with the conventional framework, insisting on the principles of lawfulness and fairness for data processing, the limitation and specification of the purpose

---

6 Protocol amending the Convention for the Protection of Individuals with regard to Automatic Processing of Personal Data, Strasbourg (10 October 2018) ETS n°223.

7 As of May 2021, Convention 108 lists 55 ratifications, of which 8 are non-members of the Council of Europe: Argentina, Cabo Verde, Mauritius, Mexico, Morocco, Senegal, Tunisia, and Uruguay.

8 UNGA, *The Right to Privacy in the digital age* (A/RES/75/176, 16 December 2020) para 7(b); see also A/RES/73/179, 17 December 2018; A/RES/73/179, 19 December 2016; A/RES/69/166, 18 December 2014.

9 UN Human Rights Committee (HRC), *CCPR General Comment No. 16: Article 17 (Right to Privacy), The Right to Respect of Privacy, Family, Home and Correspondence, and Protection of Honour and Reputation* (8 April 1988).

10 See n 60.

11 See eg Office of the High Comm'r for Human Rights, *The Right to Privacy in the Digital Age: Report of the OHCHR* (A/HRC/27/37, June 30, 2014; A/HRC/39/29, 3 August 2018).

for collecting data, the supervision by an independent and impartial authority, and appropriate means of redress whenever a person suffers from unfair or unlawful measures.[12] Both the 1980 OECD and 1990 UN guidelines already stated that the power to make exceptions to the minimum guarantees set forth by legislation on the collection and processing of data should be expressly limited by law and to the minimum extent.[13] Non-institutional instruments go along the same path, insisting on the need for public and independent oversight mechanisms assessing the transparency and accountability of State surveillance measures.[14]

Digital surveillance pertains to the category of new spaces of regulation by States, international organisations, and private actors. The lack of traditional and comprehensive rules of international law makes it symptomatic of contemporary questionings about the legitimacy of international law in the context of digitalisation. Yet, the flaws of international regulation, which once characterised the classical forms of espionage, cannot be extended to digital surveillance. The breadth of State capacities – with the cooperation of internet service providers – to undertake surveillance measures, interception, and data collection regardless of boundaries or territorial ties are now known and facing remarkable public scrutiny.

In this renewed context, it is our understanding that whether international law can legitimately answer State arbitrariness for surveillance purposes (or not) cannot be deduced from a mere assessment of existing conventional rules or consistent practice of States.

For instance, international environmental law has emerged through various political declarations pronouncing a general responsibility on the face of States not to cause environmental damage to the environment of other States,

12 See esp *UN Guidelines for the Regulation of Computerized Personal data* (Adopted by UNGA Res. 45/95 of 14 December 1990); OECD, *Recommendation of the Council concerning Guidelines Governing the Protection of Privacy and Transborder Flows of Personal Data* (23 September 1980, updated on 11 July 2013).

13 *UN Guidelines for the Regulation of Computerized Personal data* (n 12) principle 6; *OECD Guidelines Governing the Protection of Privacy and Transborder Flows of Personal Data* (n 12) principle 4.

14 The major soft-law instrument to date issued by non-governmental organizations is the 'International Principles on the Application of Human Rights to Communications Surveillance', published in 2014 under the initiative of the Electronic Frontier Foundation, also known as the 'Necessary and Proportionate Principles' or '13 Principles' and endorsed by over 300 NGO s. <https://necessaryandproportionate.org/> accessed 15 May 2021. With regard to private sector initiatives, the major information and communications technology companies endorsed the 'Global Network Initiative Principles' issued in 2015. <https://globalnetworkinitiative.org/gni-principles> accessed 15 May 2021.

to achieve sustainable development, to apply the precautionary principle, or to achieve an environmental impact assessment for activities that are likely to harm the environment.[15] These principles have found an echo in a variety of multilateral sectoral conventions and a number of bilateral treaties, as well as many soft law sectoral instruments.[16] A whole system of fundamental yet imprecise principles has emerged from these combined instruments. As Mbengue and McGarry have shown, international judicial bodies such as the ICJ, the WTO Dispute Settlement Body, ITLOS, and arbitral tribunals refined these principles and developed their normative content.[17] Yet, many of the holdings eventually rest upon the 'principles' enshrined in the laws of treaties whenever they exist rather than consolidating the autonomous existence of general principles as a formal source of law. The ICJ Judge Cançado Trindade regretted this in its separate opinion to the *Pulp Mills case* with regard to the autonomous existence of general principles of prevention and precaution.[18]

The initial assumption of this contribution is that general principles of law, as enshrined in Article 38(1)(c) of the ICJ Statute, constitute an autonomous and legitimate source of international law whose purpose and constitutive elements might be tailored to the progressive sedimentation of binding norms of international law governing state surveillance measures. An extensive and enlightened literature exists about the apprehension of surveillance measures by international law.[19] Yet, this literature does not purport to assess whether general principles of law, within the meaning of Article 38(1)(c) of the ICJ Statute, could be a relevant source for apprehending such a phenomenon.

15 Such as the 1972 Stockholm Declaration on Human Environment and the 1992 Rio Declaration on Environment and Development.

16 On this topic, we refer to the enlightening contribution of M Mbengue, B McGarry, 'General Principles of International Environmental Law in the Case Law of International Courts and Tribunals' *in* M Andenas and others (eds), *General Principles and the Coherence of International Law* (Brill 2019) 408.

17 Ibid.

18 Separate Opinion of Judge Cançado Trindade, *Pulp Mills on the River Uruguay* (*Argentina v Uruguay*) [2010] ICJ Rep 14, 156.

19 See eg, not exhaustively, M Milanovic, 'Human Rights Treaties and Foreign Surveillance: Privacy in the Digital Age'(2015) 56:1 Harvard Int'l L Journal 81; AS Deeks, 'An International Legal Framework for Surveillance', (2015) 55 Virginia Journal of International Law 291; AS Deeks, 'Regulating Foreign Surveillance through International Law' in FH Cate, JX Dempsey, *Bulk Collection: Systematic Government Access to Private-Sector Data*, (OUP 2017); A Seibert-Fohr, 'Digital Surveillance, Meta-Data and Foreign Intelligence Cooperation: Unpacking the International Right to Privacy' (25 April 2018) <https://papers.ssrn.com/sol3/papers.cfm?abstract_id=3168711> accessed 18 May 2021.

This contribution would not dare to expose a theory of general principles of law. The International Law Commission stressed that the methodology of identifying such principles remains unclear and is the subject of many divergent doctrinal controversies, notably as to whether the notion is limited to those found in domestic laws (*in foro domestico*) or extends to principles having their origin in international relations.[20]

The starting point of this contribution lies in the nebula of 'principles' surrounding State interference with the right of privacy through domestic surveillance measures. These principles currently emerge in two different yet coherent ways: first, through a fast homogenisation of States' legislation around overarching principles governing lawful surveillance; second, through the even faster development of self-standing principles in the international legal order, which are extrapolated from an existing treaty-based norm: Article 17 ICCPR.

By unravelling the flow of concordant internal legislation in every continent as well as reports, studies, and resolutions of UN bodies, and standards established by non-governmental organisations and private actors, we believe that an interpreter could unravel 'general principles of law' governing digital surveillance, having due regard to the legal necessity of such autonomous principles. This contribution will first address the relevance of general principles of law in the context of digital surveillance (1) before assessing the existence and content of such general principles (2).

1 The Relevance of General Principles in the Context of Digital Surveillance

One may wonder whether it is even pertinent to contain general principles away from other sources of international law when the ICJ itself blurs the lines and prefers to mention 'principles of general international law', 'basic principles of international law' or simply 'principle' rather than taking a stand among the sources referred to in Article 38.[21] However, by examining the extensive

20 ILC, *Report of the International Law Commission, sixty-ninth session* (2017) A/72/10 (Annex A) para 7.

21 On this particular question, see eg T Treves, 'Environmental Impact Assessment and the Precautionary Approach: Why Are International Courts and Tribunals Reluctant to Consider Them as General Principles of Law?' in M Andenas and others (eds), *General Principles …* (n 16) 379; R Wolfrum, 'General International Law (Principles, Rules, and Standards) in A Peters (ed), *Max Planck Encyclopedia of Public International Law* (OUP 2010) <https://opil.ouplaw.com/home/MPIL> paras 6–21.

doctrine on general principles of law, it appears that the current irrelevance of approaching digital surveillance as part of a general practice accepted as customary law strengthens the correlative need to open the Pandora box and consider the relevance of general principles as an autonomous source of international law (1.1). This assumption is substantiated by their constitutive elements, which seem *prima facie* perfectly suited for this purpose (1.2).

1.1 *'General Principles of Law' as an Autonomous Source of International Law*

In his landmark early contribution to the study of general principles of law, Professor Alain Pellet firmly defended the thesis according to which the autonomous scope of 'general principles of law', as defined in Article 38(1)(c) of the ICJ Statute, required methodically distinguishing them from international customs.[22] He did not reject the claim that both of these sources of international law were 'spontaneous' insofar as they resulted from a process of ascertainment of a rule through the analysis of legal facts. Yet, although answering to both a material element (a consistent practice) and a psychological one (an *opinio juris*), Pellet asserted that the content and functions of these elements differed:[23] International custom was deduced from repeated activities operated immediately by subjects of international law in the international legal order. On the contrary, general principles were extrapolated from acts and rules pertaining solely to the internal legal order, once a conviction had been reached that a necessity existed to apply such principles in international relations.[24]

According to this representation, general principles of law could only be limited to those principles which were extrapolated from domestic legal systems. Consequently, they would set aside the fundamental principles of international law (the so-called *Principes généraux* du *droit international*). In fact, adding the latter category of norms among the 'General principles of law' would be superfluous as they were deduced from existing conventions or international customs and, as such, could not have a proper reach.[25] In the same line of thoughts, fundamental principles of international law could not qualify

22 A Pellet, *Recherche sur les principes généraux de droit en droit international*, Ph.D dissertation defended on 9 February 1974, *Université de droit, d'économie et de sciences sociales de Paris* <https://www.alainpellet.eu/ouvrages> accessed 15 May 2021.

23 Ibid 339.

24 As stated by Pellet, '*La règle coutumière résulte d'une série de pratiques ayant des effets dans l'ordre international ; le principe général de droit est le résultat de la confrontation de normes internes ne comportant aucun caractère d'extranéité*' ibid 340.

25 This position has been shared, for instance, by Sir H Waldock, 'General Course on Public International Law' (1962) 106 Collected Courses of the Hague Academy of International

as 'general principles of law', but only as rules of a conventional or customary nature that are characterized by a high degree of generality.

Many authors opposed this representation and did not hesitate to include fundamental principles of international law in the category of 'general principles of law'.[26] In our opinion, defining general principles as encompassing both principles established '*in foro domestico*' and in the international sphere does not affect the autonomy of general principles for their purpose is rooted in the social necessity to regulate a factual phenomenon and the correlative global consensus of States over such a necessity. That said, general principles usually precede custom or conventional rules and, as stated by President Yusuf, 'may act as a 'lightning rod' for the creation of more defined legal rules by creating coherence around a certain value or legal position that is yet to be codified'.[27] For instance, in the *Pulp Mills* case, the ICJ referred to the 'principle of prevention' as a customary rule which 'has its origins in the due diligence that is required of a State in its territory'.[28] Before being qualified as such, this principle was rooted in 'the awareness of the need to secure the harmony between man and nature'[29] and emerged through the progressive sedimentation of international endeavours, starting with the United Nations Conferences of Stockholm (1972) and Rio de Janeiro (1992).

General principles appear as a receptacle of norms, a 'nebula in which stars are constantly being born', to quote Robert Kolb.[30] Their content can be

---

Law 68; G Gaja, 'General Principles of Law' in R Wolfrum (ed), *Max Planck Encyclopedia of Public International Law* (OUP 2012) para 19.

26 George Scelle used to consider general principles as 'general customs', induced by a general practice accepted as law by 'civilised nations', G Scelle, *Manuel élémentaire de droit international public* (Domat 1943) 401. See also eg B Cheng, *General Principles of Law as Applied by International Courts and Tribunals* (Stevens 1953) 390; M Virally, *La pensée juridique* (LGDJ 1960) 171; P Reuter, *Droit international public* (PUF 1968) 56; A Verdross, 'Les principes généraux de Droit dans le système des sources du Droit international public' in *Recueil d'études de Droit international en hommage à Paul Guggenheim* (IUHEI 1968) 525; L Henkin, 'International Law: Politics, Values and Functions' (1989) 216 Coll courses 61; J Verhoeven, *Droit international public* (Larcier 2000) 349–350; R Kolb, *Interprétation et creation du droit international* (Bruylant 2006) 240; R Wolfrum, 'General international law (principles, rules, and standards)' in *Max Planck Encyclopedia of Public International Law* (OUP 2010) para 28; PM Dupuy, 'Formation of Customary International Law and General Principles' in D Bodansky and others (eds), *The Oxford Handbook of International Environmental Law* (OUP 2012) 461.

27 A Yusuf, 'Concluding Remarks' in M Andenas and others (eds) (n 16) 456.

28 *Pulp Mills on the River Uruguay (Argentina v Uruguay)* [2010] ICJ Rep 14 para 101.

29 *Pulp Mills*, Sep op Cançado Trindade (n 18) para 56.

30 R Kolb, *Interprétation et création du droit international* (n 26) 799.

'absorbed' into another source such as custom when sufficient State practice justifies the qualification.

In the same line of thought, Pierre-Marie Dupuy merges, in a single category, the general principles of international law that only differ from customary rules based on the level of generality of their formulation and those that could only be defined as 'normative concepts', vague principles whose specific legal content will be determined on a case-by-case basis.[31]

For its part, the American Branch of the International Law Association has pointed out that the 'general principle' of the prohibition on the threat or use of force 'conform more closely than the concept of 'custom' to the situation where a norm is widely accepted even though widely violated'.[32] In another context, we believe that space law also appeared through 'normative concepts' which are not the result of extraction and transposition into the international legal order of principles *in foro domestico* but of UNGA resolutions from which various treaty regimes subsequently emerged. Such general principles could not, in the 1960s, be considered custom, or 'instant custom'. As of today, this 'nebula' of general principles keeps its autonomous existence as a principle-setter.

We believe that autonomous principles of law may also derive from particular treaty regimes. For instance, Rüdiger Wolfrum persuasively demonstrated how the principles enshrined in Article 2 of the UN Charter have been further elaborated at the international level as independent principles through the implication of ICJ cases or UNGA resolutions.[33] He also mentioned the Genocide Convention of 1951, about which the ICJ acknowledged that its underlying principles were 'recognized by civilized nations as binding on States, even without conventional obligations'.[34] The Court drew from this statement that the condemnation of genocide and the obligation of cooperation against the crime of genocide were of a universal character, thus broadening the scope of the Convention.[35]

The same process of induction is at stake as far as human rights law is concerned, which is especially important in the case of digital surveillance. As

31 PM Dupuy, 'Formation of Customary International Law and General Principles' (n 26) 461.
32 ILA (American Branch), *Report of the Committee of the Formation of Customary Law*, (1987) 101 Proceedings of the American Branch of the International Law Association 112.
33 R Wolfrum, 'General international law (principles, rules, and standards)' in R Wolfrum (ed), *Max Planck Encyclopedia of Public International Law* (n 26) paras 41–46.
34 *Armed Activities on the Territory of the Congo (New Application: 2002) (Democratic Republic of the Congo v. Rwanda)* (Jurisdiction and Admissibility) [2006] ICJ Rep. para 64.
35 Ibid.

explained by Simma and Alston, the objective nature of human rights is perceivable in the fact that human rights law principles 'have always preceded practice' through a spontaneous phenomenon.[36] Human rights, which carry an inherent normative authority and answer a need to protect individuals in the face of States' authority, may naturally qualify as 'general principles', whether or not they are otherwise expressed in customary rules.[37] In our demonstration, that would require acknowledging that general principles of surveillance could derive from particular treaty regimes, in particular from Article 17 of the ICCPR, as we will explain in section 2 of this contribution.

As an early conclusion, we believe that it does not matter whether a normative vacuum is filled through an extrapolation of principles of internal law into the international order or through the progressive empowerment of autonomous international principles.[38] The autonomous reach of general principles can be deduced from their original constitutive elements: a necessity to uncover international norms and a global consensus of States over this necessity.

1.2 *Assessing the Constitutive Elements of 'General Principles of Law' in the Context of Digital Surveillance*

General principles answer a need. Their practical necessity lies at the heart of their binding character and it is their inner generality rather than their technicity that makes them stable, long-lasting, and fit to generate particular *rules*.[39] Antônio Augusto Cançado Trindade speaks of a '*substratum* of the legal order itself' that he defines as a foundation of the *jus necessarium* which 'permeate[s] every legal system' with a continuing validity.[40]

Alain Pellet has perfectly demonstrated that general principles are relevant where new social phenomena have little or no legal framework, even more so when they deal with the relationships between States and private individuals.

---

36 B Simma, P Alston, 'The Sources of Human Rights Law: Custom, Jus Cogens, And General Principles' (1989) 12 Australian Year Book of International Law 107.

37 In its judgment handed out on 19 December 2005 in the *Armed Activities on the Territory of the Congo* case, the ICJ referred to the 'principles of international human rights law' which can be deduced, for instance, from the ICCPR or the UN Convention on the Rights of the Child of 1989. Yet, the Court deemed these 'principles' applicable to the case at hand as customary international law [2005] ICJ Rep 168 paras 215–217.

38 In the same direction see ILC, *First report on general principles of law* (Special Rapporteur M. Vázquez-Bermúdez) (A/CN.4/732, 5 April 2019) para 162.

39 A Pellet, *Recherche sur les principes généraux de droit en droit international* (n 22) 391.

40 See eg AA Cançado Trindade, *International Law for Humankind. Towards a New* jus gentium, (3rd edn, Brill 2020) 55. See also, Sep op of Judge Cançado Trindade (n 18) para 200.

Indeed, the transposition of general principles of internal law into the international sphere is all the more facilitated when there is a structural analogy of legal relations in both the internal and international sphere.[41] This is particularly relevant in our case considering the transnational nature of digital exchanges and their correlated surveillance measures. The general principles governing surveillance, which are being developed *in foro domestico* would serve the same ultimate cause in the international legal order: protecting individuals from undue interference with their right to privacy. Yet, their autonomous existence as norms of international law would not only supplant the lack of applicable conventional or customary norms but also guide the future developments of specific rules.

The 'need for norms' cannot be sufficient to characterise the existence of a general principle of law, unless from a strict *iusnaturalist* standpoint. Indeed, Article 38(1)(c) indicates that general principles are 'recognized by civilized nations'. Cançado Trindade considers that general principles represent 'the *status conscientiae* of the subjects of International Law'.[42] In his opinion, the 'recognition' criterion set forth by Article 38(1)(c) means: 'by the juridical conscience',[43] thus following the path of Verdross.[44] Recognition would no longer be an expression of will but of consent dictated by necessity. If read as an objective source of international law answering to a social need, *opinio juris* would be above the will of the State or any other subject of law.[45] As explained by Henkin,

> [p]rinciples common to legal systems often reflect natural law principles that underlie international law … [I]f the law has not yet developed a concept to justify or explain how such general principles enter international law, resort to this secondary source seems another example of the

---

41 A Pellet, *Recherche sur les principes généraux de droit en droit international* (n 22) 142–143. In the same line, see also, P Reuter, 'Le droit au secret et les institutions internationales' (1956) 2 AFDI 58.

42 AA Cançado Trindade, *International Law for Humankind* (n 40) 55, quoting A Verdross, 'Les principes généraux de Droit dans le système des sources du Droit international public' in *Recueil d'études de Droit international en hommage à Paul Guggenheim* (IUHEI 1968) 525.

43 AA Cançado Trindade, *International Law for Humankind* (n 40) 61.

44 A Verdross, 'Les principes généraux du droit dans la jurisprudence internationale', (1935) 52 coll. Courses … 206, 243.

45 AA Cançado Trindade, *International Law for Humankind* (n 40) 57. See also Separate Opinion of Judge Cançado Trindade (n 18) para 192.

> triumph of good sense and practical needs over the limitations of concepts and other abstractions.[46]

That was essentially the initial meaning of Baron Descamps's proposition to the Advisory Committee of Jurists for the drafting of the Statutes of the PCIJ: 'les règles du droit international telles que les reconnaît la conscience juridique des peuples civilisés'.[47]

We could assert that from the moment State surveillance became a universal digital activity whose reach is in no way limited by sovereign boundaries – by means of data interception, data acquisition, or exchange of data – an instant necessity to regulate such behaviours appeared.

Nevertheless, it is commonly understood by the positivist doctrine that recognition through the will of States prevails. That is not to say, nevertheless, that 'recognition' means 'acceptance', which is indicative of a custom. The notion of 'consensus', which relates to the acceptability of a principle among States, is better suited for the functions of general principles. In Pellet's words, general principles are 'acceptable to jurists trained in all the major systems of law today, although it has not yet received concrete application – which distinguishes it from a customary norm'.[48] So distinguished from the requirement of 'acceptance', there is a shared belief that the necessity to unveil normative principles legitimizes a lesser proof of recognition. In the words of Palchetti and Bonafé, 'the wider discretion enjoyed by the interpreter in the identification of this source cannot obscure the nature of general principles as a consensual phenomenon'.[49]

According to the Special Rapporteur of the ILC on General Principles of law, M. Vázquez-Bermúdez, a generally accepted position in the literature and one supported by practice is that 'the requirement of recognition is fulfilled when a principle exists within a sufficiently large number of national legal systems.[50] That is not to say that the Special Rapporteur does not support the position according to which recognition could take place at the international level outside of national legal systems. Such recognition would be the product of

46 L Henkin, 'International Law: Politics, Values and Functions: General Course in Public International Law' (1989) 216 Coll. Courses [...] 61–62.

47 PCIJ (Advisory Committee of jurists), *Procès-verbaux of the Proceedings of the Committee, June 16th – July 24th 1920, 13th meeting*, 293 and annex 3 thereto, 306.

48 A Pellet, *Recherche sur les principes généraux de droit en droit international* (n 22) 9.

49 BI Bonafé, P Palchetti, 'Relying on general principles in international law' in C Brölmann, Y Radi (eds), *Research Handbook on the Theory and Practice of International Lawmaking*, (Cheltenham, Edward Edgar 2016) 176.

50 ILC, *First report on general principles of law* (n 38) para 167.

a deduction from existing conventional or customary rules, supplemented by acts of international organisations such as UNGA resolutions[51] or policy statements of international organizations or conferences.[52] As we contended it in the previous subsection, such general principles would keep their autonomous existence as a receptacle for future norms.

So understood, we believe that general principles of law would be a suitable tool to pave the way for an appropriate – yet necessary transient – frame for digital surveillance measures in the international legal order. It is our understanding that a global momentum exists in internal legal orders so as to regulate digital data protection and that such a momentum takes into account the specific interferences that public authorities can cause to individuals through surveillance measures. Moreover, extensive instruments from UN bodies tend to induce general principles of surveillance from existing conventional rules. Whether an actual necessity of regulation backed by a global consensus over such a need exists must now be assessed.

2 The Existence of General Principles in the Context of Digital Surveillance

National security is a recognised ground for interference with the right to privacy and the principles of personal data protection, including the confidentiality of communications and connection data. It provides a wide margin of appreciation to States for implementing covert surveillance measures. The 2013 revelations about the level of intensity of unregulated surveillance measures, notably through the intelligence alliance 'Five Eyes', initiated a widespread regulatory movement of such derogatory measures.

The existence of general principles of law governing digital surveillance measures can be assessed under all of the dialectics envisioned in the previous section, from the most objectivist to the most voluntarist: ethics, the *status conscientiae* of the subjects of international law, good sense, practical need, and of course, a global consensus among internal legal orders or existing conventional or customary rules as well as acts of international organisations.

51 Ibid para 173.

52 R Wolfrum, 'General international law (principles, rules, and standards)' (n 21) para 36; See also A Verdross, 'Les principes généraux de droit dans le système des sources du droit international public' in *Recueil d'études de droit international en hommage à P. Guggenheim*, (IUHEI 1968) 526.

In our specific case, the principles governing digital surveillance measures primarily concern the relationship between States and individuals and derive from human rights in general and the right to privacy in particular. The right to privacy has evolved, both internationally and domestically, around core general principles that specifically protect individuals from undue domestic interference in data protection rights (2.1). Yet, the very nature of cross-border data flows makes it impossible to apprehend digital surveillance from a purely territorial approach. Data in the digital environment are characterised by their ubiquity, divisibility, and instant mobility. As a result, unveiling the general principles of law applying to domestic surveillance does not settle the issue. Can the general principles of domestic digital surveillance be deemed to bind States' cross-border activities? The underlying issue concerns the ties between the principles of cooperation and non-interference in domestic affairs on the one hand, and international human rights law on the other (2.2).

2.1 *The Individual Right to Privacy and the Overarching Principles of Legality, Necessity, and Proportionality*

The necessity of an international human rights framework for digital surveillance measures has long been raised within the UN system.[53] The developments of the right to privacy in the past decade, both at the international and internal level, demonstrate an unambiguous trend towards embracing domestic surveillance measures in the digital sphere among the category of interference that are governed by law. Stating the contrary would amount to consider, in Sir Lauterpacht's words, that the 'overriding rule of presumptive freedom of action of States' makes no room whatsoever for restricting their freedom to undertake surveillance activities in the digital sphere.[54]

A global consensus seems to exist over the applicability of the overarching principles of legality, necessity, and proportionality to States interference with the right to privacy through surveillance channels. Such irreducible principles of human rights law can be deduced from either existing international rules (2.1.1) or States's internal legislation (2.1.2).

53 UN Commission on Human Rights, *Report on uses of electronics which might affect the rights of the person and the limits which should be placed on such uses in a democratic society* (E/CN.4/1142/add.2, 7 October 1974) para 32.

54 Sir H Lauterpacht, *The Development of International Law by the International Court* (CUP 1982) 165.

2.1.1 Overarching Principles as Deduced from Article 17 ICCPR

Article 17 of the ICCPR forbids 'arbitrary or unlawful interference with [...] privacy' and stresses the right of everyone to 'the protection of the law against such interference'. The notion of 'arbitrariness' has been interpreted by the General comment No 16 of the Human Rights Committee as a 'guarantee that even interference provided for by law should be in accordance with the provisions, aims and objectives of the Covenant and should be, in any event, reasonable in the particular circumstances'.[55]

The 'right to privacy in the digital age' has been under the scrutiny of the United Nations General Assembly since December 2013, based on the findings that 'unlawful or arbitrary surveillance and/or interception of communications, as well as unlawful or arbitrary collection of personal data, [are] highly intrusive acts, [and] violate the rights to privacy and to freedom of expression and may contradict the tenets of a democratic society'.[56]

Under the auspices of the General Assembly, the Human Rights Council of the UN elaborated a series of general principles inferred from existing obligations under international human rights law.[57] Based on this work, the General Assembly adopted several resolutions without a vote resting upon existing international binding obligations and in particular Article 17 of the ICCPR.[58] At the heart of these resolutions lies the statement according to which 'any interference with the right to privacy should take into account its legality, necessity and proportionality'.[59] This trilogy has been consistently applied to Article 17 of the ICCPR and is reflected in several 'concluding observations' made by the Human Rights Committee in the context of country reports after a thorough review of State surveillance mechanisms.[60] Although reduced to their greatest generality and stripped of all national particularities, the General Assembly granted each of these principles a proper normative content so as to ensure

55 UN Human Rights Committee (HRC), *CCPR General Comment No. 16* ... (n 16) para 4.

56 A/RES/68/167, preamble.

57 See n 8 to n 11.

58 For instance, A/RES/75/176 (16 December 2020); A/RES/73/179 (17 December 2018); A/RES/71/199 (19 December 2016); A/RES/69/166 (18 December 2014).

59 A/RES/75/176 and A/RES/73/179, para 4.

60 For relevant (though not exhaustive) examples outside of the European Union, see the concluding observations of the Human Rights Committee concerning Nigeria (CCPR/C/NGA/CO/2*, 29 August 2019, para 41); Tajikistan (CCPR/C/TJK/CO/3*, 22 August 2019, para 42); Equatorial Guinea (CCPR/C/GNQ/CO/1, 22 August 2019, para 51); Belarus (CCPR/C/BLR/CO/5, 22 November 2018, para 44); Honduras (CCPR/C/HND/CO/2, 22 August 2017, para 39); Colombia (CCPR/C/COL/CO/7, 17 November 2016, para 33).

'the full and effective implementation of all [States] obligations under international human rights law'.[61]

As far as the principle of legality is concerned, UNGA resolutions emphasise the quality of the law, which must be accessible to the public, clear, precise, comprehensive, and non-discriminatory, whenever they seek to regulate digital surveillance measures.[62] More fundamentally, the General Assembly also considers that the principle of legality requires that independent and impartial judicial or administrative oversight mechanisms be capable of ensuring accountability for State surveillance and that any legislation provide access to an effective remedy to any individual whose right to privacy has been violated by unlawful or arbitrary surveillance.[63]

The principle of necessity refers to the legitimate aims that surveillance measures must pursue in order for the interference with the right to privacy to be considered lawful in a democratic society. As such, the combined principles of necessity and legality dictate that clear, precise, and comprehensive legislation specify the purposes for which an interference could be deemed 'necessary'. UNGA resolutions do not exhaustively list such legitimate grounds and used to refer in vague terms to 'public security' and only mentioned the prevention and suppression of terrorism as a public interest of great importance. In the preamble of its latest resolution to date (75/176), however, the General Assembly made a specific reference to national security as a legitimate ground. The United Nations High Commissioner for Human Rights added that 'Secret surveillance measures must be limited to preventing or investigating the most serious crimes or threats'.[64]

Finally, 'proportionality', as a general principle of law, designates a relationship of adequacy between the legitimate objective pursued by a State and the means that it uses to reach that objective. This meta-principle embraces every branch of international law, from *jus ad bellum* (*eg* proportionality of self-defence)[65] to *jus in bello* (*eg* unnecessary suffering of combatants),[66] maritime boundary delimitation (proportionality of the continental shelf to the length

61 A/RES/75/176, para 7(c); A/RES/73/179, para 6(c); A/RES/71/199, para 5(c).

62 See preamble of A/RES/75/176; A/RES/73/179; A/RES/71/199 and A/RES/69/166.

63 A/RES/75/176, para 7(d) and (e); A/RES/73/179, para 6(d) and (e); A/RES/71/199, para 5(d) and (e).

64 UNHCR, 'The right to privacy in the digital age – Report of the United Nations High Commissioner for Human Rights'(A/HRC/39/29, 3 August 2018) para 37.

65 See, famously, *Military and Paramilitary Activities in and against Nicaragua* (*Nicaragua v. United States of America*) (Merits) ICJ Rep 1986 para 194.

66 See *Legality of the Threat or Use of Nuclear Weapons* (Advisory Opinion) ICJ Rep 1996 para 78.

of the coast),[67] or international trade (proportionality of the suspension of concessions as countermeasures).[68] In the specific case of digital surveillance, proportionality requires that the means used to carry out surveillance measures as well as their impact on individuals and groups be strictly limited to the achievement of the legitimate aim and 'the least intrusive option available' so as not to render the essence of the right meaningless.[69] The General Assembly has further clarified the nature of possible abuses to the right to privacy, referring to 'data collection, processing, storage and sharing, profiling and the use of automated processes and machine learning'.[70]

If they are not devoid of any substantial legal content, these overarching principles nevertheless leave a great leeway for States to interpret and adopt diverging views and legislations. Yet, perceived as 'general principles of law' in the sense of Article 38 (1) (c) of the ICJ Statute, they would compel every State to move away from arbitrary and secret interference with individual rights as well as foster the development and acceptance of a number of specific principles which can already be perceived in internal law.

2.1.2 Overarching Principles as Deduced from Regional Instruments and National Laws

The trilogy of overarching principles governing state interference with the right to privacy through surveillance means is globally recognised by the community of States. The purpose of this subsection is not to address comprehensively every existing national or regional legislation governing surveillance measures but rather to demonstrate that the worldwide efforts are far from Eurocentric.

2.1.2.1 *Africa*

The right to privacy is not specifically enshrined in the African Charter on Human and Peoples' Rights. Yet, in 2014, the African Union established a Convention on Cyber Security and Personal Data Protection (Malabo Convention)[71] whose scope encompasses 'any processing of data relating to public security, defence, research, criminal prosecution or State security'.[72]

---

67 See the equally famous case, *North Sea Continental Shelf* (merits) ICJ Rep 1969 para 98.

68 DSB (WTO), *EC-Bananas III*, WT/DS27/ARB (April 9 1999) para 6.16.

69 A/HRC/39/29 (n 11) para 10.

70 A/RES/75/176 (n 8) para 7(n).

71 African Union Convention on Cyber Security and Personal Data Protection, adopted by the 23rd Assembly of Heads of States and Governments held in Malabo, 27 June 2014.

72 Ibid Article 9 (d).

As of June 2020, the Convention had been signed by 14 States out of the 55 member States of the African Union and ratified by 8 (its entry into force is subject to 15 ratifications). The Malabo Convention aims at establishing in each State Party 'a mechanism capable of combating violations of privacy that may be generated by personal data collection, processing, transmission, storage and use' and to guarantee that 'whatever form of processing is used shall respect the basic freedoms and rights of individuals while also taking into account the prerogatives of States'.[73]

The Convention's 'basic principles', which are enshrined in Article 13, develop every requirement concerning the general principles of legality (principles 2 and 5), necessity (principle 3), and proportionality (principles 3, 4, and 6).

In 2010, the Economic Community of West African States (ECOWAS) had already established a very similar framework for its 15 member States, which is currently in force and binding upon them.[74] Its scope also includes 'any processing of data related to public security, defence, investigation and prosecution of criminal offences or State security' (Article 3). It provides for explicit provisions on 'personal processing for the public service' (Article 6) based on the principle of legality (Article 24) and submits any processing of data for surveillance purposes to the authorisation of a data protection authority (Article 12). The principles of necessity and proportionality are widely developed through various more specific principles of 'purpose, relevance, and preservation' (Article 25), and accuracy (Article 26).

It is important to note that although various countries neither ratified the Malabo Convention nor are bound by the 2010 ECOWAS framework, they do recognise the overarching principles of legality, necessity, and proportionality in their national laws as far as digital surveillance is concerned. For instance, The South African *Protection of Personal Information Act 2013* which entered into force in July 2020[75] provides for a list of specific 'public interests' which may enable surveillance measures as long as the South African Information Regulator authorises such measures, based on a necessity and proportionality assessment.[76] The Kenyan *Data Protection Act* of 2019 also stresses that any processing of data which is 'necessary for national security or public interest', although exempt from the provision of the act, must comply with 'data

---

73 Ibid preamble.

74 ECOWAS, Supplementary Act A/SA.1/01/10 on personal data protection within ECOWAS, Abuja, 16th February 2010.

75 *Act No 4 of 2013: Protection of Personal Information Act, 2013*, Government Gazette, vol. 581, No 37067.

76 Ibid Section 37.

protection principles relating to lawful processing, minimisation of collection, data quality and adopting security safeguards to protect personal data'.[77]

2.1.2.2 *Asia Pacific*

As far as Asia is concerned, no regional convention exists to date, although the Organisation of the Asia-Pacific Economic Cooperation (APEC) issued a non-binding 'Privacy framework', updated in 2015, which was endorsed by its 21 member States. Although not meant to impede governmental actions with respect to the protection of national security and public safety, section 13 of the Framework addresses the trilogy of principles (legality, necessity, and proportionality) with respect to the interference with data protection rights justified by national security or public safety reasons.

At the national level, it is worth mentioning South Korea's *Personal Information Protection Act* adopted in February 2020[78] whose Article 58(4) is very similar to Article 15 of EU Directive 2002/58 and provides in general terms that the lawful grounds of exclusion of data protection (national security, public safety and security, public health ...) shall not prevent the data controller from processing the personal information 'to the minimum extent necessary to attain the intended purpose for the minimum period'. The new *Privacy Act 2020* of New Zealand also provides for a set of 'Information Privacy Principles' (IPPs) which are applicable as a principle to intelligence and security agencies except for a few exceptions.[79] IPP 1(1) generally states that personal information cannot be collected by a data processor unless the information 'is collected for a lawful purpose' and the collection of the information 'is necessary for that purpose'. It is also worth mentioning that the European Commission has decided that Japan,[80] New Zealand,[81] and soon South Korea[82] fulfil the 'adequacy' test set forth by Article 45 of the EU General Data Protection Regulation

---

77 *Data Protection Act, 2019*, Kenya Gazette Supplement No 181 (Acts No 24) Section 51.

78 *Personal Information Protection Act [Enforcement Date 05. Aug, 2020.] [Act No.16930, 04. Feb, 2020., Partial Amendment]*.

79 *Privacy Act 2020*, Public Act 2020 No 31, 30 June 2020, Part 3, S 28.

80 Commission Implementing Decision 2019/419 of 23 January 2019 pursuant to Regulation (EU) 2016/679 of the European Parliament and of the Council on the adequate protection of personal data by Japan under the Act on the Protection of Personal Information [2019] OJEU L 76/1.

81 Commission Implementing Decision 2013/65/EU of 19 December 2012 pursuant to Directive 95/46/EC of the European Parliament and of the Council on the adequate protection of personal data by New Zealand [2013] OJEU L 28/12.

82 EU Press release, 30 March 2021 <https://ec.europa.eu/commission/presscorner/detail/en/statement_21_1506> accessed 15 May 2021.

of 2016 for transfer of personal data on the basis of an adequacy decision. As such, they are regarded as 'essentially equivalent' to that ensured in the EU.

Comprehensive data protection legislation including specific measures regarding digital surveillance are also in the process of being drafted in various countries.[83] The Indian *Personal Data Protection Bill 2019* provides that whenever data processing without consent is 'necessary' for a list of 'reasonable purposes', specific regulations must lay down 'such safeguards as may be appropriate to ensure the protection of the rights of data principles', including a notice to the individuals under surveillance if it does not 'substantially prejudice the relevant reasonable purpose'.[84] Yet, these 'reasonable purposes' are defined in vague terms as they encompass the very broad 'prevention and detection of any unlawful activity including fraud'.[85]

As far as China is concerned, a draft revised version of the future *Personal Information Protection Law* has been unveiled in April 2021 which, according to the translations found, also makes room for the application of the trilogy of general principles to digital surveillance operated by State organs. Article 34 of the draft law, as enshrined in Section 3 of Chapter II on the 'Special Provisions on the Handling of Personal Information by State Organs' provides that:

> State organs handling personal information to fulfill their statutory duties and responsibilities shall conduct them according to the powers and procedures provided in laws or administrative regulations; they may not exceed the scope or extent necessary to fulfill their statutory duties and responsibilities.[86]

2.1.2.3 *Europe*

With regard to the European Union, Article 8 of the Charter of Fundamental Rights of the European Union consecrates the autonomous right to the protection of personal data. Based on this provision, read in light of Article 52(1) of

83 See the comprehensive study of SK Prasad, S Aravindakshan, 'Playing Catch Up – Privacy Regimes in South Asia' (2021) 25:1 Int'l J. of HR 79.

84 India *Personal Data Protection Bill, 2019*, Bill No. 373 of 2019, Section 14(3).

85 Ibid Section 14(2)(a).

86 Unofficial translation of the *Personal Information Protection Law of the People's Republic of China (Draft) (Second Review Draft)* effectuated by DigiChina (Stanford University) <https://digichina.stanford.edu/news/translation-personal-information-protection-law-peoples-republic-china-draft-second-review> accessed 15 May 2021.

the Charter,[87] the Court of Justice of the European Union has clearly reduced the ability of the European Union[88] as well as its member States[89] to discretionarily interfere with the fundamental right to the protection of personal data. In doing so, the Court has taken the clear stance that Article 15(1) of the *e-privacy* Directive 2002/58, which provides the right for EU Member States to adopt restrictions to electronic data protection rights, does not fall outside of the scope of EU law, as long as data is collected from digital service providers. As far as overarching principles are concerned, the Court has deemed it necessary that surveillance measures be provided by law, pursue a legitimate objective, and do not exceed the limits of what is appropriate and necessary to achieve those objectives.[90]

Outside the reach of the European Union, although the European Convention on Human Rights does not explicitly provide for a specific right to the protection of personal data, the European Court of Strasbourg inferred it from Article 8 ECHR protecting the right to privacy. In reviewing the content of the general principles applicable to the interception of digital data, the Court did not depart from its ancient rulings on secret measures of surveillance and recalled in the most general terms that '[a]ny interference with an individual's Article 8 rights can only be justified under Article 8(2) if it is in accordance with the law, pursues one or more of the legitimate aims to which that paragraph refers and is necessary in a democratic society in order to achieve any such aim'.[91]

These overarching general principles also lie at the core of the Council of Europe Convention *for the Protection of Individuals with regard to Automatic Processing of Personal Data* (Convention n°108) of 28 January 1981, ratified by all of its Member States and 8 additional States (Argentina, Cabo Verde, Mauritius, Mexico, Morocco, Senegal, Tunisia, Uruguay) which remains the

87 Article 52(1) of the Charter is the general clause concerning the limitations of the guaranteed rights: 'Any limitation on the exercise of the rights and freedoms recognised by this Charter must be provided for by law and respect the essence of those rights and freedoms. Subject to the principle of proportionality, limitations may be made only if they are necessary and genuinely meet objectives of general interest recognised by the Union or the need to protect the rights and freedoms of others'.

88 Case C-293/12 *Digital Rights Ireland Ltd* (8 April 2014) ECLI:EU:C:2014:238.

89 Joint cases C-203/15 and C-698/15 *Tele 2 Sverige* and *Tom Watson* (21 December 2016) ECLI:EU:C:2016:970.

90 *Digital Rights Ireland Ltd* (n 88) para 46 ; *Tele 2 Sverige* and *Tom Watson* (n 89) para 96.

91 *Big Brother Watch v. United Kingdom* (GC) App no 58170/13 and others (13 September 2018) para 304; *Roman Zakharov v. Russia* (GC) App no. 47143/06 (4 December 2015) para 227; *Kennedy v. United Kingdom*, App no 26839/05 (18 May 2010) para 130.

only specific and binding international instrument governing digital privacy, including States' interference through surveillance channels.[92]

2.1.2.4 *America*

Finally, as far as the American continent is concerned, the American Convention on Human Rights adopted in 1969 under the auspices of the Organisation of American States (OAS) is binding upon 24 member States with the noticeable exception of Canada and the United States. Its Article 11(2) and (3) generally forbids any arbitrary or abusive interference with this right and protects the right to the protection of the law against such interference. The Inter-American Court of Human Rights considered that the abusive interference in the sphere of privacy included those accomplished by public authorities.[93]

Extensive works have been undertaken at the regional level to monitor digital surveillance programmes, in an effort to systematise the work of the UNHRC around core principles.[94] The Inter-American juridical committee (CJI) issued in April 2021 an updated version of the *Principles on Privacy and Protection of Personal Data,* based on international norms and the different traditions among American states.[95]

Although non-binding *per se*, its twelfth Principle provides that:

> Any exceptions to whichever one of these Principles should be provided for expressly and specifically in domestic law, be made known to the public, and be limited to reasons relating to national sovereignty, national security, public security, protection of public health, the fight against criminality, regulatory compliance or other public order policies, or public interest.

---

92 If we do not take count of its amending protocol adopted in May 2018 (commonly referred to as 'Convention 108+' and whose ratification is opened only to the parties of the 1981 Convention).

93 IACtHR, *Case of the Ituango Massacres v. Colombia* (ser. C) No 148 (1 July 2006) para 194.

94 As soon as 2013, the Special Rapporteur for Freedom of Expression of the Inter-American Commission on Human Rights of the OAS urged States 'to revise their laws to set limits on the authority to monitor online communications, as well as its necessity and proportionality, in accordance with individual rights and the principles of international law' which, to the Special Rapporteur, were reflected, *inter alia*, by the reports of this regional body and the UN Human Rights Committee: IACHR, *Report of the Special Rapporteur for Freedom of Expression*, Chapter IV (Freedom of Expression and the Internet) (OEA/Ser.L/V/II.149. Doc. 50, 31 December 2013) para 151.

95 CJI/RES.266 (XCVIII-O/21) (8 April 2021) approving the *Updated Principles on Privacy and Protection of Personal Data, with annotations* (OEA/Ser. Q, CJI/doc. 638/21, 8 April 2021).

With regard to States' legislation, a recent study asserted that in 2020, 18 out of 35 American States had a specific data protection regulation and 7 others were in the process of getting one.[96] Argentina and Uruguay are considered by the European Commission as having an 'adequate level of data protection' for the purpose of Article 45 of the GDPR concerning the transfer of personal data to a third country. Both countries have also ratified Convention 108 of the Council of Europe respectively in 2019 and 2013, along with Mexico in 2018. As far as Brazil is concerned, the General Law on the Protection of Personal Data adopted in august 2018 does not apply to the processing of personal data carried out for public security, national defence, state security, or investigation and prosecution of criminal offences.[97] Yet, the law states that such processing of personal data 'shall be governed by specific legislation, which shall provide for measures proportionate and strictly necessary to meet the public interest, subject to due process, the general principles of protection and the rights of the holder provided for in this Law'.[98]

Finally, with respect to the United States, changes have been introduced to the 1978 *Foreign Intelligence Surveillance Act* (FISA)[99] as early as January 2014 so as to increase the transparency of intelligence programmes as well as implement additional protections for individuals' privacy. To that end, the 'Presidential Policy Directive 28' (PPD-28)[100] was meant to drastically reduce the scope of the so-called 'bulk metadata programs' revealed by Edward Snowden. On this Policy Directive, the infamous former EU-US adequacy decision called 'Privacy shield' stated that 'Although not phrased in [...] legal terms, [the] principles [of PPD-28] capture the essence of the principles of necessity and proportionality'.[101]

Yet, in its landmark decision '*Schrems II*' of 17 July 2020, the CJEU took the opportunity to review and subsequently annul this adequacy decision in light of the overarching trilogy of general principles.[102] Dwelling on these principles, the CJEU considered that only legislation ensuring 'effective and enforceable

96 CA Souza, CC de Oliveira, C Perrone, G Carneiro, 'From Privacy to Data Protection: The Road Ahead for the Inter-American System of Human Rights', (2021) 25:1 Int'l J. of HR 147.

97 *Lei Geral de Proteção de Dados Pessoais* (No 13.709), 14 August 2018, Article 4(III).

98 Ibid, Article 4(IV)(1).

99 50 USC 1801 *et seq.*

100 Presidential Policy Directive-28, 'Signals Intelligence Activities', 17 January 2014.

101 Commission Implementing Decision (EU) 2016/1250 of 12 July 2016 pursuant to Directive 95/46/EC of the European Parliament and of the Council on the adequacy of the protection provided by the EU-U.S. Privacy Shield, [2016] OJ L 207, para 76.

102 Case C-311/18 *Data Protection Commissioner v. Facebook Ireland Ltd, Maximilian Schrems* (16 July 2020) ECLI:EU:C:2020:559 para 176.

data subjects rights' could be deemed to match the minimum safeguards resulting, under EU law, from the principle of proportionality.[103] Considering the lack of effective and impartial redress mechanisms in US law, the CJEU found the US surveillance framework to be inadequate.[104]

As an interim conclusion, these last developments demonstrate the extent to which States have different representations of the 'overarching principles' as well as the different degrees in their implementation. We believe that this lack of homogeneity among States does not detract from the value of considering the overarching principles as 'general principles of law'. As Charles de Visscher explained, 'what is decisive in resorting to general principles of law is not the external similarity of the institutions or rules that are being compared. It is the underlying principle which is common to them and which explains them'.[105] Although the normative content of these three principles is particularly limited, their consecration as general principles of law would contribute to the homogenisation of domestic legislation and the progressive fleshing out of their content, as a general practice of States develops.

Nevertheless, the need to regulate digital surveillance measures at the international level does not stop at individual rights and safeguards against arbitrariness within State boundaries. The flow of personal digital data, and thus the means of monitoring this flow, transcends any territorial framework. The scandal of the magnitude of American surveillance programmes has revealed a need for a normative framework to assess such negative extraterritorial effects. The question then necessarily arises as to whether the overarching trilogy applies to the principles of cooperation, jurisdiction, and non-interference in the context of mass digital surveillance.

2.2 *State Jurisdiction and the General Principles of Cooperation and Non-interference*

The international legal order suffers from the absence of general rules on cooperation and non-interference in surveillance matters. This is not unrelated to the difficulties of regulating espionage activities in the pre-digital era. Traditionally seen as a perfect example of exclusive display of a State's competence, voices have always condemned intelligence gathering in light of

103 Ibid para 177 and para 184.

104 Ibid paras 191–198.

105 C de Visscher, *Théories et réalités en droit international public*, (Pedone 1970) 419. Translated from French: '*Dans ce processus, ce qui est décisif, ce n'est pas la similitude extérieure des institutions ou des règles que l'on confronte entre elles. C'est le principe sous-jacent qui leur est commun et qui les explique*'.

the principles of sovereignty, non-interference in domestic affairs, diplomatic law, and more recently international human rights, in particular the right to privacy. An overall permissiveness led to construe intelligence gathering in an ambivalent perspective.[106] As early as 1973, scholars warned that 'unless special techniques of supervision are innovated, it is probable that such fundamental doctrines as the right of privacy will be eroded'.[107] One could argue that the global capacity to undertake interception and data collection measures in the digital sphere, regardless of boundaries or territorial ties, dictates that the general principles of cooperation (2.2.1.) and non-interference (2.2.2) be deemed applicable to transboundary data flows. Yet, in contrast to the emerging global consensus that has emerged for the domestic protection of individuals within the State's territory, it seems more questionable that such limiting rules could already be deduced from internal legal orders.

2.2.1 Intelligence-Sharing Practices and the General Principle of Cooperation

Could we infer from the fundamental duty of States to cooperate a set of limiting principles protecting individuals from secretive mechanisms of digital intelligence-sharing among States?

The scandals and media interest over this question grew as the digital activities of the 'Five Eyes' intelligence-sharing network were unveiled and strongly criticized for their lack of transparency, legal framework, public scrutiny, and accountability mechanisms. Such sharing networks – The NGO Human Rights Watch believes that vastly larger networks do exist[108] – may be set up through secret memoranda of understanding and pose the risk of circumventing States domestic surveillance procedures and legal limits to take advantage of an effective yet procedurally weaker foreign surveillance mechanism. The Parliamentary Assembly of the Council of Europe spoke of a 'collusion for circumvention'.[109]

Against this background, the General Assembly clearly emphasised the fact that intelligence-sharing agreements were not exempt from respecting

106 For a classic analysis on the topic, see MS McDougal, HD Lasswell, WM Reisman, 'The Intelligence Function and World Public Order', (1973) 46 Temp. L.Q. 365. For a more recent account, see for instance, S Chersterman, 'The Spy who Came in from the Cold War: Intelligence and International Law', (2006) 27 Michigan Journal of Int'l.L 1071.

107 MS McDougal, HD Lasswell, WM Reisman (n 106) 396.

108 See the submission of Human Rights Watch as a third party before the ECtHR in the case *Big Brother Watch v. United Kingdom* (n 91) para 415.

109 Parliamentary Assembly of the CoE, 'Mass surveillance', Report, doc. 13734, 18 March 2015.

international human rights obligations regarding the right to privacy.[110] The Human Rights Committee of the UN further issued several Concluding Observations on States where it repeatedly stated that the overarching principles of legality, proportionality, and necessity, as deduced from Article 17 ICCPR, did apply to intelligence-sharing practices and required 'effective and independent oversight mechanisms'.[111]

At the European level, we believe that the ECtHR missed a true opportunity to give meaningful content to these general principles when it considered for the first time the compliance of an intelligence-sharing regime with the Convention.[112] In its *Big Brother Watch* decision of September 2018, the Court accepted that individuals could claim to be victims of an alleged violation of the right to privacy occasioned by the existence of an intelligence-sharing regime.[113] In this regard, it confirmed that Intelligence-sharing regimes must have a basis in domestic law, be accessible and foreseeable as to their effects. More specifically:

> it must be proportionate to the legitimate aim pursued, and there must exist adequate and effective safeguards against abuse. In particular, the procedures for supervising the ordering and implementation of the measures in question must be such as to keep the 'interference' to what is 'necessary in a democratic society.[114]

Very problematically, however, the ECtHR considered that in the case at hand, the interference with the applicant rights only lay in the possible reception in the United Kingdom of material intercepted in the United States but did not lie in the interception process itself 'which did not, in any event, occur within the United Kingdom's jurisdiction, and was not attributable to that State under international law'.[115] The Court's assessment relied solely on the applicable safeguards in the UK, once the data had been transferred within its jurisdiction, without prejudice of the conditions under which they were obtained. This finding is all the more surprising when confronted with the ruling of the CJEU

110 See for instance, A/RES/75/176 (n 8) preamble.

111 See for instance the Concluding Observations on the Sixth Periodic Report of Canada (CCPR/C/CAN/CO/6, 13 Aug. 2015) para 10 or the Concluding Observations on the Seventh Periodic Report of the United Kingdom of Great Britain and Northern Ireland (CCPR/C/GBR/CO/7, 17 Aug. 2015) para 24.

112 ECtHR, *Big Brother Watch v. United Kingdom* (n 91).

113 Ibid para 396.

114 Ibid para 422.

115 Ibid para 420.

in the *Schrems II* case adjudged by the CJEU in July 2020.[116] The invalidation of the EU-US adequacy decision '*Privacy Shield*' was justified by the blatant inadequacies of the US *FISA Act* with regard to the minimum requirements of the EU privacy regime. We believe that the EU standard of 'data adequacy/data equivalency', which requires any transfer of data to a third country to be subject to a level of data protection that is at least equivalent to its own,[117] should also apply to any assessment of the compliance of an intelligence-sharing mechanism with the right to privacy. Such a test of adequacy, equivalency, or appropriateness of the level of protection of data in a third country becomes more and more accepted among States and is enshrined, for instance, in the African Union Convention on Cyber Security and Personal Data Protection,[118] or the Interamerican *Updated Principles on Privacy and Protection of Personal Data.*[119] Yet, the applicability of that test to intelligence-sharing programmes remains to be seen.

In conclusion to this point, a true necessity undoubtedly exists to 'fill the gaps' of the international legal order concerning States' cooperation in intelligence-sharing. It seems, however, that no consensus can be found among States as to the applicability of the overarching principles to the general principle of cooperation. A similar finding may be drawn concerning the ability of States to undertake unilateral intelligence gathering measures in third countries.

2.2.2 Intelligence Gathering of Personal Data and the General Principle of Non-interference

The adverse effects of data processing in a digital borderless world were already identified in the early 1970s.[120] An interesting attempt at limiting the reach of intelligence practices can be found in the context of arms limitation negotiations between the United States and the Soviet Union. As noted

116 n 102.

117 Which does not mean 'identical'. Case C-311/18 (n 102) para 94.

118 African Union Convention on Cyber Security and Personal Data Protection (n 71) Article 14(6)(*a*).

119 Interamerican Juridical Committee, *Updated Principles on Privacy and Protection of Personal Data, with annotations* (n 95) Eleventh principle.

120 UN Commission on Human Rights, *Report on uses of electronics which might affect the rights of the person and the limits which should be placed on such uses in a democratic society* (E/CN.4/1142/add.2, 7 October 1974) para 4: 'One of the more recent but increasingly important developments in the field of electronics is what has been referred to as the 'marriage' of computers with communications. By this is meant, in particular, the combination of technologies which make it possible to obtain, in many cases almost immediately, information from a computer even though the person requesting it may be located in a different room, a different city, a different country or a different continent'.

by Chesterman,[121] the impossibility to reach an agreement on a verification regime such as on-site inspections resulted in the implied recognition of intelligence activities through the wording of 'national technical means of verification' in the Anti-Ballistic Missile Treaty (Article XII, § 1) and SALT 1 agreement (Article V, § 1) of 1972 which reads:

> For the purpose of providing assurance of compliance with the provisions of this Treaty, each Party shall use national technical means of verification at its disposal in a manner consistent with generally recognized principles of international law.

The scope of these 'generally recognised principles of international law' is unclear, to say the least. This disposition seems to acknowledge the consubstantial extraterritorial reach of intelligence gathering but does not allow conclusions to be drawn about any potential safeguards that such data processing should provide with regard to human rights.

In his enlightening contribution on State jurisdiction in the context of digital surveillance measures, Milan Tahraoui methodically distinguished the material ability of States to extend the reach of their surveillance powers outside of their territory, whether lawfully or not under international law ('*compétence-autorité*'), from the extraterritorial jurisdiction of State ('*compétence-juridiction*'), understood as the ability of international human rights obligations to bind States over their actions or omissions negatively affecting individuals rights outside from their territory.[122] The former remains largely accepted by States under an extensive lecture of the freedom of States deriving from the '*Lotus*' principle while the latter is tenaciously defended by the Human Rights Committee and the Human Rights office of the High Commissioner. In its General Comment No. 31 to the ICCPR, the Human Rights Committee firmly recalled how 'unconscionable' it would be that States deny the applicability of the ICCPR, under its Article 2, when exercising effective control over a situation subject to the jurisdiction of another State.[123] In the specific context of digital surveillance, several reports come together to the conclusion that Human rights law applies whenever a State exercises its power

121 S Chersterman, 'The Spy who Came in from the Cold War: Intelligence and International Law' (n 106) 1091.

122 M Tahraoui, 'Surveillance des flux de données : juridiction ou compétences de l'Etat, des notions à refonder' in M Audit, E Pataut (eds), *L'extraterritorialité* (Pedone, 2020) 41.

123 United Nations HRC, *General Comment No 31 – The Nature of the General Obligations Imposed on State Parties to the Covenant*, 2004, (CCPR/C/21/ Rev.1/Add1326).

or 'effective control' in relation to digital communication infrastructure, for example through direct tapping or penetration of communication infrastructure located outside the territory of that State.[124] Based on this premise, the High Commissioner for Human Rights strongly criticized the 'Five Eyes' countries (United States, Canada, United Kingdom, Australia, and New Zealand) for distinguishing among the human rights obligations owed to nationals or those within a State's territory, and non-nationals and those outside of it.[125] He reached this conclusion by interpreting Article 17 ICCPR in light of Article 26 guaranteeing to all persons the equal protection of the law. It is worth recalling that the United States has a longstanding position that the ICCPR only applies to individuals who are both within the territory of the State Party and within that State Party's jurisdiction.

The view of the Office of the High Commissioner for Human Rights perfectly reflects the objectivist dialectic of human rights, considering general principles of law as a reflection of *jus conscientiae*. Interestingly enough, UNGA resolutions are extremely quiet on this issue and merely 'includ[e]' extraterritorial surveillance in the list of concerns of their preambles but do not explicitly 'call upon' States to apply the overarching principles to extraterritorial intelligence gathering.[126] As far as the ECtHR is concerned, it has not condemned extraterritorial mechanisms of surveillance *per se*,[127] nor has it addressed the issue of distinguishing among internal and external communication for the purpose of mass surveillance, thus accepting such a distinction.[128] Finally, the Tallinn

124 OHCHR, *The Right to Privacy in the Digital Age* (A/HRC/27/37, 30 June 2014) para 34; Report of the Special Rapporteur on the Promotion and Protection of Human Rights and Fundamental Freedoms While Countering Terrorism, U.N. Doc. (A/69/397, 23 September 2014) para 62; Report of the UNHCR, *The right to privacy in the digital age* (A/HRC/39/29, 3 August 2018) para 12.

125 A/HRC/27/37 (n 11) paras 36–37.

126 See for instance the preamble of UNGA Resolution 75/176 of 16 December 2020.

127 *Weber and Saravia v. Germany*, App. no 54934/00, Decision on Admissibility (29 June 2006) para 88: 'The Court observes that the impugned provisions of the amended G 10 Act authorise the monitoring of international wireless telecommunications, that is, telecommunications which are not effected via fixed teléphone lines but, for example, via satellite or radio relay links, and the use of data thus obtained. Signals emitted from foreign countries are monitored by interception sites situated on German soil and the data collected are used in Germany. In the light of this, the Court finds that the applicants have failed to provide proof in the form of concordant inferences that the German authorities, by enacting and applying strategic monitoring measures, have acted in a manner which interfered with the territorial sovereignty of foreign States as protected in public international law'.

128 ECtHR, *Big Brother Watch v. United Kingdom* (n 91) paras 514–518.

Manual 2.0 'on the International Law Applicable to Cyber Operations'[129] does not consider that peacetime cyber espionage violates international law *per se* either, although noting that 'the method by which it is carried out might do so'.[130] Nevertheless, the drafters did not consider that an *opinio juris* suggested that States consider cyber-espionage 'as falling beyond the bounds of their international human rights law obligations concerning the right to privacy', thus suggesting that the overarching principles of privacy cannot be deemed to apply extraterritorially.[131]

Reconciling the law of jurisdiction with international human rights obligations is not only a matter of ethics but good sense: it answers to the necessities of the universal order of human rights.[132] The overarching general principles of law envisioned as part of domestic surveillance measures should not be undermined when it comes to foreign intelligence. As put by Alex Mills, '[j]urisdictional duties, even owed by states to each other, are part of the recognition that international law is also concerned with the relations between states and individuals'.[133] Yet it does not seem realistic to infer from the latter developments that a 'general consensus' exists among States on this matter. For the time being, a solution envisioned by scholars consists in the recourse to the notion of 'virtual control' as a means to circumvent the jurisdiction issue and apply international human rights obligations whenever a State exercises a 'virtual control' over an individual located in a foreign territory even though it does not exercise effective control over this territory.[134] Such a test could flourish where an appropriate reversal of the burden of proof benefits individuals who claim to be the victims of such control over their privacy.

•••

129 MN Schmitt (ed), *Tallinn Manual 2.0 on the International Law Applicable to Cyber Operations* (CUP, 2017).

130 Ibid rule 32, 168.

131 Ibid rule 34, 192–193.

132 A Mills, 'Rethinking Jurisdiction in International Law' (2014) *British Yearbook of International Law*, 212–213.

133 Ibid 213.

134 P Margulies, 'The NSA in the Global Perspective: Surveillance, Human Rights and International Counterterrorism', (2014) 82 Fordham Law Review 2139. See also, CMJ Ryngaert, NANM Van Eijk, 'International cooperation by (European) security and intelligence services: reviewing the creation of a joint database in light of data protection guarantees' (2019) 9:1 International Data Privacy Law, 67; A Peters, 'Privacy, Rechtsstaatlichkeit, and the Legal Limits on Extraterritorial Surveillance', in RA Miller (ed), *Privacy and Power: A Transatlantic Dialogue in the Shadow of the NSA-Affair* (CUP, 2017) 178–179.

Rethinking the legitimacy of international law can be done through a reexamination of the contemporary utility of general principles of law. This classic instrument of international law, enshrined in the necessities of the international order, may provide an appropriate solution for apprehending transnational, technical, and fast-evolving phenomena whose potentialities may fundamentally alter 'the tenets of democracy', in the General Assembly's words. Rather than seeking to devise multilateral treaty rules or following a quest for customary rules where they do not exist, it could be left to the general principles of law to ensure substantive coherence between sectoral rules, practices, and instruments, thus encouraging the progressive development of more specific and binding international standards. In this quest for substantive coherence, recognising that the overarching general principles of legality, necessity, and proportionality apply to digital surveillance measures would give its appropriate weight to the more 'refined' principles that can already be induced from a vast majority of state legislation and concordant soft-law initiatives such as the 'transparency of data processing', 'legitimacy of data processing' and 'data adequacy/equivalency test'. Keeping the whole set of recurring principles of data privacy protection in the realm of the indistinctive category of 'standards' proves to be, in our understanding, a misleading assessment of the value of data privacy principles.

CHAPTER 13

Environmental Security and Wealth: a Realist Perspective on Climate Change

Markus P. Beham

1 Introduction

'Climate' is a wide phenomenon, constituted by a variety of factors and affecting, in turn, every single aspect of our lives. The climate as such can hardly be made comprehensible in its entirety – in which the man-made contribution may naturally be portrayed as a mere fraction[1] – and negative developments are not immediately apparent as a direct result of climate change: from droughts, floods, storms, and other extreme weather events,[2] to loss in biodiversity and extinction of entire species,[3] to the submergence of entire islands.[4]

Past experience seems to suggest that certain phenomena such as greenhouse gas emissions and the ensuing Ozone depletion were less prone to scepticism than 'climate change' is today, instead being confronted by swift and effective action.[5] Whereas early environmental activism such as Rachel Carson's *Silent Spring*,[6] James Lovelock's 'Gaia hypothesis',[7] or the Club of

1 Cf. the definition contained in Article 1(2) the United Nations Framework Convention on Climate Change, according to which it 'means a change of climate which is attributed directly or indirectly to human activity that alters the composition of the global atmosphere and which is in addition to natural climate variability observed over comparable time periods'.

2 See United States Environment Protection Agency (EPA), Climate change Indicators: Weather and Climate <https://www.epa.gov/climate-indicators/weather-climate>.

3 See ES Brondizio, J Settele, S Díaz, and HT Ngo (eds), Global Assessment Report on Biodiversity and Ecosystem Services of the Intergovernmental Science-Policy Platform on Biodiversity and Ecosystem Services (IPBES Secretariat 2019).

4 Cf. the work of the ILA Committee on International Law and Sea Level Rise <https://www.ila-hq.org/index.php/committees> and of the ILC Study Group on Sea-Level rise in relation to international law <https://legal.un.org/ilc/guide/8_9.shtml>.

5 See NASA, '2019 Ozone Hole is the Smallest on Record Since Its Discovery' (21 October 2019) <https://www.nasa.gov/feature/goddard/2019/2019-ozone-hole-is-the-smallest-on-record-since-its-discovery>. On the underlying reasons see D Sprinz and T Vaahtoranta, 'The Interest-Based Explanation of International Environmental Policy' (1994) 48 International Organization 77, 104.

6 R Carson, *Silent Spring* (Houghton Mifflin 1962).

7 JE Lovelock, 'Gaia as seen through the atmosphere' (1972) 6/8 Atmospheric Environment 579.

 | DOI:10.1163/9789004508712_014

Rome[8] managed to create awareness of environmental issues to place them on the political agenda, environmental policy makers today seem less successful: an Ozone hole exists today, 'change' suggests the future.

This may also have to do with the lack in perception of climate change as a personal concern, since '[p]roblems that are immediate and proximate to people tend to elicit the most concern from citizens' with a discrepancy in the experience between individuals from developing and developed states.[9] Surveys appear to have shown that 'citizens in affluent democracies tend to think that the impacts of global warming will be geographically distant, affecting people in other countries but not necessarily themselves',[10] although there may be nuances between developed states such as between Europe and the US. Indirect effects of climate change such as public health and (climate) migration do not yet seem to have become a dominant issue within the debate.

Looking at the overall multilateral effort to push forward on regulating climate change and the environment, international environmental law appears to be in retreat. The 'First Global Report' on 'Environmental Rule of Law' compiled by UNEP emphasises 'a growing recognition that a considerable implementation gap has opened – in developed and developing nations alike – between the requirements of environmental laws and their implementation and enforcement'.[11] When it comes to environmental action, there is currently a sense of urgency paired with the frustration of being stuck in a quagmire of largely unsatisfactory regulatory attempts.

Regulation is a useful tool to combat climate change, but it may be necessary to change its trajectory. This contribution is an implementation of the ideas developed in a previous monograph by the present author which traces the interrelation between the formation of customary international law and international relations – or one might say the formation of a body of custom embedded in international relations.[12] Realism is offered as an explanatory model from which to empower the environmental agenda. As opposed to challenging sovereignty through multilateral idealism (albeit about real issues), ecopolitics might look for synergies between environmental protection and state interest to readjust the efforts to combat climate change through the law.

8 See DH Meadows, DL Meadows, J Randers, and WW Behrens III, *The Limits to Growth* (Potomac Associates 1972).

9 SB Pralle, 'Agenda-Setting and Climate Change' (2009) 18 Environmental Politics 781, 791.

10 ibid.

11 United Nations Environmental Programme, Environmental Rule of Law: First Global Report (2019) 1.

12 MP Beham, *State Interest and the Sources of International Law: Doctrine, Morality, and Non-Treaty Law* (Routledge 2018).

Instead, reframing environmental protection in realist terms as 'environmental security' and 'environmental wealth' carries potential for international regulation and the creation of transnational environmental law. So far, realism has been considered an explanatory model in opposition to international environmental regulation.[13] The present contribution starts from the assumption that its effectivity could indeed be bolstered by providing a different set of incentives – national security and economic wealth – for states to take action. Picking up from the conference theme 'building accord out of dissonance', realism is offered as an explanatory model from which to empower the environmental agenda. Duit, Feindt, and Meadowcroft, in proposing the 'environmental state' as a research agenda, wrote of 'greening Leviathan'.[14] This contribution suggests harnessing the powers of Leviathan itself for going green, to adjust environmental regulation to correspond with core state interests.[15]

Following (2.) a very brief portrayal of the notion of state interest as understood in the various schools of realism,[16] the contribution (3.) explores the idea of environmental interest to see in which areas sovereign interests and environmental protection coincide, highlighting some illustrative examples. It wraps up with (4.) a brief conclusion and outlook.

2 State Interest

What determines state actions? As Louis Henkin convincingly laid out in his seminal work *How Nations Behave*, states act according to carefully calculated

13 Or at least as a deficient model for dealing with the environment, see D Heffron, What do realists think about climate change?, Centre for Geopolitics & Security in Realism Studies (13 November 2015) <http://cgsrs.org/publications/30>; J Symons, 'Realist climate ethics: Promoting climate ambition within the Classical Realist tradition' (2019) 45/1 Review of International Studies 141.

14 A Duit, PH Feindt and J Meadowcroft, 'Greening Leviathan: The Rise of the Environmental State?' (2016) 25/1 Environmental Politics 1.

15 The ideas expressed in this contribution were first presented at the American Society of International Law (ASIL) Interest Group on International Environmental Law Conference 'States, Corporations and Commons: Dissonance and Accord' at the Aristotle University of Thessaloniki, Greece, on 11 September 2019. The conference proceedings are intended to be published in the Journal of Human Rights and Environment with the present author contributing a paper entitled 'Unfriendly Environmentally Friendly: A Realist Perspective on International Environmental Issues and Regulation'.

16 For an overview of these schools in the context of climate change see D Heffron, What do realists think about climate change?, Centre for Geopolitics & Security in Realism Studies (13 November 2015) <http://cgsrs.org/publications/30>.

interests and dependent upon the consequences of their conformity to or violation of international law.[17] The term 'interest' derives from the Latin *interesse*, which carries the meaning 'to differ' or 'to make a difference'. The expression 'state interest' – or 'national interest', as it is sometimes found in the literature – confers the idea that there must be a common set of factors that are important to the existence of the abstract entity of the state. In any school of realism, there are two principal considerations: first, national security, comprising the protection of statehood, territorial integrity, as well as sovereignty, and second, a functioning economy.

A number of structural arguments have been brought up against this view. For example, the need of states 'to include [NGOs] in their foreign policy analysis and respect their interests in the process of creating norms of international law' as a result of 'the power exercised by them through the use of media and similar means'.[18] However, these are means to an end:[19] The survival of states and, in this case, governments. These will likely set acts in the name of a state that aim at preventing civil unrest, cultivating a happy electorate,[20] attracting investment and highly skilled labour, securing development aid, gaining admission to an international organisation – the list goes on.[21] In the extreme, an authoritarian regime may ignore these considerations altogether. In addition, the NGOs in question would probably have to be of some size and reach to exert any such influence.

---

17 L Henkin, *How Nations Behave. Law and Foreign Policy* (2nd edn, Columbia University Press 1979). For a rational choice version of this approach see, prominently, JL Goldsmith and EA Posner, *The Limits of International Law* (Oxford University Press 2007). For a general overview of the various compliance theories see M Burgstaller, *Theories of Compliance With International Law* (Martinus Nijhoff 2004).

18 See G Hafner, 'Some Thoughts on the State-Oriented and Individual-Oriented Approaches in International Law' (2009) 14 Austrian Review of International and European Law 27, 35. See also AL Paulus and B Simma, 'The Responsibility of Individuals for Human Rights Abuses in Internal Conflicts: A Positivist View' (1999) 93/2 American Journal of International Law 302, 306; JJ Paust, 'The Complex Nature, Sources and Evidences of Customary Human Rights' (1995/1996) 25 Georgia Journal of International Law 147, 160–161.

19 See also P-H Imbert, 'L'Utilisation des Droits de l'Homme Dans les Relations Internationales' in Société Française pour le Droit International (ed), *Colloque de Strasbourg. La Protection des Droits de l'Homme et l'Évolution du Droit International* (Éditions Pedone 1998) 282, 283.

20 See on these two considerations *vis-à-vis* foreign policy interests J Frankel, *National Interest* (Macmillan 1970) 132.

21 See JL Goldsmith and EA Posner, *The Limits of International Law* (Oxford University Press 2005) 109–119.

Notwithstanding, the constitutionalist or Kantian argument still stands strong within international legal scholarship, spurred by Wolffian ideas of a *civitas maxima*.[22] Its moral superiority is, after all, compelling.[23] There is, of course, a certain impetus of morality determining action in the face of mass human rights violations or unrestrained warfare.[24] But this altruistic impulse seems often by itself too weak to spur any form of meaningful action.[25]

Equally, state interest is not a one-way street. Interests of other states must be taken into account at some level, in particular in a reality of international relations dominated by a universal international organisation that is the United Nations (UN).[26] Yet, this is simply another marketplace of ideas,[27] already identified and incorporated by structural realism to show how states achieve their principal interests.[28]

3 Environmental Interests

It immediately comes to attention when consulting international environmental law textbooks that they devote separate chapters and ample space to the different actors engaged in international environmental governance and regulation from international organisations to civil society.[29] One could draw the

22 See for such a Wolffian *civitas maxima* view of the international community MC Bassiouni, 'Advancing the Responsibility to Protect Through International Criminal Justice' in RH Cooper and JV Kohler (eds), *Responsibility to Protect. The Global Moral Compact for the 21st Century* (Palgrave Macmillan 2009) 31, 36–37.

23 See in this regard also A Somek, 'From the Rule of Law to the Constitutionalist Makeover: Changing European Conceptions of Public International Law' (2011) 18/4 Constellations 576, 578.

24 See HJ Morgenthau and KW Thompson, *Politics Among Nations. The Struggle for Power and Peace* (6th edn, Alfred A. Knopf 1985) 249–260; HJ Morgenthau, 'The Twilight of International Morality', (1948) 58/2 Ethics 79, 82.

25 See in this regard also M Walzer, 'The Moral Standing of States: A Response to Four Critics' (1980) 9/3 Philosophy and Public Affairs 209, 226–227.

26 See also the wording of Article 25 of the Articles on Responsibility of States for Internationally Wrongful Acts 2001.

27 Cf. MC Bassiouni, 'Revisiting the Architecture of Crimes Against Humanity. Almost a Century in the Making, with Gaps and Ambiguities Remaining – the Need for a Specialized Convention' in LN Sadat (ed), *Forging a Convention for Crimes Against Humanity* (Cambridge University Press 2011) 43, 43.

28 See KN Waltz, *Theory of International Politics* (Addison Wesley 1979).

29 See, for example, U Beyerlin and T Marauhn, *International Environmental Law* (Hart/CH Beck/Nomos 2011) 245–256; P Birnie, A Boyle, and C Redgwell, *International Law and the*

conclusion that the primary subject of international law – Leviathan – is not as dominant or involved as in other areas of law. Should international environmental lawyers not rely more strongly on states to pursue their goals?

A cursory look at the principles of environmental law – ranging from the 'no harm' rule to fair and equitable utilisation of shared resources, from permanent sovereignty over natural resources to the common heritage or concern of humankind – shows that scholarly consensus as to their customary status is strongest where there is an underlying reciprocal or individual interest in the norm.[30] States have been held to 'pursue policies that minimize adverse environmental effects on their own citizens and ecosystems' and where 'costs of compliance are relatively minor (which might explain why major emitters such as China would still agree to ratify the Paris Agreement which allows it to set its own pledges and targets.[31]

This would suggest that the above elaborations on state interest as a relevant – if not decisive – factor in the formation of law would also apply to the environment. The idea is not entirely novel. It has been recognised, after all, 'that key individuals (within government, for example) and important interest groups may be more concerned with the economic costs associated with climate change, for example, or its implications for national security'.[32] Sprinz and Vaahtoranta have proposed 'that a country's interests are defined by differences in ecological vulnerability and economic abatement costs'.[33]

Hence, realism may offer some sort of explanatory value in the formation of international environmental law. Already Daniel Bodansky used international environmental law as an example for which the explanatory model of realism

Environment (3rd edn, Oxford University Press 2009) 43–105; MA Drumbl, 'Actors and Law-Making in International Environmental Law', *Research Handbook on International Environmental Law* (Edward Elgar 2010) 3–14; P-M Dupuy and JE Viñuales, *International Environmental Law* (2nd edn, Cambridge University Press 2018) 32–38; A Epiney, 'Gegenstand, Entwicklung, Quellen und Akteure des internationalen Umweltrechts' in A Proelß (ed), *Internationales Umweltrecht* (De Gruyter 2017) 27–35; Jacqueline Peel and Philippe Sands, *Principles of International Environmental Law* (4th edn, Cambridge University Press 2018) 52–97.

30 See in U Beyerlin and T Marauhn, *International Environmental Law* (Hart/CH Beck/Nomos 2011) 283–286; MA Drumbl, 'Actors and Law-Making in International Environmental Law', *Research Handbook on International Environmental Law* (Edward Elgar 2010) 17; JE Viñuales, *International Environmental Law* (2nd edn, Cambridge University Press 2018) 39.

31 D Sprinz and T Vaahtoranta, 'The Interest-Based Explanation of International Environmental Policy' (1994) 48 International Organization 77, 78–79.

32 SB Pralle, 'Agenda-Setting and Climate Change' (2009) 18 Environmental Politics 781, 792.

33 D Sprinz and T Vaahtoranta, 'The Interest-Based Explanation of International Environmental Policy' (1994) 48 International Organization 77, 86.

produced different results than what mainstream accounts provided.[34] Many environmental threats made out throughout the previous decades and centuries touch upon national security and economic wealth, that is, ultimately, state survival. From Malthusian determinism,[35] to the Club of Rome's 'The Limits to Growth',[36] to Garrett Hardin's 'tragedy of the commons',[37] the sustainability of populations has been a central concern.

In turn, environmental regulation already corresponds with the core concerns of states under the realist model. As the 'First Global Report' on 'Environmental Rule of Law' compiled by UNEP points out, 'environmental rule of law is critical to human health and welfare',[38] issues that are connected through the underlying costs of social conflicts.[39] The report goes on to suggest engaging actors involved in 'green growth' and 'peace and security' in order to achieve an environmental rule of law.[40]

Domestic policy analysis has equally identified environmental protection as a concern of core state interests. For example, the US Fourth National Climate Assessment delivered in 2018 finds climate change first and foremost to pose 'growing challenges to human health and safety, quality of life, and the rate of economic growth'.[41]

Would it then not make sense to reframe environmental protection in realist terms? The ideas of 'environmental security' and 'environmental wealth' could serve as catalysts for future regulation and the facilitation of transnational environmental law.

3.1 *Environmental Security*

Wherever security interests are at stake, states are quick to regulate. Scholars have argued that environmental security concerns as a direct incentive for regulation might go as far back as the industrial revolution.[42] In a recent

34 D Bodansky, 'Legal Realism and Its Discontents' (2015) 28 Leiden Journal of International Law 267, 274–276.

35 Th Malthus, *An Essay on the Principle of Population* (J Johnson 1798).

36 D Meadows and others, *The Limits to Growth* (Universe Books 1972).

37 G Hardin, 'The Tragedy of the Commons' (1968) 162/3859 Science 1243.

38 United Nations Environmental Programme, Environmental Rule of Law: First Global Report (2019) 10.

39 See ibid 17–19.

40 See ibid 231–232.

41 US Global Change Research Program, Fourth National Climate Assessment. Impacts, Risks, and Adaptation in the United States, Volume II (Washington, DC, 2018) 25 <https://nca2018.globalchange.gov/downloads/NCA4_2018_FullReport.pdf>.

42 See P Hough, 'Back to the Future: Environmental Security in Nineteenth Century Global Politics' (2019) 4 Global Security: Health, Science and Policy 1, 1.

publication on environmental protection in antiquity, its earliest evidence seems to be the placing of Asclepius symbols near drinking wells to stop public urination and dumping of waste.[43] Tainting a community's means of sustenance constituted a serious threat to population survival – and, thereby, to an element of statehood. Regulating for its protection constitutes a core bargaining chip of the social contract.

The 1987 Brundtland Report stated that conflicts 'may derive also from environmental degradation and the pre-emption of development options'.[44] In 1994, Robert Kaplan expressly framed climate change as a security issue,[45] a notion most recently picked up by Anatol Lieven, holding that states 'will need to be convinced that the direct and indirect effects of climate change pose a serious threat to the security of their states and regimes'.[46] Christopher Penny went a step further, suggesting the UN Security Council take up the issue as a 'threat to international peace and security'.[47] But is has also been discussed whether concern with 'environmental security' may not predate these contributions by more than a century.[48]

How may states now be convinced to implement this notion of 'environmental security'? Jutta Brunnée finds the term to encompass two dimensions:

> On the one hand, in placing emphasis upon the environmental dimension, security means maintaining an ecological balance, at least to the extent necessary to sustain resource supplies and life-support systems. On the other hand, in emphasizing the dimension of security in the traditional sense, the term refers to the prevention and management of conflicts precipitated by environmental decline.[49]

---

43 See on this and other insights into the early history of 'environmental regulation' OD Cordovana and GF Chiai (eds), *Pollution and the Environment in Ancient Life and Thought* (Franz Steiner Verlag 2017).

44 United Nations, Report of the World Commission on Environment and Development: Our Common Future, 1987, Chapter 11, para 37.

45 See RD Kaplan, 'The Coming Anarchy. How Scarcity, Crime, Overpopulation, Tribalism, and Disease are Rapidly Destroying the Social Fabric of our Planet' The Atlantic (February 1994).

46 A Lieven, 'Climate Change and the State: A Case for Environmental Realism' (2020) 62 Survival 7, 21.

47 CK Penny, 'Greening the Security Council: Climate Change as an Emerging "Threat to International Peace and Security"' (2007) 7 International Environmental Agreements: Politics, Law and Economics 35.

48 See P Hough, 'Back to the future: environmental security in nineteenth century global politics' (2019) 4/1 Global Security: Health, Science and Policy 1.

49 J Brunnée, 'Environmental Security in the Twenty-First Century: New Momentum for the Development of International Environmental Law?' (1994) 18 Fordham International Law Journal 1742, 1742.

Although some realist scholars have held that environmental interests are not sufficient in and as of themselves to constitute security interests,[50] states have already started to frame environmental threats as security concerns since at least the 1990s: The 1995 US National Security Strategy pointed out that '[l]arge scale environmental degradation, exacerbated by rapid population growth, threatens to undermine political stability in many countries and regions'[51] and that environmental degradation, natural resource depletion, rapid population growth and refugee flows also have security implications for both present and long term American policy'.[52] It added that 'an emerging class of transnational environmental issues are increasingly affecting international stability and consequently will present new challenges to U.S. strategy'.[53]

Already in 1996, the US Environmental Protection Agency (EPA) signed a memorandum of understanding with the Department of Defense and the Department of Energy to cooperate on environmental security challenges.[54] In 1999, the EPA issued a report stating that among US national security concerns were now also 'environmental mismanagement, natural resource depletion, overpopulation, and the environmental consequences of the Cold War'.[55] The report goes on to specify examples of threats to US security interests, '[*t*]*he Chernobyl nuclear power plant explosion* and the tragic health effects that followed' and '[*t*]*he destruction of the forests of Haiti and erosion of agricultural topsoil,* contributing to untenable economic and living conditions and a flood of refugees fleeing to the United States'.[56] In addition, the report includes additional examples from the '*destruction of much of the Aral Sea and its ecosystem*'

50 See JJ Mearsheimer, *The Tragedy of Great Power Politics* (WW Norton & Compnany 2001) 371–372.

51 President WJ Clinton, A National Security Strategy of Engagement and Enlargement, February 1995, 1.

52 President WJ Clinton, A National Security Strategy of Engagement and Enlargement, February 1995, 1.

53 President WJ Clinton, A National Security Strategy of Engagement and Enlargement, February 1995, 1.

54 EPA, Environmental Security. Strengthening National Security Through Environmental Protection, September 1999, 2 <https://nepis.epa.gov/Exe/ZyPDF.cgi/91018N4S.PDF?Dockey=91018N4S.PDF>.

55 EPA, Environmental Security. Strengthening National Security Through Environmental Protection, September 1999, 1 <https://nepis.epa.gov/Exe/ZyPDF.cgi/91018N4S.PDF?Dockey=91018N4S.PDF>.

56 EPA, Environmental Security. Strengthening National Security Through Environmental Protection, September 1999, 1 <https://nepis.epa.gov/Exe/ZyPDF.cgi/91018N4S.PDF?Dockey=91018N4S.PDF>.

in Central Asia to *'forest fires in Indonesia'*.[57] The underlying security concerns are public health and (climate) migration.

In 2008, the Deputy Director of National Intelligence for Analysis and Chairman of the National Intelligence Council of the US, Thomas Fingar, delivered a 'National Intelligence Assessment on the National Security Implications of Global Climate Change to 2030' to the House Permanent Select Committee on Intelligence and the House Select Committee on Energy Independence and Global Warming stating that 'the most significant impact for the United States will be indirect and result from climate-driven effects on many other countries and their potential to seriously affect US national security interests',[58] particularly through 'growing immigration pressures'[59] and the necessity to take a leadership role in the international community.[60] While he adds that 'climate change alone is unlikely to trigger state failure in any state out to 2030', it 'will worsen existing problems – such as poverty, social tensions, environmental degradation, ineffectual leadership, and weak political institutions'.[61] Even more, it 'could threaten domestic stability in some states, potentially contributing to intra- or, less likely, interstate conflict, particularly over access to increasingly scarce water resources'.[62]

---

57 EPA, Environmental Security. Strengthening National Security Through Environmental Protection, September 1999, 1 <https://nepis.epa.gov/Exe/ZyPDF.cgi/91018N4S.PDF?Dockey=91018N4S.PDF>.

58 House Permanent Select Committee on Intelligence / House Select Committee on Energy Independence and Global Warming, National Intelligence Assessment on the National Security Implications of Global Climate Change to 2030, 25 June 2008, 4 <https://fas.org/irp/congress/2008_hr/062508fingar.pdf>.

59 House Permanent Select Committee on Intelligence / House Select Committee on Energy Independence and Global Warming, National Intelligence Assessment on the National Security Implications of Global Climate Change to 2030, 25 June 2008, 16 <https://fas.org/irp/congress/2008_hr/062508fingar.pdf>.

60 See House Permanent Select Committee on Intelligence / House Select Committee on Energy Independence and Global Warming, National Intelligence Assessment on the National Security Implications of Global Climate Change to 2030, 25 June 2008, 16–17 <https://fas.org/irp/congress/2008_hr/062508fingar.pdf>.

61 House Permanent Select Committee on Intelligence / House Select Committee on Energy Independence and Global Warming, National Intelligence Assessment on the National Security Implications of Global Climate Change to 2030, 25 June 2008, 4–5 <https://fas.org/irp/congress/2008_hr/062508fingar.pdf>.

62 House Permanent Select Committee on Intelligence / House Select Committee on Energy Independence and Global Warming, National Intelligence Assessment on the National Security Implications of Global Climate Change to 2030, 25 June 2008, 5 <https://fas.org/irp/congress/2008_hr/062508fingar.pdf>.

The effects of climate change range from desertification, to natural disasters, particularly severe weather events, and sea-level rise, all of which are detrimental to health and safety, trigger migratory movements, and, in the extreme, cause conflict scenarios.

For the states concerned, sea-level rise poses a threat to one of the constitutive elements of the state itself. At the same time, sea-level rise induced migration affects the entire international community, particularly the industrialised world. At least the states specially affected will take an interest in fighting for survival. When the International Law Commission (ILC) discussed including the topic in its programme of work, only four states[63] opposed and the US 'expressed certain reservations'.[64]

Aside the pertinent issue of climate change, there are many more areas of environmental protection that correspond with security interests, ranging from the prevention of detrimental pollution to environmental terrorism. This is reflected in many domestic safety provisions, from the necessity of administrative permits to the regulation of hazardous material or specialised criminal provisions (or prohibitions under international humanitarian law even).[65]

Protecting energy plants or resource storage facilities from water cisterns to gas storage from risk means applying the highest industry standards. This brings a possible reduction of negative effects even beyond the more extreme threats.

3.2 *Environmental Wealth*

It has been observed that 'economic problems often move environmental problems and solutions down the list of priorities'.[66] Yet environmental protection easily offers itself to be reframed in terms of cost-benefit analysis and economic gain. It is rather the case that 'environmental protection and international economic law may entertain both synergistic and conflicting relations, depending on the specific issue at stake and the context where it arises'.[67] As a 2019 *New York Times* article argued: 'In the 21st century, environmental policy

63 Cyprus, Czech Republic, Greece, and Slovakia.

64 See International Law Commission, Sea-level rise in relation to international law. First issues paper by B Aurescu and N Oral, Co-Chairs of the Study Group on sea-level rise in relation to international law, 28 February 2020, A/CN.4/740, 5.

65 Such as the Convention on the Prohibition of Military or Any Other Hostile Use of Environmental Modification Techniques ('ENMOD' Convention), 10 December 1976, or Articles 35 and 55 of Additional Protocol I to the Geneva Conventions of 1949.

66 SB Pralle, 'Agenda-Setting and Climate Change' (2009) 18 Environmental Politics 781, 788.

67 P-M Dupuy and JE Viñuales, *International Environmental Law* (2nd edn, Cambridge University Press 2018) 452.

is economic policy'.[68] After all, the expected costs of climate change will be colossal.[69] In fact, there are multiple approaches arguing for a symbiosis of environment and economy.[70] The explanatory model of realism may help conceptualise this transition towards an integrated perception of both areas of politics and, in turn, regulation.

From the attraction of innovation to the value of sustainable business conduct, even the short- to mid-term benefits of an environmentally friendly economy easily correspond with the pull of states towards economic growth. In turn, the costs of inaction may become unbearably high in the long run. The UN Secretary General, in his 2018 remarks on Climate Change pointed out that the international community is 'experiencing huge economic losses due to climate change'.[71]

As early as the 19th century, states brought about environmental regulation in international treaties in order to secure their economic interests, be it through the regulation of fisheries[72] or the – albeit largely unsuccessful – international effort to fight the spread of grape phylloxera.[73] Of course, the underlying interests were trade related, not environmental: 'Internationally-traded foods and wine were at stake in ratifying the treaties rather than the flora and fauna themselves'.[74]

Oftentimes, environmental protection was brought about as an unintended consequence. New institutions created for the furtherance of commerce such

68 J Britton-Purdy, 'The Green New Deal Is What Realistic Environmental Policy Looks Like' *New York Times* (14 February 2019) <https://www.nytimes.com/2019/02/14/opinion/green-new-deal-ocasio-cortez-.html>.

69 See, with regard to the US, for example, S Hsiang, R Kopp, A Jina, J Rising, M Delgado, S Mohan, DJ Rasmussen, R Muir-Wood, P Wilson, M Oppenheimer, K Larsen, and T Houser, 'Estimating economic damage from climate change in the United States' (2017) 356/6345 Science 1362.

70 See, *e.g.*, P Huber, *Hard Green. Saving The Environment From The Environmentalists. A Conservative Manifesto* (Basic Books 1999); D Roodman, *The Natural Wealth of Nations. Harnessing the Market and the Environment* (Routledge 1999).

71 UN, Secretary-General's remarks on Climate Change, 10 September 2018 <https://www.un.org/sg/en/content/sg/statement/2018-09-10/secretary-generals-remarks-climate-change-delivered>.

72 See, for one of the earliest examples, the Treaty concerning the Jan Mayen Seal Fishery, 28 October 1876.

73 See the Internationale Convention vom 3. November 1881 betreffend die Reblaus, Berne, 3 November 1881, RGBl. 105/1882.

74 P Hough, 'Back to the Future: Environmental Security in Nineteenth Century Global Politics' (2019) 4 Global Security: Health, Science and Policy 1, 5.

as the 1815 Rhine Commission[75] ultimately led to conservational side-effects by prohibiting the dumping of waste for navigational purposes.[76]

In international economic law, environmental regulation today is piggybacked onto lending, trade and investment agreements that are aimed at standard setting but may also create competitive advantages for individual states that can boast advanced technology and innovation.

The World Bank has long applied environmental criteria through its environmental and social policies,[77] first published in consolidated form in 1984 as Operational Manual Statement (OMS) No. 2.36, now replaced by Operational Statement (OP)[78] and Bank Procedure (BP) 4.01.[79] Today, these are implemented primarily through its Safeguard Policies[80] and the Environmental and Social Framework (ESF).[81]

Alongside the World Bank, the Global Environmental Facility (GEF) was established in the context of the 1992 Rio Earth Summit as a project financer to incentivise environmental protection.[82] It now also functions as 'financial mechanism' to the Convention on Biological Diversity (CBD), the United Nations Framework Convention on Climate Change (UNFCCC), the Stockholm Convention on Persistent Organic Pollutants (POPs), the UN Convention to Combat Desertification (UNCCD), and the Minamata Convention on Mercury.

The European Union, alongside its advanced internal environmental standards,[83] in its newer free trade agreements (FTAs) includes chapters on environmental protection.[84] While critics often hold that these pose empty threats,

75 Central Commission for the Navigation of the Rhine <https://www.ccr-zkr.org/>.

76 See the Convention révisée pour la Navigation du Rhin, 17 October 1868 ('Mannheim Convention'). See on this also P Hough, 'Back to the Future: Environmental Security in Nineteenth Century Global Politics' (2019) 4 Global Security: Health, Science and Policy 1, 7.

77 See World Bank, Environmental and Social Policies <https://projects.worldbank.org/en/projects-operations/environmental-and-social-policies>.

78 OP 4.01 – Environmental Assessment, January 1999.

79 BP 4.01 – Environmental Assessment, January 1999.

80 See World Bank, Environmental and Social Policies, The Environmental and Social Safeguard Policies <https://projects.worldbank.org/en/projects-operations/environmental-and-social-policies#safeguards>.

81 See World Bank, Environmental and Social Framework <https://www.worldbank.org/en/projects-operations/environmental-and-social-framework>.

82 Global Environment Facility <https://www.thegef.org/>.

83 See Articles 11 and 191–193 of the Treaty on the Functioning of the European Union (TFEU).

84 See European Commission, Sustainable Development <https://ec.europa.eu/trade/policy/policy-making/sustainable-development/> listing FTAs with the following regions or

the EU has shown in the case of the EU-Korea FTA that it is prepared to move forward in cases concerning labour protection.[85] At the end of 2019, the EU and Korea completed the procedure for selecting the members of the panel that will examine the ongoing dispute on workers' rights in the Republic of Korea.[86]

Increasingly, environmental concerns have been introduced into international investment agreements.[87] Article 19 of the Energy Charter Treaty requires that states 'strive to minimise in an economically efficient manner harmful Environmental Impacts occurring either within or outside its Area from all operations within the Energy Cycle in its Area, taking proper account of safety' and that they 'strive to take precautionary measures'.[88]

In the on-going debate about international investment law, the 'right to regulate' encompasses the idea of environmental measures, allowing states to an extent to identify and utilise environmental regulation as a mechanism to impose sovereignty.[89] Newer Model BITs include carve-outs for 'legitimate policy objectives such as the protection of public health, safety, environment, public morals, labour rights, animal welfare, social or consumer protection'.[90]

And there are areas that combine both security and wealth. A massive burden on the sovereign equality of states is the dependency on certain fossil

states: Canada; Central America; Colombia, Peru, and Ecuador; Georgia; Japan; Mercosur; Mexico; Moldova; Singapore; South Korea; Ukraine; Vietnam.

85 See EU-Korea FTA, Chapter 13. On 17 December 2018, the EU requested consultations under Article 13.14 of the EU-Korea FTA to discuss Korean measures, including the Korean Trade Union Act. Since these proved unsuccessful, in July 2019, the EU requested dispute settlement through a panel of independent experts. Following delays due to the Covid-19 pandemic, a virtual hearing was held in early October 2020 and the panel is expected to issue a report including recommendations shortly.

86 See European Commission, EU-Korea dispute settlement over workers' rights in Korea enters next stage, 19 December 2019 <https://trade.ec.europa.eu/doclib/press/index.cfm?id=2095>.

87 See 'Environmental Concerns in International Investment Agreements: A Survey', vol 2011/01 (2011) OECD Working Papers on International Investment 2011/01 <https://www.oecd-ilibrary.org/finance-and-investment/environmental-concerns-in-international-investment-agreements_5kg9mq7scrjh-en> accessed 2 October 2020. See on this also P-M Dupuy and JE Viñuales, *International Environmental Law* (2nd edn, Cambridge University Press 2018) 469.

88 Article 19 of the Energy Charter Treaty.

89 Cf. International Institute for Sustainable Development, A Sustainability Toolkit for Trade Negotiators: Trade and investment as vehicles for achieving the 2030 Sustainable Development Agenda <https://www.iisd.org/toolkits/sustainability-toolkit-for-trade-negotiators/5-investment-provisions/5-4-safeguarding-policy-space/5-4-1-right-to-regulate/>.

90 Article 2(2) Netherlands Model BIT (2019).

fuels. Reducing energy dependency may serve both security and economic goals. Geostrategic interests are still interwoven with the appetite for energy. The US sets the goal of 'energy dominance' but still includes coal, natural gas, and petroleum' among the mix.[91]

Energy autarky in an age of Trump could just as easily have been built on renewables or other alternatives to coal. Sarah Light has pointed to the role of the military in developing the means to saddle over to renewable energy.[92] After all, innovation is an essential tool to secure future economic success. In addition, survey evidence appears to suggest that dependency on foreign oil is perceived as a national security threat by the population.[93]

4 Conclusion and Outlook

The conference theme "Rethinking the Legitimacy of Public International Law: Democracy, Digitalization and Climate Change as Challenges for the Traditional Concept of Sovereignty?' frames sovereignty as perhaps standing in the way of climate change action. This contribution has attempted to show how the two might, in fact, align.

In a system that largely seeks to coordinate between different sovereign entities, reciprocity may serve as a catalyst for more effective regulation.[94] Without the luxury of a central legislator or a compulsory judicial mechanism, selfish-interests could serve as the compliance-pull for effective environmental protection stood firmly on the pillars of core state interest.

A population is dependent on continuity with 'future generations' constituting one of the core elements of statehood. Protecting their means of sustenance, both at the basic level of security and economically will be of the essence for state survival. As opposed to the Sisyphean task of challenging sovereignty through multilateral idealism, ecopolitics should look for synergies between environmental protection and state interest to reframe environmental issues

---

91 See President DJ Trump, National Security Strategy of the United States of America, December 2017, 22.

92 SE Light, 'Valuing National Security. Climate Change, the Military, and Society' (2014) 61 UCLA Law Review 1772, 1775; SE Light, 'The Military-Environmental Complex' (2014) 55 Boston College Law Review 879, 884.

93 SB Pralle, 'Agenda-Setting and Climate Change' (2009) 18/5 Environmental Politics 781, 793–794.

94 See B Simma, *Das Reziprozitätselement in der Entstehung des Völkergewohnheitsrechts* (Wilhelm Fink 1970).

and their regulation. Climate change need not suffer the 'tragedy of the commons' if perceived both as a security and an economic concern.

Of course, there are issues that the explanatory model of realism will not directly address or solve, from the willingness of certain states to go beyond the regulatory baselines to situations of diffuse gains. As the recent documentary *They Say It Can't be Done* argues, health and safety regulation, while necessary, serves as an entry-barrier for innovation.[95] Bill Gates in his bestseller *How to Avoid a Climate Disaster*, with an eye to the US, emphasised the issue of outdated regulatory frameworks.[96] All of this, in turn, frustrates quick solutions to environmental problems. Realism might only offer the argument that short-term economic benefits lobbied and provided for by large-scale corporations are outweighed by the threats national security and economic wealth posed by long-term inaction.

In light of the current inertia in environmental protection at the international level – with further study of the correspondence between state interests and goals of environmental protection necessary – a realist explanatory model is still a good bet to lend the reins to harness Leviathan: there is both room for 'environmental security' and 'environmental wealth'.

95 See <https://www.theysayitcantbedone.com/>.

96 See B Gates, *How to Avoid a Climate Disaster. The Solutions We Have and the Breakthroughs We Need* (Allen Lane 2021) 48–49.

CHAPTER 14

(Re-)Introducing Finiteness to Sovereignty

A New Way of Shaping the Law on Climate Change?

Kevin Grimmeiß

1 Finiteness as a Motivator for Human Behaviour

Finiteness, the fact that things come to an end, is a strong motivator for human behaviour. According to the commodity theory of social psychology, a commodity – understood as a useful thing, not necessarily a material object – will be valued to the extent that it is unavailable.[1] This phenomenon is *inter alia* exploited in marketing, where suggestions of scarcity aim at triggering purchase intentions.[2] Online booking platforms which expressly indicate the supposedly dwindling number of available hotel rooms and artificially limited supplies for highly-priced smartphones testify to this fact.

A lack of motivation on behalf of peoples and governments is also what climate activists lament in view of the increasing urgency of action to combat climate change.[3] Public international law could offer the framework for a coordinated worldwide effort in this field. But recent evidence suggests that instruments such as the United Nations Framework Convention on Climate Change[4] fail to produce the necessary state compliance.[5] At the same time, world leaders opposing global action to mitigate climate change have cited the public international law notion of state sovereignty to justify their reluctance, with U.S. President Trump referring to

1 T Brock/L Brannon, 'Liberalization of Commodity Theory' (1992) 13 Basic and Applied Social Psychology 135, 136.

2 M Eisend, 'Explaining The Impact Of Scarcity Appeals In Advertising: The Mediating Role of Perceptions of Susceptibility' (2008) 37/3 Journal of Advertising 33, 36.

3 A Markman, 'Why People Aren't Motivated to Address Climate Change' (*Harvard Business Review*, 11 October 2018) <https://hbr.org/2018/10/why-people-arent-motivated-to-address-climate-change> accessed 8 April 2021.

4 (adopted 9 May 1992, entered into force 21 March 1994) 1771 UNTS 107 (UNFCCC).

5 UNFCCC Secretariat, 'Nationally determined contributions under the Paris Agreement' (26 February 2021) <https://unfccc.int/sites/default/files/resource/cma2021_02E.pdf> accessed 27 April 2021.

 | DOI:10.1163/9789004508712_015

his withdrawal from the Paris Agreement[6] as a "reassertion of America's sovereignty".[7]

The present article will examine whether sovereignty provides a sound argument in this context. It will begin by showing that sovereignty has, since its inception, encompassed a perspective of finiteness and loss over time. Arguing that the risks of unimpeded climate change can be viewed as comparable limits today, the article will demonstrate that sovereignty and the natural conditions for life that lie at its foundation should, as a consequence, be regarded as a shared resource not attributed to one state or another. It will go on to discuss possible approaches to deal with this situation by drawing conclusions from tragedy of the commons situations. The analysis will show that regional cooperation is a viable option to handle the inherent finiteness of sovereignty and its consequences.

2 Historical Perspectives on Limits to Sovereignty

Historically speaking, the concept of sovereignty as shaped by *Bodin* and *Hobbes* was one of absolute and ultimate authority within a territory. Both scholars believed that the sovereign enjoyed all-encompassing powers and was not bound by his own laws, but only by the law of nature.[8] Today, in contrast, sovereignty is limited in multiple ways: External sovereignty towards other states is limited by various binding rules of public international law, such as the principle of non-intervention or the prohibition of the use of force. In their internal dealings, states must namely respect the human rights of their population, which impose further restrictions on their freedom to act.

Still, what governments and scholars alike seem to focus on in this context are material restrictions of sovereignty, prohibitions of specific actions. Exceeding these limits will entail the consequences prescribed by the law, such as reprisals or liability. Yet, sovereignty can also be subject to a different kind of boundary, one that sets temporal limits on sovereignty and its exercise. The limitations stemming from such circumstances are of a different character than the aforementioned ones. Exceeding them will not merely result in legal consequences that leave the substance of sovereignty untouched, but will lead to a complete or partial loss of sovereignty.

---

6 (adopted 12 December 2015, entered into force 4 November 2016) 55 ILM 740.

7 I R Pavone, 'The Paris Agreement and the Trump administration: Road to nowhere?' (2018) 11 Journal of International Studies 34.

8 S Besson, 'Sovereignty' in A Peters (ed), *Max Planck Encyclopedia of Public International Law online* (Oxford University Press 2021), para 15 et seqq.

Ideas of this kind have been part of the notion of sovereignty for a long time. From a theoretical perspective, *Bodin* had already incorporated a possibility of loss into his concept of sovereignty. In addition, on a more practical level, certain international legal phenomena have hinted at the finiteness of sovereignty in the course of the centuries.

2.1 Bodin*'s Perception of Finiteness in Sovereignty*

When *Bodin* defined sovereignty as *"puissance absolue et perpétuelle"*[9] in his *Six Livres de la République*, an understanding that still forms the basis of the modern day notion of sovereignty, he went on saying:

> La souveraineté donnée à un Prince sous charges et conditions, n'est pas proprement souveraineté, ni puissance absolue, si ce n'est que les conditions apposées en la création du Prince, soient de la Loi de Dieu ou de nature.[10]

There are two noteworthy statements in this passage with regard to the research question discussed in the present article. First, it should not go unnoticed that *Bodin* speaks of the creation of a prince, thereby referring not to a moral or legal entity, but rather to a natural person acting as sovereign. This illustrates that, at the time, sovereign and sovereignty were not yet perceived as separate concepts,[11] a finding that must be borne in mind when assessing finiteness-related phenomena of the era. Second, *Bodin* did not find restrictions or limitations on sovereignty to be incompatible with sovereignty altogether. While conceding that they could not typically be brought in line with the requirement of absolute and perpetual power and stressing that a ruler was, therefore, neither bound by his own laws nor by the laws of the land,[12] he included one important exception: that of divine law.

His statement was in line with contemporary legal thinking that saw the ruler as connected to God, from whom he derived his legitimacy. A sovereign violating this special bond by failing to comply with his duties under the law of nature would forfeit his divine right to rule and could accordingly be deposed,

9 J Bodin, *Les Six Livres de la République* (Jacques du Puys 1576), 125.

10 Ibid, 129.

11 Cf S Besson, 'Sovereignty' in A Peters (ed), *Max Planck Encyclopedia of Public International Law online* (Oxford University Press 2021), para 16.

12 In the Latin version *De Republica Libri Sex* (Jacques du Puys 1586), 78, *Bodin* accordingly states: *"Majestas est summa in cives ac subditos legibusque soluta potestas."*

albeit not by the people (to whom he owed no allegiance), but only by God.[13] The Popes, acting as Christ's vicars on earth, claimed this authority for themselves, with Pope *Gregory VII* famously declaring *"quod illi liceat imperatores deponere"* in his *Dictatus Papae* of 1075.

Feudal law contained a comparable notion. Here, too, a special bond of loyalty lay at the basis of a potential loss of power, not between a king and his God, but between a liege and his vassal. Under the feudal system, vassals were subject to numerous duties via-à-vis their feudal lords. These encompassed, *inter alia*, a duty to provide counsel, to render services or to provide soldiers and weapons.[14] Failure to comply with these obligations could entitle the seigneur to revoke a fiefdom granted. In addition, feuds automatically reverted to liege lords in cases where a liege man had not produced any eligible heirs. Against this background, feudal practice was conscious of the fact that a vassal's authority might lapse at some point in time.

Fiefdoms did not legally come with sovereignty as we know it today, even though, in the Holy Roman Empire for example, the king's rights of oversight would erode in the course of the centuries, thereby gradually giving way to the evolution of supreme authority by the former vassal in his territory. In any case, fiefdoms were always characterized by some sort of shared exercise of power, in a sense that the vassal took part in the administration of a king's rights over his lands. It is in this context that feudal law mirrored the perspective of loss in the exercise of authority over a territory that already featured prominently in *Bodin*'s notion of sovereignty.

2.2 *International Practice Alluding to the Time Limits of Sovereignty*

This is not to say, however, that time limits to sovereignty and the exercise thereof are a merely medieval phenomenon. In fact, another prominent example of temporal restrictions on jurisdiction had its heyday only in the late 19th and early 20th century: During these years, (colonial) powers exercised pressure on other countries, namely in East Asia and Africa, to grant them leases. By such international agreements, jurisdiction over a specific territory – typically of minor extent – was transferred to the lessee, but the lessor would retain sovereignty.[15] Yet, in general, no or very few rights could be deduced

13 C Barrett, 'Divine Right of Kings' in G W Brown, I McLean and A McMillan (eds), *A Concise Oxford Dictionary of Politics and International Relations* (4th edn, Oxford University Press 2018).

14 Cf for the following 'Vassal' (Encyclopedia Britannica, 2019) <https://www.britannica.com/topic/vassal> accessed 10 April 2021.

15 O Dörr, 'Cession' in A Peters (ed), *Max Planck Encyclopedia of Public International Law online* (Oxford University Press 2021), para 3.

from the lessor's position, which made the sovereignty in question resemble a *nudum ius*.[16]

Certain leases have been granted in perpetuity, as is the case with the Guantanamo Bay area leased from Cuba by the United States.[17] The same was true for the initial lease of the Canal Zone that Panama granted the United States under the Hay-Buneau-Varilla Treaty,[18] even though this lease was changed into a temporary one in 1977.[19] The latter variant was more typical. A famous case is that of Hong Kong, of which China had ceded one part to Great Britain and leased another to it (the so-called New Territories). The lease was for 99 years and expired in 1997, upon which all of Hong Kong was returned to China.[20] Leases remain relevant in international politics today, in particular with regard to military operations. Apart from the example of Guantanamo Bay given above, Russia, for instance, had leased the naval base of its black sea fleet in Sevastopol from Ukraine prior to the annexation of Crimea.[21]

Even though such temporary international leases formally left the question of sovereignty untouched, they still altered the effects of title in a most profound manner: In practice, the sovereign would more often than not be stripped of all his rights and competences in the area, being restrained to a merely formal position without real consequences. The quasi sovereign position of the lessee that corresponded with this was, however, subject to a contractually imposed time limit. Both parties shared the understanding that the jurisdiction of the lessee was ultimately of a transitional nature, which is another example of time limits in the context of sovereignty and jurisdiction.

---

16 M J Strauss, 'Territorial Leases' in A Nollkaemper and I Plakokefalos (eds), *The Practice of Shared Responsibility in International Law* (Cambridge University Press 2017), 65 et seqq.; Y Ronen, 'Territory, Lease' in A Peters (ed), *Max Planck Encyclopedia of Public International Law online* (Oxford University Press 2021), para 4.

17 Art 3 Treaty of Relations between the United States of America and the Republic of Cuba (signed 29 May 1934) USTS 866.

18 Art 3 Convention for the Construction of a Ship Canal between the United States of America and the Republic of Panama (signed 18 November 1903) USTS 431.

19 Art 2(2) Panama Canal Treaty between the United States of America and the Republic of Panama (signed 7 September 1977) 1280 UNTS 4.

20 Convention between the United Kingdom and China, Respecting an Extension of Hong Kong Territory (signed 9 June 1898).

21 I Watson and M Tkachenko, 'Russia, Ukraine agree on naval-base-for-gas deal' (*CNN*, 21 April 2010) <http://edition.cnn.com/2010/WORLD/europe/04/21/russia.ukraine/index.html?hpt=T2> accessed 13 April 2021.

2.3 *Moribund Title to Colonial Possessions*

Even more recently, the question of finiteness in sovereignty has arisen against the background of decolonization. The relevant question here is whether post-1945 legal understanding had altered colonial title to territory in a way that made it subject to expiration, namely as a result of the right to self-determination of peoples. Said right is enshrined in Art 1(2) and Art 55 Charter of the United Nations,[22] but the reference most-cited when it comes to colonial title is the fifth principle of the Friendly Relations Declaration,[23] which stipulates:

> The territory of a colony or other Non-Self-Governing Territory has, under the Charter, a status separate and distinct from the territory of the State administering it; and such separate and distinct status under the Charter shall exist until the people of the colony or Non-Self-Governing Territory have exercised their right of self-determination in accordance with the Charter, and particularly its purposes and principles.[24]

This "separate and distinct" status under public international law has prompted some legal scholars to altogether deny the territorial sovereignty of the colonial power in a non-self-governing territory.[25] The fifth principle cannot, however, be understood without a closer reading of Art 73 and 74 UN Charter, to which it expressly refers when postulating the "separate and distinct" status. Under said two articles, states administering non-self-governing territories accept as a sacred trust the obligation to promote the well-being of the inhabitants of these territories and must, to this end, *inter alia* develop self-government, take due account of the political aspirations of the peoples concerned and assist them in the development of free political institutions. Yet, these duties are – with the exception of a reporting duty in Art 73(d) UN Charter – formulated in a rather weak manner and contain several caveats. In particular, the obligation relating to self-government merely requests the political interests of the colonial people be "taken into account" and calls for

22 (adopted 26 June 1945, entered into force 24 October 1945) 1 UNTS 16 (UN Charter).

23 Declaration on Principles of International Law Concerning Friendly Relations and Co-operation among States in Accordance with the Charter of the United Nations, Annex to A/RES/25/2625 (24 October 1970).

24 Ibid, principle 5 para 6.

25 T M Franck, R Higgins, A Pellet, M N Shaw and C Tomuschat, 'The Territorial Integrity of Québec in the Event of the Attainment of Sovereignty' in A Bayefsky (ed), *Self-determination in International Law: Quebec and Lessons Learned* (Brill 2000), 282 et seq; A Pavković 'Introduction' in A Pavković and P Radan (eds), *On the Way to Statehood* (Ashgate 2008), 3.

"free political institutions", but not for sovereign statehood.[26] At the same time, it is subjected to conditions that leave wide room for interpretation. These stipulations are thus far from being a cogent revocation of colonial title to territory, even more so as state representatives such as the United States one had maintained, in the drafting process,

> that in many non-self-governing territories sovereignty or jurisdiction vest[ed] in the administering states; and nothing ha[d] been written into the Charter to change this fundamental fact.[27]

This statement testifies to a general disagreement among United Nations member states as to whether the fifth principle of the Friendly Relations Declaration had a sufficient basis in the Charter and public international law.[28] It would seem that only the reference to a separate and distinct status "under the Charter" – which in the eyes of a significant part of states did not in fact exist – enabled all member states to subscribe to the formulation.

Still, even the countries skeptical of the "separate and distinct" status acknowledged that an administering state was barred, under international law, from absorbing the non-self-governing territory or from changing its legal situation in a way that would evade its status under the Charter.[29] It is against this background that today's public international law consensus grants colonial peoples a right to an independent state within the framework of self-determination.[30],[31] As part of *ius cogens*[32] and obligations *erga*

26 H Kelsen, *The Law of the United Nations* (Praeger 1951), 559; U Fastenrath in B Simma, D-E Khan, G Nolte and A Paulus (eds), *The Charter of the United Nations* (3rd edn, Oxford University Press 2012), Art 73 para 13.

27 General Assembly Official Records, 4th Committee, 37th Meeting, 6 October 1947, 42 et seq.

28 O Šuković, 'Principle of Equal Rights and Self-Determination of Peoples' in M Šahović (ed), *Principles of International Law Concerning Friendly Relations and Cooperation* (Oceana 1972), 356.

29 G Arangio-Ruiz, *The United Nations Declaration on Friendly Relations and the System of the Sources of International Law* (Brill 1979), 138.

30 *Accordance with International Law of the Unilateral Declaration of Independence in Respect of Kosovo* [2010] ICJ Rep 403, para 79; *Reference Re Secession of Quebec*, [1998] 2 S.C.R. 217, para 131 et seq. Cf also *Legal Consequences for States of the Continued Presence of South Africa in Namibia (South West Africa) Notwithstanding Security Council Resolution 276 (1970)* [1971] ICJ Rep 16, para 52; *Western Sahara Case* [1975] ICJ Rep 12, para 56 et seqq.

31 A Cassese, *Self-Determination of Peoples* (Cambridge University Press 1996), 160; D Raič, *Statehood and the Law of Self-Determination* (Kluwer 2002), 215 et seq.

32 ILC, 'Report of the Commission to the General Assembly on the work of its fifty-third session, 23 April–1 June and 2 July–10 August 2001' 2001(II/2) YBILC 1, 85; A Cassese,

omnes,[33] it has benefitted various states in the process of their decolonization. A striking example is that of the Congo, which gained independence from Belgium in 1960. Within days of the declaration, two regions forcefully seceded while various fractions of government were struggling over power in the remaining parts of the country.[34] Even though the Congo did not meet the requirements of statehood under these circumstances, it was still recognized by many countries and admitted into the United Nations without delay.[35] Similar developments marked the decolonization of Guinea-Bissau, which the General Assembly recognized as a state despite an ongoing war of independence with Portugal,[36] as well as the cases of Algeria and Angola.[37]

In view of this state practice, colonial title to territory must be regarded as an ultimately moribund position. The right to secession flowing from the principle of self-determination does not completely do away with the sovereignty of the administering state but opens the door for its abolition. In doing so, public international law effectively subjected colonial title over territory to a principle of finiteness.

3 Environmental Factors as Limits to Sovereignty

Accordingly, there is a long and rich history of time limits to sovereignty. Today, the challenges to sovereignty are of a different kind: It is the risks of unimpeded climate change which present a serious threat to the foundations of statehood. When viewed this way, sovereignty resembles a limited resource shared by the international community as a whole.

3.1 *Climate Change as a Risk to the Natural Foundations of Statehood*

Today, the most relevant factors of finiteness in sovereignty stem from the natural foundations of human living. The state, the archetypical sovereign, is

Self-Determination of Peoples (Cambridge University Press 1996), 134 et seqq.; D Raič, *Statehood and the Law of Self-Determination* (Kluwer 2002), 218 et seq.

33 *East Timor (Portugal v Australia)* [1995] ICJ Rep 90, para 29; *Legal Consequences of the Construction of a Wall in the Occupied Palestinian Territory* [2004] ICJ Rep 136, para 155 et seq.

34 J Crawford, *Creation of States in International Law* (2nd edn, Oxford University Press 2007), 56 et seq.

35 D Raič, *Statehood and the Law of Self-Determination* (Kluwer 2002), 65.

36 T Christakis, 'The State as a 'primary fact': some thoughts on the principle of effectiveness' in M G Kohen (ed), *Secession* (Cambridge University Press 2012), 149.

37 D Raič, *Statehood and the Law of Self-Determination* (Kluwer 2002), 96 et seqq.

characterized by three qualities, namely a permanent population, a defined territory and a government.[38] Two of these criteria can only be met in human presence: The permanent population referred to is one of human beings, whereas government cannot exist without men and women taking decisions and executing them. Statehood is therefore indissolubly linked to mankind. Consequently, the natural foundations that lie at the basis of human living are at the same time preconditions for statehood. The third criterion, territory, is subject to geological processes and man-made developments. Emerging volcanic islands, for example, may expand the territory of a state, while border lines may change along with the rivers that define them. On the other hand, territory may be lost as a consequence of storm floods, such as the previously flourishing medieval town of Dunwich in Suffolk, where the shoreline has moved two kilometers landward since Roman times.[39]

Man-made climate change is expected to have consequences on state territory in a similar manner. With melting polar caps and rising sea levels, countries such as the Netherlands, large parts of which lie below sea level, will have to increase flood protection efforts significantly and might still not be able to secure all parts of their territory. The situation of certain small island nations is even direr. Rising sea levels, floods, tsunamis and other effects of climate change might cause countries such as the Maldives, Tuvalu or the Marshall Islands to fully submerge over the decades to come.[40] Here, a continuous reduction of state territory could ultimately culminate in the loss of statehood and sovereignty altogether. If climate change will proceed unimpededly, sovereignty in these regions will necessarily expire one day. The same could be true even for areas safe from rising sea levels, where meteorological conditions might worsen to the extent that they allow no human life to be sustained and no governmental authority to be displayed there anymore. These descriptions illustrate that the environmental prerequisites for sovereignty cannot always be presumed but could, eventually, cease to be met.

38 A Jellinek, *Allgemeine Staatslehre* (3rd edn, Wissenschaftliche Buchgesellschaft 1966), 180 et seq.

39 M Kennedy, 'Archaeologists map lost medieval Suffolk town of Dunwich under the sea' (*The Guardian*, 10 May 2013) <https://www.theguardian.com/science/2013/may/10/archaeologists-map-suffolk-dunwich-sea> accessed 11 April 2021.

40 J Grote Stoutenburg, *Disappearing Island States in International Law* (Nijhoff 2015).

3.2 *Sovereignty as a Limited and Shared Resource*

It is in this sense that sovereignty can be compared to a limited resource that might be depleted by climate change and other environmental risks. When looked at from this perspective, it closely resembles a shared good as well.

At first sight, the fact that public international law typically assigns sovereignty to one single international legal personality seems to be incompatible with a status as common-pool resource. However, since *Grotius*' notion of *mare liberium* has become widely accepted in the 18th century, all states are entitled to use the high seas for activities such as navigation, overflight, laying submarine cables and pipelines, constructing artificial installations and structures, for fishing and scientific research.[41] They are nonetheless precluded from establishing jurisdiction there.[42] Transboundary waters accordingly qualify as a *res communis*.[43] The concept of condominia also testifies to the existence of shared sovereignty. This special status, under which two or more states exercise sovereignty (or, in modern times, full or limited jurisdiction) together[44] instead of dividing the territory, is now largely a matter of the past. Still, what is today Vanuatu retained condominium status until 1980, when France and Great Britain gave up their joint sovereignty.[45] Certain small areas continue to be under this particular regime even today, namely the Moselle, Our and Sauer rivers where they constitute the border between Luxemburg and Germany.[46] Hence, sharing sovereignty is not a new phenomenon.

But the sense in which sovereignty can be regarded as a shared resource in the face of climate change goes beyond a restricted number of co-sovereigns and involves all of the international community. As has been established above, statehood and sovereignty do not only presuppose the three classic criteria of statehood, but through them depend on certain environmental prerequisites. Many of the processes endangering these natural conditions for sovereignty take place because of global developments: Rising temperatures and sea levels are worldwide phenomena. Greenhouse gas emissions in Europe will not only lead to rising temperatures there, but impact on the climate in Africa just as

41 Cf Art 87(1) United Nations Convention on the Law of the Sea (adopted 10 December 1982, entered into force 16 November 1994) 1833 UNTS 3.

42 T Treves, 'High Seas' in A Peters (ed), *Max Planck Encyclopedia of Public International Law online* (Oxford University Press 2021), para 1 et seq.

43 I Feichtner, 'Sharing the Riches of the Sea: The Redistributive and Fiscal Dimension of Deep Seabed Exploitation (2019) 30 EJIL 601, 606.

44 F L Morrison, 'Condominium and Coimperium' in A Peters (ed), *Max Planck Encyclopedia of Public International Law online* (Oxford University Press 2021), para 1 et seq.

45 Ibid, para 8.

46 D-E Khan, *Die deutschen Staatsgrenzen* (Mohr Siebeck 2004), 476 et seq.

well. In fact, climate change might hit hardest in those parts of the world least responsible for the pollution of the atmosphere, as is shown by the example of small island countries facing submersion. What lies at the basis of these connections is that the consequences of one state's doings will not end at the respective borders but may go well beyond. The resulting questions have been discussed in public international law for many decades, namely in the context of cross-border streams or environmental damages.[47]

As actions and consequences in the environmental field are globally interconnected, mitigating efforts by only a limited number of actors are consequently not enough to effectively combat climate change. This is exemplified by the ongoing emission of chlorofluorocarbons and hydrochlorofluorocarbons, which deplete the ozone layer. Under the Montreal Protocol on Substances that Deplete the Ozone Layer,[48] all United Nations member states have undertaken to phase out these chemicals. Despite the fact that production had already been prohibited worldwide, trichlorofluoromethane emissions increased after 2012, substantially slowing the recovery of the atmosphere.[49] Roughly half of the surplus could be traced back to factories in East China and thus to one single state which did not act to satisfy its treaty obligations.[50] Chinese emissions thereby largely nullified or devaluated the efforts of all other signatories to the Montreal Protocol.

In this regard, the atmosphere and the environment in general have much in common with the classic meadow shared by all families of a village for grazing their cattle: A fair and limited use of the grassland will enable the common resource to renew itself and continuously sustain the living of those relying on it. An overuse of the meadow will, however, result in a depletion of the resource and eventually turn the meadow into a wasteland that can no longer serve the local community. Hence, all-encompassing cooperation is necessary to ensure that the shared good will not be lost over time.

4 The Underlying Tragedy of the Commons and Its Possible Solutions

Economists discuss the problems of such interdependencies under the heading of tragedy of the commons.[51] From an economic point of view, the issue

47 *Trail Smelter Case* [1941] RIAA 1938.

48 (adopted 16 September 1987, entered into force 1 January 1989) 1522 UNTS 3.

49 M Kübler, 'Ozone layer recovery back on track after China slows CFC-11 production' (*Deutsche Welle*, 11 February 2021) <https://p.dw.com/p/3pEjo> accessed 16 April 2021.

50 Ibid.

51 G Hardin, 'The Tragedy of the Commons' (1968) 162 Science 1243.

in question is a potential overexploitation of the shared resource, which is rooted in the *homo oeconomicus* principle. Under this assumption, every actor involved seeks to maximize their own self-interest, thereby extending their individual use of the common-pool resource. This development will ultimately lead to the depletion of the good in question, a result which is generally inefficient. Economic science has offered a number of potential solutions for this problem,[52] most of which are based on the understanding that the tragedy of the commons is essentially a consequence of a lack of clearly defined property rights.

4.1 *Privatization and Nationalization*

One logical reaction to fill this void is to assign the respective good – either in whole or in individual parts – to one single person, thereby putting an end to the status as a shared resource.[53] The underlying argument is that attributing it to one actor at the exclusion of others will alter the new owner's stance with regard to his newly acquired property. It is now no longer in his interest to exploit it until depletion, for a loss of it would now affect not a vaguely-defined community, but him alone. Instead, his interests are typically best served with a sustainable management of the resource, whether the new owner of the previously shared good be a private individual or the state.

The first option, privatization, has often been the method of choice in national law. In England, for example, the process of enclosure lead to a transformation of commons into private property.[54] The other possibility, nationalization, has been applied in the international sphere as well. With regard to the group of state players involved here, assigning ownership to one single state is equivalent to privatization, whereas measures amounting to nationalization require all of the international community to be involved as beneficiaries.

The concept of common heritage of mankind comes to mind in this context. The notion, which is an accepted part of contemporary international law, has been applied to situations where areas or resources outside of the limits of national sovereignty or jurisdiction were to be distributed or protected.[55]

52 Cf for the following options M S Soroos, 'Garrett Hardin and the Tragedy of the Commons' in P Dauvergne (ed), *Handbook of Global Environmental Politics* (Edward Elgar 2005), 41 et seqq.

53 D Feeny, F Berkes, B J McCay and J M Acheson, 'The Tragedy of the Commons: Twenty-Two Years Later' (1990) 18 Human Ecology 1, 2 et seq.

54 R J P Kain, J Chapman and R R Oliver, The Enclosure Maps of England and Wales (Cambridge University Press 2004), 1 et seqq.

55 R Wolfrum, 'The Principle of Common Heritage of Mankind' (1983) 43 Zeitschrift für ausländisches öffentliches Recht und Völkerrecht 312 et seq.

It will result in a shared competence of the international community, which prohibits any claims to sovereignty or jurisdiction by individual states.[56] The moon, for example, is subject so such a regime: Under the Outer Space Treaty,[57] the exploration and use of the moon and outer space in general must be conducted for the benefit and in the interest of all countries and for peaceful purposes only.[58] Outer space, including the moon, is not open to national appropriation but free to access for all states without discrimination.[59] A similar set of rules applies to Antarctica, with the Antarctic Treaty[60] stipulating that the continent shall be used for peaceful purposes only, namely for free scientific investigation.[61] As various claims to sovereignty had already been raised in this case, the Antarctic Treaty restricted itself to barring new claims and freezing the existing ones.[62]

While the Outer Space Treaty and the Antarctic Treaty merely addressed states, the United Nations Convention on the Law of the Sea, which defined the seabed, ocean floor and subsoil beyond the limits of national jurisdiction and its resources as common heritage of mankind,[63] established an independent organization charged with the exploitation of resources in this area for the benefit of mankind.[64] This International Seabed Authority is the only entity entitled under the convention to give out licenses to contractors exploring the possibility of mining in the international seabed area. The convention additionally foresees an own organism charged with conducting exploration and mining activities,[65] the Enterprise, which has, however, not yet come into operation.[66]

4.2 *Fair Use Restrictions*

Apart from these two options, economic science has suggested that governmental regulation of use of a shared resource could mitigate the tragedy of the

56 Ibid, 332.

57 Treaty on Principles Governing the Activities of States in the Exploration and Use of Outer Space, including the Moon and Other Celestial Bodies (adopted 27 January 1967, entered into effect 10 October 1967) 610 UNTS 205.

58 Art 1(1), 3(2).

59 Art 1(2), 2.

60 (adopted 1 December 1959, entered into force 23 June 1961) 402 UNTS 71.

61 Art 1, 2.

62 Art 4.

63 Art 136 et seqq.

64 Art 153.

65 Art 170.

66 International Seabed Authority, *Secretary General Annual Report 2020* <https://isa.org.jm/files/files/documents/ISA_Annual_Report_2020_ENG.pdf> accessed 18 April 2021, 43.

commons.[67] If this set of rules imposes reasonable limits on exploitation and prevents over-use, depletion may be averted as well. This approach has also been adopted in international instruments. It namely features in the above-mentioned Framework Convention on Climate Change and the subsequent treaties.

As one such treaty, the Paris Agreement stipulates a binding goal for climate protection efforts – holding the increase in the global average temperature to well below 2°C above pre-industrial levels and pursuing efforts to limit the temperature increase to 1.5°C – and obliges all signatories to make nationally determined contributions to this end.[68] Even though the Paris Agreement sets the goal to be met through these contributions and contains certain rules regarding their content, it does not set forth concrete measures or timetables for the individual countries.[69] It differs, in this regard, from its predecessor, the Kyoto Protocol,[70] which had featured binding schedules imposing individual reduction targets on the industrialized states.[71]

This latter regime comes closer to the use restrictions suggested by economic science, for it imposes individual limits on each of the users of the shared resource, the atmosphere. The fact that states are obliged to ensure, each on their own, a clearly defined, measurable and quantifiable reduction of greenhouse gas emissions gives them a clear guideline for action. At the same time, such an individualized duty prevents states from shifting or denying responsibility, as otherwise would be typical for tragedy of the commons situations.

The Paris Agreement, on the other hand, has stopped one step short of such individually set use restrictions. Instead, the limit for a fair use of the atmosphere targets all state parties as a community and foresees a vaguely differentiated, but shared responsibility, missing out the allocation of use rights to the individual users.[72] Whilst thereby technically curbing the utilization of the atmosphere, the Paris Agreement did little to mitigate the existing tragedy of

67 Cf C M Rose, 'Rethinking Environmental Controls: Management Strategies for Common Resources' (1991) Duke Law Journal 1, 9.

68 Art 2(1)(a), Art 3.

69 B Mayer, 'International Law Obligations Arising in Relation to Nationally Determined Contributions' (2018) 7 Transnational Environmental Law 251 et seq.

70 Kyoto Protocol to the United Nations Framework Convention on Climate Change (adopted 10 December 1997, entered into force 16 February 2005) 2303 UNTS 162.

71 Contained in Annex B.

72 T Tietenberg, 'The Tradable Permits Approach to Protecting the Commons: What Have We Learned?' in E Ostrom, T Dietz, N Dolšak, P C Stern, S Stonich and E U Weber (eds), *The Drama of the Commons* (National Academy Press 2002), 197.

the commons, because the stereotypical lack of individual responsibility that leads to the over-exploitation of the common resource still endures.

4.3 *Institutionalized Local Cooperation*

Elinor Ostrom has suggested a different concept to cope with the tragedy of the commons:[73] She analyzed institutions of communal tenure in Swiss and Japanese mountain communities as well as irrigation schemes in Spain and the Philippines. Her finding was that all these mechanisms related to "long-enduring, self-organized and self-governed common-pool resources" and were accordingly successful in sustaining the shared good. This result is somewhat contrary to the orthodox approaches to the tragedy of the commons because it neither consists of a definition of property rights nor are use restrictions imposed by a central authority of government.

The examined mechanisms had certain characteristics in common which *Ostrom* identified as design principles:[74] In all cases, the common-pool resource itself as well as the persons entitled to use it were clearly defined. Furthermore, both appropriation and provision rules were congruent with local conditions. The systems additionally established collective decision-making processes, which allowed the beneficiaries to take part in the administration of the shared good. In order to supervise the boundaries established under the first design principle, there were monitoring systems in place. Graduated sanctions applied in cases of violations. For conflicts between users, low-threshold resolution mechanisms were easily available. *Ostrom* additionally found the institutions enjoyed at least a minimal degree of recognition by a superior authority, which supported the right of the community to autonomously organize the handling of the resource. Partitioning was a last design principle uncovered: Larger common-pool resources were typically managed in layers of nested enterprises, breaking down both the resource and its management to the local level.

5 Supranational Institutions as a Preferable Way to Handle Climate Change

Applying these principles to the field of public international law is not without obstacles. In fact, attempts at implementing the traditional approaches

73 See for this paragraph E Ostrom, *Governing the Commons: The Evolution of Institutions for Collective Action* (Cambridge University Press 1990), 58 et seqq.

74 Ibid, 88 et seqq.

of assigning property rights or imposing use restrictions seem to have only partially proven effective. The lack of a central authority empowered to adopt and enforce such measures on a global level is what makes the implementation of these proposals difficult. Public international law has, however, created regional supranational organizations competent to act in such a manner. Testing these institutions against *Ostrom*'s design principles will reveal that they are well-equipped to address the risks of unabated climate change.

5.1 *The Fate of Traditional Approaches to Common-Pool Resources in International Law*

It has been demonstrated above that the "classic" concepts for avoiding the tragedy of the commons have made their way into the field of international law. The International Seabed Authority is a prominent case of "nationalization" of deep-seabed resources for the benefit of the international community as a whole. In the area of climate change, the Framework Convention on Climate Change is an example for a quasi-governmental regulation of use of the atmosphere.

5.1.1 The (In-)Effectiveness of Nationalization and Use Restrictions in International Law

What is striking though is that these traditional solutions for managing shared resources seem to have failed to produce effective results in the international sphere. The Convention on the Law of the Sea received widespread criticism in the international community that resulted in a delay of twelve years until its entering into force. The goals of industrialized and newly independent states particularly clashed in the area of deep-seabed mining, with industrialized states favoring legal security and cheap access over the revenue generation and redistribution of wealth and technology sought after by developing countries.[75] This is – apart from the fact that deep-seabed mining has not been a cost-efficient option for a long time – one reason why the International Seabed Authority and its Enterprise have had little impact so far.

In the same vein, the Climate Change Convention and the treaties adopted within its framework have received strong criticism. The nationally determined contributions submitted by the signatory states so far in particular have been condemned as insufficient to reach the 2° goal.[76] In addition, the fact

75 I Feichtner, 'Sharing the Riches of the Sea: The Redistributive and Fiscal Dimension of Deep Seabed Exploitation' (2019) 30 EJIL 601, 608.

76 S Leahy, 'Most countries aren't hitting 2030 climate goals, and everyone will pay the price' (*National Geographic*, 5 November 2019) <https://www.nationalgeographic.com/science/article/nations-miss-paris-targets-climate-driven-weather-events-cost-billions> accessed 22 April 2021.

that the Paris Agreement relies on such unilateral determinations to achieve its mutually agreed aim can be regarded as a major conceptual flaw, for there is no cogent mechanism to transform said target into ambitious state measures to its accomplishment.[77] Climate clubs have been suggested as a way to mitigate this shortcoming.[78] In such voluntary associations, limited numbers of countries could agree on more aspiring greenhouse gas reduction targets as well as mechanisms to incentivize climate protection on the part of their members, namely by imposing sanctions on those who fail to comply or by conferring benefits, such as participation in newly developed climate technologies, on those who meet the goals agreed.[79]

5.1.2 Lack of Binding Decision-Making and Enforcement Mechanisms in International Law

The general problem with applying the traditional approaches to common-pool resources – privatization, nationalization and use restrictions – on the international level is an institutional one. When economists suggest such measures in theory, they presuppose a state with a comprehensive legal order. In fact, the entity economists seem to have in mind often resembles an ideal unitary authority equipped with all-encompassing powers. It is furthermore able to discern and weigh all relevant factors and to ultimately decide on an adequate rule and possesses the authority and means to fully enforce the measure adopted. This description, however, is far from what the international legal order looks like today.

The sovereign equality of states is one of the fundamental building blocks of this order, enshrined as a founding principle in the Charter of the United Nations.[80] It affords all states an equal position in public international law, irrespective of their size or economic power and, as a consequence, requires state consent for binding public international law obligations.[81] With this setup, the international community differs greatly from the institutional arrangements of democratic states, where the will of a majority will result in

77 K Raiser, U Kornek, C Flachsland and W F Lamb, 'Is the Paris Agreement effective? A systematic map of the evidence' (2020) 15 Environmental Research Letters 083006, 12.

78 C Carraro, 'Club, R&D and Climate Finance: Incentives for Ambitious GHG Emission Reductions' in R N Stavins and R C Stowe (eds), *The Paris Agreement and Beyond: International Climate Change Policy Post-2020* (Harvard Project on Climate Agreements 2016) 69.

79 Ibid, 70.

80 Art 2 no. 1 UN Charter.

81 M N Shaw, *International Law* (9th edn, Cambridge University Press 2017), 168 et seq.

norms binding everyone, even those who did not agree with them in the first place. Establishing effective public international law on global common-pool resources is consequently not as easy as assumed by the traditional economist suggestions. In fact, in international law, a very wide consensus is necessary to even reach a meaningful level of participation. The Kyoto Protocol, for example, was never ratified by the United States, the second largest emitter of greenhouse gases, while China as the largest emitter was formally bound, but not subject to a reduction obligation.[82] With the atmosphere being a shared resource, however, climate protection measures adopted by one part of the international community can easily be cancelled by additional greenhouse gas emissions by other states.

Apart from the creation of rules, national and international law also differ in the field of enforcement. As is assumed in the suggestions of managing tragedy of the commons situations by establishing property rights or imposing use restrictions, states typically dispose of means and mechanisms to enforce the rules they have set. There is usually a functioning administration in place to monitor compliance and measures such as monetary or other sanctions can be taken in cases of violations. Again, things are different in international law. The above-mentioned principle of sovereign equality bars states from exercising any sort of jurisdiction over their peers without their consent,[83] leaving them with the option of self-help. The right to take countermeasures against another state is, however, strictly limited to proportionate and reversible responses to intentional wrongful acts.[84] Other more collective forms of enforcement may be available, but only on a case-to-case basis. The power of the United Nations Security Council to authorize measures under Chapter VII of the Charter is restricted to cases of threats to and breaches of the peace as well as acts of aggression.[85] Additionally, in case of human rights treaties, compliance is often monitored by way of regular country reports, which are then analyzed by specialized bodies set up for this purpose. The Human Rights Committee established under Art 28 et seqq International Covenant on Civil and Political Rights,[86] a panel of experts that reviews periodic state reports on the implementation of the covenant, may be cited as an example here. Its power to issue

---

82 'Kyoto Protocol' (Encyclopedia Britannica, 2019) <https://www.britannica.com/event/Kyoto-Protocol> accessed 23 April 2021.

83 J Crawford, *Brownlie's Principles of Public International Law* (8th edn, Oxford University Press 2012), 448 et seq.

84 Cf *Gabčikovo-Nagymaros Project* (*Hungary v Slovakia*) [1997] ICJ Rep 7, para 83 et seqq.

85 Art 39 et seqq UN Charter.

86 (adopted 16 December 1966, entered into force 23 March 1976) 999 UNTS 171 (ICCPR).

(non-binding) recommendations to states demonstrates the extralegal role of public "shaming" in the enforcement of public international law. The committee may also decide on complaints raised by states and individuals, but only if the defendant state has explicitly recognized the committee's competence to do so.[87] This need for state consent is a general rule that also applies to conflict resolution through arbitration or international courts.

All of these findings seem to suggest that there is no entity in public international law that would be able to unilaterally impose and enforce measures such as defining property rights or applying use limits for the atmosphere on a global level. Instead, as a defining principle, state approval is required for all such restrictions. Hence, while the risks of unabated climate change clearly show that sovereignty is a finite resource that can be depleted over time, public international law seems to lack a mechanism by which these environmental limits to sovereignty could be transformed into legal rules. In fact, it would seem that public international law is inherently incapable of resolving the tragedy of the commons that lies at the heart of the problem of the global overuse of the atmosphere due to its consent-based nature.

5.2 *Institutionalized Regional Cooperation as a Means to Address Climate Change*

It must not be forgotten, however, that public international law has also spawned supranational organizations, institutions which have been empowered, by their member states, to issue binding decisions even in the absence of unanimous consent. They have proven particularly successful in the area of regional cooperation. As measured by *Ostrom*'s design principles for a successful management of the commons, they are equally well-equipped to combat climate change.

5.2.1 Supranational Law as an Instrument of Regional Integration

Despite the structural differences between national and public international law, the latter also forms the basis of institutions of supranational character, whose decision-making and enforcement powers are rather comparable to a national setup. Supranationality is characteristic of several regional integration projects such as the African Union, the East African Community or the Andean Community of Nations.[88]

---

87 Art 41(1) ICCPR; Art 1 Optional Protocol to the International Covenant on Civil and Political Rights (adopted 16 December 1966, entered into force 23 March 1976) 999 UNTS 171.

88 A Skordas, 'Supranational Law' in A Peters (ed), *Max Planck Encyclopedia of Public International Law online* (Oxford University Press 2021), para 13 et seqq; T P Miley, 'What

Among these projects, the European Union is one of the most advanced, featuring various supranational aspects:[89] Its European Commission has a central role in lawmaking, monitors member state compliance with European law and may initiate infringement procedures, which can result in severe pecuniary sanctions. In the Council, through which member state governments participate in the lawmaking process, a qualified majority often suffices for taking a decision. The role of the European Parliament as a co-legislator has become ever more important, while the compulsory jurisdiction of the Court of Justice ensures the equal application of European law in all member states.

Supranational organizations such as the European Union may accordingly have at hand the instruments necessary to sustainably manage common-pool resources. They dispose of binding decision-making processes and can enforce their rules and regulations through their own executive and judiciary institutions. What is more, their dimension of regional cooperation coincides with *Ostrom*'s approach of dealing with tragedy of the commons situations. Her suggestion of an institutionalized local cooperation actually describes – albeit on a regional level – how supranational organizations such as the European Union are set up. They represent a permanent mechanism of regional "self-management" through institutions established by their members.

5.2.2 Applying *Ostrom*'s Design Principles to the EU Emissions Trading Regime

The requirements for a successful management of the commons, however, extend to further design principles beyond this merely institutional point. In order to answer the question of whether organizations like the European Union could in fact be capable of dealing with tragedy of the commons constellations, it must be assessed whether these design principles are met as well.

An evident example in this context is the EU emissions trading system established by the Emissions Trading Directive.[90] Under this "cap and trade"

Is Wrong about Supranational Laws? The Sources of East African Community Law in Light of the EU's Experience' (2015) 75 Zeitschrift für ausländisches öffentliches Recht und Völkerrecht 579, 582 et seqq.

89 F C Mayer and S P Thies, 'European Union, Historical Evolution' in A Peters (ed), *Max Planck Encyclopedia of Public International Law online* (Oxford University Press 2021), para 13 et seqq.

90 Directive 2003/87/EC of the European Parliament and the Council establishing a scheme for greenhouse gas emission allowance trading within the Community and amending Council Directive 96/61/EC (13 October 2003), [2003] OJ L275/32.

regime,[91] emissions from certain designated areas of the economy – namely power stations, oil refineries, iron, steel, chemical and cement works, the paper industry and aviation – are capped at a certain overall regulatory limit, which decreases over time. Economic operators subjected to these rules need certificates for their emissions in order to avoid financial penalties (which depend on the amount of emissions in question). During the initial operating period of the system, distribution lay in the hands of member states, who submitted allocation plans to the European Commission for approval. They allotted most certificates free of charge, which left only a relatively low number to be auctioned off. Since 2013, there is a Union-wide cap instead of individual allocations plans and an increasing number of certificates must be allocated by member states through auctions. Emission rights can be traded freely between businesses, which leads to an internalization of previously external costs of climate change. The economic rationale behind this market-based approach is that greenhouse gas emissions will be reduced in industries where such measures can be taken most efficiently.

The emissions trading system is but one instrument to deal with climate change. Against this background, it does not apply comprehensively to all industries, but only to a certain (albeit clearly defined) group of entities who use the shared resource atmosphere. Due to many and large greenhouse gas emitters operating outside of its scope, the regime alone is currently unable to sustainably manage the use of the atmosphere, but this gap could be narrowed in future. Nonetheless, as the emissions trading system shows, the European Union would be equipped to fulfil further design principles: Following the notion of subsidiarity, European law generally leaves room for local conditions being taken into account, in particular by member states, who have to transform directives into national law. Additionally, under the emissions trading regime, special regional situations could initially be accounted for in the allotment of certificates, for which member states enjoyed wide discretion.

Beyond that, the European Union has – together with its member states – all institutions and mechanisms available to meet *Ostrom*'s design criteria. Member states and their electorate take part in the Union's decision making, whether it be in the Council or through the Parliament. In accordance with the principle of member state enforcement, compliance with the emissions trading regime and European Law in general is monitored by institutions of the individual member states who can, at the same time, be regarded as nested enterprises

91 For a description see E Fisher, E Scotford and B Lange, *Environmental Law* (Oxford University Press 2019), 616 et seqq.

charged with managing a part of the shared resource. Member states are, in turn, supervised by the European Commission. In cases of non-compliance, sanctions apply to businesses and states alike. Finally, national courts and the European Court of Justice provide resolution mechanisms for potential conflicts.

6 Regional Cooperation and Finiteness in Sovereignty

It follows from the above that managing the global commons that is the atmosphere through organizations of regional cooperation offers a high prospect of success from an economic point of view. In case of the European Union, in particular, many preconditions for a sustainable handling of climate change are already met. Public international law might underscore its importance in the struggle against climate change in this very field.

To realize that the environmental risks of unimpeded climate change could ultimately put an end to sovereignty as well is merely one step. In order to turn this understanding into decisive governmental action against global warming, it is further necessary to transform the inherent natural finiteness of sovereignty into corresponding legal and political rules. It is against this background that regional supranational organizations seem particularly suitable to handle climate change. With their law typically taking precedence over national rules and regulations, they create an additional level of authority and can accordingly be regarded as a special type of superordinate entity.

In many of the historic examples discussed at the beginning of this article, finiteness in sovereignty and jurisdiction stemmed from party consent, namely in the case of leases and ultimately also in the context of decolonization. But a perspective of loss over time could equally be inferred from the presence of a higher law and authority, be it the Pope or a liege. Regional supranational organizations with their already established superior position could play a comparable role: They could monitor whether their members respect the environmental limits that climate change imposes on the exercise of sovereignty and would, if necessary, be able to enforce these limits themselves.

CHAPTER 15

Le droit international des investissements

Exercice ou limitation de la souveraineté étatique ?

Shehrazade El-Hajjar

> C'est l'Etat qui est maintenant en position d'infériorité dans le contentieux économique transnational. Au nom de la liberté et de la protection de l'investissement international, le balancier est passé de l'autre côté.
>
> PHILIPPE FOUCHARD[1].

∴

Le droit international des investissements est aujourd'hui souvent perçu comme un droit déséquilibré, favorisant les intérêts privés des investisseurs au détriment des intérêts publics relevant des États. Cette perception explique la montée en puissance de contestations provenant de divers acteurs, notamment de certains États (ex : l'Équateur), mais également des « acteurs de la société civile »[2], y compris des juristes. Les critiques dénoncent un système qui, selon eux, porterait atteinte à la souveraineté des États. La virulence de cette contestation ne s'est que rarement concrétisée par une renonciation à l'appartenance à ce système : les dénonciations de traités relatifs à la protection des investissements sont plutôt rares. La tendance semble plutôt être à la multiplication des instruments de protection des investissements et à l'entrée en scène d'États qui s'étaient traditionnellement placés volontairement à l'extérieur de ce système (le Brésil et la Chine dans une certaine mesure). Ceci ne manque pas de remettre en question le sérieux et la réalité de la contestation étatique de ce système.

1 P. Fouchard, « L'arbitrage et la mondialisation de l'économie », *in Philosophie du droit et droit économique : quel dialogue ? Mélanges en l'honneur de Gérard Farjat*, Paris, Frison-Roche, 2000, p. 393.

2 Voir par exemple A. Depalma, « NAFTA'S powerful Little secret: obscure tribunals settle dispute, but go too far critics says », *The New York Times*, 11 mars 2001.

 | DOI:10.1163/9789004508712_016

En réalité, un aperçu rapide de l'évolution historique des systèmes de protection des investissements s'impose pour mieux comprendre les choix et concessions acceptées – avant d'être « subies » – par les États. En effet, ces choix n'ont pas été imposés, mais sont le résultat d'une évolution et d'un renforcement des modalités de protection des investissements réalisés à l'étranger. Les investissements réalisés à l'étranger ne sont évidemment pas un phénomène nouveau. Le contexte dans lequel ils s'inscrivent évolue, allant de la colonisation à la mondialisation en passant par la décolonisation. Dans chaque contexte, les rapports entre les mesures de protection et la souveraineté des États ne se posent pas dans les mêmes termes. Durant l'époque de la colonisation par exemple, la protection des investissements étrangers ne différait pas de la protection des individus : elle passait par la protection diplomatique. Dans ce cadre, un État prend fait et cause pour son ressortissant lésé et le prend en charge la défense de ses intérêts auprès d'un autre État souverain, selon une fiction selon laquelle les intérets défendus seraient ceux de l'État et non plus ceux de son ressortissant. On est donc dans le cadre du droit international « classique », où une souveraineté traite avec une autre. Ces règles classiques de protection des ressortissants contre les souverainetés étrangères s'appliquaient aux biens et droits des investisseurs. Mais ce système s'est révélé insatisfaisant, d'une part, parce que si un État choisissait de ne pas prendre fait et cause pour son ressortissant, celui-ci ne pouvait obtenir satisfaction. D'autre part, parce que cette pratique a pu ouvrir la voie à la « diplomatie du canon », où la menace du recours à la force servait de moyen de pression sur l'État hôte[3].

Cette situation insatisfaisante a poussé les investisseurs à se protéger à travers le principal outil à leur disposition : les contrats conclus avec l'État hôte. Le XXème siècle a en effet connu une prolifération des contrats d'États, dans lesquels les « investisseurs » étrangers négociaient l'insertion de clauses visant à se protéger contre la souveraineté de la partie avec laquelle ils contractaient. Ce faisant, ils cherchaient particulièrement à évincer l'application du droit de l'État hôte, et à éviter de voir leurs différends soumis aux juridictions de ce dernier. Ceci a conduit à la normalisation des clauses compromissoires, ainsi que des clauses de stabilisation ou d'intangibilité qui ont même pu être érigées en critères de définition des contrats d'États.

Ces clauses sont révélatrices des préoccupations des investisseurs, qui cherchent à se prémunir contre des juridictions qu'ils considèrent biaisées

3 Cette forme de diplomatie a notamment été utilisée en 1902 par l'Allemagne et le Royaume-Uni à l'encontre du Venezuela pour le pousser à payer ses dettes.

en faveur de l'État hôte, ainsi que d'évincer l'application d'un droit ne leur assurant pas une certaine sécurité juridique en cas de conflit. Et ce sont ces mêmes préoccupations que l'on retrouve dans les traités bilatéraux relatifs à la protection des investissements (ci-après « TBI »), qui ont commencé à se développer à partir des années 1950 et qui représentent l'apogée de la protection des investisseurs étrangers.

Les TBI ont commencé à être conclus par des pays en voie de développement souhaitant apporter des garanties aux investisseurs étrangers, notamment pour répondre à l'expression d'un certain manque de confiance des investisseursen leurs institutions. Leur objectif premier dans la conclusion de ces traités est leur développement économique, objectif qui figure généralement dans le préambule voire l'intitulé même du traité. Ils contiennent des standards répandus en droit international général, qui découlent en partie des standards et clauses contenues dans les traités relatifs à la condition des étrangers[4], retrouvés aujourd'hui dans des traités relatifs aux droits de l'Homme. Il s'agit notamment du standard du traitement juste et équitable qui coïncide avec le standard de traitement minimum du droit international en matière de traitement des étrangers[5], du standard de la pleine et entière protection et sécurité ; mais également de certains standards plus généraux, retrouvés dans d'autres instruments, tels que le principe de traitement national ou celui du traitement de la nation la plus favorisée.

Au regard de ces standards traditionnels, et de sa place dans la continuité des autres modalités de protection des intérêts des investisseurs étrangers, pourquoi ce droit fait-il l'objet de tant de contestations et pourquoi cette contestation s'inscrit-elle dans une logique de protection de la souveraineté étatique ?

Il nous semble plutôt que le droit international des investissements a été construit par un exercice de la souveraineté étatique, dont l'un des attributs est justement la faculté de contracter des engagements internationaux, pour reprendre la formulation adoptée par le Cour permanente de justice internationale[6]. Il n'en reste pas moins que les critiques soulèvent des questions raisonnables sur la viabilité du système, questions légitimées par certaines tentatives de réformes plus respectueuses des intérêts étatiques.

---

4 D. Carreau, R. Bismuth, A. Hamann et P. Juillard, *Droit international économique*, Paris, Dalloz, 6ème ed., 2017, p. 432.

5 *Ibid.*, p. 505.

6 *Affaire du Vapeur Wimbledon*, CPJI, série A n°1, p. 25, 17 août 1923.

1 La normalisation du recours à l'arbitrage, mode de règlement des différends illégitime

1.1 *Un essor dépassant les prévisions des États*

L'essor du droit international des investissements et du recours à l'arbitrage *ad hoc* ou institutionnel pour le règlement des litiges relatifs aux investissements étrangers remonte à la sentence *Asian agricultural products c. République du Sri Lanka*. Cette sentence rendue le 27 juin 1990 dans le cadre d'un arbitrage CIRDI[7], a été l'occasion pour les membres du tribunal arbitral de consacrer une solution révolutionnaire : les investisseurs peuvent désormais directement saisir un tribunal arbitral – dans ce cadre formé sous l'égide du CIRDI – sur la base d'un traité bilatéral relatif aux investissements et non sur la base d'un contrat d'État et sans compromis arbitral spécifique au litige en cause[8]. Cette solution, dite aussi « arbitrage sans lien de droit » ou « arbitrage transnational unilatéral », très favorable aux investisseurs, a constitué un premier bouleversement dans les habitudes des États, en faisant apparaître un nouvel acteur pouvant mettre en œuvre des procédures juridictionnelles internationales contre des États, sans consentement spécifique de celui-ci vis-à-vis du différend en cause.

Cette solution a ensuite été renforcée par la sentence rendue dans l'affaire *Maffezini c. Royaume d'Espagne* en 2000[9]. Cette sentence a ouvert la voie à la possibilité d'invoquer la clause de la nation la plus favorisée contenue dans un accord bilatéral, permettant le renvoi à un autre TBI conclu par l'Etat en litige avec un Etat tiers et contenant une référence à l'arbitrage CIRDI propre à fonder la compétence du Tribunal.

Ces solutions ont été à l'origine d'une multiplication sans précédent des recours directs. Cet « arbitrage sans lien de droit » est adressé à un nombre indéfinissable d'investisseurs, que l'État ne peut prétendre connaître au moment où il émet son offre d'arbitrage. Cette procédure se révèle d'autant plus imprévisible pour les États que des recours peuvent désormais être soulevés même en l'absence de liens contractuels entre l'État et l'investisseur[10].

---

7 *Asian Agricultural Products Ltd. v. Republic of Sri Lanka*, affaire CIRDI n° ARB/87/3, sentence du 27 juin 1990.

8 « *The present case is the first instance in which the Center has been seized by an arbitration request exclusively based on a treaty provision and not in implementation of a freely negotiated arbitration agreement directly concluded between the parties among whom the dispute has arisen* ».

9 *Emilio Agustín Maffezini v. The Kingdom of Spain*, affaire CIRDI n° ARB/97/7, décision sur la compétence du 25 janvier 2000.

10 M. Fekl, « Les contestations de l'arbitrage d'investissement et les négociations commerciales internationales contemporaines », *Cahiers de l'arbitrage*, n° 3, 2018, pp. 413 et s.

Ces solutions sont certainement très favorables aux investisseurs qui n'ont pas manqué d'applaudir cette protection accrue de leurs investissements à travers la facilitation de l'accès aux tribunaux arbitraux. Paradoxalement, elles n'étaient pas expressément prévues par la Convention de Washington[11] qui a créé le CIRDI : celle-ci faisait référence au consentement des parties à l'arbitrage, ce qui devrait sous-entendre un consentement au cas par cas.

Ces sentences ont entraîné un recours sans précédent à l'arbitrage CIRDI, en grande majorité sur le fondement de cet arbitrage sans lien de droit[12].

1.2 *Un mode de règlement des différends adéquat au regard des questions traitées ?*

Outre la contradiction de ces solutions avec l'esprit et même la lettre de la Convention de Washington, la nature de l'arbitrage d'investissement en tant que mode de résolution des litiges pose également problème. En effet, l'arbitrage d'investissements partage un grand nombre de liens avec l'arbitrage commercial international, notamment au niveau d'une grande partie de ses acteurs : les entreprises multinationales, les avocats et les arbitres, que l'on retrouve dans ces deux types d'arbitrages. Or, l'arbitrage commercial international revêt une nature purement privatiste, contrairement à l'arbitrage d'investissements qui touche à des matières et soulève des questions essentiellement de droit public.

La détermination de la nature privée ou publique du droit international de l'investissement ne fait sans doute pas l'objet d'un consensus. Comme nous venons d'ailleurs de le mentionner, d'un côté, sa forme (recours à l'arbitrage, acteurs communs avec le droit du commerce international) le rapproche plutôt d'une matière privée. D'un autre côté, le fond des problèmes soulevés dans le cadre de ce droit relève du droit public. De nombreux auteurs, spécialisés dans des matières très différentes, se sont d'ailleurs rejoints autour de cette thèse. Le Professeur Prosper Weil l'a soutenue dans plusieurs de ses écrits, mais particulièrement dans un article intitulé « Un nouveau champ d'influence

11 Convention de Washington pour le règlement des différends relatifs aux investissements entre États et ressortissants d'autres États Convention CIRDI (signée le 18 mars 1965), entrée en vigueur le 14 octobre 1966.

12 « Le nombre d'affaires soumises au Centre sur le fondement de conventions d'arbitrage traditionnelles est resté constant : une en 1999, une en 2000, deux en 2001 et une en 2002. Ce rythme est très comparable à celui qu'avait connu le CIRDI jusqu'au milieu des années quatre-vingt-dix. En revanche, outre ces saisines opérées sur un fondement classique, le Centre a enregistré, sur le fondement de traités, sept affaires nouvelles en 1999, neuf en 2000, douze en 2001 et seize en 2002 », *in* E. Gaillard, « L'arbitrage sur le fondement des traités de protection des investissements », *Rev. Arb.*, 2003, pp. 853–875, spéc. p. 855.

pour le droit administratif français : le droit international des contrats »[13]. Pour l'auteur, le droit des contrats d'État, qui comme nous l'avons mentionné constitue à notre sens une forme/un prédécesseur du droit international des investissements, constituait non pas simplement du droit public, mais un droit administratif « international ». Le Professeur Emmanuel Gaillard, spécialiste en matière d'arbitrage, le rejoignait sur ce point, considérant qu'« il n'est pas exagéré d'affirmer que l'on assiste aujourd'hui à la naissance d'un *contrôle de la légalité des agissements des États* au regard des exigences du droit international d'une importance [...] du rôle du Conseil d'État d'organe de conseil en véritable juge de la légalité des actes de l'administration »[14]. La reconnaissance d'une nature publique du droit international des investissements n'est pas sans intérêt. En effet, les matières publiques ont souvent et longtemps pu être exclues du champ de l'arbitrage. C'est notamment le cas du droit français dont l'article 2060 du Code civil prohibe le recours à l'arbitrage par les personnes publiques[15]. Cette interdiction avait été justifiée par des références aux intérêts en cause dans les matières publiques. Édouard Laferrière par exemple, considérait que l'État ne saurait soumettre ses litiges contractuels à des arbitres « tant à raison des conséquences aléatoires de l'arbitrage, que des considérations d'ordre public qui veulent que l'État ne soit jugé que par des juridictions instituées par la loi ». Georges Vedel a par ailleurs soutenu que les droits en cause ne sont pas purement ceux de l'État : « [les État] ne sont jamais pleinement maîtres des intérêts qui leur sont confiés. C'est une collectivité de citoyens, d'administrés ou de contribuables qui, en dernière analyse, est le véritable titulaire des droits et obligations en litiges. Par conséquent, le choix des arbitres, l'étendue des pouvoirs de ceux-ci ne peuvent être laissés à la seule volonté des parties »[16]. L'auteur soulignait déjà le manque de légitimité des arbitres pour trancher certaines questions, les sentences arbitrales ayant un impact allant au-delà des parties en cause. D'autant plus que les litiges liés aux investissements ne se cantonnent pas à des questions de pure responsabilité

13 *Études et documents du Conseil d'État*, 1971.

14 E. Gaillard, *La jurisprudence du CIRDI*, Paris, Pedone, 2004, p. 7.

15 Cette prohibition a certes été tempérée par la combinaison des décisions INSERM (TC, 17 mai 2010, *Inserm c. Fondation Letten F. Sausgstad*, n°3754), SMAC (CE, 19 avril 2013, *Syndicat mixte des Aéroports de Charente c. Sté Ryanair Ltd et autres*) et FOSMAX (TC, 11 avril 2016, *Société Fosmax Lng*, n° 4043) ce qui marque un certes assouplissement du principe d'interdiction du recours à l'arbitrage dans les matières publiques. Mais ces jurisprudences n'ont pas abouti à un abandon complet du principe, ce qui sous-entend son maintien ainsi que le maintien de certaines de ses justifications.

16 G. Vedel, « Le problème de l'arbitrage entre gouvernements ou entre personnes de droit public et personnes de droit privé », *Rev. Arb.*, 1961, pp. 116–130, spéc. p. 122.

contractuelle ou même délictuelles, mais sont l'occasion pour les arbitres de mettre en place de véritables contrôles de légalité d'actes ou de mesures adoptées par les autorités publiques contre lesquels les recours sont exercés. Ce contrôle est d'autant plus inquiétant lorsqu'il remet en cause des actes législatifs, actes souverains par excellence. Les tribunaux arbitraux, éphémères par définition, manquent sérieusement de légitimité ou d'autorité pour exercer de tels contrôles sur des actes établis par des autorités souveraines.

1.3 *Une procédure accentuant le sentiment de manque de légitimité de ce mode de règlement des différends*

D'autres éléments, plutôt liés à la procédure arbitrale en tant que telle, participent à la contestation de la légitimité et de l'opportunité du recours à l'arbitrage comme mode de résolution des litiges relatifs aux investissements étrangers. D'une part, le système de l'arbitrage présente de sérieux risques de conflits d'intérêts, constatés notamment par des nominations répétées d'un nombre restreint de personnes comme arbitres ou de personnes exerçant à la fois des missions de conseil et d'arbitre[17]. D'autre part, l'exigence de transparence n'est pas commune à toutes les procédures arbitrales, particulièrement en ce qui concerne les tribunaux arbitraux *ad hoc*. L'absence de transparence, concrétisée notamment par l'absence de publicité des sentences, est particulièrement inquiétante au regard de l'incidence de ces sentences sur les fonds publics. Certaines de ces sentences allouent des sommes exorbitantes aux investisseurs au titre de l'indemnisation des dommages subis, et peuvent avoir un effet rédhibitoire sur la volonté de l'État d'adopter des règlementations protectrices des droits économiques et sociaux des nationaux. L'*accountability* ou la responsabilité des membres des tribunaux est inexistante. La véritable possibilité de contester en appel les sentences n'est pas prévue pour un certain nombre de procédures arbitrales. Enfin, la convention de Washington, qui a mis en place le CIRDI, favorise l'exécution des sentences sans contrôle puisque les sentences arbitrales rendues sous l'égide du CRDI sont dispensées d'*exequatur*[18].

1.4 *Des solutions confirmant un manque de légitimité*

Outre un certain manque de légitimité résultant du recours à l'arbitrage en tant que mode de règlement des différends pour des questions relevant du droit public ainsi que des règles procédurales accentuant ce manque de

---

17 M. Fekl, « Les contestations de l'arbitrage d'investissement et les négociations commerciales internationales contemporaines », *op. cit.*

18 Articles 53 et 53 de la Convention de Washington précitée.

légitimité, des solutions rendues par les arbitres ont pu confirmer que ce mode de règlement des litiges ne constitue pas en l'état une solution adéquate pour le règlement de différends relatifs à des investissements étrangers. Ce sont principalement les contradictions entre certaines solutions rendues par différents tribunaux arbitraux qui ont suscité des interrogations quant à la cohérence du système. Si des différences de solutions peuvent être justifiées par la diversité des traités relatifs aux investissements, elles ne le sont pas quand les sentences sont rendues sur la base d'un même TBI et pour des faits similaires voire identiques. Deux séries de sentences illustrent cette problématique.

En premier lieu, les sentences rendues dans les arbitrages *Lauder* : deux tribunaux avaient été mis en place pour statuer sur des litiges opposant essentiellement les mêmes parties. Un premier tribunal avait été formé pour statuer sur le litige opposant Monsieur Lauder et la République Tchèque[19], et le second pour régler le différend opposant la société CME, contrôlée par Monsieur Lauder, avec la République Tchèque[20]. Ces deux tribunaux ont rendu des sentences contradictoires, l'une considérant que l'investisseur avait été exproprié et l'autre non, alors que les deux différends portaient sur les mêmes faits et que les sentences avaient été rendues en application d'un même traité.

Les tristement célèbres sentences rendues contre l'Argentine constituent également des exemples fréquemment évoquées de cette tendance à la contradiction des décisions rendues par les tribunaux arbitraux. Sur cinq sentences rendues sur la base d'un TBI conclu entre l'Argentine et les Etats, trois tribunaux[21] ont considéré que les conditions de l'état de nécessité prévu par le traité et permettant de déroger à certaines obligations conventionnelles n'étaient pas réunies, tandis que deux autres ont considéré qu'elles l'étaient[22].

La question de la légitimité des arbitres et leur capacité à statuer de manière transparente sur les affaires qui relèvent de leurs compétences pose particulièrement problème au regard des jurisprudences ayant apporté des limitations de la compétence normative des États au nom de la protection des intérêts des investisseurs.

---

19 *Lauder c. République tchèque*, Règlement d'arbitrage ad hoc de la CNUDCI, sentence du 3 septembre 2001.

20 *CME BV c. République tchèque*, Règlement d'arbitrage ad hoc de la CNUDCI, sentence finale du 14 mars 2003.

21 *CMS v. Argentina CMS Gas Transmission Company c. d'Argentine*, affaire CIRDI n° ARB/01/8, Sentence du 12 mai 2005, *Enron c. Argentine*, affaire CIRDI n° ARB/01/3, sentence du 22 mai 2007, et *Sempra Energy International c. Argentine*, affaire CIRDI n° ARB/02/16, sentence du 28 septembre 2007.

22 *LG&E c. Argentine*, affaire CIRDI n° ARB/02/1, sentence du 25 juillet 2007 et *Continental Casualty c. Argentine* affaire CIRDI n°. ARB/03/9, sentence du 5 septembre 2008.

2 La limitation de la compétence normative des États

Le développement des règles de protection des investissements étrangers est marqué par une hantise particulière des investisseurs : celle du risque politique. Ce risque est réalisé en cas de changement de la législation de l'État récepteur de l'investissement, qui aboutirait à la perte de l'investissement réalisé par l'investisseur étrangers, soit à travers une véritable dépossession (l'expropriation sous toutes ses formes en constitue l'exemple type), soit à travers la perte des avantages particuliers pris en considération par l'investisseur lorsque celui-ci choisit de s'établir dans un pays donné. Divers moyens ont été mis en place pour protéger les investisseurs contre les risques politiques dans le cadre des contrats d'État ou les TBI. Cette protection sous ses diverses formes passe par une limitation des compétences normatives des États. Or cette limitation, légitime dans le cas où l'État modifie ses règlementations de manière arbitraire, dans le but assumé ou présumé de déposséder l'investisseur, est discutable dans le cas où elle aboutit au blocage de toute modification normative, règlementaire ou législative, même dans le cas où cette intervention est légitime ou correspond à d'autres obligations internationales de l'État. C'est notamment le cas pour certaines législations environnementales ou ayant pour objet la protection de droits économiques et sociaux.

Or, le pouvoir d'édicter de nouvelles règlementations est un des attributs de la souveraineté étatique. Ce pouvoir qui constitue « l'exercice d'un droit souverain d'un gouvernement de promouvoir l'ordre, la sûreté, la sécurité et le bien-être général dans les limites constitutionnelles qui lui sont imparties »[23], est protégé par le droit international général. En effet, dans le cadre de ce dernier, un État souverain dispose de la plénitude des compétences, dans le sens du droit de prendre toutes les mesures qu'il juge nécessaires pour la protection des intérêts collectifs dont il a la charge. La CPJI le rappelle clairement dans l'affaire du *Statut juridique du Groenland Oriental*, dans laquelle elle considère que « la législation est une des formes les plus frappantes de l'exercice du pouvoir souverain »[24]. Le droit international général protège donc un domaine réservé propre à chaque État, domaine dans lequel cet État peut librement légiférer.

Au-delà de cette liberté de légiférer dans son domaine réservé, l'État est également libre de conclure les traités qu'il souhaite, et cette conclusion de traités, notamment en matière environnementale ou de protection de droits

23 Blackwell Law's dictionary.

24 CPJI, arrêt du 5 avril 1933, *Affaire du statut juridique du Groenland Oriental*, Série A/B, n° 53.

économiques et sociaux, entraîne une obligation d'exécution. Or dans ce cadre, l'État et sa souveraineté paient le prix de la fragmentation du droit international, puisqu'il arrive qu'il soit sanctionné par un tribunal arbitral sur la base d'un TBI pour avoir porté atteinte aux intérêts d'un investisseur étranger en adoptant une législation en matière environnementale ou relative aux droits de l'homme sur la base d'un traité international en la matière.

Il convient ici de présenter les différents titres qui permettent permettant la sanction des États ayant fait évoluer leurs législations. Ces titres se multiplient, et posent tous problème au regard de leurs effets sur la capacité des États à assumer d'un point de vue financier les modifications règlementaires qu'ils souhaitent adopter, mais aussi au regard d'une certaine incertitude juridique qu'ils engendrent du point de vue de l'État.

2.1 *Les clauses de stabilité ou d'intangibilité prévues dans les contrats d'États*

Avant le véritable développement des TBI avec ce qu'ils emportent de standards de protection des investisseurs étrangers, les investisseurs se basaient surtout sur les clauses contractuelles pour s'assurer une protection contre la puissance de la souveraineté étatique. Une partie de ces clauses étaient destinées, de manières différentes, à « la neutralisation du pouvoir normatif des États », pour reprendre l'expression retenue par le Professeur Pierre Mayer[25]. Dans son étude, le Professeur Mayer met en avant les différentes stratégies adoptées par les investisseurs ou cocontractants des États pour neutraliser les pouvoirs de règlementation de ces derniers, soit en se soustrayant aux juridictions de ces derniers (par le recours à l'arbitrage), soit en se soustrayant à leurs lois. Cette dernière hypothèse est généralement réalisée par des références à l'application du droit international public ou aux principes généraux du droit, mais surtout par des clauses de stabilisation ou d'intangibilité.

La clause de stabilisation est une clause impliquant l'application du droit national au contrat, mais du droit national tel qu'il existe au moment de la conclusion du contrat. Elle interdit explicitement à l'État de modifier le droit national applicable[26]. La clause d'intangibilité quant à elle, implique simplement une inapplicabilité des modifications au contrat en cause[27]. Elle

25 P. Mayer, « La neutralisation du pouvoir normatif de l'Etat en matière de contrats d'États »,*Journal du droit international*, vol. 113, 1986, pp. 5–78.

26 Voir A. De Nanteuil, *Droit international de l'investissement*, *op. cit.*, p. 36. Voir également les définitions apportées par P. Weil, « Les clauses de stabilisation ou d'intangibilités insérées dans les accords de développement économique », *in Mélanges Charles Rousseau*, Paris, Pedone, 1974, pp. 301–328.

27 *Idem.*

emporte donc moins de conséquences par rapport à l'exercice des pouvoirs normatifs de l'État, puisqu'il pourra mettre en place les modifications qu'il souhaite tant qu'il ne cherche pas à les opposer à son cocontractant. Contrairement aux autres modes de limitation des pouvoirs normatifs des États, ces clauses entrainent une limitation « objective » de ces pouvoirs, en ce qu'elles n'ouvrent pas la voie à la distinction entre des interventions législatives et règlementaires « légitimes » de l'État, et celles qui ne le sont pas et qui entraîneraient la sanction de l'État. Aucune place n'est laissée à la bonne foi de l'État, qui serait sanctionnée quel que soit le motif de son intervention normative.

Le développement du droit international des investissements à travers les TBI et les standards qu'ils contiennent n'a pas abouti à l'abandon de la prévision de ces types de clauses. Elles continuent à figurer dans les contrats et peuvent être invoquées avec succès dans le cadre d'arbitrages basés sur les TBI et non sur les contrats eux-mêmes[28]. Elles continuent donc à contribuer à mettre des obstacles aux modifications règlementaires que souhaiteraient mettre en place les États. Ces obstacles résultent du coût de l'indemnisation mise à la charge de l'Etat qui chercherait à opposer une règlementation aussi légitime soit-elle à son cocontractant, ou de la réduction de l'effectivité d'une législation qui serait inégalement opposable aux acteurs en activité dans l'État mettant en place une nouvelle législation[29]. Ils ne rendent certes pas impossible une modification, mais peuvent lui accoler un coût rédhibitoire.

2.2 *L'expropriation indirecte*

La protection des investisseurs contre les expropriations est « *au cœur de la protection que le droit international propose aux opérateurs étrangers, puisque c'est contre ce risque que ce sont développées les toutes premières règles* »[30]. Le droit international général prévoit en effet des règles relatives à la protection des personnes privées contre des expropriations réalisées par des États autres que l'État dont elles sont ressortissantes. Dans ce cadre, les expropriations ne sont autorisées que dans le respect de certaines garanties légales, particulièrement l'existence d'un intérêt public, la non-discrimination et le paiement

28 Voir notamment *AGIP c. République du Congo*, affaire CIRDI n° ARB/77/1, sentence du 30 novembre 1979, p. 735 et s.. Cette question revêt tout son intérêt au regard de la distinction entre les demandes conventionnelles et les demandes contractuelles.

29 K. Gehne and R. Brillo, « Stabilization clauses in international investment law: beyond balancing and fair and equitable treatment », pp. 14–15, disponible sur : https://telc.jura.uni-halle.de/sites/default/files/BeitraegeTWR/Heft%20143.pdf, dernière consultation le 23/07/2021.

30 A. De Nanteuil, *Droit international de l'investissement*, *op. cit.*, p. 358.

d'une indemnité « prompte, adéquate et effective ». Ces solutions ont été reprises dans les TBI, qui prévoient des clauses relatives à la protection des investisseurs contre les mesures d'expropriation directe.

Mais le droit international des investissements ne se contente pas uniquement de protéger les investisseurs contre les expropriations à proprement parler ou les expropriations « directes » : les solutions développées par les arbitres et adoptées par la suite dans les TBI sanctionnent également les expropriations indirectes. Celles-ci désignent des mesures dont le but n'est pas d'exproprier ou de nationaliser les investissements étrangers mais dont l'effet est de priver les investisseurs des droits qui s'attachent à leurs investissements. La justification de l'adoption de cette solution a été clairement formulée par les arbitres dans la sentence rendue dans l'affaire *Pope & Talbot Inc. c. The Government of Canada*[31]. Les arbitres y déclarent en effet que « les traités ne rempliraient pas leurs fonctions si les règles protectrices en cas d'expropriation pouvaient être contournées par l'édiction de mesures identiques par leurs effets mais différentes par leurs formes »[32]. Cette solution adoptée par les tribunaux arbitraux pour protéger les intérêts des investisseurs, n'est pas conforme à celles adoptées par le Droit international général ou par les législations nationales (ou régionales) en matière de protection contre les expropriations arbitraires. Dans cette confrontation entre l'intérêt général mis en avant par l'État et l'intérêt particulier de l'investisseur, celui-ci prévaut dans le cadre de ces solutions et sanctionne les États pour des mesures qui n'avaient pas pour objet la dépossession d'un bien ou d'un investissement.

Si cette solution pourrait à la limite sembler raisonnable dans le cas d'une interprétation à effet utile des clauses conventionnelles relatives à l'expropriation, d'autres solutions adoptées sur le fondement de la prohibition des mesures d'expropriations indirectes sont plus dangereuses. En premier lieu, des sentences adoptées par les arbitres peuvent aboutir à la condamnation d'États qui adoptent des mesures qui ne vont pas porter atteinte à l'investissement lui-même mais qui va simplement diminuer les bénéfices de l'investisseur. Une telle solution a notamment été adoptée dans l'affaire *Suez et Vivendi c. Argentine*[33]. Dans cette sentence, les arbitres ont considéré qu'il

31 Interim Award, UNCITRAL, 26 June 2000, paras 83–84.

32 Traduction établie par S. Manciaux, « Les mesures équivalentes à une expropriation dans l'arbitrage international relatif aux investissements », *in* F. Horchani (dir.), *Où va le droit de l'investissement ? Désordre normatif et recherche d'équilibre*, Paris, Pedone, 2006, pp.73–94.

33 *Suez, Sociedad General de Aguas de Barcelona S.A. and Vivendi Universal S.A. c. Argentine,* affaire CIRDI n° ARB/03/19, sentence du 30 juillet, para. 132.

y a expropriation lorsque l'État se prévaut de ses pouvoirs de règlementation pour mettre en place des mesures qui réduisent les bénéfices de l'investisseur sans pour autant annuler ou modifier son titre de propriété ou réduire le contrôle qu'il exerce sur ses biens[34]. Par ailleurs, les tribunaux arbitraux ont développé une jurisprudence condamnant les expropriations rampantes, dans laquelle l'expropriation est le résultat d'une série de mesure adoptée par l'État hôte. Cette solution étant dangereuse dans la mesure où il est encore plus difficile d'estimer l'impact d'une série de mesures sur des investissements. Enfin, une condamnation peut intervenir dans le cas où l'État légifère ou intervient, même pour la satisfaction d'autres obligations internationales, notamment en matière environnementale. La sentence *Metaclad c. Mexique*[35] est assez emblématique de ce type de situation : l'investisseur avait fait l'acquisition d'un permis pour exploiter une décharge, ce qui pouvait entraîner la pollution des eaux souterraines. Le gouverneur décide donc de créer une réserve naturelle englobant la décharge. Le tribunal arbitral a considéré dans sa sentence que « l'objectif poursuivi par l'État, bien que légitime, n'est pas opérant sur la qualification de l'expropriation ». Cette solution a été reprise dans d'autres sentences arbitrales hors du cadre de l'ALENA, dans lesquelles les arbitres ont considéré clairement que la source internationale de la protection de l'environnement ne fait pas de différence sur la qualification de l'expropriation[36].

Ces différentes solutions n'empêchent techniquement pas les États d'adopter de nouvelles règlementations en matière environnementales ou de protection de droits économiques et sociaux. Simplement, elles les condamnent à payer des indemnisations dans le cas où les règlementations adoptées portent atteinte, directement ou indirectement, à des investissements. C'est pour cette raison que l'on considère que les États paient le prix de la fragmentation

34 Des mesures d'expropriations existent « *host states invoke their legislative and regulatory powers to enact measures that reduce the benefits investors derive from their investments without actually changing or cancelling investor's title to their assets or diminishing their control over them* ».

35 *Metaclad c. Mexique*, affaire CIRDI n° ARB/97/1, sentence du 30 août 2000.

36 *Compañía del Desarrollo de Santa Elena, S.A.* c. Costa Rica, affaire CIRDI n° *ARB/96/1, sentence du 17 February 2000, para. 72* : « *While an expropriation or taking for environmental reasons may be classified as a taking for a public purpose, and thus may be legitimate, the fact that the Property was taken for this reason does not affect either the nature or the measure of the compensation to be paid for the taking. That is, the purpose of protecting the environment for which the Property was taken does not alter the legal character of the taking for which adequate compensation must be paid. The international source of the obligation to protect the environment makes no difference* ».

du droit international, dans la mesure où l'adoption de telles mesures présente un cout rédhibitoire qui peut décourager les États de faire évoluer ses législations. Mais qualifier ces solutions d'atteinte à la souveraineté de l'État dépend de la position que l'on adopte au sujet des considérations économiques : soit celles-ci constituent une réelle contrainte susceptible de porter une véritable atteinte à la souveraineté des État, soit elle ne constituent qu'un simple facteur que l'État prend en compte dans le cadre d'un calcul économique libre réalisé dans le plein exercice de sa souveraineté. Cette dernière lecture fait obstacle à toute critique de la jurisprudence arbitrale qui serait basée sur l'idée sur la défense d'une certaine « espérance légitime » que pourraient avoir les États en ce qui concerne l'interprétation des clauses prévues dans les TBI.

Il reste à noter que la décentralisation du règlement de litiges aux investissements étrangers continue à engendrer de nouvelles problématiques, notamment en ce qui concerne la théorie de l'expropriation indirecte. Les solutions relatives à cette notion ont en effet fait l'objet de deux tendances contraires. D'une part, une évolution positive à travers la réaffirmation du critère de la discrimination comme élément de définition des cas d'expropriation. Dans la sentence *El Paso Energy International Company c. Argentine*[37], les arbitres ont considéré que « des mesures règlementaires générales et non discriminatoires prises conformément aux règles de bonne foi et des garanties procédurales, n'impliquent pas une compensation »[38]. Cette solution a par la suite été confirmée par la sentence *Saluka Investments BV (The Netherlands) c. The Czech Republic*[39]. Mais parallèlement à ces sentences, d'autres arbitres, loin d'adopter cette approche équilibrée entre la protection des investisseurs contre les mesures d'expropriation, ont renforcé les limitations à la pleine compétence normative des États. La sentence *Occidental Petroleum*

---

37 *El Paso Energy International Company c. Argentine*, affaire CIRDI n° ARB/03/15, sentence du 31 Octobre 2011.

38 Traduction de l'auteur. Version originale : « *In sum, a general regulation is a lawful act rather than an expropriation if it is non-discriminatory, made for a public purpose and taken in conformity with due process. In other words, in principle, general non-discriminatory regulatory measures, adopted in accordance with the rules of good faith and due process, do not entail a duty of compensation* ».

39 *Sentence partielle, Cour permanente d'arbitrage, decision du 17 Mars 2000*: « It is now established in international law that *States are not liable to pay compensation* to a foreign investor when, in the *normal exercise of their regulatory powers*, they adopt in a *non-discriminatory* manner *bona fide* regulations that are aimed at the general welfare ».

corporation c. Equateur[40], est assez emblématique de cette tendance libérale des arbitres à l'encontre des compétences souveraines des États. En effet, dans cette sentence, le tribunal ne s'est pas contenté de condamner l'État à des dommages-intérêts, mais est allé jusqu'à déclarer la nullité d'un règlement fiscal émis par l'Équateur. L'adoption de cette solution dépasse largement les pouvoirs des arbitres, qui n'ont ni compétence ni légitimité pour annuler un acte souverain, mais peuvent seulement apprécier les conséquences de l'adoption de cet acte sur les droits des investisseurs. La généralisation de cette solution n'est guère à redouter, mais son adoption est assez révélatrice des dangers du recours à un tribunal arbitral pour résoudre des litiges liés à l'exercice de compétences souveraines.

2.3 *Le traitement juste et équitable, vecteur d'une obligation de sécurité juridique*

Dans le cadre de l'impératif de stabilité et de sécurité juridique nécessaire à la protection des intérêts des investisseurs, certains traités ont commencé à englober dans leurs préambules l'obligation pour les États récepteurs d'assurer un cadre règlementaire stable. Cette obligation sert de base pour sanctionner les modifications législatives que peuvent adopter des États. En l'absence de telles stipulations, les arbitres ont eu recours à la clause de traitement juste et équitable pour imposer aux États une obligation de stabilité juridique.

La clause de traitement juste et équitable est une clause plutôt standard[41], qui figurerait même dans le cadre du droit international général sous le titre du « standard minimum »[42]. Cette clause regroupe un assez large éventail d'obligations, dont bon nombre ne font pas débat : interdiction du déni de justice ; interdiction des mesures arbitraires ; interdiction des mesures discriminatoires ; respect de la bonne foi ; respect des procédures légales ... D'autres obligations, fruits de l'interprétation de la clause par les tribunaux arbitraux, sont plus problématiques[43]. Celle qui nous intéresse en particulier est l'obligation de respecter les attentes légitimes des investisseurs. La sentence *Tecmed c. Mexique*[44] est la première à avoir fait de la notion « d'attente légitime » des investisseurs une composante du standard du traitement juste et équitable.

---

40 *Occidental Petroleum Corporation and Occidental Exploration and Production Company c.* Equateur, affaire CIRDI n°. ARB/06/11,sentence du 5 octobre 2012.

41 A. De Nanteuil, *Droit international de l'investissement, op. cit.*, p. 334.

42 *Ibid.*, p. 335.

43 M. Fekl, « Les contestations de l'arbitrage d'investissement et les négociations commerciales internationales contemporaines », *op. cit.*

44 *Tecmed c. United Mexican States*, affaire CIRDI n°ARB/00/2, sentence du 29 mai 2003.

Cette notion, qui implique l'obligation d'assurer la stabilité du cadre règlementaire, a été reprise par un certain nombre de tribunaux arbitraux, notamment dans cinq sentences rendues dans les différends liés à l'Argentine, qui ont rattaché l'obligation de maintien d'un environnement juridique stable au standard de traitement juste et équitable[45].

Ces solutions sont critiquables du fait de la charge imprévue qu'elles font porter aux États. Pour être acceptables, elles devraient être rééquilibrées à deux égards. D'une part, les attentes légitimes des investisseurs devraient être basées sur des promesses claires et particulières faites aux investisseurs, matérialisées par exemple par des contrats, des lettres d'intention, des promesses spécifiques faites dans des réunions[46]... D'autre part, seules des mesures ayant un caractère arbitraire ou déraisonnable devraient pouvoir faire l'objet de sanction. La sentence *Charrane*[47], rendue sur la base de la Charte de l'Énergie, intègre les assouplissements nécessaires à l'obligation de respect des attentes légitimes des investisseurs. Les arbitres y considèrent en effet qu'une modification unilatérale de la règlementation par l'Etat hôte ne constitue pas à elle seule une atteinte aux espérances légitimes des investisseurs.

Ces différentes solutions relatives à la question du pouvoir de règlementation des États, mettent en relief les problèmes soulevés par la résolution arbitrale des litiges qui s'ajoutent à ceux découlant du manque de légitimité des arbitres pour résoudre ce type de litiges touchant à la souveraineté étatique.

3 Une nécessité de faire évoluer les procédures

Les différentes critiques adressées au DII, dont nous n'avons rapporté que les plus répandues chez les professionnels de ce droit comme chez les profanes, ont été dans une certaine mesure entendues par les tribunaux et les États appelés à conclure de nouveaux TBI. Cette évolution se traduit en premier lieu par une tentative de rééquilibrer le système par un recalibrage de la jurisprudence des tribunaux arbitraux à travers une admission des demandes

45 CMS c. Argentine, sentence du 12 May 2005, précitée, para. 274: « *a stable legal and business environment is an essential element of fair and equitable treatment* ».

46 Voir Newcombe and Paradell, *Law and Practice of Investment Treaties: Standards of Treatment*, Kluwer Law International, 2009 pp. 281–282: "State conduct should be "specific and unambiguous", as well as "targeted at a specific person or identifiable group".

47 *Charanne B.V. and Construction Investments S.A.R.L. c. Royaume d'Espagne,*, arbitrage SCC n° 062/2012, sentence finale du 21 janvier2016.

reconventionnelles. Mais elle résulte surtout de la prise de conscience des États de la nécessité de faire évoluer les dispositions conventionnelles, particulièrement en ce qui concerne les procédures de règlement des différends.

3.1 *L'admission des demandes reconventionnelles*

Un thème récurrent des critiques adressées au droit international des investissements est le déséquilibre de ce système en faveur de l'investisseur. Une manifestation de ce déséquilibre se matérialise par le fait que les investisseurs soient systématiquement demandeurs et les États défendeurs, particulièrement depuis le développement de l'arbitrage unilatéral à partir de la sentence *Asian agricultural products c. République du Sri Lanka*. Cette forme d'arbitrage présume en effet l'accord des États à l'arbitrage, mais pas celui des investisseurs. Les États ne pourront donc théoriquement se retrouver en situation de demandeurs que si l'investisseur donne son consentement à la formation d'un tribunal arbitral. Mais cette hypothèse ne pourra pas être réalisée sur le fondement d'un TBI. En effet, ces derniers ont été pensés et rédigés comme des traités classiques, c'est-à-dire des traités ne prévoyant des obligations qu'à la charge des États, et quasiment pas d'obligations à la charge des investisseurs. Pour cette raison, un État ne trouvera en principe pas dans le TBI une base permettant de présenter des demandes à l'encontre d'un investisseur.

C'est dans ce contexte qu'a commencé à apparaître une question relative à la possibilité pour un État, en situation de défendeur, d'introduire des demandes reconventionnelles permettant de relativiser ou d'excuser des éventuels manquements de sa part à ses obligations conventionnelles. Un État pourrait-il dans le cadre d'un arbitrage d'investissement se prévaloir d'une exception d'inexécution envers un investisseurs ayant violé des dispositions du droit interne de l'État, particulièrement en matière fiscale, environnementale ou sociale ? Cette question prend une certaine importance avec le développement d'une responsabilisation des entreprises multinationales, à travers notamment le contexte des exigences liées à la *Corporate social responsibility*.

La réponse à cette question semble dépendre de plusieurs facteurs. La formulation des dispositions conventionnelles y joue bien entendu un rôle fondamental. Celui-ci permet-il de recourir à l'arbitrage pour tous les litiges relatifs à un investissement ? Ou bien ce recours n'est-il autorisé que pour des violations des dispositions de ce traité ? En cas de silence du traité sur la question des demandes reconventionnelles présentées par les États, celles-ci sont-elles autorisées ?

Certains tribunaux semblent être ouverts à cette critique et à la nécessité d'accepter des demandes reconventionnelles. Cette solution permet à la fois de contribuer à la responsabilisation des Etats et d'atténuer la fragmentation du droit international. La sentence rendue dans l'affaire *Urbaser c. Argentine*[48] semble particulièrement significative à cet égard. Dans cette affaire, l'investisseur, concessionnaire de service lié au traitement de l'eau et des égouts, a subi des pertes du fait des mesures prises par l'Argentine suite à la crise économique de 2001–2002. Ces pertes les ont poussé à mettre fin à la concession et saisir un tribunal arbitral. Celui-ci accepta une demande reconventionnelle introduite par l'Argentine relative aux droits de l'Homme, particulièrement le droit à l'eau. Le tribunal a considéré dans cette sentence que les instruments internationaux relatifs aux droits de l'Homme pouvaient être invoqués à l'encontre des entreprises multinationales, à condition que les dispositions de ces instruments soient suffisamment précises à ce niveau. Or, ce n'était pas le cas en l'espèce, ce qui a abouti au rejet de la demande reconventionnelle. La sentence n'en demeure pas fortement intéressante, notamment par rapport à la distinction établie par le tribunal en ce qui concerne les obligations positives et les obligations négatives ou abstentions qui pourraient être mis à la charge des investisseurs. Selon ce tribunal, les abstentions sont directement opposables aux investisseurs, tandis que les obligations positives telles que l'obligation d'assurer un accès à l'eau, ne le sont pas sauf dispositions claires. Même si la demande reconventionnelle n'a pas abouti en l'espèce, cette sentence donne des indications aux États quant à la voie à suivre dans la rédaction de nouveaux TBI pour tenter de rééquilibrer la donne au niveau des obligations à la charge des deux parties dans des litiges liés aux investissements.

La nouvelle génération de TBI connaît d'ailleurs une certaine augmentation de clauses renvoyant à des normes relatives aux droits fondamentaux ou au droit de l'environnement[49]. Cette voie ne s'est pas encore généralisée, mais marque une certaine évolution positive. Il est par ailleurs intéressant de noter qu'un certain nombre de ces essais d'intégration de « considération extra-économiques » dans les TBI sont destinés à garantir la liberté normative des États[50].

---

48 Urbaser c. Argentine affaire CIRDI n°ARB/07/26, sentence du 8 décembre 2016.

49 K. Gordon and J. Pohl, « Environmental concerns in international investment agreements: a survey », *OECD Working papers*, n° 2011/1, OECD Publishing, p. 34.

50 Voir en ce sens, A. De Nanteuil, *Droit international de l'investissement*, *op. cit.*, pp. 337 et s.

3.2 *La tentative de réforme des tribunaux arbitraux*

Comme nous l'avons précédemment exposé, les principales critiques adressées au système du DII concernent le recours à l'arbitrage pour régler des différends confrontant des personnes privées à des entités souveraines sur des questions touchant à des prérogatives souveraines. Ce système serait d'autant plus critiquable qu'elles impliquent des instances telles la Cour internationale d'arbitrage de la Cour de Commerce international de Paris ou l'Institut d'arbitrage de la chambre de commerce de Stockholm, institutions créées d'abord pour le règlement de litiges arbitraux et qui suivent plutôt une logique privatiste.

Cette critique a également fait l'objet d'une réception plutôt positive de la part des États, et des tentatives de mise en place d'une cour permanente pour le règlement des litiges relatifs aux investissements, sachant que le CIRDI ne constitue pas une « cour » pour le règlement des différends, mais plutôt un organe administratif qui facilite le processus de recours à l'arbitrage pour le règlement des différends. Une telle Cour permettrait théoriquement une harmonisation des solutions, la mise en place d'un véritable recours en appel (qui n'existe pas dans toutes les procédures d'arbitrages actuelles) et plus de transparence dans la nomination des membres du tribunal.

Au niveau global, une initiative notable est avancée par l'UNCITRAL sous l'égide de l'ONU, qui a mis en place un groupe de travail pour s'attaquer à la question[51]. Mais la tentative la plus aboutie est celle mise en place par l'Union européenne avec son « *investment court system* » (ICS), une institution semblable à l'organe de règlement de différends de l'OMC.

Depuis le Traité de Lisbonne[52], l'Union européenne a centralisé la gestion des investissements interétatiques, et notamment conclusion de traités relatifs aux investissements avec les États non-européens. Ceci l'a notamment amenée à conclure de nouveaux traités en matière de commerce et d'investissement, ce qui a permis un renouvellement de la réflexion sur les procédures de règlements des différends en la matière. En particulier, l'Accord économique et commercial global (généralement connu sous l'acronyme « CETA ») conclu avec le Canada le 30 octobre 2016, a permis une avancée sur la question en créant « une institution permanente, de nature hybride, pour statuer sur les litiges qui pourraient naitre entre les investisseurs d'une des parties à

51 « La CNUDCI se penche sur la réforme du régime de règlement des différends entre (…) – Représentation permanente de la France auprès des Organisations Internationales et des Nations unies à Vienne », www.delegfrance.org, consulté le 25/05/2021.

52 Traité de Lisbonne modifiant le traité sur l'Union européenne et le traité instituant la Communauté européenne, signé le 13 décembre 2007, *JOUE*, n° C 306.

l'accord et l'autre État »[53]. Le traité prévoit en effet la mise en place d'un tribunal de 15 membres dont 5 nommés par le Canada, 5 par l'Union européenne et 5 par des États tiers, pour une période de 5 ans. Ce Tribunal prendra en charge l'instruction des affaires à travers des divisions composées de 3 membres. Le traité prévoit par ailleurs l'institution d'un tribunal d'appel qui pourra être saisi en cas « d'erreurs dans l'application ou l'interprétation du droit applicable ; d'erreurs manifestes dans l'appréciation des faits, y compris l'appréciation du droit interne pertinent ; ou pour les motifs classiques d'annulation de sentences énoncés par la Convention CIRDI » (vice dans la constitution du Tribunal ; excès de pouvoir manifeste du Tribunal ; corruption d'un membre du Tribunal ; inobservation grave d'une règle fondamentale de procédure ; défaut de motifs).

Par ce traité, les parties répondent donc aux principales préoccupations relatives au manque de cohérence des solutions adoptées dans des litiges relatifs aux investissements étrangers ainsi qu'en l'absence de contrôle des sentences arbitrales rendues en la matière. Mais l'efficacité de cette évolution au niveau de la procédure quant au rééquilibrage du système ne pourra être vérifiée qu'à partir du règlement d'un certain nombre de différends.

•••

Le droit international des investissements constitue, bien que dans une mesure moindre que ne le laissent entendre les critiques, un système déséquilibré en faveur de la protection des droits et intérêts des investisseurs. Mais de là affirmer catégoriquement que ce système est attentatoire à la souveraineté des États, il y a un pas qu'on ne devrait pas franchir. Ce système est certainement attentatoire aux intérêts des États, mais il reste indéniable que ces derniers ont fait le choix d'adopter des normes insuffisamment précises. Le fait qu'ils continuent à s'engager dans un tel système en maintenant globalement les mêmes standards et les mêmes normes, et qu'ils n'exercent pas leur droit souverain de s'en retirer, démontre leur choix de continuer à favoriser l'attractivité de leurs territoires au regard des investisseurs par rapport à d'autres considérations extra-économiques d'intérêt public.

53 C. Kessedjian, « Les différends entre investisseurs et États hôtes par un tribunal arbitral permanent. L'exemple du CETA », *Revue trimestrielle de droit européen*, 2017, pp. 633 et s.

CHAPTER 16

Remise en cause et volonté de réforme du droit international des investissements

Réflexions à partir des Third World Approaches to International Law (TWAIL)

Yannick Mihnzou Kouassi

Ces[1] dernières années, les parutions consacrées au droit des investissements comportent généralement un chapitre relatif au futur du droit des investissements : « *The Future of International Investment Law* »[2], « *The Future of Investment Arbitration* »[3] et d'autres titres aux accents quelque peu pessimistes tels que : « *Does Investment Arbitration Have a Future ?* »[4]. À ces ouvrages s'ajoutent des dizaines d'autres articles s'interrogeant tous sur l'avenir du droit international des investissements[5].

---

1 L'auteur voudrait remercier les professeurs Évelyne Lagrange et Edoardo Stoppioni pour leur relecture et commentaire du manuscrit. Toute erreur ou omission relève naturellement de sa seule responsabilité.

2 C. Schreuer, « The Future of International Investment Law », *in* M. Bungenberg and *al.* (eds), *International Investment Law*, Beck/Hart/Nomos, 2015, pp. 1904–1911 ; K-H. Böckstiegel, « The future of International Investment Law-Substantive Protection, and Dispute, Settlement », *in* M. Bungenberg and *al.* (eds), *International Investment Law, op. cit.*, pp. 1863–1872 ; E. Gaillard, « L'avenir des traités de protection des investissements », *in* C. Leben (dir.), *Droit international des investissements et de l'arbitrage transnational*, Paris, Pedone, 2015, pp. 1027–1047 ; J. Alvarez et K. Sauvant, *The Evolving International Investment Regime: Expectations, Realities, Options*, Oxford University Press, 2011 ; W. M. Reisman, « The Future of International Investment Law and Arbitration », *in* A. Cassese, *The Future of International Law*, Oxford University Press, 2012, pp. 275–286.

3 A. Reinisch, « The Future of Investment Arbitration », *in* C. Binder and *al.* (eds), *International Investment Law for the 21st Century, Essays in Honour of Christopoh Schreuer*, Oxford University Press, 2009, pp. 894–916 ; C. Rogers and R. Alford, *The Future of Investment Arbitration*, Oxford University Press, 2009.

4 K. Hober, « Does Investment arbitration have a future? », *in* M. Bungenberg and *al.* (eds), *International Investment Law, op. cit.*, pp. 1873–1878.

5 N. Butler et S. Subedi, « The Future of International Investment Regulation: Towards a World Investment Organisation? », *Neth. Int'l Law Rev*, vol. 64, 2017, pp. 43–72 ; K. Miles, « Investor-State Dispute Settlement: Conflict, Convergence, and Future Directions », *Eur. Ybk Intl Ec. L*, vol. 7, 2016, pp. 273–308 ; G. Kahale III, « Rethinking ISDS », *Brooklyn J. Int'l Law*, vol. 44, 2018, pp. 12–50.

 | DOI:10.1163/9789004508712_017

Ces préoccupations sur l'avenir de la matière sont au moins le marqueur d'un malaise, et ce d'autant qu'elles s'inscrivent dans un contexte, certes pas nouveau, mais qui demeure particulier. Sur le plan politique, la signature de l'Accord économique global entre l'UE et ses États membres d'une part et le Canada de l'autre, a donné lieu en 2016 à de nombreux mouvements sociaux et positionnements politiques dénonçant certaines des options prises dans ce traité. En France, lors de l'adoption de la loi de ratification de ce traité par l'Assemblée nationale, certains députés de la majorité présidentielle au pouvoir ont même voté contre la loi de ratification[6]. Plus significativement encore, en Belgique, la Wallonie a d'abord refusé de ratifier ce texte ; exigeant par là-même la saisine de la CJUE à l'effet de vérifier la conformité dudit traité au droit primaire de l'UE[7]. Aussi, la conclusion d'accords de libre-échange est-elle décidément devenue un sujet majeur au même titre que la santé ou la sécurité lors des débats électoraux[8]. De plus en plus d'articles de presse consacrés au droit des investissements en peignent un portrait peu flatteur, à l'instar de ce titre du *New York Times* : « *Nafta's Powerful Little Secret; Obscure Tribunals Settle Disputes, but Go Too Far* »[9].

Sur le plan juridique, ces divers mouvements auxquels s'ajoutent de nombreuses autres raisons ont conduit certains États à dénoncer des conventions internationales relatives à la protection des investissements. La Bolivie, l'Équateur[10] et le Venezuela ont ainsi dénoncé la Convention de Washington[11]

6 « CETA : qui sont les députés de la majorité qui ont voté contre le traité ? », *Sud Ouest*, 24/07/2019, <https://www.sudouest.fr/2019/07/24/ceta-qui-sont-les-deputes-de-la-majorite-qui-ont-vote-contre-le-traite-6373987-710.php>.

7 Le 30 avril 2019, la CJUE a conclu à la compatibilité entre le droit primaire de l'UE et le mécanisme de règlement des différends mis en place par le CETA. V. Avis 1/17, 30 avril 2019, ECLI:EU:C:2019:341.

8 G. Poingt, « Pour ou contre le « libre-échange » : les propositions des candidats aux européennes », *Le Figaro*, 17/05/2019 <https://www.lefigaro.fr/economie/le-scan-eco/dessous-chiffres/pour-ou-contre-le-libre-echange-les-propositions-des-candidats-aux-europeennes-20190517>.

9 A. Depalma, « Nafta's Powerful Little Secret; Obscure Tribunals Settle Disputes, but Go Too Far, Critics Say », *NY Times*, 11/03/2011 <https://www.nytimes.com/2001/03/11/business/nafta-s-powerful-little-secret-obscure-tribunals-settle-disputes-but-go-too-far.html>; « Ceta : les tribunaux d'arbitrage cristallisent les réticences », *Les Echos*, 24/10/2016, <https://www.lesechos.fr/2016/10/ceta-les-tribunaux-darbitrage-cristallisent-les-reticences-220250>.

10 Après avoir dénoncé la convention CIRDI en 2009, l'Équateur a fait un pas vers une nouvelle adhésion à cette convention en la signant le 21 juin 2021. V. G. Prieto, « Ecuador returns to the ICSID Convention: A brief assessment of its decade-long international investment law 'exit strategy'», *EJIL:Talk!*, 19/06/021 < https://www.ejiltalk.org/ecuador-returns-to-the-icsid-convention-a-brief-assessment-of-its-decade-long-international-investment-law-exit-strategy/>.

11 Respectivement en 2007, 2009 et 2012.

et certains de leurs Traités Bilatéraux de protection des Investissements (TBI). À partir de 2012, l'Afrique du Sud, quant à elle, a dénoncé une dizaine de ses TBI. En 2011, le gouvernement australien a annoncé qu'il n'intégrerait plus de dispositions relatives au règlement des différends dans ses accords[12]. En 2016, l'Inde a notifié à 57 de ses partenaires commerciaux sa volonté de dénoncer les TBI qui la liaient à ceux-ci. En mai 2020, 23 États membres de l'UE ont conclu un accord ayant pour finalité l'extinction de plus de 200 traités bilatéraux d'investissement entre les États membres de l'Union européenne.

Dans le même temps, des initiatives de réforme ont été entreprises par plusieurs institutions internationales. Ainsi, la Commission des Nations Unies pour le droit commercial international (CNUDCI) a-t-elle mis en place un groupe de travail ayant pour mission de conduire les réflexions sur une éventuelle réforme du système de règlement des différends entre État et investisseur[13]. De son côté, le Centre international pour le règlement des différends relatifs aux investissements (CIRDI) a entrepris une refonte de ses règlements[14].

Pourtant, on pouvait difficilement s'attendre à un tel mouvement de remise en cause tant le droit international des investissements (DII) a connu un développement exponentiel et semblait avoir emporté la conviction de tous les États. En effet, 2654 traités de protection[15] sont toujours en vigueur, impliquant un réseau de 234 États, territoires ou espaces économiques. Au 31 décembre 2019, la CNUCED recensait 1023 affaires relatives à des différends issus d'un investissement[16]. En quelques décennies[17], la pratique du droit des

12 J. Cazala, « La défiance étatique à l'égard de l'arbitrage investisseur État exprimée dans quelques projets et instruments conventionnels récents », *JDI*, n° 3, 2017. Notons tout de même que le Gouvernement australien est quelque peu revenu plus tard sur cette décision en indiquant que l'insertion de clauses de règlements des différends dans les traités de protection des investissements se ferait désormais au cas par cas.

13 CNUCDI, *Rapport de la Commission des Nations Unies pour le droit commercial international*, Doc. A/72/17, 2017, paras 263–264 <https://undocs.org/fr/A/72/17>.

14 L'ensemble de la documentation relative à ce processus peut être consulté sur <https://icsid.worldbank.org/resources/rules-and-regulations/icsid-rules-and-regulations-amendment-working-papers>.

15 CNUCED, « The Changing IIA Landscape: New Treaties And Recent Policy Developments », *IIA Issues Note*, juillet 2020, p. 1, disponible sur : <https://unctad.org/en/PublicationsLibrary/diaepcbinf2020d4.pdf>.

16 CNUCED, « Case, name and number », <https://investmentpolicy.unctad.org/investment-dispute-settlement>.

17 S. Alexandrov, « The "Baby Boom" of Treaty-based Arbitrations and the Jurisdiction of ICSID Tribunals. Shareholders as "Investors" and Jurisdiction *Ratione Temporis* », *Law & Prac. Int'l Cts. & Trib.*, vol. 4, 2005, p. 19 ; J. Pauwelyn, « At the Edge of Chaos? Foreign Investment Law as a Complex Adaptive System, How It Emerged and How It Can Be Reformed », *ICSID Rev.*, vol. 29, 2014, p. 379.

investissements a permis de revisiter certains concepts du droit international ou même d'en créer de nouveaux, au point même où certains auteurs estiment que des règles coutumières ont pu émerger[18].

Comment expliquer que, malgré son succès, le DII se trouve freiné par un vent de contestation et de remise en cause qui implique même des États traditionnellement en faveur du régime de protection des investissements ? Nous répondrons à cette question à partir d'une approche tiers-mondiste qui impliquera de recourir aux outils d'analyse des *Third World Approaches to International Law* (TWAIL) mais aussi de la théorie de la dépendance telle que développée dans les années 1960–1970. Certes, ces approches sont loin d'être en elles-mêmes homogènes[19]. Toutefois, on sait combien l'histoire et les rapports de domination sont centraux dans les analyses que font les auteurs relevant de ces approches[20]. À partir de ces outils, la thèse soutenue ici consistera à montrer que le DII continue, d'une part, de reproduire les rapports de domination (I) et, d'autre part, que les tentatives de réforme ont peu de chance de bouleverser ce paradigme aussi longtemps qu'elles n'auront pas placé l'humain au centre des préoccupations (II).

Mais avant d'y arriver, au regard des débats qui ont parfois lieu sur les méthodes et outils d'analyse utilisés par les *TWAIL*[21] et, dans un environnement marqué de plus en plus par une suspicion presque systématique, il faut s'empresser de relever que l'objectif de cet article n'est ni pamphlétaire ni militant, et encore moins destiné à débusquer quelque complot qui aurait été ourdi par le droit international des investissements. Il vise modestement à présenter une vision alternative[22], en tout cas une approche qui diffère de

---

18 S. M. Schwebel, « The Influence of Bilateral Investment Treaties on Customary International Law », *Proceedings ASIL*, vol. 98, 2004, pp. 27–30 ; C. McLachlan, « Is There an Evolving Customary International Law on Investment? », *ICSID Rev.*, vol. 31, 2016, pp. 257–269 ; M. Audit et M. Forteau, « Investment Arbitration without BIT: Toward a Foreign Investment Customary Based Arbitration ? », *J. Intl. Arb.*, issue 5, 2012, pp. 581–604.

19 J. T. Gathii, « TWAIL : A Brief History of Its Origins, Its Decentralized Network, and a Tentative Bibliography », *Trade Law & Dev*, vol. 3, 2011 ; A. Bianchi, *International Law Theories: An Inquiry into Different Ways of Thinking*, Oxford University Press, 2016, p. 205.

20 A. Bianchi, *International Law Theories: An Inquiry into Different Ways of Thinking*, *op. cit.*, p. 205.

21 A. Geslin, « L'apport des postcolonial studies à la recherche en droit international », *in* A. Geslin, C. M. Herrera et M.-C. Ponthoreau (dir.), *Postcolonialisme et droit : Perspectives épistémologiques*, Kimé, 2020, p. 179.

22 V. notamment C. L. Lim (ed.), *Alternative Visions of the International Law on Foreign Investment: Essays in Honour of Muthucumaraswamy Sornarajah*, Cambridge

l'approche classique autour de laquelle toute la discipline est construite et évolue. À partir de cette grille de lecture, des options nouvelles peuvent apparaître qui pourraient permettre de répondre plus efficacement au vent de contestation auquel fait face la discipline. En définitive, si en présentant cette vision alternative, la tâche peut prendre des airs de déconstruction, il ne s'agit en réalité que d'orienter l'édifice vers d'autres horizons qu'il a, jusqu'à présent, insuffisamment pris en compte[23].

1 Les « péchés »[24] du droit international

Comme toute l'histoire du droit international[25], celle du DII est bien souvent présentée comme l'histoire du progrès, du développement, voire celle d'un humanisme de l'investisseur qui, désirant contribuer au développement des pays pauvres[26], sollicite un certain nombre de garanties pour mettre en œuvre

University Press, 2018, 530 p. L'ouvrage commence par la contribution de K. Vandevelde sur la vision libérale du droit international des investissements et se poursuit avec les autres contributions sur l'approche alternative qui, comme il a été déjà souligné est loin, elle-même d'être tout à fait homogène.

23 En cela, mutatis mutandis, nous rejoignons I. Wallerstein lorsqu'il écrit : « Les concepts de droits de l'homme et de démocratie, la prétendue supériorité d'une civilisation occidentale fondée sur des valeurs et des vérités universelles, et l'assujettissement incontournable aux lois du "marché", tout cela nous est servi comme "tombant sous le sens". Mais ce ne sont en rien des évidences qui relèvent du sens commun. Ce sont des idées complexes qui réclament une analyse attentive, afin de les dépouiller des leurs paramètres nocifs et superflus, afin d'évaluer avec pondération ce qui en elles peut être retenu et mis au service du bien commun plutôt que de l'intérêt de quelques-uns seulement », *L'universalisme européen : De la colonisation au droit d'ingérence*, Demopolis, 2008, pp. 6–7.

24 L'expression est empruntée à B. S. Chimni, « An outline of a Marxist Course on Public International Law », *Leiden J. Int'l Law*, vol. 17, n° 2, 2004, p. 2. M. Sornarajah utilise une formulation similaire lorsqu'il écrit que « [*t*]*he original sin in investment arbitration was committed in AAPL v. Sri Lanka* », *Resistance and Change in the International Law on Foreign Investment, Cambridge University Press*, 2015, p. 139.

25 *Ibid.*

26 « Pays pauvres », « pays en voie de développement », « tiers-monde » : nous n'entendons pas ici différencier chacune de ces expressions. Nous les utiliserons donc de façon interchangeable en ce qu'elles désignent la même réalité économique, politique et sociale, c'est-à-dire celle qui correspond globalement à la situation de l'ensemble des pays issus, d'une manière ou d'une autre, du processus de colonisation menée par l'Europe de l'Ouest (et dans une certaine mesure les États-Unis) et qui, pour la majorité ont acquis leur indépendance, pour une partie au XIXeme siècle et pour l'autre à partir du milieu du XXeme siècle.

les bonnes intentions qui l'animent. Le Professeur R.-J. Dupuy soulignait ainsi, dans la sentence *Texaco c. Libye*, que les contrats de concession conclus avec des sociétés étrangères « revêtent [...] une importance réelle dans le développement du pays où ils sont exécutés [...]. Le cocontractant de l'État se trouve de la sorte associé à la réalisation du progrès économique et social du pays d'accueil »[27] tant et si bien que leur soustraction à l'emprise du droit de l'État-hôte s'avère nécessaire pour « donner les garanties de sécurité indispensables aux sociétés étrangères qui, apportant à des pays en voie de développement leur concours financier et technique, assument des risques importants »[28]. La logique est alors implacable : il faut protéger l'investisseur en raison de sa contribution au développement économique de l'État où il a choisi d'investir. La réitération de cet argument notamment dans les préambules des traités de protection des investissements[29] et dans la pratique arbitrale qui en découle[30],

Pour une discussion de ces expressions dans la littérature des TWAIL, v. notamment B. S. Chimni, « Third World Approaches to International Law: A Manifesto », *Int'l Community Law Rev.*, vol. 8, 2006, pp. 4–7.

27 *Texaco-Calasiatic (TOPCO) c. Gouvernement de Libye* (29 janvier 1977), reproduit *in JDI*, 1977, p. 360.

28 *Ibid.*, pp. 360–361. L'arbitre se réfère sur ce point à la sentence *Sapphire* rendu en 1963 : « Il est de l'intérêt des deux parties à de tels accords que les litiges pouvant les diviser soient tranchés selon des principes généraux universellement reconnus et soient soustraites aux particularités des droits nationaux ».

29 Le préambule du TBI entre le Maroc et le Japon (2020) souligne ainsi que :« the reciprocal promotion and protection of [investments] will be conducive to stimulation of business initiative and increase prosperity in both Contracting Parties ». Une formulation analogue figure dans le TBI entre l'Arménie et la Lettonie (2005): « the treatment to be accorded to [the investments] will stimulate the flow of private capital and the economic development of the Contracting Parties ».

30 La contribution de l'investissement au développement de l'État-hôte a été retenu par certains tribunaux arbitraux comme l'un des critères de qualification de l'investissement : *Fedax N. V. c. Venezuela*, aff. CIRDI n° ARB/96/3, sentence sur les objections à la compétence, 11 juillet 1997, para 43: « The basic features of an investment have been described as involving a certain duration, a certain regularity of profit and return, assumption of risk, a substantial commitment and a significance for the host State's development »; *Consortium RFCC c. Maroc*, aff. CIRDI n° ARB/00/6, décision sur la compétence, 16 juillet 2001, para 60 : « La doctrine considère généralement que l'investissement suppose des apports, une certaine durée d'exécution du marché et une participation aux risques de l'opération. La lecture du préambule de la Convention [CIRDI] permet d'y ajouter le critère de la contribution au développement économique de l'État d'accueil de l'investissement ». La même formule est reprise dans l'affaire *Salini Costruttori S.P.A. et Italstrade S.P.A. c. Maroc*, aff. CIRDI n° ARB/00/4, decision sur la competence, 23 juillet 2001, para 52.

finit par donner l'impression que le DII et le système de règlement des différends qui l'accompagne relèveraient de l'évidence même[31].

Si le DII, nonobstant les mouvements de remise en cause relevés plus haut, a connu et sans doute connaît encore un succès indéniable qui en a fait l'une des spécialités les plus dynamiques du droit international, sa réussite était loin de relever de l'évidence. Ce succès relève en réalité d'un accident de l'histoire, sinon de la témérité de deux arbitres dans la sentence *AAPL c. Sri Lanka* en 1990[32]. M. Flory, observant les activités du CIRDI en 1977, faisait remarquer que « [p]ratiquement les activités du Centre restent très modestes puisqu'en dix ans, une seule affaire lui a été soumise [...], ce qui semble indiquer qu'une solution effective aux contentieux en matière d'investissement privé n'a pas encore été trouvée »[33]. Même l'Allemagne, qui pourtant avait conclu avec le Pakistan le premier TBI, se montrait très réservée sur les options envisagées d'abord par l'OCDE puis par la Banque Mondiale pour la protection des investissements étrangers[34]. La naissance et la dissémination du DII relèvent plutôt d'un processus incrémental dont les origines remontent à la confrontation coloniale. Cette origine coloniale du DII ayant déjà été largement soulignée dans les théories des *TWAIL*[35], il convient de se focaliser ici sur les processus par lesquels le système hérité de la colonisation s'est maintenu après l'accession des territoires colonisés à l'indépendance.

---

31 K. Miles, *The origins of international investment law*, Cambridge University Press, 2013, p. 19 ; J. Salacuse, *The Law of Investment Treaties*, Oxford University Press, 2015, p. 46 ; C. Brown, « The Evolution of the Regime of International Investment Agreements: History, Economics and Politics », *in* M. Bungenberg and *al.* (eds), *International Investment Law, op. cit.*, p. 154.

32 M. Sornarajah, *Resistance and Change in the International Law on Foreign Investment, op. cit.*, pp. 139–143; N. Perrone, *Investment Treaties and the Legal Imagination: How Foreign Investors play by their Own Rules*, Oxford University Press, 2021, pp. 108–111.

33 M. Flory, *Droit international du développement*, Paris, Presses Universitaires de France, 1977, p. 205. Voir aussi, C. Lipson, *Standing Guard: Protecting Foreign Capital in the Nineteenth and Twentieth Centuries*, University of California Press, 1985, pp. 167–168 ; L Poulsen, *Bounded Rationality and Economic Diplomacy: The Politics of Investment Treaties in Developing Countries*, Cambridge University Press, 2015, p. 57.

34 L. Poulsen, *Bounded Rationality and Economic Diplomacy, op. cit.*, p. 56. Tout porte même à croire que le système d'arbitrage État-investisseur tel qu'il se présente aujourd'hui dans le cadre du CIRDI n'était pas envisagé à l'origine selon A. Lowenfeld, « The ICSID Convention: Origins and Transformation », *Ga. J. Int'l & Comp. Law*, vol. 38, 2009, pp. 55–56.

35 A. Anghie, *Imperialism, Sovereignty and the Making of International Law*, Cambridge University Press, 2004, 356 p ; J. T. Gathii, « TWAIL : A Brief History of Its Origins, Its Decentralized Network, and a Tentative Bibliography »; *op. cit.*, pp. 38- 46; K. Miles, *The origins of international investment law, op. cit.*, pp. 1–70.

1.1 *Colonisation, décolonisation et persistance des structures juridiques*

Si le droit international a légitimé la colonisation, c'est en son sein que les peuples colonisés ont trouvé les ressources pour revendiquer leur indépendance. Mais c'est encore par le droit international que cette indépendance deviendra simplement « nominale »[36] et aura même tendance à s'effacer pour faire place à l'ordre ancien, toujours présent. Comme le souligne Anthony Anghie, en réalité, l'état du droit international à l'origine continue de se déployer dans son état actuel. Ainsi, le paradigme originel qui opposait l'Europe civilisée au reste du monde primitif persiste dans tous les mécanismes et notions qui parcourent le droit international. C'est ce que cet auteur appelle la « dynamique de la différence » qu'il définit comme « *the endless process of creating a gap between two cultures, demarcating one as 'universal' and civilized and the other as 'particular' and uncivilized, and seeking to bridge the gap by developing techniques to normalize the aberrant society* »[37]. En conséquence, le droit international évolue autour de grandes notions qui servent à perpétuer cette division : d'abord autour de la notion de souveraineté qui permettait de distinguer les puissances européennes, souveraines des autres territoires et peuples à qui cette qualité était niée (*terra nullius*) puis autour de concepts comme la démocratie, les droits de l'homme, la bonne gouvernance, la protection de l'environnement ... [38]. Toutes ces notions servent, en réalité, à démarquer les uns, vertueux, des autres, « voyous »[39] ; perpétuant ainsi le manichéisme presque congénital du droit international[40]. Pour N. Tzouvala,

---

36 M. Bedjaoui, « Observations sur le texte d'Antony Anghie », *in* M. Toufayan, E. Tourme-Jouannet et H. Ruiz Fabri (dir.), *Droit international et nouvelles approches sur le tiers-monde : entre répétition et renouveau*, Société de législation comparée, 2013, p. 83. Voir aussi *id.*, *Pour un nouvel ordre économique*, Paris, Unesco, 1978, pp. 78–84 ; L. Poulsen, *Bounded Rationality and Economic Diplomacy*, *op. cit.*, p. 50 ; A. Bianchi, *International Law Theories: An Inquiry into Different Ways of Thinking*, *op. cit.*, pp. 212–213.

37 A. Anghie, *Imperialism, Sovereignty and the Making of International Law*, *op. cit.*, p. 4.

38 *Ibid.*, pp. 3–4, 243–244 et 258–263. V. aussi K. Mickelson, « South, North, International Environmental Law, and International Environmental Lawyers », *Y. B. Int'l Envtl. Law*, n° 11, vol. 78, 2000, pp. 54–81.

39 Pour reprendre un terme cher à la politique étrangère américaine. L'expression « république bananière » est aussi utilisée. Ainsi dans un communiqué publié sur Twitter à la suite de l'assaut contre le Capitole, l'ancien Président George Bush écrit : « *This is how elections are disputed in a banana republic – not in our democratic republic* ». Pour désigner notamment plusieurs États africains, Donald Trump avait pour sa part utilisé une expression, propre à son registre de langue, que la pudeur interdit de reprendre ici.

40 A. Anghie, *Imperialism, Sovereignty and the Making of International Law*, *op. cit*, pp. 316–317.

le « standard de civilisation » constitue le pivot du droit international, gravitant autour de logiques contradictoires : d'une part, une logique de différenciation biologique, culturelle ou raciale (*logic of biology*) et de l'autre, une logique d'accompagnement, d'assimilation des peuples non européens pour assurer leur évolution vers la civilisation (*logic of improvement*)[41].

Si le droit international tel que présenté aujourd'hui se trouve profondément enracinée dans l'histoire européenne, sa dissémination en dehors des frontières européennes s'est largement faite au moyen de l'entreprise coloniale européenne. Les puissances européennes ont, en effet, conclu de nombreux traités avec les autorités qui gouvernaient les territoires qui bientôt seraient sous domination coloniale . Il s'agissait, de traités que les représentants européens (gouvernements ou compagnies privées) concluaient avec les chefs ou rois africains ou asiatiques[42] non seulement pour asseoir leur domination sur ces peuples mais aussi, dans la course aux empires, signaler leur présence aux autres puissances européennes. Charles Henry Alexandrowicz[43] a consacré de bonnes pages à l'analyse de ces « traités de verroterie »[44]. Il a ainsi montré que certains de ces traités faisaient écho aux capitulations bien connues depuis le Moyen Âge dans lesquelles des souverains s'engageaient unilatéralement ou bilatéralement à garantir certains droits et privilèges à des étrangers résidant sur leur territoire. Alexandowicz souligne ainsi que, dès le VIIIème siècle, les commerçants musulmans résidant dans les États hindous de la côte ouest de l'Inde jouissaient notamment de privilèges juridictionnels[45]. Il mentionne également les Arabes résidant à Canton, qui avaient leurs propres quartiers, où les autorités chinoises leur permettaient de s'organiser selon les lois et coutumes de leur pays d'origine sous la responsabilité de leurs Cadis (juges)[46]. La philosophie de cette institution reposait sur des traditions asiatiques très anciennes qui consistaient à laisser aux commerçants étrangers le soin de s'organiser selon leurs propres lois en matière juridique (pour les questions qui ne touchent que les membres de la communauté) ou religieuse sous la responsabilité de leurs chefs de communauté[47].

---

41 N. Tzouvala, Capitalism as Civilisation : A History of International Law, Cambridge University Press, 2020, p. 2.

42 G. Uzoigwe, « Partage européen et conquête de l'Afrique : aperçu général », *in* A. Boahen (dir.), *Histoire générale de l'Afrique*, Paris, Unesco, 1987, III, p. 49.

43 C. H. Alexandrowicz, *The European-African Confrontation*, Sijthoff, 1973.

44 M. Bedjaoui, « Observations sur le texte d'Antony Anghie », *op. cit.*, p. 82.

45 C H Alexandrowicz, *The European-African Confrontation, op. cit.*, p. 22.

46 *Ibid.*, p. 90.

47 *Ibid.*

Lorsque les puissances européennes se sont lancées véritablement dans le commerce avec l'Afrique et l'Asie à partir du XVème siècle, des capitulations leur ont été abondamment accordées ou ont été conclues. D'abord unilatérales, ces capitulations n'avaient d'autres justifications que la générosité de celui qui les accordait et étaient plutôt vues comme le signe d'une immense considération. Ces capitulations-là ont d'abord eu pour cadre l'Empire Ottoman qui, à partir de 1535 a octroyé généreusement aux citoyens européens spécialement Français de nombreux avantages et privilèges. Ces actes unilatéraux ont eu pour effet d'admettre les Français à s'établir et à pratiquer leur culte sur le territoire de l'Empire. Ils leur permettent également d'être soumis à la juridiction de leur État d'origine[48].

En même temps se sont développés aussi des capitulations sous forme de traité bilatéraux avec des engagements réciproques des parties. C'est le cas par exemple du traité conclu en 1631 entre les Provinces-Unies (Pays-Bas) et la Perse qui accorde aux ressortissants de chaque État-partie des privilèges sur le territoire de l'autre État-partie. Ce traité, régissant presque tous les aspects des rapports entre les deux États, garantissait aux ressortissants perses au Pays-Bas des privilèges qui font écho au traitement national et au traitement de la nation la plus favorisée. Il offre aussi aux perses établis au Pays-Bas la liberté de pratiquer leur culte et surtout les Pays-Bas s'engagent à accueillir un représentant du Shah de Perse ; lequel représentant était doté de pouvoirs juridictionnels à l'égard de ses compatriotes[49]. Ailleurs, après la perte de contrôle de l'Empire Ottoman sur le Maghreb, la France va ainsi conclure un traité avec l'Algérie en 1666 au terme duquel cette dernière devrait envoyer à Marseille « deux hommes de qualité » pour régler les différends relatifs à l'application du traité[50]. De même les traités conclus entre la France et la Tunisie et la Lybie respectivement prévoient l'échange d'envoyés pour statuer sur les violations des traités[51].

48 D. Servière et S. Torrès, « Aperçu historique sur le Protectorat et les Capitulations », *Échos d'Orient*, n°108, 1915, p. 439. Mais l'existence de ces actes est contestée par certains historiens. V. notamment G. Zeller, « Une légende qui a la vie dure : les capitulations de 1535 », *Revue d'histoire moderne et contemporaine*, n° 2, 1955, pp. 127–132.

49 C. H. Alexandrowicz, «Treaty and Diplomatic Relations between European and South Asian Powers in the Seventeenth and Eighteenth Centuries», *R.C.A.D.I.*, vol. 100, 1960, pp. 261–265.

50 C. H. Alexandrowicz, *The European-African Confrontation*, *op. cit.*, p. 20.

51 C. H. alexandrowicz, « Le rôle des traités dans les relations entre les puissances européennes et les souverains africains », *Rev. Int'le de Droit Comp.*, vol. 22, 1970, n° 4, p. 704.

Ces capitulations reposaient, dans leur forme unilatérale, sur la volonté d'élever le bénéficiaire à une dignité presque égale à celle de celui qui l'offrait et, dans leur forme bilatérale, sur un principe de réciprocité. Ainsi, lorsque l'Empereur ottoman offrait des capitulations aux Français, il s'agissait de les élever à une dignité qui puisse leur permettre de traiter d'égal à égal avec ses propres sujets. C'est pourquoi, « [l]e terme de capitulations [...] indiquait des concessions faites par le magnanime et libéral Padischah à ceux qu'il daignait honorer de son amitié et de sa protection bienveillante [...] »[52]. Autrement dit, lorsque François Ier sollicite ces capitulations auprès de Soliman et les obtient, ce n'est pas qu'il estime que les ressortissants français ou protégés français auraient quelque supériorité sur les ottomans[53]. C'est plutôt la manifestation de la solidité de l'amitié entre les deux souverains. Le geste est ainsi apprécié par les Français comme un honneur et un privilège dont ils pouvaient s'enorgueillir devant les autres puissances européennes. En tout cas, les capitulations étaient au moins un signe de considération pour le bénéficiaire. C. H. Alexandrowicz écrit ceci : « *[j]urisdictional privileges granted to foreigners were no evidence of the inferior civilisation of the receiving country and the superior civilisation of the country whose nationals enjoyed theses privileges* »[54]. Dès lors, en aucun cas, les capitulations n'étaient la manifestation d'une civilisation que l'on considérerait comme inférieure et arriérée et qui ne mériterait donc pas que l'on se soumette à ses lois[55]. Pourtant ce glissement, autour duquel le droit international des investissements s'est construit, n'a pas tardé à s'opérer et a totalement bouleversé la philosophie de cette institution et de celles qui ont en découlé.

52 D. Servière et S. Torrès, « Aperçu historique sur le Protectorat et les Capitulations », *op. cit.*, p. 438. Les auteurs se réfèrent à une étude parue dans la revue *Questions actuelles* en 1901 et qui portait sur le *Protectorat français en Orient.*

53 Bien au contraire, ce sont plutôt les ottomans qui avaient le sentiment de supériorité. C'est pourquoi ces capitulations-là prenaient une forme unilatérale car un traité aurait supposé reconnaître les français comme leurs égaux. Ainsi, « [l]e terme de traité est impropre, parce que, s'il concédait à la France de précieux et incomparables privilèges en Orient, il ne lui imposait guère d'autres obligations que celle de rester fidèle à l'amitié de la Porte. D'ailleurs, l'orgueil musulman s'accordait mal d'un pareil terme qui semblait mettre sur un pied d'égalité le glorieux et tout-puissant souverain du monde avec un de ces princes chrétiens si longtemps méprisés, fût-ce même le roi de France ». D. Servière et S. Torrès, « Aperçu historique sur le Protectorat et les Capitulations », *op. cit.*, p. 438. V. aussi P. Villiers, Ph. Jacquin et P. Ragon, *Les européens et la mer : De la découverte à la colonisation (1455–1860)*, Ellipses, 1997, p. 18.

54 C. H. Alexandrowicz, *The European-African Confrontation*, *op. cit.*, p. 83 et 90.

55 *Ibid.*, p. 23 et p. 82.

En effet, sous l'influence du positivisme ambiant du XIXème siècle, la capitulation finit par être envisagée comme la manifestation de la supériorité des européens sur les peuples colonisés. Ce renversement s'opère à deux niveaux. D'abord, le concept de souveraineté devient le pivot du droit international et sert de démarcation entre les européens civilisés et les non-européens barbares. Ensuite, c'est désormais l'État de l'étranger qui exige que son ressortissant ne soit plus soumis aux juridictions du territoire d'accueil en raison de sa supériorité. L'argument des positivistes comme H. Wheaton ou J. Westlake était simple : les États non européens ne faisaient pas partie du monde civilisé. Or, la souveraineté constitue l'une des manifestations de la civilisation. Dès lors, il était inenvisageable de traiter avec eux sur un pied d'égalité, encore moins de soumettre les ressortissants européens aux institutions « barbares » des territoires sur lesquels ils se trouvaient[56]. Toutefois, cette différence pouvait être comblée en imposant à ces peuples la conception européenne du droit et des institutions[57]. Dans tous les cas, « [w]*hatever the pratices of the 'uncivilized tribes', in a situation where these practices conflict with the assessment made by the civilized* [...] *it is the latter which prevails* »[58]. Cette posture

56 Sur la formulation de cet argument des positivistes, une question peut surgir sur le point de savoir si l'argument a été d'abord théorisé avant d'être mis en pratique ou bien s'il a plutôt été théorisé pour servir de justification à une pratique préexistante. À cette question, A. Angie répond que « [...] *positivism legitimized conquest and dispossession*». Il ajoute que « [*p*]*ositivists developed and elaborate vocabulary for denigrating non-European people, presenting them as suitable objects for conquest, and legitimizing the most extreme violence against them, all in furtherance of the civilizing mission, the discharge of the white man's burden* ». Sur les compagnies à charte, il note que « [d] octrines were developed to give trading companies some measure of legal personality by characterizing them as extensions of the Crown by virtue of royal charter ».

Mais cet auteur observe que le positivisme, école de pensée dominante dans le droit international de cette é poque, ne se contentait pas justifier ou de légitimer (position défensive), il visait aussi en même temps non seulement sa propre transformation mais aussi la transformation des situations concrètes qu'il entendait régir. Il avait ainsi une dimension prospective, offensive. On comprendra dès lors, pourquoi après avoir justifié la colonisation, c'est encore au sein du droit international qu'il a façonné que les arguments seront présentés pour la décolonisation (position offensive). A. Anghie, *Imperialism, Sovereignty and the Making of International Law*, *op. cit.*, pp. 37–38.

57 A. Anghie cite ainsi Henry Wheaton qui écrivait en 1886 ceci : « *Is there a uniform law of nations ? There certainly is not the same one for all the nations and states of the world. The public law, with slight exceptions, has always been, and still is, limited to civilized and Christian people of Europe or to those of European origin* », *Imperialism, Sovereignty and the Making of International Law*, *op. cit.*, p. 54.

58 *Ibid.*, p. 55.

s'est illustrée particulièrement dans une série de traités[59] conclus au XIXème siècle. On voit un exemple dans le traité de Nankin de 1842 qui inaugure l'ère des « traités inégaux »[60] en mettant fin à la première guerre de l'Opium, par lequel le Royaume-Uni se réserva des avantages considérables pour ses commerçants[61].

En Afrique, si les premiers rapports avec les Européens, fondés sur des traités[62], tendaient à favoriser le for du défendeur (*actor sequitur forum rei*), à

---

59 C'est sur ce point que l'argumentation positiviste perd en crédibilité. En effet, en avançant que les peuples non européens n'étaient pas civilisés, on leur niait du même coup la personnalité juridique qui leur permettrait d'accomplir des actes juridiques. Dès lors, la conséquence serait que les accords conclus avec les chefs et rois asiatiques et africains soient frappés de nullité. Mais tel ne fut pas le cas. Ces traités ont été reconnus comme valides. Et des réclamations ou titres ont pu être fondés sur ces actes. Les seules contestations sérieuses venaient parfois de puissances rivales qui, dans leur propre intérêt remettaient en cause la validité des actes accomplis entre la puissance européenne et les rois ou chefs asiatiques ou africains. Voir A. Anghie, *Imperialism, Sovereignty and the Making of International Law, op. cit.*, pp. 67–82. Pour une étude de référence en langue française, V. M. Hébié, *Souveraineté territoriale par traité : Une étude des accords entre puissances coloniales et entités politiques locales*, Graduate Institute Publications, 2015, spéc. pp. 300–428.

La CIJ s'est fait l'écho de ces contradictions dans l'avis consultatif sur le Sahara occidental en s'abstenant de prendre position sur la question. Elle a donc prudemment avancé que : « Des vues divergentes ont été exprimées devant la Cour au sujet de la nature et de la valeur juridique des accords conclus entre un État et des chefs locaux. Mais la Cour n'est pas invitée [...] à se prononcer sur le caractère juridique ou la légalité des titres auxquels l'Espagne doit d'être devenue Puissance administrante au Sahara occidental », *Sahara occidental*, avis consultatif, 1975, *CIJ Rec.*, p. 12, para 82.

60 Sur la notion de traités inégaux, voir entre autres I. Detter, « The Problem Of Unequal Treaties », *Int'l. & Comp. Law Quarterly*, vol. 15, 1966, pp. 1069–1089 ; M. Craven, « What Happened to Unequal Treaties? The Continuities of Informal Empire », *Nordic J. Int'l Law*, vol. 74, 2005, pp. 382, 2005.

61 Par exemple, l'article II de ce traité dispose que « *His Majesty the Emperor of China agrees that British Subjects, with their families and establishments, shall be allowed to reside, for the purpose of carrying on their commercial pursuits, without molestation or restraint at the Cities and Towns of Canton, Amoy, Foochow-fu, Ningpo, and Shanghai, and Her Majesty the Queen of Great Britain, etc., will appoint Superintendents or Consular Officers, to reside at each of the above-named Cities or Towns, to be the medium of communication between the Chinese Authorities and the said Merchants, and to see that the just Duties and other Dues of the Chinese Government as hereafter provided for, are duly discharged by Her Britannic Majesty's Subjects* ». C. Déry, *Diplomatie, Rhétorique et canonnières, relations entre la Chine et l'Angleterre, de l'Ambassade Macartney à la guerre de l'Opium, 1793–1842*, Presse Universitaire de Laval, 2007, pp. 3–6 et pp. 101–104.

62 Encore que, le recours à la technique du traité, en principe fondée sur la réciprocité ne reflétait pas la réalité des rapports pour la raison presqu'évidente que très peu « d'indigènes » – si ce n'est aucun – ne résidaient dans les métropoles européennes et ne

admettre des juridictions de composition mixte ou la compétence de chaque souverain sur ses sujets[63], la phase active de la colonisation au XIXème siècle va graduellement éroder ces principes jusqu'à voir s'imposer une prépondérance du recours aux juridictions coloniales jusque dans des litiges entre « indigènes »[64]. Ainsi, bien que « [t]*he mixed court solution or the principle of "actor sequitur forum rei" left African Rulers with a measure of influence in matters of mixed dispute* », l'on relève dans le même temps que « [w]*hen their internal sovereignty tended to be restricted, this influence declined* »[65]. On le voit, alors que les premières capitulations étaient fondées sur la seule générosité de celui qui les offrait, la prise de possession définitive des continents africain et asiatique va transformer ces instruments en des symboles vexatoires et signes de soumission.

Plus tard, le recours à la protection diplomatique ou à l'arbitrage comme moyen de règlement des différends relatifs aux investissements étrangers a reproduit ce paradigme « civilisationnel ». Dans le contexte des nombreux différends issus des contrats pétroliers entre certaines compagnies pétrolières occidentales et certains États (ou entités) d'Afrique du Nord ou du Moyen orient, ce paradigme s'est trouvé illustré. Nonobstant les différences factuelles entre ces affaires, elles avaient en commun de poser la question du droit applicable à ces types de contrat[66]. Ainsi, dans la sentence *Abu Dhabi*, Lord Asquith, après avoir reconnu qu'en principe le droit applicable au contrat en cause était évidemment le droit de l'État contractant, ajoutait

---

pouvaient donc demander à bénéficier des stipulations de ces traités. On ne peut que souscrire, *mutatis mutandis*, à l'affirmation de M. Kumm selon laquelle : « *One difference between traditional consular jurisdiction and the postcolonial context of BITS was that in the latter case the requirement of reciprocity was formally recognized: If Germany and Pakistan concluded such a bilateral investment treaty it would mean that Pakistani investors in Germany would profit from its guarantees in the same way as German investors in Pakistan. But of course, this recognition was mostly a formality. In a world where there is a clear division between capital-importing and capital exporting states, the formal recognition of reciprocity merely covered up the reality of privileging investors from capital exporting countries* », « Empire of Capital? Transatlantic Investment Protection as the Institutionalization of Unjustified Privilege » *ESIL-SEDI*, vol. 4, 2015, n°3, disponible sur < https://esil-sedi.eu/fr/an-empire-of-capital-transatlantic-investment-protection-as-the-institutionalization-of-unjustified-privilege/> consulté 24 août 2021.

63 C. H Alexandrowicz cite ainsi un Traité de 1883 entre la France et les Chefs Brass (région du Niger actuel) dont l'article V disposait que « [l]es chefs Brass rendront justice aux réclamations des blancs ». *The European-African Confrontation*, p. 85.

64 *Ibid.*, pp. 83–91.

65 *Ibid.*, p. 88.

66 C. Leben, « La théorie du contrat d'État et l'évolution du droit international des investissements », *R.C.A.D.I.*, vol. 302, 2003, pp. 221–234.

aussitôt : « *But no such law can reasonably be said to exist. The Sheikh administers a purely discretionary justice with the assistance of the Koran; and it would be fanciful to suggest that in this very primitive region there is any settled body of legal principles applicable to the construction of modern commercial instrument* »[67]. Il y avait comme un certain standard de civilisation juridictionnelle que les Européens cherchaient à trouver chez les peuples non européens. Le défaut de ce standard – naturellement évalué de façon unilatérale – justifiait donc que les ressortissants européens ne soient pas soumis à la compétence des règles et des autorités locales. Les solutions proposées pour les types de contrats en cause ici variaient[68]. Si de toute évidence, le droit de l'État d'origine de l'investisseur ne pouvait pas s'appliquer au contrat et que celui de l'État contractant est, selon les termes de Lord Asquith, encore primitif, alors une solution plus subtile est envisagée : le recours aux principes généraux du droit comme droit applicable au contrat. Or ces principes généraux sont presque toujours dégagés des systèmes juridiques des pays d'origine des investisseurs ; ce qui en réalité revient à appliquer au contrat le droit de l'État d'origine de l'investisseur. C'est ce que Lord Asquith, dans la sentence *Abu Dhabi* précitée, a systématisé en avançant que « *albeit English municipal law is inapplicable as such, some of its rules are in my view so firmly grounded in reason, as to form part of this broad body of jurisprudence – this " modern law of nature "* »[69]. Pour A. Anghie, au final, « [...] *a non-European state was deemed to be civilized if it*

---

67 « Petroleum Development (Trucial Coast) Ltd./The Sheikh of Abu Dhabi », *Int'l. & Comp. Law Quarterly*, 1952 pp. 250–251.

A. Anghie, qui analyse plus tard ces affaires (pp. 223–244) écrit que « [*f*]*or the European states, the local systems of justice were completely inadequate, and there was no question of submitting one of their citizens to these systems. Non-European were thus forced to sign treaties of capitulation which gave European powers extra-territorial jurisdiction over the activities of their own citizens in these non-European states. This derogation from the sovereignty of non-European state was naturally regarded as a massive humiliation by that state, which sought to terminate all capitulations at the earliest opportunity* », A. Anghie, *Imperialism, Sovereignty and the Making of International Law*, *op. cit.*, p. 85 ; D. R. Shea note pour sa part que, « [...] *the basic opposition to concepts such as the Calvo Clause was grounded on the* [...] *fear of the investor powers that their citizens would suffer if subjected exclusively to local standards of justice* », D. R. Shea, *The Calvo Clause : A Problem of Inter-American and International Law and Diplomacy*, University of Minnesota Press, 1955, p. 286.

68 P. Weil, « Problèmes relatifs aux contrats passés entre un État et un particulier », *R.C.A.D.I.*, vol. 128, 1969, pp. 148–204.

69 Petroleum Development (Trucial Coast) Ltd./The Sheikh of Abu Dhabi, *Int'l. & Comp. Law Quarterly*, 1952 p. 251.

could provide an individual, a European foreigner, with the same treatment that the individual would expect to receive in Europe »[70].

Ces préjugés avaient même fini par être intégrés par les États latino-américains au point qu'ils estimaient avoir atteint un niveau de civilisation qui leur permettrait de pouvoir juger les étrangers présents sur leur territoire sans que ces derniers réclament le recours à la protection diplomatique[71]. À la 3ème conférence de l'*Inter-American Bar Association* en 1944, un projet de résolution fut présenté qui était ainsi formulé : « *due to the similarity of their republican institutions, their unshakeable will for peace, their profound sentiment of humanity and tolerance, and their absolute adherence to the principles of international law, of the equal sovereignty of states and of individual liberty without religious or racial prejudices,* the nations of this Continent have attained a similar reasonable standard of justice which renders diplomatic protection unnecessary in their case »[72]. On le voit, tout le système de protection des étrangers et de leurs biens est fondé sur ce paradigme civilisationnel.

C'est dans ce cadre historique, économique et juridique que s'est inévitablement inscrit le système d'arbitrage État-investisseur. La décolonisation ne semble pas avoir mis fin à ces préjugés. Elle semble même les avoir renforcés avec l'instabilité institutionnelle et économique que connaîtront ces nouveaux États et qui ne feront que continuer à justifier et même renforcer le régime de protection des investisseurs étrangers. Comme l'a très pertinemment relevé R. Bachand, « [...] l'une des raisons principales, si ce n'est la raison la plus importante, ayant poussé les pays occidentaux à s'adresser aux pays du tiers-monde pour la conclusion de traités d'investissement était justement que les premiers ne faisaient pas confiance aux systèmes judiciaires

70 A. Anghie, *Imperialism, Sovereignty and the Making of International Law, op. cit.*, p. 84.

71 D. R. Shea, *The Calvo Clause: A Problem of Inter-American and International Law and Diplomacy, op. cit.*, p. 9. Plusieurs autres raisons pouvaient aussi expliquer ce positionnement notamment la crainte que le prétexte de la protection diplomatique soit un moyen pour les occidentaux de s'ingérer dans leurs affaires internes. Cette crainte était justifiée au regard des interventions militaires parfois très musclées des occidentaux dans la région. Ainsi, on estime qu'entre la guerre hispano-américaine en 1898 et la grande dépression des années 30, les États-Unis avaient initié plus de 44 interventions militaires en Amérique latine et dans les Caraïbes. Entre 1820 et 1914, l'on recense au moins quarante interventions armées britanniques en Amérique latine. V. M. H. Mourra, « The Conflicts and Controversies in Latin American Treaty-Based Disputes » *in* M. H. Mourra et T. Carbonneau, *Latin American Investment Treaty Arbitration: The Controversies and Conficts*, Wolters Kluwer, 2008, pp. 7–8; C. Lipson, *Standing Guard, op. cit.*, p. 54.

72 Cité *in* A. Freeman, « Recent Aspects of the Calvo Doctrine and the Challenge of International Law », *AJIL*, vol. 40, 1946, p. 121.

des seconds qui étaient réputés pour rendre des jugements discriminatoires à l'égard, notamment des investisseurs occidentaux »[73].

Il paraît aujourd'hui paradoxal de constater que les vertus reconnues à l'arbitrage comme mode de règlements des différends relatifs aux investissements étrangers sont largement remises en cause. L'indépendance, l'impartialité, l'expertise, le professionnalisme ou encore la célérité de la procédure, vertus traditionnellement invoquées pour soutenir l'arbitrage d'investissement, sont largement battues en brèche[74]. Ainsi, les mêmes griefs formulés à l'égard des juridictions des pays en voie de développement peuvent être formulés en substance à l'égard de l'arbitrage d'investissement. Cependant, le régime de protection des investisseurs étrangers par le recours à l'arbitrage continue de demeurer le principe en la matière.

1.2 *Colonisation, décolonisation et dépendance économique*

Les processus de décolonisation, d'abord en Amérique latine, puis en Asie et en Afrique n'ont pas eu pour effet de défaire ou remodeler la structure de l'économie mondiale. C'est cette pérennisation des rapports de production, de l'exploitation, des inégalités qu'ont mis en relief les théoriciens de la dépendance. Ils considèrent, en effet, que pendant la colonisation, les États colonisateurs se sont octroyés des privilèges et monopoles qu'ils s'emploient encore à garantir et perpétuer[75] après les indépendances. Ainsi, les règles du DII n'auraient pour objectif que de protéger en quelque sorte le *statu quo ante*.

La théorie de la dépendance naît dans le contexte sud-américain des années 1970[76]. Mais on pense trouver déjà les fondements de cette

73 R. Bachand, « Indétermination du droit, légitimité des institutions et droit international de l'investissement » *in* M. Arès et É. Boulanger (dir.), *L'investissement et la nouvelle économie mondiale : Trajectoires nationales, réseaux mondiaux et normes internationales*, Bruylant, 2012, p. 96.

74 Voir les critiques formulées à l'égard de l'arbitrage des investissements dans le cadre de la réforme en cours devant la CNUDCI spécialement les documents A/CN.9/WG.III/WP.151 et A/CN.9/WG.III/WP.153. L'ensemble des documents relatifs à cette réforme est disponible sur <https://uncitral.un.org/fr/working_groups/3/investor-state>.

75 A. Anghie, *Imperialism, Sovereignty and the Making of International Law*, *op. cit.*, pp. 214–216.

76 Elle a été officiellement portée sur les fonds baptismaux en 1972 lors du congrès du Conseil latino-américain des sciences sociales à Mexico. Voir l'hommage que Samir Amin rend à André Gunder Frank dans les colonnes du quotidien *Le Monde*, 30/04/2005, <https://www.lemonde.fr/disparitions/article/2005/04/30/andre-gunder-frank-economiste-allemand_644945_3382.html>.

théorie dans les travaux de Raoul Prebisch présentés dans les années 1950[77]. La dépendance se présente comme « une relation d'interdépendance asymétrique entre deux unités nationales ou sociales »[78]. Ainsi, pour les théoriciens de la dépendance, l'échange international est en défaveur des pays sous-développés ; c'est même presque une lapalissade. Mais loin d'être le fruit d'un déséquilibre conjoncturel, c'est plutôt toute l'architecture, la structure internationale, qui est viciée à la base. R. Preiswerk résume parfaitement cette théorie : « [...] le sous-développement et la pauvreté de la majorité des populations du Tiers Monde [...] ne s'expliquent plus par un retard, par une infériorité quasiment congénitale, mais par une condition créée au cours des derniers siècles à travers la mise en place de certaines structures politiques et économiques internationales »[79]. Les travaux de Immanuel Wallerstein[80], Samir Amin[81] et André Gunder Frank[82] sont d'un grand secours pour bien appréhender toute la profondeur de cette analyse[83].

---

77 R. Preiswerk, « Relations interculturelles et développement », *in* P. Bungener (dir.), *Le savoir et le faire*, Graduate Institute Publications, 1975, disponible sur <http://books.openedition.org/iheid/3913>.

78 *Ibid.*

79 *Ibid.*

80 Économiste, sociologue et historien américain, I. Wallerstein (1930–2019) a consacré de nombreux travaux à l'origine et à l'expansion du capitalisme ainsi qu'aux problèmes économiques des États africains nouvellement indépendant.

81 Franco-égyptien, S. Amin (1931–2018) s'est illustré à la fois dans le milieu académique – professeur agrégé d'économie en 1966 à Paris – mais aussi en tant que militant. Considéré comme précurseur du mouvement altermondialiste, il a consacré de nombreux ouvrages aux pays africains où il intervenait comme conseiller ou expert auprès de nombreux gouvernements.

82 Germano-américain, Gunder Frank (1929–2005) fut Élève de Milton Friedman à l'Université de Chicago d'où il sera plus tard évincé. La situation du Chili dans les années 70 devait être le terrain où la vision des deux hommes allaient s'opposer vigoureusement. Ses positions économiques et politiques auxquelles s'ajoutent son refus de rejoindre l'armée américaine lors de la guerre de Corée lui valurent des refus de visa d'entrée aux États-Unis. Le Canada, où il avait pourtant enseigné quelques années, en fera de même en 1975 et 1977. Jusqu'en 1973, il séjourne, enseigne et participe à la mise en place de certains programmes gouvernementaux au Chili d'où il s'enfuira après le renversement du gouvernement socialiste de Salvador Allende.

83 Plusieurs autres auteurs, à des degrés divers peuvent être classés dans le courant de la dépendance. Ce sont notamment Emmanuel Arghiri, Celso Furtado, Rui Mauro Marini, Anibal Quijano et Dieter Senghaas. Nous faisons le choix ici de partir du cadre général que constitue la théorie du système-monde que Wallerstein mène à sa plus brillante expression. Ensuite avec André Gunder Franck et Samir Amin, on en verra les implications respectivement pour l'Amérique latine et pour l'Afrique et l'Asie.

Influencé notamment par les travaux de Fernand Braudel, Immanuel Wallerstein envisage l'évolution du monde non pas de façon sectorielle mais dans sa globalité, comme un système unique, un tout[84]. Cette posture le conduit à avancer sa théorie bien connue de « système-monde » que l'on trouve déjà sensiblement chez Samir Amin[85], selon laquelle les différentes phases de l'évolution de l'économie mondiale sont marquées par une sorte de stratification des acteurs. Dans un tel système, on distingue des acteurs centraux, des acteurs semi-périphériques et des acteurs périphériques. Le centre est ainsi caractérisé par des acteurs disposant d'appareils étatiques puissants[86] qui, dans la division des tâches qu'implique inévitablement le « système-monde », se réservent celles qui « exigent les plus hauts degrés de spécialisation et les plus forts capitaux »[87]. La périphérie est, pour sa part, à l'autre bout de l'échelle, caractérisée par des États faibles[88], « faiblesse pouvant aller de l'inexistence totale (dans le cas d'une situation coloniale) à l'autonomie presque nulle dans une situation néo-colonialiste »[89]. Sur le plan des échanges, les États de la périphérie se spécialisent dans l'exportation de matières premières qu'ils vendent à vil prix[90]. Quant à la semi-périphérie, elle se présente comme une zone « tampon » entre les deux extrémités et se compose d'États qui, soit appartenaient précédemment au centre, soit ont évolué de la périphérie vers

84 Il écrit ainsi : « Nous avons affirmé que les différents champs d'analyse – les « disciplines » universitaires – constituent un obstacle et non une aide pour comprendre le monde. Nous avons affirmé que la réalité sociale dans laquelle nous vivons et qui détermine nos choix sociaux, n'est pas constituée d'une multitude d'États nationaux dont nous sommes les citoyens, mais d'une entité plus grande que nous appelons « système-monde », I. Wallerstein, *Comprendre le monde : Introduction à l'analyse des systèmes-mondes*, La Découverte, 2006, p. 7 ; voir aussi, *id.*, « Sous-développement et dépendance », *Esprit*, 1974, p. 213.

85 Mais contrairement à I. Wallerstein, Samir Amin, sera réticent, dans sa vision du « système-monde » à y intégrer des semi-périphéries. Pour lui en effet, certes l'émergence de semi-périphéries n'est pas définitivement exclue mais force est de constater que « le système capitaliste mondial est mû par une tendance forte à la polarisation, tout comme dans le mode de production capitaliste la tendance est à la polarisation entre les deux classes fondamentales, bourgeoisie et prolétariat », S. Amin, *L'eurocentrisme : Critique d'une idéologie*, Anthropos, 1988, p. 140.

86 I. Wallerstein, *Le système du monde du xvème siècle à nos jours : Capitalisme et économie-monde*, Paris, Flammarion, 1980, p. 39.

87 *Ibid.*, p. 315.

88 L'auteur se refuse même à employer le terme État pour les entités de cette zone du fait justement de cette faiblesse, p. 314.

89 *Ibid.*

90 *Ibid.*, p. 274.

la semi-périphérie[91]. Il s'ensuit que la composition de chaque zone n'est pas définitivement fixée. Les zones n'étant pas étanches, des glissements peuvent s'opérer vers l'une ou l'autre des zones. Ce qui conduit inévitablement à la concurrence pour se maintenir dans sa zone ou gravir l'échelon supérieur[92]. Ainsi, les États centraux qui ont plus à perdre, car risquant la déchéance, se feront une concurrence pour accéder au privilège d'exploiter les zones périphériques. Il leur faut donc acquérir de nouveaux privilèges tout en maintenant ceux dont ils disposent déjà. Wallerstein est on ne peut plus explicite dans *L'universalisme européen*, lorsqu'il écrit ceci : « [j]'ai tenté de démontrer ici comment les réalités du pouvoir au sein du système-monde moderne ont depuis cinq cents ans façonné une série d'idées qui les légitiment, permettant ainsi aux détenteurs de ce pouvoir de les garder entre leurs mains »[93].

Pour Samir Amin, l'une des manifestations du sous-développement réside dans « la domination économique du centre, qui s'exprime dans les formes de spécialisation internationale et dans la dépendance des structures du financement de la croissance à la périphérie »[94]. En d'autres termes, d'une part, la division internationale du travail incline les pays pauvres, c'est-à-dire ceux de la périphérie, à se spécialiser dans l'exportation « de produits de base »[95] et, d'autre part, ces économies restent largement tributaires des flux de capitaux étrangers. Ainsi, le centre détenant les structures de financement[96], le financement des économies périphériques provient essentiellement des pays du centre, donc de l'étranger. Certes, l'investissement étranger peut stimuler l'économie à court terme par l'injection de nouveaux capitaux et de nouvelles technologies. Mais à long terme, en raison du rapatriement des bénéfices plutôt que leur réinvestissement, l'investissement étranger devient improductif

---

91 *Ibid.*, pp. 315–316.

92 Wallerstein le formule ainsi : « Les avantages des États centraux n'ont cessé de croître tout au long de l'histoire ; mais l'aptitude d'un État donné à se maintenir au centre de l'économie-monde n'est pas garantie. [...] En fait il se pourrait même très bien que, dans ce type de système, il ne soit pas structurellement possible d'éviter, dans la longue durée historique, une sorte de roulement des élites, c'est-à-dire que le pays qui domine à une époque donnée risque, tôt ou tard, d'être supplanté par un autre », I. Wallerstein, *Comprendre le monde : Introduction à l'analyse des systèmes-mondes, op. cit.*, p. 316.

93 I. Wallerstein, *L'universalisme européen : de la colonisation au droit d'ingérence, op. cit.*, p. 111.

94 S. Amin, *Le développement inégal : Essai sur les formations sociales du capitalise périphérique*, Les Éditions de Minuit, 1973, p. 174 ; *id., L'accumulation à l'échelle mondiale*, Anthropos, 1970, pp. 358–376.

95 S. Amin, *Le développement inégal : Essai sur les formations sociales du capitalise périphérique, op. cit.*, p. 214 et p. 250.

96 *Ibid.*, p. 225.

pour l'économie locale[97]. C'est ce qui expliquerait le déficit chronique de la balance des paiements à la périphérie. L'une des solutions que propose alors le centre pour y faire face consiste dans le recours à l'aide extérieure. Or, justement, celle-ci « a pour effet de remettre la responsabilité de l'orientation du développement aux fournisseurs de fonds. Elle accentue les mécanismes de la domination économique, comme ceux de la domination politique tout court »[98]. De plus, la localisation de la technologie, du savoir-faire et du financement au centre conduit à une concurrence entre économies périphériques pour les attirer et ainsi aboutit à « réduire leur pouvoir de négociation »[99]. Samir Amin est gagné par une sorte de fatalisme au terme de son analyse en posant que « chaque tentative sérieuse de la périphérie de se libérer de la domination politique du centre conduit à des conflits [...] »[100], d'autant plus que l'ensemble des ressources est monopolisé par les économies du centre et qui articulent « l'efficacité de leurs actions »[101]. Ces monopoles constituent même des « conditionnements »[102] qui inévitablement vont se maintenir dans l'« avenir »[103]. Une approche similaire est visible chez André Gunder Frank.

Avec Gunder Frank, on assiste à la remise en cause de la vision d'un développement linéaire, d'un développement qui serait fait d'étapes successives qui placeraient donc les pays sous-développés au bas de l'échelle. Pour lui, « le sous-développement n'est pas originel ou traditionnel »[104] dans la mesure où, d'une part, les pays dits sous-développés ne partagent aucune des caractéristiques du passé des pays dits développés et, d'autre part, les pays dits développés « n'ont jamais été sous-développés, bien qu'ils aient pu être

---

97 Il écrit : « [...] si les investissements productifs sont financés par le capital étranger, ils doivent nécessairement conduire tôt ou tard à un reflux des profits en sens inverse tel que la croissance se bloque » et « [l]'histoire montre que la dynamique de l'investissement étranger conduit à un retournement de la balance des flux, le reflux des profits finissant par l'emporter sur le flux d'entrée du capital » S. Amin, *Le développement inégal : Essai sur les formations sociales du capitalise périphérique, op. cit.*, p. 215 et p. 216.

98 *Ibid.*, p. 215.

99 S. Amin, *Le développement inégal : Essai sur les formations sociales du capitalise périphérique, op. cit.*, p. 184.

100 *Ibid.*, p. 337 ; voir aussi S. Amin, *Modernité, religion et démocratie : critique de l'eurocentrisme, critique des culturalismes*, Paragon, 2008, pp. 167–171.

101 S. Amin, *Les défis de la mondialisation*, L'Harmattan, 1996, p. 114 ; Voir aussi S. Amin, « Sous-développement et dépendance en Afrique noire contemporaine », *Partisans*, n° 64, 1972, pp. 29–34.

102 S. Amin, *Les défis de la mondialisation, op. cit.*, p. 117.

103 *Ibid.*

104 A. G. Frank, *Le développement du sous-développement : l'Amérique latine*, François Maspero, 1972, p. 20.

non-développés »[105]. Il arrive ainsi à sa position définitive : « [...] le sous-développement contemporain est en grande partie le produit historique des relations passées et présentes, économiques et autres, entre les pays satellites sous-développés et les pays métropolitains actuellement développés »[106]. Il durcit encore ses conclusions en avançant que, contrairement à la sagesse commune qui veut que le développement des pays sous-développés puisse être provoqué entre autres par l'afflux de capitaux étrangers, le développement de ces pays se fera « indépendamment de la plupart de ces relations de diffusion »[107]. En lecteur attentif de Karl Marx, André Gunder Frank considère que « [l]es institutions et les relations économiques, politiques, sociales et culturelles que nous y observons [dans les pays sous-développés] aujourd'hui sont donc le produit du développement historique du système capitaliste [...] »[108]. Ces considérations ont trouvé un écho dans la *théologie de la libération*, qui a profondément marqué l'environnement politico-religieux de l'Amérique latine, et ont été à la base de nombreux mouvements sociaux, politiques et économiques. Elles ont aussi inspiré des luttes pacifiques ou armées en vue du renversement de toutes les forces qui maintenaient ces pays et leurs populations dans des conditions jugées intolérables.

Face au pessimisme des auteurs que nous venons de voir quant à la possibilité que les structures internationales puissent bénéficier aussi aux populations issues des anciens territoires colonisés, n'existerait-il pas une voie par laquelle le droit international pourrait lui-même se transformer et devenir ainsi un instrument d'émancipation et non d'asservissement.

2 La possible rédemption du droit international des investissements

Les réformes en cours du droit international des investissements, et spécialement celles relatives au mode de règlement des différends, affichent comme objectifs, entre autres, de redonner de la légitimité au système, de garantir l'indépendance et l'impartialité des juges et arbitres, d'assurer la constance et la cohérence des décisions rendues et de rationaliser le coût et la durée des procédures[109]. On aurait pu s'attendre à ce que ce vent de réforme soit

105 *Ibid.*

106 *Ibid.*

107 *Ibid.*

108 *Ibid.*, p. 21.

109 Voir les documents de la 37ème session du Groupe de Travail III de la CNUDCI sur la réforme du système de règlement des différends entre États et investisseurs, notamment les documents A/CN.9/WG.III/WP.150 ; A/CN.9/WG.III/WP.151 ; A/CN.9/WG.III/

principalement initié, porté et soutenu par les pays d'Amérique latine du fait de leur posture traditionnelle à l'égard du droit international des investissements ou même par certains États africains jaloux de leur souveraineté, mais force est de constater que ce mouvement de réforme est aussi soutenu par les pays développés, notamment ceux de l'Union européenne.

Il faut donc chercher à comprendre ce changement de paradigme de l'UE alors même que la Commission européenne avance – peut-être fièrement – que « *International investment rules were invented in Europe* »[110] et qu'on aurait donc pu s'attendre à ce qu'elle défende cet héritage. Une fois relevée la vraie nature des réformes en cours, il apparaîtra que ce mouvement manque sa cible : l'humanisation du droit international des investissements.

2.1 *La vraie nature des réformes en cours*

En mai 2020, 23 États membres de l'UE ont conclu un accord à l'effet de dénoncer les traités de protection des investissements conclus entre eux[111]. Il s'agit d'un mouvement de dénonciation collective jamais enregistré en droit international des investissements. Si des raisons institutionnelles et judiciaires ont pu conduire à cet événement, il nous semble qu'une raison structurelle a pu justifier cette démarche et même guider toute la politique de l'UE vis-à-vis des principes du droit international des investissements.

Nonobstant la pérennité de la configuration de l'économie mondiale entre le Nord et le Sud, une nouvelle tendance se fait de plus en plus ressentir. Les flux d'investissement ne se font plus seulement en direction du sud mais on observe aussi des flux du sud – des pays en voie de développement ou émergents – en direction des pays développés[112]. Les cas les plus emblématiques concernent, par exemple, les investissements angolais dans l'ancienne puissance coloniale, le Portugal[113], ou encore l'acquisition par la Chine du port

WP.152 et A/CN.9/WG.III/WP.153. Ces documents sont disponibles sur <https://uncitral.un.org/fr/working_groups/3/investor-state>.

110 Commission européenne, « Investment in TTIP and beyond – The path for reform: Enhancing the right to regulate and moving from current ad hoc arbitration towards an Investment Court » disponible sur <https://trade.ec.europa.eu/doclib/docs/2015/may/tradoc_153408.PDF>.

111 Accord portant extinction des traités bilatéraux d'investissement entre États membres de l'Union européenne (5 mai 2020) SN/4656/2019/INIT.

112 V. les chiffres publiés par l'OCDE dans son rapport « Statistiques de l'OCDE sur l'investissement direct international », 2020, pp. 26–334, disponible sur <https://doi.org/10.1787/6fb1b099-fr>.

113 N. Onishi, « Portugal Dominated Angola for Centuries. Now the Roles Are Reversed », *NY Times*, 22/08/2017 <https://www.nytimes.com/2017/08/22/world/europe/angola-portugal-money-laundering.html>. Voir aussi J. Ambrose, « Where in Britain does China spend its money? », *The Guardian*, 11/07/2020 <https://www.theguardian.com/world/2020/jul/11/where-in-britain-does-china-spend-its-money>.

du Pirée en Grèce[114]. Quoique ces flux restent encore marginaux[115], ils ont conduit les traditionnels pays d'origine des investisseurs à prendre conscience de l'impact que peuvent avoir les règles du droit international des investissements sur leur aptitude à mettre en œuvre des politiques publiques[116]. Alors que ces règles ont été pendant longtemps promues par les États développés et appliquées aux États sous-développés, l'éventualité que ces mêmes règles puissent être appliquées aux États développés les conduit à envisager et soutenir aujourd'hui une réforme du système. Le *New York Times* notait déjà en 2001, presque avec surprise, à propos des tribunaux arbitraux institués dans le cadre du NAFTA : « *Their meetings are secret. Their members are generally unknown. The decisions they reach need not be fully disclosed. Yet the way a small group of international tribunals handles disputes between investors and foreign governments has led to national laws being revoked, justice systems questioned, and environmental regulations challenged. And it is all in the name of protecting the rights of foreign investors under the North American Free Trade Agreement* »[117]. Or, pendant longtemps, des tribunaux similaires (tribunaux ou commissions mixtes de réclamation) ont siégé et rendu des décisions, parfois même dans des affaires aux fondements douteux comme certaines de celles ayant opposé des ressortissants européens et étatsuniens aux États d'Amérique latine tout au long des XIXème et XXème siècles. Pourtant, ces affaires-là n'ont pas semblé émouvoir ou choquer outre mesure.

On se souvient que dans le contexte du Nouvel Ordre Économique International (NOEI), des propositions de réforme similaires à celles envisagées aujourd'hui avaient été proposées et qu'elles s'étaient heurtées à l'opposition

114 P. Kapantais, « Grèce : le Pirée, bientôt premier port de Méditerranée », *Le Parisien*, 17/06/2020 <https://www.leparisien.fr/economie/grece-le-piree-bientot-premier-port-de-mediterranee-17-06-2019-8094810.php>.

115 J. Clifton and D. Díaz-Fuentes, « Is the European Union Ready for Foreign Direct Investment from Emerging Markets? », *in* K. Sauvant, G. McAllister and W. Maschek (eds), *Foreign Direct Investments from Emerging Markets: The Challenges Ahead*, Palgrave Macmillan, 2010, pp. 335–358.

116 Quelques procédures ont été déjà initiées contre certains pays européens : *Ping An Life Insurance Company of China c. Belgique*, aff. CIRDI, n° ARB/12/29, 2012 (Suite de la crise financière de 2008, le Gouvernement belge avait renfloué, nationalisé puis vendu à un tiers la compagnie dans laquelle l'entreprise chinoise avait investi). V. aussi (quoique l'investisseur soit issu d'un autre pays européen), *Vattenfall AB c. Allemagne*, aff. CIRDI, n° ARB/12/12, 2012 (Affaire découlant de l'adoption par l'Allemagne de mesures visant à abandonner l'énergie nucléaire).

117 A. Depalma, « Nafta's Powerful Little Secret; Obscure Tribunals Settle Disputes, but Go Too Far, Critics Say », *op. cit.*

des États développés[118]. L'un des points d'achoppement était alors relatif à la question de savoir s'il appartenait ou non aux juridictions nationales, dans l'hypothèse d'une expropriation, de déterminer le montant de l'indemnisation à verser à l'investisseur en cas de désaccord sur ce montant. Lorsque la Charte des droits et devoirs économiques de 1974[119], votée à l'initiative des pays du tiers monde[120], a vu le jour, elle posait que, dans le cas où à la suite d'une nationalisation, la détermination de l'indemnisation provoquerait un différend entre les parties, « [...] celui-ci sera réglé conformément à la législation interne de l'État qui prend des mesures de nationalisation et par les tribunaux de cet État, à moins que tous les États intéressés ne conviennent librement de rechercher d'autres moyens pacifiques sur la base de l'égalité souveraine des États et conformément au principe du libre choix des moyens ». On le voit, la Charte, tout en admettant le principe de l'indemnisation en cas d'expropriation, renvoyait son contentieux aux soins des tribunaux de l'État auteur de l'expropriation. Commentant l'article 2 c) de la Charte, le ministre mexicain des affaires étrangères de cette époque, Emilio Rabasa, expliquait le but de cet instrument :

« [...] *as the charter says, if any dispute arises it should be settled in accordance with the domestic law of the nationalizing State and by its tribunals; that is, it should be internal legal order which establishes the procedures and means of compensation. What is not to be tolerated, and what the overwhelming majority of countries have therefore completely rejected, is that instead of or in addition to the national legal system, other bodies or extranational procedures should be called on to rule on what a State should do in such cases. To accept such a system as binding would be to place States on an equal legal and political footing with foreign corporations, and that would mean that those corporations would receive nothing more or less than the treatment which should be reserved solely for States* »[121]. C. Leben écrit à ce sujet qu' « [i]l y a [...] dans la Charte une

118 U. Özsu, «Neoliberalism and the New International Economic Order: A History of 'Contemporary Legal Thought » *in* C. L. Tomlins et J. Desautels-Stein (eds.) *Searching for Contemporary Legal Thought*, Cambridge University Press, 2017, pp. 341–344.

119 Résolution 3281de l'Assemblée générale des Nations Unies, Charte des droits et devoirs économiques des États, A/RES/3281(XXIX), 12 décembre 1974.

120 En plus du « Groupe des 77 » et du bloc des pays d'obédience socialiste, ce texte a été aussi voté approuvé par 8 membres de l'OCDE dont l'Australie, la Finlande, la Grèce, l'Islande, la Nouvelle-Zélande, le Portugal, la Suède, la Turquie.

121 Reproduit *in* F. V. Garcia-Amador, « The Proposed New International Economic Order: A New Approach to the Law Governing Nationalization and Compensation », *Law. Am.*, vol. 12, 1980, pp. 41–42.

aversion à l'égard de tout type de juridiction internationale susceptible d'imposer son interprétation de telle ou telle question du droit international. [...] Dans l'hypothèse d'un litige entre un État et des personnes privées, celles-ci doivent s'adresser aux juridictions de l'État »[122]. Pour R. B. Lillich, l'ensemble de ces textes « [...] *attack the basic procedural principal of diplomatic protection for nationals abroad* »[123]. On comprendra aisément pourquoi les principaux États exportateurs d'investissement ont voté contre la Charte des droits et devoirs économiques des États ou s'abstinrent[124].

De façon relativement concomitante, une série de sentences arbitrales est intervenue à partir du milieu du XXème siècle qui va miner ces mouvements et réaffirmer la référence au droit international et aux mécanismes internationaux de règlement des différends telle que traditionnellement soutenue par les États européens et les États-Unis[125]. Il s'agit notamment des sentences *Abu Dhabi* (1951), *Ruler of Qatar* (1953), *Aramco* (1958), *Sapphire* (1963), *Aminoil* (1982) et les sentences rendues dans les affaires libyennes, *BP* (1973), *Texaco* (1977) et *Liamco* (1977)[126]. L'une des questions auxquelles les arbitres étaient appelés à répondre était relative à détermination de la loi applicable aux contrats en cause. Dans l'affaire des *Emprunts serbes*, la CPJI avait rappelé un principe traditionnel en droit international : « Tout contrat qui n'est pas un contrat entre des États en tant que sujets du droit international a son fondement dans une loi nationale »[127]. Pourtant, on remarquera que, sur divers

122 C. Leben, « Un survol historique », *in* C. Leben (dir.), *Droit international des investissements et de l'arbitrage transnational*, Paris, Pedone, 2015, p. 51. Voir ausi A. Bianchi, *International Law Theories: An Inquiry into Different Ways of Thinking*, *op. cit.*, pp. 212–213.

123 R. B. Lillich, « The Diplomatic Protection of Nationals Abroad: An Elementary Principle of International Law Under Attack », *AJIL*, vol. 69, 1975, p. 359, cité par C. Lipson, *Standing Guard*, *op. cit.*, p. 89.

124 Ont voté contre : la Belgique, le Danemark, la RFA, le Luxembourg, le Royaume-Uni et les États-Unis. Se sont abstenus : l'Autriche, le Canada, l'Espagne, la France, l'Irlande, Israël, l'Italie, le Japon, la Norvège et les Pays-Bas.

125 C. Lipson, *Standing Guard*, *op. cit.* ; K. Miles, *The origins of international investment law*, *op. cit.*

126 Dans le cours qu'il a dispensé à la Haye en 2003, le professeur Leben analyse divers problèmes soulevés par les sentences arbitrales issues de ces affaires, C. Leben, « La théorie du contrat d'État et l'évolution du droit international des investissements », *op. cit.*, pp. 197–386. Ces affaires ont reçu une immense audience en doctrine et ont largement été commentées. On se contentera de renvoyer ici à la riche bibliographie présente dans le cours de cet auteur.

127 *Affaire concernant ce paiement de divers emprunts serbes émis en France* (France/Serbie) (Arrêt) CPJI Rec. Série A n° 20/21, p. 41.

fondements théoriques (lacune ou primitivité des règles locales, internationalisation du contrat) et en présence de clauses, certes plus ou moins ambiguës mais d'où il ressortait tout de même une certaine priorité pour le droit interne, les arbitres écarteront systématiquement l'application de la seule législation locale au profit des principes généraux de droit ou tout simplement du droit international ou encore d'un tiers ordre juridique situé quelque part entre le droit interne et le droit international. Pour A. Anghie, ces diverses solutions relèvent toutes d'une stratégie visant en réalité à appliquer aux contrats en cause les principes défendus par les pays d'origine de ces investisseurs. Ainsi, « [...] *when international law was established as governing these arrangements, it was an international law 'found in the general principles of civilized nations'*»[128]. Ce sont justement ces principes défendus alors par les « États civilisés » que ces derniers eux-mêmes remettent en cause. Or, pour leur part, les États en voie de développement ont toujours contesté, avec plus ou moins de succès, ces principes. S'ils les ont finalement adoptés et même promus ce n'est qu'en raison de nombreux facteurs et de complexes processus de décisions mêlant nécessité économique et posture idéologique[129].

C'est pourquoi, le fait que les États traditionnellement en faveur de la protection internationale des investissements rejoignent le mouvement de remise en cause et de réforme peut s'analyser au fond comme une tentative pour ces États – face au risque plus élevé aujourd'hui[130] de se trouver soumis eux aussi aux règles dont ils ont longtemps fait la promotion – de reprendre en main le système. C'est en quelque sorte l'histoire du Dr Frankenstein qui se joue. Pourtant l'arbitrage d'investissement a été construit contre une forte critique et méfiance à l'égard des systèmes judiciaires des États en développement[131].

---

128 A. Anghie, *Imperialism, Sovereignty and the Making of International Law*, pp. 229–230.

129 L. Poulsen et E. Aisbett, « Diplomats Want Treaties: Diplomatic Agendas and Perks in the Investment Regime », *J. Int'l Dispute Settl.*., 2016, vol. 7, n° 1, pp. 83–91; L. Poulsen, *Bounded Rationality and Economic Diplomacy, op. cit.*, pp. 55–56; C. Lipson, *Standing Guard, op. cit.*, p. 92.

130 À vrai dire, cette prise de conscience date déjà de la fin des années 1990 au moins pour les États-Unis avec les premières affaires procédures arbitrales initiées dans le cadre de l'ALENA, quoique la multiplication des traités de protection des investissements en parallèle ne permettait pas de bien prendre la mesure du mouvement.

131 G. Van Harten, « Five Justifications for Investment Treaties: A Critical Discussion », *Tr. L. Dev.* 2010, vol. 2, n° 1, pp. 33–35; R. Bachand, « Indétermination du droit, légitimité des institutions et droit international de l'investissement » *in* M. Arès et É. Boulanger (dir.), *L'investissement et la nouvelle économie mondiale : Trajectoires nationales, réseaux mondiaux et normes internationales, op.cit.*, p. 93 ; M. Sornarajah, *The International Law on Foreign Investment, op. cit.*, pp. 112–113.

Outre les critiques contre l'indépendance et l'impartialité de leurs tribunaux, l'on a pointé du doigt aussi le défaut d'expertise, et la longueur des procédures dans ces pays[132]. Il fallait donc soustraire les investisseurs de la compétence de telles juridictions pour les soumettre à l'arbitrage international.

Or, aujourd'hui force est de constater que ces mêmes critiques peuvent être faites à la fois à l'égard de l'arbitrage d'investissement mais aussi à l'égard des systèmes judiciaires des États qui ont fait la promotion des mécanismes du droit international des investissements. Sur l'arbitrage d'investissement, les critiques sur l'indépendance et l'impartialité des arbitres[133], la durée des procédures[134] et l'expertise des arbitres[135] ne manquent pas. Quant aux organes judiciaires des États développés, dans l'affaire Loewen par exemple, le traitement infligé par les juridictions de l'État du Mississipi (États-Unis) à M. Loewen et son entreprise ne diffère pas de celui qui est reproché aux États en développement et qui a servie de justification du système de règlement des différends entre États et investisseurs. D'ailleurs, l'investisseur a saisi par la suite un tribunal arbitral pour critiquer le traitement qui lui a été réservé[136]. Dans la même veine, un récent sondage a montré que seulement 22% des Français ont confiance en l'appareil judiciaire quand 51% sont inquiets à son égard, 3% lui manifestent de la sympathie et 12% déclarent lui être hostiles[137].

En résumé, le renversement graduel de la trajectoire traditionnelle des investissements et les failles que montrent les appareils judiciaires des États développés contribuent à leur faire prendre conscience de l'impact réel que peuvent avoir sur eux les règles internationales qui structurent la protection

---

132 V. par exemple, Banque Mondiale, *Investment Law Reform: A Handbook for Development Practitioners*, 2010, p. 49, disponible sur < https://openknowledge.worldbank.org/handle/10986/25206 > consulté le 04/08/2021.

133 V. notamment le fameux rapport de *Corporate Europe Observatory* et *Transnational Institute* paru en 2012 et au titre évocateur « Profiting from injustice : How law firms, arbitrators and financiers are fuelling an investment arbitration boom » disponible sur <https://www.tni.org/files/download/profitingfrominjustice.pdf> consulté le 04/08/2021.

134 CNUDCI, *Éventuelle réforme du règlement des différends entre investisseurs et États (RDIE) : coût et durée*, Doc. A/CN.9/WG.III/WP.153, 31 août 2018, disponible sur <https://undocs.org/fr/A/CN.9/WG.III/WP.153> consulté le 04/08/2021.

135 F. Zarbiyev, *Le discours interprétatif en droit international contemporain : Un essai critique*, Bruylant, 2015, pp. 96–99.

136 *Loewen Group, Inc. et Raymond L. Loewen c. États-Unis*, aff. ALENA (CIRDI) n°ARB(AF)/98/3, sentence, 26 juin 2003, paras 3–8, 54–70.

137 <https://www.ifop.com/publication/le-regard-des-francais-sur-la-police-et-la-justice/> 27/05/2021, consulté le 04/08/2021. Pour des études en sens contraire, voir notamment OCDE, « Government at a Glance 2021 », pp. 212–213, disponible sur <https://doi.org/10.1787/1c258f55-en>.

des investissements étrangers. C'est ainsi que peut s'analyser l'empressement et l'implication des pays développés dans le processus actuel de réforme du droit international des investissements, c'est-à-dire, au fond, une tentative de reprise en main par ces États d'une créature qui se retourne contre son maître. Comme le note justement M. Kumm « *What is new about ISDS in the context of the 21st century is that the problem of geographic bias disappears. Liberal constitutional democracies themselves are subjected to claims by foreign investors making use of ISDS mechanisms, be it investors based in other liberal constitutional democracies or investors from developing countries that, as "emerging markets", have morphed into exporters of investment capital themselves. If we think of ISDS, like consular jurisdiction, as an institution of Empire, today's Empire would not be the Empire of France, Britain, the US or even "the West". It would be the global Empire of capital. In that Empire those enjoying special protection would not be nationals of any country, but foreign investors. And among the colonized would be the citizens of the traditional western heartlands, who find themselves confronted with the unintended consequences of their own hypocrisy* »[138]. De la même manière, M. Sornarajah fait oberver que « *[t]he rules the developed states crafted to protect the foreign investment of their nationals will soon come to haunt them. As a result, they may be bent on backtracking on these rules and creating, as developing countries argued for in the past, significant sovereignty-based defences to liability and redrawing the boundaries of investment protection* »[139].

Mais, même en rejetant ces considérations pour plaider la bonne foi de ces États, l'analyse des options prises dans les processus de réforme révèle-t-elle une optique nouvelle ou au contraire tout change pour qu'au final rien ne change ?

2.2 *Une humanisation du droit international des investissements*

La formule est à la fois une critique et une proposition que font les TWAIL. La critique consiste à souligner les choix que fait le droit international entre différents intérêts. Entre la libéralisation des biens, des services et des capitaux d'une part, et la libre circulation de la main d'œuvre d'autre part, le droit international va favoriser les premiers[140]. Entre la sacralisation des droits

138 M. Kumm, « Empire of Capital? Transatlantic Investment Protection as the Institutionalization of Unjustified Privilege », *op. cit.*

139 M. Sornarajah, *The International Law on Foreign Investment*, Cambridge University Press, 2021, p. 9.

140 R. Bachand, « Indétermination du droit, légitimité des institutions et droit international de l'investissement » *in* M. Arès et É. Boulanger (dir.), *L'investissement et la nouvelle*

de propriété et le droit à la santé, les droits de propriété seront privilégiés au détriment de millions de femmes et d'hommes incapables de soutenir les coûts des médicaments[141]. Entre la protection de l'environnement et la santé des populations d'une part, et la sauvegarde des droits des investisseurs d'autre part, ces derniers prévaudront parfois[142]. Les traités d'investissement imposent des obligations aux États d'accueil au bénéfice des investisseurs alors qu'en contrepartie ces derniers n'ont que très rarement des obligations vis-à-vis de l'État sur le territoire duquel ils investissent[143]. Pour B. S. Chimni, il s'agit là tout simplement de la codification des aspirations de la « bourgeoisie impérialiste »[144].

Dans le droit international des investissements, cette tendance à la suprématie des droits des investisseurs s'est illustrée dans la crise économique argentine de 2001. Alors prise dans la tempête de la grave crise économique de 2001 où des dizaines de procédures ont été intentées à son encontre, cet État s'est trouvé plusieurs fois condamné à payer des centaines de millions de dollars alors même que la situation économique était désastreuse et le fonctionnement régulier des services publics de base, interrompu. La situation était tellement désastreuse que l'on a pu rapporter que des populations affamées traquaient « les rats, chats, crapauds, grenouilles ou abatt[aient]

économie mondiale : Trajectoires nationales, réseaux mondiaux et normes internationales, op.cit., p. 83.

141 M. Arès et É. Boulanger, « Le régime international de l'investissement : où en sommes-nous ? » *in* M. Arès et É. Boulanger (dir.), *L'investissement et la nouvelle économie mondiale : Trajectoires nationales, réseaux mondiaux et normes internationales, op. cit.*, p. 21.

142 B. S. Chimni, « An outline of a Marxist Course on Public International Law », *op. cit.*, p. 10.

143 *Ibid.*, p. 21. Voir aussi M. Mbengue, « Les obligations des investisseurs », *in* L. Dubin, P. Bodeau-Livinec, J.-L. Iten et *al.*, *L'entreprise multinationale et le droit international*, Paris, Pedone, 2017, pp. 295–337 ; A. von Walter, « Balancing Investors' and Host States' Rights – What Alternatives for Treaty-makers ? », *Eur. Ybk Int'l Ec. Law.*, 2011, pp. 141–143 ; T. Mortimer et C. Nyombi, *Rebalancing International Investment Agreements in Favour of Host States*, Emerald, 2018.

Si la tendance générale des traités de protection des investissements confirme nos propos, il faut toutefois admettre que les traités récents inscrivent de plus en plus d'obligations à la charge des investisseurs. C'est le cas notamment du récent traité entre l'Inde et le Brésil (art. 11 et 12).

144 B. S. Chimni, « An outline of a Marxist Course on Public International Law », *op. cit.*, p. 10. Et plus généralement sur la question des intérêts, voir le recent ouvrage de N. Perrone, *Investment Treaties and the Legal Imagination: How Foreign Investors play by their Own Rules, op. cit.*

des chevaux malades pour les manger »[145]. Pourtant, dans ce contexte, seuls quelques tribunaux arbitraux ont admis que la responsabilité de l'Argentine ne pouvait pas être engagée au regard des circonstances[146].

La critique va donc se transformer en proposition en vue de mettre le droit international au service des millions de femmes, d'hommes et d'enfants pauvres. Pour le dire autrement, il s'agit de mettre l'humain au cœur du droit international ; faire du droit international un droit à visage humain, un droit qui reflète les aspirations des plus pauvres. Ainsi « [o]*rdinary life must become the focus of the entire discipline of international law* »[147]. Cette proposition

145 R. Bachand, « CMS contre Argentine : Premières réflexions sur une sentence arbitrale qui deviendra célèbre », *Note de Recherche*, p. 9. Disponible sur : <http://www.ieim.uqam.ca/IMG/pdf/Bachand_CMS.pdf>.

Aussi, dans sa défense devant les juridictions allemandes (17 % de la dette souveraine argentine était soumis au droit allemand), l'Argentine avait invoqué l'État de nécessité. Les juges de Francfort ont alors décidé de se référer à la Cour constitutionnelle fédérale sur la question de savoir s'il existait une règle de droit international public qui pouvait faire échec au paiement par l'Argentine de sa dette envers les créanciers privés sur la base de l'article 100 (2) de la Loi fondamentale allemande (Article 100 (2) : Les règles générales du droit international public font partie du droit fédéral. Elles sont supérieures aux lois et créent directement des droits et obligations pour les habitants du territoire fédéral). Dans sa décision en date du 8 mai 2007 (2 BvM 1/03), la Cour décida à la majorité que l'Argentine était tenue de respecter ses obligations. Toutefois, dans son opinion dissidente, la juge Lübbe-Wolff estimait pour sa part « qu'imposer à un État de payer ses créanciers privés alors que l'exécution de ses obligations risquerait d'engendrer une rupture dans le fonctionnement de ses services publics essentiels, constituerait une violation des droits de l'homme (jus cogens) dans la mesure où aucun intérêt essentiel de cette nature ne serait en jeu du côté des créanciers privés ». C. Kleiner, « Les affaires relatives à la dette souveraine argentine : un contentieux collectif et transnational en quête de règles et de tribunal », *AFDI*, vol. 61, 2015, p. 760.

146 C'est le cas notamment de l'affaire *LG&E c. Argentine*, aff. CIRDI, n° ARB/02/1, Décision sur la responsabilité, 3 octobre 2006, où le tribunal arbitral a estimé que « *the conditions in Argentina in December 2001 called for immediate, decisive action to restore civil order and stop the economic decline. To conclude that such a severe economic crisis could not constitute an essential security interest is to diminish the havoc that the economy can wreak on the lives of an entire population and the ability of the Government to lead. When a State's economic foundation is under siege, the severity of the problem can equal that of any military invasion* ». para 238. Pourtant quelques mois plus tard, le tribunal de *CMS c. Argentine*, aff. CIRDI, n° ARB/01/8, Sentence, 12 mai 2005, appelé à se prononcer sur la question de savoir si la crise était suffisamment grave pour justifier l'invocation par l'Argentine de l'état de nécessité, a jugé que certes « *the situation was difficult enough to justify the government taking action to prevent a worsening of the situation and the danger of total economic collapse. But neither does the relative effect of the crisis allow here for a finding in terms of preclusion of wrongfulness* » para 322.

147 B. S. Chimni, « The Past, Present and Future of International Law: A Critical Third World Approach », *Melb. J. Int'l Law* vol. 8, 2007, p. 515 ; *id.*, « A Just World Under Law: A View

est fort pertinente en ce qu'elle souligne un biais répandu dans les articles, ouvrages, conférences et colloques où le droit est commenté, analysé, apprécié ou critiqué mais où l'on fait peu de cas de l'impact que ces règles ont sur la vie quotidienne des individus. Bien que la théorie classique pose que les individus ne sont pas des sujets immédiats du droit international (ce qui est discutable aujourd'hui)[148], il importe de ne pas ignorer que ce sont eux qui en dernier lieu subissent ou bénéficient de la règle, qu'elle soit relative à une délimitation de frontière maritime, à la licéité de l'utilisation de l'arme nucléaire ou même à l'immatriculation de la Station spatiale internationale. Le progrès, la prospérité, le bien-être tant célébrés[149] doivent être pour tous. C'est pourquoi « *[i]t is time that the abstractions of international law are rooted in the empirical world of ordinary life and its travails. These would yield insights and judgements that can then be deployed to shape international laws and institutions that benefit*

From the South », *Proceedings ASIL*, vol. 100, 2006, pp. 17–24 ; D. Fidler, « Revolt Against or From Within the West?: TWAIL, the Developing World, and the Future Direction of International Law », *Chinese J Int'l Law*, vol. 2, 2003, pp. 29–76 ; V. Nmehielle, « A Just World Under Law: An African Perspective on the Status of the Individual in International Law », *Proceedings ASIL*, vol. 100, 2006, pp. 252–257 ; S. Gordon, « Indigenous Rights in Modern International Law from a Critical Third World Perspective », *Am. Ind. Law Rev.*, vol. 31, 2007, pp. 401–424 ; M. Fagbongbe, « The Future of Women's Rights from a TWAIL Perspective », *Intl. Com. L. R.*, 2008, pp. 401–409 ; K. Neri, « Le droit international économique comme moyen de 'décoloniser' le droit international ? L'exemple des préférences commerciales », et M. Mbengue, « 'La loi des nations est faite de fer' ? Reconnaissance et 'décolonisation' du droit international des investissements », *in* A. Geslin et E. Tourme Jouannet (dir.), *Le droit international de la reconnaissance, un instrument de décolonisation et de refondation du droit international ?*, Confluence des droits, 2019, pp. 119–149 et pp. 97–117 ; N. Lamp, « How Should We Think about the Winners and Losers from Globalization? Three Narratives and Their Implications for the Redesign of International Economic Agreements », *EJIL*, vol. 30, 2019, pp. 1359–1397 ; A. Geslin, « L'apport des postcolonial studies à la recherche en droit international », *in* A. Geslin, C. M. Herrera et M.-C. Ponthoreau (dir.), *Postcolonialisme et droit : Perspectives épistémologiques, op. cit.*, pp. 171–178.

148 A. Peters, *Beyond Human Rights: The Legal Status of the Individual in International Law*, Cambridge University Press, 2016.

149 A. Geslin résume bien cette ambivalence du droit international quand elle note que « [...] à rebours du discours qu'il porte – de protection des faibles, d'émancipation, d'égalité, d'universalité des droits, de neutralité, etc. – [le droit international] reproduit en fait des rapports de domination, perpétue la soumission des peuples et maintient les discriminations au profit des puissants, quelque forme que prenne cette puissance, qu'elle soit politique, économique, militaire, culturelle, ou cognitive », A. Geslin, « L'apport des postcolonial studies à la recherche en droit international », *in* A. Geslin, C. M. Herrera et M.-C. Ponthoreau (dir.), *Postcolonialisme et droit : Perspectives épistémologiques, op. cit.*, p. 161.

humanity »[150]. Il est aussi temps de sortir d'une approche trop souvent formelle consistant à soutenir que « *Elections were held and duly elected governments concluded the treaties* » ou de signer des contrats [151]. Il est rare que l'on s'interroge sur les conditions dans lesquelles ces actes ont été conclus[152] et sur l'impact négatif qu'ils peuvent avoir sur la vie des populations[153]. L'humanisation du droit international nécessite de « dépass[er] le silence »[154] imposé à ceux qui subissent les conséquences d'une libéralisation sans limites sur leur mode de vie, leur culture et leur identité. Elle passe ainsi, dans le domaine qui nous intéresse ici, par le respect de l'identité et l'avis des populations locales face à des projets d'investissement parfois imposés par des gouvernements en collisions avec des entreprises multinationales[155]. Mais cette quête n'est-elle pas utopique dans la mesure où les aspirations de ces populations marginales sont formulées « dans le langage même qui a permis de les assujettir » ou qui a au moins justifié leur assujettissement, c'est-à-dire le droit international[156] ?

---

150 B. S. Chimni, « The Past, Present and Future of International Law: A Critical Third World Approach », *op. cit.*, p. 515.

151 G. Van Harten, « Five Justifications for Investment Treaties: A Critical Discussion », *Trade Law and Dev.*, vol. 2, 2010, p. 29. V. aussi N. Perrone, *Investment Treaties and the Legal Imagination: How Foreign Investors play by their Own Rules, op. cit.*, p. 173.

152 V. notamment l'affaire *Siemens c. Argentine* à la suite de laquelle il a été prouvé que le contrat en cause avait été obtenu grâce au versement de pot de vin. S. Rubenfeld, « Former Siemens Executive Pleads Guilty in Argentina Bribery Case », *The Wall Street Journal*, 15/03/2018 < https://www.wsj.com/articles/former-siemens-executive-pleads-guilty-in-argentina-bribery-case-1521156057 >.

153 V. les affaires que N. Perrone passe en revue dans son ouvrage, *Investment Treaties and the Legal Imagination: How Foreign Investors play by their Own Rules, op. cit.*, pp. 172–198.

154 E. Stoppioni, « Droits économiques et sociaux et organisations internationales financières et commerciales : repenser les formes d'un silence assumé », *Europe des Droits & Libertés*, 2020/1, pp. 117. N. Perrone écrit pour sa part : « *Foreign investor rights define the relations between investors, states, and the local communities, determining 'who will adapt to whom' so to make the investment work. Investment treaties and ISDS can contribute in various ways to this objective; these include silencing some social effects and making invisible some of the actors involved* » *Investment Treaties and the Legal Imagination: How Foreign Investors play by their Own Rules, op. cit.*, p. 24.

155 M. Kumm, « Empire of Capital? Transatlantic Investment Protection as the Institutionalization of Unjustified Privilege », *op. cit;* N. Perrone, *Investment Treaties and the Legal Imagination: How Foreign Investors play by their Own Rules, op. cit.*, pp. 172–198. Ce dernier écrit: «*foreign investors are entitled to receive compensation in cases of expropriation, disappointment of their legitimate expectations, and violations of due process. This treatment is in stark contrast whit that granted to local communities in most instances, as they are rarely aware or consulted about the decision to open their area for business, support a project, or grant regulatory givings* », p. 182.

156 L. Assieu-Andrieu, « Coutume et usage », *in* D. Alland et S. Rials (dir.), *Dictionnaire de la culture juridique*, Paris, PUF, 2003, p. 318.

En tout état de cause, un obstacle se dresse devant la réalisation de ce projet : l'État postcolonial (du tiers-monde)[157] et l'élite aux commandes qui reproduisent et intègrent les schémas de domination et dont les éventuelles tentatives de « renverser la table » relèvent plus de la rhétorique qu'elles ne sont tendues vers des actions décisives[158]. Contrairement à ce qu'avait pu penser le Président Bedjaoui[159], les structures idéologiques et les postures intellectuelles laissées par le colonisateur paraissent plus difficiles à extraire que sa présence physique d'autant plus que ces structures et postures sont invisibles. La situation est encore plus inextricable quand les pays du tiers-monde eux-mêmes demandent le renforcement des règles qui, selon les TWAIL, les maintiennent au stade où ils se trouvent[160]. Il faut donc voir aussi la part de responsabilité des dirigeants locaux dans la souffrance des populations du tiers-monde. Mohamed Salah-Sfia parle de « victime-complice »[161].

157 O. Okafor, *Re-Defining Legitimate Statehood : International Law and State Fragmentation in Africa*, Martinus Nijhoff, 2000.

158 Il suffit de regarder par exemple les différents arguments soulevés par certains dirigeants africains pour maintenir le Franc CFA, la monnaie héritée de la colonisation française.

159 Comparant les contextes historiques et socio-politique de l'émergence des différentes générations d'auteurs tiers-mondistes, il avait laissé l'impression que le contexte de la première génération d'auteurs marqué par la présence physique du colonisateur dont il fallait se débarrasser était beaucoup plus difficile que le contexte dans lequel apparait la seconde génération des TWAIL au début des années 1990. M. Bedjaoui, « Observations sur le texte d'Antony Anghie », *in* M. Toufayan, E. Tourme-Jouannet et H. Ruiz Fabri (dir.), *Droit international et nouvelles approches sur le tiers-monde, op. cit.*, p. 83. Cependant, voir ce qu'il disait déjà en 1979 dans son ouvrage *Pour un nouvel ordre économique international, op. cit.*, pp. 84–87.

160 Dans une tribune publiée le 3 février dans les colonnes du *Monde*, par exemple, le président Sénégalais, associé au président français, la chancelière allemande, le secrétaire général des Nations Unies et la présidente de la Commission européenne, on pouvait lire : « *No doubt, globalization and international cooperation have helped billions of people escape poverty* ». Et, après avoir indiqué les défis auxquels la crise sanitaire a exposé le monde, il est indiqué : « *To meet these challenges, multilateralism is not just another diplomatic technique. It shapes a world order and is a very specific way of organizing international relations based on cooperation, the rule of law, collective action, and shared principles* ». Ce texte est reproduit dans sa version anglaise sur <https://emmanuelmacron.medium.com/we-must-build-a-more-inclusive-multilateralism-e49764ccae8> consulté le 13 février 2021. Le texte français est disponible sur <https://www.lemonde.fr/idees/article/2021/02/03/l-appel-de-l-onu-de-l-ue-et-de-trois-chefs-d-etat-face-au-covid-19-nous-devons-batir-un-multilateralisme-plus-solidaire_6068589_3232.html>.

161 Cité par I. Wallerstein, « Sous-développement et dépendance », *op. cit.*, p. 228.

C'est de ce fatalisme et de cette ambiguïté que rend compte A. Geslin lorsqu'elle convoque G. Spivak et L. Goldon et que s'établit entre ces deux auteurs une sorte de dialogue. Le premier s'interroge sur le point « de savoir si les subalternes peuvent parler », et le second de lui répondre : « les subalternes peuvent[-ils] être entendus – et par qui »[162]. En tout cas, B. S. Chimni avertit que ce changement de paradigme ne doit pas se faire par une approche verticale mais plutôt horizontale qui mettrait toutes les cultures, toutes les façons de vivre sur un pied d'égalité[163].

Si, au regard de tout ce qui vient d'être dit la transformation du droit international peut paraître utopique, l'on note toutefois quelques évolutions dans la prise en compte d'autres intérêts que ceux de l'investisseur sont à signaler. Déjà l'on peut se satisfaire de la reconnaissance, dans l'affaire *Urbasser* d'un droit à l'eau[164], de la prise en compte des dégâts environnementaux causés par l'investisseur dans l'affaire *Burlington*[165]. Dans l'affaire *Bear Creek Mining*, le Pérou soutenait l'obligation pour l'investisseur de consulter les populations locales[166]. Dans le même temps, l'affaire *South American Silver* illustrait l'opposition des populations locales qui devait conduire la Bolivie à mettre fin au projet de l'investisseur[167]. Le droit positif ne restent pas en marge puisque

---

162 A. Geslin, « L'apport des postcolonial studies à la recherche en droit international », *op. cit.*, pp. 171–172.

163 B. S. Chimni, « The Past, Present and Future of International Law: A Critical Third World Approach », *op. cit.*, p. 513. Comme le souligne notamment A. Geslin, à l'instar des modes de vie de chaque peuple qui doivent être préservés, il faut aussi admettre que le droit international contemporain qui est indiscutablement d'origine européenne, n'est en réalité qu'une conception parmi tant d'autres des relations « entre entités politiques se reconnaissant relativement indépendantes les unes des autres ». Et le triomphe de cette approche n'était pas évident (A. G. Franck le montre bien en soulignant que la Chine aurait pu le faire à une certaine époque). Elle a fini par s'imposer parfois par des moyens très brutaux ou des manœuvres pas toujours orthodoxes. C'est donc, dans une perspective décoloniale que le droit international doit tendre pour inclure les autres approches non-européennes.

Sur la question spécifique des approches du développement v. notamment N. Monebhurrun, *La fonction du développement dans le droit international des investissements*, L'Harmattan, 2016, pp. 29–32.

164 *Urbaser S.A. et al. c. Argentine*, aff. CIRDI n° ARB/07/26, sentence finale, 8 décembre 2016.

165 *Burlington Resources Inc. c. Équateur*, aff. CIRDI n° ARB/08/5, décision sur les demandes reconventionnelles, 7 février 2017.

166 *Bear Creek Mining Corporation c. Perou*, aff. CIRDI n° ARB/14/21, sentence finale, 30 novembre 2017.

167 *South American Silver Limited c. Bolivie*, aff. CPA n° 2013–15, sentence finale 22 novembre 2018.

quelques traités de protection des investissements témoignent de ces évolutions notamment le TBI entre l'Inde et le Brésil qui dispose en son article 12 que « [*i*]*nvestors and their investments shall strive to achieve the highest possible level of contribution to the sustainable development* [...] *the local community* »[168]. Certes, ces données restent encore parcellaires, mais elles fournissent au moins une indication sur la direction que le droit international des investissements devrait prendre.

3 Conclusion

Les outils d'analyse proposés par les TWAIL et les théoriciens de la dépendance permettent de mettre en exergue la réalité du paradigme autour duquel est construit le DII. Construit autour d'une binarité qui met d'un côté les « civilisés » et de l'autre les « non civilisés », le droit international continue de perpétuer ce paradigme. Ce *statu quo* s'explique par le maintien des structures juridiques et économiques que l'accession à la souveraineté internationale des 'non civilisés' n'a pas réussi à ébranler. Mais, alors que les tentatives de remise en cause observées jusqu'à présent émanaient essentiellement des pays en développement, force est de reconnaître que le mouvement de contestation actuelle s'inscrit dans un cadre global. C'est donc là, indéniablement le signe de ce que les pays développés, qui ont de tout temps défendu ces règles, prennent conscience de l'impact qu'elles peuvent avoir sur leurs capacités d'action, par exemple pour protéger la santé de leurs citoyens. Mais en même temps, les pistes de réforme proposées ne semblent pas aller dans un sens qui ferait sortir le DII de l'opposition binaire pour en faire un véritable outil d'émancipation au service de l'humain où la productivité et la compétitivité des investissements étrangers ne priment pas la protection de l'environnement et des droits des communautés dont la vie, la culture et l'identité sont impactées par les investissements.

168 Encore que de telles dispositions ne sont pas formulées sous forme d'obligations et leur contenu précis reste discutable.

PART 5

Conclusions

CHAPTER 17

Concluding Remarks

Christian Tomuschat

1 Introduction: The Objectives of the Symposium

The title chosen for the German-French symposium on issues of international and concomitantly constitutional law was ambitious: *Democracy and Sovereignty: Rethinking the Legitimacy of Public International Law*. In order to engage in dialogue about the issues raised within this conceptual framework physical obstacles first had to be overcome. Most of the participating French lawyers were prevented by the well-known health crisis from attending physically in Tutzing (Bavaria) so that a hybrid meeting had to be organized, which eventually could take place in fact.

The major challenges were of another caliber. Hardly could one expect that the encounter would serve to clarify all the ideas and doubts surrounding the concepts that lie at the basis of international law, for which the sovereign State still remains the foundational unit, due to its consecration in the Charter of the United Nations (Art. 2(1)) and, not by accident, in hard empirical facts. The Charter itself does not mention democracy as a paradigmatic criterion of statehood but confines itself to setting forth 'sovereign equality' of States as a *Grundnorm* of international law from which most of the other basic principles of the present-day international legal order – in particular the ban of the use of force and the prohibition of intervention – derive. Yet, the introductory words of the Charter, 'We, the Peoples of the United Nations', made clear from the very outset that the world's constitutional instrument did not emerge just from a consensus achieved at the elitist level of the governments concerned but that the World Organization had deeper roots at the grassroots level, being tied to the aspirations and needs of the peoples themselves. Thus, notwithstanding the linguistic gap, it was clear from the very outset that the democratic principle belonged to its core substance. The United Nations was not the product of an ad hoc arrangement among the big powers, serving first and foremost the interests of these powers. Although reserving for themselves a privileged position in the powerful Security Council, they realized that a regulatory framework for the whole world required broad bases of legitimacy for which the cooperation of all of the nations of the globe was necessary. By opening the World Organization for all 'peace-loving states' (Art. 4), they conferred on

 | DOI:10.1163/9789004508712_018

the state, a historical and to some extent 'cold' concept, a flavour of humaneness that ensured its vitality and durability for future generations. In Western Europe, in contrast to the universal level, initial difficulties caused by members nurturing reservations with regard to the concept of democracy did not exist when the Council of Europe was founded in 1949. In its preamble, the Statute of the Organization embraced in a straightforward manner the concept of 'genuine democracy' for its peoples.

As a necessary consequence of the political philosophy shared by its founders, the word 'democratic' appeared soon in the linguistic usage of the United Nations in a number of instruments which reflected the principled lines of development of the World Organization. Art. 21(3) of the 1948 Universal Declaration of Human Rights proclaimed in forthright terms that '[t]he will of the people shall be the basis of the authority of government', and Art. 25 ICCPR translated this political statement into binding international law by granting everyone, without any distinction, the right and the opportunity 'to take part in the conduct of public affairs'. The paramount intellectual and emotional attractiveness of the concept of state increased even more when in later years, states were conceived of as the factual embodiment of the exercise of the right of self-determination of a people. Self-determination was included in the Declaration on Principles of International law, adopted by the UN General Assembly in 1970, which listed the seven fundamental principles of the international legal order. As recently observed by the International Court of Justice (ICJ) self-determination had hardened as a genuine principle of positive international law already ten years earlier through the adoption of the Independence Declaration of 1960[1] that put a definitive end to any legitimacy of colonialism.[2]

As a consequence of these developments, in political rhetoric the idea that States should be structured as democratic systems of governance has achieved an overwhelming success. Even most of the few countries still formally designed as monarchies – kingdoms or sultanates – have in substantive terms become democracies with regard to their mechanisms of decision-making.[3] Thus, at first glance, it appears that the two concepts of sovereign State and democracy match one another without any trace of disparities.

1 UNGA Resolution 1514 (XV), 14 December 1960.

2 ICJ, Legal Consequences of the Separation of the Chagos Archipelago from Mauritius in 1965, Advisory opinion, 25 February 2019, Reports 2019, 95, 132.

3 This applies to all of the remaining European monarchies and also to the Kingdom of Bhutan. Only few absolute monarchies remain: Brunei Darussalam, Saudi Arabia, the United Arab Emirates.

Notwithstanding this image of harmony, the challenges remain tremendous. What is a democracy? What kind of mechanisms ensure its specific character? And what are the powers conferred by international law pursuant to the concept of sovereignty? Even cursory reflection encounters a seemingly endless chain of questions. The symposium could not provide for a complete inventory of all of the relevant issues and did not strive to do so but confined itself to selecting a number of exemplary key questions that were suitable to shed some light on the overall problématique of the democratic State in its internal setting and in its relationship within the international legal order. The structuring general idea was to re-examine democracy and sovereign statehood in their mutual relationship, enquiring whether through the strengthening of the democratic principle over the years since the founding of the United Nations the traditional framework of rules defining the limits of sovereign powers had opened up new spaces for the realization of essentially democratic objectives. Notwithstanding this guiding idea, the symposium was not specifically issue-focused. It aimed to present a broad panorama covering State sovereignty and democracy, wishing to incite the participants to address selected issues of paradigmatic relevance. Defying this cautious approach, in his introduction Stefan Oeter (p. 1) succeeded in providing a vast overview of the topics that are not only discussed in titerary debates, but currently dominate the agenda of all future-oriented institutions.

2 The Contributions

2.1 *The Democratic State and Its Citizens*

The democratic State is not a *res perfecta* once and for all, immutable and resilient. An ideal point of departure is described by Angelika Nussberger and Júlia Miklasová (p. 269) in their presentation on the work of the Venice Commission that has guided the adaptation of the constitutions of the former eastern European States to the standards of Western-type democracy after their emancipation from the cage of socialist narrowness and has continued thereafter to provide advice to the work of the institutions of the Council of Europe in Strasbourg, including the European Court of Human Rights. According to a traditional saying the basic principle is simple: Democracy means government of the people, by the people and for the people. Going a significant step further, the Venice Commission views the state as a governmental mechanism shaped additionally by the substantive standards of protection of human rights and fundamental freedoms and the rule of law. This conception has validly stood the test of time and is in no need of review, still being recognized as a guiding signal for the whole of Europe.

And yet, faithful implementation of these elementary paradigmatic propositions is nowhere automatically guaranteed. Moreover, the human element may not be left aside. Legal craftsmanship of the best constitutionalists cannot make up for deficits in the attitude of citizens who bear the responsibility of protecting their polity. In his contribution, Lando Kirchmair (p. 95) insists on the necessity of truthfulness for those who are entrusted with discharging official functions, claiming that in a democratic system truthfulness constitutes an essential pillar. He goes even so far as to require a constitutional prohibition to tell lies. It is certainly true that the strength of the public polity depends in the last analysis on the preparedness of its members to defend their common project. But it is precisely the task of the architects of a constitutional framework to ensure that human errors and deficits are removed or compensated by appropriate procedures. To hope that under a democratic system human being could be elevated to a higher level of moral authority is an illusion. Constitution-making remains a human undertaking with all the possible weaknesses that may attach to it. Kirchmair addresses even the question of whether false and truncated information in international relations could amount to a breach of the general principle of non-intervention, which is characterized by the criterion of coercion. His reflections evince that the individual human being at the basis of all political processes remains the pivotal element of any political system, and rightly emphasize the importance of moral consciousness in political processes but do not lead to realistic solutions for daily practice.

2.2 *The Internal Mechanisms in a Genuinely Democratic State*

Several contributions address the internal mechanisms designed to make democratic processes, in particular elections, trustworthy manifestations of the political will of the people, the only legitimate source of all political legitimacy. It has become common opinion in Europe and has found its reflection in the jurisprudence of the European Court of Human Rights (ECtHR) that elections presuppose, in order to become a reliable basis of legitimacy, a vast area of pluralist freedom where political opinions can be expressed without any hindrance or intimidation. In this regard, Stephanie Schiedermair (p. 145) gives an account of the regimes governing freedom of journalism while Robert Uerpmann-Wittzack (p. 169) focuses on freedom of association as a vehicle to permit citizens to establish groups that are able collectively to pursue specific goals, thereby offering the electorate significant political choices on election day.

The two contributions, both well-researched and well-documented, do not surprise the reader. They describe the established guarantees in the relevant European instruments on the one hand while portraying, on the other hand, in particular the threats to which these freedoms are currently subjected not only in Russia and Turkey, but also in two member States of the European Union, namely Hungary and Poland. It is for the reader extremely instructive to find together in one piece a description of the manifold obstacles that authoritarian regimes have erected with a view to preventing or suppressing any public criticism of their conduct. On the other hand, they must find it intriguing that the fact of being both a member of the Council of Europe and the European Union does not prevent two States from engaging in practices that closely resemble the former communist methods of repression.

A delicate topic is examined by Daniel Ventura (p. 291) who aims to clarify to what extent protective rules on data protection have emerged in general international law apart from Council of Europe Convention No 108[4] and the general clause laid down in Art. 17 CCPR ('arbitrary or unlawful interference with ... privacy'). Basing himself on the largely concordant formulations in a great number of binding and non-binding international instruments, he attempts to prove that the generally recognized standards for the handling of personal data have grown into the status of general principles, norms that differ from customary law. His reflections on the different categories of legal sources listed in Art. 38 of the ICJ Statute highlight once again the schism in the debate on the origin of general principles, in domestic law or directly in international law, adding interesting accents to the deliberations currently going on at the ILC. One may regret, however, that the author has dealt with his topic exclusively as a configuration where the individual stands alone against State authority without considering the more collective dimension of the freedom of civil society vis-à-vis the different branches of institutionalized government, which must lead to innovative reflections on the relationship between the actual power-wielding agents and the people in whose name they act.

Observation of elections and assistance to elections have become a routine model of international cooperation. Christina Binder (p. 212) gives a detailed description of the efforts undertaken in particular by the organs of the United Nations, the OSCE and the Council of Europe in this field. The reader notes with interest that quite a number of States are refusing any such supervisory activity in their territories. It stands to reason that any kind of observation mission

4 Convention for the Protection of Individuals with regard to Automatic Processing of Data, 28 January 1981, ETS No. 108.

increases the reliability and trustworthiness of the electoral results. Claims that observation of elections by foreign organizations amounts to undue interference in domestic matters, frequently put forward in earlier years, have by now totally lost their plausibility. One may call it a big success for the democratic movement that the observation of elections is, in most cases, no longer regarded as a stigma for the State concerned in the international community. Binder rightly emphasizes that the correctness of the electoral process for it alone does not ensure the democratic legitimacy of a governmental system, and also Oeter strongly underlines this requirement: any government must show its attachment to the rule of law after its election in its daily practice, which becomes eventually the determinative test. In general terms one may rightly observe that if the correct conduct of an election is not guaranteed, the governmental system concerned is at great pains to affirm its legitimacy.

Unfortunately, a specific topic which currently attracts ever more attention in the public debate on democracy is not covered in any of the written contributions although it was extensively discussed at the symposium on the basis of an oral presentation, namely the risk of alienation of the representatives discharging public functions in the fields of legislation, administration and the judiciary from their grassroots level, the citizenry. In his introduction, Oeter had already warned of 'elitist' government (p. 9). Such alienation, which inevitably leads to mistrust and diffidence, can be avoided to some extent by appropriate mechanisms of accountability. Participants saw here a rising problem in particular with regard to Africa. In fact, office-holders must be susceptible of being perceived truly as persons discharging a mandate that was entrusted to them for a limited period of time within the framework of the relevant legislation. It becomes a lethal threat for genuine democracy if office holders exercise their functions as if those functions were their personal assets or if 'expertocracy' supplants decision-making from the ground.

The reader misses also a short regard on economic and social rights, which do not enjoy the same prominence in the conventional regimes outside the European Union although, in particular, health care and old age pension systems have become essential factors of a democratic system of government committed to the vital needs of everyone. The European Social Charter, notwithstanding its weakness as a set of rules and principles that lack direct applicability, stands symbolically for the welfare component which re-enforces governmental legitimacy both by its presence and its output performance. Even the Venice Commission, departing from its primary adherence to the 'negative' freedoms under the rule of law has from time to time, as appropriate, advised States as to the advisability to include social and economic rights in their constitutional instruments.

2.3 *The Great Tasks of a Democratic Government in Our Time*

It was self-evident that the participants had to turn their eyes also to the great tasks with which in our time democratic governments are prominently confronted. Markus Beham (p. 322) believes that still today public interest in environmental issues needs active stimulation by drawing attention to environmental security and environmental wealth – and does not really take note of the fact, notwithstanding a knowledgeable detailed overview of the ongoing efforts, that such issues have everywhere in the world risen to the top of the agenda of any government. Indeed, in all countries of this globe all responsible office-holders have become aware of the fact that to preserve mankind's natural heritage has become a question of life and death from which no escape is possible. To speak of 'environmental inertia' does not seem accurately to reflect the activities of the mechanisms that have started rolling, albeit not with the desirable speed. Dealing with the same challenges, Kevin Grimmeiß (p. 338) introduces the long-forgotten concept of finiteness into the debate. Sovereignty embodies normative power over human beings but should not be mistaken for man's dominance over the natural resources that provide the foundations of any biological life on earth. For centuries, humankind lived in the belief that the natural resources of this globe were inexhaustible. Given today's knowledge as provided by scientific research, humankind must endeavour to establish limits to its continuous desire to exploit all available riches up to their eventual exhaustion and even destruction. Grimmeiß advocates for a supranational regime that could through mandatory regulations determine a binding framework for all human activities. Unfortunately, as could be expected, he is not able to put forward suggestions as to how such a framework could be established under the prevailing conditions of the world order where consent still remains the basic parameter of legal action. Finiteness will certainly become the leitmotiv for future legislation at universal level if humankind wishes to tackle the upcoming crisis of climate and biodiversity in a rational fashion.

It stands to reason that the effectiveness of new visions to reform the economy in countries formerly under colonial rule had to come under close scrutiny. Shehrazade El-Haijaar (p. 360) and Yannick Mihnzou Kouassi (p. 380) examine both the regime of investor-State dispute settlement under which individual economic operators may sue foreign States for the protection of their investments. Most of the legal regimes available for that purpose have been established under the auspices of the ICSID Convention of 1965,[5] which had come

5 Convention on the Settlement of Investment Disputes between States and Nationals of Other States, 18 March 1965, 575 UNTS 159.

into existence as fruit of a World Bank initiative. The applicable substantive guarantees are generally contained in bilateral treaties (BITS) between the national State of the investor and the State where the investment was made while the enforcement mechanisms have been entrusted to arbitration panels that are composed specifically for each and every individual case. Both authors are unanimous in criticizing this system which indeed is currently in a process of deep review. For them, the system must be seen as a remnant of former colonial predominance which curtails the sovereign powers of the young States that in order to attract foreign capital feel compelled to grant far reaching guarantees of stability. They argue, in agreement with a large group of legal writers, that the standard of 'fair and equitable treatment' generally applied by the arbitral tribunals lacks precise contours and has many times been blown up beyond any reasonable limit. Indeed, the system as it stands requires to be overhauled with fairness for both sides. It is certainly desirable to establish a higher level of judicial review where awards rendered at the lower level could be appealed. The critical line of the two authors follows closely the reform efforts that have already been set in motion.

2.4 *The External Relations of Democratic States*

The symposium lastly turned to new orientations under the auspices of democracy in external relations. Laurence Burgorgue-Larsen (p. 60), drawing on her vast experience with the practice of human rights courts not only in Europe but also in the Americas and in Africa, focuses on the way in which the international bodies deal with national judgments that – necessarily – precede the decisions at international level. International human rights courts are obviously caught in a dilemma. On the one hand, they are called upon to defend the integrity and regional uniformity of 'their' treaty, on the other hand, lacking themselves any direct democratic legitimacy. they have to leave the domestic fora enough room for taking into consideration the specificities of the situation on the ground in the overall national context, where the will of a parliamentarian majority requires attention and respect. The margin of appreciation has become for the European Court of Human Rights in this regard the major instrument to accommodate national concerns. In respect of the traditional arsenal of civil rights supporting the democratic character of the State, on the other hand, the author finds 'common intransigence': no lowering of the common standards is deemed legitimate in the jurisprudence of the different human rights courts. Regarding sexual self-determination, a highly delicate province of human rights, major conflicts of views have often emerged. The author underlines that eventually the advisory opinion of the

Inter-American Court of Human Rights of November 2017 on same-sex marriage[6] has introduced a common understanding – which however, is not self-evident for Europe and Africa. The consensus has evident regional limits.

Several contributions enter the field of foreign relations outside the field of human rights. No common denominator can be easily detected for their quest to reconcile national self-determination and the key principles of the international legal order. Edith Vanspranghe (p. 119) complains that at the international level perfect equality of States is not in fact ensured. Obviously, no one needs to be taught that in terms of factual power States are not and cannot be equal – from China down to Liechtenstein. But the author fails in lamenting that coalitions of States elevate certain substantive criteria to conditions of membership. On the level of the UN only 'peace-loving' has been set as a benchmark – which every civilized State wishing to belong to the international community must be able to attain. Yet, it is eminently wrong to criticize the European Union for requiring a broad range of criteria for admission to membership. The EU is a group of like-minded countries desirous to share and defend a number of values particularly dear to them. Postulating freedom of choice for individual States, the author denies the same freedom to others who have joined to form such alliances according to their sovereign wishes.

A similar issue is addressed by Emanuel Castellarin (p. 183) who asks whether policies of development assistance can be allowed to promote political goals that correspond to the western ideal of a liberal democracy or whether the relevant international bodies should be ideologically 'neutral'. In fact, hitherto development policies have mainly followed the former path without considering this choice as problematic. Development has been generally linked to promotion of democracy. As a consequence, financial assistance has often been subjected to 'democratic conditionality'. The author evaluates the linkage of financial assistance with the realization of democratic objectives from a critical viewpoint, mentioning at the end of his contribution that China has opted for a different viewpoint, disregarding the constitutional order of the country concerned provided that its assessment of the economic and financial situation provides satisfactory outcomes.

Finally, democracy can also be fostered by means of pressure below the level of military force and not amounting to coercion. Ioannis Prezas (p. 235) discusses possible ways and means to enforce democracy by sanctions that can either be collective, issued by an international organization, or unilaterally by

6 IACtHR, Gender Identity, and Equality and Non-Discrimination of Same-Sex Couples, Advisory Opinion, OC-24/17, 24 November 2017.

a (powerful) State. A great majority of developing nations has since many years denounced the unilateral imposition of sanctions, in particular in the field of trade and finances, as being in breach of the principle of non-intervention while Western countries view such policies as an outflow of their sovereign powers that may be used for any good purpose as long as the forbidden zone of intervention is not reached. All the relevant resolutions of the General Assembly[7] and the Human Rights Council[8] have been adopted by majorities against large groups of opponent countries. In this perspective, it is easily understandable that the demarcation line between sovereign freedom and unlawful intervention is highly controversial and has hitherto found no definitive answer in the jurisprudence of the International Court of Justice.

3 Conclusions

Does democratic governance open up new horizons in international law? The contributions assembled in the present volume do not provide the reader with a persuasive answer. It rather appears that the great shift regarding the paradigmatic foundations of international law occurred some decades ago through the process of decolonization unleashed by the resounding call for freedom that had found its dynamic expression in the Atlantic Charter of 14 August 1941.[9] As from that determinative step forward in the history of humankind, the new States could assert their concerns and needs directly in the international arena after the criminal alliance of aggression had been defeated. They were accepted as equals in law – and they have resolutely made use of this opportunity by pledging their cooperation for all projects of the United Nations aiming to overcome and shed the remaining legal and de facto elements of Western superiority. It is indeed true that the international legal order must be freed from all hidden obstacles that in fact deprive the developing nations from the full enjoyment of their newly won sovereign rights.

Unfortunately, the present times do not provide appropriate conditions for a wide and generous exercise of sovereign powers within the limits of general international law. A growing awareness has arisen that in order to ensure the survival of humankind a strict management of the earth's resources is necessary. States do not only need to act with careful respect for their neighbours but will additionally have to include in their political strategies the welfare of

7 UNGA Res. 75/181, 16 December 2020 (adopted 131 to 56).
8 HRC Res. 27/21, 26 September 2014, adopted 31 to 14, with two abstentions.
9 https://history.state.gov/milestones/1937-1945/atlantic-conf.

humankind as a whole. This is not a task incumbent on governmental authorities only, but must also be embraced by societies in all countries of this globe. In this respect, a new belief in the common citizen is required. Although the democratic idea in its purity requires to follow the aspirations from the ground, it seems undeniable that in some instances a reversal may be necessary: societies need to listen for education.

In this new order of the world, the countries that have attained a high standard of well-being will have to make great sacrifices in order to alleviate in particular the fate of those who currently live in poverty and misery and who, without any external assistance, would have to face up to a bleak future. All democracies will need to embrace the new philosophy of scarcity and discipline on this globe. This outcome may sound excessively pessimistic for those who still believe that sovereignty means unbridled freedom of action. Yet, recognition of unavoidable realities opens up at the same time avenues for rational and responsible joint efforts by all nations under the auspices of genuine democracy.

CHAPTER 18

Conclusions

Evelyne Lagrange

A quoi ressemblerait le droit international s'il était le droit d'une société d'Etats tous démocratiques ? A un droit de coopération bienheureuse entre Etats, à un droit cosmopolitique, à un droit protégeant l'espace national d'une délibération démocratique arcboutée sur la souveraineté populaire ou nationale, à un droit portant en germe l'annihilation de tout écart par rapport à un idéal-type d'Etat démocratique, au prix des expérimentations et révolutions politiques ? Pour avoir des racines historiques profondes, une telle spéculation n'irait pas sans risque. Le contexte politique qui interdit, au seuil des années 2020, de tenir pour acquise l'expansion continue du domaine de la démocratie libérale, voire de toute forme de régime démocratique, n'y invite guère. Les intervenants à ce double colloque de Tutzing, « junior » et « senior », marqué du sceau d'une pandémie (2020-…) qui aura favorisé la mise en scène du contraste entre différents régimes et modes de gouvernement confrontés au même péril, ne se sont d'ailleurs guère aventurés vers les origines et conséquences ultimes d'une telle *utopie*.

Une utopie, c'est ainsi que la question serait en effet spontanément envisagée dans une perspective européenne, voire ouest-européenne, qui articule étroitement le gouvernement du peuple, par le peuple, pour le peuple et la garantie des droits et libertés individuels : cet idéal « universel » ne s'est pas encore universellement concrétisé ; selon certains indicateurs, sans doute discutables, la démocratie serait même en recul, y compris dans ses bastions historiques comme les Etats-Unis (IDEA, Global State of Democracy Report, 2021). L'exaltation de ce modèle démocratique entretient en vérité une profonde ligne de fracture au sein de la société internationale contemporaine. Un peu plus d'un an après le colloque franco-allemand, alors que le Président américain Joe Biden conviait une sélection d'une centaine d'Etats à participer à un sommet sur la démocratie, les ambassadeurs russes et chinois auprès des Etats-Unis d'Amérique publiaient dans *National Interest* (26 novembre 2021) une tribune aussi rare que virulente pour dénoncer tout ensemble l'éviction de la Russie et de la République populaire de Chine de la liste des invités, les ingérences et interventions (armées) conduites au nom de la défense ou de la promotion de la démocratie et les dérives constatées dans les « démocraties libérales ». « Positivement », les auteurs s'efforçaient de promouvoir une définition de

 | DOI:10.1163/9789004508712_019

la démocratie suffisamment élastique pour s'adapter à toutes les cultures et pratiques nationales ou presque. Relativisme des valeurs et « réalisme politique » s'alliaient ainsi ouvertement contre l'un des projets emblématiques de la société internationale d'après la fin de la guerre froide – diffuser un modèle de démocratie, la démocratie libérale – au point de le dépeindre pratiquement comme une *dystopie*.

Les participants à ce colloque franco-allemand avaient déjà pris acte de cet antagonisme en se concentrant, précisément, sur les toutes dernières décennies, de l'alliance prometteuse du droit international et de la démocratie (à partir de 1989–1990) au désenchantement contemporain, nourri par la « déconsolidation démocratique », l'écrasement des printemps arabes et la consolidation de « démocratures » ou « démocraties illibérales » – avant l'abandon et l'effondrement d'un embryon d'Etat démocratique en Afghanistan (août 2021) érigé à la force des armes, scellant semble-t-il l'échec du changement de régime par voie d'intervention armée extérieure. Il est vrai que cette thématique avait été proposée par la Société allemande pour le droit international en écho à une inquiétude croissante face aux effets sur le fonctionnement de la société internationale et de ses institutions de la fragilisation interne et de la perte de leadership d'Etats tenus pour les précurseurs de la démocratie libérale. Les deux phénomènes sont parfois liés (ainsi des Etats-Unis sous la présidence de Donald Trump), mais pas systématiquement. En tout cas, des Etats autoritaires ou des caricatures de démocraties, qui parfois se targuent de réussites économiques bien réparties et d'efficacité (sanitaire par ex.), et parfois affichent des bilans calamiteux, remplissent le vide pour pousser non seulement leurs intérêts mais leur modèle, à l'instar de la République populaire de Chine, et leur conception du droit international, repliée sur un souverainisme assumé. Tous ces phénomènes se cumulant, ils pourraient mettre en péril le pacte international scellé en 1945 puis revivifié en 1990 et avec lui, le multilatéralisme dans les institutions internationales et en dehors, tels que les Européens en particulier tendent à les comprendre et valoriser – quoique des voix discordantes et résolument critiques sachent se faire entendre, jusque dans le cercle élargi des échanges académiques franco-allemands. Le lien entre démocratie et droit international est rien moins que simple.

•••

Les principes fondamentaux proclamés en 1945 et revivifiés en 1990 ont été largement, mais non exclusivement, inspirés et défendus par les démocraties libérales : un droit protecteur des Etats, des peuples, de la personne humaine ; un droit porteur de promesses : la paix, la liberté, le progrès économique et social de tous les peuples, exaltés dans le préambule de la Charte des Nations Unies et son article 1. Ces mêmes Etats ont modelé ou remodelé les institutions internationales censées donner corps à ces principes. A leur tour, ces institutions ont favorisé l'exportation du modèle de la démocratie libérale édifié sur trois piliers : les élections libres, le contrôle juridictionnel (y compris celui qu'exercent les cours constitutionnelles), la garantie des droits fondamentaux, avec une préférence pour les droits civils et politiques plutôt qu'économiques et sociaux, augmentés d'une orientation (néo-) libérale des politiques économiques[1]. De là à dire que le droit international contemporain a été modelé par et *pour* les démocraties libérales, au service de leurs intérêts et de l'extension de leur influence, comme le *jus publicum europaeum* avait été édifié par et pour les Etats européens, il y a un pas que certains n'hésitent pas à franchir, au mépris peut-être de la complexité de l'histoire des régimes et institutions internationales, y compris pendant la guerre froide[2], et de la capacité des autres Etats à s'approprier ou à subvertir des mécanismes internationaux de légitimation du pouvoir. Face aux oligarchies internationales, ceux qui sont surtout forts de leur nombre peuvent tirer parti de l'idéal de la démocratie ou de la démocratisation … dans le système international. De petits Etats et moyennes puissances démocratiques peuvent même avantageusement en tirer parti pour pousser leurs projets de réforme des pratiques sinon de la composition des organes[3].

S'en tenant à ce que le droit international contemporain doit *prima facie* à l'influence des démocraties libérales (grandes puissances et petits Etats confondus), maints intervenants au colloque ont abondamment démontré et illustré comment et combien les exigences démocratiques sont entrées dans des régimes internationaux de plus en plus techniques et sophistiqués, de promotion, de protection et même d'approfondissement de la démocratie. Celle-ci a aujourd'hui des gardiens en-deçà et au-delà des cours constitutionnelles nationales qui veillent notamment à la régularité des opérations électorales, depuis les « chiens de garde » que sont les ONG (internationales ou non) jusqu'aux organes politiques, d'experts ou juridictionnels d'organisations internationales universelles ou régionales. Plutôt que de réduire de très riches interventions en un long inventaire, qu'il nous soit permis d'insister sur l'ambivalence du legs

1 v GF Sinclair, *To Reform the World. International Organizations and the Making of Modern States* (OUP 2017).

2 v S Kott, *Organiser le monde. Une autre histoire de la guerre froide* (Seuil 2021).

3 v E Benvenisti, G W Downs, 'The Empire's New Clothes: Political Economy and the Fragmentation of International Law', (2007) 60 (2) *Stanford Law Review* 595–631.

des démocraties libérales au droit international en ayant en tête qu'elles ne sont plus aujourd'hui toutes concentrées dans l'espace euro-atlantique.

En premier lieu, ces Etats sont présupposés être disposés ou du moins mieux disposés à admettre que le droit international remplisse un rôle complémentaire, mais contesté, du droit constitutionnel pour limiter le pouvoir de l'Etat, y compris à l'égard des personnes privées, et à accepter de plier devant des contre-pouvoirs internationaux, fût-ce des cours internationales. Pour autant, ils sont eux aussi sujets à la tentation politique de retourner l'argument soit de la raison d'Etat, soit de la volonté majoritaire, soit de la constitution nationale contre les institutions internationales qui se posent en gardiennes du droit international, des droits fondamentaux de la personne humaine et des principes fondamentaux de la démocratie. Alors que le refus d'exécution d'une décision de justice internationale pouvait par le passé scandaliser, mais s'imposer, comme le fait d'une superpuissance renvoyant aux limites des institutions internationales[4], il peut *a priori* aujourd'hui s'interpréter de manière plus nuancée dans le jeu réciproque de contre-pouvoirs mettant aux prises des cours internationales et des juridictions nationales. Ce jeu ne peut cependant se défendre ou du moins se comprendre qu'à l'examen attentif des motifs soustendant le refus d'exécution et qu'au regard d'un système de relations organisé autour de l'équilibre ou de l'équilibrage des pouvoirs au sein de l'Etat d'abord, entre les organes dans l'Etat et les organes en dehors de l'Etat ensuite, alors que les juridictions nationales se trouvent confrontées à un « choix tragique »[5]. Or, il est parfois réduit à l'affirmation brutale ou caricaturée de la souveraineté nationale contre le droit international, ou de la suprématie de la constitution nationale sur les engagements internationaux de l'Etat. Le jeu subtil se retourne alors en une fâcheuse source d'inspiration pour d'autres Etats ou gouvernements cherchant fondamentalement à s'affranchir de toute contrainte juridique et de tout contre-balancement du pouvoir.

En deuxième lieu, les Etats d'Europe occidentale et d'Amérique du Nord, plus quelques autres, étaient déjà des démocraties, plus ou moins avancées, et s'engageaient déjà, plus ou moins activement, dans une coopération

4 A l'instar du refus des Etats-Unis d'Amérique d'exécuter l'arrêt rendu par la Cour internationale de Justice dans l'affaire *Activités militaires et paramilitaires au Nicaragua et contre celui-ci* (*Nicaragua c. Etats-Unis d'Amérique*) [1986].

5 Pour reprendre une expression utilisée par J. Weiler dans un éditorial à la fois vigoureux et las inspiré par la non-exécution en Italie de l'arrêt rendu par la Cour internationale de Justice dans l'affaire des *Immunités juridictionnelles de l'Etat* (*Allemagne c. Italie*) [2012], une inexécution rapprochée de la jurisprudence du Bundesverfassungsgericht.

institutionnalisée au plan régional et universel qu'ils étaient encore des Etats colonisateurs et ségrégationnistes, si ce n'est esclavagistes. Plus tard, ils se résignèrent à la perte de leurs possessions coloniales, à la reconnaissance du droit des peuples à disposer d'eux-mêmes et à la réalisation (plus) effective de l'égalité de tous sans distinction de race, de sexe, de genre ou de religion. Ils le firent en s'accommandant passablement de la disparition des peuples derrière l'écran d'Etats à régimes forts, laissant perdurer des discriminations massives couvertes par le déni, finalement ébranlé par des mouvements comme *Black Lives Matter*, et pérennisant les profits tirés de l'exploitation des ressources des territoires anciennement colonisés sans justes contreparties. Le droit international économique, en ce qu'il organise, régule et légitime des échanges et rapports inégaux, a favorisé l'enrichissement des économies libérales et la consolidation de ces Etats, y compris dans leur versant « providentiel » – pour leurs propres populations s'entend. Mais à l'inverse, il a aussi permis, dans une mesure très variable, tant le développement économique d'Etats qui étaient cantonnés à la périphérie des échanges commerciaux internationaux que la création des conditions d'émergence d'une classe moyenne dans les Etats anciennement communistes et/ou colonisés qui s'élargit et réclame pour elle aussi les bénéfices de la démocratie, de la *rule of law* et des protections du droit international.

En troisième lieu, les démocraties libérales entretiennent un rapport équivoque à maintes normes fondamentales dans l'ordre international. En dépit de la place accordée au droit dans des Etats qui pratiquent le culte de la constitution et à la paix par le droit sur la scène internationale, il n'est plus à démontrer qu'un régime démocratique n'est pas nécessairement respectueux de la lettre et de l'esprit du *jus contra bellum* ni d'ailleurs du droit international en général, même s'il sera généralement enclin à développer un argumentaire juridique étoffé de grands principes au soutien de ces initiatives. L'intérêt qu'il trouve à plier devant la règle de droit selon sa puissance relative est une variable structurelle de l'ordre international. La capacité de ses gouvernants à intégrer le droit à leurs politiques peut, ensuite, fluctuer au gré des majorités, en dépit de facteurs de stabilisation (la culture administrative et diplomatique, l'existence d'une politique juridique extérieure plus ou moins codifiée ...). A un niveau de détail plus fin, il est manifeste que les démocraties libérales sont dans l'ensemble assez peu enclines à aménager certaines des normes internationales qui les protègent, certes, mais qui protègent aussi bien des gouvernements ennemis de leurs propres peuples (immunités de juridiction, principe de non-intervention, consensualisme ...). Il y a à cela, au-delà du souci de protéger le *souverain* et ses représentants, une raison évidente : dans une société internationale qui ne se compose pas que d'Etats alliés, démocratiques, pacifiques et acquis au principe de la *rule of law*, il est raisonnablement prudent de conserver des règles internationales qui paraissent axiologiquement neutres et de faire un usage circonspect des mécanismes les plus altruistes en apparence. Alors même que le corpus de normes impératives, très restreint, reflète aujourd'hui des normes que les démocraties libérales considèrent comme fondamentales dans les registres juridique, moral et politique, elles sont plutôt réticentes à l'évolution du corpus aussi bien que des règles d'identification de ces normes, de crainte qu'elle durcisse le standard au regard duquel leurs propres politiques et interventions unilatérales pourraient être appréciées.

Ces différentes postures pourraient en principe être justifiées ou compensées par l'existence de procédures de contrôle internes à un Etat *de droit* démocratique sur ses propres actes susceptibles d'aller à l'encontre de ses obligations internationales ou de contredire ses positions de principe, parfois retranscrites dans la constitution nationale. Mais en pratique persiste, y compris dans les Etats de droit les mieux assis, un « domaine réservé », mystérieux, dans lequel le juge national souvent ne s'aventure pas, ou alors à reculons, et sur lequel le parlement national n'exerce pas toujours de droit de regard, ou alors avec retard : celui des relations dites extérieures. L'Allemagne constitue cependant probablement un contre-exemple à cet égard.

Pour ramasser ce propos : la contribution des démocraties libérales au droit international public est à la fois considérable et impure, comme elles ; une partie des tensions internes aux normes et institutions internationales sont – même abstraction faite des stratégies d'instrumentalisation et du jeu des intérêts et de la puissance – le reflet de leur actif comme de leur passif ou, si l'on préfère, des contradictions internes aux régimes démocratiques qui ont largement promu leur développement. Peut-être même ces tensions sont-elles la conséquence de l'inachèvement du projet démocratique au plan national, que l'on envisage la démocratie au sens institutionnel ou social du terme : le bilan « par classe » des bénéfices tirés de l'expansion continue des normes de droit international mériterait d'être dressé. A l'inverse pourtant, l'insertion des Etats démocratiques dans le système multilatéral contemporain peut – sous certaines conditions – être envisagée comme une promesse ou une possibilité de perfectionnement du système démocratique stato-national[6], et pas seulement comme une opportunité de maximiser les chances de réalisation ou protection des intérêts nationaux *stricto sensu.*

•••

6 V. pour une analyse nuancée R Keohane, S Macedo, A Moravcsik, 'Democracy-Enhancing Multilateralism' (2009) 63 (Winter) *International Organization* 1–31.

Un tel regard peut sembler excessivement rétrospectif alors que l'ambition du colloque était d'éclairer la démocratie – la notion, le concept, le principe, l'idéal, le mode effectif de gouvernement – en tant que pierre angulaire ou socle de l'ordre international, pour l'avenir. Il convient cependant pour ce faire non seulement de garder en tête cette impureté, propre à toute construction sociale, mais également de revenir sur ce que l'on entend par « démocratie ».

L'exigence démocratique se traduit fondamentalement par le droit pour un peuple de décider de sa propre destinée au moyen de procédures de vote, dans un cadre pluraliste, et le droit pour les citoyens de participer à ces procédures de telle manière qu'ils puissent se dire co-auteurs des normes qui leur seront appliquées – avec à tout le moins une limite, le respect des droits fondamentaux des personnes comme des minorités, et un gardien des limites, le juge constitutionnel sous l'éventuel contrôle d'un juge international.

Si l'on repart de là, la légitimation démocratique du système international dépend, en tout premier lieu, de la généralisation et de la qualité du contrôle exercé par les peuples ou leurs représentants élus sur les engagements internationaux de l'Etat – mais peut-être aussi sur d'autres actes du type reconnaissance, réactions à l'illicite, vote des représentants à l'ONU, etc. Toutefois, les limites d'une telle proposition tiennent, d'une part, à la capacité du corps électoral à percevoir et accepter la dimension transactionnelle d'un grand nombre de normes internationales et la logique des règles du jeu international, y compris la réciprocité pour la plupart d'entre elles ; d'autre part, à la pauvreté des règles secondaires du droit international relatives aux conditions d'expression du consentement de l'Etat (on retombe ici, en passant par une autre porte, sur les inconvénients d'une conception rigide et datée de l'autonomie des ordres juridiques, nationaux et international) ; ensuite, à la possible inadaptation du contrôle démocratique national sur des normes régulatrices à la fois techniques et changeantes ; enfin, à la difficulté d'articuler les cycles électoraux ou référendaires d'un côté et, de l'autre, le temps des normes internationales dont l'élaboration est souvent très lourde mais devrait parfois aussi être très rapide pour répondre à ce que les Etats perçoivent comme une urgence. Quoique le perfectionnement du contrôle démocratique exercé sur les engagements internationaux d'un Etat et leur mise en œuvre puisse à l'avenir limiter le sentiment de dépossession qui nourrit la « fatigue démocratique », il est douteux qu'il suffise à lui seul à restaurer la légitimité du système international et à le libérer du soupçon qu'il se retourne contre la démocratie, tout simplement parce que tout ne se joue pas au moment de la délivrance du consentement de l'Etat, après approbation ou autorisation parlementaire ou populaire. A ce stade, en effet, tout est souvent joué ou presque. *Take it or leave it.*

Même si l'on doute avec Alain Pellet que la « démocratie internationale » soit une notion opératoire et pertinente dans un système interétatique[7], *a fortiori* si elle n'est que le reflet d'une logique majoritaire transposée aux relations institutionnalisées entre Etats, même si l'on admet avec Joseph Weiler que le peuple sans qui il ne serait pas de démocratie est introuvable dans les différentes strates du système international[8], il n'est plus possible aujourd'hui de faire l'économie d'un triple questionnement :

- du processus normatif international complexe qui associe, avec des rétroactions, une pluralité d'Etats et d'institutions internationales de natures très diverses (quelle transparence ? quelle inclusivité ? quels garde-fous contre les phénomènes de capture ?) ;
- de l'articulation entre les institutions internationales exerçant un pouvoir normatif ou de contrôle et les pouvoirs constitués au plan national (ainsi que des *checks and balances* entre eux, dont la subsidiarité, la marge nationale d'appréciation, le dialogue des juges peuvent – sous certaines conditions – être des variantes) ;
- de la représentativité et du fonctionnement des institutions internationales, notamment celles qui déterminent les grands paramètres de politiques publiques facialement « nationales » mais souvent coordonnées ou standardisées, quand elles ne sont pas purement et simplement conditionnées par une organisation internationale prêteuse ou prestataire de services.

Plus exactement, faire l'économie de ces questionnements reviendrait à admettre comme une fatalité le « fait oligarchique », d'une part, et d'autre part, un état d'anarchie internationale qui favorise comportements opportunistes et perméabilité des institutions internationales aux puissances privées[9].

Le défi va bien au-delà de réaménagements institutionnels dont l'élaboration est déjà si laborieuse. En effet, le besoin de (re-)légitimation démocratique du droit international doit être envisagé à l'aune des critiques dirigées contre son instrumentalisation par les puissants comme du renouvellement de ses objets. Il a beaucoup été question de la protection internationale des droits fondamentaux en raison du lien fort justement établi, dans les démocraties libérales, entre démocratie et *rule of law*, démocratie et indépendance des juges, démocratie et pluralisme politique, sociétal, identitaire, etc. et de la quête de protections en dehors de l'Etat contre l'Etat lui-même ou contre la

7 A Pellet, 'Legitimacy of Legislative and Executive Actions of International Institutions', in R Wolfrum, V Röben (eds), *Legitimacy in International Law* (Springer 2008) 63–82.

8 J Weiler, 'The Geology of International Law. Governance, Democracy and Legitimacy' (2004) 64 *ZaöRV* 547–562.

9 R Rivier, 'Communauté internationale et oligarchie' (2020) 1 *Droits* 111–151.

tyrannie de la majorité, voire contre les menaces d'origine privée qui pèsent sur le fonctionnement et la vitalité des institutions démocratiques. D'autres enjeux, non moins pressants, ne peuvent être appréhendés sans que soient garantis précisément la liberté d'information, la liberté d'expression, le pluralisme, la liberté d'association et les droits des lanceurs d'alerte d'une part, la participation la plus large et équilibrée aux processus décisionnels nationaux et internationaux d'autre part. Ce sont notamment les menaces pour la vie privée ou la vie démocratique que l'accumulation et la manipulation de données par des acteurs publics ou privés représentent, l'urgence environnementale – changement climatique, effondrement de la biodiversité, pollutions massives des sols, de l'air et de l'eau, stérilisation des sols, adaptation des pratiques individuelles et collectives au changement accéléré des écosystèmes –, et les questions de justice sociale : à la persistance d'inégalités insoutenables (malgré le recul de la pauvreté avant l'épidémie de COVID-19 dans un certain nombre d'Etats) est opposée la redistribution de richesses ou l'invention de modes de production « prédistributifs »[10] (par opposition au modes de production destructifs dans un contexte de raréfaction de certaines ressources avec une redistribution marginale des revenus). Le mérite est revenu aux jeunes chercheurs de les aborder de front.

Sauf à considérer que l'urgence environnementale puisse encore être retraduite dans les schèmes classique des intérêts étatiques, de la sécurité nationale, etc., voire doive l'être pour être prise en considération, les peuples ont, ensemble, fatalement, à rendre des arbitrages qui engagent leur(s) destinée(s). Une pléiade d'institutions internationales s'empare de ces enjeux mais telles qu'elles ont été constituées il y a des décennies ou récemment suivant un patron daté, sont-elles vraiment mieux à même que les Etats de gérer et de préserver des biens communs, de concevoir des arrangements viables pour leur gestion, d'accompagner la raréfaction de ressources vitales pour l'humanité ? Suffit-il d'accroître en leur sein la participation des ONG ou celles des communautés directement affectées par leurs politiques pour remédier aux biais des procédures internationales ?[11] Il est permis de douter que l'humanité puisse (re)prendre en main sa destinée sans repenser aussi les prérogatives de l'Etat souverain, sans repousser les frontières de la démocratie telles qu'elle a été

10 L'épithète est emprunté à J Linarelli, ME Salomon, M Sornarajah, *The Misery of International Law. Confrontations with Injustice in the Global Economy* (OUP 2018).

11 Sur ces tendances, v J von Bernstoff, 'New Responses to the Legitimacy Crisis in International Institutions: The Role of 'Civil Society' and the Rise of the Principle of Participation of 'The Most Affected' in International Institutional Law' (2021) 32 (1) *EJIL* 125–157.

expérimentée jusqu'ici (à savoir dans un cadre stato-national ou supranational à l'échelle régionale), sans s'efforcer de réinventer les modalités procédurales et temporelles de la participation du public, *des publics*, à l'élaboration des normes d'usage ou de non-usage puis à la surveillance de leur respect de part et d'autre des limites des juridictions nationales[12]. Les frontières nationales ne sont certes pas frappées de complète obsolescence mais elles ne sauraient servir de cadre adéquat à une délibération démocratique réservée aux nationaux sur des questions fondamentalement transnationales, sauf à se satisfaire de réponses partielles à des questions tronquées[13].

En se contentant de revivifier l'idée que le droit international contemporain puisse et doive protéger les principes fondamentaux de la démocratie libérale dans une version héritée du XVIIIe siècle, on renouerait avec une utopie appartenant au passé.

---

12 V. en ce sens les réflexions développées au Collège de France par S Besson, '*Reconstruire l'ordre institutionnel international*', (3 décembre 2020) Collège de France, leçon inaugurale.

13 V. not. sur les limites du cadre stato-national les réflexions stimulantes de M. Kumm, 'The Best of Times and the Worst of Times. Between Constitutional Triumphalism and Nostalgia' in P Dobner, M Loughlin (eds), *The Twilight of Constitutionalism?* (OUP 2010) 201–219.

Index

www.ingramcontent.com/pod-product-compliance
Lightning Source LLC
LaVergne TN
LVHW010623300926
849162LV00001B/44